Studies in Church History

46

GOD'S BOUNTY?
THE CHURCHES AND THE NATURAL WORLD

GOD'S BOUNTY?
THE CHURCHES
AND THE NATURAL WORLD

PAPERS READ AT
THE 2008 SUMMER MEETING AND
THE 2009 WINTER MEETING OF
THE ECCLESIASTICAL HISTORY SOCIETY

EDITED BY

PETER CLARKE

and

TONY CLAYDON

PUBLISHED FOR
THE ECCLESIASTICAL HISTORY SOCIETY
BY
THE BOYDELL PRESS
2010

First published 2010

A publication of the Ecclesiastical History Society
in association with The Boydell Press
an imprint of Boydell & Brewer Ltd
PO Box 9, Woodbridge, Suffolk IP12 3DF, UK
and of Boydell & Brewer Inc.
668 Mt Hope Avenue, Rochester, NY 14620, USA
website: www.boydellandbrewer.com

ISBN 978–0–95468–096–1

ISSN 0424–2084

A CIP catalogue record for this book is available
from the British Library

Details of previous volumes are available from Boydell & Brewer Ltd

This book is printed on acid-free paper

Printed in Great Britain by
CPI Antony Rowe, Chippenham and Eastbourne

CONTENTS

PREFACE

'The Church and the Natural World' was greeted warmly by the Ecclesiastical History Society when Professor William Sheils chose it as the theme for his presidency of the society for 2008–09. As the papers in this volume show, the topic proved to be both timely (given the depth of public ecological concern in the early twenty-first century) and hugely informative about a great range of religious history. The contributions included here comprise the eight plenary papers given at the Summer Meeting in 2008 and the Winter Meeting in 2009, and a selection of the communications offered at the Summer Meeting.

The Editors are grateful to the members of the society who chaired communications sessions during the Summer Meeting, and who gave their time and expertise to reviewing those communications submitted for publication. We also thank the authors for their speed and good humour in responding to requests for revision, and wish to express our deep gratitude to the Assistant Editor, Dr Tim Grass, without whose efficiency in co-ordinating and copy-editing this collection would never have seen the light of day. We thank the Ecclesiastical History Society for funding Tim's essential post.

The society wishes to thank the staff of the National University of Ireland, Galway, for hosting the Summer Meeting in such a spectacular part of these islands, and is particularly grateful to Dr Barbara Bombi (the Conference Secretary), Dr Alison Forrestal and the university's conference office staff, for organizing both the meeting and the excursions to the ecclesiastical and other wonders of Connacht. It is also indebted to Dr Williams's Library and to its Director, Dr David Wykes, for accommodating the Winter Meeting in London.

We are proud to present this latest volume of Studies in Church History, a series which during its distinguished history has (we believe) proved a most valuable aid to the study of human religiosity.

Peter Clarke
University of Southampton
Tony Claydon
Bangor University

CONTRIBUTORS

William SHEILS (*President*)
  Professor of History, University of York

Andrew ATHERSTONE
  Tutor in History and Doctrine, and Latimer Research
  Fellow, Wycliffe Hall, Oxford

Michael BENTLEY
  Professor of Modern History, University of St Andrews

Peter BILLER
  Professor, Department of History, University of York

Brenda BOLTON
  Formerly Senior Lecturer in History, Queen Mary and
  Westfield College, University of London

Christopher CLARK
  Professor of History, University of Connecticut

Simon DITCHFIELD
  Reader in History, University of York

Sarah FOOT
  Regius Professor of Ecclesiastical History, University of
  Oxford

Keith A. FRANCIS
  Associate Professor of History, Baylor University, Waco,
  Texas

Raymond GILLESPIE
  Professor of History, National University of Ireland
  Maynooth

Michael R. GLADWIN (*EHS postgraduate bursary*)
  Postgraduate student, University of Cambridge

Olga GUSAKOVA (*EHS postgraduate bursary*)
  Postgraduate student, Institute of General History, Russian
  Academy of Sciences, Moscow

Tadhg Ó HANNRACHÁIN
  Senior Lecturer, School of History and Archives, University
  College Dublin

Robert G. INGRAM
   Associate Professor of History, Ohio University

Suzy KNIGHT (*EHS postgraduate bursary*)
   Postgraduate student, Queen Mary, University of London

Cŏnor KOSTICK
   Post-Doctoral Fellow of the Irish Research Council for the
   Humanities and Social Sciences, Trinity College, Dublin

Gesine OPPITZ-TROTMAN (*Michael J. Kennedy Postgraduate Prize*)
   Postgraduate student, University of East Anglia

Sarah PARSONS (*EHS postgraduate bursary*)
   Postgraduate student, University of Exeter

Alasdair RAFFE
   Research Associate, Department of History, University of
   Durham

Stanley P. ROSENBERG
   Director, Centre for Scholarship and Christianity in
   Oxford; Associate Member, Wycliffe Hall, Oxford

Tamsin ROWE (*EHS postgraduate bursary*)
   Postgraduate student, University of Exeter

Peter Manley SCOTT
   Senior Lecturer in Christian Social Thought and Director
   of the Lincoln Theological Institute, University of
   Manchester

Mark SMITH
   University Lecturer in English Local and Social History,
   University of Oxford

Andrew SPICER
   Professor of Early Modern European History, Head of
   History and History of Art, Oxford Brookes University

R. N. SWANSON
   Professor of Medieval History, University of Birmingham

Elizabeth C. TINGLE
   Senior Lecturer in History, University of Plymouth

Alexandra WALSHAM
   Professor of Reformation History and Head of
   Department, University of Exeter

Paul WHITE
> Research Associate, University of Cambridge; Editor, Darwin Correspondence Project

Jonathan WILLIS (*EHS postgraduate bursary*)
> Postgraduate student, University of Warwick

ABBREVIATIONS

ActaSS   *Acta sanctorum*, ed. J. Bolland and G. Henschen
            (Antwerp etc., 1643–)
ACW   Ancient Christian Writers, ed. J. C. Quasten and J.
            C. Plumpe (New York etc, 1946–)
AHR   *American Historical Review* (New York, 1895–)
BAV   Biblioteca Apostolica Vaticana, Vatican City
BJRL   *Bulletin of the John Rylands Library* (Manchester,
            1903–)
BL   British Library, London
BN   Bibliothèque Nationale de France, Paris
Bodl.   Bodleian Library, Oxford
CChr   Corpus Christianorum (Turnhout, 1953–)
CChr CM   Corpus Christianorum, continuatio medievalis
            (1966–)
CChr SL   Corpus Christianorum, series Latina (1953–)
ChH   *Church History* (New York/Chicago, 1932–)
CICan   *Corpus iuris canonici*, ed. E. Richter and E. Fried-
            berg, 2 vols (Leipzig, 1879–81)
CUL   Cambridge University Library
CYS   Canterbury and York Society (London, etc., 1907–)
EETS   Early English Text Society (London/Oxford,
            1864–)
ESTC   English Short Title Catalogue, <http://estc.bl.uk>
EHD   *English Historical Documents* (London, 1953–)
EHR   *English Historical Review* (London, 1886–)
ET   English Translation
HistJ   *Historical Journal* (Cambridge, 1958–)
HThR   *Harvard Theological Review* (New York/Cambridge,
            MA, 1908–)
JBS   *Journal of British Studies* (Hartford, CT, 1961–)
JEH   *Journal of Ecclesiastical History* (Cambridge, 1950–)
JHI   *Journal of the History of Ideas* (London, 1940–)
JMedH   *Journal of Medieval History* (Amsterdam, 1975–)

LCC	Library of Christian Classics, 26 vols (London, 1953–69)
LPL	Lambeth Palace Library, London
MGH	Monumenta Germaniae Historica inde ab a. c. 500 usque ad a. 1500, ed. G. H. Pertz et al. (Hanover, Berlin etc., 1826–)
MGH AA	Monumenta Germaniae Historica, Auctores antiquissimi (1877–1919)
MGH LdL	Monumenta Germaniae Historica, Libelli de Lite Imperatorum et Pontificum, Saeculis XI et XII conscripti (1891–97)
MGH Quellen	Monumenta Germaniae Historica, Quellen zur Geistesgeschichte des Mittelalters (1955–)
MGH S	Monumenta Germaniae Historica, Scriptores (1826–)
MGH SRG	Monumenta Germaniae Historica, Scriptores rerum Germanicarum in usum scholarum seperatum editi (1871–)
MGH SRM	Monumenta Germaniae Historica, Scriptores rerum Merovingicarum (1937–)
MGH SS	Monumenta Germaniae Historica, Scriptores (in folio) (1826–)
MGH Schriften	Schriften der MGH (1938–)
NAS	National Archives of Scotland, Edinburgh
n.d.	no date
NPNF I	A Select Library of Nicene and Post-Nicene Fathers of the Christian Church, ed. P. Schaff, 14 vols (New York, 1887–92 and subsequent edns)
ns	new series
ODNB	Oxford Dictionary of National Biography, ed. H. C. G. Matthew and Brian Harrison (Oxford, 2004)
os	old series
P&P	Past and Present: A Journal of Scientific History (London/Oxford, 1952–)
PL	Patrologia Latina, ed. J. P. Migne, 217 vols + 4 index vols (Paris, 1841–61)
PS	Parker Society, 54 vols + index vol. (Cambridge, 1841–55)

RHC Oc	Recueil des historiens des croisades: Historiens occidentaux, 5 vols (Paris, 1844–95)
RS	*Rerum Brittanicarum medii aevi scriptores*, 99 vols (London, 1858–1911) = Rolls Series
RSCHS	*Records of the Scottish Church History Society* (Edinburgh, 1923–)
s.a.	*sub anno*
SC	Sources Chrétiennes (Paris, 1941–)
SCH	Studies in Church History (London/Oxford/Woodbridge, 1964–)
ScHR	*Scottish Historical Review* (Edinburgh/Glasgow, 1904–)
SCH S	Studies in Church History: Subsidia (Oxford/Woodbridge, 1978–)
SHS	Scottish History Society
s.n.	*sub nomine*
Speculum	*Speculum: A Journal of Medieval Studies* (Cambridge, MA, 1925–)
ss	supplementary series
s.v.	*sub verbo*
VCH	*Victoria History of the Counties of England* (London, 1900–)

INTRODUCTION

'My kingdom is not of this world.'[1] Christ's response to Pilate has resounded through almost two millennia of Christian history, challenging theologians and preachers to identify the relationship between the material and the spiritual and to locate the boundary between the natural and the supernatural. As Robert Bartlett has recently demonstrated, the concept of the supernatural only really began to be developed in the high Middle Ages following Peter Lombard's glossing of the creation story and his distinction between seminal causes, which belong to nature, and those causes which are reserved to God alone, beyond nature rather than supernatural in his formulation.[2] This distinction was to have a profound effect on Scholastic thought in the following centuries, but for ordinary Christians the challenge was, and remains, that of discerning the meaning and purposes of their actions while on earth in the context of that heavenly destiny to which they believe themselves and all humanity to be called. Of course, the distinction between this world and the heavenly kingdom has never been as sharp as the words of Christ quoted above seemed to imply, but the contrasts remained profound. The most famous expression of the contrast between earthly and heavenly values is to be found in the words of the Sermon on the Mount, in which the normal structures of power were inverted: 'the meek shall inherit the earth' served to remind both the powerful and the powerless of the transitoriness of earthly fortune.[3] More recently, as technological progress has fostered higher standards of material prosperity in the developed world and enabled greater population growth in less developed countries, the relationship between the natural and the divine, the material and the spiritual, has been reconfigured.

[1] John 18: 36.
[2] Robert Bartlett, *The Natural and the Supernatural in the Middle Ages* (Cambridge, 2008), 6–7.
[3] Matt. 5: 5.

For many Christians the distinction has become irrelevant, and the care and conservation of the planet and its resources, both animate and inanimate, have become central to their understanding of their spiritual obligation. This draws on a long tradition of stewardship in Christian thinking, going back to the parables of Jesus; but it is also informed by non-Christian traditions such as Buddhism and Jainism, in which humanity and other living organisms are mutually interdependent, so that the natural world is to be preserved and protected in its own right, as well as by the ethical and political stance of secular pressure groups such as Greenpeace, which embrace both believers and non-believers in responding to issues related to global conservation. The essays in this volume attempt to place these current ecological concerns of Christians in historical perspective. In so doing they contribute both to historical scholarship and to the current debate on global issues.

They do this in a number of ways: by examining the varying understanding of creation itself which Christian thinkers and groups developed; by looking at the ways in which Christians sought to influence the divine plan through their own actions, whether by communal ritualistic practice or through individual supplication; by examining attempts to discern through natural events and surviving phenomena traces of the divine in the world; by interrogating the relationship between knowledge of this world, science and theological understanding; by recalling those attempts to create ideal societies here on earth, whether monastic, and thereby essentially withdrawn from society as exempla of the divine plan, or utopian and committed to setting out a model for living in this world for others to follow; and finally by recalling the importance of the theme of stewardship rather than ownership, use rather than possession, which runs through Christian history. These lines of inquiry are not independent of each other, and in many essays we can see two or more of these questions arising, but they do help us to organize our thoughts. The creation story itself provides us with the greatest and most fundamental of contradictions: what were we to make of this divine gift marred by human sinfulness? Which left the greater mark on the world? Did we live in a bountiful universe which God left us to improve and develop, as many of the Christian liturgical readings of whatever church or denomination reminded those who attended the weekly services, or was it, in the words of that famous medieval prayer to the Virgin, the *Salve Regina*, a 'vale of tears' in which humanity as 'poor banished children of Eve' were destined to 'mourn and weep'?[4]

Clearly the orthodox had alternative – and potentially conflicting – views of creation available to them in their liturgies and theologies, and Foot's evocation of the prayers and poems of holy men and women of the early Middle Ages amply demonstrates the ambivalence felt by Christians when they surveyed the world around them, with God as not only the 'author of all marvels' but also 'the terrible one' who could wreak vengeance on his sinful people by letting hail fall 'in malice against men'. In such uncertainty, what secured the world for God was sanctity, a status which individuals could achieve through obedience to God's purposes and which was recognized by the Church as witnessing to the divine in nature and to God's purposes for the world. As Gusakova's study of Anglo-Saxon hagiographies demonstrates, through their example and intercession individual saints helped to restore order to nature and overcome sin. In some cases this not only involved restoring nature but taming it, a fact which helps to explain the somewhat unexpected emphasis on hawking, a popular knightly pastime, in the miracle stories of Thomas Becket discussed by Oppitz-Trotman.

Not everyone could achieve sanctity, and for ordinary Christians the liturgy and public formularies were an important aid to the overcoming of sin, especially when the natural world appeared threatening. Two early modern cases are discussed here: on sea voyages in the sixteenth and seventeenth centuries both English Protestant and Breton Catholic seafarers invoked the Almighty to assist them in their perilous labours, and in the labours of childbirth Italian women of the sixteenth century had a trust in the biblical plant, the Rose of Jericho (Ecclesiasticus 24: 13–14), as a birthing aid. Despite opposition from clerical and medical authority, faith in the efficacy of the rose could be found surviving in parts of Italy into the 1970s. Survival in this case can be attributed to unofficial folkloric belief, but in Protestant Britain commemoration of, and thanksgiving for, divine favour continued to have official support

---

[4] The *Salve Regina* quickly became one of the most popular intercessions to the Virgin, and was later incorporated into the Tridentine service of Benediction.

into the later twentieth century. Special occasions of public fasting and thanksgiving for divine assistance in facing both natural and man-made disasters were called for and endorsed by ecclesiastical and secular authority and remained a feature of public life in Britain until after the Second World War. But it was not always danger or disaster which produced liturgical forms. Rowe's account of the medieval blessings of trees in order to make them fruitful produced liturgical forms in which the prayers alluded directly to the Genesis story in their concern to 'cast out the ancient enemy and the snares of the first sin', thereby linking the abundance of nature with Christ's redemptive sacrifice. If it was orthodox to see the fruits of nature as part of God's bounty, it took heretics to develop the bleakest view of creation, such that even some of their supporters rejected it or were uncomfortable with it. This was especially true of those thirteenth-century Cathars discussed by Biller. They denied that any growth or fertility in the natural world was attributable to divine action, asserting that all could be explained in materialist terms and needed no Creator to initiate those seminal causes identified by Lombard. The world in which these Cathars lived, or at least its natural features, was not God-given.

This was, of course, an extreme view, and Christians continued, and in some cases continue, to seek for evidence of divine traces in this world, or to ask God and the heavenly hosts to intercede in daily life. Traces of the divine presence on earth are not confined to Christian traditions, but within Christianity they are found everywhere. Some, of course, were seen as sources of divine power of universal importance; such was the cave at Subiaco where Benedict of Nursia lived prior to his calling together the community which became the foundation of western monasticism. As Bolton shows, six centuries later Pope Innocent III sought to exploit this site to bring together eastern and western Christianity and to link them to the Jewish Scriptures by reference to Elijah's cave. Jerusalem and the Holy Land were even more important as sites of universal divine power, but as Kostick demonstrates, these were, and remain, heavily contested sites which could, and still can, appeal to the darker side of Christian devotion, the contested claims to the city making Jerusalem the site of some of the bleaker episodes in relations between Christians and members of the other Abrahamic faiths. Elsewhere the divine significance of particular places was more local in character.

As is well known, Irish Catholics populated their local landscapes with topographical references to local saints and sites of miraculous occurrences, thus linking, as Gillespie says, their local and particular environment to a wider cosmic order embracing both heaven and earth. And this use of the natural world was also deployed in the missionary environment, as Ditchfield points out in his study of the Jesuits in the Americas, where traditional stories and local flora and fauna were employed to link the lives of native peoples to the Christian cosmic order, most notably through the use of the 'passion flower' used by missionaries in Latin America to explain the Crucifixion and the redemption which it secured, much as St Patrick was said to have used the shamrock to introduce the native Irish to the mystery of the Trinity. Such 'devotional landscapes' or natural signs of heavenly grace were less obviously attractive to Protestant reformers but, as Walsham shows, the pre-Reformation tradition of the sacred footprint survived the Protestant Reformation in England, despite the best efforts of many preachers to eradicate such traces of idolatry. In the religiously contested region of early modern Lancashire, both Protestants and Catholics published competing versions of a strange indentation in the wall of Brindle parish church for their own polemical purposes. Later on, during the revival associated with the early Methodists, such phenomena, in which preachers and others appeared to have left physical imprints on the landscape or buildings where they had been forced to minister to their flocks, became part of the stories surrounding John Wesley and other Methodist preachers.

Divine traces in the landscape may have been problematic to Protestants, but from the start both Calvinists and Lutherans emphasized the importance of the natural world in revealing the glory of God, although, for Calvinists especially, it remained very much secondary to the Word of God in Scripture. The papers of Willis on Elizabethan England and Spicer on seventeenth-century Scotland reveal the tensions inherent in this juxtaposition of the 'book of nature' and the Word of God. In Elizabethan England music, and especially harmony, was generally recognized as tangible proof of the divine in nature, but the power of such 'music of the spheres' was problematic, for it could be seductive as well as instructive, and had to be firmly subordinated to Scripture if it was to direct its hearers to divine truth. As well as revealing the divine in the world, nature was part of God's plan for humanity, and the resources of the earth were, for Calvinists especially, a God-given gift over which humanity had dominion, a circumstance which carried with it, as Spicer recalls, the responsibility to develop and improve its abundance. In the religiously contested and economically expanding context of South Lanarkshire in the 1690s, the use of open spaces for worship by the miners caused problems for a Kirk which, whilst wanting to deny the 'holiness' of any one particular place for worship, deeming it a remnant of popish superstition, feared the growth of that same superstition from unregulated worship in the landscape.

Leadhills represented peculiar circumstances; more generally the 'book of nature', which was to be read alongside Scripture, had a long and honourable place in both Catholic and Protestant traditions as an aid to understanding the divine will, encapsulated well in William Blake's frequently quoted couplet: 'to see a world in a grain of sand / and a heaven in a wild flower'.[5] Mention of Blake leads naturally to the Romantic poets, whose positive responses to nature had a major influence on all Christian denominations.[6] Thus, within the British experience, we can see both the grandeur of the natural world in the mountains of the Alps as central to the devotional writing of the later nineteenth-century Evangelical, Frances Ridley Havergal (with the snow on the Jungfrau recalling the psalmist's prayer to be 'washed whiter than snow') and also the miniaturist beauty of flowers being deployed as spiritual comfort and as a means of bringing the gospel to the sick and hospitalized through the evangelical Bible Flower Mission, which distributed bouquets and small garlands throughout the cities of Britain. This evangelical engagement with nature and the natural world carried on into the mid-twentieth century in the work of the Cambridge historian Herbert Butterfield. Formed in the Methodist tradition, even after he had left it theologically Butterfield remained

[5] W. Blake, 'Auguries of Innocence' I, stanza 1, in *William Blake, the Complete Poems*, ed. W. H. Stevenson, 2nd edn (London, 1989), 589.

[6] See, for example, D. W. Bebbington, *Evangelicalism in Modern Britain: A History from the 1730s to the 1980s* (London, 1989), 80–81; for Coleridge, see Peter J. Kitson, 'Coleridge's *Lectures, 1795; On Politics and Religion*' and Pamela Edwards, 'Coleridge on Politics and Religion', both in F. Burwick, ed., *The Oxford Handbook to Samuel Taylor Coleridge* (Oxford, 2009), 127–43, 235–54.

absorbed by what he thought of as the God-given beauty of the natural world, and Bentley's analysis of his unpublished notebooks reveal a man caught in the tension between the legitimate scientific analysis of the universe as an object of empirical study and the wonder of the world he beheld; 'I stood still and held my breath as I watched the moon not far above the willows ... I tried to see it as something still, something which stood steadfast while time speeds ahead'. Similar wonder at both the great vistas of open countryside and the contemplation of the intricate structure of small plants and organisms had been expressed by a Victorian clergyman, John Christopher Atkinson, half a century earlier. Each provided him with spiritual sustenance and an understanding of God's purposes, and in considering the structure of plants he was also led to contemplate the relationship between scientific knowledge and theological understanding.

Atkinson had, of course, read Darwin, and the great debate which publication of the *Origin of Species* reopened about the relationship between scientific knowledge and theological understanding is necessarily one of the major themes of the volume. But the relationship between scientific knowledge, or reason, and theology has a history as long as the Christian tradition. As Rosenberg's paper demonstrates, Augustine's later work on the creation story, produced a conception of the world which was contingent, rational and capable of being understood; a product of the Creator and maintained by his providence, it was nevertheless wholly distinct from its Creator and knowable to human reason. This represents a shift from Augustine's earlier view of the catastrophic nature of the Fall, and was to be influential in the development of early modern scientific thought, influencing Galileo among others. Early modern scholars, both Catholic and Protestant, sought rational proofs or demonstrations of the existence of God. On the eve of the Galilean revolution the Hungarian Cardinal Pázmány produced an account of a geocentric universe ordered for the benefit of mankind in his *Kalauz*, a volume based essentially on patristic sources and sharing many concerns – but also some significant differences – with Calvin's account of nature. Each thought that the world existed essentially for the benefit of humankind, but agreed that such authority over nature brought with it responsibilities, though it is to be questioned whether Calvin would have followed Pázmány's description (following

Macrobius) of the world as God's temple, in which humanity should live like priests in a church. Over a century after Pázmány published his study, Thomas Newton, later Bishop of Bristol, declared at the outset of his Boyle Lectures in 1756: '[T]here is nothing inconsistent in science and religion'. The Boyle Lectures, founded by the celebrated scientist and studied here by Ingram, were delivered annually from 1692 with the aim of proving the truth of the Christian religion against notorious infidels. In the early years this was usually done by the application of Newtonian principles (Isaac's) and some formulation of the argument from design, as the quotation from Thomas Newton suggests, but, as Ingram's article indicates, from the 1750s there was something of a retreat from dependence on this argument from deductive reason to a historically based analysis in which nature and natural events were viewed as examples of God's care for his world, especially in the context of miracles and prophecy. In this analysis God continually accommodated providence to humanity's historical condition, and in this way the mysterious became knowable.

In the early nineteenth century new parts of the globe also became knowable to the Christian old world and were settled by its peoples. The landscape of the Australian colonies provided challenges from the local fossil record for those clergyman-geologists who moved from Europe to work there. Gladwin's paper examines two key figures here, demonstrating the tight bond which existed between Evangelicalism and science, though that bond was at that time usually deployed to harmonize science and religion in support of Mosaic cosmogony. Publication of Darwin's *Origin of Species* challenged that harmonious relationship. The famous confrontation between Samuel Wilberforce and Thomas Huxley has produced a caricature of the conflict between science and religion which has come down to the present in the recent works of Richard Dawkins and others[7] but, as some essays here suggest, the picture was more complex than that. If for Wilberforce nature was 'a parable of grace, and grace an interpreter of nature', this

---

[7] See, for example, Richard Dawkins, *The God Delusion* (London, 2006) and the debate which it has generated, both in the press and academic circles; for a theologian's response to Dawkins, see especially Keith Ward, *Why There Almost Certainly Is a God* (London, 2008).

was a view shared by many clerics, Atkinson included, whose views tended to the Darwinian without removing a Creator from the account. And Darwin's own relationship with the Church remained pluralistic; although publicly not attending its services, he continued, as White shows, to support the work of the Established Church in his home parish and was active in its pastoral work, at least for as long as it served the whole community. From the 1870s however the contributions of the Darwin family to the parish church dropped off and from 1880 Charles was actively supporting the work of a young Brethren evangelist by renting to him what later became known as the Gospel Room, which remained a home of nonconformist worship for more than half a century. What attracted Darwin to this young preacher was his pastoral work in improving the behaviour of the locality, especially in respect of drunkenness, and it is to this pastoral mission that we now turn.

From the time of Paul, Christians have sought to organize their worldly existence in line with the divine plan, and this has sometimes led them to build communities founded on their understanding of specific biblical precepts. The social dimension of the gospel had, of course, always been part of Christian living and it has its contemporary expression in the huge variety of Christian aid and welfare agencies, both local and global, which are prompted by a desire, if not to bring about the kingdom of God on earth, at least to alleviate the injustices and inequities which are the consequences of fallible and corrupt human agency. As we can see from White's article and that by Sheils, from the mid-nineteenth century the work of the Church in assisting social and civil improvement became increasingly valued by clergy and non-believers alike, but it is to specific experiments in creating Christian societies separated from a fallen world that Clark draws our attention. The impetus to share a common life originated in the apostolic Church, was given formal structure within monasticism during the Middle Ages, and has been carried through to the modern world in a variety of utopian experiments in which edification, in both its material and spiritual senses, provided the foundations on which these communities thrived, or failed to do so. Recent work on these communitarian experiments has shifted the focus from their charismatic leadership to the experience of the members, demonstrating, as Clark shows, that although they were premised on what were to their founders the immutable precepts of Scripture, it was adaptability rather than stasis which became the hallmark of successful Christian communitarian living.

If these communities represent one aspect of the attempt in Christian living to come to terms with modernity, the question of stewardship represents another. Of course the question of the right stewardship of earthly and human resources is not just a modern preoccupation but goes back to the parable of the talents.[8] During the Middle Ages, as Swanson shows in his discussion of tithes, God's bounty required of humanity an acknowledgment of its true purposes, which in theoretical terms involved some contribution to the economy of *caritas* which underpinned medieval Christianity. This was achieved through tithing, a fact often overlooked in the discussions of historians who focus on the significance of tithes for confrontation between laity and clergy. If tithing stressed reciprocity, we can see from Spicer's paper that growth and development were also regarded as important responsibilities in the early modern world; the subsequent success of western Christianity in this respect and the global dominance of the West in other respects has led some to believe that development has become exploitation, or something close to it. As the richer countries use up an ever-increasing proportion of the earth's resources and the gap between rich and poor widens, the emphasis has moved away from development towards conservation and protection, be it of the ice cap or the rainforest, and it is this shift which lies at the heart of the recent growth of ecotheology.

This frames the paper with which our volume ends. Scott's paper asks us to consider what the natural world might represent to theologians at a time when global pressures threaten the future existence of our planet as we know it. It reviews recent ecological theology, identifying it with other strands of liberation theology concerned with questions of social justice or those about sexuality and identity, placing it firmly in the modern or postmodern world. Notwithstanding their current importance, these questions have been the traditional concerns of Christians since the time of the

---

[8]   Matt. 25: 14–30; Luke 19: 12–28.

apostles; who am I, how do I relate to those about me and to the world in which I live, and (above all) how do my answers inform my relationship with God? What lessons does contemplation of the natural world hold for my understanding of God's purposes and my own place in creation, and how should I respond? Globalization and the dramatic effects of the exploitation of the natural resources of the planet and the atmosphere which encloses it have added urgency to these questions, such that, as Scott indicates, it seems legitimate for some theologians to ask what it might mean for our understanding of theology and of humanity's place in the world to contemplate a continuing planet without humankind.

This is a bleak question with which to end this introduction, and it is right to remember that the natural world has often been contested space for Christians, to be embraced as God's bounty or to be despised as the consequence of humanity's turning away from God. For most, of course, nature occupied a space somewhere between these extremes, and the essays in this volume testify both to the variety of responses which the churches, Christian congregations and individual believers have made to those questions, and to the continuities which crossed both denominational and temporal boundaries. As technological advances add urgency to those questions it is hoped that this volume will help to provide some historical and theological perspective on current concerns about our stewardship of the planet. It seems appropriate to leave the last word with a Christian thinker and poet who himself wrestled with the consequences of modernity and technological innovation towards the end of the nineteenth century, the Jesuit Gerard Manley Hopkins:

> The world is charged with the grandeur of God.
>   It will flame out, like shining from shook foil;
>   It gathers to a greatness, like the ooze of oil
> Crushed. Why do men then now not reck his rod?
> Generations have trod, have trod, have trod;
>   And all is seared with trade; bleared, smeared with toil;
>   And wears man's smudge and shares man's smell: the soil
> Is bare now, nor can foot feel, being shod.
>
> And for all this, nature is never spent;
>   There lives the dearest freshness deep down things;
> And though the last lights of the black West went

Oh, morning, at the brown brink eastward, springs –
Because the Holy Ghost over the bent
 World broods with warm breast and with ah! bright wings.[9]

William Sheils
University of York

[9] 'God's Grandeur', in *The Poetical Works of Gerard Manley Hopkins*, ed. N. H. Mackenzie (Oxford, 1990), 139.

FORMING THE *SAECULUM*: THE DESACRALIZATION OF NATURE AND THE ABILITY TO UNDERSTAND IT IN AUGUSTINE'S *LITERAL COMMENTARY ON GENESIS*

by STANLEY P. ROSENBERG

AUGUSTINE'S view of the *saeculum* continues to be contested ground; his textual and terminological ambiguities, his own intellectual developments, and possible contradictions have fed contrasting interpretations.[1] Understanding Augustine's view of the *saeculum* – that which exists as part of the created order, which is neither in itself sacred and identified with a specifically Christian status nor profane reflecting antichristian or pagan institutions and mores – is obviously critical to unravelling his political theology, which has largely been the focus of discussions since the magisterial work of R. A. Markus in 1970, but it has another purpose too. It contributes to a chapter in the history of science by clarifying the evolution of a view of the natural world which would influence medieval and early modern developments.

Augustine took keen and consistent interest in the opening chapters of Genesis: he certainly treated it as one of the most important texts in his canon. His interest plausibly goes back to the time of his conversion when he probably heard Ambrose's sermons on the *Hexameron*; these could have both helped him resolve some

---

[1] R. A. Markus provides insight on the developing state of the question in his *Christianity and the Secular* (Notre Dame, IN, 2006). These published lectures respond to the debate spawned by his earlier work, *Saeculum: History and Society in the Theology of St. Augustine* (Cambridge, 1970, rev. edn 1988). Critics include Michael Hollerich, 'John Milbank, Augustine and the Secular', *Augustinian Studies* 30 (1999), 311–22, and Oliver O'Donovan, 'Romulus's City: The Republic without Justice in Augustine's Political Thought', paper delivered at the Society for the Study of Theology annual conference, Durham, 1 April 2008. Two others contributing critically to this debate are John Milbank and Charles Taylor. While Milbank is best known for his *Theology and Social Theory: Beyond Secular Reason* (Oxford, 1990), the density of the argument encourages one to look at his 'An Essay against Secular Order', *Journal of Religious Ethics* 15 (1987), 199–244, and '"Postmodern Critical Augustinianism": A Short *Summa* in Forty Two Responses to Unasked Questions', *Modern Theology* 7 (1991), 225–37. Charles Taylor's work has seen many versions but is brought together, if rather discursively, in his *A Secular Age* (Cambridge, MA, 2007).

of his earlier tensions about Christianity and offered the alternative to the Manichaean cosmology which he had begun to doubt in the period preceding his move to Milan.[2] A substantial part of his writing was devoted to interpreting the first part of Genesis, including a cycle of sermons on the book.[3] The number of times that Augustine marshals arguments from Genesis is striking. For example, he cites Genesis 1:1 at least seven hundred times. This prodigious use of a single sentence is second only to that of the first chapter of John's Gospel (itself a cosmological text), which includes some thousand citations of verses 1–18.[4] If one added to these figures the total of Augustine's uses of the first three chapters of Genesis, the number would increase drastically, as, perhaps, would our appreciation of how important this passage was to him.

Augustine's attention to Genesis provides a controlling text against which we can test for continuities and discontinuities in his thought; his continued interest in the text over a span of thirty-seven years, from the beginning of *De Genesi contra Manichaeos* around 389 to the completion of *De civitate Dei* in 426, assists us with tracking his intellectual development. As for the theme of this study, one can detect in his explorations of Genesis an attempt to work out the implications of the doctrine of *creatio ex nihilo*, though it should be noted that Augustine used both *factio* and *creatio* to describe this activity.[5] Testing Augustine's ideas in this way demonstrates that his views of natural reason and the nature of

---

[2] See J. Patout Burns, 'Ambrose Preaching to Augustine: The Shaping of Faith', in J. Schnaubelt and F. Van Fleteren, eds, *Augustine: Second Founder of the Faith*, Collectanea Augustiniana 1 (New York, 1990), 373–86.

[3] *Sermones* 229.Q–V. The tone, emphases, theology, and terminology suggest an early date but these *sermones* are only available in extracts and lack any internal evidence for dating. More broadly, attempts to date most of Augustine's sermons are at best cautious approximations. A recent translation of Augustine's sermons has been included in the series, *The Works of Saint Augustine, a Translation for the 21st Century.* For these particular sermons, see Augustine, *Sermons 184–229Z*, trans. Edmund Hill, ed. John E. Rotelle (New Rochelle, NY, 1992).

[4] These figures do not include sermons and letters discovered since H. I. Marrou offered these calculations in *St. Augustine and his Influence through the Ages*, trans. Patrick Hepburne-Scott (London, 1957), 83.

[5] The text of *De Genesi ad litteram* [= *De Genesi*] is from the critical edition of P. Agaësse and A. Solignac, *La Genèse au sens Littéral en Douze Livres, Traduction, Introduction et Notes*, 2 vols, Bibliothèque Augustinienne 48–49 (Paris, 1972). Translations are based (with some emendations) on the work of John Hammond Taylor SJ, *The Literal Meaning of Genesis*, 2 vols, ACW 41–42 (New York, 1982). Examples of Augustine's various renditions of the phrase are found in *De Genesi* 7.21.31, 10.4.6, 10.9.16.

the world underwent substantial change in the decade preceding the writing of *De civitate Dei.* This development provided him not only with the intellectual vision – the desacralization of society and history which Markus argues – enabling him to respond to the theological and apologetic crisis spawned by the sack of Rome by the Gothic tribes in 410 but also offered a substantially different reading of the value of the cosmos and the ability of the human mind to understand it.[6] While Augustine certainly offered strong criticisms of those who indulge their curiosity about nature, which are often presented as emblematic of Augustine's view of nature, rehearsing this criticism of curiosity alone does not adequately represent Augustine's theological vision.

LATE ANTIQUITY'S ENCHANTED WORLD

A brief excursus on the cosmologies that dominated Augustine's period will set in counterpoint Augustine's distinctly different views of nature and the importance of his work. Augustine inherited a world that was, in a sense, alive for both pagans and Christians. Four major views of the cosmos contributed to this situation. The origin and development of these positions cannot be adequately detailed here, but it is worth noting them in order to show how they contrast with the early development of *creatio ex nihilo* as a distinctively Judaeo-Christian cosmology,[7] and the expansion of this understanding under Augustine. First was the Neoplatonic chain of being in which emanations within the cosmos including the material world are (relatively) corrupted or depleted derivatives of essential being. Second was the tradition beginning with Aristotle and re-envisioned by the Stoics, which treated physical bodies as being infused with souls. For the Stoics, the *logos* permeated all bodies and so all the world amounted to a type of organism. Thirdly, Manichaean rationalism presented a world that resulted from, and continued as the battleground for, cosmic conflicts between ranks of divine beings. Fourthly, popular

---

[6] Markus (*Saeculum,* 11, 43) touches on this in arguing for the significance of Augustine's reflections on the time in *De Genesi* as foundational to his later reflections on history in *De civitate Dei.*

[7] For the early period, see G. May, *Creatio ex Nihilo: the Doctrine of 'Creation out of Nothing' in Early Christian Thought,* trans. A. S. Worrall (Edinburgh, 1994).

pagan religion treated the world as animated by a whole hierarchy of divine beings, which had to be managed and placated.
Just to confuse things, these positions became interwoven in pagan
religion and science as seen in the tradition of the third-century
philosopher Iamblichus (whose spiritualizing tendencies attracted
Julian the Apostate)[8] and later in the fifth century in the works
of Proclus.[9]

As a result, late antique science became increasingly reattached
to various mythologies. Motion required soul and so the whole of
the celestial realm reflected the proliferation of souls as the various
writers accounted for motion of celestial bodies as the activity of
embodied spirits. The world was animated and therefore subject
to the whims of beings. Such a world was not a natural world, as
later science would come to understand and describe it. It was
a world filled with caprice, and as such it is not really intelligible; so it cannot be rationalized and predicted. This view permeated Augustine's congregations.[10] Not just a pagan and a popular
view, however, the animation of the cosmos can even be found in
Augustine's early writings.[11] This would change.

PREOCCUPATIONS WITH GENESIS

Of his ninety-three books, *De Genesi ad litteram libri duodecim*
(often referred to as *De Genesi ad litteram* and referred to below
simply as *De Genesi*) is one of the few works arguably written
for the sake of his own exploration as opposed to responding to
a particular problem or query. Begun in 401 or soon after, it is a
work of his maturity coming after the intellectual growth of the
390s and his elevation to the episcopate; it picks up difficult questions regarding the proper interpretation of Genesis as he sets out
the challenges raised by conceptions of time and eternity, creation,
and the Trinity. It differs markedly from his earliest attempts to
interpret Genesis 1–3, demonstrating that he has taken major steps

---

[8]   Ammianus Marcellinus, 23.5.1; 25.2.7.
[9]   On Iamblichus, see John F. Finamore, *Iamblichus and the Theory of the Vehicle of the
Soul* (Chico, CA, 1985). On Proclus, see L. Siorvanes, *Proclus: Neo-Platonic Philosophy
and Science* (New Haven, CT, 1996). The *Corpus Hermeticum* played an important role
in this milieu.
[10]   Cf. *Enarrationes in Psalmos* 93.3; *Sermo* 223a.2; *Sermo* 360b.8 (Dolbeau 25.8).
[11]   cf. *De diversis quaestionibus* 79.1.

away from the Neoplatonic interpretations that helped him find his way into the Church.[12] Discussions of Genesis which come after the completion of *De Genesi* differ little from it. Unusually among his works, *De Genesi* has no immediate polemical purpose.

Though important to many of his early works, Augustine particularly focused on Genesis in about 389 in *De Genesi adversus Manichaeos*. This work attempted to confront the Manichaean doctrines and cosmology by interpreting Genesis allegorically. Soon after that, he attempted a literal interpretation of Genesis 1–3, *De Genesi ad litteram liber imperfectus,* but he soon abandoned this effort.[13] This failure did not dim his interest. In the *Confessiones,* begun some four years after his failed attempt, he again contemplated applying his reading of the implications of Genesis. At about the same time, he began work on *De doctrina Christiana,* which both expanded his earlier study of interpretation in *De magistro* and developed a theory of symbols, language and interpretation (semiotic) that was both deeply dependent on his cosmology and foundational to his view of human society. Augustine then turned his attention to writing two of his most important works; *De trinitate* and *De Genesi,* his most extensive commentary on Genesis. By his own account, Augustine began *De trinitate* first but finished *De Genesi* first: it is generally thought that the latter was written between 401 and 419.[14]

Augustine's cosmology and his theology of history are closely linked and alteration of the latter suggests that one should watch for development in the former. As others have already detected, as late as 408 Augustine still retained the influence of Eusebius's providential view of history, maintaining the notion of a Christianized Roman empire as part of salvation history, with all the hopes and dreams concerning the possibilities that ought to be

---

[12] Though note that Robert O'Connell argues for continuity in the work supporting his thesis on the Plotinian fall of the soul in his *The Origin of the Soul in St. Augustine's Later Works* (New York, 1987).

[13] *Retractio* 1.17.

[14] See Agaësse and Solignac, *La Genèse au sens Littéral,* 1: 25–31. Elizabeth Clark posits a beginning date of 401 and an ending date of 416 in 'Vitiated Seeds and Holy Vessels: Augustine's Manichean Past', in eadem, *Ascetic Piety and Women's Faith* (New York, 1986), 291–349. Peter Brown concurs with this dating, as noted by R. Teske in 'Peter Brown on the Soul's Fall', *Augustinian Studies* 24 (1993), 103–31.

achieved by a Christian emperor.[15] This was a view that Augustine's younger colleague and sometime 'pupil' (at least as he thought of himself), Orosius, firmly maintained and developed in his *Historiarum adversum paganos*, which has led some to the position that Augustine's own mature thought on the two cities came relatively late, only developing as he wrote the latter half of the work and making its first appearance in Book 11 of *De civitate Dei* written c. 417.[16] Close attention to his cosmology and interpretations of Genesis 1–3, however, shows hints of the changes to come appearing before *De civitate Dei* took shape. He foreshadows his mature position when writing on pride and the two loves of the two cities in *De Genesi* 11.15.20, probably to be dated between 410 and 413 and hence predating the writing of *De civitate Dei*.[17]

What transpired in the five-year period between 408 and 413 which could account for this significant change? Obviously, the sack of Rome in 410 by Alaric and the Goths had sent shockwaves through the Roman world affecting pagans and Christians. This in turn led (or gave opportunity for) pagan intellectuals to blame Christians for their abandonment of the gods that had previously protected Rome; Christians, following Eusebius's providential historicism, were shaken and could not understand how God could allow the destruction of Rome; yet this did not lead to any sort of broad rethinking on the part of Christian intellectuals about the relationships between the Church and Roman society. Can this event alone, then, account for the profound reshaping of the contours of Augustine's thought? No other Christian intellectuals altered their views so substantially, let alone offered a substantive response. As there are no other examples of intellectuals changing their position in response to the event, the validity of predicating a change in his views based on the sack is weakened. The citation of *De Genesi* 11 above provides an indication: there is a significant degree of continuity between the exegesis of Genesis 1–3 in Books

---

[15] Markus, *Saeculum* (1988 edn), 138; this change is found in *epistula* 93, which can be securely dated to 408.

[16] B. Lacroix argues for a late change in Augustine's position: 'La date du xiᵉ livre du *De civitate Dei*', *Vigiliae Christianae* 5 (1951), 121–22. T. E. Mommsen argues otherwise: 'Orosius and Augustine', in Eugene F. Rice, ed., *Medieval and Renaissance Studies* (Ithaca, NY, 1959), 325–48.

[17] Cf. R. A. Markus, '*De civitate Dei*: Pride and the Common Good', in Schnaubelt and Van Fleteren, eds, *Augustine: Second Founder*, 245–59.

11–12 of *De civitate Dei*, which directly focuses on the opening chapters of Genesis, and Augustine's study of the text in *De Genesi*, dictated before he began the later sections of *De civitate Dei*.[18]

Augustine dictated his first commentary on Genesis primarily for uneducated Catholics but this is not the case with *De Genesi*. This he offered for the educated and, it would seem, to pursue his own concerns and nagging questions. He claims that this commentary is an attempt at 'working out' his ideas and that many of his interpretations are tentative.[19] *De Genesi* attempts, then, to work out the intellectual foundations for understanding the world. Augustine does this using a literal exegetical approach which is critical to appreciating the way in which his work helped legitimize the value of nature. Rather than approaching the opening chapters allegorically as he had previously, he chose a method that made him wrestle more particularly with the meaning to be discovered in the passage in its own right. *Ad litteram* should not be confused with modern notions of literal interpretation, however. For Augustine, this implied paying attention not to the meaning of the words in their own right but to searching for the intent of the author. Hence, if the sacred author intended to offer material that should be read historically, a literal reading required historical interpretation; if allegory was intended, one should interpret the passage allegorically. In the case of Genesis 1, Augustine interpreted this *ad litteram* as betokening the revelation to the angels of God's purpose and design in the creation of the heavens and the earth. He focused on concepts which the written signs were employed to convey. This is, of course, central to Augustine's semiotic and hermeneutical approach found elsewhere in his works, which emphasizes that spoken and written words are approximations chosen to represent and convey the concepts in the mind of the speaker or author.[20]

As a number of historians of science have repeated,[21] Augustine notes the danger of churchmen speaking boldly on matters pertaining to the physical from a position of ignorance and thereby

---

[18] Perhaps *De Genesi* 11 may be dated as early as 409 if his comments in 11.15 are spurred by the questions of the priest Victorianus, but there is little evidence for this.

[19] Ibid. 4.28.45.

[20] Cf. *Sermo* 288; *De doctrina Christiana* 2.3.4.

[21] e.g. David Lindberg, 'Science and the Early Church', in idem and R. Numbers, eds, *God and Nature* (Madison, WI, 1986), 19–48.

discrediting the faith. He advocates the need for exegetes of Scripture to beware of driving away those pagans who generally know something about the earth, heavens and 'the other elements of the world' by proffering foolish and ignorant opinions about the nature of the world.[22] Foolish opinions arising about the nature of the world, Augustine believes, result from poor interpretation of difficult chapters.[23]

COSMOLOGICAL FOUNDATIONS

Cosmology was the substructure to wide swathes of Augustine's theology (cosmology here defined as metaphysical speculations regarding the cosmos). Augustine posits a cosmology with a three-fold structure.[24] The pattern of creation existed first and foremost in the mind of the maker. The eternal and unchangeable ideas in the Word of God precede the work of creation; these are the blueprint. The accounts in Genesis begin with this second aspect of creation. Genesis 1 describes the creation of the underlying and enduring principles; these are spiritual and metaphysical realities and not material reality, and so precede the physical creation. Augustine interprets Genesis 1 as speaking not of the actual creation of the phenomenal world, but of the causal reasons – the *rationes incommutabiles*. These *rationes* inform the material creation. This creation was immediate, in which these *rationes* were created simultaneously without any intervals of time. 'One will ask how they were created originally on the sixth day. I shall reply: "Invisibly, potentially, in their causes, as things that will be in the future are made, yet not made in actuality now."'[25] He describes this as the potential creation of the whole world. The actual production of the physical world is the third aspect of creation and is represented in the second creation story of Genesis 2. At this stage comes the creation of the *rationes seminales*, the seminal reasons implanted in the world. These have physical properties and guide the continuing

---

[22] *De Genesi* 1.19.39.
[23] Ibid. 3.6.8.
[24] Ibid. 5.12.28.
[25] 'Quaeret: tunc quomodo? Respondebo: inuisibiliter, potentialiter, causaliter, quomodo fiunt futura non facta': ibid. 6.6.10.

structure and development of the cosmos.[26] Augustine typically uses the language of production to describe this third stage.

COSMOS, PROVIDENCE AND KNOWLEDGE

This cosmology provides Augustine with the means for explaining the ongoing governance of activity in nature. Not all *rationes* are always evident and some are only employed for a particular purpose in time, which helps Augustine to fit miracles into his cosmology; this notion was adapted by some interpreters at the time of the Scopes trial to suggest that Augustine held a notion not incompatible with evolution.[27] By means of seminal reasons informed by causal reasons, 'God moves His whole creation by a hidden power, and all creatures are subject to this movement: the angels carry out His commands, stars moving in their courses, the winds blow on earth … meadows come to life as their seeds put forth the grass, animals are born and live their lives according to their proper instincts'. All are subject to God's providence exercised through such natural means. 'It is thus that God unfolds the generations which He laid up in creation when first He founded it; and they would not be sent forth to run their courses if He who made creatures ceased to exercise His provident administration over them.'[28] The Creator's ongoing power and governance sustains it. There is an order to the cosmos and motion not because of an animated substrate but because it operates according to a structure both imposed and maintained by an external Creator.

Hence, the divinely ordered world is rational and describable. Augustine argues, 'the sacred writer, therefore, was not ignorant of the nature and order of the elements when he described the creation of visible things that move by nature throughout the universe

---

[26] Ibid. 6.5.8.

[27] See, e.g., the report offered by Kevin Guinagh, 'Saint Augustine and Evolution', *Classical Weekly* 40.4 (4 November 1946), 26–31. Debates about Augustine's views on evolution began as early as 1871, before the prosecution of John Scopes in 1925; the 1920s saw a series of such disputes.

[28] 'Mouet itaque occulta potentia uniuersam creaturam suam eoque motu illa uersata, dum angeli iussa perficiunt, dum circumeunt sidera, dum alternant uenti, … dum uireta pullulant suaque semina euoluunt, dum animalia gignuntur uarioque adpetitu proprias uitas agunt … explicat saecula, quae illi, cum primum condita est, tamquam plicita indiderat: quae tamen in suos cursus non explicarentur, si ea ille, qui condidit, prouido motu administrare cessaret': *De Genesi* 5.20.41; cf. 4.12.22; 9.15.27.

in the midst of the elements'.[29] This is a contingent world and begins to present us with a notion of a world which is 'natural' but nonetheless deeply dependent on divine activity. It is a world, a *saeculum* brought forth by the Son and made knowable by the Son. Augustine writes,

> To them [the angels], therefore, it was known from the beginning of the ages [*saecula*]; for no creature is before the ages, but only from the beginning of the ages. From their creation the ages began, and they began with the beginning of the ages. For their beginning is the beginning of the ages. The only-begotten Son, however, existed before the ages, and through him the ages were created.[30]

There evolves from this an intimate connection between providence, nature and natural law. He describes a twofold working of providence: voluntary and natural. Natural providence is God's hidden governance of the world. It is the means by which he gives growth to trees and plants and by which heavenly and earthly bodies follow an established order – natural phenomena. Voluntary providence, on the other hand, consists of the *deeds* of angels and men. By it creatures are instructed, fields are cultivated, societies are governed, the arts are practised, and so on.[31] In humans, this twofold providence affects both the body and the soul. Natural providence controls the coming into being, development and growth of bodies. Voluntary providence controls the provision made for food, clothing and well-being. Both types of providence, likewise, affect the soul: 'by nature it is provided that it lives and has sensation; by voluntary action it is provided that it acquires knowledge and lives in harmony.'[32] It is this latter form of providence on which Augustine focuses in *De civitate Dei* 19. The creation and governance of society is a result of voluntary providence and derives from the creation of the *saeculum*.

---

[29] 'non igitur ignorabat naturas elementorum eorumque ordinem, qui cum uisibilium, quae intra mundum in elementis natura mouentur': ibid. 3.6.8.

[30] 'Ab ipsa enim exorta sunt saecula et ipsa a saeculis quoniam initium eius initium saeculorum est; unigenitus autem ante saecula, per quem facta sunt saecula': ibid. 5.19.38.

[31] Ibid. 8.9.17.

[32] 'Similiter erga animam naturaliter agitur, ut uiuat, ut sentiat; uoluntarie uero ut discat, ut consentiat': ibid.

There is here an intrinsic relationship between illumination and natural law.[33] Just as causal reasons act as intermediaries in creation and are a source of knowledge for the angelic hosts, natural laws guide the courses of natural phenomena and human volition. This point is clear when Augustine states that 'the ordinary course of nature in the whole of creation has certain natural laws in accordance with which even the spirit of life, which is a creature, has its own appetites, determined in a sense, which even a bad will cannot elude'.[34] In *De Genesi* 4 he argues that the human mind, like the angelic, acquires knowledge of the corporeal world via bodily senses so as to arrive at limited knowledge of the causes themselves.[35] This ability is based, however, on an inverse structure: because the eternal reasons exist first in the Word, they are knowable.[36] Certainly such knowledge is fragile and fragmented, lacking certainty, as is seen in Book 10 of the *Confessiones*, but it is nonetheless a form of knowledge. This interconnection between knowledge and the cosmos was a significant step and offers evidence for the relative importance and value of the physical world in his thought.

By making this move Augustine played a critical role in developing an understanding of natural reason and this too evolved out of his cosmology. The second-century Apologists like Justin and Clement of Alexandria accounted for pagan knowledge of the cosmos and aspects of the divine by attributing it to plagiarism, initiating a tradition of accounting for the ability of pagan thinkers (especially Plato) to reflect ideas consistent with Christian beliefs as resulting from acts of pilfering from the sacred books. A younger Augustine, influenced by Ambrose, accepted this view.[37] The mature Augustine rejected the chronology used to demonstrate plagiarism as faulty and, more significantly, had no theological need to attribute pagan knowledge to such awkward construc-

---

[33] Cf. *Sermo* 8.1.

[34] 'Omnis iste naturae usitatissimus cursus habet quasdam naturales leges suas'*: De Genesi* 9.17.32; cf. *De trinitate* 10.3.

[35] 'Mens itaque humana prius haec, quae facta sunt, per sensus corporis experitur eorumque notitiam pro infirmitatis humanae modulo capit et deinde quaerit eorum causas': *De Genesi* 4.32.49.

[36] 'Neque enim cognitio fiere potest, nisi cognoscenda praecedant; quae item priora sunt in uerbo, per quod facta sunt omnia': ibid.

[37] *De doctrina Christiana* 2.108.

tions. Having previously altered his views and concluded that even the fallen retain some shard of the *imago Dei*, Augustine admitted in applying Paul's comments in Romans 1: 20–21 that the Platonists (in particular) may well have understood some things correctly even if pagans generally experienced a greater degree of privation and consequent misinformation.[38] His allowance that perhaps Plato was able to understand 'the invisible things of God by the things he has made' is particularly noteworthy.[39] Thus by this period the noetic consequence of the Fall for Augustine is significant but not as comprehensive and catastrophic as some interpreters of his works assert.[40] The Fall was indeed catastrophic enough to alter original human nature and require the bestowal of divine grace for salvation, to be sure, but it did not lead to the complete destruction of the *imago Dei* and all its attending aspects such as some corrupted knowledge of the *saeculum*. As with other parts of his thought, Augustine's development of his privation theory after 396 played a foundational role in his understanding of human reason both by establishing a relative degree of goodness as a created thing and by setting limits to its goodness and, hence, trustworthiness, in proportion to its level of corruption.

These insights were penetrating, extensive and influential. By interpreting the *saeculum* in this manner, Augustine eviscerated it of an animated presence. The activity and value of the *saeculum* was made a derivative of its creation rather than dependent on a being inhabiting it. The Creator both made the matter and gave it form.[41] This gives nature a relative degree of intelligibility and worth. It also offers its derivatives such as human *institutiones*, which are a result of voluntary providence, a degree of viability.[42]

CONCLUSION

Many follow Peter Brown's assertion that an intellectual landslide cascaded through Augustine's mind and reshaped his world as a

---

[38] *De civitate Dei* 8.11–12, cf. 11.21.

[39] Quoting Romans 1.20: *De civitate Dei* 11.21.

[40] Such a view might be interpreted as present in his earlier works.

[41] A favourite text, cited often by Augustine, is Wisdom 11.20: 'He arranged all things by measure, number and weight'; e.g. *De Genesi* 4.5.12.

[42] Note the connection to *De doctrina Christiana* 2.25.40 and the *locus classicus* for the discussion, *De civitate Dei* 19.

consequence of his exegesis of Romans 7 and 9 dictated at the request of his former mentor, Simplicianus.[43] This essay argues that another, separate cascade began soon afterwards, and took significant form while Augustine was writing his great commentary on Genesis, *De Genesi ad litteram.*[44] This further revolution contributed substantially to the reshaping of his intellectual world. Arguably, in his completed commentary, Augustine decisively set aside a number of visions of the world with which he had been grappling: Manichaean dualism; Neoplatonic chains of being; and Stoic metaphysics (which might also include Cicero's rejection of *creatio ex nihilo*[45]) to name a few. We can detect the results, the scree, of this further landslide in the altered terrain of *De civitate Dei.* Markus argued that Augustine's efforts in *De civitate Dei* amounted to a secularization of history, the empire, and the Church. This analysis presented here both supports his position and argues that the secularization of history and empire derived from the prior secularization of the world (and not just the secularization of time). Prior to writing *De civitate Dei,* Augustine had already done the revolutionary work of de-animizing or disenchanting the cosmos – in essence, he had desacralized it. During the period preceding and shortly after the sack of Rome, he produced the critical speculative work that reshaped his cosmos. While the sack may have spurred Augustine to new interpretations of society, he did this with the benefit of his speculative work on Genesis. This explains Augustine's unique ability to respond to the altered landscape after 410; he had already altered the substructure shaping his own vision.

The interpretation of the cosmos, which Augustine emphasized, developed and 'settled', largely in the first decade of the fifth century, would also have wide-ranging implications for the understanding of nature which would evolve in the Western Christian tradition. He offered a natural world that is contingent, rational, capable of being understood, and worthy of one's attention. As a product derived from the eternal reasons in the mind of

[43] P. Brown, *Augustine of Hippo, a Biography* (Berkeley, CA, 1967, rev. edn 2000), 139–50. Note Carol Harrison's critique: *Rethinking Augustine's Early Theology: An Argument for Continuity* (Oxford, 2006). John Rist offers a careful and critical review of Harrison's work in *New Blackfriars* 87 (2006), 542–44.

[44] The citations above advancing this argument also demonstrate that indications of the changes were forming as he wrote *Confessiones* and *De doctrina Christiana.*

[45] Cf. Cicero, *De diuinatione* 2.37; *De fato* 18; *Tusculanae disputationes* 1.43.102.

the Creator, and maintained by his providence, creation is wholly distinct from the Creator, possessing value and hence legitimacy.

A postscript: *De Genesi ad litteram* was widely copied and used in the medieval West,[46] and Galileo both used and cited it. Its role in shaping the development of early modern science has not yet been adequately discussed, perhaps because many recent narratives focus on the earlier works of Augustine (such as *Contra academicos*) and the anti-Pelagian writings. These overly narrow approaches present an Augustine who has not developed or changed his views and focus too much on the more apologetic works of Augustine as a controversialist (which are perhaps, for this reason, not fully representative). Hence many are preoccupied with the aspects of his thought which emphasize the catastrophic nature of the Fall by making human reason so frail as to be uncertain, and they note the occasional caustic comment about curiosity. Such sentiments, however, do not represent the full range of Augustine's thought or the possibility that his views helped shape later generations' attitudes toward nature. This, however, is a subject for further study.

Centre for Scholarship and Christianity in Oxford

---

[46] Cf. Michael Gorman, 'The Oldest Manuscripts of St. Augustine's *De Genesi ad litteram*', *Revue Bénédictine* 90 (1980), 7–49, esp. 30–33.

PLENTY, PORTENTS AND PLAGUE: ECCLESIASTICAL READINGS OF THE NATURAL WORLD IN EARLY MEDIEVAL EUROPE

by SARAH FOOT

Noli pater
Father do not allow thunder and lightning,
Lest we be shattered by its fear and its fire.
We fear you, the terrible one, believing there is none like you.
All songs praise you throughout the host of angels.
Let the summits of heaven, too, praise you with roaming lightning,
O most loving Jesus, O righteous King of Kings.

(Thomas Owen Clancy and Gilbert Márkus, *Iona:*
The Earliest Poetry of a Celtic Monastery, 85)

EARLY medieval attitudes to the natural world were distinctly ambivalent. At one level the natural world represented the marvel of God's creative power; filled with beauty, it supplied everything necessary for human existence, meriting praise, as in the hymn sung by the herdsman from Whitby, Cædmon:[1]

> Now we must praise the Maker of the heavenly kingdom, the power of the Creator and his counsel, the deeds of the Father of glory and how He, since he is the eternal God, was the Author of all marvels and first created the heavens as a roof for the children of men and then, the almighty Guardian of the human race, created the earth.

On the other hand, the natural world was a dangerous, frightening and erratic place, the violence of whose forces could bring unforeseen devastation, destruction and death to people and beasts at will, a view encapsulated in the Old English elegiac poem *The Wanderer*:[2]

---

[1] Bede, *Historia ecclesiastica* 5.24, ed. and trans. Bertram Colgrave and R. A. B. Mynors, *Bede's Ecclesiastical History of the English People* (Oxford, 1969), 416–17.
[2] *The Wanderer*, lines 102–105, ed. and trans. Richard Hamer, *A Choice of Anglo-Saxon Verse* (London, 1970), 180–81.

The falling tempest binds in winter's vice
the earth and darkness comes with shades of night,
and from the north fierce hail is felt to fall
in malice against men.

The early Irish poem, attributed to St Columba and probably indeed originating within his circle, quoted at the outset expresses this ambivalence well. As a prayer for divine protection from anticipated meteorological calamity, it articulates wonder and fear at the splendour of lightning, while simultaneously expressing confidence in God's power to protect humanity from the force of the elements he created.

This paper explores ecclesiastical readings and representations of the natural world in the early Middle Ages, looking at the ways in which churchmen attempted to reconcile these ambiguities of delight and terror through three specific themes: the abundance of creation; omens of impending catastrophe; and — this one concept serving as useful shorthand for any natural disaster — plague. The discussion is restricted to western Europe and to the sixth to tenth centuries, the period of the Christianization of Europe through the missionary efforts of monks and other clergy from Rome, Ireland and — after its own conversion — Anglo-Saxon England. Concentration on this period enables us to explore how Christianity shaped the articulation of contemporary ideas about humanity's relationship with the natural world before the arrival in the West of Greek and Arabic scientific texts that challenged earlier medieval worldviews.[3] In the earlier Middle Ages, it was not possible to separate natural phenomena, governed by physical and natural laws, from mystical or supernatural phenomena which defied rational explanation; all was governed by the hand and will of the Almighty. Interestingly, no word in Old English denoted nature in our sense of the natural world; there is an Old English noun for nature as in essence, or character, and one describing the whole world, the

---

[3] Karen Jolly, 'Father God and Mother Earth: Nature-Mysticism in the Anglo-Saxon World', in Joyce E Salisbury, ed., *The Medieval World of Nature: A Book of Essays* (New York, 1993), 221–52, at 224–25. For discussion of the 'discovery' of nature in the twelfth-century renaissance, see M.-D. Chenu, 'Nature and Man — the Renaissance of the Twelfth Century', in *Nature, Man and Society in the Twelfth Century: Essays on New Theological Perspectives in the Latin West*, ed. and trans. J. Taylor and L. K. Little (Chicago, IL, 1968), 1–48.

created environment (*gesceaft*, meaning creation), but no one term encompassed the natural world, the tangible landscape as opposed either to a world created by God or to man-made entities.[4] This does not mean that there was no contemporary understanding of natural laws. The Anglo-Saxon scholar and historian Bede, for example, showed an impressive capacity to observe and report natural phenomena such as the phases of the moon, movements of planets and the sequence of tides.[5] But in the holistic worldview prevalent in early medieval Christian Europe, the hand of God was always implicitly manifest in guiding the forces of nature.[6]

PLENTY

Praising God for the wonders of his creation, the beauty of the earth and the abundance therein came naturally to the medieval ecclesiastical mind, steeped as it was in the verses of the Psalter which lay at the heart of all medieval monastic liturgies.[7] As Augustine of Hippo explained in his commentary on the Psalms:[8]

> This fabric of creation, this most carefully ordered beauty, rising from the lowest to the highest, descending from the highest to the lowest, never broken, but all kinds of different things tempered together, all praises God. Why does the whole earth praise God? Because when you look at it and see its beauty, you praise God in it. The beauty of the earth is, as it were, the voice of the dumb earth. Look and you will see its beauty.

In the introduction to his liturgical calendar called *The Reckoning of the Course of the Stars* (written between 575 and 581), the sixth-century Gallo-Roman historian and bishop, Gregory of Tours,

---

[4] Jennifer Neville, *Representations of the Natural World in Old English Poetry* (Cambridge, 1999), 1–3.

[5] T. R. Eckenrode, 'The Growth of a Scientific Mind: Bede's Early and Late Scientific Writings', *Downside Review* 94 (1976), 197–212.

[6] For discussion of the emergence of the term *supernaturalis* from the thirteenth century onwards, see Robert Bartlett, *The Natural and the Supernatural in the Middle Ages* (Cambridge, 2008), 12–17.

[7] Verses such as Ps. 19: 1; 24: 1; or 136: 4–9.

[8] Augustine, *Enarrationes in psalmos* 144.13, ed. D. E. Dekkers and J. Fraipont, CChr SL 40 (Turnhout, 1956), 2098; quoted by Thomas Owen Clancy and Gilbert Márkus, *Iona: The Earliest Poetry of a Celtic Monastery* (Edinburgh, 1995), 92.

listed natural phenomena as a further seven wonders of the world. Comparable to the wonders of the ancient world – the works of men – the works of nature were fundamentally different; for whilst the former decay and fall into ruin, the wonders of creation – the tidal movement of the sea, the fruits of the earth, the manifestations of God's heavenly powers – being constantly renewed, never perish.[9] For Gregory, contemplation of the mystery and miracle of continuously renewed and revitalized creation provided some consolation for the mutability of earthly existence.[10]

While much early medieval Christian literature expresses love of nature and praise for God's creation, the popular mind associates these themes overwhelmingly with Ireland and the Celtic world in general.[11] Characterized not by elaborate or sustained descriptions of scenery but by almost haiku-like brevity, such literature is typified in an Irish poem, 'The Blackbird':[12]

> Blackbird, it is well for you
> wherever in the thicket be your nest,
> hermit that sounds no bell,
> sweet, soft fairylike is your note.

Longer, but no less evocative is the celebrated verse, 'The Hermit', which begins:

> I have a bothy in the wood –
> none know it but the Lord my God;
> one wall an ash, the other hazel,
> and a great fern makes the wall.

Having described his hut (and the blackbird singing on its gable), the hermit goes on to praise the wonders, and above all the plenty of the natural world around him, singing of 'Trees of apples huge and magic'; and 'Crops in fistfuls from clustered hazel', eggs, honey and berries.[13] Much has been made of these lyrical evocations of the natural world and its abundant goodness, but we need to

---

[9] *De cursu stellarum ratio* 9, ed. B. Krusch, MGH SRM I.2 (Hanover, 1885), 860; trans. Giselle de Nie, 'The Spring, the Seed and the Tree: Gregory of Tours on the Wonders of Nature', *JMedH* 11 (1985), 89–135, at 89.

[10] De Nie, 'The Spring', 130–31.

[11] Kuno Meyer, *Selections from Ancient Irish Poetry* (London, 1911), xii–xiii.

[12] James Carney, *Medieval Irish Lyrics* (Dublin, 1967), 82–83 (no. 34).

[13] Carney, *Medieval Irish Lyrics*, 68–69 (no. 27, stanzas 5 and 9).

be cautious before reading back too many of our own idealistic images, and particularly any contemporary environmental
concerns, into this literature. At one time this Irish poetry was
considered a distinct genre, written by hermit poets, who lived
unlike us, in close proximity to nature, communing with its fecund
abundance in summer, or alternatively facing the closeness of the
natural world as a curse:[14]

> Grey branches have wounded me,
> they have torn my hands;
> the briars have not left
> the making of a girdle for my feet.

Donnchadh Ó Corráin has, however, recently cast doubt on this
notion and shown that these were in fact men just like us, 'literary
men whose lives were lived out, as teachers and administrators, in
the great monastic towns … cultivated and scholarly men writing
to meet the needs and taste of a cultural elite'.[15] The poem just
quoted with its apparent evocation of the joys of a solitary hermit
was more plausibly written to celebrate the foundation of a new
monastic community.

Commenting on another specific, charming verse called
'Writing out of doors', in which the poet looks over his lined
book at a wall of woodland, listens to the trilling of the birds, and
enjoys the clear-voiced cuckoo singing in a cloak of bush-tops,
Patrick Ford has taken Ó Corráin's argument yet further. After
examining the place of that verse in its manuscript context – the
margin of a copy of Priscian's grammar now in Sankt Gallen, at the
foot of a page on which the text tackles infixed pronouns – Ford
has demonstrated that the point of the verse is to show the use of
the first person singular pronoun in its various cases at different
points in the poetic metre. It has nothing, therefore, directly to do
with the rural idyll it pretends to depict, but arose rather in a busy
and noisy monastic school room.[16]

---

14 *Buile Suibne*, quoted by Clancy and Márkus, *Iona*, 91.
15 Donnchadh Ó Corráin, 'Early Irish Hermit Poetry?', in idem et al., eds, *Sages,
Saints and Story Tellers: Celtic Studies in Honour of Professor James Carney* (Maynooth,
1989), 251–67, at 254.
16 Patrick Ford, 'Blackbirds, Cuckoos, and Infixed Pronouns: Another Context for
Early Irish Nature Poetry', in Ronald Black et al., eds, *Celtic Connections: Proceedings*

Pastoral themes occur similarly in poetry written in Frankia during the Carolingian renaissance, some of it echoing the same notions of rural idyll, such as Alcuin's elegy on his life at Aachen which begins:[17]

> O my cell, my sweet beloved dwelling,
> forever and ever, o [sic] my cell, farewell.
> Trees with rustling boughs surround you on all sides
> a little wood always lush with blooming foliage.

Yet this image of a *locus amoenus*, an idealized pleasant place, results not from Alcuin's direct observation but emerges rather from his melancholy imagination; the theme of the poem is loss and temporal mutability. Here pastoral imagery functions metaphorically for the spiritual and didactic pleasures of the court that Alcuin can no longer enjoy.[18] This poem, and Alcuin's lament for a nightingale, cannot be read simply as pastoral eclogues,[19] although other poems, such as Alcuin's imaginative text 'Conflict between Spring and Winter' or Sedulius Scottus's debate between the rose and the lily, do offer straightforward praise for the beauty of the earth, for summer's fertility and the provision of abundant plenty.[20] Walahfrid Strabo more directly praised the produce of the earth in his lengthy poem on the cultivation of a monastic garden written while he was Abbot of Reichenau, where acute observation characterizes his descriptions of individual plants.

But not all images of the natural world in this literature depict the fecundity of the earth, nor is the natural world uniformly conveyed in favourable terms as a place of plenty or comfort. In a plea for patronage, Sedulius Scottus lamented:[21]

---

of the 10th International Congress of Celtic Studies. 1: Language, Literature, History, Culture (East Linton, 1999), 162–70.

[17] O mea cella, in Poetry of the Carolingian Renaissance, ed. and trans. Peter Godman (Norman, OK, 1985), no. 9, lines 1–5, 7–8 (124–25); see also Godman's comments (18–19).

[18] Ibid., lines 25–28.

[19] Ibid., no. 13 (144–45); here, as Godman explained (20), 'the nightingale, recalling a series of delicate analogies between Creator and creation, becomes symbolic of the relationship between man and God'.

[20] Alcuin, Conflictus veris et hiemis: ibid., no. 14 (144–49); Sedulius Scottus, 'Debate of the rose and the lily': ibid., no. 45 (282–87).

[21] Scottus, 'Plea for patronage': ibid., no. 46 (286–87).

The gust of the north wind are blowing and there are signs
of snow;
they terrify us with their sudden threatening movements;
the earth itself trembles, stricken by great fear,
the sea murmurs and the hard stones groan, as the wind
from the north
sweeps on its violent way through the expanses of heaven
with thunder-claps and terrible rumblings.

Anglo-Saxon religious poetry offers similarly stark contrast
between the disagreeable aspects of life on earth and the joys of
heaven, especially those of the lost paradise of Eden. Greenness is
one of the recurrent themes of this verse, often used as a synonym
for fertility and fecundity,[22] as for example in the poem *Genesis
A*. When Noah stepped back onto the earth again after the flood,
God told him to enjoy its greenness:

> Be fruitful now and increase and enjoy your glory and security
> with gladness; fill the earth and multiply all things. Into your
> authority is given the patrimony and the contents of the ocean
> and the birds of heaven and the wild beasts and the earth all
> verdant and its teeming wealth.

As Noah followed his instructions, tilling and sowing the earth
diligently, so 'the green earth with its year-bright gift brought
its bright fruits to him'.[23] In the Old English calendar poem
the *Menologium*, the loss of greenness in November symbolizes
the beginning of winter: 'fettered at the Father's bidding, so the
garment of grounds, the green of meadow must fade from us'.[24]
The month of May, however, marks the beginning of summer,
promising fertility and so eventual fruitfulness; its 'sun-brightsome
days, and warming weathers' mean that 'the meads / bloom with

[22] Hugh Magennis, *Images of Community in Old English Poetry* (Cambridge, 1996),
147–48.
[23] *Genesis A*, lines 1512–17, 1560–61: trans. Kathleen Barrar, 'A Spacious, Green and
Hospitable Land: Paradise in Old English Poetry', *BJRL* 86.2 (2004), 105–25, at 112.
See also Ananya Jahanara Kabir, *Paradise, Death and Domesday in Anglo-Saxon Literature*
(Cambridge 2001), 141–45.
[24] *Menologium*, lines 205–207a, trans. Kemp Malone, 'The Old English Calendar
Poem', in E. Bagby Atwood and Archibald A. Hill, eds, *Studies in Language, Literature,
and Culture of the Middle Ages and Later* (Austin, TX, 1969), 193–99, at 198.

blossoms, and the bliss mounts up, / over middle-earth'.[25] August fulfils the promised abundance, 'with lovely wealth'.[26]

A tenth-century text, the Old English rune poem, takes the letters of the runic alphabet, the *futhorc*, explaining in verse what each one means, often with reference to the natural world and its produce. Day symbolizes the Almighty: 'Day is sent by the Lord, beloved by mankind, the glorious light of the Creator, a source of joy and hope to the haves and have-nots, of benefit to everyone'.[27] The rune called *ger*, the word for year, means not the calendar of the months but rather the cycle of the productive, fruitful year and thus harvest: [28]

> Harvest is a joy to men, when God
> the holy king of heaven, makes the earth bring forth
> bright fruits for rich and poor alike.

Yet earth itself, the final, twenty-ninth character of this alphabet, *ear*, here symbolizes not the good soil with its potential for fruitful life as, for example, in the parable of the sower,[29] but the death of the grave:[30]

> Earth is loathsome to every man,
> when irresistibly the flesh,
> the dead body begins to grow cold,
> the livid one to choose earth as its bedfellow;
> fruits fail, joys vanish, man-made covenants are broken.

That ambivalence about the natural world and uncertainty as to whether it was necessarily always a force for good is never far away.

In many early medieval saints' lives, the natural world functioned as a device through which an individual's sanctity might be made manifest. Sometimes nature ministered to a saint, as for example when an eagle fed the wandering Cuthbert and the boy travelling with him;[31] a pair of ravens, previously chastized for taking for

---

[25] *Menologium*, lines 90b–92a (195–96).
[26] Ibid., lines 140b–143a (197).
[27] *The Old English Rune Poem*, ed. and trans. Maureen Halsall (Toronto, ON, 1981), 92–93 (no. 24).
[28] Ibid. 88–89.
[29] Matt. 13: 3–9, 18–23.
[30] *Old English Rune Poem*, no. 29, trans. Halsall, 92–93; for commentary, ibid. 160–63.
[31] Anon, Life of St Cuthbert 2.5, ed. and trans. Bertram Colgrave, *Two Lives of St Cuthbert* (Cambridge, 1940), 86–87.

their own nest materials from the thatch of the roof that Cuthbert had made over a guest house on Farne, made their apology by bringing him some lumps of lard with which to grease his boots;[32] or sea-otters dried his feet with their fur after he had spent all night submerged beneath the waves in prayer.[33] Various Irish saints demonstrated control over wild animals which others feared; for example, Brigit acted as mistress of foxes and other creatures; Columba, when confronted in solitary prayer by a wild boar, charged it to drop dead (which it obligingly did); and in several stories flocks of sheep, herds of pigs, cattle or horses might appear or disappear at a saint's command.[34] The natural world frequently played a direct role in conversion-narratives, demonstrating to hesitant unbelievers the power of the Christian God, often through the miraculous provision of plentiful supplies of food. When Wilfrid, travelling to Rome in 678/9, preached en route to pagans in Frisia, 'the catch of fish that year proved unusually large and the year was more than usually fruitful in every kind of produce'.[35] Similarly, a few years later when Wilfrid preached to the still-pagan population in Sussex, he rescued the people from a terrible famine that had assailed the populace, for 'on the very day on which the people received the baptism of faith, a gentle but ample rain fell; the earth revived, the fields once more became green, and a happy and fruitful season followed'.[36] Earth where saints had once been martyred could prove especially fruitful: Gregory of Tours told of a tree that grew on the place near Arles, where the martyr Genesius had been decapitated, whose bark had healing properties,[37] and described the beneficial effects of the grass planted over the tomb of St Gall (to keep it cool in the

[32] Ibid. 3.5 (100–03).

[33] Ibid. 2.3 (80–81). On this incident, see also, in this volume, Olga Gusakova, 'A Saint and the Natural World: A Motif of Obedience in three early Anglo-Saxon Saints' Lives', 42–52.

[34] Lisa Bitel, *Isle of the Saints: Monastic Settlement and Christian Community in Early Ireland* (Ithaca, NY, 1990; paperback edn, Cork, 1993), 33–34.

[35] Stephen, *Life of Bishop Wilfrid*, ch. 26, ed. and trans. Bertram Colgrave, *The Life of Bishop Wilfrid by Eddius Stephanus* (Cambridge, 1927), 52–53.

[36] Bede, *Historia ecclesiastica* 4.13 (ed. and trans. Colgrave and Mynors, 372–75).

[37] Gregory of Tours, *Liber in gloria martyrum*, ch. 67, trans. Raymond van Dam, *Gregory of Tours, Glory of the Martyrs* (Liverpool, 1988), 91; quoted by Giselle De Nie, 'Caesarius of Arles and Gregory of Tours: Two Sixth-Century Gallic Bishops and Christian Magic', in Doris Edel, ed., *Cultural Identity and Cultural Integration: Ireland and Europe in the Early Middle Ages* (Dublin, 1995), 170–96, at 191.

heat).[38] On another occasion, a former sacred fountain, converted to Christian use for the sacrament of baptism, behaved most oddly so that when the faithful arrived on Easter morning the water in the spring was piled up high 'like wheat poured into a measure'; the people brought amphorae, filled them up and carried the water to irrigate their fields and vineyards to ensure their future prosperity, yet the heap never diminished.[39]

Such images of saints' capacity to harness the beneficial attributes of the natural world to their own ends should not lead us to forget the fundamental early medieval perception that irrational and unpredictable forces governed the natural world. [40] Rather than wait for disaster to strike, Christian rituals could ward off misfortune pre-emptively, as seen most obviously in the practice of holding annual Rogation Day processions to pray in advance for a good and abundant harvest. Antiphons to be chanted in these processions fall into several categories: general prayers asking God's mercy for sin, or help in unspecified difficulty; petitions embodying specific requests such as deliverance from rain; prayers for use in a specific emergency, such as an outbreak of plague; prayers offering general comfort and expressing trust in the Lord; or texts of praise, joy and thanksgiving, especially those prayers sung in honour of the relics of saints carried in Rogation processions.[41]

Other sorts of interference in the natural order to ensure good weather and sufficient crops met with varying degrees of tolerance in the early medieval Church. The practice of erecting weather crosses is attested in various parts of Europe from sixth-century southern Gaul in the days of Caesarius of Arles – who permitted his own wooden staff to be made into a cross and erected in a

---

[38] Gregory of Tours, *Vitae patrum* 6.7, trans. Edward James, *Gregory of Tours: Life of the Fathers* (Liverpool, 1985), 41; quoted by Valerie Flint, *The Rise of Magic in Early Medieval Europe* (Oxford, 1991), 270.

[39] Gregory of Tours, *Liber in gloria martyrum*, ch. 23 (trans. van Dam, 42); quoted by Flint, *The Rise of Magic*, 268.

[40] A sentiment encapsulated most succinctly in the Old English poem, *The Fortunes of Men*, which describes the birth of an infant and then states: 'God alone knows what, while the child grows, the winter will bring' (lines 8–9), going on to list the various different fates that might befall the hapless adult; 'Such things are not man's to control' (line 14): G. P. Krapp and E. V. K. Dobbie, eds, *The Exeter Book*, Anglo-Saxon Poetic Records 3 (New York, 1936), 154.

[41] Terence Bailey, *The Processions of Sarum and the Western Church* (Toronto, ON, 1971), 94–97, 128–31.

high place, after which the Lord allowed the crops to be protected from it by hail – to tenth- and eleventh-century Germany, where prayers for blessing weather crosses against the aery powers and evil spirits to whom power is given to harm the land and for those crosses which protect against ice and spirits appear in monastic formularies.[42] How did the Church respond when portents and divine prognostications foretold impending disasters?

PORTENTS

Astronomical phenomena such as eclipses of sun and moon, shooting stars, comets, or unexpected planetary movements and abnormal occurrences in the natural environment, including bizarre behaviour among animals and plants, all found regular mention in early medieval annals.[43] Irish annals reported in 691 that the moon turned to the colour of blood on the feast of the nativity of St Martin (11 November),[44] that a huge dragon was seen with great thunder after it at the end of autumn in 735,[45] and under several years solar and lunar eclipses or the appearance of a comet (in 917, comets plural).[46] Did these events find place in the written record because contemporaries saw them as portents, or did they record acute astronomical observation, mirroring the substantial ecclesiastical interest in the workings of the natural world attested elsewhere?[47] Turning to the English sources, we find similar preoccupations; under the year 776 the Anglo-Saxon Chronicle recorded laconically: 'In this year a red cross appeared in the sky after sunset. And that year the Mercians and the people

---

[42] Flint, *Rise of Magic*, 189.

[43] Bartlett, *Natural and Supernatural*, 51–70.

[44] *The Annals of Ulster (to AD 1131)*, s.a. 692, ed. Seán Mac Airt and Gearóid Mac Niocaill (Dublin, 1983), 154–55; also recorded in the *Chronicon Scotorum*, Annals of Tigernach and Annals of Clonmacnoise: Aidan Breen and Daniel McCarthy, 'Astronomical Observations in the Irish Annals and their Motivation,' *Peritia* 11 (1997), 1–43, at 13.

[45] *Annals of Ulster*, s.a. 735 (ed. Mac Airt and Mac Niocaill, 188–89); also recorded in the *Annals of Tigernach* in the same year: Breen and McCarthy, 'Astronomical Observations', 13.

[46] Listed and discussed by Breen and McCarthy, 'Astronomical Observations', 10–19.

[47] For this early Irish interest in the workings of nature, see Marina Smyth, *Understanding the Universe in Seventh-Century Ireland* (Woodbridge, 1997).

of Kent fought at Otford. And marvellous adders were seen in Sussex.'[48] Whether the red cross was thought a portent indicating the outcome of the battle or prefiguring the occurrence of snakes among the South Saxons we cannot know. Given the annalist's failure to record who won the battle (it was the men of Kent), the second might seem more plausible than the first. Compare the more verbose account of the Annals of Fulda for the year 889:[49]

> A terrible time began in this year. For an attack of whooping-cough from Italy troubled many; there were more floods than usual; civil wars disturbed the regions all around; and plague here and there and unexpected famine were exceptionally bad. The harvest was destroyed by hailstorms and men suffered the lack of crops in misery. But above all else there was a detestable portent in the lands of the Thuringians. For water fell from the heavens not, as usual, in raindrops, but all together like a waterfall, and in three *villae* the houses were carried away in a moment by the shock and three hundred human corpses were collected after they had been swept on to the fields by the force of the waters.

In this last example the misfortunes of the people are clearly attributable to the vileness of the weather, but although the monsoon-like rainfall is explicitly called a portent (*prodigium*) what it portended beyond more suffering is left unstated. Plentiful other examples from Frankish annals of what Scott Ashley has neatly labelled 'portents manqué' might also be cited: strange earth movements in 822; an occasion in 824 when a huge chunk of ice fell out of a summer sky; or the report made by the anonymous biographer of Louis the Pious (known, for his interest in such things, as the Astronomer) that in 828, in which year a fading of the moon occurred twice, in July and December, 'a certain supply of grain was brought to the emperor from the region of Gascony smaller than wheat but not polished as peas which was said to have fallen from the sky'.[50] These pieces of raw material might have served to

---

[48] Anglo-Saxon Chronicle, s.a. 776, trans. Dorothy Whitelock, *EHD I, c. 500–1042*, 2nd edn (London, 1979), no. 1. All further references to this work cite Whitelock's translation and follow her corrected dates.

[49] *Annals of Fulda*, s.a. 889, trans. Timothy Reuter (Manchester, 1994), 118.

[50] *Royal Frankish Annals*, s.a. 822, 824, trans. Bernard Walter Scholz, *Carolingian Chronicles* (Ann Arbor, MI, 1972), 110, 117; Astronomer, Life of Louis the Pious, ch.

construct omens, to explain or account for later events, but they were never in fact thus employed.[51]

In other annals, manifestly written after the events they described, portents specifically explained later misfortunes. A celebrated entry recorded in the Anglo Saxon Chronicle for the year 793 reported that dire portents appeared in that year over Northumbria, sorely frightening the people: 'immense whirlwinds and flashes of lightning and fiery dragons were seen in the air. A great famine immediately followed those signs and a little after that, in the same year, on 8 June, the ravages of heathen men miserably destroyed God's church on Lindisfarne, with plunder and slaughter'.[52] Clearly the celestial signs presaged the first incursion of Danish raiders on English soil, an event to cause ripples of shock as far away as the court of Charlemagne. By the time this annal was written in the form in which we now know it, the meaning of the signs had become apparent.[53] What, however, should we make of an entry in the Annals of Ulster for 664 – another highly significant date in early British history?[54]

> Darkness on the Kalends (1st) May at the ninth hour and in the same summer the sky seemed to be on fire. The plague reached Ireland on the Kalends (1st) August. [A battle and the deaths of various people.] And an earthquake in Britain.

This is the first accurate record of an Irish observation of a solar eclipse. Bede made several references to this eclipse, linking its occurrence in May 664 with a sudden outbreak of pestilence that raged with grievous destruction for a long time far and wide and struck down a great multitude of men.[55] Was this eclipse a portent and if so, how was it read at the time and remembered later?

42.4, trans. Allen Cabaniss, *Son of Charlemagne: A Contemporary Life of Louis the Pious* (Syracuse, NY, 1961); Scott Ashley, 'The Power of Symbols: Interpreting Portents in the Carolingian Empire', *Medieval History* 4 (1994), 34–50, at 37.

51 Ashley, 'Power of Symbols', 37.

52 Anglo-Saxon Chronicle, s.a. 793 (MSS D and E).

53 The earliest comment came from Alcuin, the English cleric at Charlemagne's court in letters to the king of Northumbria and to the Bishop of Lindisfarne written after the attack in June: trans. Whitelock, *EHD I*, nos 193–94.

54 *Annals of Ulster*, s.a. 664 (ed. Mac Airt and Mac Niocaill, 134–35).

55 Bede, *Historia ecclesiastica* 3.27, 4.1, 5.24 (ed. and trans. Colgrave and Mynors, 310–11, 328–29, 564–65); cf. Bede, *Chronica minora*, s.a. 664, ed. T. Mommsen, *Chronica minora saec. IV, V, VI, VII*, MGH AA 12 (Berlin, 1898), 313; *Chronica majora*, s.a. 664:

As every student of Anglo-Saxon history knows, 664 was a date of enormous significance for the future of Christianity in England. For in this year, after the eclipse on 1 May, while the summer sky seemed to be on fire (lit up with aurorae, the northern lights) and the plague advanced across the country, in a heightened atmosphere of fear and anxiety a synod met at Whitby. There King Oswiu of Northumbria, arguably motivated in part by fear of the various calamities affecting his realm, elected to throw his weight behind the traditions of the Roman church in the matter of the method of calculating the date of Easter.[56] This decision rescued the English church from darkness, as Pope Vitalian asserted in a letter he wrote to Oswiu soon after the synod.[57] Both Bede and Stephen (the biographer of Bishop Wilfrid, a figure who played the key role at the synod in arguing the pro-Roman case), chose to omit discussion of the eclipse from their accounts of the synod itself, perhaps to make the strength of the Roman argument appear to have been the central factor determining the ultimate outcome. Yet the words put in Oswiu's mouth as rationale for his volte-face – that he would not go against the Prince of the Apostles, lest, when he arrive at the gates of heaven, St Peter would not open them for him – rather suggest that Oswiu had indeed read the signs, especially the total darkness that had fallen over Whitby at the start of May, as indications that the last days were at hand and the king's putative encounter with the saint all too imminent.[58] Did other factors as well as darkness suggest impending judgement? We should return to the reference to an earthquake in the same year in the Annals of Ulster. No English source reports any earth tremors in this already momentous year and David Woods has persuasively shown that the Ionan chronicler (on whose annals this entry depends) took a reference to a disturbance in Britain, namely the contentious synod at Whitby after which the

ibid. Compare also Anglo-Saxon Chronicle, s.a. 664 (MSS A, B and C): 'In this year there was an eclipse of the sun and Eorcenberht, king of the people of Kent died. … And the same year there was a great pestilence'; Anglo-Saxon Chronicle, s.a. 664 (MS E): 'In this year there was an eclipse of the sun on 3 May, and in this year a great pestilence came to the island of Britain, and in that pestilence Bishop Tuda died … And Eorcenberht king of the people of Kent died'.

56 McCarthy and Breen, 'Astronomical Observations', 29.

57 Bede, *Historia ecclesiastica* 3.29 (ed. and trans. Colgrave and Mynors, 318–21); McCarthy and Breen, 'Astronomical Observations', 29–30.

58 McCarthy and Breen, 'Astronomical Observations', 28–29.

Irish party left Northumbria with Bishop Colman and returned to Ireland, and mentally elided this with his recollection of the genuine earthquake felt on Iona in 685.[59] 664 was a year of great significance, but the earth did not move (or only metaphorically).

To ignore portents might be thought unwise.[60] Einhard, writing some years after the death of the Emperor Charles the Great, catalogued the various signs of the emperor's impending demise with the benefits of hindsight: frequent eclipses of the sun and moon and a dark mark on the face of the sun; the collapse of an arcade between the church and palace at Aachen; the burning down of a wooden bridge over the Rhine at Mainz; frequent earthquakes at Aachen and a lightning-strike on the church there, so that the apple on the peak of the roof fell down onto the bishop's house next door. Most alarmingly, an inscription recording Charles's own name in the interior of the church began to fade from view. Yet, Einhard said that Charles 'either rejected all these things or acted as if none of them had anything to do with him'.[61] His son, Louis the Pious, was distinctly less blasé about portents and prodigies; his biographer, the Astronomer (again writing some time after the event), reported him disturbed in mind by strange signs: an earthquake at Aachen; unheard-of signs in the night; a girl who fasted for twelve months; abundant and unaccustomed lightnings; the falling of stones with hail; and plague of men and beasts. 'Because of these singular occurrences, the most pious emperor advised that fasts should be observed frequently and that God be appeased by urgent prayers of the priests and by liberality of alms, declaring that by these prodigies a great future calamity was most assuredly portended for the human race.'[62] Similarly, although displaying a substantial interest in watching Halley's comet (which was visible for twenty-five days during Lent and Easter in 837) and instructing the Astronomer closely to observe its form, Louis was aware that this was a prodigy that affected him and his people jointly and that comets were usually thought to portend the death of a

---

[59] David Woods, 'An Earthquake in Britain in 664?', *Peritia* 19 (2005), 256–62.

[60] Bartlett, *Natural and Supernatural*, 51–70.

[61] Einhard, Life of Charlemagne, ch. 32, trans. Paul Dutton, *Carolingian Civilization: A Reader*, 2nd edn (Peterborough, ON, 2004), 46–47; Ashley, 'Power of Symbols', 38.

[62] Astronomer, Life of Louis the Pious, ch. 37.2 (trans. Cabaniss, 77); cf. *Royal Frankish Annals*, s.a. 823 (and 825 for the end of the girl's fast) (trans. Scholz, 114, 118).

prince.[63] Contemporaries debated the comet's significance; Lupus of Ferrières thought that there was probably more to fear in it than to explain, since other writers had shown how comets portend pestilence, famine and war, but he also observed that they could sometimes presage the future greatness of a king.[64] Einhard did not equivocate: 'The apparition of the star was not casual but was a warning to mortals to strive to avoid the danger to come by penitence and appeals to the mercy of the Lord.' If only, Einhard said, the devastation a fleet of the northmen brought upon parts of the realm was the disaster this star portended, 'But I fear that what was signified by so deadly a portent is to be visited by a heavier punishment.'[65] According to the Astronomer, Louis certainly took the warning seriously, taking spiritual remedies – watching, fasting, almsgiving and the saying of masses – to ward off this potential threat and revitalize the spiritual and moral life of his people.[66] To his biographer, at least, the emperor's respect for heavenly portents was well-founded. He recorded in considerable detail the 'failure of sun [which] occurred in a preternatural manner on the third day of the Major Litany' in 840 (i.e. the day before Ascension), this time assessing rightly what it portended, namely the emperor's death.[67]

For the Astronomer portents were easy to read. We should, however, carefully distinguish those explanations of heavenly signs interpreted after the event from contemporary responses such as those of Oswiu and his circle in 664 or of Einhard and Lupus who were writing while Halley's comet was still visible in the sky. That God might chose to vent his anger on his sinful people by punishing them with elemental fury, was an ever-present possibility in the early medieval mind. If such signs did not portend

---

[63] Astronomer, Life of Louis the Pious, ch. 58.1 – 58.2 (trans. Cabaniss, 112–14).

[64] Lupus of Ferrières, letter to Altuin, monk at St Alban's, near Mainz, trans. Graydon W. Regenos, *The Letters of Lupus of Ferrières* (The Hague, 1966), 23 (no. 8).

[65] Einhard, letter to the Emperor Louis, after June 837, trans. Dutton, *Carolingian Civilization* (Broadview, ON, 1993), 301. Cf. Annals of Xanten, s.a. 837, ed. Bernhard von Simson, MGH SRG 12 (Hanover, 1909), 10: 'An enormous whirlwind kept breaking out and a comet was seen, sending out a great heat trail to the east which to human eyes looked as if it was three cubits long. And the heathen ravaged Walcheren, from where they carried off many women as captives, along with a huge amount of treasure of various kinds.'

[66] Astronomer, Life of Louis the Pious, ch. 58.1 – 58.2 (trans. Cabaniss, 112–14).

[67] Ibid., ch. 62.3 (trans. Cabaniss, 121); Ashley, 'Power of Symbols', 41–45.

divine anger, some wondered whether they might rather result from the activities of evil magicians, hence the practice reported – and condemned – in various early medieval sermons of shouting at the moon during an eclipse.[68] Several penitentials (handbooks for clergy, listing appropriate penances for the performance of particular sins) specified penances for those who cried 'Conquer, moon!' at the time of eclipses, and those who when the moon was darkened, busied themselves with shouting and witchcraft.[69] The church's argument against these recourses to shouting, shooting spears at the moon or throwing fire into the air was to remind their flock that eclipses were natural phenomena.[70]

In this context we might mention the Anglo-Saxon texts called brontologies, or prognostics by thunder, which explained what would happen if thunder occurred in a given month. Thus thunder in January is bad for men, sheep and trees; 'If thunder occurs in the month of March, it is to be feared by those who are expecting mortality or judgement'; 'If thunder occurs in the month of July, fish are in peril'; August thunder is deadly for serpents, but in December thunder can presage prosperity and good health.[71] Studying the manuscripts in which these Latin and Old English texts occur, Roy Liuzza has argued that they seem to be preserved by monastic communities for practical, utilitarian reasons; they lie on a fluid boundary between educated Latin traditions and relics of popular folklore. While they might seem rather close to the sorts of magic or superstitious practices that the early medieval church tried to eradicate, their perceived pragmatic value seems to have ensured their survival and recopying for the benefit of future generations.

[68] Caesarius of Arles, Sermon 13, ed. and French trans. M.-J. Delage, *Sermons au peuple par Césaire d'Arles*, SC 175 (Paris, 1971), 426–27; cited by Bartlett, *Natural and Supernatural*, 54–55. And compare also Bartlett's discussion of the sermons of Hrabanus Maurus in the 820s: ibid. 56–58.

[69] Bartlett, *Natural and Supernatural*, 55. Compare also the so-called *Indiculus superstitionum* (a list of superstitions and pagan practices apparently compiled in the circle of the Anglo-Saxon missionary Boniface in the 740s), §21: 'Of the eclipse of the moon – what they call "Triumph, Moon!"', trans. Dutton, *Carolingian Civilization*, 2nd edn, 3 (no. 1); Alain Dierkens, 'Superstitions, christianisme et paganisme à la fin de l'époque mérovingienne: A propos de l'*Indiculus superstitionum et paganiarum*, MS. Vat. Pal. lat. 577, fol. 7', in Hervé Hasquin, ed., *Magie, sorcellerie, parapsychologie* (Brussels, 1984), 9–26.

[70] Bartlett, *Natural and Supernatural*, 57–58.

[71] Roy M. Liuzza, 'What the Thunder Said: Anglo-Saxon Brontologies and the Problem of Sources', *Review of English Studies* ns 55, no. 218 (2004), 1–23, at 8–11.

The weather and indeed all the natural world did indeed appear extraordinarily dangerous to early medieval ecclesiastical commentators. Let us turn to our final ecclesiastical reading of the natural world and consider natural disasters.

PLAGUE

Plague fulfils alliterative needs here, but it stands, as already suggested, as a shorthand for any sort of natural disaster. Just as much as heavenly signs, extremes of weather (rain, flooding, frost, heavy snow, hail and thunder, severe drought), attacks of sickness and disease (affecting humans or animals) and all sorts of bizarre behaviour among animals or peculiar plant growth occur in regularly in medieval ecclesiastical narrative sources, usually without explanation. Two examples may serve to give a flavour of this sort of ecclesiastical reading of nature. In his *Histories* Gregory of Tours reported that in 591,

> there was a terrible drought which destroyed all the green pasture. As a result there were great losses of flocks and herds, which left few animals for breeding purposes. ... This epidemic not only afflicted the domestic cattle, but it also decimated the various kinds of wild animals. Throughout the forest glades a great number of stags and other beasts were found lying dead in places difficult of access. The hay was destroyed by incessant rain and by the rivers which overflowed, there was a poor grain harvest, but the vines yielded abundantly. Acorns grew, but they never ripened.[72]

The entry in the Annals of Xanten for the year 873 offers another vivid example:[73]

> Later, in the middle of the month of August, the ancient plague of the Egyptians once again appeared throughout the land from the east, namely countless swarms of locusts, like bees leaving the hive, which as they flew through the air gave

[72] Gregory of Tours, *Histories* 10.30, trans. Lewis Thorpe, *Gregory of Tours: The History of the Franks* (Harmondsworth, 1974), 592–93.
[73] Annals of Xanten, s.a. 873 (ed. von Simson, 33).

out a faint noise, like little birds. And when they rose, the sky could only just be seen, as if through a sieve.

That so many of the disasters described in narrative texts related to the weather is unsurprising; any disruption to the agricultural cycle whether caused by freak weather, plagues of insects or man-made disaster made economies so closely dependent on the produce of the soil particularly vulnerable.[74] Less immediately explicable is the remarkable extent to which imagery of winter dominated Old English poetry from this period. Scholars have frequently observed how slight and unsatisfactory are the depictions of summer in this verse, and how conventional and lifeless the accounts of spring, whereas evocations of winter are much more intense and effective.[75] Rather than attribute this to a prevailing gloom and despondency among early English poets, some have wondered whether contemporary climatic conditions might account for this tendency to dwell on winter above all other seasons. Was it, in fact, colder in the early medieval period than it is now?

Between 750 and 950, chronicle sources from across Europe mention nine extraordinarily harsh winters which stood out to contemporaries as much colder and significantly more dangerous to human life as well as to agriculture than the winters to which they were accustomed.[76] The winter of 763–64, for example, was remarkably cold across all of western Europe and Asia Minor, its severity attracting widespread comment in annals from Ireland, England and Frankia. The Chronicle of Moissac reported that a great freeze oppressed Gaul, Illyricum and Thrace; everything froze so that olive and fig trees withered, as did the sprouts of the new crops and in the following year hunger oppressed these regions and many died from lack of food. The weather became a topic for discussion in letters, too; Pope Paul I wrote to Pippin, the Frankish king, complaining that no one had been able to cross the Alps from Gaul to Italy because of the fierceness of the cold; and

[74] Jussi Hanska, *Strategies of Sanity and Survival: Religious Responses to Natural Disasters in the Middle Ages*, Studia Fennica Historica 2 (Helsinki, 2002), 10–12.

[75] Jennifer Neville, 'The Seasons in Old English Poetry', in Léo Carruthers, ed., *La Ronde des Saisons*, Cultures et civilisations médiévales 16 (Paris, 1998), 37–49, at 37.

[76] Michael McCormick, Paul Edward Dutton and Paul A. Mayewski, 'Volcanoes and the Climate Forcing of Carolingian Europe, A.D. 750–950', *Speculum* 82 (2007), 865–95. The years in question were 763–64, 821–22, 823–24, 855–56, 859–60, 873–74, 913, 927–28, 939–40.

Gutberht, Abbot of Wearmouth and Jarrow, wrote to Lul, Bishop of Mainz, to apologize for not having sent more books to assist the mission in Germany on account of the impact of the past winter 'which horribly oppressed the island of our people by cold and freezing and storms of wind and rain'.[77] Although, of course, these were subjective assessments, the unanimity of the response across Europe implies that contemporaries perceived this as a particularly bad year. Michael McCormick and others have recently demonstrated through study of palaeo-climatic data that these nine years that attracted contemporary comment were objectively colder than normal, extreme winters being the result of volcanic activity which led to the sun's rays being shielded from the earth by clouds of volcanic dust, thereby reducing average temperatures quite significantly.[78]

We might want, therefore, to attribute some of the wintry gloom prevalent for example in the Old English poetry to the fact that, in comparison with our own climate, this era experienced more severe cold. Also relevant, as Earl Anderson has argued, is the fact that the concepts of spring and autumn were only introduced into England, and so into the Old English language, with the advent of Christianity. Older Germanic culture conceived of only two seasons: winter, the wet season, and summer, which encompassed the seasons we would call spring and autumn as well as the summer itself. It took the church to introduce the notion of a four-season year, adding *Lencten* and *Hærfest* to the two existing seasons, so that writing late in the tenth century both Byrhtferth, Abbot of Ramsey, and Ælfric, Abbot of Eynsham, felt it necessary in different texts to explain what might seem to us self-evident, that four seasons are numbered in one year.[79]

Uncertainty about the weather, whether justified by the relative harshness of the climate or not, may in part explain the relative lack of good agricultural news in early medieval annals in contrast to poems and saints' lives which, as we saw earlier, frequently celebrated the plentiful abundance of God's bounty. Perhaps the

---

[77] Ibid. 878.

[78] Ibid.

[79] Ælfric, *De temporibus anni* 4.36–40, ed. H. Henel, EETS os 213 (London, 1942), 36; *Byrhtferth's Enchiridion*, ed. P. S. Baker and M. Lapidge, EETS ss 15 (Oxford, 1995), 12, 112; both cited by Earl R Anderson, 'The Seasons of the Year in Old English', *Anglo-Saxon England* 26 (1997), 231–63, at 231–32.

litany of disasters that seem so to dominate chronologically-organized narrative sources reflected contemporary anxieties about the future supply of that munificence, fears that may have had some justification. Lay responses to the unpredictability of the climate were not entirely passive and some of the Church's ambivalence in its responses to nature reflects deep-seated ecclesiastical anxieties about enduring pagan and superstitious responses to the natural world. A text surviving from Boniface's missionary circle in eighth-century Germany lists a range of superstitious acts seemingly still being practised after the conversion, many concerning agriculture or the weather.[80] Early in the ninth century Agobard, the Suffragan Bishop of Lyons, wrote a treatise entitled 'On hail and thunder', in which he described in some detail the extent of popular belief in weather magic among his flock. In these regions, he wrote,

> almost everyone – nobles and commoners, city and country folk, old and young – believe that hail and thunder can be caused by the will of humans. For as soon as they have heard thunder or seen lightning, they will say, 'The wind has been raised.' When asked why it is called a raised wind some with shame, their consciences troubling them a little, others boldly, as is the way of the ignorant, answer that the wind was raised by the incantations of people who are called *tempestarii*. Hence it is called a raised wind.[81]

Agobard went on to describe how the people believed in a magic land (*Magonia*) from which ships travelled in clouds; these ships carried crops that had been knocked down by hail and perished in storms and the cloud-sailors paid the storm-makers before taking grain and other crops back to their own land. Once the bishop found a crowd about to stone to death four people, whom the mob believed had fallen from one of these cloud-ships.[82] Against this foolish superstition, Agobard tried to explain that, 'if the almighty God, through the power of his arm, whips the wicked with new waters, hail and rains and whose hand it is impossible to flee, then

---

[80] *Indiculus superstitionum*, trans. Dutton, *Carolingian Civilization*, 2nd edn, 3–4 (no. 1); Dierkens, 'Superstitions'.

[81] Agobard, *De grandine et tonitruis*, ch. 1, trans. Dutton, *Carolingian Civilization*, 2nd edn, 220 (no. 33).

[82] Ibid. chs. 2–3 (221).

these people are entirely ignorant of God who believe that human beings can do these things.'[83] Astutely he recognized that fear was the major driver of this behaviour, specifically the fear induced by thunder and flashes of lightning, which led the people, instead of calling on God for assistance, to issue curses.

Across Europe, the Church attempted to focus such fears into Christian rituals. Earlier in the spring of that same year, 591, mentioned earlier, Gregory of Tours also recorded 'a terrible epidemic killed off the people in Tours and Nantes. Each person who caught the disease was first troubled with a slight headache and then died.' He explained that in order to avert the wrath of God and make things better, Rogations were held with fasting and strict abstinence, while the poor received alms.[84] Following a long drought on the island of Iona, Adomnán described in his Life of Columba how the elders of the community took the saint's white tunic and books copied in his own handwriting and carried them round the plain that had been ploughed and sown, three times raising and shaking in the air the tunic that Columba had been wearing at the hour of his death. They stood also on the hill of angels (where the heavenly host had been wont to confer with the holy man) and read aloud from his writings. Immediately, it began to rain.[85] Bishop Chad responded swiftly to bad weather: if a high wind arose he would start to pray for God's mercy on humanity; if the wind worsened, he would fall on his face to pray, but in a 'violent storm of wind and rain or if lightning and thunder brought terror to earth and sky he would enter the church and with still deeper concentration earnestly devote himself to prayers and psalms until the sky cleared'.[86] In ninth-century Gaul, the Annals of Xanten described how the church took direct prayerful action against the plague of locusts in 873: 'And in many places the pastors of the churches and all the clergy opposed them with

[83] Ibid. ch. 7 (221). See Paul Dutton, 'Thunder and Hail over the Carolingian Countryside', in Del Sweeney, ed., *Agriculture in the Middle Ages: Technology, Practice, and Representation* (Philadelphia, PA, 1995), 111–37.

[84] Gregory of Tours, *Histories* 10.30, trans. Thorpe, 592–93. Cf. ibid. 4.5 (199–200: Rogations instituted by St Gall during Lent in response to plague); 9.21 (510: plague at Marseilles, spread to Lyons but averted through Rogations).

[85] Adomnán, Life of St Columba 2.44, trans. Richard Sharpe, *Adomnán of Iona: Life of St Columba* (London, 1995), 199–200; Flint, *Rise of Magic*, 187.

[86] Bede, *Historia ecclesiastica* 4.3 (ed. and trans. Colgrave and Mynors, 342–43); William D. McCready, *Miracles and the Venerable Bede* (Toronto, ON, 1994), 25.

reliquaries and crosses, imploring God's mercy to defend them from this plague'.[87]

No less fear-inducing was plague itself. In his History of the Lombards, written c. 790, Paul the Deacon provided a lengthy and extremely detailed account of the plague that broke out in Liguria in rural northern Italy in the 560s. Presaged by peculiar marks among the dwellings, doors, utensils and clothes of the people, marks that could not be washed away, the plague itself arrived when 'there began to appear among the groins of men and in other rather delicate places, a swelling of the glands, after the manner of a nut or date, presently followed by an unbearable fever, so that on the third day the man died'. Having described the flight of the population from villages and fortified places, the neglect of the flocks in hills and fields, and the inevitable decease of the few who remained to bury the dead, Paul offered an apocalyptically vivid picture of a post-plague landscape brought back to its ancient silence: 'pastoral places had been turned into a desert, and human habitations had become places of refuge for wild beasts'.[88] In the 660s, as already mentioned, plague descended suddenly on Britain and Ireland, an outbreak hitherto little discussed by historians but now analysed in substantial detail by John Maddicott. Two major outbreaks occurred: one from 664 to c. 666, the other from c. 684 to c. 687.[89] Both spread over a wide area, and had devastating effect.[90] Medieval writers debated the causes of plague. To Gregory of Tours, natural and divine causes ran in parallel and might overlap; there were natural explanations for plague but it could also result from sin and God's anger;[91] Adomnán was less ambiguous: the plague in Britain and Ireland resulted from sin, and only the grace of God mediated through St Columba had saved

---

[87] Cf. *Annals of Fulda*, s.a. 873 (trans. Reuter, 71), describing the 'worms like locusts' in considerable detail, the damage they did in Germany and in Italy, and the consequent famine in both places.

[88] Paul the Deacon, *History of the Lombards*, 2.4, trans. W. D. Fouke, *History of the Langobards, by Paul the Deacon* (Philadelphia, PA, 1907), 56–58; quoted in full by J. R. Maddicott, 'Plague in Seventh-Century England', *P&P*, no. 156 (1997), 7–54, at 36.

[89] Maddicott, 'Plague', 11.

[90] Bede, Life of Cuthbert, ch. 8 (ed. and trans. Colgrave, 180–81); Adomnán, Life of Columba 2.46 (trans. Sharpe, 203); Maddicott, 'Plague', 14.

[91] Gregory, *Histories* 4.5, 31; 5.34; 6.14; 8.17 (trans. Lewis, 199–200, 225–26, 296, 346, 449); Maddicott, 'Plague', 18; McCready, *Miracles*, 27.

the Dalriadan Irish and Picts, also sinners.[92] Yet although Bede saw plague as a manifestation of the will of God,[93] he did not equate plague as a punishment for sin and error, perhaps, as Maddicott has suggested, because to do so would fit badly with his wider argument about the last quarter of the seventh century. Then he saw the victory of the Roman party at Whitby (in, it will be remembered, the same year that plague first struck Britain), and the arrival of Archbishop Theodore at Canterbury, as inaugurating a golden age in the English Church.[94] Bede did not, however, shrink from describing the devastation it brought, painting a picture of the depopulation of villages and estates similar to Paul the Deacon's account of the earlier Italian plague.[95]

CONCLUSION

Early medieval ecclesiastical readings of the natural world were, as already suggested, deeply ambivalent. Although the beauty of creation might elicit expressions of joy, wonder and praise, the unpredictability and potential hostility of the natural environment could as often evoke fear, and so encourage in lay minds a return to the potential security offered by more ancient, non-Christian rituals. Many of the Church's responses aimed to harness such tendencies towards a resumption of pagan or superstitious practice towards more obviously Christian ends. While the prelapsarian paradise could be depicted as a place of unambiguous delight, the world in which humanity found itself compelled to live was more complicated. Although Bede did begin his Ecclesiastical History with an idealized description of Britain and Ireland as places of natural abundance, he did so, as Calvin Kendall has argued, by describing them outside time and thus comparable to the paradise in Genesis.[96] Elsewhere human experience of the joys of creation

[92] Adomnán, Life of Columba 2.46 (trans. Sharpe, 203); Maddicott, 'Plague', 18.

[93] Bede, *Historia ecclesiastica* 4.7–8 (ed. and trans. Colgrave and Mynors, 356–59); Bede, Life of Cuthbert, ch. 27 (ed. and trans. Colgrave, 246–49).

[94] Maddicott, 'Plague', 19–20.

[95] Bede, Life of Cuthbert, ch. 33 (ed. and trans. Colgrave, 258–61); Maddicott, 'Plague', 37–38.

[96] Calvin B. Kendall, 'Imitation and the Venerable Bede's *Historia ecclesiastica*', in Margot King and Wesley Stevens, eds, *Saints, Scholars, and Heroes*, 2 vols (Collegeville, MN, 1979), 1: 161–90, at 180; Magennis, *Images of Community*, 129.

was often more than somewhat muted; nature and the natural landscape presented as the antitheses of security and content.

Since the connection between the Almighty and the world he created was understood to be so close that, as St Augustine argued, the natural world represented a kind of great book upon which humans could gaze and there read the greatness of his glory,[97] the ambivalence of the early medieval Church's readings of nature was necessary. Given the impossibility in this period of differentiating the natural world and the phenomena of nature from divine intervention, readings had to incorporate both recognition of the wondrous miracle of creation and an acceptance that God spoke to his people through manipulating the heavens and all the forces of nature. The implicit threat that all these texts convey is one of judgement: the forces of nature – storms, comets, plagues or plentiful harvests – thus reminded human observers of the inevitability of the judgement that would await them in the afterlife. When asked why he always stopped what he was doing during storms in order to pray, Bishop Chad told his followers:

> the Lord moves the air, raises the winds, hurls the lightnings and thunders forth from heaven to rouse people to fear him and call them to remember the future judgement. So we should respond to his heavenly warnings with fear and love, and as often as he disturbs the sky as if to strike but spares us, we should implore God's mercy so that we never deserve to be struck down.[98]

Similarly, in his commentary on Ezra and Nehemiah, Bede explained how in 'disturbance of the sky, the stirring up of the elements and the deterioration into violent winds, floods of rain, heavy snowstorms, parching drought or even the death of men or animals, the judge himself threatens the force of his anger through open signs' and warned that these signs should be read rightly and sin corrected.[99]

[97] Augustine, 'Sermon on Matthew' 11.25–26, ed. G. Morin, *Sancti Augustini sermones post Maurinos reperti* (Rome, 1930), 360; trans. Neville, *Representations*, 165–66.

[98] Bede, *Historia ecclesiastica* 4.3 (ed. and trans. Colgrave and Mynors, 342–45).

[99] Bede, *On Ezra and Nehemiah* 10.9, trans. Scott de Gregorio (Liverpool, 2006), 145–46; cf. McCready, *Miracles*, 25–26.

Fear of the imminence of the end of time runs throughout the period we have been exploring. For Gregory the Great, pope at the end of the sixth century, the terror that would presage the end of the world was all too close, and the natural world bore witness to its proximity:[100]

> You know how frequently we have heard reports from other parts of the world of countless cities being destroyed by earthquakes. Plagues we suffer without relief; we do not yet clearly see the signs in the sun, the moon, the stars, but we gather from the change in the air that these are not far off ... As so many of the things foretold have already occurred, there is no doubt that the few that still remain will soon follow: for the experience of what has come to pass gives us certainty about what is to come.

We saw how the signs, especially celestial comets and unusual planetary motions, were read as threats of approaching judgement in Carolingian Frankia. A similar preoccupation might be thought to lie behind much Old English poetry, which might not necessarily surprise us when we recall with Jennifer Neville how much of this was written down in the latter part of the tenth century, when the fateful year 1000 was approaching. She has suggested that the preoccupation of this literature with winter may reflect contemporary fears of the approach of the end of the world. Accounts of the passing of the seasons in Old English verse often failed to portray them in a cyclical mode, so showing that however terrible the winter, in the end spring will always return; rather poets dwelt on the storms, cold and especially the frost of winter to depict scenes of desolation, implying that the end of the world approached. As the poet of *The Wanderer* wrote, 'this middle earth weakens and fails every day'.[101] The transience and fragility of earthly existence focused minds firmly on the world to come; even at its most achingly beautiful, the natural world conveyed threat as well as promise. This essential and necessary ambivalence finds expression in the Old English poem known as *Judgement*

---

[100] Gregory, *Homilies on the Gospels*, book 1, homily 1.5, ed. Raymond Etaix, CChr SL 141 (Turnhout, 1999), 9 (trans. Robert A. Markus, *Gregory the Great and his World* (Cambridge, 1997), 51); cf. Luke 21: 25–33.

[101] Neville, 'The Seasons', 44–48.

Day II, a vernacular paraphrase of a poem of Bede's on the day of judgement which begins with one of the most extended natural descriptions of early English poetry. It does so, however, only to point to the imminence of the coming of judgement.[102]

> Lo I sat alone within a grove
> Concealed with sheltering cover in the middle of a wood where
> the streams of water murmured and ran
> midst an enclosure (just as I say).
> Pleasant plants also grew and blossomed there,
> midst the throng in this incomparable meadow,
> and the trees swayed and murmured
> through the force of the winds. The clouds were agitated
> and my poor mind was wholly troubled.
> Then suddenly, afraid and despairing,
> I raised up in song this frightening poem
> (Just as you said), remembering my sins,
> the vices of my life and the long period
> of the sombre coming of death in this earth.

Ecclesiastical readings of the natural world in the early Middle Ages encompassed both pleasant plants and sombre death on earth.

Christ Church, Oxford

---

[102] Graham D. Caie, *The Old English Poem Judgement Day II* (Woodbridge, 2000), 84–85.

A SAINT AND THE NATURAL WORLD: A MOTIF OF OBEDIENCE IN THREE EARLY ANGLO-SAXON SAINTS' LIVES

by OLGA GUSAKOVA

S AINTS' interactions with the natural world (with beasts and birds as well as the elements) as represented in hagiographical literature constitute an integral part of a much wider theme concerning Christian perceptions of nature and the place of humankind in it. While being in line with the general Christian ideas on creation, hagiographical accounts of the saints' relationship with nature may reveal different aspects of such ideas and perform diverse narrative functions in various traditions and texts. This paper will look at the Anglo-Saxon hagiographical tradition which was enriched in its development by Irish, Continental and Eastern influences. Thus analysis of Anglo-Saxon saints' Lives is an essential part of a broader study of medieval hagiographical literature, both Eastern and Western.

Three early Latin Anglo-Saxon saints' Lives (an anonymous Life of St Cuthbert,[1] Bede's prose Life of the saint[2] and a Life of St Guthlac by Felix of Crowland[3]) were chosen for the purpose of this study. These works were closely connected on the textual level. The anonymous Life of St Cuthbert, created by a Lindisfarne monk between 699 and 705,[4] is the earliest surviving example of Latin hagiography in Anglo-Saxon England. Bede the Venerable (672/3–735), who composed his prose Life of St Cuthbert about 721, based his work to a great extent on this earlier work. Felix of Crowland wrote his Life of St Guthlac in the 730s–40s[5]

---

[1] Anon., Life of St Cuthbert, ed. and trans. Bertram Colgrave, *Two Lives of St Cuthbert* (Cambridge, 1940; repr. 1985), 60–139.

[2] Bede, *Sancti Cutberti, Lindisfarnensis episcopi, liber de vita et miraculis*, PL 94: 729–89; ET by J. F. Webb, in eadem and D. H. Farmer, eds, *The Age of Bede* (London, 1988), 41–104.

[3] *Vita sancti Guthlaci auctore Felice*, ActaSS Apr. 2, 38–49; ET by C. W. Jones, *Saints' Lives and Chronicles in Early England* (Ithaca, NY, 1943), 125–60.

[4] A. Gransden, *Historical Writing in England c. 550 to c. 1307* (London, 1974), 67.

[5] Ibid. 70.

and used some material from Bede's Life of St Cuthbert, either copying passages almost verbatim or borrowing motifs and details. This paper examines episodes describing relations between saints and nature in the three works in order to see the development of the perception of such relations by different authors and to reveal the narrative functions that such episodes performed in each text.

Discussion of medieval attitudes towards the natural world and their representation in literature and art has covered a wide range of aspects in recent decades. The development and transformation of the perception of humankind's relations with nature in various periods in the Middle Ages,[6] as well as in the works of particular authors,[7] has attracted the attention of researchers. One of the central ideas to be found in recent scholarship, as Salter notes in his book *Holy and Noble Beasts: Encounters with Animals in Medieval Literature*, is the anthropocentric tendency of medieval descriptions of the animal kingdom.[8] Quite in this trend is Hobgood-Oster's recent book *Holy Dogs and Asses: Animals in the Christian Tradition*,[9] which argues that the dominant forms of Christianity became increasingly anthropocentric over the centuries. The relationship between the natural world and saints as ideal or extraordinary humans has also been a focus of scholarly attention.[10] It has been suggested that saints in their relations with nature restore a prelapsarian order in which human dominion is peacefully and willingly accepted by the rest of creation.[11] While analysing the three Anglo-Saxon saints' lives this paper will be looking at how these ideas were embodied in the texts and used by the authors for their narrative purposes.

[6] e.g. J. Salisbury, *The Beast Within: Animals in the Middle Ages* (New York, 1994).

[7] e.g. L. Nijhuis, '"Sumum menn wile þincan syllic þis to gehyrenne": Ælfric on Animals – His Sources and their Application', in K. Cawsey and J. Harris, eds, *Transmission and Transformation in the Middle Ages: Texts and Contexts* (Dublin, 2007), 65–76.

[8] D. Salter, *Holy and Noble Beasts: Encounters with Animals in Medieval Literature* (Rochester, NY, 2001), 2.

[9] L. Hobgood-Oster, *Holy Dogs and Asses: Animals in the Christian Tradition* (Urbana, IL, 2008).

[10] For recent comprehensive research, see D. Alexander, *Saints and Animals in the Middle Ages* (Woodbridge, 2008).

[11] Salisbury, *Beast Within*, 173; Benedicta Ward, 'The Spirituality of St Cuthbert', in G. Bonner, D. Rollason and C. Stancliffe, eds, *St Cuthbert, his Cult and his Community to AD 1200* (Woodbridge, 1989), 65–76, at 72; G. Mursell, *English Spirituality: From Earliest Times to 1700* (London, 2001), 42.

Forms and characteristics of the animals found in medieval literature may differ according to the genre or the type of text. Moreover, as Salter has noted, 'the narrative function of animals and the range of meanings attributed to them – whether symbolic, allegorical or metaphorical – vary dramatically from text to text and frequently from page to page'.[12] Thus the same stories may play different roles in various texts. Cavill, in his article 'Some Dynamics of Story-Telling: Animals in the Early Lives of St Cuthbert', presents a thorough analysis of the adjustments Bede made to the animal stories he borrowed from the anonymous Life of St Cuthbert and of their semantics. He suggests that sometimes Bede was uneasy with the material in the anonymous Life and that he 'deprives animals of their place in an order that glorifies God in his saints *by nature*' (Cavill's italics) making them more functional and less natural and central than in the anonymous Life. Cavill argues that the changes made by Bede 'demonstrate his lack of sympathy for the popular Celtic understanding of animals as independent and natural and basically good' while Bede 'wants to control and domesticate' them.[13] I hope to show that changes Bede made to the animal stories were all aimed at constructing a certain model of the saint's relations with the natural world and that such a model had a strong didactic connotation in the text.

★ ★ ★

Both Lives of St Cuthbert contain several episodes of the saint's relations with nature. One of the most famous of those stories relates how Cuthbert when visiting the monastery at Coldingham was ministered to by two sea animals (otters in Bede's version) that wiped and warmed the saint's feet after his prayer in the sea.[14] Though Bede made no significant alterations to the sequence of the events in this episode, some changes both in style and seman-

---

[12] Salter, *Holy and Noble Beasts,* 4.

[13] P. Cavill, 'Some Dynamics of Story-Telling: Animals in the Early Lives of St Cuthbert', *Nottingham Medieval Studies* 43 (1999), 1–20.

[14] Anon., Life of St Cuthbert 2.3; Bede, *Sancti Cutberti* 10. For the Irish ascetic practice of praying in water and its influence on the Anglo-Saxon tradition, see C. Ireland, 'Penance and Prayer in Water: An Irish Practice in Northumbrian Hagiography', *Cambridge Medieval Celtic Studies* 34 (Winter 1997), 51–66.

tics have been noticed.[15] Bede also altered the biblical references, replacing an allusion to Daniel and lions with a reference to the Transfiguration.[16] However, the motif of servitude of animals to a saint was not introduced by Bede but was already present in the anonymous version that styles the sea animals' behaviour as *servitium* (service) and *ministerium* (ministry).

Another story relates how the saint, when preaching in distant regions accompanied by a boy, happened to be in want of food for dinner. Cuthbert assures the boy: 'the Lord will provide food for those who hope in him'. Then they saw an eagle in the sky and Cuthbert said: 'This is the eagle which the Lord has instructed to provide us with food to-day.' When after a short time the bird caught a fish, the boy brought it to the saint but was reproved by him: 'Why did you not give our fisherman a part of it to eat since he was fasting?'[17] When Bede tells the same story,[18] he changes a few words that might, however, be significant for an understanding of his ideas. Thus Cuthbert tells the boy to have constant faith and hope in the Lord and adds: 'He who serves God shall never die of hunger.' Bede twice calls the eagle a servant (or rather a maiden servant, *ministra*)[19] whereas in the anonymous Life it was a fisherman (*piscator*). Thus Bede reinforces the motif of servitude in this passage.

Two other episodes of Cuthbert's relations with the natural world demonstrate how Bede transformed material taken from the earlier text. Chapter five of the third book of the anonymous Life tells the story of the ravens. Once when Cuthbert was dwelling on Inner Farne he saw two ravens disturbing the roof of a guest house to take the straw for their nest. He bade them stop.

> But when they disregarded him, at last his spirit was moved
> and sternly bidding them in the name of Jesus Christ to depart

---

[15] Cavill argues that Bede had less interest in naturalistic details and made the otters more functional than they were in the anonymous Life: 'Dynamics of Story-Telling', 8–18.

[16] Benedicta Ward suggests that by changing the biblical reference Bede presented Cuthbert as 'the New Adam, once more at peace with all creation': 'Spirituality of St Cuthbert', 72.

[17] Anon., Life of St Cuthbert 2.5 (Colgrave, ed. and trans., *Two Lives*, 85–87).

[18] Bede, *Sancti Cutberti* 12.

[19] For discussion of the grammatical connotations, see Cavill, 'Dynamics of Story-Telling', 7.

from the island, he banished them. Without any pause or delay, they deserted their homes according to his command, but after three days, one of the two returned to the feet of the man of God as he was digging the ground, and settling above the furrow with outspread wings and drooping head, began to croak loudly, with humble cries asking pardon and indulgence. And the servant of Christ recognising their penitence gave them pardon and permission to return. And those ravens at the same hour having won peace, both returned to the island with a little gift. For each held in its beak about half of a piece of swine's lard which it placed before his feet. He pardoned their sin and they remain there until to-day.[20]

Bede adds to the episode the introductory words: 'This is the place to recount another of the blessed Cuthbert's miracles similar to one of our father Benedict's,[21] in which human pride and obstinacy are openly put to shame by the humble obedience of birds.' Of note here is the juxtaposition of human pride on the one hand and obedience of birds on the other, though this remark does not have a direct relevance to the plot of the story, which does not include any account of human pride or disobedience. However these words are echoed in the concluding passage that Bede adds to the original story:

'What care should not men take,' he [Cuthbert] would say, 'to cultivate obedience and humility when the very birds hasten to wash away their faults of pride by prayers, tears and gifts.'

The birds stayed on the island many years to set men a good example of reform, building their nests but never presuming to do harm to anyone. Let no one think it ridiculous to learn a lesson in virtue from birds. Does not Solomon instruct us: 'Go to the ant thou sluggard, consider her ways and be wise'?[22]

Thus Bede represents the incident as an example of repentance and obedience that birds set for human beings. The changes Bede made to the episode of the ravens all seem to be purposely aimed at strengthening its pedagogic message. The explanatory remarks

---

[20] Anon., Life of St Cuthbert 3.5 (Colgrave, ed. and trans., *Two Lives*, 101–03).
[21] Bede refers here to the episode found in Gregory the Great, *Dialogues* 2.8.
[22] Bede, *Sancti Cutberti* 20 (Webb, *Age of Bede*, 69–70).

frame the story and it is especially important that Cuthbert himself declares the moral and explains the meaning of the miracle.

The idea of learning a lesson from birds is in line with another story where the sea sets an example of obedience for humans. Once Cuthbert asked the monks visiting him on his island to bring him some wood twelve feet in length. The anonymous biographer relates the miracle as follows:

> He had asked the brethren for this beam but would not have obtained it – and may God not impute this to them for evil – had he not received aid from our Lord Jesus Christ in answer to his prayers; for that same night the sea, uplifting its waves in honour of the servant of God, landed a floating timber exactly twelve feet in length ... And waking in the morning, the brethren saw it and gave thanks to God, marvelling that the sea in honour of Christ had accomplished more than men, in obedience to the hermit ...[23]

The motif of the obedience of nature is already present here. Of note also is a parallelism of phrases: 'in honour of the servant of God' and 'in honour of Christ', suggesting that while serving a saint, nature serves God. Bede reinforces these motifs with several details. Firstly, he adds the introductory passage:

> Not only the inhabitants of the air and ocean but the sea itself ... showed respect for the venerable old man. No wonder; it is hardly strange that the rest of creation should obey the wishes and commands of a man who has dedicated himself with complete sincerity to the Lord's service. We, on the other hand, often lose that dominion over creation which is ours by right through neglecting to serve its Creator.[24]

Here, most clearly in Bede's Life of St Cuthbert, the model of obedience of nature to a saint is expressed and explained. Humankind's dominion over the natural world is guaranteed only through obedience to God. This explanation has a close parallel in the writ-

---

[23] Anon., Life of St Cuthbert 3.4 (Colgrave, ed. and trans., *Two Lives*, 101).
[24] Bede, *Sancti Cutberti* 21 (Webb, *Age of Bede*, 70).

ings of Augustine of Hippo,[25] one of the most influential authors for Bede.[26]

After these introductory words Bede relates the miracle. Here again he stresses the contrast between obedient nature and humans who neglect to perform due obedience to a saint. The monks came to visit Cuthbert without the piece of wood he had asked them for.

> He gave them a very warm welcome, commending them to God with the usual prayer, then asked: 'Where is the wood?' Then they remembered. They confessed they had forgotten and asked him to pardon their negligence. The kindly old man soothed their anxiety with a gentle word and bade them stay till next morning: 'For I do not believe God will forget my wish.' ... The following morning when they went out there was a piece of wood of the correct length thrown up by the tide ... They marveled at the sanctity of a man whom the very elements obeyed, and blushed with shame at their own slackness in needing to be reminded by inanimate nature what obedience is due to saints.[27]

Bede strengthens the didactic function of this episode both by adding his explanatory remarks and by stressing the psychological motivations of the monks' behaviour and emphasizing their negligence.

It seems reasonable to conclude that the motif of obedience and servitude of nature to a saint, already present in the anonymous Life, was reinforced by Bede with stylistic, grammatical and compositional means to emphasize the didactic message of the stories. Moreover, in Bede's text saints' relations with nature are built into a wider hierarchical model of world order where human beings who obey God receive obedience from the rest of creation.

[25] See Augustine, *Homilies on the First Epistle of John* 8.7–8 (NPNF I, 7: 509): 'Mark what I say: God, man, beasts: to wit, above you, God; beneath you, the beasts. Acknowledge Him that is above you, that those that are beneath you may acknowledge you. Thus, because Daniel acknowledged God above him, the lions acknowledged him above them. But if you acknowledge not Him that is above you, you despise your superior, you become subject to your inferior.'

[26] C. Stancliffe, 'Cuthbert and the Polarity between Pastor and Solitary', in Bonner, Rollason and Stancliffe, eds, *St Cuthbert*, 21–44, at 40. For Augustine's influence on many aspects of Anglo-Saxon spirituality, see Mursell, *English Spirituality*, 15.

[27] Bede, *Sancti Cutberti* 21 (Webb, *Age of Bede*, 70–71).

★ ★ ★

While Bede used the anonymous Life of St Cuthbert as a source for his own *Life* of the saint, a lot of material from his work was in turn taken by Felix of Crowland when writing the Life of St Guthlac.[28] At the same time, however strong the influence of Bede was on Felix's writings, it was neither the only nor the predominant one. Another very influential literary source was the Evagrian Latin translation of the Life of St Antony, on which the portrayal of Guthlac to a great extent was modelled.[29] If St Cuthbert combines the ideals of pastor and solitary,[30] Felix presents St Guthlac as a hermit and a *miles Christi*, not a pastor.[31] Accordingly, even while borrowing some passages from Bede, Felix applies them for the purposes of his own text. This also seems true for the accounts of the saint's relationship with nature.

Felix relates a story of two crows 'who in fits of devilry would destroy whatever they could smash, throw in the water, tear to bits, steal, or contaminate', and he notes that Guthlac bore it submissively:

> His pious endurance not only demonstrated his great patience to men but was manifest to the birds and the beasts. His unrivaled charity increased his every grace so much in proportion that the wild fowl of the wilderness and the restless fish in the marshy fen would come swimming and flying at his voice as if to a shepherd. From his hand they would receive the kind of food proper for their species.[32]

Then a passage from Bede's Life of St Cuthbert concerning the obedience of all creation to the humans who serve God is cited almost verbatim. Felix also adds two biblical references: 'If ye be

---

[28] *Felix's Life of Saint Guthlac*, intro. and trans. B. Colgrave (Cambridge, 1956), 18.

[29] See B. P. Kurtz, 'From St Antony to St Guthlac: A Study in Biography', in *University of California Publications in Modern Philology* 12.2 (Berkeley, CA, 1926), 103–46; J. Roberts, 'Hagiography and Literature: The Case of Guthlac of Crowland', in M. P. Brown and C. A. Farr, eds, *Mercia: An Anglo-Saxon Kingdom in Europe* (London, 2001), 69–86, at 72–74.

[30] For the analysis of this theme, see Stancliffe, 'Polarity'.

[31] J. R. Black, 'Tradition and Transformation in the Cult of St. Guthlac in Early Medieval England', *The Heroic Age: A Journal of Early Medieval Northwestern Europe* 10 (2007) [online journal], <http://www.mun.ca/mst/heroicage/issues/10/black.html>, accessed 10 March 2009.

[32] *Vita sancti Guthlaci* 38 (Jones, *Saints' Lives*, 144–45).

willing and obedient, ye shall eat the good of the land' (Isaiah 1: 19) and 'If your faith abounds like the mustard seed' (Matthew 17: 20; Luke 17: 6).

Though Felix borrows Bede's words (that in their turn were based on Augustine) to explain Guthlac's relations with nature, the difference in the two narratives is evident. Whilst Cuthbert banished the ravens for their disobedience, Guthlac submissively bears all the troubles caused by the crows. The logic of the narrative suggests that the motif of the animals' obedience to Guthlac was used to show his personal piety rather than to emphasize a hierarchical model of the world as in Bede's Life of St Cuthbert. The motif of obedience is stressed once again in the first biblical reference added by Felix, though the second reference shifts the focus to the theme of faith.

In another episode Guthlac was visited by two swallows who settled on his shoulders as if this were their accustomed resting place. A monk who saw the incident was astounded and asked Guthlac why a wild fowl was not afraid of him.

> St Guthlac responded to that question that those who were linked to God in pureness of heart were all joined together in God – that those who refused to be known to men sought to be known to the beasts and frequently to the angels; for if they were frequented by men they could not be frequented by angels.

Then Guthlac showed the birds where to build their nest and they obeyed his signal. They would come to the saint every year to seek directions for their home. Felix concludes this passage by citing another phrase from Bede: 'It would not be foolish for anyone to learn the quality of obedience from the birds, as Solomon says: "Go to the ant, thou sluggard; consider his ways, and be wise."'[33] Though Felix's reference to Bede here is evident, Guthlac's explanation of the unusual behaviour of the birds presents a union of all creatures in God rather than a strictly hierarchal model. Here again the episode highlights some spiritual characteristics of the saint and adds details to his portrait as an anchorite: as Guthlac later reveals on his deathbed, from the second year of his life as a

---

[33] Ibid. 39 (Jones, *Saints' Lives*, 145–46).

hermit he was visited every morning and evening by an angel of consolation,[34] which probably explains why he speaks here about angels.

Another story relates how a 'thievish black son of a crow' has taken a glove left in a boat by a monk visiting the saint. 'St Guthlac with a fatherly voice reprimanded the bird as if it were conscious of its own guilt, and the bird, leaving the glove on the ridgepole of the hut, flew off on the dying breeze as if in shame.'[35] The chapter that incorporates this episode is focused on the saint's gift of prophecy (Guthlac knew that crows were in possession of the gloves though he had not seen it) rather than on his relations with nature. Perhaps this explains why Felix passes over the bird's obedience to the hermit without any additional comment.

In the Life of St Guthlac two of the three episodes concerning the saint's relationship with nature have textual parallels in Bede. Felix borrows both the explicit explanation of the right world order and the didactic message that the obedience of nature might serve as an example for human beings. But he shifts the focus in his animal stories, using them to emphasize Guthlac's piety and his spiritual achievements as a hermit or a prophet.

CONCLUSION

In the three early Anglo-Saxon saints' Lives examined in this paper, episodes concerning saints' interactions with the natural world describe wild beasts, birds and even the elements as obedient to the saints. Thus, in their relations with nature, saints restore the right world order, lost by other human beings through sin. The motif of the obedience and even servitude of nature to a saint is already present in the anonymous Life of St Cuthbert. Bede in his prose Life of the saint reinforces the motif by different narrative devices. He explains that the proper relations in the hierarchy 'God – human being – natural world' are based on the principles of obedience, while an act of disobedience destroys the balance. Moreover, Bede creates a strong didactic context for the stories of Cuthbert's interactions with nature, and his focus is again on the notion of obedience, for with their obedience to the saint birds,

---

34 Ibid. 50 (Jones, *Saints' Lives*, 155).
35 Ibid. 40 (Jones, *Saints' Lives*, 146).

animals and the elements set an example for Cuthbert's brethren and for the audience of the Life. In Felix's Life of St Guthlac the relationship between saint and nature fits the same general model of obedience. However the narrative functions of the animal stories seem rather to show Guthlac's spiritual characteristics and to add to his portrait as a hermit. It might be suggested that Felix borrowed Bede's remarks as a ready pattern for describing saints' interactions with the natural world but used them for his own narrative purposes.

It has been noted that recent scholarship points out the problem of anthropocentric attitudes towards nature found in medieval literature. In the Anglo-Saxon hagiography analysed here, an anthropocentric pattern is revealed throughout the stories, in which animals and the elements set an example of obedience for human beings. Such images aim to stimulate reflection upon pious Christian behaviour rather than to explore nature. However, the ideal model of the world, in which saints serving God receive obedience from the rest of creation, is not anthropocentric but theocentric. In such a model, it is not human dominion over nature which is central but the obedience of all creatures to God.

Institute of General History, Russian Academy of Sciences, Moscow

'BLESS, O LORD, THIS FRUIT OF THE NEW TREES': LITURGY AND NATURE IN ENGLAND IN THE CENTRAL MIDDLE AGES*

by TAMSIN ROWE

IN Bede's dialogue on the book of Genesis, a pupil asks his master, 'Why did [God] bless man and the animals, but not the trees or the plants?' And the master replies: 'He blessed these things in order to increase their generation. [But] trees do not have the sense of perceiving or understanding ... Therefore he did not say to the trees: *Come forth and multiply*.'[1] This dialogue raises important issues about the benediction of different elements of the natural world. While God did not bless the trees and the plants at the Creation, nevertheless during Bede's time liturgical compilers were producing a body of material for just such a purpose. By the tenth century, benedictional texts for trees, fruits, nuts, seeds and herbs from different liturgical traditions were routinely included in the service-books of the western Church, petitioning God to multiply their number or else to bestow physical or spiritual well-being on those who used them.

Benedictions were 'the chief sacramental actions of the Church next to the Sacraments themselves', and the office of blessing was reserved for clerics.[2] Formulae existed to 'render holy' a whole range of people, places, days and things – everything, in fact, from the eucharistic host to a cup of beer in which a mouse or weasel had drowned. It was in these more unusual blessings that Keith Thomas infamously identified 'the magic of the medieval Church'.[3]

* I would like to thank the Editors of Studies in Church History and Sarah Foot, Sarah Hamilton and Sarah Scutts for commenting on this paper.

[1] Bede, *Quaestionum super Genesim ex dictis partum dialogus* (PL 93: 259): 'Discipulus: Quare non benedixit arbores et herbas, sed hominem et animalia? Magister: Ideo namque ista benedixit propter propagandi prolem ... quia arbores sensum non habent sentiendi uel intelligendi, animalia sentiunt, et non intelligunt, homo quidem sentit et intelligit: ideo arboribus non dixit: *Crescite et multiplicamini*.'

[2] *New Catholic Enyclopedia* (Detroit, MI, 2003), s.v. 'Benedictions'; L. K. Little, *Benedictine Maledictions: Liturgical Cursing in Romanesque France* (New York, 1993), 92.

[3] K. Thomas, *Religion and the Decline of Magic* (London, 1971), 27–28.

Rituals for crops, fruits and medicinal herbs in particular were seen to bear a resemblance to spells or 'pagan' practices.[4] Indeed, in the 1950s the Dominican scholar Marie-Dominique Chenu argued that liturgical ritual had absorbed 'certain images and practices borrowed from a religion of nature ... not without degrading effect'.[5] But what kinds of images and practices did he mean, and what place did they occupy within the institutional Church?

This paper is primarily an attempt to understand liturgical benedictions in light of existing discussions of the medieval Church and the natural world. It is divided into three sections. The first outlines the interpretative contexts in which nature rituals have been viewed, specifically those of pastoral care and the 'desacralization of nature' identified in the renaissance of the twelfth century. The second introduces the sources upon which the argument is based, and explores some of the problems associated with historical studies of medieval liturgy. Finally, section three considers the contents of selected blessings for fruits and herbs, and attempts to draw together some of the strands of the discussion towards an understanding of their historical importance.

★   ★   ★

Modern scholarship routinely distances itself from the sharp distinctions made between folkloric and orthodox beliefs during the late nineteenth and early twentieth centuries. Historians now acknowledge that the ostensibly profane usage with which nature is associated in certain surveys of the central medieval period still formed part of a learned and pious response to the universe. While prognostic texts and charms have, over the last twenty years, been reassessed in a more forgiving light than Chenu felt able to cast,[6]

---

[4]   Valerie Flint argued that these sorts of rituals were used by the Church to 'rescue' certain forms of magic beneficial to conversion: *The Rise of Magic in Early Medieval Europe* (Princeton, NJ, 1991), 4.

[5]   M.-D. Chenu, 'The Symbolist Mentality', in *Nature, Man and Society in the Twelfth Century: Essays on New Theological Perspectives in the Latin West*, ed. and trans. J. Taylor and L. K. Little (Chicago, IL, 1968), 99–145, at 129; originally published as *La théologie au douzième siècle* (Paris, 1957).

[6]   R. M. Liuzza, 'Anglo-Saxon Prognostics in Context: A Survey and Handlist of Manuscripts', *Anglo-Saxon England* 30 (2001), 181–230; K. L. Jolly, *Anglo-Saxon Charms in the Context of Popular Religion* (Ann Arbor, MI, 1987); A. Hall, *Elves in Anglo-Saxon England: Matters of Belief, Health, Gender and Identity* (Woodbridge, 2007).

less has been said about the liturgical blessings that often provided the inspiration for these forms.[7]

Existing studies tend to relate to the 'pastoral' origins of the rituals, inferred from their relationship to agricultural subsistence.[8] While this is not an unreasonable approach, I think it is also important to look beyond the obvious links between nature and lay spiritual provision. The idea that blessings represented a form of surrogate 'magic' given by the Church to the laity (an assumption inherent in Valerie Flint's thesis) can divert attention from their strong institutional credentials. Liturgical rituals were devised and reproduced in monastic centres, and in many instances retained there. Karen Jolly's recent study of a unique collection of 'field prayers' in the *Durham Collectar* demonstrated how one late tenth-century community actively engaged in 'liturgical experimentation' by placing new formulae for the blessing of crops alongside existing ones.[9] But few scholars have considered the significance of the latter in their own right, or acknowledged that the books in which they were circulated can shed real light on their historical function.[10] Reflecting on the purpose of the formulae from this perspective permits a re-evaluation of the relationship between the Church and the natural world.

The earliest recorded blessings came out of the mass-book (or sacramentary) tradition on the Continent, working their way into episcopal manuals (pontificals) by the ninth century.[11] But by the eleventh we find these formulae appearing in other types of sources, such as prayer-books and *libri vitae* (books principally containing the names of members and affiliates of religious houses, but often including other miscellaneous material), as well as in

[7] With the exception of D. A. Rivard, *Blessing the World: Ritual and Lay Piety in Medieval Religion* (Washington, DC, 2008).

[8] André Vauchez calls them 'parallel liturgies'. He argues that they were designed 'to permeate the daily existence of the faithful with religion': *The Spirituality of the Medieval West: the Eighth to the Twelfth Century*, trans. C. Friedlander (Kalamazoo, MI, 1993), 29.

[9] K. L. Jolly, 'Prayers from the Field: Practical Problems and Demonic Defense in Anglo-Saxon England', *Traditio* 61 (2006), 95–147.

[10] Derek Rivard's broad survey of medieval benedictions does not go into regional or chronological nuances.

[11] A. Hughes, *Medieval Manuscripts for Mass and Office: A Guide to their Organization and Terminology* (Toronto, ON, 1982); E. Palazzo, *A History of Liturgical Books: From the Beginning to the Thirteenth Century*, trans. M. Beaumont (Collegeville, MN, 1998); N. K. Rasmussen, *Les pontificaux du haut moyen âge: genèse du livre de l'évêque* (Leuven, 1998).

more formal liturgical contexts. The twelfth and thirteenth centuries tell yet another story, seeing more obvious regional diversification, and the development of 'Uses' (the Pontifical of the Roman Curia in Rome, and the Sarum Missal in England, for example) with which came greater standardization of content.[12]

The taxonomy of the central medieval liturgy is such that it is not possible to attribute blessings for nature to one particular group of users across the period. This inevitably has an impact on how we interpret them. Chenu claimed that the twelfth century witnessed a fundamental shift in the Church's attitude towards the natural world, reducing the latter's role as an intermediary between man and God in a process termed the 'desacralization of nature'.[13] Theological developments in the twelfth century even now shape the study of nature and the supernatural in the Middle Ages, as Robert Bartlett's recent work on the same theme attests.[14] However, only Chenu really attempted to link these to liturgical culture, intimating that advances in Scholastic thought precipitated changes in service-books, including the removal of rituals associated with nature. He saw the old 'syncretic' liturgies inherited from the Carolingian period – those that combined ceremonies of mixed functions and levels of solemnity – giving way in the twelfth century to separate lay and professional ('pure') traditions.[15]

The general character of the liturgical corpus certainly changed around this time, but the reasons for this were deeper and more wide-ranging. The idea that any were related to Scholastic unease about man's relationship with nature is debatable. We have to bear in mind that Chenu was decidedly unsympathetic toward the pre-Thomist Church, and his views on the dissolution of the syncretic liturgy rest to a large degree on the assumption that it was (in his words) 'degrading'. In fact, the evidence is not there to support so unequivocal a correlation between changes in the liturgy and new theological constructions of nature. Liturgical diversification – in this case the inclusion of blessings in medical books, prayer-

---

[12] This is something I will explore further in my Ph.D. thesis, 'Blessings for Nature in English Liturgical Books, c. 900 1200'.

[13] M.-D. Chenu, 'Nature and Man: The Renaissance of the Twelfth Century', in Taylor and Little, eds, *Nature, Man and Society*, 1–48, at 5.

[14] R. Bartlett, *The Natural and the Supernatural in the Middle Ages* (Cambridge, 2008).

[15] M.-D. Chenu, 'Monks, Canons, and Laymen in search of the Apostolic Life', in Taylor and Little, eds, *Nature, Man and Society*, 202–38, at 229.

books and *libri vitae* – actually predated the Scholastic movement. Moreover, the inclusion of blessings for seeds and fruit (some significantly extended) in the thirteenth-century Sarum Missal also suggest that a linear interpretation is inadequate.[16]

While Chenu's partial – and notoriously opaque – modes of expression make him a difficult scholar with which to engage, he nonetheless broaches many of the areas in which further research seems necessary. How did liturgy and ecclesiastical culture interact? Were the Church's changing perceptions of nature reflected in its service-books, or did liturgical changes occur independently of theological developments? Even though these questions ultimately lie beyond the scope of this paper, some groundwork can be put in place. The present analysis focuses on examples of blessings for fruits and herbs drawn from two books produced in England in the eleventh century: the *Liber Vitae* of Winchester New Minster[17] and the *Portiforium* of Bishop Wulfstan II of Worcester.[18] These sources not only illustrate the consonance of liturgical blessings with the Church's attitude towards the natural world, but also highlight the fluidity of these blessings in the written context, and the challenges they pose to the 'desacralization' narrative.

★　★　★

Fruits and the harvest have enjoyed religious significance for thousands of years, with the ritual dedication of first-fruits playing an important part in ancient Greek, Roman and Jewish cultures as well as in medieval Christianity. In his *Treatise on the Apostolic Tradition*, the third-century anti-pope and martyr, Hippolytus of Rome, urged people to take their fruit to be blessed by a bishop, and provided liturgical forms for the occasion.[19] However, the forms that became the staples of the western liturgy are first recorded in the seventh century. Four benedictions (two for new fruit, one for apples and one for fruit-trees) are included in the Old Gelasian Sacramentary, a Roman mass-book modified for use in Gaul.[20]

---

[16] *The Sarum Missal*, ed. J. Wickham Legg (Oxford, 1916), 455–56.

[17] London, BL, MS Stowe 944.

[18] Cambridge, Corpus Christi College, MS 391; *The Portiforium of Saint Wulstan*, ed. A. Hughes, 2 vols (London, 1958–60).

[19] Hippolytus of Rome, *Apostolic Tradition* 3.28.

[20] The Old Gelasian survives in a single manuscript: Vatican City, BAV, Reg. Lat. MS 316; see *Liber Sacramentorum Romanae Æcclesiae: Vaticanus Reginensis Latinus 316, Fos.*

This text survives in just a single manuscript from the mid-eighth century. Although it was superseded on the Continent by the so-called Eighth-Century Gelasian, which was introduced during the reign of the first Carolingian king, Pippin (c. 751–68), and then by the Gregorian *Hadrianum* and its later Supplement (attributed to the influential abbot, Benedict of Aniane), its blessings were preserved by a process of liturgical synthesis.[21] By the time the first extant book with an English connection – the Leofric Missal A – was produced around 900, a hybrid rite had developed. Late Anglo-Saxon books typically contain a concoction of Old and Frankish Gelasian, Italian and insular rites, structured around a Supplemented *Hadrianum*. Although our blessings for fruits and herbs originated in different traditions at different stages, by this time they routinely travelled together, forming part of a larger assembly of texts that recent editors have described as 'blessings for various occasions' or 'blessings for things'.[22] That examples were copied into the Winchester *Liber Vitae* and Wulfstan's *Portiforium* suggests medieval writers were able to unfasten this group from its original liturgical context – an important point to bear in mind when we are examining function and typology.

The earliest parts of the *Liber Vitae* of Winchester New Minster can be dated to 1031, and they contain (among other things) texts associated with liturgical commemoration, and lists of kings, bishops and eminent laymen associated with the community. This, and the fact that the book continued to be used until the sixteenth century, means that it has appealed to historians of various topics and periods.[23] However, the selection of liturgical benedictions which were copied into folios 50–54 has scarcely been recognized.

3–245, ed. L. C. Mohlberg (Rome, 1968), 233. See also A. Chavasse, *Le Sacramentaire Gélasien (Vaticanus Reginensis 316)* (Tournai, 1958), 461–69.

[21] For full discussions of the development of the Frankish liturgy, see R. McKitterick, *The Frankish Church and the Carolingian Reforms, 789–895* (London, 1977); Y. Hen, *The Royal Patronage of Liturgy in Frankish Gaul to the Death of Charles the Bald, 877* (London, 2001). Gelasian blessings were preserved in so-called 'developed' Gregorians: R. W. Pfaff, 'Massbooks', in idem, ed., *The Liturgical Books of Anglo-Saxon England* (Kalamazoo, MI, 1995), 7–34, at 11.

[22] It is possible that these terms are influenced by the Post-Tridentine *Rituale Romanum*. See, e.g., *The Bobbio Missal: A Gallican Mass-Book [MS. Paris Lat. 13246]*, ed. E. A. Lowe, A. Wilmart and H. A. Wilson, 3 vols (London, 1917–24); *The Leofric Missal*, ed. N. Orchard, 2 vols (London, 2002).

[23] See *The Liber Vitae of the New Minster and Hyde Abbey, Winchester*, ed. S. Keynes (Copenhagen, 1996); idem, 'The *Liber Vitae* of the New Minster, Winchester', in

Among these are two blessings for herbs and two for apples which I discuss below. Analogous texts appear in our second source, the *Portiforium of St Wulfstan*, a small-size prayer book containing an assortment of liturgical material. The *Portiforium* almost certainly belonged to Wulfstan II, who was Bishop of Worcester between 1062 and 1095. Indeed, scholars have reason enough to believe that it was the very 'book of prayers' to which William of Malmesbury claimed the bishop was devoted.[24] Like the *Liber Vitae*, the *Portiforium* has attracted attention for a number of reasons – notably its musical contents[25] – but not its benedictions.

Various blessings for 'apples' or 'fruits' were in circulation at the time our sources were compiled. Three examples are included in the appendix to this paper. The first *benedictio* in Wulfstan's *Portiforium* is a version of the Old Gelasian formula, which was copied into English books from the Leofric Missal right through to the Sarum Missal of the late thirteenth century. The *Liber Vitae* also has this formula as its main text. In addition, it carries an alternative blessing – rather briefer – that I have only been able to trace back to the *Durham Collectar* of the early tenth century.[26] In addition this paper deals with two formulae for the benediction of 'herbs' – a catch-all term in the medieval period for herbs, grasses, flowers and fruits.[27] These blessings do not have precedents, as far as I am aware, in the Gelasian or Gregorian liturgies, but they are possibly associated with earlier charms or medical texts of Germanic origin.

Given that there is little unique or original about the blessings in our two sources, why do they matter? One of the chief qualms historians have had with using the liturgy as a historical source is that it does not represent the beliefs of the age in which it was

D. Rollason et al., eds, *The Durham* Liber Vitae *and its Context* (Woodbridge, 2004), 149–63, esp. 156–60.

[24] N. P. Brooks, 'Introduction: How do we know about St Wulfstan?', in J. S. Barrow and N. P. Brooks, eds, *St Wulfstan and his World* (Aldershot, 2005), 1–21, at 14; William of Malmesbury, *Vita Wulfstani*, ed. M. Winterbottom and R. M. Thomson, *William of Malmesbury: Saints' Lives* (Oxford, 2002), 7–157, at 110.

[25] S. Rankin, 'Some Reflections on Liturgical Music at Late Anglo-Saxon Worcester', in N. Brooks and C. Cubitt, eds, *St Oswald of Worcester: Life and Influence* (London, 1996), 325–48.

[26] Durham, Cathedral Library, MS A.IV.19, fol. 47ʳ. See *The Durham Ritual (Durham Cathedral Library A.IV.19)*, ed. T. J. Brown (Copenhagen, 1969).

[27] R. E. Latham, *Revised Medieval Latin Word-List from British and Irish Sources* (London, 1965), s.v. 'Herba'.

written because it was necessarily copied from earlier work.[28] Two points might be offered in response to this. The first is that medieval culture was, by nature, anthological.[29] It survived and thrived in commentaries and *florilegia* in which copying was commonplace. Benedict of Aniane's description of the supplemented *Hadrianum* as a gathering of 'spring flowers ... in a beautiful bouquet' reflects the wider intellectual context and need not be an insurmountable impediment.[30] Secondly, we have to bear in mind that the books of the early and central medieval liturgy were handwritten, and arranged or modified according to those who commissioned or owned them.[31] The blessings for fruits and other secular objects constituted a distinct group that could, like many things, be lifted out of the traditional service-book context – that of the sacramentary or pontifical – and incorporated into other texts, such as the *Liber Vitae* and Wulfstan's *Portiforium*. And although analogous formulae appear time and again, they are irreducible to form; one seldom finds these blessings organized in the same way twice. It is the interplay between compilation and invention that lies at the very heart of the construction of medieval culture, and reveals the changes that historians of the liturgy seek. Bearing these conclusions in mind, the next part of the paper discusses the light which blessings can shed on the attitude of the medieval Church towards the natural world, before considering their relevance to the problems raised in the secondary literature.

★　★　★

Chenu himself acknowledged that even 'the most stereotyped formulas for blessing cannot hide their modest attention to "meanings" inscribed in created things'.[32] It is to these 'meanings' that we turn first. What do the blessings say, how do they say it, and

---

[28] For example, Y. Hen, *Culture and Religion in Merovingian Gaul, A.D. 481–751* (Leiden, 1995), 49–50.

[29] J.-C. Schmitt, 'Religion, Folklore and Society in the Medieval West', in L. K. Little and B. H. Rosenwein, eds, *Debating the Middle Ages: Issues and Readings* (Oxford, 1998), 376–87, at 382.

[30] Hen, *Royal Patronage*, 77–78.

[31] R. W. Pfaff, 'Prescription and Reality in the Rubrics of Sarum Rite Service Books', in idem, ed., *Liturgical Calendars, Saints and Services in Medieval England* (Aldershot, 1998), 197–205, at 204.

[32] Chenu, 'Symbolist Mentality', 129.

why? Benedictional formulae adhere to a common template, opening with a formal address to God and very often drawing on a biblical episode linked to the function they intend to perform. The middle portion of the formula usually describes that function, and outlines the anticipated outcome. Finally, the blessing is enacted in the Lord's name. As Robert Scribner pointed out, this kind of 'Catholic liturgical practice … involved both an other-worldly salvific purpose and an inner-worldly instrumental purpose'.[33]

In terms of their 'salvific purpose', our rites touch on the concepts of both original sin and redemption. Most fruit blessings contain some reference to the Book of Genesis. The main formula for apples (the first in the Appendix) asks that God 'repel and cast out the ancient enemy and the snares of the first sin' (*depulsis atque abiectis uetustate antiqui hostis atque primi facinoris insidiis*) – indicating the fruit eaten from the tree of knowledge (Genesis 3: 2–6). Here we can see how an important biblical allusion was used to locate the blessing in a wider spiritual context. Moreover, Christ's redemption from original sin was also worked into the blessings for fruits and herbs. Antoine Chavasse alluded to the importance of the Incarnation in the Gelasian texts – a point that can be extended to the other formulae as well.[34] The second blessing for herbs (item 4 in the Appendix) describes Christ coming to 'cure' the sins of mankind, which was a common trope in the central Middle Ages.[35] Belying their brevity, these texts are grounded in the fundamentals of Christian doctrine, and it would not be difficult to envisage them fulfilling some form of didactic purpose.

As I mentioned above, Scribner also draws attention to the 'anthropocentric cosmology' embedded in Catholic blessings.[36] Blessings for fruit appeal for divine grace to bestow health on body as well as soul (*animae et corporis*). While some are designed, in Bede's words, to 'increase generation', ours tend to focus on the qualities of the newly harvested fruits.[37] This concern for worldly issues is complementary to the spiritual aspect, and likely to have

---

[33] R. W. Scribner, *Popular Culture and Popular Movements in Reformation Germany* (London, 1987), 40.

[34] Chavasse, *Le Sacramentaire Gélasien*, 468–69.

[35] A. Meaney, 'The Practice of Medicine in England about the Year 1000', *Social History of Medicine* 13 (2000), 221–37, at 223.

[36] Scribner, *Popular Culture*, 40; Jolly, 'Prayers from the Field', 102.

[37] Chavasse, *Le Sacramentaire Gélasien*, 468–69.

been aimed at both lay and religious communities. Nature benedictions are certainly imbued with a collective spirit: Wulfstan's herb blessing was designed to be read out 'for the sake of the health of the faithful' (*ob salutem fidelium*), while the second formula for apples (item 2 in the Appendix) permits 'anyone who partakes of' the fruit (*hi qui utuntur ex eo*) to benefit from it.

In the blessings for herbs recipients gain access to the remedial 'occult virtue' of nature.[38] Audrey Meaney recently discussed the quasi-medical function of benedictions found in the early eleventh-century remedy book, *Lacnunga*, and noted a contemporaneous shift towards sole reliance on blessings made in God's name in the *Homilies* of Ælfric.[39] The liturgical formulae themselves support this view. In the first *benedictio* for herbs the medical element is actually discussed in more explicit terms than in *Lacnunga*. The formula asks 'that … sickness might disappear, faintness be dispelled, the heat of fever die down, pains in the body be resisted, and all vexing "stabbings" of the enemy depart far away' (*languor diffugiat, calor febrium obeat, dolores laterum et cruciatus uiscerum obsistant, omnisque infestatio iaculantis inimici procul recedat*). In eleventh-century England, it seems the benediction of nature 'with God's words'[40] was upheld both in liturgical books and in medical manuscripts coming out of a monastic context. It was ideologically and spiritually important both inside and outside the Church.[41]

★ ★ ★

This paper started by asking what light the deployment of liturgical blessings in the medieval period can shed on current historiographical interpretations of religion and nature. In particular, it sought to focus on the relationship between context and chronology, and whether the so-called 'desacralization of nature' of the twelfth century had any direct impact on church practices. Charms and natural blessings are highly visible constituents of tenth- and

---

[38] B. Ward, *Miracles and the Medieval Mind: Theory, Record and Event, 1000–1215* (London, 1982), 11.

[39] Primarily in Ælfric's St Bartholomew's Day Homily; see Meaney, 'The Practice of Medicine', 233.

[40] Ibid. 232.

[41] The audience for Ælfric's *Homilies* is much debated; for a helpful summary, see J. Wilcox, 'Ælfric in Dorset and the Landscape of Pastoral Care', in F. Tinti, ed., *Pastoral Care in Late Anglo-Saxon England* (Woodbridge, 2005), 52–62.

eleventh-century English service-books. However, the types of books in which they appear change and evolve. As I have demonstrated, the deployment of these blessings outside of the traditional sacramentary and pontifical traditions appeared to begin – or if not begin, then certainly occur – in the eleventh century. This, we might infer from Meaney's work, was an indication of the importance attached to them by different members of the ecclesiastical community. The twelfth-century evidence reinforces the strong link that exists between the purpose of liturgical blessings and the period in which they were copied. Moves towards 'professionalized' service-books in that period meant that the benedictional contents became increasingly standardized. This was less a form of 'desacralization' than a result of practical changes in book production. Ultimately, the suggestion made by Chenu and others that ecclesiastical attitudes towards nature underwent a wholesale shift under the influence of Scholasticism is not easily reconciled with the nuances of the service-book evidence.

More research needs to be carried out into the eleventh- and twelfth-century liturgy in England before we can make any firmer assumptions about the medieval Church's attitude towards the sacramental role of nature. As such, this paper represents only a small proportion of the groundwork to a much larger topic.[42] It does, however, raise questions about the nature of liturgical production and the function of benedictions which cast doubt on Keith Thomas's rather undiscriminating approach to 'the magic of the medieval Church'. I hope to have offered an alternative perspective on the relationship between nature blessings and existing themes in medieval religious and cultural history, and, most importantly, revealed fresh meanings in sources too often dismissed as unoriginal and uninteresting.

University of Exeter

---

[42] Currently being explored in my Ph.D. thesis.

APPENDIX: LITURGICAL BLESSINGS FOR APPLES AND HERBS[43]

LV: *Liber Vitae* of New Minster, Winchester
PW: The *Portiforium* of St Wulfstan

1. *Benedictio pomorum* [*LV* and *PW*]
Deprecamur omnipotens deus, ut benedicas hunc frutum nouum pomorum, ut qui interdictae arbore loetalis pomi in primo parentis iustae funeris sententia multati sumus, per illustratione unici filii tui redemptoris nostri ihesu christi, et spiritus sancti benedictione sanctificata omnia atque benedicta depulsis atque abiectis uetustate antiqui hostis atque primi facinoris insidiis, salubriter ex huius diei anni anniuersaria sollempnitate diuersis terrae edendum germinibus sumamus.

2. *Alia* [*LV*]
Benedic, domine, hunc fructum nouorum arborum, ut hi qui utuntur ex eo sint sanctificati. per dominum nostrum iesum christum filium tuum.

3. *Benedictio herbarum* [*LV* and *PW*]
Omnipotens aeterne deus, rerum conditor et dominator totius creaturae tuae, qui verbo cuncta ex nichilo faciens ad perfectionem tui operis tertio die herbam uirentem et lignum pomiferum faciens fructum aridam producere iussisti, hos uirentium herbarum flores ob salutem fidelium undecumque collecto per inuocationem sancti tui nominis benedicere et sanctificare tua pietate dignare, et presta nobis quamuis indignis ut quicumque aegritudine qualibet laborantes haec sumpserint, omnis ab eis morbus te miserante euanescat, languor diffugiat, calor febrium obeat, dolores laterum et cruciatus uiscerum obsistant, omnisque infestatio iaculantis inimici procul recedat qui cum coeterno filio tuo et spiritu sancto.

4. *Alia* [*LV* and *PW*]
Domine ihesu christi fili dei uiui, qui ex sinu paternae maiestatis ad medelam et ad curandus nostrorum scelerum cicatrices

---

[43] All formulae from the *Portiforium* are transcribed from the manuscript by the author and collated with Hughes's edition. Those from the *Liber Vitae* are transcribed by the author.

descendens, in te credentibus polliceri et dignatus, si quid petieritis patrem in nomine meo fiet uobis; adesto nunc nobis eandem in te fidem habentibus, et interuenientibus meritis et intercessionibus genetricis tuae perpetuae uirginis mariae, cum omnibus sanctis, pariterque tui precursoris interuentione cuius hodierna die sacro irradiamur natalicio; hos expositarum herbarum flores quos serenitate et rore affluenti enutristi, benedic et sanctifica ut sint per inuocationem tui sancti nominis quibusque infirmitate laborantibus abstersio languoris, salus remediumque animae et corporis, per. [*sic*]

5. *Benedictio herbarum* [*Lacnunga* CXCI]

Omnipotens sempiterne deus qui ab initio mundi omnia instituisti et creasti tam arborum generibus quam herbarum seminibus quibus etiam benedictione tua benedicendo sanxisti eadem nunc benedictione holera aliosque fructus sanctificare ac benedicere digneris ut sumentibus ex eis sanitatem conferant mentis et corporis ac tutelam defensionis eternamque uitam per saluatorem animarum dominum nostrum iesum christum qui uiuit et regnat deus in secula seculorum. Amen.[44]

---

[44] T. O. Cockayne and C. Singer, *Leechdoms, Wortcunning and Starcraft in Early England*, 3 vols (London, 1961), 3: 79.

GOD'S BOUNTY, *PAUPERES* AND THE CRUSADES OF 1096 AND 1147

by CONOR KOSTICK

Cease, therefore, your discords, let your quarrels fall silent, your wars become quiescent, and let the disagreements of all controversy be put to sleep. Start the journey to the Holy Sepulchre, get that land off the criminal race and make it subject to you, that land the possession of which had been given by God to the sons of Israel, which – as the Scripture says – is *flowing with milk and honey.*[1]

ROBERT the Monk was present at the famous Council of Clermont in 1095, at which Pope Urban II launched the First Crusade by announcing that there would be a major expedition against the pagans to assist the Christians of the East. According to Robert, Urban reminded his listeners of the journey of the Children of Israel from Egypt; a journey in which God's bounty several times saved Moses and his followers from famine and thirst. The report of another eyewitness at Clermont, Baldric (or Baudri) of Dol, reinforces the likelihood that the Book of Exodus was in the thoughts of those who listened to Urban. Shortly after the announcement that Adhémar, Bishop of Le Puy, had volunteered to go on the expedition, the Provençal count Raymond of Toulouse made it clear he was willing to join the crusade and share the responsibility for it with Adhémar. Baldric's version of the message of Raymond's envoys to the assembly included the lines: 'Behold! God be thanked, two men voluntarily offered to proceed with the Christians on their journey. Behold! Religious and secular power, the clerical *ordo* and the laity, harmonise in order to lead the army of God. Bishop and count, we

---

[1] Robert the Monk, *Historia Iherosolimitana*, RHC Oc. 3. 717–882, at 728. 'Cessent igitur inter vos odia [vos discordiae], conticescant jurgia, bella quiescant et totius controversiae dissensiones sopiantur. Viam sancti Sepulcri incipite, terram illam nefariae genti auferte, eamque vobis subjicite, terra illa filiis Israel a Deo in possessionem data fuit, sicut Scriptura dicit, quae lacte et melle fluit' (referring to Exod. 3: 8, 17; 13: 5; 33: 3).

imagine ourselves like another Moses and Aaron.'[2] Again, then, we have a conscious echoing of the epic undertaking by Moses.

How literally did the audience for this message interpret the references to a land of milk and honey? How much did they anticipate that like the Children of Israel, they could depend upon God's bounty to sustain them for this extraordinary journey? When the crusading message spread through northern Europe, did listeners believe that the logistical difficulties of such an ambitious journey could be overcome by divine aid given that the enterprise was such a holy one? Those princes who responded to the appeal of the crusade took a very pragmatic and practical approach to the questions of supply. Robert of Normandy, for example, raised the funds he needed by mortgaging his duchy for ten thousand silver marks. Duke Godfrey of Lotharingia sold the county of Verdun, the towns of Stenay and Mouzay, his personal lands at Baisy and Genappe, and the castle of Bouillon for a great sum of coin to meet his needs.[3] But how did the poorest sections of society and those least able to sustain themselves for a two-thousand-mile march think that they would obtain the food they needed? Did they really believe that God's bounty would be directly provided to them like manna from heaven?

Obtaining an insight into the mentality of the lower social orders in this era is a tricky business, given that we have no direct testimony from serfs, peasants, free farmers or the urban poor, instead we have to rely on those of the clergy who took an interest in the outlook of the poor. In the case of both the First Crusade and the Second Crusade there were, however, at least some clergy who not only believed that those with the least wealth were the most deserving of God's bounty, but it was the efforts of the poor above all that earned divine approval for the First Crusade. An important example of a crusader and a writer with just such a perspective was Raymond of Aguilers, a canon of the cathedral church of St Mary of Le Puy, in the Auvergne region of France. Raymond joined the First Crusade (1096–99), probably in the company of Bishop

---

[2] Baldric of Dol, *Historia Hierosolymitana*, RHC Oc. 4: 1–111, at 16: 'Ecce, Deo gratias, jam Christianis ituris, duo ultronei processere viri; ecce sacerdotium et regnum; clericalis ordo et laicalis ad exercitum Dei conducendum concordant. Episcopus et comes, Moysen et Aaron nobis reimaginantur.'

[3] A. V. Murray, *The Crusader Kingdom of Jerusalem, A Dynastic History 1099–1125* (Oxford, 2000), 38–42.

Adhémar of Le Puy, the papal legate.[4] He was raised to the priest-hood during the course of the expedition and subsequently joined the chaplaincy of Count Raymond IV of Toulouse.[5]

The key term used by Raymond to encompass the lower social orders was *pauperes*. Loosely, this meant 'the poor', but quite apart from the fact that, as Karl Leyser has observed, at this time *pauperes* could also mean 'defenceless',[6] in the context of the crusade it could be used for all of Christ's followers, including combat-ants. Raymond's use of the term is in fact a good illustration of an observation made by Colin Morris, that 'such groups as the knights (*milites*) and poor (*pauperes*) might seem to us to be socio-logical phenomena, but to twelfth-century writers they were theo-logical and moral conceptions, significant for the function they fulfilled in the divine purpose for the world'.[7] Many of Raymond's uses of the term *pauperes* were relatively straightforward, such as where they were juxtaposed to the *divites*, the rich.[8] But Raymond was writing in a framework that saw the mighty pagan powers being confronted by a Christian force that, although in appear-ance lowly and weak, was powerful through the assistance of God. From this theological point of view the entire movement could be considered to be one of *pauperes* and Raymond had no difficulty describing Christian warriors on horseback as *pauperes*;[9] in this sense Raymond of Aguilers' use of *pauperes* anticipates similar uses of the term by the scholar and civil servant Peter of Blois (c. 1180) and Innocent III (1198–1216).[10]

With these nuances of the term in mind, what then can we determine about the *pauperes* of the First Crusade and their beliefs in regard to God's bounty? One piece of evidence that emerges

---

[4] Raymond of Aguilers, *Historia Francorum qui ceperunt Iherusalem*, ed. John France (unpublished Ph.D. thesis, University of Nottingham, 1967), 11–12, 17 (237, 238). I am grateful to Professor France for permission to quote from his thesis. References to the PL edition (PL 155: 0591–0668A) are in brackets.

[5] Raymond of Aguilers, *Historia Francorum*, ed. France, 202 (0633D); 100 (0612C).

[6] K. Leyser, *Communications and Power in Medieval Europe: The Gregorian Revolution and Beyond*, trans. T. Reuter (London, 1994), 82 n. 26.

[7] C. Morris, *The Papal Monarchy: The Western Church from 1050 – 1250* (Oxford, 1989), 34.

[8] Raymond of Aguilers, *Historia Francorum*, ed. France, 46 (0601D).

[9] Ibid. 68–69 (0606A).

[10] See Morris, *The Papal Monarchy*, 316–50; I. S. Robinson, *The Papacy 1073–1198: Continuity and Innovation* (Cambridge, 1990), 365–66.

very directly from the sources is that *pauperes* responded to the appeal to join the crusade in enormous numbers. Very soon after the Council of Clermont, the pope himself was anxious to dampen down an unexpected enthusiasm for the crusade among non-combatants. Urban wrote a letter to the clergy and people of Bologna, 19 September 1096, in which he tried to restrain women, children and clergy from joining the Christian armies.[11] Ekkehard, later Abbot of Aura (1108–25), was an eyewitness to the departure of people in Bavaria on the expedition and observed of the very first contingents that along with a great many legions of knights were as many troops of footsoldiers and crowds of those who worked the land, women and children.[12] Ekkehard also noted that some of the commoners as well as persons of higher rank admitted to having taken the vow through misfortune.[13] Furthermore, a great part of them proceeded laden with wives and children and all their household goods.[14]

Guibert of Nogent, an eyewitness to the departure of crusaders from northern France, observed the recruiting activity of the itinerant preacher Peter the Hermit, and the social composition of Peter's army amused him. Noting, like Ekkehard, that entire families of *pauperes* with carts full of their belongings joined the various contingents, he wrote that after the Council of Clermont 'the spirit of the *pauperes* was inflamed with great desire for this [expedition] so that none of them made any account of their small wealth, or properly saw to the sale of homes, vineyards and fields'.[15] This passage is evidently a description of property-owning farmers turning their fixed assets into ready wealth for the journey, even at much reduced prices. A little later, he adds: 'There you would have seen remarkable things, clearly most apt to be a joke; you saw certain *pauperes*, whose oxen had been fitted to a two-wheel cart

[11] Urban II, 'Letter to the Clergy and People of Bologna', in H. Hagenmeyer, ed., *Epistulae et Chartae ad Historiam Primi Belli Sacri spectantes quae supersunt aevo aequales ac genuinae: Die Kreuzzugsbriefe aus den Jahren 1088–1100* (Innsbruck, 1901), 137–38.

[12] Ekkehard of Aura, *Frutolfs und Ekkehards Chroniken und die Anonyme Kaiserchronik*, ed. F.-J. Schmale and I. Schmale-Ott (Darmstadt, 1972), 140.

[13] Ibid.

[14] Ibid.

[15] Guibert of Nogent, *Gesta Dei per Francos*, ed. R. B. C. Huygens, CChr CM 77a (Turnhout, 1996), 119: 'pauperum animositas tantis ad hoc ipsum desideriis aspiravit ut eorum nemo de censuum parvitate tractaret, de domorum, vinearum et agrorum congruenti distractione curaret'.

and iron-clad as though they were horses, so as to carry in the cart a few possessions together with small children.'[16] Independently but with a similar turn of phrase, the northern French historian and the Bavarian chronicler found it noteworthy that peasant families participated in the crusade. Guibert also provided clear evidence that people from the very lowest layers of the eleventh-century social spectrum responded to the idea of the crusade. He noted that the meanest, most common men (*homines extremae vulgaritatis*) appropriated the idea of the expedition for themselves.[17]

The use of the term *pauperes* in these passages seems to cover a broad grouping of the lower social orders, from relatively wealthy farmers – owners of a team of oxen – through to those from the very bottom of society: serfs and even slaves. Christopher Tyerman, in his impressive survey of the various social groupings who took the cross during the crusades, doubts that serfs participated in such expeditions. Because, he argues, serfs had no freedom of action or choice, they could not participate in the movement independently of their masters. In addition, their lack of resources leads him to conclude that 'it does seem to have been the case that … serfs did not become crusaders'.[18] But this precludes the possibility that some serfs took advantage of the crusading message to leave their homes without permission from their lords, hoping to survive on charity and the distribution of captured booty. Tyerman is right, though, to raise the question of how such very lowly crusaders expected to sustain themselves? Did they anticipate being able to depend on the charity of the Christian communities they passed? But there still remained over a thousand miles to walk through lands owned by those hostile to the crusaders.

A critical passage with regard to the Second Crusade provides evidence that insubordinate serfs did indeed leave their fields for the expedition and that their solution to the problem of supply was indeed to rely upon their faith in God and manna from heaven. Gerhoch, provost of Reichersberg, was an eyewitness to the depar-

---

[16] Ibid. 120: 'Videres mirum quiddam, et plane joco aptissimum, pauperes videlicet quosdam bobus biroto applicitis, eisdemque in modum equorum ferratis, substantiolas cum parvulis in carruca convehere.'

[17] Ibid. 300.

[18] C. Tyerman, 'Who Went on the Crusades?', in B. Z. Kedar, ed., *The Horns of Hattīn* (Jerusalem, 1992), 14–26, at 24.

ture of the German contingent of the Second Crusade in 1147. He explicitly noted that there was among the army,

> no lack … of peasants and serfs (*servi*), the ploughs and serv-ices due to their lords having been abandoned without the knowledge or against the will of their lords. Having little or nothing of gold or silver, inadvisably having begun that very long expedition, hoping in such a holy business that like long before in such an ancient time happened to the people of Israel, that nourishment would either rain down from heaven or be everywhere provided by God.[19]

Other sources suggest that a similar participation by serfs occurred during the First Crusade. The anonymous author of the *Historia Peregrinorum euntium Jerusolymam* reported that so great a commotion of men and women took place in all the regions of the world wishing to join the holy journey that 'the father did not dare restrain the son, nor the wife the husband, and the *dominus* did not dare to restrain the *servus*'. Because of the fear and love of God, everyone was free to join the journey.[20] Marwan Nader assumes *servus* here stands for a serf,[21] which is entirely possible, but even if its alternative meaning of 'servant' was meant by the compiler of the history, the point still stands that the usual bonds of authority could be undermined by the appeal of the crusade. Similarly, the *Annals of Augsburg* say that along with warriors, bishops, abbots, monks, clerics and men of diverse professions, 'serfs and women' (*coloni et mulieres*) joined the movement.[22] Cosmas of Prague wrote that in 1096 so many people departed for Jerusalem that there

---

[19] Gerhoch, *De Investigatione Antichristi Liber I*, in MGH LdL 3, ed. E. Dümmler et al. (Hanover, 1897), 304–95, at 374–75: 'non rusticanorum ac servorum, dominorum suorum relictis aratris ac servitiis, ignorantibus quoque nonnulli vel invitis dominis, parum aut nichil auri vel argenti habentes inconsulte expeditionem illam longissimam arripuerant, sperantes in tam sancto negotio sicut olim antiquo illi Israhelitarum populo, vel pluente desuper celo vel undecunque celitus ac divinitus amminiversitates eundem exercitum in eadem sancta via, ut estimabant, comprehenderunt'.

[20] *Historia Peregrinorum euntium Jerusolymam*, in RHC Oc. 3: 167–229, at 174: 'Pater non audebat prohibere filium, nec uxor prohibere virum, et dominus non audebat prohibere servum.'

[21] M. Nader, *Burgesses and the Burgess Law in the Latin Kingdom of Jerusalem and Cyprus (1099–1325)* (Aldershot, 2006), 20.

[22] *Annales Augustani*, ed. G. H. Pertz, MGH SS 3 (Hanover, 1839), 134.

remained very few *coloni* in the *urbes* and *villae* of Germany and Eastern France.[23]

From a modern perspective it seems the height of folly for those with nothing, nor with the arms to procure plunder, to embark on the crusades. But there were many contemporaries, especially those imbued with the kind of theology expressed by Raymond of Aguilers, who wore their poverty as a badge of pride. It was their poverty that made them worthy for the divine aid that they anticipated would meet their needs on the journey. This spiritual self-belief and enthusiasm for the crusade was derived in part from very harsh conditions in the homelands of the *pauperes*. If we look at the state of western Europe at the time of the first two crusades, it becomes clearer why the appeal of moving to a land of milk and honey might displace thousands of poor people from the land in search of a better life.

The graphs at the end of this paper show how many references exist to plagues and famine in a large collection of annals of the eleventh and twelfth centuries. Absolute economic data for this era is extremely difficult to obtain as we lack marriage, birth and death records. Only the most basic outline of trends in demography, agriculture or manufacturing is available. There is a strong consensus among economic historians that in general this was an era of population increase, with growing numbers of towns, an expansion of the land under cultivation, and improvements in agricultural productivity.[24] But at the same time, this growth was faltering and human existence precarious in the face of periodic outbreaks of plague, famine, or both. There is a way to study this *relative* hardship of one year compared to another and obtain a sense of the years that would have been particularly difficult, which is to survey the western European annals and note the number of references to plagues and famine. The annals used in the compilation of the charts presented here are those published in the thirty-eight volumes of the Monumenta Germaniae Historica Scriptores series. By making a note of each time an annalist described the appear-

[23] *Cosmae Chronica Boemorum*, ed. G. H. Pertz et al., MGH SS 11 (Hanover, 1854), 103.
[24] N. J. Pounds, *An Economic History of Medieval Europe*, 2nd edn (London, 1994); C. Postan and P. Mathias, eds, *The Cambridge Economic History of Europe, 2: Trade and Industry in the Middle Ages* (Cambridge, 1987), 204–39; L. T. White, *Medieval Technology and Social Change* (Oxford, 1964).

ance of plague or famine, it proved possible to create these charts and obtain a good sense of the periods of economic and social distress across the eleventh and twelfth century.

There are problems in assembling the data. Often an annalist would incorporate an earlier work wholesale, for example the many annalists who began their own works as continuations of the widely circulated annals of Sigebert of Gembloux or Ekke-hard of Aura. Thus information from the entries in the *Annals of Rosenfeld* or the *Annals of Würzburg* has not been used here, as at this point both were copies of the *Annals of Hildesheim.* Assisted by the works of F. Curschmann (who in 1900 was the first to discuss the background of famine against which the early crusades took place), W. Wattenbach and F.-J. Schmale, such repetitions can be eliminated, so that each entry, as much as possible, represents a unique observation.[25] The other distortion to the data that is worth bearing in mind is that there was an increase in the numbers of annals being written across Europe in the twelfth century, so we might expect an increase in the number of entries concerning famine and plague, even if the frequency of incidents of hardship remained about constant. Despite these reservations, the graphs show something very striking and conclusive. There were years of extreme hardship and dislocation at exactly the times when the First and Second Crusades were being preached. Thus, for example, in 1091 not one annalist mentioned the presence of famine and only two noted a plague. In 1092 one annalist recorded a famine, one an outbreak of plague. In 1093 we have mention of famine by one annalist and plague by two. But in 1094 – the year before the First Crusade was launched – we have a shocking upsurge of mentions of plague, twenty in all, with one annalist mentioning famine. But as a result of the plague, famine increased; we have six entries to that effect in 1095 as well as plague in four.

In fact, the period around the First Crusade stands out as a particularly difficult one; only that around 1145 – shortly before Bernard of Clairvaux began to promote the Second Crusade – is worse. The *Annals of the Four Masters* are not included here, as they are not in the Scriptores series, but they reported that

---

[25] F. Curschmann, *Hungersnöte im Mittelalter* (Leipzig, 1900); F. Wattenbach and F.-J. Schmale, *Deutschlands Geschichtsquellen im Mittelalter: Vom Tode Kaiser Heinrichs V. bis zum Ende des Interregnum* (Darmstadt, 1976).

in Ireland up to a quarter of the population died of famine in 1095.[26] By 1097, however, the crisis was over. It has plausibly been suggested that the 'plague' mentioned in these reports refer to an outbreak of ergot poisoning among the rye crop, which would fit the pattern of a sharp outbreak of mortality that disappeared by the time of the following harvest. In addition, ergotism also fits with the account of Ekkehard – an eyewitness – who graphically portrayed the effects of a plague that caused limbs to wither through an invisible fire.[27]

The impression given by these graphs is of a correlation between the times when preaching the crusade obtained a massive popular response among the *pauperes* and times of extreme economic difficulty. This connection is confirmed for the First Crusade by the historical sources. According to the brief entry in the *Annals of St Blaisen*, it was plague that created the movement to Jerusalem.[28] Similarly, in addition to the previously cited comment by Ekkehard that many took the vow through misfortune, he reported in his chronicle that it was easy to persuade the *Francigenae* to go to the Orient because for some years previously *Gallia* had been afflicted by civil disorder (*seditio*), famine and excessive mortality.[29] Guibert of Nogent reported that the preaching of the crusade took place at a time of famine, which had the consequence that the crowds of the poor learned to feed often on the roots of wild plants.[30] The famine reduced the wealth of all and was even threatening to the mighty (*potentes*).[31] Guibert condemned those magnates who stored food for profit during a year of famine, writing that they considered the anguish of the starving *vulgus* to be of little importance.[32]

[26] *Annals of the Four Masters*, ed. J. O'Donovan (Dublin, 1856), 949.

[27] Ekkehard, *Frutolfs und Ekkehards Chroniken*, ed. Schmale and Schmale-Ott, 140: 'Tactus quisquam igne invisibili quacumque corporis parte tam diu sensibili, immo incomparabili tormento etiam inremediabiliter ardebat, quosque vel spiritum cum cruciatu vel cruciatum cum ipso tacto membro amitteret. Testantur hoc hactenus nonnulli manibus vel pedibus hac pena truncati.' For ergot poisoning, high temperatures and gangrenous limbs, see M. McMullen and C. Stoltenow, *Ergot* (Fargo, ND, 2002). See also J. Sumption, *Pilgrimage* (London, 2002), 75; J. Riley-Smith, *The First Crusaders* (Cambridge, 1997), 16.

[28] *Annales Sancti Blasii*, ed. G. H. Pertz et al., MGH SS 17 (Hanover, 1861), 277.

[29] Ekkehard, *Frutolfs und Ekkehards Chroniken*, ed. Schmale and Schmale-Ott, 140.

[30] Guibert of Nogent, *Gesta Dei per Francos*, ed. Huygens, 118.

[31] Ibid.

[32] Ibid. 119.

The exact manner in which the upsurge of hardship connected with the mentality of the *pauperes* and the crusading message is impossible to determine. When Ekkehard reported that the crusaders were easily persuaded to depart because of hardship, he explained that 'certain prophets' carried out this agitation.[33] Presumably these were figures like Peter the Hermit, the itinerant and popular leader of the 'People's Crusade' that departed in advance of the main princely contingents of the First Crusade.[34] But what was Peter's message to the 'poor' about their difficult circumstances that was so well received? A clue is provided by the fact that that immediately after making his report Ekkehard adds that in the same year extraordinary events occurred, such as a woman giving birth after a two-year pregnancy to a boy who could talk and lambs being born with two heads.[35] Other contemporaries observed contingents of the lower social orders following women who held a cross that had fallen from heaven; there were followers of a woman who had a divinely inspired goose; and there were even crusaders who followed a she-goat.[36] In other words, the sense of dislocation seems to have fuelled an eagerness among some to grasp at the miraculous as a sign that they should join the movement to Jerusalem. And the fact that the first section of Peter's army left Cologne shortly after Easter (12 April) 1096, long before the harvest, implies an urgency that – in contrast to the princes who left in the autumn – placed the question of supply in God's hands.[37]

Attempting to reconstruct the mentality of the lower social orders in the eleventh and twelfth century is extremely challenging, given the lack of direct testimony from the historical sources. Nevertheless, some monastic authors were sufficiently attentive to the deeds

[33] Ekkehard, *Frutolfs und Ekkehards Chroniken*, ed. Schmale and Schmale-Ott, 140.

[34] For Peter the Hermit, see J. Flori, *Pierre l'Ermite et la Première Croisade* (Paris, 1999); also H. Hagenmeyer, *Peter der Eremite* (Leipzig, 1879); E. O. Blake and C. Morris, 'A Hermit Goes to War: Peter and the Origins of the First Crusade,' in W. J. Shiels, ed., *Monks, Hermits and the Ascetic Tradition*, SCH 22 (Oxford, 1984), 79–107; M. D. Coupe, 'Peter the Hermit – A Reassessment', *Nottingham Medieval Studies* 31 (1987), 37–45.

[35] Ekkehard, *Frutolfs und Ekkehards Chroniken*, ed. Schmale and Schmale-Ott, 141.

[36] Baldric of Dol, *Historia Hierosolymitana,* RHC Oc. 4: 17; Albert of Aachen, *Historia Iherosolimitana*, ed. S. B. Edgington (Oxford, 2007), 58.

[37] F. Duncalf, 'The Peasants' Crusade,' *AHR* 26 (1920–21), 440–53, argues in favour of good logistical planning by Peter and his followers, but see C. Kostick, *The Social Structure of the First Crusade* (Leiden, 2008), 95–103.

of farmers and serfs at the time of the departure of the First and Second Crusades that we have historical evidence to reinforce the picture created by compiling data on famines and plagues. The statement from Gerhoch that serfs abandoned their fields in the expectation that nourishment would rain down from Heaven is particularly important in demonstrating that some of the poor crusaders did indeed take seriously the idea that the miraculous manifestation of God's bounty would sustain them on the journey. Given the background of a dramatic upsurge of plague in 1096 and famine in 1146, it is perhaps not so hard to believe that people with little or no wealth could be attracted by the papal message that the time had come to emulate the sons of Israel and march to a land flowing with milk and honey.

Trinity College, Dublin

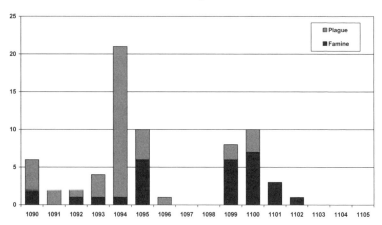

Figure 1: Famine and Plague at the time of the First Crusade

Famine and Plague 1140 - 1150

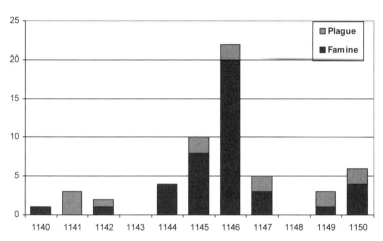

Figure 2: Famine and Plague at the time of the Second Crusade

Famine and Plague 1000 - 1200

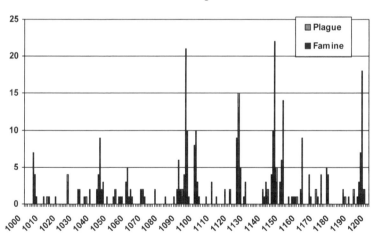

Figure 3: Famine and Plague in perspective

BIRDS, BEASTS AND BECKET: FALCONRY AND HAWKING IN THE LIVES AND MIRACLES OF ST THOMAS BECKET*

by GESINE OPPITZ-TROTMAN

IN the late twelfth century, the practice of hawking and falconry was symbolically ambiguous, associated powerfully with the secular life yet also open to mystical interpretation. This paper suggests that the authors of St Thomas Becket's miracle collections, as well as his contemporary biographers, appropriated this ambiguity as a means of reconciling some of the contradictions of Becket's career. Henry II was himself an avid enthusiast for hunting with birds, and records show a marked increase in the number of transactions involving birds of prey, and the number of falconers employed to handle them, during his reign (1154–1189).[1] Of all the types of birds used for hunting, the most prized was the gyrfalcon, *Falco rusticolus*, still valued as the bird of kings even at the end of the fifteenth century in *The Boke of St. Albans*.[2] Robin Oggins reveals that 'almost two thirds of recorded purchases of gyrfalcons were for more than £2, at a time when a knight's annual income could be as low as £20'.[3] Such birds were valuable enough to be used as payment in kind. By 1177 Henry II was owed ninety-seven hawks and eight gyrfalcons; at the end of his reign he was still expecting payment totalling one hundred and thirty birds.[4]

Henry II's friend and chancellor Thomas Becket revelled in this culture. William fitzStephen relates that Becket, as chancellor, gave

---

* I would like to thank Nicholas Vincent for his helpful comments and suggestions.

[1] Robin S. Oggins, *The Kings and their Hawks* (New Haven, CT, 2004), 54–63; my paper is indebted to Oggins's detailed research into the practice of hawking and falconry under Henry II. Cf. John Cummins, *The Hound and the Hawk: The Art of Medieval Hunting* (London, 1988).

[2] Rachel Hands, ed., *English Hawking and Hunting in the* Boke of St. Albans: *A Facsimile Edition of sigs. a2–f8 of the Boke of St. Albans* [1486] (Oxford, 1975), 54, lines 1172–74.

[3] Oggins, *Kings and their Hawks*, 12.

[4] Ibid. 60–61.

birds routinely as diplomatic gifts.[5] Herbert of Bosham, Thomas's most loyal supporter in exile, reported with regret that many of the clergy doubted whether a 'pastor of hounds and hawks' could make an effective church leader,[6] and Frank Barlow notes that an unknown monk, writing in the margin of Lactantius' *Divinae Institutiones* somewhere in the Angevin domains, rebuked Thomas for, among other things, the unchristian extravagance of purchasing wild animals.[7] It is clear that Thomas Becket was an enthusiastic hawker from an early age, an enthusiasm he probably acquired from his family's acquaintance with the well-connected and appropriately named knight, Richer de l'Aigle, whom he accompanied on hawking and hunting expeditions while still a schoolboy.[8] Traditionally a royal sport (although this may be an impression informed by the somewhat diffuse nature of non-royal sources for hawking), it would have given the ambitious young clerk – '*a plebeo quodam clerico*', as his enemies described him – a taste of the chivalrous life.[9] As has already been suggested, this pastime, which he enjoyed with the king as part of their close friendship, became one of the foremost indications of what later sceptics would perceive as Becket's secular outlook.

Before we encounter hunting in the miracle collections, it may be appropriate to discuss the training of birds in relation to the manipulation of nature. As Oggins writes, 'the practical need and desire to control nature can be seen in such phenomena as writings on hawk medicine and changes in falconry-training techniques (e.g. the introduction of the hood)'.[10] This fascination with the disciplining and training of nature may have reflected the

[5] William fitzStephen, 'Vita Sancti Thomae, Cantuariensis Archiepiscopi et Martyris', in James Craigie Robertson, ed., *Materials for the History of Thomas Becket, Archbishop of Canterbury (Canonized by Pope Alexander III. A.D. 1173),* 7 vols (London, 1876), 3: 1–154, at 23. See also *The Lives of Thomas Becket*, ed. and trans. Michael Staunton (Manchester, 2001), 51.

[6] Michael Staunton, *Thomas Becket and his Biographers* (Woodbridge, 2006), 79; Robertson, ed., *Materials*, 3: 183.

[7] Frank Barlow, *Thomas Becket* (London, 1986), 62.

[8] Anonymous I, 'Vita Sancti Thomae, Cantuariensis Archiepiscopi et Martyris', in Robertson, ed., *Materials*, 4: 1–179, at 3–12; *Lives*, ed. and trans. Staunton, 43.

[9] On the bias of the extant material, see Oggins, *Kings and their Hawks*, 109. For the description of Thomas, see Edward Grim, 'Vita S. Thomae, Cantuariensis Archiepiscopi et Martyris', in Robertson, ed., *Materials*, 2: 353–450, at 429.

[10] Robin S. Oggins, 'Falconry and Medieval Views of Nature', in Joyce E. Salisbury, ed., *The Medieval World of Nature* (London, 1993), 47–60, at 47.

education and breeding of hawking enthusiasts. John of Salisbury suggested in his *Policraticus* that knowledge of hunting 'constitute[d] the liberal studies of the higher class'.[11] William fitzStephen implicitly linked chess and falconry in this regard.[12] The practice of hawking also presupposed the exploration of a natural hierarchy of species. The wish to accentuate such a hierarchy in nature led to the practice of flying birds of prey at much larger targets than they would normally attack in the wild, reinforcing a perception of natural social hierarchy.[13] The fascination with elite birds such as gyrfalcons, as well as the obsessive emphasis on their pure breeding, furthered a social elite's attempts to find in nature a vindication of their power in society, similarly reliant on blood-lines.

Despite these inevitable secular uses, the training of hawks and falcons was assigned religious meaning by some. For Adelard of Bath, the struggle to impose on nature in this way could echo the struggle to curb evil predispositions. In his dialogue on birds, his nephew quizzes him on appropriate behaviour for men flying birds of prey. He replies:

> Drunkenness is the mother of forgetfulness, anger causes injuries, visiting prostitutes transmits parasites to birds when they are touched, a bad breath makes them haters of men and fills them with bad air, so that they suffer rheum. Moreover, a preoccupation that is not under control will result in the birds being carried through the midst of rain or gales, or treated with excessive violence, or not being carried enough.[14]

Here the struggle to train a hawk is one with the struggle for self-improvement. This was an association completely different

---

[11] John of Salisbury, *Policraticus: The Stateman's Book*, ed. Murray F. Markland (New York, 1979), 6. Nederman's more recent edition abridges this part of the first book: John of Salisbury, *Policraticus: Of the Frivolities of Courtiers and the Footprint of Philosophers*, ed. and trans. Cary J. Nederman (Cambridge, 1990).

[12] fitzStephen, 'Vita Sancti Thomae', 20.

[13] Raptors would be trained to attack heron and crane, far larger and more dangerous targets than they would naturally have attempted. See Frederick II of Hohenstaufen's standard work describing this grisly process: *The Art of Falconry, being the De Arte Venandi cum Avibus of Frederick II of Hohenstaufen*, ed. and trans. C. A. Wood and F. M. Fyfe (Stanford, CA, 1981), 256–57.

[14] Adelard of Bath, *De avibus tractatus*, in *Adelard of Bath: Conversations with his Nephew; On the Same and Different, Questions on Natural Science and On Birds,* ed. and trans. Charles Burnett (Cambridge, 1998), 238–76, at 241.

from that of worldly triviality, which lay behind the Church's condemnation of clergymen's participation in the sport. In medieval manuscript marginalia, falconry and hawking were more frequently used to help draw a contrast between good and bad clergy: the bad churchman is sometimes shown bearing a hawk or falcon; alternatively, a vicious monkey may assume the appearance of a falconer. John of Salisbury himself wrote: '"Where are they that take their diversion with birds of the air?" asks the prophet … they have gone down to hell.'[15] Walter Map and others described it as an 'idle sport', full of worldly vanity.[16] Mira Friedmann notes that 'in religious and moralistic writings of the Middle Ages references to sin and especially to carnal desire are often illustrated with pictures of falcon-bearers … not mentioned anywhere in the text'.[17] Yet one could not enter into the practice so idly as Map and others suggested, since it involved considerable commitment. Adelard emphasized that the true falconer would be someone 'free from preoccupations', absolutely devoted to what he was doing.[18] Indeed, perhaps this is why in a version of *The Bestiary* the hawk's perch is compared to 'life under monastic rule, because it is suspended high above earthly things', and the hawk itself 'is the image of the holy man, who seizes the Kingdom of God'.[19] The very remoteness of the hawk in the air is connected with the monastic way.[20] Here, too, we find a fascinating description of the hawk's mystical significance:

> Hawks are usually carried on the left hand, so that they fly to the right to seek their prey when they are let off their leash: 'His left hand is under my head, his right hand doth embrace

---

[15] John of Salisbury, *Policraticus*, ed. and trans. Markland, 6.

[16] Walter Map, *De nugis curialium: Courtiers' Trifles*, ed. and trans. Montague R. James, revised by C. N. L. Brooke and R. A. B. Mynors (Oxford, 1983), 477.

[17] Mira Friedmann, 'The Falcon and the Hunt: Symbolic Love Imagery in Medieval and Renaissance Art', in Moshe Lazar and Norris J. Lacy, eds, *The Poetics of Love* (Fairfax, VA, 1989), 157–75, at 158.

[18] *Adelard of Bath*, ed. and trans. Burnett, 241.

[19] *The Bestiary: being an English Version of the Bodleian Library, Oxford, MS Bodley 764*, ed. and trans. Richard Barber (Woodbridge, 1999), 156 and 155. This manuscript dates from between 1220 and 1250.

[20] Birds had also played an important role in divination since antiquity, an influence deriving in part from Cicero; while they came not as high as demons, birds were believed to be nearer God than men, and were thus treated as augurs: Valerie I. J. Flint, *The Rise of Magic in Early Medieval Europe* (Oxford, 1991), 103, 116–26.

me' [Song of Solomon 2: 6]. The left represents temporal things, the right everything that is eternal ... all those who in the depths of their hearts desire eternal things fly to the right. There the hawk will catch the dove; that is, he who turns toward the good will receive the grace of the Holy Spirit.[21]

Thus the very practice of hawking was linked to revelation or conversion, an aspect underlined in the work's emphasis on the etymology of *accipiter* ('hawk'), from *capere*, to seize, with its mystical connotations.[22] Not only, as elsewhere in *The Bestiary*, is the bird given emblematic functions, but the sport of hawking is figured as a mediation of the temporal and spiritual worlds, a movement across them, almost in the manner of a miracle. This gives a sense of the potential ambiguity of the falcon, hawk, or sportsman in the religious literature of the time, but also of how this ambiguity might have proved appealingly dynamic to the compilers of miraculous reports at Christ Church, Canterbury, for whom the problem of Thomas Becket's secular career must have loomed large.

Shortly before he was appointed Archbishop of Canterbury, Thomas, then chancellor and confidant of the king, was taken ill at the convent of St Gervais at Rouen. There he received visits from the English and the French kings. William fitzStephen mentions that the prior of Leicester, Asketil, also visited the convalescent. He found him playing chess, and challenged him boldly on his choice of dress, which he suggested was more appropriate for a falconer than for an ecclesiast and future archbishop.[23] His comment prefigured the rift between Thomas and members of the English clergy. Here, as during this later conflict, Thomas was challenged on the ostentation of his chancellorship, central to some of the main royalist attacks on the archbishop in exile.[24] The outward sign, in this instance, of what Asketil perceived as character unsuited to ecclesiastical obligation is the long sleeved cape Becket wore in

---

[21] *The Bestiary*, ed. and trans. Barber, 156.

[22] Ibid. 154.

[23] fitzStephen, 'Vita Sancti Thomac', 25–26; *Lives*, ed. and trans. Staunton, 58–59.

[24] See especially Gilbert Foliot's famous letter, 'Multiplicem nobis', sent on behalf of the royalist bishops to Becket in September 1166: *The Correspondence of Thomas Becket, Archbishop of Canterbury 1162–1170*, ed. and trans. Anne Duggan, 2 vols (Oxford, 2000), 1: 498–537 (no. 109); *The Letters and Charters of Gilbert Foliot*, ed. Dom Adrian Morey and C. N. L. Brooke (Cambridge, 1967), 229–43 (no. 170).

the manner of a falconer. Asketil's anxiety reflected the clergy's increasingly ambivalent relationship to the sport in the twelfth century. At the Third Lateran Council (1179), Pope Alexander III would forbid prelates to burden their subjects with the costs of hunting, building on the trend since the sixth century to legislate against clergymen involved in hawking and falconry; his canon implicitly acknowledged the incompatibility of the sport with the attempt to manifest godly humility.[25]

It may strike one as puzzling, therefore, that in the miracle collections assembled after Becket's martyrdom hawking and falconry receive any attention at all, even as *jocunditas*, the kind of 'lighthearted' miracle disparaged by their Victorian editor Edwin Abbott as 'degenerate'.[26] We must nevertheless bear in mind that the cult of St Thomas had its foundations in a spontaneous popular movement begun virtually from the moment of his death, with the Canterbury poor collecting his still warm blood from the stones of the cathedral. Benedict of Peterborough, the first collector of the miracles, was overwhelmed by their sheer number; William of Canterbury was enlisted initially to help him cope, before succeeding him. The construction of Thomas's sainthood could not always entail straightforward suppression of the inappropriately miraculous. Such control was probably not often available to the hagiographers at the tomb. Instead, the very association of the falcon or hawk with secular preoccupations could be used cleverly to help construct the myth of Thomas's preordained greatness and sanctity. One of the few anecdotes pertaining to Thomas's early life concerns an incident in which he almost died, having fallen into a stream near a watermill while chasing a disobedient hawk. This event became one of the foremost providential signs of Becket's

---

[25] The fourth canon of the Third Lateran Council stated: 'Nor should [clergy] set out with hunting dogs and birds, but they should proceed in such a way that they are *seen to be seeking* [*quaerere videantur*] not their own but the things of Jesus Christ': Norman Tanner, ed. and trans., *Decrees of the Ecumenical Councils*, 2 vols (London, 1990), 1: 213 (Canon 4; my emphasis). This underlined the decision made in 517 at the Council of Epaon, where it was ordered that a bishop could be suspended from communion for three months for owning a falcon or hunting dog, a priest two months and a deacon one: Charles de Clercq, ed., *Concilia Galliae*, 2 vols (Turnhout, 1963), 2: 25 (canon A.517); collated in 'Decretum Magistri Gratiani', *CICan*, 1: 126 (Decreti Prima Pars Dist[inctio] 34 c.2).

[26] Edwin A. Abbott, *St Thomas of Canterbury: His Death and Miracles*, 2 vols (London, 1898), 2: 24.

grace in his hagiography, an indication that God had ordained his greatness.

The accident is described by nearly all of Becket's biographers.[27] It occurred while the young Thomas was out with Richer de l'Aigle, his patron. Following the knight, crossing a footbridge over a rapid stream, Thomas's horse slipped, taking him with it into the current. Edward Grim tells a different version in which a falcon, catching a duck, plunged into the water, with Thomas jumping in to rescue his bird.[28] The Scandinavian *Saga* relates how the two hunters were crossing at the dangerous point in order to retrieve a disobedient falcon, which had flown across to the other side of the river.[29] As we shall see below, aspects of the story were reflected in a miracle of the 1170s. However, some of the biographers, Grim foremost amongst them, perceived this event itself as miraculous. For as Thomas was being swept by the current towards the mill-wheel, it miraculously stopped of its own accord. The accounts of Garnier and Anonymous I are somewhat more prosaic, recording that the miller happened to pass by and, albeit oblivious to what was happening, stopped the mill himself. Yet all biographers attach a great importance to the tale, with Anonymous I asking: 'Who could believe that this happened by chance, and was not the work of divine providence mercifully arranging such a sudden and unexpected rescue for this endangered boy, the future prelate of his Church?'[30] We are told that Becket's mother 'lamented the danger less than she rejoiced for his wonderful and unexpected liberation. And from this she drew hope for the future, that it was not in vain that divine mercy had snatched him from death.'[31]

It is potentially significant that this accident occurred as Thomas traversed a narrow way. John of Salisbury, probably the most active after 1166 in promoting an image of Thomas's trib-

---

[27] Anonymous I, 'Vita Sancti Thomae', 6–7; Grim, 'Vita S. Thomae', 360–61; *Garnier's Becket, Translated from the 12th Century* Vie Saint Thomas Le Martyr De Cantorbire *of Garnier of Pont-Sainte-Maxence*, ed. and trans. Janet Shirley (London, 1975), 7, lines 206–30; *Thómas Saga Erkibyskups: A Life of Archbishop Thomas Becket, in Icelandic*, ed. and trans. Eiríkr Magnússon, 2 vols (London, 1875), 1: 33.

[28] Grim, in Robertson, ed., *Materials*, 2: 360–61.

[29] *Thómas Saga Erkibyskups*, ed. and trans. Magnússon 1: 33.

[30] Anonymous I, 'Vita Sancti Thomae', 6–7; cf. *Lives*, ed. and trans. Staunton, 44.

[31] *Lives*, ed. and trans. Staunton, 44.

ulations as reflecting those of Christ himself,[32] wrote earlier in his *Policraticus*, which Thomas may have read during his escapades around Toulouse as the dashing, worldly chancellor,[33] of the 'steep and narrow' path, whose 'stumbling stone ... encourages and strengthens' those seeking God.[34] Perhaps, then, the pursuit of the hawk formed the very epitome of vain, worldly pursuit, causing Becket to fall from the narrow path of religious truth.[35] In this sense, the story prefaces Becket's 'conversion', which became the overriding emphasis in posthumous hagiographical accounts.[36] The biographers' treatment of the anecdote confirms, perhaps, that hawking was a sport which stood for the worldliness of the younger Becket.[37] However, it also indicates that the very worldliness for which the hunting bird might become a symbolic shortcut could play a part in a more coherent project that told stories of conversions, divine interventions, revelations and prefigurations. In short, the hawk or falcon could acquire an importance for the hagiographical project itself. Hunting with birds thus occupied a curious place in the Becket hagiography. It operated as a sign of Becket's worldliness, and yet could be implicated in narratives that constructed St Thomas's holiness.

There are numerous miracles involving birds and animals in the miracles of St Thomas, but only ten directly involve birds of prey or related sports, a small but significant group among the two collections that together comprise more than seven hundred reports. These involve various kinds of hunting birds receiving injuries or flying away, but they are also used to introduce broader sections on cures. In one miracle account, bearing an important

---

[32] Cf. John McLoughlin, 'The Language of Persecution: John of Salisbury and the Early Phase of the Becket Dispute (1163–66)', in W. J. Sheils, ed., *Persecution and Toleration*, SCH 21 (Oxford, 1984), 73–87.

[33] E. F. Jacob, 'John of Salisbury and the *Policraticus*', in F. J. C. Hearnshaw, ed., *The Social and Political Ideas of Some Great Political Thinkers: A Series of Lectures delivered at King's College University of London* (London, 1923), 53–84, at 77–78.

[34] John of Salisbury, *Policraticus*, ed. and trans. Nederman, 90–91.

[35] Cf. Matt. 7: 13–14; Num. 22: 24.

[36] See Michael Staunton's important essay, 'Thomas Becket's Conversion', *Anglo-Norman Studies* 21 (1998), 193–211.

[37] Anonymous I and Alan of Tewkesbury both relate how, at an inn at Gravelines after the flight from England in 1164, the disguised Thomas almost gave himself away because of his great interest in a falcon which he saw on a knight's wrist: Alan of Tewkesbury, 'Vita S. Thomae', in Robertson, ed., *Materials*, 2: 335; Anonymous I, in ibid. 4: 56–7.

resemblance to some versions of Becket's accident as a young man, a Norman knight, Robert Silvester, is obliged to rescue his hawk from a river, having seen 'the prey,' a duck, 'preying on the predator'.[38] The knight then puts his injured bird in a cage and promises to send a waxen votive (in the image of the hawk) to St Thomas's shrine. Elsewhere, William of Canterbury explains to us why the saint deigns to clear up such small matters as the cure of a sparrowhawk (a relatively lowly species). He suggests that it is because the saint wants by these small gifts to encourage people to make greater requests.[39]

In another instance, the cure of a hawk for a woman who had petitioned the saint for help coincided with an experience of paralysis in the hands after she failed to fulfil her oath, apparently believing the cure to have been effected by natural remedies.[40] This is quite significant, in that many practical hawking and falconry treatises gave advice as to how to treat illnesses in the birds. Indeed, the twelfth century witnessed a real increase in the number of such treatises on the treatment of birds of prey, with no fewer than eight such texts surviving.[41] Adelard of Bath, for example, suggested a remedy for a type of worms that would involve the forced feeding of dragonwort in the sealed gut of a hen or pigeon.[42] The partially paralyzed woman of the miracle, one Mabilia, had forced pigeon-heart into the apparently dead bird's beak. The similarity of method may imply that manuals such as Adelard's were in circulation at this time, had passed into common knowledge pertaining to the keeping of hawks and other birds, or at least that such manuals relied on knowledge gleaned from common experience. The woman was rebuked by the saint for her faith in such remedies, but as in the interaction between natural medicine and pilgrimage to shrines, her behaviour suggests that a combination of the two was not considered entirely inappropriate,

[38] William of Canterbury, 'Miraculorum Gloriosi Martyris Thomae, Cantuariensis Archiepiscopi', in Robertson, ed., *Materials*, 1: 137–546, at 388: 'quia praeda praedonem praedaretur'. There are also several miracles involving the dangers posed to the unwary by mill-wheels: see, e.g., ibid. 348; 499.

[39] Ibid. 388–89.

[40] Ibid. 389.

[41] These are listed by Baudoin van den Abeele, *La fauconnerie au Moyen Âge: connaissance, affaitage et médecine des oiseaux de chasse d'après les traités latins* (Paris, 1994), 21–26.

[42] *Adelard of Bath*, ed. and trans. Burnett, 259.

even if, in the light of her sheer ingratitude, the saint thought she should be punished.

The cure of the royal gyrfalcon Wiscard is easily the most significant of the miracles dealing with falconry. In William of Canterbury's collection it is isolated from the other hawking miracles, perhaps to indicate that it was not just another miracle of hawks or birds, but a sign of Thomas's reconciliatory virtues; the saint's forgiving nature was an important aspect of his cult. According to the miracle, the royal falconer, against the king's wishes, flew his prize falcon against a large bird which mortally wounded its attacker. The falconer, apparently fearing for his life, fled to Tours with the dying animal, and followed advice to seek St Thomas's help. In the first place, this was a show of mercy to the royal falconer, rather than to Henry himself, although William of Canterbury considered that the saint probably meant the favour for both. The saint appeared to Ralph, the falconer, in a dream, telling him to pierce twelve swellings on the bird's body. Ralph assumed that because he could find twelve such injuries, they evidenced the dream's truth. Having done as he was told, Ralph witnessed the bird's immediate recovery. When the king was informed of this, William continued, he thanked the martyr for saving the companion of his sporting hours.[43]

It was as the king's favourite companion in such sport that Thomas Becket excelled before he was appointed to Canterbury. Perhaps it is a measure of how closely the pastime connected the two men that Henry II used it to insult and humiliate the archbishop publicly prior to the fateful Council of Northampton in October 1164, from which Thomas was to flee across the Channel. Having been summoned, not by the king but by the sheriff of Kent, Thomas was left waiting in his lodgings on the first day of the council, as the king went hawking with his noblemen along the banks of the river Nene, not returning until the evening. Anne Duggan thought this nothing out of the ordinary, but it must surely have stung Becket to some degree that the king was using their old pursuit as a way of antagonizing and alienating him still further.[44] Gerald of Wales relates a probably apocryphal anecdote

---

[43] Robertson, ed., *Materials*, 1: 528–29.
[44] Anne Duggan, *Thomas Becket* (London, 2004), 62.

relating to the king's early life, but one which seems almost irresist-ible in the context of Henry's relationship to Becket:

> Henry II … or his son Richard …[45] in the early part of his reign flew his best hawk at a heron … When the hawk … had almost reached the heron … the king, as if certain of the capture, said '… that heron will not escape even if God himself should command it.' When the king had spoken …, the heron immediately turned round, *and almost miraculously … broke open the hawk's head with its beak, causing its brain to be cast out.* The heron, completely unharmed, threw the dying hawk down at the king's feet.[46]

For Henry, Becket would be the hawk that did not return to its lure. Having befriended, trained and appointed Thomas to a task he assumed he would perform, Henry would spend much of his reign chasing his errant companion, until he finally returned, only to fall out of the sky, dead, at the angry king's feet.

University of East Anglia

---

[45] By offering a choice of kings, Gerald is making a feeble attempt at discretion.

[46] Gerald of Wales, *The Jewel of the Church: A Translation of* Gemma Ecclesiasticus *by Giraldus Cambrensis*, ed. and trans. John J. Hagen (Leiden, 1979), 124, my emphasis. A key symbolic feature of Becket's martyrdom was the spilling of his brains. See Martin Aurell, 'Le Meutre de Thomas Becket: Les Gestes d'un Martyre', in Natalie Fryde and Dirk Reitz, eds, *Bischofsmord im Mittelalter* (Göttingen, 2003), 187–210, at 204. He supposes the knights' brutal de-crowning of Becket reflected their disdain for his clerkly status, as signified by his tonsure. As Aurell points out, this act had the unexpected effect of sealing Becket's symbolic victory, and God's through him, for in martyrdom one crown was exchanged for another, and the king's hubris made apparent with a humbling blow.

CATHARS AND THE MATERIAL WORLD

by PETER BILLER

ON 6 August 1221 Dominic 'migrated to Christ' in the Dominican convent in Bologna. He had no bed of his own and he had lent his only tunic to someone. As he slept in the convent, he was lying on a borrowed bed and dressed in borrowed clothes.

This was the story later told by Moneta of Cremona, the friar who had lent his bed and clothing to the dying holy man.[1] Moneta features in another story, collected by a friar who was commissioned by a general chapter of the Order in 1256 to collect miracles and tales illustrating the wonderful early progress of the Order. Progress included the entry of important men.[2] At Bologna there was 'Master Moneta, who was then famous throughout Lombardy for his lecturing in the arts'.[3] The Dominican friar Reginald was preaching with great success in Bologna. Fearing the power of Reginald's sermons, Moneta tried to keep his students away from them. But he failed to protect himself. He happened to hear Reginald's preaching and was captivated by the first words he heard, falling to his knees and making his religious profession on the spot. Thus the great university master became humble and entered the Dominican Order. 'The quality of his holiness after his entry into the Order cannot easily be described', the account concludes, 'nor how much progress he made in word and teaching and in the confutation of heresies'.[4]

---

[1] Stephen of Salagnac and Bernard Gui, *De quatuor in quibus Deus Praedicatorum ordinem insignivit* 3.2, ed. T. Kaeppeli, Monumenta Ordinis Praedicatorum Historica 22 (Rome, 1949), 33. For a modern account of these events, see M.-H. Vicaire, *Saint Dominic and His Times*, trans. K. Pond (London, 1964), 373–74.

[2] Gerald of Frachet, Prior Provincial of Provence. His *Vitae Fratrum* was written in 1259–60; ed. B. Reichert, Monumenta Ordinis Praedicatorum Historica 1 (Louvain, 1896).

[3] Ibid. 4.10 (ed. Reichert, 169): 'magister Moneta, qui tunc in artibus legens in tota Lombardia famosus erat'.

[4] Ibid. 4.10 (ed. Reichert, 170): 'Ingressus autem ordinem, qualis in omni sanctitate fuerit, quantum in verbo et doctrina et heresium confutacione profecerit, non de facili scribi posset.'

This was in 1219, and Moneta died around 1260.[5] We know little about him between these dates, apart from the fact that he fought valiantly against heretics, and that around 1241 he wrote a treatise against Cathars and Waldensians.[6] Cathars occupy most of the space in this massive work. Moneta begins it by dividing them theologically into two main groups. One comprised those who believed in two Gods, creators of two alternative worlds, the evil God creating the visible material world. The other group contained those Cathars that believed in one God who, after creating matter, had allowed the Devil to shape it. These two forms of theological dualism led to the rejection of the good God's or the one God's creation of flesh and bodies, the notion that Mary and Christ took on real human flesh, the sacrament of marriage and the resurrection of the body.

The presence of such heretical dualism in Latin Christendom can be seen as significant in the genesis of a profound shift in Catholic Christianity. One aspect of this was increasing spiritual and mystical emphasis on the humanity and flesh of Christ and the emergence of the feast of Corpus Christi.[7] Another aspect was the Franciscan and Dominican friars' promotion in the new universities of a natural science of God's creation – the natural world – based upon recently translated works of Aristotle.[8] This broader picture and the theme of 'The Churches and the Natural World' provide the setting for this paper and its object. This is to look at and characterize more closely one of the consequences of Cathar dualist theology: the notion that the natural world that we can see was created by the bad God or the Devil. We shall do this

[5] See, on him, T. Kaeppeli and E. Panella, *Scriptores Ordinis Praedicatorum*, 4 vols (Rome, 1970–93), 3: 137–39.

[6] Moneta of Cremona, *Adversus Catharos et Valdenses Libri Quinque*, ed. T. A. Ricchini (Rome, 1743). On the manuscripts, see Kaeppeli and Panella, *Scriptores*, 2: 138 9, 4: 201; *Quellen zur Böhmische Inquisition im 14. Jahrhundert*, ed. A. Patschovsky, MGH Quellen 2 (Weimar, 1979), 87–88.

[7] C.W. Bynum, *Jesus as Mother: Studies in the Spirituality of the High Middle Ages* (Berkeley, CA, 1982), 130–31, 134; eadem, *Holy Feast and Holy Fast: The Religious Significance of Food to Medieval Women* (Berkeley, CA, 1987), 64, 252–53; eadem, *Fragmentation and Redemption: Essays on Gender and the Human Body in Medieval Religion* (New York, 1991), 143–44; M. Rubin, *Corpus Christi: The Eucharist in Late Medieval Culture* (Cambridge, 1992).

[8] R. French and A. Cunningham, *Before Science: The Invention of the Friars' Natural Philosophy* (Aldershot, 1996), expound the view of this interest in the natural world as a response to heretical dualism.

by looking at what Moneta wrote and what was said by Cathar believers questioned by inquisitors in Languedoc.

The approach adopted here needs explanation. Moneta presents textual puppets. A 'heretic' states a doctrine, and cites in its support *auctoritates* (passages from scripture) and *rationes* (arguments), and a 'Catholic' then rejects the doctrine, citing counter-authorities and stating counter-arguments. It all seems rather remote from lived religion. This quality of apparent abstractness has its part to play in a debate that is now raging among scholars about the nature of Catharism, a dispute which has suggested this selection of evidence.

At issue is the question whether we should retain or abandon the notion of two great high medieval sects, Catharism and Waldensianism, possessing a degree of identity or coherence. The demolition corps used to concentrate on arguing about a document emanating from a Cathar council of around 1170. This had to be a forgery, otherwise Catharism seemed both organized and ecclesial: too solid an entity. Now the front has widened, and the troops are led by an Australian historian who works in the United States, Mark Pegg. Pegg has produced two books of remarkable power and skill in which he has attempted to dismantle our picture of Catharism.[9]

According to Pegg, they were not called 'Cathars', nor were their preachers called 'perfects' (*perfecti*). They did not have an international organization. Cathar followers''adoration' of a 'perfect' was no more than a construction on the part of the inquisitors. They took something which was no more than a local custom of civility in Languedoc, namely doing lots of bowing when one met people, and constructed it into a formal ritual. Records of replies by heresy suspects are misleading. This is because questions were thought up by friars, who were trained in sequential logic, and then put to simple people whose minds were innocent of that mental mode of connectivity, innocent that is, until the moment of questioning. Although Pegg does not say this, the suggestion is analogous to the notion in modern physics that enti-

---

[9]   M. G. Pegg, *The Corruption of Angels: The Great Inquisition of 1245–1246* (Princeton, NJ, 2001); *A Most Holy War: The Albigensian Crusade and the Battle for Christendom* (Oxford, 2008). See the reviews of *The Corruption of Angels* by B. Hamilton, *AHR* 107 (2002), 925; P. Biller, *Speculum* 78 (2003), 1366–70.

ties are changed by the fact of measurement. Further, it is the friars who had abstract theological ideas in their minds, rather than the simple folk they were questioning. We should be sceptical, therefore, when the record shows such deponents, under questioning, making apparently abstract theological statements. There is no real early evidence of people in Languedoc believing in dualism and therefore rejecting God's creation of this present, material, visible, natural world. Above all, Pegg argues, modern historians have not shaken off an understanding of medieval heresy that is rooted in a nineteenth-century idealist way of envisaging a religion, as a coherent set of ideas, disembodied and disengaged from the real people who lived it. The historian's task is that of demolishing historians' idealist mythical constructions of these sects. In their place he or she should recover and describe the infinitely varying colours and shapes of the real individual's momentary contacts with a wide variety of thoughts and actions, some of which were named and conceptualized by Dominican friars and shoe-horned into an organized system of ideas labelled 'heresy'.

This onslaught on the conventional picture of Catharism means that our first question must be both more elementary and more fundamental than it might have been in a more confident period thirty or forty years ago. Is rejection of divine creation of the natural world actually there, and if so what forms does it take? In what ways do the surviving texts construct the reality which (we used to think) we can discern through them?

Here we shall begin by applying these questions to two texts that are very close in time and that seem to play well to Pegg's tune. One is the representation of Cathar theology in Moneta's text, from around 1241. Its exploitation by modern historians could be evidence for one of Pegg's indictments, that idealist historians' accounts of the beliefs of heretics are disembodied and detached from human beings and context. The contention can be tested. The other text is a manuscript containing the interrogations of over five thousand people in the Lauragais area of Languedoc in 1245–6. This moves the investigation onto Pegg's own ground: it is the evidence exclusively used in his first book. These two texts also test the point about internationalism: one is from Lombardy, the other from Languedoc. Finally, on virtually every folio in the manuscript of interrogations, we can read two highly trained friar inquisitors, John of St Pierre and Bernard of Caux, putting five theological questions to suspects. Pegg used the rest of this manuscript to produce a colourful picture of various locales in Languedoc, and in this luminous canvas these theological propositions – including denial of divine creation of the natural world – were simply alien intrusions coming from the minds of these friar inquisitors. Is this a persuasive view?

Let us look first at Moneta. A French Dominican memorializing him in the later thirteenth century described Moneta's five-book treatise as a 'most strong and enormous summa' (*validissima et maxima summa*) against heretics.[10] Its length, over 500,000 words, prevented it from becoming a best-seller, but it is extant in fifteen manuscripts, and we know that one, in a Benedictine monastery in Garsten near Steyer, was still being read in the 1390s.[11]

Earlier we summarized Moneta's preliminary account of Cathar faith. Let us return to this account to sample the words he uses.

> There are some of them who assert that there are two principles, without beginning and end. One they say is the father of Christ and all the just and the God of light, the other … the God of darkness. They believe he [the God of darkness] created those four elements that we see, namely earth, water, air and fire, and all the things that are on this earth or this water or this air, likewise also the visible sky and all its adornment, that is to say the sun, the moon and the stars. They believe that this is the God about whom Moses spoke in chapter 1 of Genesis, *In the beginning God created heaven and earth.* … They believe that the transitory and visible things of this world (*visibilia ista et transitoria*) come from him by creation. Conversely, they believe that the God, who is father of Christ and the just, is the creator only of permanent and eternal things, and that he created his own other four elements, and all the things that are in them, and his own heavens, and that he ordained [these other heavens] with a sun other than this visible one, and another moon and other stars …[12]

---

[10] Stephen of Salagnac and Bernard Gui, *De quatuor in quibus* 3.2 (ed. Kaeppeli, 33). A terminus is given by the death in 1291 of the author of this part, Stephen of Salagnac.

[11] P. Biller, *The Waldenses, 1170–1530: Between a Religious Order and a Church,* Collected Studies 676 (Aldershot, 2001), 258–61, 273, 276, 290, 295.

[12] Moneta, *Adversus Catharos* 1, Descriptio fidei haereticorum (ed. Ricchini, 3): 'Quidam illorum duo asserunt principia sine initio et sine fine. Unum dicunt patrem

Postponing his account of the beliefs of the other Cathars, Moneta now gets down to highly organized and systematic exposition and refutation. The heretic puts forward a proposition which is stated, he supports it with an authority (*auctoritas*), that is to say, a quotation from scripture, which is quoted, and he also supports it with logical arguments (*rationes*). Then, in alternating chapters, the Catholic opponent puts counter-statements of doctrine, counter-quotations from Scripture, and counter-arguments, some of them derived logically from axioms.

A fair number of comparable anti-Cathar treatises were written in northern Italy during the middle decades of the thirteenth century.[13] Though shorter than Moneta's, they are similar in style. Dualist heretical and Catholic beliefs are counterposed in a very formal fashion. One of them is a dispute presented as a dialogue between a Catholic and a heretic, virtually a script providing dialogue for a play. The protagonists whack each other over the head with scriptural quotations and arguments. Two of these treatises were written by convert heretics (Rainier Sacconi and Andrew of Florence), and it comes as no great surprise to find one written by a layman (Salvo Burci of Piacenza), given the levels of lay literacy in Italy. These Catholic treatises had their heretical counterparts, for the heretics of northern Italy also wrote theological treatises. These treatises were rooted in the realities of their time and place. Given the relative ineffectiveness of inquisi-

Christi et omnium justorum et Deum lucis, alium … Deum tenebrarum. Isti credunt eum creasse quatuor elementa ista quae vidimus, scilicet terram, aquam, aerem et ignem, et omnia quae in terra hac vel in aqua ista vel in aere isto sunt, similiter et caelum istud visibile et omnem ornamentum eorum [*recte*: eius], scilicet solem, lunam et stella. Credunt etiam quod iste sit Deus de quo ait Moyses, Genes. cap. 1, *in principio creavit Deus caelum et terram etc.* … Isti credunt visibilia ista et transitoria esse ab illo per creationem. E converso credunt Deum patrem Christi et justorum esse creatorem permanentium tantum et aeternorum, et credunt quod ipse alia sua quatuor elementa creaverit et omnia quae in eis sunt et suos caelos, et quod ordinaverit sole alio quam sit iste visibilis, et alia luna et aliis stellis.'

[13] See for the following, L. Paolini, 'Italian Catharism and Written Culture', in P. Biller and A. Hudson, eds, *Heresy and Literacy, 1000–1530* (Cambridge, 1994), 83–103. Notable among modern editions of these treatises are F. Šanjek, 'Raynerius Sacconi O. P. Summa de Catharis', *Archivum Fratrum Praedicatorum* 44 (1974), 42–60; *Disputatio inter Catholicum et Paterinum Hereticum*, ed. C. Hoécker, Edizione Nazionale dei Testi Mediolatini 4, series 1, 3 (Tavarnuzze, 2001); Salvo Burci, *Liber Suprastella*, ed. C. Bruschi, Istituto Storico Italiano per il Medio Evo, Fonti per la Storia dell'Italia Medievale, Antiquitates 15 (Rome, 2002); Andreas Florentinus, *Summa contra hereticos*, ed. G. Rottenwöhrer, MGH Quellen 23 (Hanover, 2008).

tion in Italy up to 1250, much of the struggle between Catholic Christianity and heresy was carried on in preaching and debate. Catholics and heretics argued with each other.

Turning back to Moneta's treatise, let us read it further with these things in mind, and ask about the relation between these arguments and the textual dialogue in Moneta's treatise or in the *Dispute between a Catholic and a Paterine Heretic*.[14] Would Moneta's treatise have been of any use to Catholics engaged in such debates if it had not accurately represented heretical positions? Questioning Moneta's text, we begin to notice some of the variations in the words he uses to attribute statements to a heretic. Most commonly we read 'the heretic says that' or 'the heretic argues that'. But we also encounter 'as a certain Cathar wrote'; 'they want to show this by many testimonies, which can be found in the writings of a heretic called Tetricus'; 'as a heretic wrote in a certain treatise of his'; 'Note that a heretic wrote and taught that'; and 'a heresiarch called Desiderius ... sometimes preached and wrote'.[15] At one point Moneta even supplies a text we could add to Anthony Grafton's history of academic citation:[16] 'As the heretic Tetricus wrote in one part of a certain book of his, in chapter 2'.[17] While Moneta's accuracy cannot be checked here, because Tetricus's work does not survive, it receives striking confirmation in another example. Moneta ascribes to the heretics the proposition that the serpent tempting Eve had sex with her using his tail,[18] in words which closely paraphrase the still extant text, once possessed and used by the Cathars, *The Questions of John (Interrogatio Iohannis)*.[19]

---

[14] From the second half of the twelfth century, 'Patarene' denoted Italian Cathars: *Disputatio inter Catholicum et Paterinum Hereticum*, ed. Hoécker, xvi-xvii.

[15] Moneta, *Adversus Catharos* 1.3.2, 1.6.3, 1.8.3, 3.3.4, 4.1.9 (ed. Ricchini, 42, 71, 94, 248, 292): 'sicut quidam Catharus scripsit'; 'volunt autem hoc habere pluribus testimoniis, quae in scriptis cujusdam haeretici Tetrici nomine reperi [possunt]'; 'ut haereticus dixit in quodam suo tractatu'; 'nota haereticum dixisse et scripsisse quod'; 'haeresiarcha qui Desiderius vocatur ... aliquando ...praedicavit et scripsit'.

[16] A. Grafton, *The Footnote: A Curious History* (Cambridge, MA, 1997).

[17] Moneta, *Adversus Catharos* 1.6.2 (ed. Ricchini, 79): 'sicut Thetricus haereticus in quadam parte cujusdam libri sui cap. II'.

[18] Ibid. 1.1.2 (ed. Ricchini, 111).

[19] E. Bozóky, *Le livre secret des Cathares, Interrogatio Iohannis: Apocryphe d'origine Bogomile*, Textes Dossiers Documents 2 (Paris, 1980), 60.

After invoking the memory of Dominic, Moneta began his work with a statement that is both consciously written within a rhetorical tradition and at the same time a heartfelt plea:

> One thing however I beg of the readers of this work … where they will have seen me positing certain arguments against the Church or replies on behalf of heretics, they should not tear into me, saying that these did not originate with the heretics, but that I used my own ingenuity to invent the sort of things that could nourish and help heretical wickedness. For I got these things from their own mouths and writings.[20]

Two things have become clear. First of all, we should avoid slipping from observation of the abstractness of the contents of this theological treatise into envisaging it as abstracted from reality. It was rooted in the reality of theological debates in Lombard cities. Secondly, while we can attribute the clarity of organization of the treatise to the powerful clarity of Moneta's own mind, the case of its contents is different. As we have seen, there is every reason to believe Moneta's opening remarks. That is to say, there is every reason to read his presentation of heretics' doctrines, authorities and arguments as acute and sharp quotations, paraphrases and summaries of what contemporary Italian heretics were actually writing and saying. Book 1, chapter 8, part 1 is entitled 'Heretics' proof that transitory things are not from God'. 'Let us see with what testimonies they are led to believe this', writes Moneta. 'As the Lord says, Matthew 24, verse 35, *Heaven and Earth will pass away*. From this they say, that because it will pass away, this visible heaven [the sky] is not from the good God'.[21] Reading the quotation and its interpretation, we are reading what the heretics said and wrote.

As we wander through Moneta's pages we see that the scriptural texts picked up by Cathar and Catholic debaters threw up

---

[20] Moneta, *Adversus Catharos* 1, Praefatio (ed. Ricchini, 2): 'Unum autem peto a lectoribus huius operis … ubi etiam viderint me ponere argumenta aliqua contra Ecclesiam aut responsiones pro haereticis, non me lacerent, dicentes ea non ab haereticis duxisse originem sed me proprio ingenio adinvenisse hujusmodi quae possent nutrire et augere haereticam pravitatem – quia vel ex ore eorum vel ex scripturis illa habui.'

[21] Ibid. 1.8.1 (ed. Ricchini, 80, 81): 'Probatio haereticorum quod transitoria non sunt a Deo. … Ut dicit Dominus, Matth. 24. v. 35, *Caelum et terra transibunt*.' I have not compared the printed text with manuscripts to see whether the enumeration of the verse comes from the eighteenth-century editor.

a miscellany of things concerning the natural world. Topics that were supplied by Scripture and invited argument about creation by a good or evil God included hunger and the enjoyment of food;[22] the rising and the setting of the sun;[23] sparrows;[24] poisonous creatures and harmful animals;[25] fields, seed and fruit;[26] the sky, the earth and the sea;[27] the distinction of four seasons;[28] the habitability or not of parts of the globe;[29] and the disposition of the bodies of a woman and of a man.[30] Although Moneta writes in a studiedly Olympian fashion, his prose can convey visceral disgust, as for example when he presents heretics using St Paul's letter to the Philippians (3: 8), 'I regard as excrement', as the basis for heretics seeing things as *foetida et inmunda*, 'stinking and dirty.'[31] Occasionally we can pick up something that is deeply felt. Debate about one of the four elements provides a momentary glimpse of two bitter contemporary realities, poverty and the burning of heretics. The heretic asks, 'How can it be that this fire comes from good creation, fire that burns the house of a little poor woman, and also in fact [the bodies] of holy men?'[32]

Moneta reports that heretics wanted to prove their case not only by scriptural authorities but also by logical arguments. The first of the latter cited by Moneta begins with a dictum from Aristotle's *On Generation and Corruption*, that the principles of contraries are contraries, and uses this to show that an evil principle created this world. Since good and evil are contraries, they have contrary principles. Since, therefore, the Highest Good is the cause of good, the principle of evil will be the highest evil.[33] Of more concern for us is the argument about the mutable materiality of the world rather

---

[22] Ibid. 1.1.2 (ed. Ricchini, 22).
[23] Ibid. 1.8.2 (ed. Ricchini, 84).
[24] Ibid. 1.8.2 (ed. Ricchini, 86).
[25] Ibid. 2.1.1 (ed. Ricchini, 116).
[26] Ibid. 1.8.2 (ed. Ricchini, 87).
[27] Ibid. 1.8.3 (ed. Ricchini, 89).
[28] Ibid. 2.2.5 (ed. Ricchini, 122).
[29] Ibid. 2.2.5 (ed. Ricchini, 122).
[30] Ibid., 2.2.5 (ed. Ricchini, 123).
[31] Ibid. 1.8.1 (ed. Ricchini, 82).
[32] Ibid. 2.3.1 (ed. Ricchini, 124).
[33] Ibid. 1.1.3 (ed. Ricchini, 23). These axiomatic arguments are investigated more fully in P. Biller, 'Northern Cathars and Higher Learning', in P. Biller and [R.] B. Dobson, eds, *The Medieval Church: Universities, Heresy and the Religious Life. Essays in Honour of Gordon Leff*, SCH S 11 (Woodbridge, 1999), 25–53.

than its moral evil. 'They adduce a certain proposition. If a cause is invariable, so are its effects. Since therefore these visible things are variable, it cannot be that their cause is the holy and true God, who is invariable'.[34]

While Moneta states arguments used by heretics of his time and his Lombard milieu, the statements themselves draw us towards France. A strange, but never refuted, letter reported by Matthew Paris stated that Lombard and Tuscan heretics sent their cleverest students to Paris to learn logic. The axiomatic genre of theological argument had been in vogue in the theology faculty in the nascent University of Paris in the second half of the twelfth century. The axiomatic propositions reported by Moneta were repeated by Guillaume of Auxerre, who was a master in the theology faculty in Paris and knew of dualist heretics in the diocese of Auxerre.[35] We are just able to perceive a web of connections between identical propositions, proving that the material world was not created by the good God, which were held in common by the dualist heretics of Lombardy and of France. Given that the Cathars tried to be secret, we are lucky to be able to find such clear evidence about the links between them in different kingdoms.

Let us turn to the manuscript containing interrogations of 1245–6 of deponents from the Lauragais in Languedoc: Toulouse, Bibliothèque municipale, MS 609, (henceforth Toulouse 609).[36] On 27 May 1245 Pons Rainard of Mas-Saintes-Puelles took an oath and was questioned. He had seen heretics in the house of Peter of Saint André, namely John Cambitor and his companion, and with them William Vital; Bernard, the Lord of Mas-Saintes-Puelles; Arnold of Rosergue; Raymond of Causit and many others whom he could not recall. And all of them, together with him the witness, then adored the said heretics. And this was about fourteen years ago or thereabouts. He confessed five other similar sightings and actions, all dated. Then he confessed that he believed the heretics were good and had good faith, and that they told the truth and were friends of God. 'And he heard the heretics saying that

---

[34] Moneta, *Adversus Catharos* 1.8.1 (ed. Ricchini, 83): 'inducunt quamdam propositionem: si causa invariabilis, et effectus ejus. Cum ergo ista visibilia sint variabilia, non potest esse quod caussa [*sic*] eorum sit Deus sanctus et verus, qui invariabilis est.'

[35] Biller, 'Northern Cathars', 28–33, 50–53.

[36] The fundamental study of this manuscript is Y. Dossat, *Les crises de l'inquisition Toulousaine au XIIIe siècle (1233–1273)* (Bordeaux, 1959), chs 2–3.

God had not made visible things, and that the sacred host was not the body of Christ, and that baptism of water was worth nothing, and that there was no salvation in marriage. And he the witness believed just as they said.'[37] The deposition concludes with a statement about a previous confession to an inquisitor, confession of an item Pons had forgotten, and abjuration of heresy.

The manuscript contains depositions from over five thousand people. Many of the depositions were not like this – they simply record denials and there was no further questioning. But where deponents had had a fair degree of involvement with heretics, the questioning usually went like Pons Rainard's. Most of what the scribes recorded was the answers deponents gave. But we know how the questions went from these answers and also from a standard question-list that was drawn up in the same decade. Did you see a heretic? In the case of a 'yes' to this question, the follow-ups were: Who was he or she? In whose house did you see the heretic? Who else did you see there? Did you engage in the ritual of adoration? How long ago was this?[38]

Before we analyse the question about God's creation of visible things, we need to bear in mind the relationship between action and belief in inquisitors' questions. Presented in its simplest form, the history of inquisitors' questions in Languedoc has two stages. In the first stage, inquisitors asked questions about actions only, beginning with the question about seeing a heretic, and going on to 'Did you hear a heretic?' The one nod in the direction of belief in the 1240s question-list came at the end: 'Did you believe the heretics to be good and to have good faith?' In the second stage, in the early fourteenth century, inquisitors were still asking, 'Did you see a heretic?', but the question 'Did you hear a heretic?' was now followed by the further question, 'What did he say?' This could open the floodgates, and depositions could now contain a lot of memories of heretics' sermons.

This potted history needs immediate qualification. At any given time, one inquisitor might well differ from another in the

---

[37] Toulouse 609, fol. 1ᵛ: 'Et audivit hereticos dicentes quod Deus non fecerat visibilia, et quod hostia sacrata non est corpus Christi, et quod baptismus aque nichil valet, et quod in matrimonio non est salus. Et ipse testis credebat sicut ipse dicebant.'

[38] *Texte zur Inquisition*, ed. K.-V. Selge, Texte zur Kirchen- und Theologiegeschichte 4 (Gütersloh, 1967), 71–72; ET in W. L. Wakefield, *Heresy, Crusade and Inquisition in Southern France, 1100–1250* (London, 1974), 250–58.

extent and type of their curiosity, as we see in the early fourteenth century with the contrast between the more laconic records of Bernard Gui and the immensely detailed ones of Jacques Fournier. And although actions predominated in inquisitors' minds at this earlier period, in the 1240s, we do see the two main inquisitors of Toulouse 609, John and Bernard, showing a penchant for a little group of questions about doctrine. Here they are again, at the end of the confession of Raymond del Pont of Mas-Saintes-Puelles, where they appear transparently through the answers, though the scribe has compressed answers to two questions (on baptism and marriage) into one statement. 'And he heard them saying errors: about visible things, that God had not made them; about the sacred host, that it is not the body of Christ or the Lord; about baptism and marriage, that they do not have power for salvation; about resurrection of the flesh, that it will not be.'[39] There is no doubt about the source and role of this little quintet of questions. They were formulated by the two friar inquisitors. If the inquisitors thought a witness had had sufficient contact with heretics for hearing, understanding and memory of doctrine to be possible, these were the five questions they put to them. The questions were always the same.

Two modern historians of inquisition texts, John Arnold and Caterina Bruschi, have commented very acutely on the reading of depositions like these. Writing within a range of ideas drawn from Michel Foucault, John Arnold has said that inquisitors' questions developed and marked out a field of knowledge.[40] This does not lead to simple reduction of the truthfulness of what a deponent was recorded as saying, when he or she was questioned within this field. If inquisitors asked about A but not about B, the records of their interrogations will tell us about A, and the exclusion of B does not mean that A has been conjured up out of the air. In her discussion of formulaic questions put by inquisitors, Caterina

---

[39] Toulouse 609, fol. 7ᵛ: 'et audivit eos dicentes errores: de visibilibus, quod Deus non fecerat ea; de hostia sacrata, quod non est corpus Christi vel Domini; de baptismo et matrimonio, quod non valent ad salutem; de resurrectione carnis, quod non erit.'

[40] J. H. Arnold, *Inquisition and Power: Catharism and the Confessing Subject in Medieval Languedoc* (Philadelphia, PA, 2001); idem, 'Inquisition, Texts and Discourse', in C. Bruschi and P. Biller, eds, *Texts and the Repression of Medieval Heresy* (Woodbridge, 2003), 63–80, at 69.

Bruschi has divided the content of replies into two parts.[41] One part is the responses to the formulaic questions, when these are couched in the words of the questions that have been put. The other part contains variations in words and additions in substance. The second part she calls the 'surplus'. The more formulaic and repetitive the questions and the answers to them are, the more significant is this 'surplus'. Bearing these comments in mind, let us now look more closely at replies to John's and Bernard's five questions about doctrine.

If these five questions were like boxes in a questionnaire, how free were deponents to choose to tick or cross? 209 deponents put a tick, admitting that they had heard the heretics expressing these errors.[42] Among these, quite a lot said that they had only heard one or two of the errors.[43] A further handful initially said they had not heard the errors and then said they had done so.[44] This retraction suggests that, if any lying was going on, it was in this direction, that is to say, minimizing what a deponent had heard. Nevertheless, 174 put a cross in the box, saying said they had not heard heretics expressing these errors.[45] And usually the inquisitors left the matter at that.

---

[41] C. Bruschi, '"Magna diligentia est habenda per inquisitorem": Precautions before Reading Doat 21–26', in Bruschi and Biller, eds, *Texts*, 81–110, at 94.

[42] In the following, a number inside parentheses indicates the number of times something is attested. Toulouse 609, fols 1ʳ (2), 1ᵛ (2), 2ʳ (2), 2ᵛ, 3ʳ, 4ᵛ, 5ʳ, 5ᵛ, 6ʳ, 7ᵛ, 8ʳ, 10ʳ, 10ᵛ (2), 11ʳ, 12ᵛ, 13ᵛ (2), 14ᵛ, 15ʳ, 16ʳ, 18ʳ⁻ᵛ, 19ᵛ, 20ʳ, 21ʳ, 21ᵛ–22ʳ, 22ʳ, 22ᵛ, 24ᵛ, 31ʳ, 32ʳ, 33ʳ (2), 33ᵛ (2), 34ʳ, 34ᵛ, 36ʳ, 40ʳ, 41ᵛ (2), 43ᵛ, 45ʳ, 50ʳ, 50ᵛ (2), 51ᵛ, 52ʳ, 55ᵛ, 56ʳ (2), 56ᵛ, 58ᵛ, 60ᵛ, 62ʳ (2), 62ᵛ, 63ᵛ, 64ʳ, 64ᵛ, 65ᵛ, 66ᵛ, 67ʳ, 67ᵛ, 69ʳ, 70ʳ, 71ᵛ, 72ʳ⁻ᵛ, 72ᵛ, 73ʳ (2), 73ᵛ (5), 74ʳ (5), 74ᵛ (5), 75ʳ (4), 75ᵛ (2), 76ᵛ, 77ʳ, 77ᵛ (2), 79ʳ (2), 80ʳ, 87ᵛ, 88ᵛ, 90ᵛ, 91ᵛ, 94ʳ, 96ʳ, 98ʳ, 99ᵛ, 100ʳ, 101ʳ, 101ᵛ, 102ʳ, 103ʳ, 110ᵛ (2), 111ʳ, 112ᵛ, 114ʳ (2), 117ᵛ, 120ʳ (2), 121ᵛ, 122ʳ, 123ᵛ, 125ʳ, 126ᵛ, 127ʳ, 130ʳ, 130ᵛ, 131ʳ, 132ᵛ, 133ʳ (2), 134ʳ, 136ʳ, 137ʳ, 140ʳ, 141ᵛ, 142ᵛ, 143ʳ (2), 144ᵛ, 146ʳ, 147ᵛ, 148ʳ, 149ʳ, 149ᵛ, 150ᵛ, 151ᵛ, 152ʳ, 153ᵛ, 154ʳ, 154ᵛ, 155ᵛ, 156ʳ (2), 156ᵛ (3), 158ʳ, 158ᵛ, 159ʳ, 159ᵛ, 160ᵛ, 164ʳ, 167ᵛ, 168ʳ, 171ʳ, 173ʳ⁻ᵛ, 174ʳ, 175ʳ, 184ᵛ, 187ʳ, 187ᵛ, 188ʳ, 192ᵛ–193ʳ, 193ᵛ, 194ʳ (3), 195ʳ, 196ᵛ, 197ʳ, 198ʳ, 198ᵛ, 201ʳ, 203ʳ (2), 204ᵛ, 210ᵛ, 215ʳ, 215ᵛ, 216ᵛ, 219ᵛ (2), 220ʳ, 220ᵛ, 221ᵛ, 224ᵛ, 225ʳ, 225ᵛ, 228ʳ, 235ᵛ, 236ᵛ, 243ʳ, 246ᵛ, 251ʳ.

[43] Ibid. fols 4ᵛ, 12ᵛ, 19ᵛ, 20ʳ, 24ᵛ, 33ʳ (2), 41ᵛ, 50ʳ, 50ᵛ (2), 52ᵛ, 62ʳ, 63ᵛ, 64ʳ, 66ᵛ, 67ᵛ, 70ʳ, 71ᵛ, 75ʳ (2), 76ᵛ, 79ʳ, 110ᵛ, 111ʳ, 122ʳ (2), 122ᵛ, 123ʳ, 126ᵛ, 130ʳ, 131ʳ, 132ᵛ, 133ʳ, 136ʳ, 137ʳ, 143ʳ, 144ᵛ, 146ʳ, 147ᵛ, 149ʳ, 155ᵛ, 156ʳ (2), 156ᵛ, 158ʳ (2), 158ᵛ, 164ʳ, 194ʳ, 204ᵛ, 243ʳ.

[44] Ibid. fols 10ᵛ–11ʳ, 21ᵛ–22ʳ, 196ᵛ; see also 210ᵛ.

[45] Ibid. fols 1ᵛ, 3ᵛ, 5ʳ, 6ᵛ (2), 7ʳ (2), 8ᵛ, 9ᵛ, 10ʳ, 12ᵛ, 13ʳ, 14ʳ (2), 14ᵛ, 16ᵛ, 17ʳ, 17ᵛ, 18ʳ, 18ᵛ, 19ʳ (2), 19ᵛ, 20ʳ (3), 21ʳ, 21ᵛ, 23ʳ, 24ʳ, 25ʳ, 25ᵛ, 26ʳ (2), 29ʳ, 29ᵛ, 30ᵛ, 31ʳ, 32ᵛ, 35r, 37ᵛ, 38ᵛ, 39ʳ (2), 40ᵛ (2), 45ᵛ, 49ʳ (2), 50ᵛ (2), 51ʳ, 51ᵛ (3), 52ʳ (2), 56ᵛ, 57ʳ (2), 59ʳ, 69ᵛ, 70ʳ, 73ʳ (2), 73ᵛ (2), 74ᵛ, 76ʳ, 76ᵛ, 77ʳ, 78ʳ (3), 78ᵛ (2), 79ʳ, 83ʳ, 83ᵛ, 84ʳ, 87ʳ, 87ᵛ (2), 88ʳ (4), 91ᵛ, 92ᵛ, 93ʳ, 94ᵛ, 95ʳ, 97ᵛ, 101ᵛ, 105ʳ, 105ᵛ, 108ᵛ, 109ʳ, 110ᵛ, 113ʳ, 115ʳ (3), 118ʳ (2), 118ᵛ, 121ʳ, 121ᵛ (2), 123ᵛ, 130ʳ, 132ʳ (2), 134ᵛ (2), 135ʳ, 135ᵛ, 137ʳ (2), 137ʳ⁻ᵛ, 137ᵛ (2), 138ʳ, 141ᵛ (2), 142ʳ, 146ᵛ, 152ʳ,

The variation of response and the ready permission of negatives does not fit the suggestion that theologically minded friars were forcibly injecting these propositions into the minds of the deponents, but it accords well with John Arnold's comments. This quintet of questions constitutes the field of knowledge demarcated by the inquisitors. Relative freedom of response – in this set of depositions, at any rate – indicates that *within* this field we are getting to know things. Beyond ticks and crosses there are other things, however, variations and additions that fall within Caterina Bruschi's notion of 'surplus'. Asked the same question, 'Did you hear the heretics saying that that God had not made visible things?', a deponent could simply say, 'Yes', and be recorded affirming this in the same words as the question. But some added something, saying that they had heard the doctrines 'many times'.[46] A deponent could specify that the heretics 'preached' (rather than or as well as 'said'),[47] or identify the heretics in question. Peter Safaia of Laurac had received two female heretics into his house, Bruna his lady and her companion Rixenda. They stayed there for a week around 1234 and he heard them *predicantes*, 'preaching', the doctrines, beginning with God not having made visible things.[48]

Most significant, of course, are the precise words they produced. One deponent responded to the question about *visibilia*, visible things, with *transitoria*, transitory things. We are reminded of the couplet *visibilia et transitoria* with which Moneta opened his account. Some deponents switched from the negative about God to a positive: 'the devil had made all these visible things'.[49] Another remembered that 'flesh and blood will not possess the kingdom of heaven'.[50] Some replies included snatches of remembered phrases.

157[r], 160[v], 161[v], 162[r], 163[r] (2), 163[v], 164[v], 167[v], 168[r], 169[r], 171[r], 171[v], 172[r], 174[v], 182[r], 185[r], 188[r], 189[v], 190[r], 190[v], 192[r], 193[r] (2), 193[v], 194[v], 195[r] (2), 195[v], 203[v], 204[v], 207[v], 213r, 214[v], 220[r], 221[v], 222[v], 225[v], 231[r] (2), 232[r], 232[v], 235[v], 236[r] (2), 252[r]. Here I have noted those whose denials list the errors or refer to 'errors' (*errores*), suggesting questioning on the individual doctrines. Not noted are those who denied hearing heretics 'preaching' (*predicantes*), a reply that suggests that they deponents had only been asked the general question, 'Did you hear them preaching?', and had not been taken through the individual doctrines.

[46] Ibid. fol. 45[r]: 'multociens'; for other examples, see fols 55[v], 75[v], 134[r], 224[v], 251[r].
[47] Ibid. fols 188[r], 246[v].
[48] Ibid. fols 192[v]–193[r].
[49] Ibid. fol. 158[r]: 'diabolus fecerat omnia ista visibilia'; for other examples, see fols. 2[r], 64[r], 150[v].
[50] Ibid. fol. 4[v]: 'caro et sanguis regnum Dei non possidebunt'.

William of Pont had 'heard heretics saying that God had not made the sky and the earth'.[51] Sabdalina of Gourvielle had heard heretics saying that 'God did not make things come into flower and produce seed, but the earth did this of itself'.[52] A deponent could include in the reply a bit of crisply and clearly remembered theology. One deponent had heard heretics saying that 'nothing of those things that God had made could be corrupted or pass away':[53] the theological core of what Moneta reported, namely heretics' arguments about the incompatibility between the attributes of the Good God and the corruptibility and passing away of material things in this world. The recollections cited so far are like a few isolated jigsaw pieces that fit the larger picture of Moneta's account of absolute dualist relegation of God from anything to do with this material world. But not all. The reply made by Lady Willelma of Montgis-card to the question about visible things was a trifle longer than usual, and it made a very distinctive addition. 'Questioned about the errors, she said that she had heard the heretics well, stating that all visible things had been made with the will and in the face of God, nevertheless he himself had not made them'.[54] This looks like a jigsaw piece from a different picture, Moneta's representation of the less radical theology of those heretics who maintained that there was one God, who had permitted the devil to form and shape all matter, which was thereafter under his rule.

The formulaic question which followed this formulaic question about doctrine was, 'Did you believe as the heretic said?' Although most replies to this were 'yes' or 'no', a few could fall into Caterina Bruschi's 'surplus' category. They could be self-aware waverers, like Na Flors of Mas-Saintes-Puelles who believed just as often as she disbelieved.[55] Sometimes the only doctrine remembered was the rejection of divine creation of visible things,[56] or it was singled out among the other doctrines as the one that was not recalled.[57]

---

[51] Ibid. fol. 15^v: 'audivit hereticos dicentes quod Deus non fecit celum et terram'.
[52] Ibid. fol. 63^v: 'Deus non faciebat florere nec granare, sed terre hoc faciebant per se'.
[53] Ibid. fol. 103^r: 'nichil de his que Deus fecerat potuerant corrumpi nec preterire'.
[54] Ibid. fol. 65^v: 'de erroribus requisita, dixit quod bene audivit hereticos loquentes quod omnia visibilia facta fuerant de voluntate et vultu Dei, tamen ipse non fecerat ea'.
[55] Ibid. fol. 22^r.
[56] Ibid. fols 19^v, 24^v, 64^r, 111^r, 132^v, 133^r, 149^r, 156^r, 158^v, 194^r, 235^v, 243^r.
[57] Ibid. fols 21^v, 33^r, 71^v.

The formulation of memory and belief could be emphatic. Thus some deponents stated that they had heard the doctrines often, or that that they believed them *firmiter*, very strongly.[58] Lady Ermessen of Saint Martin-de-Lalande was questioned on 11 June 1245, and clearly wanted to underline the strength of her belief. She believed all the doctrines stated by the heretics, 'and if there was more in the confession she had previously made to Friar Ferrier, she approved the whole of that (*totum*)' too.[59]

The deponents also include a stream of people who had received heretics and thought them to be good, while not believing the doctrines they stated,[60] a position expressed in a striking aphorism by Peter of *Garmassia*[61] of Fanjeaux. 'He believed their works were good and their faith bad'.[62] Deponents could reject all five doctrines, or just one. Sometimes the one with which they really did not agree was the proposition that God had not made this visible world. For example, Garnier of Mas-Saintes-Puelles had heard what the heretics said and believed what they said, 'apart from this, that he never believed that God had not made visible things'.[63] And some of the deponents said that they had disputed with the heretics about theology.[64]

The variety, theological sharpness and liveliness of response to belief in, and criticism of, the heretics' theological preaching is startling. It is startling that we can still discern it in these most laconic and formulaic of Languedoc depositions. But it is not surprising. Some of the deponents were very old, and in 1245 or 1246 these old people were recalling heretics fifty years before.[65] One deponent's first contact with heretics had been about seventy years before his interrogation, that is, around 1175.[66] We are hearing personal histories of people who had had contact with heretics

---

[58] Ibid. fols 55ᵛ, 140ᵛ, 173ᵛ.

[59] Ibid. fol. 36ʳ: 'et si plus inveniretur in confessione facta fratri Ferrario, totum approbabat'. For another example of belief in *totum*, see fol. 134ʳ.

[60] Ibid. fols 3ʳ, 12ᵛ, 16ʳ, 34ᵛ, 52ʳ, 56ʳ (2), 58ᵛ, 62ᵛ, 63ᵛ, 70ʳ, 75ʳ, 80ʳ, 117ᵛ, 123ʳ, 156ʳ, 159ᵛ, 160ᵛ, 188ʳ, 192ᵛ–193ʳ, 228ʳ, 236ᵛ.

[61] Unidentified place-name.

[62] Toulouse 609, fol. 157ᵛ: 'opera tamen eorum credebat esse bona et fidem malam'.

[63] Ibid. fol. 13ᵛ: 'preter hoc quod nunquam credidit quod Deus non fecisset visibilia'; for other examples, see fols 1ʳ, 4ᵛ, 150ᵛ, 156ʳ, 243ʳ.

[64] Ibid. fols 42ʳ, 130ᵛ.

[65] Ibid. fols 133ᵛ, 136ʳ, 142ᵛ, 177ʳ, 213ᵛ, 225ʳ, 243ʳ.

[66] Ibid. fol. 159ʳ.

stretching backwards from 1245–6, deep into the twelfth century. Younger deponents were the children and grandchildren of parents and grandparents who had received and listened to heretics. In many cases a parent, aunt or uncle or grandparent had been a vested heretic, before the crusade of 1209 living in communi ties with other vested heretics, roughly comparable to Catholic communities of religious. The doctrinal instruction that took place inside these religious communities and the preaching within the houses of adherents were supported by theological books, which do not survive.

Outside both sorts of houses there were several ways in which the heretics' theology was ventilated. The disputations referred to in the hearings of 1245–6 have a history which goes back to 1165. There were large formal disputations between Catholics and here-tics, with appointed judges to decide who won the debates, and long ones, like the fortnight at Montréal in 1205, when heretics and Catholics exchanged their positions in written texts. And there were little and informal ones, a disputation in a carpenter's work-shop, or just informal chats in front of a church after mass. Theo-logical argument seems to have taken the place of football and television in Languedoc.[67] Friends, believers in the heretics rather than heretics themselves, or unspecified 'others' could be alleged to be the main source of knowledge of doctrines. One deponent who had not heard heretics saying these things had nevertheless 'heard it said that heretics said' them.[68] This could be a lie, but if so it will have been plausible to suggest that one could just pick the stuff up anywhere. And one source of clear information, of course, was Catholic anti-heresy preaching. Two sorts of evidence are extant about this preaching, its textual sources, and statements by those who had heard it. Two Latin Bibles of the mid-thirteenth century, now in the Bibliothèque Nationale de France, contain a few leaves with references to passages in the Bible which can be used to hit the heretics. Twenty quotations are presented to use in argument against denial of God's creation of the material world.[69] The manu-

---

[67] Disputations: ibid. fol. 25^r.

[68] Ibid. fol. 222^v: 'audivit dici quod heretici dicebant'; see also ibid. fols 111^r, 114^v, 152^r.

[69] C. Douais, *La somme des autorités à l'usage des prédicateurs méridionaux au xiiie siècle* (Paris, 1896), 36–37.

scripts are tiny pocket-books, one measuring 19 cm x 13 m, the other 17 cm x 12 cm: in physical terms, archaeological evidence of the itinerant Catholic clerics wandering round Languedoc preaching against heretics. At the same time there are deponents questioned in 1245–6 who claimed that they had not heard the doctrines expounded by heretics, but they did know them through the clergy preaching against heretics.[70] One deponent specified the cleric – 'he had heard the error that "God had not made visible things" from the bishop of Toulouse'.[71] In an account of the Albigensian crusade written by the Cistercian Peter of les Vaux-de-Cernay, the Count of Toulouse is reported as uttering a witticism about things not going well for him and God not creating this world.[72] Making such a quip only made sense in a culture and society where this heretical doctrine was an utter commonplace. It was in the air. And in 1245–6 it had been in the air for a very long time.

As we have said, in later decades inquisitors' questions began to lighten up. Here is an example from an inquisition in Toulouse in 1273. Inquisitors' questioning of Petronilla, the wife of William of Castanet of Verfeil, in the diocese of Rodez elicited two sources of her beliefs, a godmother and her own husband.

> 'One day [she said], she visited her godparents Daide of Bras and Petronilla, who are from Villefranche, and she slept in their house and ate. And in the morning – it was a Sunday and the people had gone to church – the same witness remained alone with the said Petronilla, her god-parent, and when she had shown her the house, and the corn, and the wine, and the other things which she had, she said that all these things were of the devil …[73]

---

[70] Ibid. fol. 110[r]: 'audivit tamen clericos exprimentes errores quos heretici dicunt de visibilibus, de baptismo, de hostia sacrata, de resurrectione carnis' ('He heard, however, clergy expressing the errors that heretics say about visible things, about baptism, about the consecrated host, about the resurrection of the flesh'). For other examples, see fols 1[v], 16[v], 17[r], 18[v], 31[v], 232[r].

[71] Ibid. fol. 235[v]: 'sed audivit ab episcopo Tholosano <hereticos dicere> quod deus non fecerat visibilia'.

[72] *The History of the Albigensian Crusade: Peter of les Vaux-de-Cernay's Historia Albigensis*, trans. W. A. and M. D. Sibly (Woodbridge, 1998), 22–23.

[73] Paris, BN, MS Collection Doat 25, fols 7[v]–8[r]: 'quadam die visitavit compatrem suum Deodatum de Brass, et commatrem suam Petronillam, qui sunt de Villa Franca,

The inquisitors of 1273 were continuing to use the laconic and action-focused 1240s question-list, but by now inquisitors' lower workload was giving them more contact hours with each deponent, so they were getting more out of each of them. By the early four-teenth century the question-list of the 1240s had been superseded by more belief-friendly ones, and although some inquisitors had very full timetables, one of them, Jacques Fournier, could spend many days on a particular deponent.

To an even greater degree than in the case just cited from 1273, the recollections presented to Fournier by deponents in 1319–20 are given detailed and colourful settings, of the sort familiar to readers of Emmanuel Le Roy Ladurie's *Montaillou*,[74] and doctrine is recollected in greater detail.[75] Visibility – the evil God's or Devil's creation of all visible things – becomes a subject in itself. There is emphasis on the evil creation of all the human senses with which material things are perceived. And there is more detailed listing of things in the natural world. Thus Raymond Valsiera remembered one of the family of Autier heretics preaching that 'the malign God had made all things which can be perceived by the physical eyes or by other physical senses, such as the sky and earth, and all animals, air and water, and all the things that are in them'.[76] Heretics were reported in Toulouse 609 saying, as we have seen, that 'nothing of those things that God had made could be corrupted or pass away', and now they are being reported to Fournier as saying that 'God only made that which lasts and perseveres forever … but that God had not made those things that are corrupted and destroyed'.[77]

---

et in domo ipsorum iacuit, et comedit, et facto mane, cum esset dies dominica, et populus ivisset ad ecclesiam, ipsa testis remansit sola cum dicta Petronilla, commatre sua, et cum ostendisset ei domum et bladum, et vinum, et alia quæ habebat, dixit quod omnia ista erant diaboli'.

[74] E. Le Roy Ladurie, *Montaillou: Cathars and Catholics in a French Village, 1294–1324*, trans. B. Bray (London, 1978).

[75] *Le registre d'inquisition de Jacques Fournier évêque de Pamiers (1318–1325)*, ed. J. Duvernoy, Bibliothèque Meridionale 3rd ser. 41, 3 vols (Toulouse, 1965), together with J. Duvernoy, *Le registre d'inquisition de Jacques Fournier évêque de Pamiers (1318–1325): Corrections* (Toulouse, 1972).

[76] *Registre*, ed. Duvernoy, 1: 281–2: 'Deus vero malignus fecerat omnia que occulis corporalibus sentiri possunt, vel aliis sensibus corporalibus, sicut sunt celum et terra, et omnia animalia, aer et aqua, et omnia que sunt in eis.'

[77] Ibid. 2: 422: 'illud solum quod durat et perseverat semper … fecerat Deus, set illa que corrumpuntur et destruuntur Deus non fecerat'; cf. ibid. 2: 35 for a similar formula.

There are glimpses of the way that heretics' sermons had packaged rejection of divine creation of the natural world. Striking is their emphasis on animals and weather that people did not like, such as wolves, flies, lizards, snakes, storms and hailstones.[78] Fertility looms larger. Whereas fertility was only briefly glimpsed in one recollection in Toulouse 609, that the good God did not make things flower and seed (*florere et granare*), it came up often in depositions in front of Fournier and an inquisitor acting slightly earlier (1308–9), Geoffroi d'Ablis. The same phrase is used – *florere et granare*[79] – but in longer statements, which also give several glimpses of an illustrative image used by heretics when preaching. This was that seed placed on a bare stone did not germinate; this only happened when placed in earth and because of earth:[80] we shall return to this. The good God was entirely removed from fertility in this world. Arnaut Sicre heard the heretic saying that 'the celestial father did nothing at all in this world, not for things to flower or seed, nor for beings to conceive or give birth, nor to produce babies'.[81] In the heaven of the good God there was no fertility, a point whose expression mixes poetry and lack of logic. There 'corn may be born and grow and will flower, yet will not produce seed; and vines may throw out shoots, and yet they will not produce fruit; and trees will have leaves and blossom, and yet they will not produce fruit'.[82]

At this point let us terminate the survey of evidence of heretical rejection of the good God's creation of the natural world. Recapitulating what we have found, let us sort it into three strands. One of these is a past reality. We get keyhole glimpses of it: the application of Parisian axiomatic logic to the fundamental theology of

---

[78] Ibid. 1: 304, 378; 2: 36, 58, 113–14.

[79] Ibid., 1: 230, 283; *L'Inquisiteur Geoffroy d'Ablis et les Cathares du Comté de Foix (1308–1309)*, ed. A. Pales-Gobilliard, Sources d'Histoire Médiévale Publiées par l'Institut de Recherche et d'Histoire des Textes 15 (Paris, 1984), 134; *Le livre des sentences de l'inquisiteur Bernard Gui*, ed. A. Pales-Gobilliard, Sources d'Histoire Médiévale Publiées par l'Institut de Recherche et d'Histoire des Textes 30, 2 vols (Paris, 2002), 1: 680, 684, 704, 740.

[80] *Registre*, ed. Duvernoy, 1:.230; *Inquisiteur Geoffroy d'Ablis*, ed. Pales-Gobilliard, 104.

[81] *Registre*, ed. Duvernoy, 2:.58: 'pater celestis nichil omnino faciebat in hoc mundo, nec florere nec granare, nec concipere, nec parere, nec fetus producere'.

[82] Ibid. 2: 36: 'blada nascentur et crescent et florebunt, et tamen non granabunt; et vine emitent palmites, et tamen non fructificabunt; et arbores habebunt folia et flores, et tamen non fructificabunt'.

the position; books of heretical theology; formal and street-corner disputations in Languedoc; scholastic debates between learned and treatise-writing Catholic and heretical theologians in Lombard cities; and sermons over many decades in the houses of heretics' followers in Languedoc. The second strand is those constraints on the different sorts of evidence that shape the keyholes through which we peer. Moneta's reporting of listening to heretics and reading their books has to stand in for the absence of any records of the debates and the loss of the heretics' theological treatises, while we have to negotiate the subtle problems of inquisitors' questions and the ways in which they developed over time in order to assess how they shaped what deponents said. The third strand is that of modern historical scholarship and the debate about Catharism as an entity, where deconstructionists present difficulties in the evidence and past 'reality' as muddy and impenetrable.

This survey suggests three concluding points. First, there are many overlaps and verbal similarities between the texts we have been surveying, while the differences we see seem to flow naturally from the different parts of past heretical reality from which the evidence comes and the different ways in which different types of text skew things. The notion that the theology has been entirely imposed by a collective clerical fantasy beggars belief.

Secondly, throughout the inquisition records there is evidence of opposition to this particular doctrine. Many people liked the heretics and their doctrines, but did not like this one. Further, when the preaching of rejection of the natural world concentrated on fertility, it almost automatically slipped sideways. It moved away from God's or a God's role (that is, absence of a role) to autonomous fertility, and, in the case of agrarian pastoral production, it moved from autonomous fertility towards statements about good things on the earth. 'Things do not grow because of the good God' becomes 'things grow because of the goodness of the earth'. Preaching in this way, heretics either stimulated or perhaps simply provided the occasion for the expression of materialist views, while the more open inquisitions of post-1273 and 1319–20 ensured the entry of these views into written records. Growth: no God had anything to do with it, just seed, manure and rain.[83]

83 See W. L. Wakefield, 'Some Unorthodox Popular Ideas of the Thirteenth

Let us allow the third and final point to emerge through one example of this, a scene reported by one deponent questioned by Jacques Fournier. Around the feast of John the Baptist the witness, Adémar of Bédeilhac, was together with Arnold of Bédeilhac the Elder; Bernard John, the parish priest of Bédeilhac; and others he could not remember. They were sitting under an elm tree. They had been talking about a miraculous spring in the diocese of Couserans, and a miracle which had taken place in olden times, when some fish frying in a pan had jumped out of the frying pan and into the fountain. The witness Adémar said that he then said, 'Similarly we see God performing miracles every day'. 'In winter we see that all the trees are dry and leafless, and then they flower in summer, and they bear fruit'.[84] Arnold then replied that this came about because of the nature of the earth. Debate about the natural world was being stimulated by heretical preaching, and in this instance something more can be seen in this conversation under an elm tree. It is using one's eyes to look at the natural world, and seeing something of beauty in the transition of trees through the seasons.

University of York

Century', *Medievalia et Humanistica* ns 4 (1973), 23–35, on the expression of these views in the depositions contained in MS Collection Doat 25.

[84] *Registre*, ed. Duvernoy, 3: 52: 'similiter vidimus cotidie quod Deus facit miracula … nos vidimus quod in yeme omnes arbores sunt sicci et sine foliis, et in estate floriuntur, et granantur'.

SUBIACO – INNOCENT III'S VERSION OF ELIJAH'S CAVE

by BRENDA BOLTON

IN Biblical history and Christian literature alike, caves or grottoes, those works of nature, 'as if cut painstakingly but elegantly in the rocks or the cliff side without any tool',[1] have always played their significant part. Had not Benedict of Nursia, father of western monasticism, spent three years in eremitical solitude in just such a grotto beneath Monte Taleo in the Simbruini range of the Apennines?[2] It was no surprise then that it was to this, the Sacro Speco or Holy Cave, that Innocent III (1198–1216) came in person during the summer of 1202.[3] Drawn to Subiaco in no small part by his reading of Book II of Gregory the Great's *Dialogues*,[4] in which his distinguished papal predecessor had described Benedict's *Life and Miracles*,[5] Innocent's visit was notable on several counts. As the first of the 'newly mobile' popes of the thirteenth century, his willing absence from the stifling Roman summer was enforced 'not by man but by nature'[6] while, as *abbas universalis* with power over

---

[1] As witnessed by Godric of Finchale (c. 1106) in the Valley of Jehoshaphat. See Reginald of Durham, *Libellus de vita et miraculis S. Godrici*, Surtees Society 15 (1847), 57–58; Andrew Jotischky, *The Perfection of Solitude: Hermits and Monks in the Crusader States* (University Park, PA, 1995), 68.

[2] *Chronicon Sublacense*, ed. Raffaele Morghen, Rerum Italicarum Scriptores 24/6 (Bologna, 1927), 4, lines 3–7.

[3] From before 6 August until c. 10 September: *Regesta Pontificum Romanorum*, ed. Augustus Potthast (Berlin, 1874), 149 (nos 1716–22); *Chronicon Sublacense*, ed. Morghen, 34, lines 23–27; Uwe Israel, 'Der Papst und die Urkunde an der Wand: Innozenz III. (1198–1216) in Subiaco', *Quellen und Forschungen aus italienischen Archiven und Bibliotheke* 84 (2004), 69–102.

[4] *Grégoire le Grand: Dialogues*, ed. A. de Vogüé, trans. P. Antin, 3 vols, SC 251, 260, 265 (Paris, 1978–80).

[5] Johannes Fried, 'Le passé à la merci de l'oralité et du souvenir: Le baptême de Clovis et la vie de Benoît de Nursie', in *Les tendances actuelles de l'histoire du Moyen Âge en France et en Allemagne: Actes des colloques de Sèvres (1997) et Göttingen (1998)*, ed. J. -C. Schmitt and O. G. Oexle, Histoire Ancienne et Médiévale 66 (Paris, 2003), 85–104.

[6] Agostino Paravicini Bagliani, *Il corpo del Papa*, Biblioteca di cultura storica 204 (Turin, 1994), 257–59; idem, *The Pope's Body*, trans. D. S. Peterson (Chicago, IL, 2000), 171–73.

all Benedictines,[7] he regulated the two vastly different communities of monks which he found at Subiaco. From this exceptional place of refreshment and inner contemplation – bringing men closer to the mysteries of both God and nature – a unique contemporary letter has also survived.[8] The particular spirituality of the location confirmed the pope's view that the Sacro Speco itself should be the catalyst for the reform of Benedictine monasticism throughout Christendom.[9] As a direct result of his visit, therefore, Innocent was instrumental in fashioning a building campaign which marked a clear break with previous western tradition.[10] Henceforth, as in the East, monks and pilgrims alike were invited to meditate on the empty cave as a *memoria* – the dramatic scene of a particular but temporary event, namely Benedict's brief but crucial eremitical retreat there.

It was precisely the spiritual significance of this 'very narrow cave', where Benedict dwelt before adopting the coenobitic life,[11] which turned Innocent's thoughts towards the Holy Land and to that great Old Testament prophet, Elijah. Knowing both his Bible and the works of Gregory, his famous predecessor,[12] Innocent must rapidly have made the connection between the fathers of eastern and western monasticism. In fact, in his *Life* of Benedict, Gregory twice compares the saint to Elijah, both men witnessing evil deeds performed at a distance[13] and restoring a child to life.[14] Furthermore, the pope was well aware of Elijah's close association with two particular caves, one on Mount Carmel near Acre, the other on Mount Horeb in Sinai. In the first cave, Elijah, the

---

[7] Ursmer Berlière, 'Innocent III et la réorganisation des monastères bénédictins', *Revue Bénédictine* 32 (1920), 22–42, 145–59, at 26–29.

[8] Karl Hampe, 'Eine Schilderung des Sommeraufenthaltes der römischen Kurie unter Innozenz III. in Subiaco 1202', *Historische Vierteljahrsschrift* 8 (1905), 509–35.

[9] C. Giumelli, ed., *The Benedictine Monasteries of Subiaco* (Milan, 1982)

[10] Marina Righetti Tosti-Croce, 'The Architecture of the Sacro Speco', in ibid. 75–94, 234–36; eadem, 'Il Sacro Speco di Subiaco e l'architettura dei Crociati in Terra Santa', in *Il Medio Oriente e l'Occidente nell' arte del XIII secolo*, ed. H. Belting, Atti del XXIV Congresso Internazionale di Storia dell'Arte, 2 vols (Bologna, 1982), 2: 129–39.

[11] Gregory, *Dialogues* 2.1.4 (SC 260: 132–33).

[12] Christoph Egger, '"The Growling of the Lion and the Humming of the Fly": Gregory the Great and Innocent III', in *Pope, Church and City: Essays in Honour of Brenda M. Bolton*, ed. F. Andrews, C. Egger and C. M. Rousseau, The Medieval Mediterranean 56 (Leiden, 2004), 13–46, at 21–27.

[13] 3 Kings 18: 3–4: Gregory, *Dialogues* 2.13.4 (SC 260: 178–79).

[14] 3 Kings 17: 21: Gregory, *Dialogues* 2.31.1 (SC 260: 226–27).

hermit who had defeated the priests of Baal, was perceived as the ultimate monastic founder figure,[15] whilst in the second, Elijah, the prophet, eventually received God's message in 'the still small voice' after forty days and nights.[16] From the fourth century onwards, pilgrims venerated the cave on Mount Carmel as the hermitage par excellence and the cave itself caught the imagination of later centuries in both east and west.[17] This was to be particularly so following the loss of Jerusalem in 1187.

More prosaically, the spectacular setting and altitude of Subiaco permitted Innocent and his Curia some respite from the fierce heat of the Roman summer.[18] For similar reasons, the emperor Nero (54–68 AD) had selected this site for an imposing summer villa, creating three artificial lakes by damming the River Aniene.[19] In his *Dialogues*, Gregory the Great attributed to Benedict the foundation of no fewer than twelve monasteries at Subiaco[20] but, by Innocent's day, only S. Scolastica survived, situated on the plateau above the lake.[21] It was, however, the cave complex, comprising the Sacro Speco and the Grotta dei Pastori, located a full mile higher up the mountain above S. Scolastica, which was regarded as the true cradle of monasticism.[22] Whilst Benedict's retreat was the Speco or upper cave, it was to the geological and structural axis of the grotto below that the shepherds of the Aniene valley came to hear his sermons.[23]

Until the end of the eleventh century, communication between the two caves was effected by a narrow path cut into the steep ridge running along the mountain side. Following the permission willingly granted by Abbot John V (1060–1121) to the monk Palumbo to live in the manner of Benedict at the Speco,[24] the

---

[15] 3 Kings 18: 40: Jotischky, *Perfection of Solitude*, 67–69.

[16] 3 Kings: 19: 8–13.

[17] Jotischky, *Perfection of Solitude*, 106–08.

[18] Israel, 'Innozenz III.', 69–72.

[19] The last was destroyed by an earthquake in 1305.

[20] Gregory, *Dialogues* 2.3.13 (SC 260: 148–51).

[21] F. Caraffa, *Monasticon Italiæ, I: Roma e Lazio*, Centro storico benedettino italiano (Cesena, 1981), 174–75 (no. 229).

[22] P. Carosi, *Il primo monastero benedettino*, Studia Anselmiana 39 (Rome, 1956), 28, 32–36.

[23] Gregory, *Dialogues* 2.1.8 (SC 260: 136–37).

[24] *Chronicon Sublacense*, ed. Morghen, 14, lines 7–8: 'in Specu ubi beatissimus pater Benedict habitaverit'.

cave complex was made more accessible both within and without. Significantly, John instituted a solemn liturgical procession for the Monday of Passion Week at which the whole community, some barefoot, moved from S. Scolastica to their final destination at the Speco, singing psalms, bearing crosses and carrying holy water.[25] Likewise, for the feast of St Benedict (21 March), a similar but yet more elaborate procession made its way to the Speco, a *capsa* or reliquary and an *ycona* or representation of the saint himself being borne aloft.[26] It is even possible that Pope Paschal II (1088–99) responded to the abbot's fervent request that he should visit Subiaco.[27] Small wonder, then, that John should have been hailed as a second Benedict on his death.[28] Not only had he transformed the natural structure of the rock into a crypt but he also linked the upper and lower grottoes by a short flight of steps, the so-called Scala Sancta,[29] and repaired the steep road leading up to the Speco.[30] These would later prove to be vital contributory elements in Innocent's plan for developing the sanctuary.

The papal visit to Subiaco was the precursor of wider changes, the peaceful nature of which Paravicini Bagliani has graphically demonstrated.[31] Innocent could now freely choose when and how often to leave Rome and initiated a regular summer exodus of papal officials from the city. Whilst the Pope was concerned to recover those parts of the Patrimony of St Peter previously held by German imperial troops,[32] the new mobility of the Curia was motivated as much by the need to itinerate and demonstrate papal

---

[25] Ibid. 15, lines 14–16.

[26] Ibid. 15, lines 16–24, at line 19.

[27] Ibid. 17, lines 19–24.

[28] Ibid. 19, line 28.

[29] Ibid. 17, lines 2–3.

[30] Ibid. 18, lines 15–16.

[31] Agostino Paravicini Bagliani, 'La mobilità della corte papale nel secolo XIII', in S. Carocci, ed., *Itineranza Pontificia: la mobilità della curia papale nel Lazio (secoli XII–XIII)*, Istituto storico italiano per il Medio Evo, Nuovi Studi Storici 61 (Rome, 2003), 3–78, at 5–16.

[32] Celestine III had by 1192 secured control of Subiaco and its region. See B. Bolton, 'Celestine III and the Defence of the Patrimony', in J. Doran and D. J. Smith, eds, *Pope Celestine III (1191–1198). Diplomat and Pastor* (Aldershot, 2008), 317–53, at 335.

authority[33] as by the desire to escape torrid Rome with its endemic malarial sickness for fresher climes.[34] Evidence abounds to demonstrate Innocent's desire for *recreatio corporis*.[35] Later, in 1207, twice more in 1208, and 1209, he is recorded as suffering heat exhaustion, while in 1203 and 1212 he spent the entire summer out of Rome for similar reasons.[36]

The documentary and visual evidence for Innocent's visit to Subiaco are both unusually rich and detailed, representing a remarkable survival for such a relatively brief period.[37] An anonymous *breviator* or curial official, close to Hugolino, cardinal deacon of S. Eustachio (1198–1206),[38] addressed an outspoken private letter to a sick friend, probably Raynaldo of Capua.[39] The author records the pope's intimate leisure moments, demonstrating both the delights and tribulations of life in this rural setting. No other piece of late twelfth- or early thirteenth-century writing better conveys the beauties of nature in the wild, or indeed their drawbacks.

Innocent and the Curia did not, in fact, stay at the monastery of S. Scolastica but encamped close by, above Nero's lake, some living under canvas whilst others lodged in the painted chamber of the hospice. Although appreciative of the magnificent blue lake and the breezes which it created, the eye-witness seems to have found

---

[33] Eadem, 'The Caravan Rests: Innocent III's Use of Itineration', *Omnia Disce: Medieval Studies in Memory of Leonard Boyle, OP*, ed. A. J. Duggan, J. Greatrex and B. Bolton (Aldershot, 2005), 41–60, at 57–59.

[34] Paravicini Bagliani, *Il corpo del Papa*, 257–59; idem, *The Pope's Body*, 171–73; Bolton, 'Caravan Rests', 57–59.

[35] Innocent, *Sermones de tempore* 18 (PL 217: 393–98, at 393).

[36] Paravicini Bagliani, 'La mobilità della corte papale', 16–17; Bolton, 'Caravan Rests', 58–59.

[37] Paris, BN, MS Lat. 11867, fol. 141ᵛ; Hampe, 'Eine Schilderung des Sommeraufenthaltes', 528–35.

[38] Cardinal Bishop of Ostia (1206–27), Pope Gregory IX (1227–41): W. Maleczek, *Papst und Kardinalskolleg von 1191 bis 1216: Die Kardinäle unter Cölestin III. und Innocent III.*, Publikationen des Historischen Instituts beim Österreichischen Kulturinstitut in Rom, Abhandlungen 6 (Vienna, 1984), 126–33.

[39] Raynaldo de Celano, papal procurator (1199), bishop-elect of Capua (1204) and bishop (1208–12). See Norbert Kamp, *Kirche und Monarchie im staufischen Königreich Sizilien. Prosopographische Grundlegung: Bistümer und Bischöfe des Königreiches 1194–1266*, Münstersche Mittelalter-Schriften 10, 4 vols (Munich, 1973–75), 1: 112–16; Hampe, 'Eine Schilderung des Sommeraufenthaltes', 522–24; idem, *Mitteilungen aus der Capuaner Briefsammlung*, Sitzungsberichte der Heidelberger Akademie der Wissenschaften 13 (Heidelberg, 1910), 27–31 (no. 1), 41–44 (no. 5).

much about which to complain, disliking the sombre mountains and the often stifling lack of air. The rows of trees of different sorts, linked together by twisted lengths of vines, which surrounded it, all combined to charm and bemuse the senses. For men and horses alike, however, the steep mile-long descent down to the lake and the laborious ascent back again meant that these excursions were more often than not made on foot with all the consequent dangers and difficulties. Indeed, so worn out were the *curiales* by the climb along the rocky track through the ruins of the villa that this completely negated the joys of the cool water below. Above all, they suffered from swarms of insects, described and recorded in every tiny detail, and by far the most annoying feature of their stay. Flies were everywhere, buzzing, biting, stinging, being inhaled and even masticated with food, whilst the daytime nuisance caused by cicadas was at night replaced by that of crickets. The *curiales* seem to have felt that they had been brought to Subiaco to be punished by nature, so as not to take too much pleasure from their surroundings!

Only Innocent rose above these considerations and irritations. The letter reveals his vivid appreciation of the beauty and tranquillity of the natural world. The pope's particular pleasure was to rejoice in the differential currents which flowed into the lake and around the small islets, creating on the one hand a limpid depth and, on the other, the effect as of a bubbling saucepan. Into this he dipped his hands and gargled with the cold water, thus washing away not only the external impurities but also benefitting internally from the pleasing icy draught. His task was to sustain the morale of the *curiales*. Indeed, whenever they were troubled, they ran to 'the new Solomon'[40] as to the spring of living water, and sat in familiar fashion at his feet, delighting in his words of grace and listening to his eloquence and wisdom, as contemplative Mary had done. The anonymous letter-writer records that they tarried long in this way, joyfully drinking water from the springs of the Saviour, and thus enabling each man to satisfy his copious needs – spiritual, contemplative and historical.

Close to this idyllic setting, however, at the monastery of S. Scolastica on the lower slopes of Monte Taleo, abuses were rife

---

[40] Hampe, 'Eine Schilderung des Sommeraufenthaltes', 530; Michele Maccarrone, *Studi su Innocenzo III*, Italia Sacra 17 (Padua, 1972), 380 n. 2.

and secular influence appeared deeply intrusive.[41] The pope's visitation thus assumed an urgent pastoral purpose. As elsewhere, the possession of personal property had contributed to this decline and, in his letter, *Cum ad monasterium*,[42] Innocent restated Gregory the Great's graphic account of the monk whose corpse remained unburied on a dunghill as the sign of his perdition.[43] In a face-to-face meeting with the Subiaco community, Innocent's sermon, based on a text from Matthew 5: 'Blessed are the pure in heart',[44] presented the monks with a dramatic and moral challenge, whilst the provisions of *Cum monasterium* were so thoroughgoing that they entered into canon law as part of a code of reformed monasticism.[45] The papal visit to Subiaco resulted directly in a novel experiment by which, in 1203, heads of certain Benedictine houses exempt from the control of their local bishop were summoned to meet together in six provincial chapters.[46] This initiative achieved only limited success and it was not until the Fourth Lateran Council of November 1215 that Innocent created a more permanent organ of monastic reform by instituting a triennial General Chapter for the Benedictines on the model of that held annually by the Cistercian Order.[47]

Above the lake at Subiaco, the remote and atmospheric location of the Sacro Speco ensured its isolation from less welcome developments elsewhere. By 1202, six monks occupied a small conventual building of which no trace survives.[48] Although subordinate to the lower monastery of S. Scolastica, Innocent's attitude to this

---

[41] *Chronicon Sublacense*, ed. Morghen, 35, lines 9–10; Brenda Bolton, '*Via Ascetica*: A Papal Quandary', in W. J. Sheils, ed., *Monks, Hermits and the Ascetic Tradition*, SCH 22 (Oxford, 1985), 161–91, at 178–79.

[42] 4 September 1202, *Die Register Innocenz' III.* 5. Band: *5. Pontifikatsjahr, 1202/1203: Texte*, ed. O. Hageneder et al., Publikationen des Historischen Instituts beim Österreichischen Kulturinstitut in Rom 2/1/5 (Vienna, 1993), 156–60 (no. 81 (82)). [Henceforth *Register 5*].

[43] Gregory, *Dialogues* 4.57.11 (SC 265: 190, lines 81–3); *Register 5*, 158, lines 29–31; *Chronicon Sublacense*, ed. Morghen, 34–36, at 35, lines 35–38.

[44] Innocent, *Sermones de sanctis* 31 (PL 217: 589–96).

[45] *Decretales Gregorii IX*, 3.35.6 (*CICan*, 2: 599–600).

[46] Maccarrone, *Studi*, 226–46, 328–34 (Appendices 1–2).

[47] *Decrees of the Ecumenical Councils*, ed. N. J. Tanner, 2 vols (Georgetown, DC, 1990), 1: 240–41 (Canon 12).

[48] V. Federici, *I monasteri di Subiaco*, 2 vols (Rome, 1904), 2: 50 (no. 234).

tiny community, led by Prior John,[49] was in vivid contrast to his strictures in *Cum ad monasterium*. Seeing the Sacro Speco as the perfect example of a monastic community, he ensured its autonomous existence with a gift that was to be uniquely illustrated, not once, but three times. Two letters laid the foundation for future papal munificence. The first granted the monks of the Speco an annual subsidy of six pounds of silver to be paid in perpetuity from the papal treasury.[50] The second, a special privilege to Prior John and the brothers,[51] confirmed the source of their income as Castrum Porziano, a concession repeated by subsequent popes in 1217, 1227 and again in 1255.[52] This privilege, the first enregistered document of Innocent's sixth pontifical year, is illustrated with a famous miniature in the left-hand border which elaborates the initial letter 'I' of *Inter holocausta*.[53] A full-length, full-face portrait of Innocent, designated 'dominus papa', also shows a cardinal, identified as 'dominus cardinalis Iohannes' at his right hand, and two small figures at the pope's feet, displaying inscribed scrolls. This, the earliest image of Innocent, drawn, according to Cheney, some time between 20 May 1204 and 26 July 1205,[54] not only 'depicts the event which is the subject of this very letter'[55] but also associates the pope with the privilege given to the Sacro Speco and reveals in a unique way his patronage of the tiny community. The presence there of Cardinal John is also of real significance. Now considered to be John of S. Paolo, medical doctor, Benedictine monk, former abbot of the eponymous Roman monastery and cardinal, in all likelihood it was he who intervened to assist the community at the Speco to impetrate or request the privilege.[56]

---

[49] John de Taliacotio (Tagliacozzo). See Israel, 'Innozenz III.', 80–81, n. 33.

[50] 30 August 1202: *Register 5*, 152–53 (no. 78 (77)).

[51] 24 February 1203: *Die Register Innocenz' III. 6. Band: 6. Pontifikatsjahr, 1203/1204: Texte und Indices*, ed. O. Hageneder et al., Publikationen des Historischen Instituts beim Österreichischen Kulturinstitut in Rom 2/1/6 (Vienna, 1995), 3–4 (no. 1) [Henceforth *Register 6*].

[52] Israel, 'Innozenz III.', 89 n. 69.

[53] Vatican City, Archivio Segreto Vaticano, Reg. Vat. 5, fol. 72^r; *Register 6*, Plate 1.

[54] C. R. Cheney, 'The Office and Title of the Papal Chancellor 1187–1216', *Archivum historiae pontificiae* 22 (1984), 369–76, at 374–76

[55] Ibid. 375.

[56] John of S. Paolo, Cardinal Priest of S. Prisca (1193–1205), Cardinal Bishop of Sabina (1205–14). Maleczek, *Papst und Kardinalskolleg*, 114–17; L. Gaffuri, 'Giovanni di San Paolo', *Dizionario bibliografico degli Italiani*, 56 (Catanzaro, 2001), 212–17; Cheney, 'Papal Chancellor', 376.

The fresco on the north wall of the lower church at the Sacro Speco represents the Promulgation of the Privilege.[57] Set out as an epigraph,[58] the monks reflected their gratitude for this gift by enshrining its complete text in a location near to the Speco itself.[59] All twenty four lines are visible, written alternately in red and black. On the left side, a seated St Benedict blesses with his right hand whilst supporting the privilege with his left. His companion, Romano, Abbot of S. Scolastica (1193–1216), kneels, with both hands raised in a gesture of praise. Innocent stands on the right side of the fresco, wearing Byzantine-style vestments and holding the text with both hands. The involvement of pope and abbot alike in this phase of decoration, combined with the obvious esteem in which the monks held them as spiritual patrons, merited their depiction too, in a place as close as possible to the cave of the founder. Following later alterations to the building, including the staircase descending to the Grotta dei Pastori, half of Innocent's face was lost, but the surviving portion shows a square yellow nimbus, edged in red and set against a blue background, surrounding his head. Romano displays the same attribute, a clear indication that the fresco must have been completed before 1216, the year in which both men died.[60]

Innocent and Romano, however, by no means limited their activities to the commissioning of the fresco. Instead, they shared responsibility for an extensive building campaign to highlight further the example of Benedict as founder and exalt the very origins of Benedictine monasticism.[61] By 1202, the Sacro Speco was still only accessible from the steep and winding track leading to the lower gate of the complex. First, the flight of steps by which Abbot John V had connected the upper and lower grottoes was

---

[57] Maria Laura Cristiani Testi, 'Frescoes at the Sacro Speco', *Benedictine Monasteries of Subiaco*, 95–132, 236–38, at 110–13.

[58] L. Gulli, 'A proposito dell'epigrafe dipinta sotto l'effigie di Innocenzo III al Sacro Speco Sublacense', *Bullettino dell'istituto storico italiano per il Medio Evo* 65 (1953), 103–06.

[59] Israel, 'Innozenz III.', 72: 'einer ... Form der Urkunden-Promulgation'.

[60] Gerhart Ladner, 'The so-called Square Nimbus', in idem, *Images and Ideas in the Middle Ages: Selected Studies in History and Art*, 2 vols, Storia e letteratura 155–56 (Rome, 1983), 1: 115–70, at 161; Cristiani Testi, 'Frescoes at the Sacro Speco', 111.

[61] Righetti Tosti-Croce, 'Architecture of the Sacro Speco', 78–86; eadem, 'Il Sacro Speco di Subiaco e l'architettura dei Crociati in Terra Santa', 131–35.

extended.[62] This created 'a fixed transit point', and explains the location of the text of the Privilege in the central space before which all entering the monastery would have to pass. Rather than carve out an articulated architectural space as in certain other grottoes, the two caves at Subiaco, already venerated for seven centuries, were now enveloped within a completely new structure in which the Scala Sancta formed a crucial element.[63] Entering the complex close to the Grotta dei Pastori, a flight of stairs led up to the landing, on the wall of which was the fresco of the Privilege. A second flight descended to Benedict's cave and then rose up again to the Capella di S. Gregorio, the small apsidal hall which was also part of Innocent's building campaign.[64]

While buildings in the West connected to saints' cults were usually located at places of martyrdom or burial, thus often risking too close an association with relics,[65] at Subiaco, Innocent turned instead to the eastern model for inspiration. This focused on wells, springs, cisterns and caves where *ad memoriam* structures were erected to commemorate transitory episodes from biblical or apostolic times.[66] Innocent, Romano and the architects seem to have based their reconstruction of the Subiaco caves on the church of St Mary of the Valley of Jehoshaphat, near Gethsemane in the Kidron Valley.[67] In particular, the monumental staircase descending to the grotto which had been the temporary tomb of the Virgin before her Assumption bears a striking similarity to the structure of the rebuilt Scala Sancta at Subiaco.[68] Popes from Pascal II in 1113 to

[62] Eadem, 'Architecture of the Sacro Speco', 82.

[63] Ibid. 82; eadem, 'Il Sacro Speco di Subiaco', 130–34.

[64] Eadem, 'Architecture of the Sacro Speco', 80–82, with a very clear diagram at 82.

[65] Brenda Bolton, 'Signs, Wonders, Miracles: Supporting the Faith in Medieval Rome', in Kate Cooper and Jeremy Gregory, eds, *Signs, Wonders, Miracles: Representations of Divine Power in the Life of the Church*, SCH 41 (Woodbridge, 2005), 157–78, at 157–65.

[66] André Grabar, *Martyrium: recherches sur le culte des reliques et l'art chrétien antique*, 2 vols (Paris, 1946), 1: 68–70; Righetti Tosti-Croce, 'Architecture of the Sacro Speco', 85–86.

[67] C. N. Johns, 'The Abbey of St Mary in the Valley of Jehoshaphat, Jerusalem', *Quarterly of the Department of Antiquities in Palestine* 8 (1939), 117–36; B. Bagatti, M. Piccirillo and A. Prodomo, *New Discoveries at the Tomb of the Virgin Mary in Gethsemane* (Jerusalem, 1975); D. Pringle, *The Churches of the Crusader Kingdom of Jerusalem: A Corpus*, 3: *The City of Jerusalem* (Cambridge, 2007), 287–306 (no. 337).

[68] Ibid. 298–300, plates 156–161; Righetti Tosti-Croce, 'Architecture of the Sacro Speco', 86; eadem, 'Il Sacro Speco di Subiaco', 133.

Adrian IV in 1154 granted privileges to this important Benedictine abbey church whilst deeply appreciating the liturgical significance of its setting in Gethsemane.[69] On the processional route for Palm Sunday, the Abbot of Jehoshaphat accompanied the Patriarch of Jerusalem from the Temple Precinct to Bethany and thence to the Golden Gate.[70] The abbey was the beneficiary of rich land holdings and possessions across Palestine. Destroyed in 1099, the church of Jehoshaphat had been rebuilt by pious donations from the nobles of the Latin kingdom and, in 1161, received for burial the body of Queen Melisande.[71] The Romanesque abbey church was described in 1165 by John of Würzburg,[72] and again after 1172 by Theodoric who, following John to the Holy Land, adapted his text by adding further details: 'The church is entered through a certain portico with more than 40 steps going down into the crypt ... from here, one may go up into the church by as many steps as one went down into the crypt.'[73] The upper church was destroyed again, probably in 1192 by Saladin,[74] and soon afterwards the crypt became a *mash'had* or place of Muslim prayer: 'The tomb of Maryam is in the Wâdî Jahannum. You descend (to the tomb) by six-and-thirty steps'.[75]

While the precise personal connections which brought details of the architectural layout of St Mary of the Valley of Jehoshaphat to Innocent's attention must remain unresolved, certain suggestions can nevertheless be made. In the first place, this Benedictine monastery enjoyed many contacts all over the south of Italy,

[69] *Regesta pontificum romanorum*, ed. P. Jaffé, 2 vols (Leipzig, 1885), 2: 784 (nos 6336–37); *Chartes de Terre Sainte provenant de l'abbaye de N.-D. de Josaphat*, ed. H.-F. Delaborde (Paris, 1880), 61–67 (nos 27–28), 72–78 (no. 31). See now *Papsturkunden für Kirchen im Heiligen Land*, ed. Rudolf Hiestand, Vorarbeiten zum Oriens Pontificius 3, Abhandlungen der Akademie der Wissenschaften in Göttingen, Phil.-hist. Klasse 3/136 (Göttingen, 1985), 117–19 (no. 14). For a discussion on papal letters and privileges for St Mary of the Valley of Jehoshaphat, see ibid. 36–38.

[70] Pringle, *Churches*, 292.

[71] Ibid. 290.

[72] *Peregrinationes Tres. Saewulf. John of Würzburg, Theodoricus*, ed. R. B. C. Huygens, CChr CM 139 (Turnhout, 1994), 127–30; Pringle, *Churches*, 290–92.

[73] *Peregrinationes Tres*, ed. Huygens, 169–71; Pringle, *Churches*, 291–92.

[74] Roger of Howden, *Gesta Regis Henrici II*, ed. W. Stubbs, RS 41, 2 vols (1867), 2: 24: 'Vallis de Japhes, abbatia et castellum'; Pringle, *Churches*, 292–93.

[75] G. Le Strange, *Palestine under the Moslems* (London, 1890), 210; Pringle, *Churches*, 293.

in Calabria, Puglia and most of all in Sicily.[76] Between 1194 and 1207, whilst some of his former community sought refuge at Jehoshaphat's dependent abbey of St Paul in Antioch,[77] Abbot Amatus, together with the rest of his chapter, appears to have resided at Messina, where the abbey's eponymous priory was situated[78] and not at Acre as was once supposed.[79] In exile, Amatus also busied himself with improving the possessions which his abbey held at Paternò in Sicily, following a disastrous earthquake in 1185.[80] If the communicating two-level structure of upper church and crypt-grotto at Jehoshaphat was a Benedictine architectural initiative, then comparisons and methods used elsewhere – particularly Amatus's knowledge of these from personal experience – would certainly have become available to Romano and his architects. The closeness of the Benedictine family is indicated, not only by the experience and wide contacts of John of S. Paolo but also by a surviving inscription suggesting that Roffredo, Abbot of Montecassino (1188–1209), was present at Subiaco in 1202, accompanying Innocent and perhaps even advising on the work in progress.[81]

A quite exceptional conjunction of nature and culture took place at Subiaco where a small-scale topographical reorganization of an Apennine landscape (or 'cavescape'?) had far-reaching consequences. The fusion of two historic episodes, the harsh experience of the personal *conversatio*, perfected by the young Benedict in eremitical solitude at the Sacro Speco, and the stimulation of the Grotta dei Pastori from whence he preached and attracted his first recruits to the coenobitic life, became a reality under Innocent's firm direction. Only a pope could have authorized the transformation of the Sacro Speco and Grotta dei Pastori into a unified complex, and Innocent possessed the vision to realize the theat-

[76] Ibid. 290.

[77] *Chartes de Terre Sainte*, ed. Delaborde, 92–94; Garufi, 'Il Tabulario', 16–17.

[78] C. A. Garufi, 'Il Tabulario di S. Maria di Valle Giosafat e la data delle sue falsificazione', *Archivio Storico per la Sicilia orientale* 5 (1908), 161–83, 315–49, at 327 (no. 125); Hans Eberhard Mayer, *Bistümer, Klöster und Stifte im Königreich Jerusalem*, MGH Schriften 26 (Stuttgart, 1977), 310.

[79] Pringle, *Churches*, 293.

[80] C. A. Garufi, 'Un contratto agrario in Sicilia nel secolo XII', *Archivio Storico per la Sicilia orientale* 5 (1908), 11–22, at 16–18.

[81] Jacques Stiennon, 'Studio critico sopra un'inscrizione dell'abbazia di Santa Scolastica a Subiaco', *Bullettino dell'istituto storico italiano per il Medio Evo* 65 (1953), 93–102, at 100–02.

ricality of the location. In the surroundings of that place too, the pope and his *curiales* were seen to experience the spiritual power of nature in a completely uninhibited way. The empty cave enshrined the unique memory of Benedict, 'pater et patronus noster',[82] not only on account of the vow taken by the monks there, but also as the place where spirituality was so abundant.[83] Place was all-important to Innocent III as Elijah's cave had been to him!

Queen Mary and Westfield College, University of London

---

[82] Innocent, *Sermones de sanctis* 31 (PL 217: 596B).
[83] Ibid.: 'non solummodo propter votum, sed etiam propter locum'.

PAY BACK TIME? TITHES AND TITHING IN LATE MEDIEVAL ENGLAND

by R. N. SWANSON

IN seeking aspects of the pre-Reformation Church which might be expected automatically to invoke connections with God's bounty, tithes and tithing are obvious candidates. In an essentially agricultural society, where the overwhelming majority of the population worked on the land, God's bounty in providing crops and food animals, and tithing as the response to the moral and theological imperative to acknowledge that bounty, surely ought to be almost a commonplace. Tithes had biblical origins as a divine precept,[1] and an obligation which Christians were deemed to have inherited from the Jews.[2] Theologians might be expected to discuss tithes in terms of divine generosity and human reciprocity, and priests to urge their flocks to acknowledge their resulting debt to God by accepting the obligation to pay tithes on their produce to support his ministers.

In reality, evidence of such concerns in late medieval England, the focus of this brief survey, is elusive;[3] the clearest acknowledgement of an obligation to repay divine bounty may be Yarmouth's custom of dedicating a tithe-like share of the sea-fishing catch to the Church as 'Christ's part'.[4] Generally, the sources overwhelmingly endorse the view that 'the primary meaning of tithing was social and economic rather than religious'.[5] There is no lack of

---

[1] e.g. Lev. 27: 30–33; Deut. 14: 22.

[2] However, for an assertion that the obligation to tithe was abrogated by Christ's birth, see *Registrum Johannis Trefnant, episcopi Herefordensis, A.D. MCCCLXXXIX–MCCCCIV, ed.* W. W. Capes, CYS 20 (1916), 304–06, at 306.

[3] In limiting the survey to England, it is also restricted to works produced by English authors. Adding material produced by Continental authors and known to have been available in England (including a range of confessional and instructional material, and canon law texts) would clearly affect the scope. It might also affect the argument, but any impact should be reflected in the English-generated evidence.

[4] R. N. Swanson, 'Standards of Livings: Parochial Revenues in Pre-Reformation England', in C. Harper-Bill, ed., *Religious Belief and Ecclesiastical Careers in Late Medieval England* (Woodbridge, 1991), 151–96, at 166–67.

[5] R. C. Palmer, *Selling the Church: The English Parish in Law, Commerce, and Religion, 1350–1550* (Chapel Hill, NC, 2002), 32.

evidence about tithes and tithing, with lay grumbles at visitations about harsh tithing by parish priests (matched by clerical grumbles about non-paying parishioners), and frequent cases in church courts as priests and parishioners clashed over their respective rights and obligations.[6] These were contentious issues, but there was seemingly very little discussion of basic principles, and very little attempt to address matters through formulations derived from perceptions of a direct relationship between God as provider of resources and man as their consumer with an obligation to render thanks. As in Johannes de Burgo's *Pupilla oculi*, dating from 1385, tithing was a matter of rules and regulations, not theory and principle.[7] Discussion seems to be notably and inexplicably absent from sermons, where it might be expected to be a key factor in priestly concerns for parochial discipline. The only collection providing substantial comment seems to be *Jacob's Well*, from the fifteenth century, which may not actually be a sermon collection in any case.[8]

Tithes may be only rarely discussed in relation to God's bounty, but the limited discussion which does exist is suggestive, and reveals lines of argument which, while speculative, may mean that the issue of how humans might express their thanks for divine generosity has wider repercussions than are immediately obvious in the religious life of pre-Reformation England.

Three didactic works from the fourteenth and fifteenth centuries point the way towards possible formal theological analyses. In the *Fasciculus morum*, written in the early 1300s, disputes concerning tithes and tithe-paying were subsumed within a discussion of the sin of pride, requiring payers to humble themselves in relation to the Church. Tithes were here treated explicitly as a response to God's bounty: 'tithes are owed to the giver of all things by natural

---

[6] Tithe disputes are scattered through, e.g., *Kentish Visitations of Archbishop William Warham and his Deputies, 1511–1512*, ed. K. Wood-Legh, Kent Records 24 (1984); for legal processes, see R. H. Helmholz, *The Oxford History of the Laws of England*, 1: *The Canon Law and Ecclesiastical Jurisdiction from 597 to the 1640s* (Oxford, 2004), 435–65.

[7] Johannes de Burgo, *Pupilla oculi* (Paris, 1518), 9.3.

[8] *Jacob's Well: An English Treatise on the Cleansing of Man's Conscience: Part 1*, ed. A. Brandeis, EETS os 115 (1900); discussion of tithing at 37–47. On the text as a sermon collection, see V. O'Mara and S. Paul, *A Repertorium of Middle English Prose Sermons*, 4 vols, Sermo 1 (Turnhout, 2007), 1: xxxii; tithing discussion summarized ibid. 4: 2285–88.

law, for it is just that he who gives everything receive back a part'.[9] The return to God is, however, a return to the Church – and it is the obligation to give which counts. Tithe payers have no discretion about whether they deem individual clerics worthy to receive the tithes or not: such moral issues are between the priest and God, but the payment is solely to God, with the priest acting on God's behalf 'for safekeeping and faithful distribution'. Failure to pay what is owed to God is therefore an act of sacrilege; anyone who avoids payment 'cheats not man but God, and is consequently excommunicated by God and by common [church] law'.[10]

Tithing here represents a debt to God, not to man; but it is a debt which brings its own rewards – in receiving his due, God offers further bounty in exchange. Faithful tithe-payers may become members of a restored tenth order of angels; in any event, according to canon law they will receive the fourfold reward of abundance of crops, bodily health, forgiveness of sins and ultimately heaven.[11] For this author, though, alms for the poor are a separate issue: the tithe is for God; alms are to be given from what remains after tithes have been paid.[12]

The second discussion appears under the heading of 'Decima' in John of Bromyard's monumental compilation of material for preachers, the *Summa predicantium*. The precise date of this fourteenth-century work is uncertain, but is not significant here.[13]

As the *Summa* was intended to assist preachers, it is unsurprising that many of the comments in its discussion deal with practicalities, and particularly the need to reprove bad tithing. There is, nevertheless, a clear sense of the reciprocity between God and humans in tithing. While tithes may be received by the clergy, they

[9] *Fasciculus morum: a Fourteenth-Century Preacher's Handbook*, ed. S. Wenzel (University Park, PA, 1989), 80–81.

[10] Ibid. 82–83. Cf. Brandeis, *Jacob's Well*, 45, which condemns false tithing as theft from God, which by analogy with the actions of Judas the false tither 'sleeth aȝen crist'.

[11] These benefits also appear in the later *Jacob's Well*: ibid. 42.

[12] Wenzel, *Fasciculus morum*, 82–83.

[13] I cite the two-volume edition published at Venice, 1586. On dating, see L. E. Boyle, 'The Date of the *Summa praedicantium* of John Bromyard', *Speculum* 48 (1973), 533–37, repr. in idem, *Pastoral Care, Clerical Education, and Canon Law, 1200–1400* (London, 1981), ch. 10. An earlier date is suggested in K. Walls, *John Bromyard on Church and State: The* Summa Predicantium *and Early Fourteenth-Century England. A Dominican's Books and Guide for Preachers* (Market Weighton, 2007), 189–96, which may merit serious consideration.

are in fact paid to God, in recognition of his universal dominion as creator of all things, and the bountiful lord (*largus dominus*) who has allowed humans (*nobis*) to benefit from nine-tenths of creation, claiming only a tenth for himself.[14] Poor tithing accordingly can be condemned as theft and ingratitude for such divine goodness, an unjust repayment of bad for good, after the manner of Cain.[15]

Like others, Bromyard refers to the fourfold rewards offered in return for good tithing.[16] His approach to the relationships established by tithes is explicitly transactional. Thus, God's claim is not treated as moral or spiritual. He is not merely the lord of creation, but its landlord: tithes are the annual rent owed by mankind in exchange for the divine concession.[17] In similarly concrete fashion, Bromyard cuts through challenges to tithing based on claims that the clergy fail to spend the income as they should by dismissing such arguments as irrelevant: it is the obligation to tithe which matters, with the rewards from God placed at the heart of the transaction. After all, when buying land, the purchaser's core concern is to gain possession of the property, not how the seller might spend the purchase money.[18]

The third and final discussion appears in *Dives and Pauper*, and dates from the early fifteenth century. Constructed as a dialogue, this instructional text comprised a lengthy discussion of the Ten Commandments, offering guidance on one element of the by-then traditional syllabus of Catholicism. Issues arising from tithing are considered in relation to the seventh commandment, 'Thou shalt not steal'. Tithing first appears as part of the discussion of sacrilege understood as occurring from the nature of 'the thing that is stolen or misused'. Drawing on canon law, tithes are portrayed as part of a debt to God; their withholding amounts to robbing the poor of their goods, for which the sinner will be answerable at the Final Judgement, as well as suffering here on earth.[19]

For the work's author, tithes are identified as the 'vows of Christian people, ransom for sins, and the patrimony, heritage, and aid

---

[14] Bromyard, *Summa,* 1, fols 180[rb], 178[vb].
[15] Ibid. 1, fols 179[va], 179[ra]. For Cain as a bad tither, see also below, 129).
[16] Ibid. 1, fols 179[rb]–179[va].
[17] Ibid. 1, fol. 178[vb].
[18] Ibid. 1, fol. 180[va].
[19] *Dives and Pauper*, ed. P. H. Barnum, 2 vols in 3, EETS os 275, 280, 323 (1976–2004), 1/2: 165–66.

for poor people, and the tributes of needy souls'.[20] They are due to God not because he needs them, but as straightforward acknowledgement of his lordship and bounty as 'the giver of all good', being demanded 'for our profit, not for his profit'.[21]

This, though, is a limited definition of bounty: tithes are due only on things from which humans benefit, so not from things which are not beneficial – or indeed which it is not 'worshipful' to tithe (among which the author includes dogs and cats).[22] Moreover, following from awareness of, and asserting the distinction between, the predial tithes derived from natural increase, and the privy or personal tithes due from wages and the profits of trade, it is a fundamental point that not everything has to be tithed. Tithe is not an automatic fiscal payment, due from every transfer of goods and wealth – otherwise eventually all landed property would end up in ecclesiastical hands, the poor would face levies on the charity offered to them, and every will might be tithed, creating a situation where 'the Church would be too rich and the people too poor'.[23] (Even so, tithes were demanded on an extensive catalogue of agricultural products, as evident in the lists included in one of the 'sermons' of *Jacob's Well*, which did argue that the recipients of gifts and bequests should pay tithes on such transfers, even if the donor had already paid tithes.)[24]

Dives and Pauper does not consider in detail how tithes should be spent, but spending is not wholly ignored. The author's main concern is to address the suggestion that lay people can refuse tithes to unworthy clerics. While he accepts that tithes should not be paid to a cleric who misspends church goods, or is a notorious lecher, the obligation to tithe does not disappear in such cases. Hostiensis is cited to suggest that in such circumstances the tithes should be paid to the person above the cleric in the hierarchy, almost as an ecclesiastical line manager, who would then assume the duty to spend the receipts for the benefit of the Church and the poor.[25]

---

[20] Ibid. 1/2: 165–66.
[21] Ibid. 166.
[22] Ibid. 167.
[23] Ibid. 167–68.
[24] *Jacob's Well*, ed. Brandeis, 37–41; comment on gifts and bequests at 41.
[25] *Dives and Pauper*, ed. Barnum, 1/2: 168–69; the legal debate on payment continues to 170.

These texts all originate as clerical works, but obviously with lay instruction in mind. Evidence for equivalent doctrinal formulations addressed directly to the laity, seeing tithes as repayment to God for divine bounty in the fruits of nature, is elusive in the surviving sources. It seems to occur most coherently in England in the cycles of northern mistery plays, notably in plays recounting the tale of Cain and Abel.[26] Here Abel is represented as the good tithe-payer, offering to God in return for the good he has received. In contrast (and most emphatically in the 'Towneley' version of events), Cain is the poor tithe-payer: the agricultural worker whose experience of God's bounty is hard labour and poor harvests, with the expectation that the best results of his toil will literally go up in smoke. He pays grudgingly, having little to thank God for, and seeking to evade his obligations by offering the worst of the harvest and miscounting his sheaves.

Especially in the 'Towneley' text, Abel's language stresses God's bounty, informing Cain that 'God giffys the all thi lifyng', and offering his own tithe in thanks to 'my Lord, that all has sent'.[27] In the 'Towneley' text he also invokes an idea of earthly goods as loaned by God.[28] This resonates with the language of some late-medieval wills, which redistribute property declared to have been 'loaned' to the testator by God and now bequeathed in charity, especially to the poor. Such testamentary provision arguably provides a parallel to the language of tithe distribution, as an equitable act of agency by the payer to benefit those in need. Such associations open up new linkages which tie tithe-paying into a vocabulary of need and deserts, and the mutuality of *caritas*, which also gives the tithe-payer (or allows him to claim) some degree of control over the destination of his offering.

The contrast of Cain and Abel focuses on payment to God, on what can be interpreted – and was, in canon law – as a contractual

---

[26] *The Towneley Plays, Volume One: Introduction and Text*, ed. M. Stevens and A. C. Cawley, EETS ss 13 (1994), 14–19; *The N-Town Play: Cotton MS Vespasian D. 8*, vol. 1: *Introduction and Text*, ed. S. Spector, EETS ss 11 (1991), 37–39; L. T. Smith, *York Plays* (New York, 1885), 36–37.

[27] *Towneley Plays*, ed. Stevens and Cawley, 15, 17. Cf. *N-Town Play*, ed. Spector, 37: 'Lord … All is had þorwe grace of þe'.

[28] *Towneley Plays*, ed. Stevens and Cawley, 15:

> '… all the good thou has in wone
> Of Godys grace is bot a lone.'

obligation to the Church as God's principal channel of agency on earth. However, the resonances of Abel's language (and possibly Cain's direct challenge to a God who actually does not give him much bounty, for all his labour) raise the question of the precise contractual nature of the obligation, and by extension the issue of who should actually receive the tithes in the age of the New Covenant. The question of disbursement may be the most problematic element of tithing if considered in terms of God's bounty. The complexities of tithing make the agriculturists who paid them merely intermediaries: while paying individually, they act on behalf of the collectivity of humans in transferring the produce to the clergy. Yet the clergy themselves are also, even if only partially, mere intermediaries. While they are the beneficiaries of the payments, they do not in theory have exclusive right to the produce. Others have a claim, in the traditional division which asserted that a fraction of the tithes (but not a fixed portion) should go to the poor.[29]

Here tithing intermingles with wider concepts of God's bounty as something which should be available to all. Bounty of itself lacks purpose: it needs an object and objective. God's bounty, the natural world, can certainly exist of itself, but once humans become involved and move beyond self-sufficiency and subsistence, complications set in – the legend of the Fall. Human relations become economic relations, as the natural world is tamed into producing produce – no less natural, but now controlled – which is traded and exchanged. Those processes of exchange can be legitimated through a humane concern which is also a moral and spiritual imperative, the demands of *caritas*, requiring people to care for each other, especially the poor, through processes of distribution of natural products and produce. *Caritas* needs no emphasis as a theoretical underpinning of medieval Catholicism as a social force, which sought among other things to guarantee the rights of the poor. Such understandings, applied in terms of God's bounty, are exemplified in the preamble to an ordinance issued by the Mayor of London in 1382, regulating distribution of bread and beer to ensure that the poor had access to supplies in the market. He, with his aldermen, issued the ordinance, but it was 'our Lord God omnipotent' who 'of his merciful goodness' – his

---

[29] B. Tierney, *Medieval Poor Law: a Sketch of Canonical Theory and its Application in England* (Berkeley, CA, 1959), 70–71, 73–74, 122.

bounty (*bountee*) – had 'given to his people the gracious market in grains and brewing (*breez*) which runs generally throughout this land'.[30] Disruption of that market, particularly by disrupting free exchange and excluding the poor, by implication provoked divine displeasure, and had to be curtailed.[31]

If the links between God's bounty and tithes do tend (as certainly suggested in *Dives and Pauper*) to integrate distribution to the poor, the ramifications extend. As most incumbents' incomes derived principally from tithes, with the obligation for their disbursement, this clearly resonates with ideas that the Church's goods were all in theory the goods of the poor, and should be used accordingly.[32] The implications and implementation of that attitude appear perhaps most strikingly in late medieval England in the will of Richard Caister, the early-fifteenth century Vicar of St Stephen's in Norwich who gained a reputation for sanctity. Basing his actions explicitly on the tenet that 'the goods of the Church, according to the canons, are the goods of the poor', he bequeathed his property to be distributed among the poor, with his own parishioners taking precedence.[33] Caister was exceptional, but the assumptions of his will would have underpinned relations between clergy and laity more generally, and they would especially affect understandings of clerical behaviour. In particular they may be implicit in some criticisms of clerical extravagance, even as voiced by other clerics. Equivalent concerns underlie Thomas Wimbeldon's complaint in the 1380s that greedy, proud and spendthrift priests were wasting 'þe goodis of pore men and of Cristis heritages'.[34]

Going even further, the expectation that relief of 'the poor' should be one of the prime uses of tithes opened up the possibility

---

[30] F. Rexroth, *Deviance and Power in Late Medieval London* (Cambridge, 2007), 341 (see also 343).

[31] Ibid. 343–44.

[32] For this idea, see Tierney, *Medieval Poor Law*, 40–43. The theory was also used to defend the Church against royal exactions: *De speculo regis Edwardi III seu Tractatu quem de mala regni administratione conscripsit Simon Islip, cum utraque ejusdem recensione manuscripta*, ed. J. Moisant (Paris, 1891), 98–99; *Political Thought in Early Fourteenth-Century England: Treatises by Walter of Milemete, William of Pagula, and William of Ockham*, ed. and trans. C. J. Nederman (Turnhout, 2002), 85.

[33] N. P. Tanner, *The Church in Late Medieval Norwich, 1370–1532*, Pontifical Institute of Mediaeval Studies, Studies and Texts 66 (Toronto, 1984), 231–32.

[34] *Wimbledon's Sermon: Redde rationem villicationis tue: A Middle-English Sermon of the Fourteenth Century*, ed. I. K. Knight (Pittsburgh, PA, 1967), 78.

of debate and conflict over their being granted to the ordinary clergy at all. Hints of that strand may inhere in the occasional conflicts in which the laity's control of the produce paid as tithes was used or threatened as a weapon to discipline unpopular or ineffective clergy – although this also had its sanction in canon law produced during the struggles of the Gregorian reform period. It was, nevertheless, a logical argument that, as the laity paid the tithes – even if only as intermediaries – they should determine who should have them, and could judge whether the recipient was qualified to receive them. Hence, maybe, the arguments about tithes as free-will offerings, sometimes formulated in ways which did not challenge the obligation to pay tithes, but asserted that who they were paid to could be a matter of choice. This stance underlies the article condemned as erroneous at the anti-Wycliffite Blackfriars Council in 1382: 'that tithes are pure alms, and that on account of the sins of their curates parishioners may withhold them, and confer them on others at will'.[35] In so far as a general 'Lollard' approach can be reconstructed, it seems to have comprised an acceptance of the liability to pay tithes moderated by the claim that the payer could determine who was their most suitable recipient (and that, especially, the poor might have a greater claim than the parish clergy, particularly if the latter were deemed ineffective or disqualified by character flaws).[36] In the Norwich heresy trials of 1430, Thomas Plowman of Sizewell admitted that he had not paid tithes to churches or curates for the past seven years, but had given them to the poor instead – 'which he asserted that he believed it was licit to do'.[37] While there is here no explicit

[35] Thomas Netter, *Fasciculi zizaniorum magistri Johannis Wyclif cum tritico*, ed. W. W. Shirley, RS 5 (1858), 496; cf. *Registrum Trefnant*, ed. Capes, 279–80, 365. Similar ideas underlay the dispute over personal tithes in London provoked by comments of the Franciscan William Russell, but the argument that such tithes were not due by divine precept removes that case from a context of justification in terms of God's bounty: see C. A. Robertson, 'The Tithe-Heresy of Friar William Russell', *Albion* 8 (1976), 1–16, esp. 4–5; also J. Röhrkasten, *The Mendicant Houses of Medieval London, 1221–1539*, Vita Regularis: Ordnungen und Deutungen religiosen Lebens im Mittelalter, Abhandlungen 21 (Münster, 2004), 308–10.

[36] A. Hudson, *The Premature Reformation: Wycliffite Texts and Lollard History* (Oxford, 1988), 341–45; see esp. 344, an argument that clergy should place themselves among the poor and feeble to validate their right to tithes. See also M. Aston, *Faith and Fire: Popular and Unpopular Religion, 1350–1600* (London, 1993), 121–22; A. Hudson, ed., *Selections from English Wycliffite Writings* (Cambridge, 1978), 10, 21.

[37] *Heresy Trials in the Diocese of Norwich, 1428–31*, ed. N. P. Tanner, Camden Society

formulation in terms of God's bounty, nevertheless the occasional indication that such donation to the poor is more pleasing to God than tithe-paying does suggest such inferences. However, as the author of *Jacob's Well* noted, arguments that tithes should go to the poor were not always motivated by charity. He suggested that people advocating such arrangements were often bad tithe-payers, arguing simply out of malice against the Church.[38]

★   ★   ★

In late medieval England, tithe-paying appears primarily as a matter of contention, one of the many potential flashpoints in the complex relations between clergy and laity. Beyond calling on the Old Testament verses which established the obligation for the Jews, the theoretical validation of tithing is rarely considered, either by contemporaries or later commentators. However, the evidence considered here suggests that there was awareness of a need for theoretical justification which established tithing as an obligation which repaid God for his bounty, and through that repayment contributed to the economy of *caritas* which underpinned 'the social miracle' of medieval Catholicism.[39]

University of Birmingham

4th ser. 20 (1977), 103; see also ibid. 61, 141, 183; *Lollards of Coventry, 1486–1522*, ed. S. McSheffrey and N. Tanner, Camden Society 5th ser. 23 (2003), 72.

[38] *Jacob's Well*, ed. Brandeis, 44. One argument here was possibly that free-will charitable distributions, without clerical oversight, made it easier to avoid full payment.

[39] For the concept of the 'social miracle', see J. Bossy, *Christianity in the West, 1400–1700* (Oxford, 1985), ch. 4, esp. 57.

DEVOTION, POPULAR BELIEF AND SYMPATHETIC MAGIC AMONG RENAISSANCE ITALIAN WOMEN: THE ROSE OF JERICHO AS BIRTHING AID

by SUZY KNIGHT

THE natural world offered Renaissance men and women an abundance of raw materials which could be used to protect and to heal. Healers and wise women used particularly potent plants, gemstones and animal parts, in conjunction with magical ritual and Christian prayer, as preventative and cure. Pertaining largely to an oral and unlettered culture, much of this natural lore has been lost. Fortunately, the Renaissance demand for vernacular translations of classical works brought about a revived interest in botany, whilst cheap print and a wider reading public fostered the proliferation of a new genre of self-help manuals and books of secrets, and it is within these works that some of the oral traditions have been captured in ink.[1] Whilst it may be true that many of the new authors of the Renaissance used print to disparage and demystify many of these popular beliefs, it is often only through the disapproving lens of the vernacular manual that we are able to catch glimpses of folk beliefs in practice. This paper will examine one such tradition: the use of the Rose of Jericho as birthing aid.

When Paolo di Iacopo, a Florentine rope-maker, died intestate in 1535, the Office of Wards drew up an inventory of his family's possessions. Listed among their most treasured objects, including rosaries made of amber and ivory and an illuminated Book of

---

[1] For books of herbals, see Agnes Arber, *Herbals, Their Origin and Evolution: A Chapter in the History of Botany 1470–1679* (Cambridge, 1953); Karen Reeds, *Botany in Medieval and Renaissance Universities* (New York, 1991). For Renaissance Italian self-help manuals, see Rudolph Bell, *How to Do It: Guides to Good Living for Renaissance Italians* (Chicago, IL, 1999). For the vernacular book of secrets and its impact on science, medicine and attitudes towards nature, see William Eamon, 'Science and Popular Culture in Sixteenth-Century Italy: The "Professors of Secrets" and their Books', *Sixteenth Century Journal* 16 (1985), 471–85; idem, *Science and the Secrets of Nature: Books of Secrets in Medieval and Early Modern Culture* (Princeton, NJ, 1994).

Hours, is the curious entry for 'a Rose of Jericho for women in labour'.[2] Stored with precious devotional items and noted in the household inventory, this was clearly no ordinary plant. The name of the Rose of Jericho sounds very familiar, whether because it is one of the plants described in the famous passage from Ecclesiasticus (24: 13–14) in praise of wisdom, or because it has been used as the title of various novels, songs and poetry anthologies. Despite its familiar name, the appearance, properties and history of this plant have been almost forgotten. The Rose of Jericho was used in the Renaissance as an important birthing aid, yet it has merited only passing mention in recent historical scholarship on pregnancy and childbirth in early modern Europe.[3] My paper will draw on the work of folklorists and botanists who, since the middle of the nineteenth century, have revived interest in this curious plant.[4] This paper will examine how the Rose of Jericho's unusual biology led it to be invested with powerful spiritual and magical meaning. It will also explore the complex belief systems of Renaissance Florentine women, which comfortably combined folk belief and natural magic with Catholic doctrine, particularly within the ceremonies and rituals surrounding childbirth.

[2] 'jᵃ roxa di Jericho da dona di parto': Florence, Archivio di Stato di Firenze, Magistrato dei Pupilli del Principato [hereafter: ASF, MPP], 2646, fols 330ʳ–341ʳ [estate of Pagholo di Jacopo, funaiuolo, 10 May 1535], at fol. 339ᵛ.

[3] See Jacqueline Musacchio, *Art and Ritual of Childbirth in Renaissance Italy* (New Haven, CT, 1999), 141; Jacques Gélis, *History of Childbirth: Fertility, Pregnancy and Birth in Early Modern Europe* (Cambridge, 1991), 117; 145–46.

[4] See Charles Morren, 'The Rose of Jericho', in *The Annals of Horticulture and Year-Book of Information on Practical Gardening* (London, 1850), 333–34; Moncure Conway, 'The Sacred Flora', *Harper's New Monthly Magazine*, vol. 42, no. 247 (December 1870), 87–95; Grace Crowfoot and Louise Baldensperger, *From Cedar to Hyssop: A Study in the Folklore of Plants in Palestine* (London, 1932), 119–25; Guglielmo Lützenkirchen and Maria Doretta Simoni, 'Utilizzazione magica e terapeutica dell'Anastatica hierochuntica', *Storia e medicina popolare* 9 (1991), 192–204; and Alessandra Gasparroni, 'La rosa di Gerico. Tratti di un'indagine fito-magico-religiosa dalla tradizione ai nuovi contesti', *Etnoantropologia* 1 (2007), 143–49.

BIRTHING AMULETS[5]

Florentine mothers-to-be used birthing amulets and rituals for three main reasons: protection, alleviation and tradition. Renaissance women sought protection from miscarriage, death in childbed and stillbirth.[6] They sought alleviation from the pains of labour, which preachers told them to expect as part of the punishment they had inherited from Eve.[7] The use of amulets and rituals was also an important part of the female traditions surrounding childbirth and certain patterns of behaviour were inherited from mothers and grandmothers. The physician Antonio Guianerio recognized the importance of these traditions when he advocated performing certain familiar ceremonies in order to please the mother-to-be and to satisfy the wise women present at the birth, all of whom clearly expected ritual.[8]

Childbirth was an event ordinarily controlled and attended solely by women, however. It relied on a vast repository of female pregnancy lore, much of which combined devotion, popular belief

[5] The word 'amulet' will be used here to describe an object that is treasured for its powers to protect against harm or encourage good fortune and health. For textual amulets used in birthing rituals, see Don Skemer, *Binding Words: Textual Amulets in the Middle Ages* (University Park, PA, 2006), 235–50.

[6] For the dangers and fears relating to pregnancy and childbirth during the period, see Roger Schofield, 'Did the Mothers really Die? Three Centuries of Maternal Mortality in "The World We Have Lost"', in L. Bonfield et al., eds, *The World we have Gained* (Oxford, 1986), 230–60; Adrian Wilson, 'The Perils of Early Modern Procreation: Childbirth with or without Fear?', *British Journal for Eighteenth-Century Studies* 16 (1993), 1–19; Linda A. Pollock, 'Embarking on a Rough Passage: The Experience of Pregnancy in Early Modern Society', in *Women as Mothers in Pre-Industrial England: Essays in Memory of Dorothy McLaren*, ed. Valerie Fildes (London, 1990), 39–67, at 45. For the maternal death-rate in fifteenth century Florence, see David Herlihy and Christiane Klapisch-Zuber, *Tuscans and their Families: A Study of the Florentine Catasto of 1427* (New Haven, CT, 1985), 270–79.

[7] e.g. Bernardino da Siena, *Predica volgari sul Campo di Siena,1427,* ed. Carlo Delcorno, 2 vols (Milan, 1989), 2: 29, 824.

[8] This was in his *Tractatus de matricibus*, cap. 24 in *Opera omnia* (Pavia, 1481), at fols 2.3ʳ⁻ᵛ, quoted in Wendy R. Larson, 'Who is the Master of this Narrative? Maternal Patronage of the Cult of St Margaret', in Mary C. Erler and Maryanne Kowaleski, eds, *Gendering the Master Narrative: Women and Power in the Middle Ages* (Ithaca, NY, 2003), 94–104, at 94. For Guianerio, see Helen Rodnite Lemay, 'Anthonius Guainerius and Medieval Gynecology', in Julius Kirshner and Suzanne F. Wemple, eds, *Women of the Medieval World* (Oxford, 1985), 317–36.

and sympathetic magic.[9] One ritual was the practice of girding a woman in labour with leaves of the miraculous vervain plant that had been gathered on the morn of St John the Baptist's feast day.[10] Another involved reciting a combination of prayers and incantations into the expectant mother's right ear.[11] The Church promoted its own birthing aids and rituals. Popes Urban V (1362–70) and Paul II (1464–71) had advocated pregnant women wearing Agnus Dei (small wax discs stamped with the image of the Lamb of God and blessed by the pope) to protect themselves from harm, whilst individual churches recommended certain relics in their possession.[12] For Florentine women, the Virgin's Holy Girdle, kept at Santo Stefano in nearby Prato, was by far their most important birthing relic.[13] These women, therefore, followed a holistic approach to protecting themselves from the dangers of pregnancy, combining natural magic with orthodox and unorthodox Christian ritual, and this is precisely why the mysterious Rose of Jericho was so attractive as a birthing aid.

THE ROSE OF JERICHO

I was exalted like a cedar in Libanus, and as a cypress tree
   on mount Sion.
I was exalted like a palm tree in Cades, and as a rose plant
   in Jericho …
      (Ecclesiasticus 24: 13–14, Douay-Rheims translation)

---

[9] See Thomas Forbes, *The Midwife and the Witch* (New Haven, CT, 1966), 64–79; and Franco Cardini, 'Tra scienza e magia', in Gabriele Borghini et al., eds, *Una Farmacia preindustriale in Valdelsa: la spezieria e lo spedale di Santa Fina nella città di San Gimignano, Secc. XIV–XVIII* (San Gimignano, 1981), 153–71. For the displacement of midwives by male physicians in the early modern period, see Adrian Wilson, *The Making of Man-Midwifery: Childbirth in England 1660–1770* (London, 1995); Lianne McTavish, *Childbirth and the Display of Authority in Early Modern France* (Aldershot, 2005).

[10] A practice branded superstitious by Fra Scipione (Girolamo Mercurio), the former Dominican friar turned physician in his *De gli errori popolari d'Italia* (Verona, 1645), 382; cited in Bell, *How to Do It*, 108.

[11] Bell, *How to Do It*, 114. For other examples of female ritual, see *The Trotula: An English Translation of the Medieval Compendium of Women's Medicine*, ed. Monica H. Green (Philadelphia, PA, 2002).

[12] For a detailed history of the Agnus Dei, see John Cherry, 'Containers for Agnus Dei', in *Through a Glass Brightly: Studies in Byzantine and Medieval Art and Archaeology Presented to David Buckton*, ed. C. Entwistle (Oxford, 2003), 171–84.

[13] For the importance of this relic to Florentine women, see Brendan Cassidy, 'A Relic, some Pictures and the Mothers of Florence in the Late Fourteenth Century', *Gesta* 30 (1991), 91–99.

This passage from Ecclesiasticus would have been familiar to Renaissance Christians from the popular Little Office of the Virgin, but the scented rose-bushes it described were no longer growing in Jericho when the crusaders and pilgrims visited the Holy Land in the Middle Ages.[14] What was offered in their place was the *Anastatica hierochuntica*, a plant that is neither a rose, nor a native of Jericho. *Anastatica* is a small cruciferous annual that grows in the deserts of the Middle East and North Africa. It has a very peculiar seed-dispersal system that allows it to reproduce even in the most extreme desert conditions. When its seeds reach maturity, the plant dries out completely and curls into a ball to protect them. The Rose of Jericho will remain thus until it rains when its flesh rehydrates and uncurls, allowing its seeds to be released into a more fertile environment.[15] This reaction to humidity can be simulated to dramatic effect by soaking the base of the plant in water, causing the Rose of Jericho to completely open and uncurl. This process of closing and opening, dying and coming back to life, doubtless seemed miraculous to those who witnessed it for the first time. The Rose of Jericho was interpreted as a natural demonstration of the mystery of Christ's Resurrection; an interpretation expressed by its botanical name *Anastatica* – the Resurrection plant.[16]

According to Ludolph von Suchem, a German prelate who visited the Holy Land in the mid-fourteenth century, Roses of Jericho were sold to pilgrims as souvenirs by the Bedouin.[17] Relic- and souvenir-collecting was an essential part of pilgrim culture and those natural objects that had special spiritual significance were particularly prized.[18] The Rose of Jericho, with its biblical

[14] See Laurent de Saint-Aignan, 'Recherches sur la Rose de Jéricho', *Annales de philosophie chrétienne* 93 (1877), 348–63, at 348.

[15] Jacob Friedman and Zipporah Stein, 'The Influence of Seed-Dispersal Mechanisms on the Dispersion of *Anastatica Hierochuntica* (Cruciferae) in the Negev Desert, Israel', *Journal of Ecology* 68 (1980), 43–50.

[16] It was given this name by Johann Friedrich Gronov (1611–1671): Lutzenkirchen and Simoni, 'Utilizzazione magica', 195.

[17] For Ludolph von Suchem's description, see his 'Description of the Holy Land', in *Library of the Palestine Pilgrims' Text Society*, ed. Aubrey Steward and C. R. Conder, 14 vols (London, 1887–97), 12: 91, cited in Crowfoot and Baldensperger, *Cedar to Hyssop*, 123.

[18] For souvenir-collecting by pilgrims, see Diana Webb, *Pilgrims and Pilgrimage in the Medieval West* (London, 1999), 124–32. For souvenirs from the Holy Land, see Kathryne Beebe, 'Knights, Cooks, Monks and Tourists: Elite and Popular Experience of the Late-Medieval Jerusalem Pilgrimage', in Kate Cooper and Jeremy Gregory, eds,

pedigree and miraculous properties, was a highly valued souvenir and specimens were brought back to Western Europe. Its image can be found on crusaders' tomb sculptures, in the architecture of churches sponsored by Templar Knights and as the attribute of pilgrims in some paintings of the period.[19] This paper is not concerned, however, with examining the Rose of Jericho as a symbol of masculine religious zeal and bravery. Instead it will consider *Anastatica* in its role as Renaissance pregnancy aid.

It is clear from the archival evidence that by the late fifteenth century, the Rose of Jericho had been reinterpreted by Italian women as an important birthing amulet. These women had also renamed it, preferring to call it the Rose of the Virgin Mary, by far its most popular name within the household inventories.[20] The family of the apothecary Jacopo di Marco, who died in 1497, kept 'a Rose of the Virgin Mary' in a little box made of cypress wood.[21] The Quaratesi family inventory of 1527 includes a 'Rose of Our Lady for women in childbirth', whilst a 'Rose of the Virgin Mary' is listed amongst the estate of a Venetian courier named Lorenzo di Bastiano, who died in 1549.[22] In all these cases the Rose was preserved among the most precious of the family's belongings.

This Tuscan name for *Anastatica* is confirmed in the monumental herbal of Pietro Andrea Mattioli. His vernacular translation of, and commentary on, Dioscorides's *Materia medica* was so successful that it went through several editions in Italian, French, Spanish, German, Czech and Latin and led to Mattioli's appointment as

Elite and Popular Religion, SCH 42 (Woodbridge, 2006), 99–109, at 106; Hilda F. M. Prescott, *Jerusalem Journey: Pilgrimage to the Holy Land in the Fifteenth Century* (London, 1954), 141–60.

[19] See Herbert Haines and Richard James Busby, *A Manual of Monumental Brasses* (Oxford, 1861), cxi. A Rose of Jericho features in Matthias Grünewald's St Cyriacus panel, which forms part of the Heller Altarpiece (1509–11), at the Städel Museum, Frankfurt.

[20] Other areas in Italy refer to them as roses of St Anne or St Margaret: Gasparroni, 'rosa di Gerico', 145.

[21] 'jª chassettina d'arcipresso entrovi … jª rosa della Vergine Maria': ASF, Magistrato dei Pupilli Avanti il Principato [hereafter: MPAP], 180, fols 49ʳ–52ᵛ [estate of Jachopo di Marcho di Marcho, speziale in [Piazza] Verzaia, 1496], at fol. 50ʳ.

[22] 'iª rosa della Nostra Donna sopra a done di parto': ASF, MPAP, 190, fols 71ʳ–74ᵛ [estate of Piero d'Antonio Quaratesi, 14 May 1527], at fol. 72ʳ; 'iº schatolino entrovi iª rosa della Vergine Maria': ASF, MPP, 2649, fols 586ʳ–590ʳ [estate of Lorenzo di Bastiano, coriere di Vinezia, 21 April 1549], at fol. 588ᵛ.

physician to Archduke Ferdinand of Austria.[23] It was purely by chance that the mysterious practices surrounding the Rose were written down by Mattioli at all. His rival, Valerio Cordo, had misidentifed the Rose of Mary with the genus *Amomum* in his own herbal and Mattioli could not resist exposing this error on paper in order to exalt himself; in doing so he provided the modern reader with valuable insight into this almost forgotten ritual.[24]

Mattioli lists the plant in his index as the 'Rose of St Mary brought back from Jericho'.[25] He goes on to say that these plants 'are called Roses of St Mary by our Italian women and are brought here from Jericho by pilgrims visiting the most sacred Sepulchre of our Lord Jesus Christ'.[26] The Rose of Jericho as a symbol already had its associations with the Virgin Mary in Western Christian tradition. The Rose of Jericho as *Anastatica* was linked to Mary through Middle Eastern legends, all of which revolved around the plant having been touched in some way by the Virgin. The Bedouin who sold von Suchem his Rose of Jericho told him that these plants had sprung up along the path that Mary took on the Flight into Egypt.[27] Another legend said that the Roses of Jericho had been infused with miraculous power when they were touched by the Virgin's hands, as she used them to hang Christ's laundered swaddling-bands to dry.[28] Today *Anastatica* is called in Arabic *Kaff el'Adra* or *Kaff Mariam*, translating as the Virgin's or Mary's Hand.[29] Eastern tradition had turned the Rose of Jericho as a species into a secondary relic of the Virgin, an object which, like the Holy Girdle of Prato, had been infused with blessings by having come into contact with Mary.

---

[23] For an introduction to Mattioli and his work, see Bell, *How to Do It*, 45–46.

[24] 'Valerio Cordo nel suo volumetto delle compositioni de medicamenti, scrive dell'Amomo assai inconstantemente. Imperoché nella compositione dell'aurea Alessandrina afferma per certo che l'Amomo non è altro, che questa pianta di Hierico': Pietro Andrea Mattioli, *Il Dioscoride dell' eccellente Dottor P.A. Matthioli co i suoi discorsi, con l'aggiunta del sesto libro de i rimedi di tutti i veleni de lui novamente tradotto & con dottissimi discorsi per tutto commentato* (Venice, 1548), 31.

[25] 'Rose di S Maria portate di Hierico': ibid., unpaginated.

[26] 'che le nostre Donne d'Italia chiamano Rose di santa Maria, portateci di Hierico da i peregrini, che vanno al santissimo sepolchro del nostro Signore GIESU CHRISTO': ibid. 31.

[27] von Suchem, *Description of the Holy Land,* 91; cited in Crowfoot and Baldensperger, *Cedar to Hyssop*, 123.

[28] Lutzenkirchen and Simoni, 'Utilizzazione magica', 197.

[29] See Crowfoot and Baldensperger, *Cedar to Hyssop*, 123.

It was also in the East that the Rose of Jericho was first used as a birthing aid. Then, as now, Muslim women in the Middle East used it to speed up childbirth.[30] A specimen would be soaked in water and as it started to open up, so the women believed that their labour would begin. The Franciscans who conducted the pilgrimage tours of the Holy Land soon began to promote this usage. By the sixteenth century, they too had started selling Roses of Jericho and claimed that they only opened on Christmas Eve or when women were in labour, and at no other time.[31] Here we witness the conflation of the Islamic belief about the Rose of Jericho with the expectation that this wonder of nature must express some spiritual truth. Rather than being a demonstration of Christ's Resurrection, the friars now interpreted the strange properties of the plant as a living manifestation of the miracle of the opening and closing of the Virgin's womb. Whilst northern Europeans focused on this aspect, calling *Anastatica* the Christmas Rose, it was the help that it promised to women in labour that captured the imagination of Italian mothers.[32]

Mattioli related how Italian women used the Rose of Jericho in exactly the same way as Middle Eastern Muslims: 'women are accustomed to put them into water when they are in labour, believing that once that plant is opened, they will give birth straightaway'.[33] Used in this way, the *Anastatica hierochuntica* would have slotted easily into Italian pregnancy lore, since it combined familiar elements found in both Christian and folk birthing aids. It was a secondary relic of the supreme mother, the Virgin Mary, whose sin-free pregnancy and pain-free delivery of Christ was offered up to women as the unattainable paragon. Recourse to such a relic, infused with the blessings of Mary, would have been a powerful birthing aid in its own right. Yet the Virgin's Rose also functioned according to principles of sympathetic magic that

[30] Ibid.

[31] See Pierre Belon, *Les observations de plusieurs singularitez & choses memorables, trouvées en Grece, Asie, Iudée, Egypte, Arabie, & autre pays estranges, Redigeés en trois livres*, 3 vols (Paris, 1555), 2: 144.

[32] Lutzenkirchen and Simoni, 'Utilizzazione magica', 198–200. It is this aspect of the Rose's legend that is the basis of David Hess's story about this plant: *The Rose of Jericho*, trans. and ed. Caroline Norton (London, 1870).

[33] 'nell'hora del partorire usano di tenere le donne nell'acqua; credendosi, che, come tal pianta s'apre, subito partoriscano': Mattioli, *I discorsi*, 31.

played such a great part in the ritual and ceremony of childbirth.[34] According to the principle that like could affect like, the Rose of Jericho – which behaved as the womb was thought to, closing to protect its seeds and opening to release them – could have a beneficial effect on the wombs of pregnant women.[35] It could also be used as one of the sympathetic rituals that surrounded childbirth. Ceremonial openings of windows and drawers and the untying of hair and birthing girdles were thought to speed up labour by encouraging a mimetic effect in the womb.[36] Ritualistic hydration of a Rose of the Virgin, therefore, would have been familiar in terms of these other sympathetic rituals.

CONCLUSION

Although it is thanks to Mattioli's herbal that we have this insight into the use of the Rose of Jericho by Renaissance Italian women, Mattioli certainly did not approve of the ritual. To the passage detailing his countrywomen's use of the Rose of the Virgin in the 1554 edition of his *Discorsi*, he added this sardonic judgement: 'such is the superstition that reigns among Christians'.[37] It was a judgement that was to appear in all subsequent editions.[38] The sixteenth century saw the female-controlled oral culture of pregnancy and childbirth, as well as other areas of popular healing, cross-examined on paper. Male authors started to re-examine the classical medical texts that were the source of much pregnancy lore, translating them into the vernacular.[39] Those rituals without a classical basis,

[34] For a Renaissance Italian interpretation of sympathetic magic, see Giambattista della Porta, *Natural Magick* (London, 1658), 16–17.

[35] This notion appears in Giovanni Marinello's late sixteenth-century treatise *Delle medicine partinenti all'infermità delle donne* (Venice, 1563), 235–40; quoted in Bell, *How to Do It*, 73.

[36] For the continuation of these ceremonies in present-day Abruzzo, see Gasparroni, 'La rosa di Gerico', 149.

[37] 'tanta inter christicolae irrespit superstitio': Mattioli, *I discorsi* (Venice, 1554), 35.

[38] *I discorsi* (Venice, 1557), 38; *I discorsi* (Venice, 1568), 58; *Commentaires de M. Pierre André Matthiole médecin sennois, sur les six livres de Ped. Dioscoride Anazarbeen de la matière médicinale: avec certaines tables médicinales, tant des qualités & vertus des simples médicamens, que des remèdes pour toutes maladies, qui peuvent avenir au corps humain, comme aussi des sentences, mots & matières traictées esdicts commentaires* (Lyons, 1572), 41; *I discorsi* (Venice, 1597), 50.

[39] Bell, *How to Do It*, ch. 3; *Medicina per le donne nel cinquecento: Testi di Giovanni Marinello e di Girolamo Mercurio*, ed. Maria Luisa Altieri Biagi et al. (Turin, 1992).

like the use of the Rose of Jericho, were either branded as superstition or not included at all. Those treatises that did discuss the Virgin's Rose were largely botanical, and tended to follow, more or less forcefully, the stance that Mattioli had taken.[40]

It was not only its lack of classical pedigree that caused the use of the Rose of Jericho as birthing aid to be dubbed superstitious. Like many other female rituals of the time it was problematic in the way it straddled the spheres of orthodox and folk belief. Yet its use as a birthing aid was not destroyed by the condemnation or the silence of these male critics; they merely caused the Rose of Jericho to slip back into the oral tradition of female pregnancy lore from whence it had come. Whilst the Rose of Jericho may be little known within the historiography of early modern childbirth, recent research has shown that it continued to be used in some parts of Italy as a birthing aid as recently as the 1970s.[41] Interpreted by the mothers of Florence as a secondary relic of the Virgin, a natural demonstration of the birth of Christ and the centrepiece of sympathetic birthing ritual, the Rose of Jericho embodied all the complexities that existed within the belief systems and childbirth rituals of Renaissance women. While its use may have been branded by some as ignorance and superstition, to the women of Italy who relied on it for assistance for over five hundred years it was truly a gift of God's bounty.[42]

Queen Mary, University of London

---

[40] See the judgements of Belon, *Observations*, 2: 144; Johannes Sturmius, *De rosa hierochuntina liber unus: in quo de eius natura, proprietatibus motibus, et causis pulchrè disseritur* (Louvain, 1608), quoted in Saint-Aignan, 'Recherches', 356–61; John Parkinson, *Theatrum botanicum: The Theater of Plantes or an Universall and Complete Herball* (London, 1640), 1384; Thomas Browne, *Pseudodoxia epidemica*, ed. Robin Robbins (Oxford, 1981), 148–50, 775–76. See also Caroline Norton's comments in the introduction to Hess, *Rose of Jericho*, vi–vii.

[41] See Gasparroni, 'rosa di Gerico'.

[42] Caroline Norton had encountered the tradition in nineteenth-century Italy 'among the lower classes' and followed by 'the simpler sort of peasant woman': Hess, *Rose of Jericho*, vii.

WHAT DID NATURAL HISTORY HAVE TO DO WITH SALVATION? JOSÉ DE ACOSTA SJ (1540–1600) IN THE AMERICAS[*]

by SIMON DITCHFIELD

AT the southern foot of the Palatine Hill in Rome, a little more than one hundred metres due west of the triumphal arch erected by the emperor who is associated more than any other with the Christian conversion of the Old World – Constantine the Great – there stands another arch. Relocated from its original position at the eastern foot of the Palatine, more or less directly across from the biggest remaining ruin in the forum – that of the Basilica of Maxentius – it formed the monumental entrance to one of the most important botanic gardens in sixteenth-century Europe – the *Orti farnesiani*, which were given their definitive shape between 1565 and 1590.[1] I propose that this second arch has reason to be considered as occupying a similar symbolic significance for the conversion of the New World.

As their name suggests, the gardens were established by the Farnese family, whose fortunes had been made by the election of Cardinal Alessandro as Pope Paul III in 1534. In view of the theme of this chapter it is highly appropriate that not only is this pontiff associated with that other watershed of early modern Roman Catholicism – the Council of Trent – which the pope finally convened after several false starts in 1545, but he also officially approved the Society of Jesus in 1540. Furthermore, it was his grandson, also called Alessandro Farnese, who commissioned the architect Jacopo Barozzi di Vignola both to oversee the design of the initial architectural framework for the *Orti farnesiani* (which

[*] This article was researched and written while I was holder of a British Academy Research Leave fellowship (2006–08). I am very pleased to acknowledge the financial generosity of the Academy.

[1] For the *Orti farnesiani* in this period see, in particular, the articles by Marcello Fagiolo, Alessandro Viscogliosi, and Paolo Nocchi and Ezio Pellegrini, in Giuseppe Morganti, ed., *Gli Orti farnesiani sul Palatino, Atti del convegno internazionale (Roma 28–30 novembre 1985)* (Rome, 1990); cf. idem, *Gli Orti farnesiani sul Palatino* (Milan, 1999).

was then carried out mainly by Jacopo Del Duca) and that of the mother church of the Jesuits – il Gesù.[2]

This plot of land had been originally purchased with a view to its value as a source of rather different produce – buried classical statuary (the famous Laocoön group which Julius II had put on display in the Belvedere courtyard in the Vatican had been found not too far away on the adjacent Esquiline Hill). Bankrolled by the Farnese and blessed with the global contacts conferred by the family patronage of the Jesuits, which were exploited with particular effect by Odoardo Farnese in the first three decades of the seventeenth century, the *Orti* soon became home to one of the finest collections of trees, shrubs and plants from the East Indies and New World in the Old, in proud competition with such rival botanic gardens as those at Pisa, Leiden and Aranjuez.[3] Nor was competition absent within Rome itself, which John Evelyn described as the 'Worlds sole cabinet' precisely to allude to the fact that in its various collections all the world was represented there.[4] The Jesuit Giovanni Battista Ferrari, who held the chair in Hebrew at the Roman College for twenty-eight years, was also author of the most important treatise of the period on Italian flower gardens, which devoted an illustrated chapter to the plants of New World origin in the garden in Rome belonging to his patron, the Princess Anna Colonna Barberini.[5]

[2] In fact, the earth dug for the foundations of the Gesù was used in the restructuring of the terrain against which the eastern perimeter wall of the Orti was built: Viscogliosi, 'Gli Orti farnesiani – cento anni di trasformazioni (1537–1635)', in Morganti, ed., *Gli Orti farnesiani sul Palatino*, 299–339, at 310–11.

[3] In 1625 the exotic planting there was catalogued in T. Aldino [Pietro Castelli], *Exactissima descriptio rariorum quarundam plantarum quae continentur Romae in Horto Farnesiano* (Rome, 1625). New World highlights included acacia (*Acacia Farnesiana*), yucca (*Yucca flaccida*) and passion flower (*Passiflora edulis*).

[4] John Dixon Hunt, 'Curiosities to Adorn Cabinets and Gardens', in O. Impey and A. MacGregor, eds, *The Origins of Museums: The Cabinet of Curiosities in Sixteenth- and Seventeenth-Century Europe* (Oxford, 1985), 267–79 (quotation at 272). Cf. A. MacGregor, *Curiosity and Enlightenment: Collectors and Collections from the Sixteenth to the Nineteenth Century* (New Haven, CT, 2007), 36–39.

[5] A. Ferrari, *Flora overo cultura dei fiori* (Rome, 1638; Latin edn 1633), ch. 21, 'Piante indiane negli Horti Barberini', 372–93. My sincere thanks to Amanda Lillie for drawing this treatise to my attention and to supplying me with a photocopy of the work. For a full discussion of Ferrari's sources and wide influence, see A. V. Segre, 'Horticultural Traditions and the Emergence of the Flower Garden in Italy (c.1550 – c. 1660)' (unpublished D.Phil. thesis, University of York, 1995), 19–45.

However, Ferrari was just one of a numerous kind. In a recently reprinted catalogue by the antiquarian booksellers Quaritch of some 237 titles by or about the Society of Jesus published between 1548 (the year in which Loyola's *Spiritual Exercises* was first printed) and the suppression of the Society in 1773, we find works by Jesuits on subjects as diverse as optics, the use of plain mirrors in surveying, geometry, atomic theory, the art of lacquer, hydrostatics and mechanics, the Gregorian calendar, perspective, horticulture, book-keeping, astronomy, magnetism and hydraulics.[6] These topics are, of course, over and above the more mainstream works of hagiography, martyrology, theology, history and catechesis, which make up the bulk of the catalogue. Not a few of the books listed also contained descriptions of the natural world.

The very breadth and miscellaneous nature of Jesuit interests has rendered problematic the term 'Jesuit science', which looks as if it will soon follow the term 'Jesuit art' into the lexical recycling bin. This is because it is currently more fashionable to emphasize how the Jesuits 'made their contribution as individuals rather than as members of a group', so that it was not uncommon to find members of the Society if not openly supporting at least creatively engaging with or even appropriating some of the insights of the likes of Descartes, Galileo and Newton.[7] That said, we are still left with the conundrum crisply expressed by Steven Harris: 'What did science have to do with salvation?' Or for that matter, flowers with faith?[8] Before attempting to answer this question, it is necessary to say something more about the wider context within which

---

[6] Detlev Auvermann and Anthony Payne, *The Society of Jesus, 1548–1773: A Catalogue of Books by Jesuit Authors and Works Relating to the Society of Jesus Published between 1548, with the First Printing of Ignatius of Loyola's* Spiritual Exercises, *and the Suppression of the Society in 1773* (London, 2006). This is a reprint, with a new introduction by Alastair Hamilton, of Catalogue 1226, which was originally issued by Bernard Quaritch (Kendal, 1996).

[7] A. Hamilton, 'Introduction', in Auvermann and Payne, *Society of Jesus*, final page of unpaginated text.

[8] According to Harris, in just under two hundred years 'the Society produced a corpus of some 5,000 *published* titles touching on virtually every branch of the natural and mathematical sciences', let alone the mountain of *unpublished* related correspondence by such figures as Athanasius Kircher (1602–80), for whom we have at least two thousand surviving letters: Stephen J. Harris, 'Confession-Building, Long-Distance Networks, and the Organisation of Jesuit Science', *Early Science and Medicine* 1 (1996), 287–318, at 288.

my principal case study – the Castilian Jesuit missionary José de Acosta – needs to be located.

All the kinds of activity just listed were considerably facilitated by the fact that during the period between 1550 and 1670 Rome was perhaps the premier destination and distribution centre for knowledge and goods from all over the known world and so significant even for the majority of the five thousand Jesuit 'scientists' who did not actually live in the city.[9] (As it happens, Acosta's two years in Rome, 1592–94, were mostly spent in miserable isolation since his colleagues believed him to be the King of Spain's stooge and Philip II himself began to have doubts about the Jesuit's loyalty.[10]) The second half of the sixteenth century saw the Eternal City relaunch itself as a pilgrimage destination after the disastrous Sack of Rome of 1527, with the Holy Year of 1575 (in which the pope granted a special Jubilee indulgence) marking the start of a half-century when Rome became a veritable boom town and magnet for all kinds of adventurers from artisans to artists, and printers to prostitutes.[11] As Montaigne noticed in a visit in 1580, Rome 'by its nature [is] a city pieced together out of foreigners'.[12] In addition, Rome was also a major hub of learned information. Over and above its university, the Sapienza, there was the Jesuit high school, seminary and research institute rolled into one, the Roman College (founded 1551; rebuilt 1582–84) as well as the seminaries founded to train foreign students as missionaries. These included the German College (1552); the Greek College

[9] For what follows, I have drawn upon P. Burke, 'Rome as a Centre of Information and Communication for the Catholic World', in P. M. Jones and T. Worcester, eds, *From Rome to Eternity: Catholicism and the Arts in Italy, ca. 1550–1650* (Leiden, 2002), 253–69.

[10] Claudio M. Burgaleta, *José de Acosta SJ: His Life and Thought* (Chicago, IL, 1999), 63–64. Writings by Acosta relating to his Rome visit may be found in *Obras del P. José Acosta*, ed. Franciscos Mateos (Madrid, 1954), 353–86.

[11] See, for example, the contemporary account of Gregory Martin, *Roma sancta (1581)*, ed. George Bruner Parks (Rome, 1969); Richard E. Spear, 'Scrambling for Scudi: Notes on Painters' Earnings in Early Baroque Rome', *Art Bulletin* 85 (2003), 310–20; Michael Bury, *The Print in Italy 1550–1620* (London, 2001), 121–69; Tessa Storey, *Carnal Commerce in Counter-Reformation Rome* (Cambridge, 2008). For a comprehensive account of the material conditions of the city during this period, see Jean Delumeau, *Vie économique et sociale de Rome dans la seconde moitié du XVIe siècle*, 2 vols (Rome, 1957–59).

[12] *Montaigne's Travel Journal*, trans. and intro. Donald Frame (San Francisco, CA, 1983), 97 ('car de sa nature c'est une ville rapiecée d'estrangiers': *Journal de Voyage de Michel de Montaigne,* ed. François Rigolot (Paris, 1992), 127).

(1577); the English College (1578); the Maronite College (1584) and the Irish College (1628). Half a century ago, Jean Delumeau, in his still-unsurpassed study of the economic and social life of the city, noted how it was 'the most active postal centre of the Italian peninsula and perhaps of Europe'.[13] This was ensured by the presence not only of permanent representatives of all the major Roman Catholic powers but also of innumerable convents and monasteries, not a few of which were residences of the heads of congregations or of orders with truly transnational reach.

Of these, without any shadow of a doubt, the Society of Jesus occupied a pre-eminent position. Although Loyola lived very much a peripatetic existence in his pre-Paris years, during which he tellingly referred to himself as the anonymous 'pilgrim', after the approval of his order in 1540 he never left Rome; the city became the headquarters of the Jesuits to an extent which was not the case for other genuinely transnational male religious orders such as the Dominicans, Franciscans or Augustinians, whose regional network of semi-autonomous congregations made for a more federated and less pyramidal structure. Indeed, it has been remarked how: 'Such a strong and geographically stable centre was both cause for and the consequence of the paper-trail-based system of administration. Since administration was intended to be centralised, communication between the centre and the periphery had to be both extensive and intensive.'[14]

Already in 1545 Loyola showed an astute grasp of publicity when he arranged to have a long letter which the Jesuit missionary Francis Xavier had written the previous year from India translated into French and published to considerable acclaim.[15] This was the first letter from the East Indies ever to be published in Europe and was also printed in German the same year. Down to 1573 it

---

[13] Delumeau, *Vie économique*, 1: 37.

[14] M. Friedrich, 'Communication and Bureaucracy in the Early Modern Society of Jesus', *Schweizerische Zeitschrift für Religions- und Kulturgeschichte* 101 (2007), 49–75 (quotation at 51). My thanks to Benjamin Ziemann for drawing my attention to this important article and for sending me a copy.

[15] This letter, dated Cochin, 15 January 1544, may be most conveniently consulted in English as document 20 in *The Letters and Instructions of Francis Xavier*, ed. and trans. M. Joseph Costelloe (St Louis, MO, 1992), 63–74.

was followed by more than fifty editions of letterbooks from the Indian mission alone.[16]

That the clarity and purpose of Loyola's secretary Juan de Polanco mirrored that of his master is suggested by the following instructions from Loyola to the Jesuit superior in Goa, India, dating from 1554:

> Some leading figures who in this city [Rome] read with much edification for themselves the letters from India, are wont to desire, and they request me repeatedly, that *something should be written regarding the cosmography of those regions where ours* [i.e. the Jesuits] *live*. They want to know, for instance, how long are the days of summer and of winter; when summer begins; whether the shadows move towards the left or towards the right. Finally, *if there are things that may seem extraordinary, let them be noted*, for instance, details about animals and plants that are neither not known at all, or not of such a size etc. And this news – *sauce for the taste of a certain curiosity that is not evil and is wont to be found among men* – may come in the same letters or in other letters separately.[17]

According to the *Constitutions of the Society of Jesus*, which were first published in 1558, just two years after the founder's death, the local superiors should write to their provincial superior every week if possible, and the provincials: 'should likewise write to the general every week if he is near. If they are in a distant realm … …. [then] once a month'.[18] Even though this represents the ideal rather than the reality, it was recognized by members of the Society that, to use the words of an important manual of letter writing distributed in 1620 by the Roman secretary to the father general, Francesco Sacchini, to the provincial of Germany Superior: 'Since the epistolary communication between the General and the Provincials is

---

[16] Harris, 'Confession-Building', 304; cf. Donald F. Lach, *Asia in the Making of Europe,* 1: *The Century of Discovery,* Book 1 (Chicago, IL, 1965), 318–21.

[17] Italics mine; in the original, italicized portions read: 'que se scriviese algo de la cosmographia de las regions donde andan los nuestros. … si otras cosas ay que parescan estraordinarias, se dé aviso … Y esta salsa, para el gusto de alguna curiosidad que suel haver en los hombres, no mala': Ignatius to Gaspar Berze, 24 February 1554, letter 4193 in *Monumenta Ignatiana: Epistolae et Instructiones,* 12 vols (Madrid, 1903–11), 6: 358.

[18] Saint Ignatius of Loyola, *Constitutions of the Society of Jesus,* ed. George E. Ganss (St Louis, MO, 1970), 292–93 (quotation at 292, paragraphs 673–76); cf. John W. O'Malley, *The First Jesuits* (Cambridge, MA, 1993), 62–63.

the backbone of our order's administration, and since this communication relies on letters, it is important that the writing of these letters is done with the utmost care and accuracy.'[19] The same manual mentions at least sixteen different kinds of documents going exclusively from the provinces to Rome.[20] The effectiveness with which the Society was able to generate, sustain and manage such a paper trail may easily be seen by the fact that the Roman headquarters of the Jesuits oversaw the editing and regular publication of annual letters in thirty volumes, which related the activities of the Society in all its provinces covering the period from 1581 to 1614.[21] By the seventeenth century, according to Harris, the letters were accompanied by 'regular shipments of such exotic – and often therapeutic – natural wonders as guaiacum, bezoar and snakestone'.[22]

My starting point for the reading and reflection for this chapter was a pair of texts written by the Spanish Jesuit, José de Acosta (1540–1600): *De procuranda indorum salute* ('How to Provide for the Salvation of the Indians') of 1589, and the *Historia natural y moral de las Indias* ('Natural and Moral History of the Indies') published the following year. What had initially attracted my attention, in particular, was that the first of these works was prefaced by the first two books of the second so that its full title ran: 'Two books concerning the nature of the New World and six books about the promulgation of the Gospels amongst the barbarians or, in other words, about the obtaining of the salvation of the Indians'. In other words, not only was Acosta interested in both natural history and the conversion of the Indians, but he manifestly believed that the connection between the two topics was such that they effectively constituted a single work.

Acosta was born to prosperous parents in the important Castilian commercial centre of Medina del Campo, in the same year as the

[19] Cited in Friedrich, 'Communication and Bureaucracy', 50 n. 2.
[20] Ibid. 56
[21] John Correia-Afonso, *Jesuit Letters and Indian History* (Bombay, 1955), 38. After a long gap, the second series, published in the 1650s, covered the years 1650–54.
[22] Steven J. Harris, 'Networks of Travel, Correspondence and Exchange', in Katharine Park and Lorraine Daston, eds, *The Cambridge History of Science*, 3: *Early Modern Science* (Cambridge, 2006), 341–62, at 351–52.

Society's foundation (1540).[23] No fewer than four of his brothers became Jesuits and two out of his three sisters became nuns – surely something of a record? In 1552, just a few weeks before his twelfth birthday, perhaps fearing his parents' opposition, José ran away to the University town of Salamanca to join the Jesuits. But within a month he was back in Medina where he joined the novitiate of the Society. He remained there for the next five years, by the end of which he was working as a scholastic, a Jesuit student teaching humanities to young pupils. Aged fifteen, the evidently academically precocious Acosta wrote and staged a Latin play, 'Jephthah Sacrificing his Daughter', and at nineteen such was his perceived eloquence that he was chosen to preach at the inauguration of the Jesuit college at Segovia.

The next formative experience of his life appears to have been the six months or so he spent at the Jesuit college in Coimbra, Portugal, in 1557–8. This college was not only a renowned centre for the study of Greek language and thought, particularly the philosophy of Aristotle (new critical editions of whose work were being prepared there), but was also a place where young Jesuits were recruited and trained for missionary work in the East Indies. Acosta then spent the next eight years studying first philosophy and then theology at the premier Jesuit college in Spain, at Alcalá de Henares. During this time he also gained his first experience of missionary work in the villages surrounding Alcalá.

This work focused in particular on the reconciliation of warring local families but Acosta also engaged in another form of reconciliation, which was centred on the confessional. Revealingly, the Jesuits considered confession not as a spiritual work of mercy so much as another form of the ministry of the Word. This may be explained by the fact that 'the forum of the confessional allowed the confessor not only to reconcile but to give advice … In short,

---

[23] Besides the biography by Burgaleta cited above (n. 10), the most up-to-date account of his career with a list of his published works and a bibliography down to 1999 may be found in Charles E. O'Neill and Joaquín M. Domínquez, eds, *Diccionario histórico de la Compañía de Jesús: biográfico-temático*, 4 vols (Rome, 2001), 1: 10–12. An excellent brief summary of Acosta's biography and significance may be found in Kenneth Mills, William B. Taylor and Sandra Lauderdale Graham, *Colonial Latin America: A Documentary History* (Wilmington, DE, 2002), 134–37. This is followed by a brief extract from *De Procuranda* (ibid. 138–43) translated from *De Procuranda Indorum Salute*, ed. Luciano Pereña, 2 vols (Madrid, 1984, 1987), by Professor Mills.

... it allowed a sort of private sermon to the penitent.'[24] The link between the ministry of the confessional and that of the Word was also made explicit in a convention widely practised by the Jesuits. In one of the quarterly letters that the superior of the college there was obliged to send to the father general in Rome, a task which had evidently been delegated to Acosta on account of his fine Latin, the young Jesuit measured the efficacy of sermons by the number of confessions – or, as he put it significantly, conversions – that ensued. (For the Jesuits, the confessional provided the opportunity not only for the ministry of reconciliation but also the delivery of what was effectively a private sermon to the penitent.) This helps to explain why Acosta later placed so much emphasis on the need for missionaries in the New World to speak local languages.

Acosta was ordained in 1567 and two years later wrote several letters to the Jesuit father general Francisco de Borja requesting to be sent to the Indies, a vocation which he had been nurturing since 1561.[25] The following passage from the last of these, dated 23 April 1569, gives us significant insight into a feature of his thought shared by all his writings about the New World: on the one hand, the need to view the Indies (East and West) as a whole; on the other, the necessity of appreciating the distinctiveness of the various societies found there.

> I do not have any inclination to go to any particular part, except that it might be a help for me to be amongst people that are not too brutish and have some capacity [for reason], although there might be things that weigh against that. Of course, the way to the West Indies from Spain having begun to open, it has occurred to me that I might be able to play my part somewhere there if I were to be sent to do what I do here, that is, to read theology or some other sort of ministry. *But if obedience requires me to go to the other Indies, to stay in Goa or other some such place, I find a certain repugnance towards that*

---

[24] For this and what follows I have drawn directly on Burgaleta, *José de Acosta*, 26.

[25] What follows is based on the transcription of the letter in José de Acosta, *De Procuranda Indorum Salute*, ed. and trans. G. Stewart McIntosh, 2 vols (Tayport, 1996), 1: v–vi [hereafter cited as '*De Procuranda*, ed. McIntosh' to avoid confusion with the Madrid edition which gives the Latin text with parallel text in Spanish, which will be referred to as '*De Procuranda*, ed. Pereña'].

as the situation there must be similar to what it is here. But in all things please understand that I will find peace of mind being directed by your good self ...[26]

Two years later, in 1571, Acosta was to have his wish granted and he set sail for Peru in what was only the third expedition of Jesuits to the Americas. The first expedition had only been three years previously, so the Society might be said to have taken part in what was the second wave of missionary work, the first (which began in Central America in the 1520s) having been staffed by such mendicant orders as the Augustinian friars, the Dominicans and the Franciscans.

On arrival in Peru, which he reached by sea via Panama, after several months spent on the Caribbean island of Santo Domingo, he taught at the Jesuit college in Lima but thirteen months later he was sent by his provincial to visit the interior of the viceroyalty in order to encourage and oversee the new colleges in places like Cuzco and to visit the burgeoning world capital of silver mining, Potosì (in present-day Bolivia), a visit which he discusses at some length in Book IV of his *Historia* (chapters 6–9). This enabled him to gain considerable direct experience of the Indians' life as well as the particular challenges it posed to their evangelization. In 1575 Acosta became rector of the College in Lima and the following year was made Provincial of the Society in Peru, a post he retained for four years, during which time the Jesuits were put under sustained pressure by the secular authorities to run parishes (*doctrinas*, parishes for indigenous peoples) and therefore to compromise their autonomy from episcopal authority as regular clergy'. This policy was motivated by the acute shortage of priests in the province of Peru and led Acosta to petition the father general in Rome to modify the Society's prohibition against running parishes on the grounds that in East Asia and Japan, where similar conditions applied, the Jesuits already staffed *doctrinas*.[27] As

---

[26] *De Procuranda*, ed. McIntosh, 1: vi (in the original, the italicized portion reads: 'Y si a es otras Indias me enviase la obediencia, en quedarme en Goa o por allí, hallo alguna repugnancia por parecerme que debe de ser poco más aquello lo de acá': *Obras del P. José de Acosta* ed. Mateos, 251–52, at 252).

[27] Burgaleta, *José de Acosta*, 40. The degree to which this was very much a burning issue can be seen in the extent to which Book III of *De Procuranda* was given over to addressing the practicalities facing the Jesuits in running parishes, in particular relating to the acceptance of tribute (a form of tithe paid to parish priests, more often than

has already been mentioned, for Acosta the *sine qua non* for effective missionary work was command of the relevant languages. When he took over as provincial in 1576 there were some seventy-seven Jesuits under his supervision, no more than a handful of whom were fluent in the native languages. By 1581, when Acosta finished his time as provincial, there were 113 Jesuits, no fewer than 50 of whom were fluent in the various indigenous languages, principally Quechua and Aymara.[28] Emblematic of Acosta's vision of the concrete form which the apostolate in the Americas might take was the settlement at Juli on the south-western shore of Lake Titicaca near Peru's current border with Bolivia. Described by one recent biographer as 'the apple of Acosta's eye', this *doctrina* had been founded by the Dominicans in 1547 but was relinquished by them in 1572.[29] Two of the main problems with the Dominican missionary strategy were that firstly, they catechized only in Spanish, and secondly, the friars were frequently transferred from convent to convent so that they were not well placed to sustain long-term programmes of instruction which took local conditions and requirements into account. With the arrival of the Jesuits in 1576 all this changed and over time the settlement became the prototype *reducción* (a village composed of resettled native people) for the larger and more well-known successors in Paraguay made famous by Roland Joffé's film *The Mission* (1986).

In Juli (as later in Paraguay), Spanish settlers were not allowed to reside (although they could visit, usually for a maximum of three days) and the substantial indigenous population – numbering some fourteen thousand when the Jesuits arrived – was supervised by around a dozen Jesuit priests, brothers and scholastics

not in kind) from their Indian parishioners. As things turned out, however, the Jesuits only took permanent charge of two *doctrinas*: Juli in Lake Titicaca and Santiago del Cercardo on the outskirts of Lima: cf. Sabine MacCormack, 'Grammar and Virtue: The Formulation of a Cultural and Missionary Programme by the Jesuits in Early Colonial Peru', in John W. O'Malley et al., eds, *The Jesuits II: Cultures, Sciences and the Arts 1540–1773* (Toronto, ON, 2006), 576–601, at 581.

[28] Burgaleta, *José de Acosta*, 43; cf. *De Procuranda*, ed. McIntosh, 2: 16–17, 24–26.

[29] Burgaleta, *José de Acosta*, 45; cf. Aliocha Maldavsky's observation that indigenous language-learning was regarded as a mere skill, not genuine scholarly knowledge, and: 'If indigenous language-learning had an application in a geographical place (i.e. in the *doctrinas*), it did not necessarily play a consistent role in a Jesuit's education or career over time.' See her important article: 'The Problematic Acquisition of Indigenous Languages: Practices and Contentions in Missionary Specialisation in the Jesuit Province of Peru (1568–1640)', in O'Malley et al., eds, *Jesuits II*, 603–15 (quotation at 611).

(for whom a language school was set up). Aymara, Quechua and Puquina were taught at this school with great success.[30] Central to longer term effectiveness of the Society's missionary strategy here was the establishment of good relations with the local elite. They were careful to seek the permission of the *kurakas* – or *caciques* in Spanish – for their preaching, catechesis, processions and confraternities. Juli was divided into four parishes, each of which was governed by native *kurakas* from the ethnic groups that inhabited the parish and attended by a Jesuit priest who was bilingual in the relevant language. Indian children under the age of sixteen (both male and female) were catechized every morning and, unusually, all the inhabitants were encouraged to participate in the sacraments (with the exception of Holy Orders). As a result, most of the baptized Indians over seven years old received the eucharist every two months and on the principal feasts of the liturgical year. Juli became known, in due course, as *pueblo santo* or the Amerindian Rome.[31]

In 1581, probably for reasons of health (he was overweight and had suffered for many years from heart problems which the high altitudes of the Peruvian Andes cannot have helped), Acosta requested to return to Europe, but he did not actually leave Peru until 1586. In the intervening period he carried out what was undoubtedly his most important task during his sixteen years in Peru when he acted as official theologian to the Third Provincial Council of Lima (1582–83). This had been convoked by the Archbishop of Lima, Toribio de Mogrovejo, and owing to its importance for the subsequent development of the Roman Catholic Church in Latin America has come to be known as the 'Trent

---

[30] In his annual letter to Rome of 1578, Acosta mentioned that there were eleven Jesuit priests at Juli plus three 'brothers' (temporal coadjutors, i.e. lay, unprofessed brothers). 'Los padres todos saben la lengua de los Indios, si no es uno que la va aprendiendo agora, y algunos dellos saben las dos lenguas, quichua y almará y algunos tambien la puquina, que es otra lengua dificultosa y muy usada en quellas provincias': *Obras del P. José de Acosta*, ed. Mateos, 294–97 (quotation at 294). Interestingly, Juli was located in an Aymara-speaking area, so there must have been a permanent staff of Quechua (and Puquina) speakers: see Alan Durston, *Pastoral Quechua: The History of Christian Translation in Colonial Peru, 1550–1650* (Notre Dame, IN, 2007), 340 n. 32.

[31] Burgaleta, *José de Acosta*, 47–50. Acosta himself referred on the same page of the annual letter cited above (n. 30) to just *three* parishes, with eight fathers supervising the largest, St Thomas, and two each (both with two brothers as assistants) attached to the parishes of St John the Baptist and the Assumption.

of the Americas'.[32] The catechism, confessors' manual and collection of short sermons approved by the Council, which had been composed by Acosta, remained the standard catechetical tools until well into the nineteenth century. They were all subsequently translated into the two principal languages of Peru and Bolivia, Aymara and Quechua, and were the first books to be printed in the province (at the press of the Jesuit College in Lima).[33]

On his way home, Acosta stopped off in Mexico for almost a year, spending part of the time as the guest of his brother, Bernardino de Acosta, who had lately been appointed rector of the Jesuit college at Oaxaca. José took advantage of his time in Mexico to study the culture and religion of the Aztecs. He also had occasion to meet with another Jesuit with direct experience of the *East* Indies: Alonso Sánchez, who was on his way to the court of Philip II to represent the interests of Spanish settlers in the Philippines. At the time, Sánchez was causing the Society no little embarrassment since he was advocating a military invasion of China and Japan in order to effect their conversion to Christianity. Acosta was specifically charged by the father general, Claudio Aquaviva, to get Sánchez to drop his advocacy of the plan, which, as we shall see, aside from its lunatic impracticality, was directly counter to the Society's 'way of proceeding'.[34] Taken together, therefore, José de Acosta had some eighteen years' experience in the Caribbean, Central and South America as well as the opportunity of extended conversation with someone who had similar eyewitness testimony to share about the East Indies.

Such is the biographical background, in outline, to Acosta's *De procuranda indorum salute* and *Historia moral y natural,* which I am going to consider in its conflated form of eight books (i.e. the six books of *De procuranda* prefaced by the first two books of the *Historia*). It was Aquaviva who recommended to Acosta that he preface the *De procuranda* in this way, since like Loyola he believed

[32] Rubén Vargas Ugarte, *Concilios Limenses 1551–1772,* 3 vols (Lima, 1951–54), 1: 261–375; Enrique T. Bartra, ed., *Tercer Concilio Limense 1582–1583* (Lima, 1982). Cf. *Toribio de Mogrovejo: misionero, santo y pastor: actas del congreso académico internacional. Realizado en Lima del 24 al 28 de abril de 2006* (Lima, 2006).

[33] For the table of contents of the *Doctrina Christiana* (which contained all three) in English, see Burgaleta, *José de Acosta,* 146–49 (Appendix 4).

[34] Two documents written by Acosta on this topic in 1587 are reprinted in *Obras del P. José de Acosta,* ed. Mateos, 331–45.

in building on man's natural curiosity.[35] The remaining five books of the history had been written while its author was in Peru. The Latin language of the first two indicates straightaway the identity of its principal audience: missionary priests. In his dedication to the father general, Everard Mercurian (dated Lima, 24 February 1577), Acosta made clear at the very outset his principal motive for composing the treatise:

> I could never come to persuade myself that all this innumerable number of peoples of the Indies could be frustrated in the Divine call of the Gospel, or that many other servants of God had been sent out to this endeavour for nothing, and then to be followed by those of the Compañia ourselves … I must confess, [to having] a singular confidence in these people's salvation.[36]

The preface was then given over to Acosta's insistence on the need for any missionaries to take note of the particular circumstances of the people they are dealing with, since: 'there is such great variety amongst the nations which populate the New World'.[37] He then went on to sketch out his famous three-tiered model of barbarism which measured cultural difference in terms of a people's capacity to create urban society and to possess a written language.

> The first class are those who do not depart greatly from true reason and the common way of life. They have a stable form of government, legal system, fortified cities, magistrates who are obeyed and well established, prosperous commerce and *what is most important, the use and knowledge of letters*, for where there

---

[35] 'servirà la salsa para algunos gustos': cited in *Obras del P. José de Acosta*, ed. Mateos, xxxvii. Cf. the intelligent commentary on the issues raised by the *Historia* in Gregory L. Shepherd, *An Exposition of José de Acosta's 'Historia natural y moral de las Indias', 1590: The Emergence of an Anthropological Vision of Colonial Latin America* (Lewiston, NY, 2002).

[36] *De Procuranda*, ed. McIntosh, 1: 1 ('Frustra vero gentes innumerabiles ad Evangelium vocari divinitus, frustra tum alios Dei servos tum nostros ad hoc opus mitti, ut mihi persuaderem adduci nunquam potui … quod fatendum est, peculiarem quandam iampridem conceptam de harum gentium salute fiduciam, omnibus difficultatibus superiorem, in me semper adverterem': José de Acosta, *De Procuranda*, ed. Pereña, 1: 48).

[37] Ibid. 1: 3 ('quod barbarorum gentes innumerabiles sint, ut caelo, locis, habitu, ita ingenio, moribus, institutis latissime dissidentes': *De Procuranda*, ed. Pereña, 54).

are books and engraved monuments there the people are more human and civilised.[38]

Acosta included in this category the Chinese, whose characters he said he had seen (probably in Mexico, courtesy of Sánchez). In the second class:

I include Barbarians who did not achieve the use of writing nor the knowledge of philosophy or civil rights, but nevertheless *have their commonwealth and government defined by leaders, and where they have fixed settlements and custodians of law and order, armed forces and captains, and finally some form of religious worship* [italics mine]. Amongst this order are our Mexicans and Peruvians, whose empires and republics, laws and institutions, are truly worthy of admiration. And with reference to orthography, they supplied their lack of it with such ability and ingenuity, that it has allowed them to remember their histories, their laws, their way of life and, what is more interesting, the calculation of seasons, accounts and numbers, through the signs and monuments they have invented, and through what they call *quipos* (coloured and knotted cords) and other methods that do not follow the same method as our writings. Our accountants cannot work their arithmetical figures with more accuracy when there is something to multiply or divide, than those Indians can do with their cords and knots.[39]

Finally, the third and lowest class of Barbarians:

are the savages similar to wild animals, who hardly have any human feelings – *without law, without agreements, without government, without commonwealth, who move from place to place, or if they live in one place they are more like animals' caves or animal cages* [italics mine]. Such are those that our people call *Caribes*, always hungry for blood, cruel to foreigners, they devour human flesh, walk naked and barely cover their private parts. Aristotle talked about this class of barbarian when he stated

[38] Ibid. 1: 4, italics mine ('*quod omnium caput est, litterarum celebris usus*': *De Procuranda*, ed. Pereña, 1: 60, 62).
[39] Ibid. 1: 4–5, slightly modified ('habent tamen magistratus suos certos, habent rempublicam, habent frequentes et certas sedes, ubi politiam suam servant, habent militae et duces et ordinem et religionis suae celebritatem quandam': *De Procuranda*, ed. Pereña, 1: 62).

that they could be hunted like wild beasts and dominated by force.[40]

Thus it followed, according to Acosta, that 'we should not make the same norms for all the Indian nations, if we do not want to make a big mistake'.[41] These first two books – which were republished in Spanish as books I and II of the *Historia* – were concerned with the place of the Indies in relation to the configuration of the heavens, the region's climate and its living conditions. In particular, they were directed at confuting the belief expressed by such classical authors as Aristotle that no one could live in the middle ground between the two poles which was referred to as the 'Torrid Zone' – so called owing to its excessive heat. He compared the ancients with the moderns in unfavourable terms, noting not only: 'we must conclude that much was unknown to the ancients', but also 'that today a good part of the world is still to be discovered'.[42] Acosta also observed how, owing to the compass and the magnet, the sailors of his time possessed greater skill than those of the ancients.[43] His belief in the inadequacy of ancient sources to answer the question as to the identity and origin of the various Indian peoples he encountered was reflected in the highly original way in which he explained the human and animal settlement of the New World.

Essentially he posited a land link between the Americas and the Eurasian land mass somewhere in the north. He followed up this argument, which subsequent discoveries have shown to be true, with a dismissal of the belief that the Indians in fact constituted a lost tribe of Israel, on the straightforward grounds that he had encountered no case of Hebrew-related writing script amongst the

---

[40] Ibid. 1: 5 ('sine lege sine rege, sine certo magistratu et republica, sedes identidem commutantes aut ita fixas habentes, ut magis ferarum specus aut pecorum caulas imitentur': *De Procuranda*, ed. Pereña, 1: 66).

[41] Ibid. 1: 6 ('Neque enim de omnibus indorum gentibus eodem modo pronuntiare oportet, nisi graviter errare malimus': *De Procuranda*, ed. Pereña, 1: 68).

[42] José de Acosta, *Natural and Moral History of the Indies*, ed. Jane E. Mangan (Durham NC, 2002), 51 ('Por tanto devemos colegir, que a los antiguos les quedò gran parte por conocer, y que a nostros oy dia nos esta encubierta no pequeña parte del mundo': José de Acosta, *Historia natural de las Indias en que se tartan las cosas notables del cielo, y elementos, metales, plantas, y animals, … y los ritos, y ceremonias, leyes, y govierno y guerras de los Indios* (Seville, 1590), bk 1, ch. 15).

[43] Acosta, *Historia natural de las Indias*, bk 1, ch. 16 (*Natural and Moral History*, ed. Mangan, 53).

Indians he had known.[44] Acosta concluded by arguing that since even the Indians' own tales about their origins did not resolve the issue one should just take the pragmatic line that: 'though they came from civilised and well-governed countries [originally] it is not difficult to believe that they forgot everything in the course of a long time and little use'.[45] As if to clinch this point he went on to say further down the same page: 'for it is well known that even in Spain and Italy groups of men are sometimes found who, except for their shape and faces, have no other resemblance to men'.[46]

Having demonstrated in Book I the inadequacy of ancient literature when trying to account for the natural and human world of the Indies, Acosta used Book II to describe the kind of climate a missionary might actually encounter in South America. The overall impression he gave the reader was of a natural world turned upside down, where climatic features seemed paradoxical and things were frequently the direct opposite of what one might logically expect. He began by explaining how far from being dry and burned up as Aristotle had imagined the 'torrid zone' or tropics, it was in fact very wet (II.3) and that, in contrast to the Old World, the rains come in summer when the sun is at its nearest (II.5, 7). Book II concluded with the judgement that the climate of the Indies was most agreeable, its gentle and moderate weather making it much more pleasant than the Old World. He was particularly keen on Chile which, perhaps because he never went there, he idealized as the region of South America most like Spain for its climate, flora and fauna.[47]

This optimistic and positive assessment of the natural environment of the Indies, composed while Acosta still lived in Peru, contrasts with the treatment he gave in Books III and IV of the *Historia* that were subsequently written on his return to Spain. However, in the context of the *De procuranda* they served the purpose of putting the prospective missionary in a suitable frame

---

[44] Ibid., bk 1, ch. 23 (*Natural and Moral History*, ed. Mangan, 69).

[45] Acosta, *Natural and Moral History*, ed. Mangan, 72 (Acosta, *Historia natural de las Indias*, bk 1, ch. 24).

[46] Ibid. 72 ('pue es notorio, que aun en España y en Italia se hallan mandas de hombres, que si no es el gesto y figura, no tienen otra cosa de hombres': Acosta, *Historia natural de las Indias*, bk 1, ch. 24).

[47] Acosta, *Historia natural de las Indias*, bk 2, ch. 4 (*Natural and Moral History*, ed. Mangan, 79).

of mind so that – to borrow the title of chapter 1 of Book I: 'We must not despair of the salvation of the Indians'.[48] After asserting unambiguously: 'There is therefore no lineage of peoples which is excluded from the faith and from the gospel',[49] Acosta went on to emphasize that although the task was far from easy, people were after all slow to change the devotional habits of a lifetime and the communication of Christian teaching would have to cope with the challenge posed by 'the jungle of over thirty languages'.[50] 'Give me apostolic men for the Indians and I will give you apostolic fruit from the Indians'.[51] In the previous chapter, Acosta had, by way of encouragement, drawn on a historical example from the evangelization of Ireland. He quoted what St Bernard of Clairvaux had said about St Malachy, the eleventh-century pioneer of the Gregorian reform in Ireland, when he was consecrated Bishop of Connor in 1124:

> When he began to undertake the functions of his office, it appeared to this man of God that he had not been sent to men but rather to beasts, for he had never encountered the likes of them amongst all the groups of Barbarians. They were so insolent in their ways, so savage in their ceremonies, so unbelieving in their faith, so wild with respect to law and order …[52]

Acosta drew the following lesson: 'Now there cannot be anyone who is such an enemy of the Indians who would not admit that things are better here than in Hibernia, or that the state and customs of our Peru are not quite so bad as that!'[53] He later cited Bede's Ecclesiastical History to similar effect: 'Let anyone read about the

---

[48] *De Procuranda*, ed. McIntosh, 1: 7 ('Quod non sit desperanda salus indorum': *De Procuranda*, ed. Pereña, 1: 74).

[49] Ibid. ('Neque enim genus aliquod hominum exclusum est in Evangelii fideique communicatione': *De Procuranda*, ed. Pereña, 1: 74).

[50] 'for even in the regions that I have gone through I think that there are more than thirty of them': *De Procuranda*, ed. McIntosh, 2: 22 ('cum idiomatum tam multiplex sylva sit, ut in his locis, quae ipse emersus sum, existimem plusquam triginta linguas numerari': *De Procuranda*, ed. Pereña, 1: 236).

[51] Ibid. 1: 54 ('Da mihi certe apud indos apostolicos viros reddam ipse vicissim ex indis apostolicos fructus': *De Procuranda*, ed. Pereña, 1: 236).

[52] Ibid. 1: 51 (*De Procuranda*, ed. Pereña, 1: 224).

[53] Ibid. ('Hoc statu, his moribus nemo, opinor, causae indicae tam iniquus sit, qui non feliciorem vel potius minus infelicem provinciam istam nostram agnoscat': *De Procuranda*, ed. Pereña, 1: 224).

customs of the ancient English. They will find they were much wilder than our Indians.'[54]

The crucial point for the Jesuit was that the missionaries be men of humility and chastity and that violence only be used as a last resort. Indeed, for Acosta the main problem was not the Indians, who were simply children who needed teaching, but the Spaniards. As he put it succinctly: 'There is really only one miracle that is needed for these people of the New World ... *that our* [i.e. the missionaries'] *way of life should match the faith being preached*'.[55] This comment was immediately followed in the original manuscript copy by the passage: 'and in our age and in these lands it would be such a rarity that it could be held to be a miracle to find a life that is not in disaccord with the preaching'.[56] At the close of Book II Acosta laid the blame for the lack of true conversions amongst the Indians firmly at the door of the settlers, whose 'dreadful example and wanton way of life' was fiercely censured.[57] In Book III, Acosta's criticisms of the Spaniard settlers, particularly their abuse of the *encomendero* system, whereby indigenous peoples were forced to work for the settlers effectively as indentured labourers, had been considerably toned down by the censors within the Society of Jesus in Rome, to whom he had sent the manuscript of *De procuranda*. General Aquaviva instructed Gil González Dávila, the Jesuit provincial in Toledo: 'take out what is said about the Conquistadors' way of doing things and their cruelty'.[58]

On more than one occasion, he referred to the Indians as 'the new plants' of the Gospels who needed to be nurtured, not brutalized.[59] Acosta closed Book III with a plea for moderation:

[54] Ibid. 2: 14 ('Legat qui volet antiquos anglorum mores, duriores nostris indis inveniet': *De Procuranda*, ed. Pereña, 2: 40).

[55] Emphasis mine; ibid. 1: 77 ('ad fidem efficacissimum ac pene singulare miraculum necessarium est, mores cum fidem congruentes': *De Procuranda*, ed. Pereña, 1: 320).

[56] 'et nostra aetate in his praesertim locis adeo rarum ut vere miraculum haberi possit vita praedicationi non impar': *De Procuranda*, ed. McIntosh, 1: 77 n. 5.

[57] In the original manuscript this bad example was specified in the following terms: 'avarice, violence, tyranny, for although confessing that they know Christ, nevertheless they radically deny Him through their acts (avaricia, violentia, tyrannis, cuoniam etsi Christum se nosse confitentur, factis tamen maxime negant)': ibid. 1: 94 n. 1.

[58] Ibid. 1: xiv. On the same page McIntosh listed the chapters whose text received the most significant censure.

[59] e.g. *De Procuranda*, ed. McIntosh, 1: 122, 131 ('tyrones teneraque stirpes', 'novis Evangelii cultoribus': *De Procuranda*, ed. Pereña, 1: 460, 492).

'in points where their customs do not oppose our religion or justice, I do not think it is a good idea to change them for change's sake'.[60] He then quoted at length from Pope Gregory the Great's famous letter to Mellitus (in which the pope encouraged Mellitus to build on and adapt to local pagan practices and thereby, incrementally, introduce Christian practices), which closed with the advice: 'because anyone who strives to ascend to the highest place, relies on ladders or steps. He is not lifted up in one leap.'[61] Book IV was then spent outlining in greater detail the desirable qualifications of the missionary which, in summary, were threefold: integrity of life, sound doctrine and facility of speech.[62] The final two Books (V and VI), which were devoted, respectively, to the kind of catechizing necessary and to how the sacraments were to be best administered, reinforced the insight which unified the whole work – and indeed Acosta's entire *oeuvre* – that one should only act according to the indigenous peoples' capabilities and that where local customs did not go against Christian teaching they should be left alone: 'harsh laws should not be passed that are completely out of context for the Indies, but rather the Indians should be left to live their lives within their own customs and institutions as much as Christian law permits and then, from within that framework, direct them and improve them'.[63]

Such an argument will be familiar to those who have ever read or studied about the slightly later Malabar or Chinese Rites controversies, in which Jesuit concessions made to local customs came in for censure from Rome after generating (in the former case) disputes within the Society and (in the latter) attacks by their missionary rivals.[64] Although, as Acosta's treatment has shown, such

[60] *De Procuranda*, ed. McIntosh, 1: 157 ('attamen si qua in re illorum mores a religione et iustitia non discrepant, non existimo facile immutandos': *De Procuranda*, ed. Pereña, 1: 596).

[61] *The Letters of Gregory the Great*, ed. John R. C. Martyn, 3 vols (Toronto, ON, 2004), 3: 802–03 (quotation at 803); letter 11.56, 18 July 601 ('quia is qui locum summum ascendere nititur necesse est ut gradibus vel passibus non autem saltibus elevetur': bk 11, ep. 76, PL 77: 1215–17).

[62] 'vita integra, doctrina idonea, copia sermonis': *De Procuranda*, ed. Pereña, 2: 46 (*De Procuranda*, ed. McIntosh, 2: 16).

[63] *De Procuranda*, ed. McIntosh, 2: 156.

[64] On the Chinese Rites controversy, see Paul Rule, 'The Chinese Rites Controversy: Confucian and Christian Views on the Afterlife', in Peter Clarke and Tony Claydon, eds, *The Church, the Afterlife and the Fate of the Soul*, SCH 45 (Woodbridge, 2009), 280–300.

an approach had its roots way back near the beginnings of the history of Christian conversion, there was something unprecedented, not only about the way Acosta and his fellow Jesuits from Alessandro Valignano and Matteo Ricci to Alexander of Rhodes and Roberto de Nobili applied it to their own missionary work, but also about how these insights were turned back onto the 'Other Indies' (*Otras Indias*), the areas which needed to be won or won back for the faith in the Old World. This term was coined by Polanco as part of a deliberate rhetorical strategy to render the European missions more popular with his brethren, so many of whom were keen to follow in Francis Xavier's footsteps and achieve martyrdom in the *real* Indies, as can be seen from the numerous letters to the father general requesting to go to the Indies (the famous *litterae indipetae*) still preserved in the Society's central archive in Rome.[65] By the end of the seventeenth century, this notion of the 'other Indies' had become so internalized in Jesuit missionary discourse that it makes perfect sense to regard the Society's missions to the Old and New Worlds as complementary exercises in which the strategies deployed were often indistinguishable from one another.[66]

It has already been noted how Acosta not only compared the Indians in the New World with British and Irish from an earlier age, but also to contemporary peasants in the Old.[67] As Anthony Pagden has reminded us, at about this time, the Duke of Alba had discovered a community of people not far from Salamanca,

[65] Rome, Archivum Romanum Societatis Iesu, Fondo gesuitico 732–759, containing 14,067 letters from 5,167 Jesuits covering the period 1583–1770. One of the earliest uses of *otras Indias* can be found in a letter from the Jesuit missionary Silvestro Landini, writing from Corsica on 7 February 1553: 'Non ho mai provato terra, che sia più bisognosa delle cose dil Signor di questa ... *Questa isola sarà la mia India*, meritoria quanto quella dil preste Giovanni [Prester John]': Adriano Prosperi, '"Otras Indias": missionari della controriforma tra contadini e selvaggi', in idem, *America e Apocalisse e altri saggi* (Pisa, 1999), 65–87 (quotation at 67).

[66] See, e.g., Trevor Johnson's discussion of the Jesuit missions in the Upper Rhine Palatinate at the turn of the seventeenth and eighteenth centuries in which the missionaries made use of such sacramentals as *Xavierwasser*, water that had been in contact with relics of the saint: 'Blood, Tears and Xavier-Water: Jesuit Missionaries and Popular Religion in the Eighteenth-Century Upper Palatinate', in Bob Scribner and Trevor Johnson, eds, *Popular Religion in Germany and Central Europe, 1400–1800* (Basingstoke, 1996), 183–202, 272–75.

[67] For a stimulating discussion of how the voyages of discovery stimulated the search for the 'indigenous' in the field of natural history in the Old World, see Alix Cooper, *Inventing the Indigenous: Local Knowledge and Natural History in Early Modern Europe* (Cambridge, 2007), esp. 156–66, 'The Indies in Switzerland'.

who had apparently taken refuge from the invading Moors. They went naked, spoke an incomprehensible language, worshipped the Devil and did not appear to possess any technical skills whatsoever.[68] The story aroused great contemporary interest and was even the subject of the play *La Batuecas del duque de Alva* (1638) by the founder of Spanish drama, Lope de Vega (1562–1635).[69] It was in such a context that the publishing firm of De Bry published their extensively illustrated accounts of the New World, including selections from Acosta along with translations (into Latin) from an assemblage of Dutch, English, Italian, Spanish, Portuguese, German and French travel accounts. Recent research has emphasized the degree to which, in a deliberate attempt to market their volumes to both Protestant and Roman Catholic readers, the firm of De Bry downplayed nuance in the accounts of the New World which were their sources, whether it be Thomas Harriot's *Briefe and true report of the new found land of Virginia* or Acosta's account of Peru in his *Historia natural y moral*. Instead, by means of judicious editing and, especially, through the juxtaposition of striking images, the publishers played up the exotic otherness of the New World.[70]

The root of the Jesuit interest in and conviction of the efficacy of taking local, particular factors – natural or cultural – into consideration when trying to sow the universal message of the Gospel lay not, at least in the first instance, with their famous doctrine of accommodation, but with the engine which drove it – the *Spiritual Exercises*. To borrow Philip Endean's crisp formulation, 'Jesuits became Jesuits through the Exercises'.[71] Annotation 18

[68] Anthony Pagden, *The Fall of Natural Man: The American Indian and the Origins of Comparative Ethnology*, revised edn (Cambridge, 1986), 197. In a similar vein, the Dominican Gregorio García included an account of a group of Visigoths who almost a millennium before had fled into the mountains near Almuñeca from the invading Arabs and had only preserved 'a bell and a few other symbols' from their old religion: *Historia ecclesiástica y seglar de la Yndia oriental y occidental predicación del sancto Evangelio en ella por los Apóstoles* (Baeza, 1626), fols 19ᵛ–20ᵛ.

[69] I am very grateful to Erin Rowe for identifying the precise play which was inspired by this incident. There exists a modern edition of the play in question: *Las Batuecas del duque de Alba* (Charleston, NC, 2007).

[70] '[T]he De Bry collection above all vied to be recognisable, conforming itself to widespread expectations of the overseas world as uncivilised and un-Christian. Commercial considerations strictly curtailed the De Brys' representational and ideological latitude': Michiel van Groesen, *The Representations of the Overseas World in the De Bry Collection of Voyages (1590–1634)* (Leiden, 2008), 388.

[71] Philip Endean, 'The Spiritual Exercises', in Thomas Worcester, ed., *The Cambridge*

stated unequivocally: 'The *Exercises* are to be adapted to the capabilities of those who want to engage with them, i.e. age, education or intelligence are to be taken into consideration.' So important did this sensitivity to local needs and customs become that the *Constitutions* of the Society, which were first drawn up in 1558, made explicit reference to this fact, noting: 'In general, they [the Jesuit scholastics] ought to be instructed in the way of proceeding proper to a member of the Society, who has to associate with so great diversity of persons throughout such varied regions.'[72]

As the number of works by Jesuit priest-naturalists and priest-physicists identified by Steven Harris suggests, Acosta was in good company as his brethren were wont to incorporate details about the peoples and lands visited by missionaries in all four of the then known continents. This included not only such works as Acosta's, which were explicitly narratives of natural history, but also works of hagiography such as Joao de Lucena's massive life of Francis Xavier, which was stuffed full of incidental ethnographic and natural details.[73] Such circumstantial detail was also prominent in the historiography of the Jesuit missions in general, from Matteo Ricci and his *Della entrata della Compagnia di Giesù e Christianità nella Cina* (brought to publication in Latin translation by his confrère Nicolaus Trigault in 1615, Book I of which was wholly given over to a comprehensive description of the human and natural geography of the region), to Daniello Bartoli, whom Leopardi considered to be nothing less than 'the Dante of Italian prose'. Bartoli's unfinished, geographically ordered multi-volume history of the Order, *Dell'historia della Compagnia di Giesù* (1653–1673), was positively crammed with information about local customs and natural curios.[74]

However, we must be careful not to be seduced by such erudite and not infrequently exotic fruits of prodigious intellectual labour and information-gathering into trying to shoehorn them into any

---

Companion to the Jesuits (Cambridge, 2008), 52–67 (quotation at 52).

[72] *Constitutions of the Society of Jesus*, ed. Ganss, 204 (paragraph 414); cf. O'Malley, *First Jesuits*, 255–56 and index entries under 'accommodation'.

[73] João de Lucena, *Historia da vida do Padre Francisco Xavier* (Lisbon, 1600; Italian trans., Rome, 1613; Spanish trans., Seville, 1619).

[74] The volume on Asia and Japan was the first to be published, followed by those on Japan (1660); China (1663); Europe, including England (1667); and Italy (1673). That on America is conspicuous by its absence; cf. Leopardi, *Zibaldone*, 2396.

evolutionary narrative implied by such labels as the 'lost or quiet [Roman Catholic] scientific revolution'.[75] Jesuit priest–naturalists, botanists and ethnographers may well have added substantially to the stock of our knowledge about the New World and its inhabitants, but we must never forget that their motives were very particular. As the latest research has confirmed, not a few Jesuit natural philosophers by the later seventeenth century would have concurred with Galileo's affirmation that the book of nature was written in the language of mathematics.[76] However, the uses to which they directed such an insight was to uncover the providential plan encoded by God and their interest in the natural world lay, above all, in what Christian lessons it could teach.[77] One such animal which was understood as bearing a liberating Christian message in the New World was the *hoitzitziltotl* (hummingbird), which was believed to use its beak or claws to hang from tall trees, whence it fell into a catatonic state, only to come around and be resurrected six months later. As the Jesuit Juan Nieremberg put it:

> It is a small bird, but through an amazing providence it dies to live again. It thinks it will die happy on the wood from which it will rise up again. This is a sign for us of wisely dying to the world in the tree of a cross, from which we shall be immortal, if it has died to the world by crucifixion.[78]

A flower from the New World with a particularly rich set of meanings, according to Nieremberg, was the *granadilla* (passion flower), whose appearance suggested that it might represent not only the whip and the pillar of the Passion but also Christ's red wounds and blood, the three nails of the Crucifixion, the crown of thorns and the lance that pierced Christ's side.[79] Acosta dutifully

---

[75] This appears to be the premise of Antonio Barrera-Osorio, *Experiencing Nature: The Spanish American Empire and the Early Scientific Revolution* (Austin, TX, 2006).

[76] e.g. Marcus Hellyer, *Catholic Physics: Jesuit Natural Philosophy in Early Modern Germany* (Notre Dame, IN, 2005).

[77] The classic work in this tradition was Juan Eusebio Nieremberg's *Historia naturae, maxime peregrinae libris XVI distincta: In quibus rarissima naturæ arcana, etiam astronomica, & ignota Indiarum animalia, quadrupedes, aves, pisces, reptilia, insecta, zoophyta, plantæ, metalla, lapides, & alia mineralia, fluviorumque & elementorum conditiones, etiam cum proprietatibus medicinalibus, describuntur* (Antwerp, 1635).

[78] Nieremberg, *Historiae naturae*, 12, as cited in Jorge Cañizares-Esguerra, *Puritan Conquistadors: Iberianizing the Atlantic 1550–1700*, (Stanford, CA, 2006), 271 n. 91.

[79] Cañizares-Esguerra, *Puritan Conquistadors*, 147–48.

enumerated these meanings before adding: 'There is something to be said for this belief, although in order to imagine it one needs a touch of piety to help one see it all.'[80] Yet even if he did not go so far as some of his fellow Jesuits in his emblematic readings of the natural New World, Acosta had no doubt that natural history had everything to do with salvation. In the preface to his *Historia natural y moral*, he noted:

> The aim of this work is that, by disclosing the natural works that the infinitely wise Author of all Nature has performed, praise and glory may be given to almighty God, who is marvellous in all places. And that, by having knowledge of the customs and other matters pertaining to the Indians, they may be helped to continue and remain in the grace of the high calling of the Holy Gospel, to which he who enlightens from the lofty peaks of his eternity deigned to bring these blind people in these latter days.[81]

In recent years, perhaps one of the most important developments in the history of early modern thought in Western Europe has been the appreciation that 'science' did not emerge in the teeth of religious opposition. On the contrary, it is now widely acknowledged how several of the most important pioneers in the study of natural history during this period were members of religious orders; particularly, as we have seen, the Jesuits. I offer this case study to show how an author from the Society sought to account for the environmental and social particularities of the New World and to use this understanding to explain to his readers how divine Providence favoured the making of Roman Catholicism as this planet's first world religion.

University of York

---

[80] Acosta, *Natural and Moral History*, ed. Mangan, 219 (Acosta, *Historia natural de las Indias*, bk 4, ch. 27).

[81] 'Prologue to the Reader', *Natural and Moral History*, ed. Mangan, 12.

FOOTPRINTS AND FAITH: RELIGION AND THE LANDSCAPE IN EARLY MODERN BRITAIN AND IRELAND

by ALEXANDRA WALSHAM

THE idea that divine beings, holy people and magical creatures leave behind permanent marks of their immortality on the surface of the earth is common to many cultures and spiritual systems. Throughout history curious hollows, cavities, and coloured stains on stone and rock have been explained as tangible evidence of the presence and intervention of deities, saints, prophets, angels and demons. The folk motif of the miraculous impression of a foot, hand or limb finds frequent expression within Buddhism, Hinduism, Islam, Judaism and Christianity.[1] Footprint shrines and cults abound in the Middle East, India, south-east Asia and China, from the Dome of the Rock in Jerusalem and Qadam Sharif in Delhi to Phra Sat in Thailand. Variously revered as the footmark of Buddha, Siva, Adam and St Thomas the Apostle, Sri Pada in Sri Lanka is perhaps the most compelling emblem of the polyvalency of this intriguing phenomenon and its capacity to range across the full spectrum of religious traditions.[2] Modern science might rationalize such puzzling features as the consequence of geological processes, the fossilization of prehistoric remains, or human ingenuity; but the impulse to see them as supernatural signs and to venerate such sites as hallowed places persists tenaciously. Falling into the category of the non-corporeal contact relic, the indelible footprint is at once an enduring physical extension of the person or creature alleged to have made it and a graphic token of their absence and erasure from a space they had once occupied

[1] Stith Thompson, *Motif-Index of Folk-Literature*, 5 vols (Copenhagen, 1955–58), 1, entries A972–A972.6; Janet Bord, *Footprints in Stone* (Loughborough, 2004) is a useful popular survey of this phenomenon, only some features of which are discussed in the current essay.

[2] See Markus Aksland, *The Sacred Footprint* (Oslo, 1990); Perween Hasan, 'The Footprint of the Prophet', *Muqarnas* 10 (1993), 335–43; Anthony Welch, 'The Shrine of the Holy Footprint in Delhi', *Muqarnas* 14 (1997), 166–78; Jacob N. Kinnard, 'The Polyvalent Pādas of Visnu and the Buddha', *History of Religions* 40 (2000), 32–57.

or visited.[3] It reflects an irrepressible tendency to view the world through anthropocentric spectacles – to see it as redolent with human analogy and symbolic meaning and chronically to confuse the boundaries between nature, culture and art.[4]

This essay uses the sacred footprint as a focus for exploring the relationship between the religious changes associated with the long Reformation and the landscape of early modern Britain and Ireland. It is a footnote to a wider investigation of how the onset and entrenchment of Protestantism affected contemporary perceptions of the natural environment, of how it shaped the ways in which sixteenth- and seventeenth-century people interpreted trees, woods, springs, stones, rocky outcrops, mountain peaks and other distinctive topographical landmarks of this cluster of north Atlantic islands. The current discussion exemplifies the key themes of this more extended study in miniature.[5]

★   ★   ★

The tradition of the sacred footprint appears to have been an integral part of the indigenous religious culture of the ancient inhabitants of Britain and Ireland. Although little direct evidence of pagan belief and practice survives, we catch a fleeting glimpse of it in early medieval canons and penitentials condemning idolatrous rites and magical practices linked with trees, springs and conspicuous stones. Bishops like Ælfric inveighed against the wickedness of making offerings to rocks and heathen worship of wooden carvings of human limbs and denounced the scraping up of soil from a person's footprint for use in spells as a form of superstition and diabolism. Simultaneously, however, by a series of intricate adaptations and subtle accommodations, Christianity absorbed the hallowed footprint within the framework of the new monotheistic religion.[6] At Monte Gargano in Italy, for instance, the heathen associations of one such imprint in a dark cave were gradually

3   Kinnard, 'Polyvalent Pādas', 38.
4   See Richard Bradley, *The Archaeology of Natural Places* (London, 2000).
5   See my *The Reformation of the Landscape: Religion, Identity and Memory in Early Modern Britain and Ireland* (Oxford, forthcoming). For two earlier discussions of aspects of these themes, see Keith Thomas, *Man and the Natural World: Changing Attitudes in England 1500–1800* (Harmondsworth, 1983); Simon Schama, *Landscape and Memory* (London, 1995).
6   Valerie I. J. Flint, *The Rise of Magic in Early Medieval Europe* (Oxford, 1991), esp.

displaced by the claim that the mark had been left by an apparition of the Archangel Michael, with whom it had become associated by the ninth century.[7] Across Europe, legends linking similar sites with the movements of Christ, the Virgin Mary and the ever growing company of saints proliferated between 400 and 800 AD. Such stories became associated not only with the places in Palestine and Rome where Jesus and his apostles had lived, suffered and died, but also with later missionaries like St Martin of Tours and St Hilary who subsequently planted the faith further afield. British and Irish hagiography illustrates the process by which the countryside was reinvested with supernatural significance and power. Native saints such as Agnes, Samson, Patrick, Columba and Finbar leave lasting monuments of their pious presence in the guise of prodigious foot-prints and castings of various other anatomical features.[8] According to an eleventh-century *vita* of St David, the stone upon which his mother, St Non, leant in the travails of childbirth received the marks of her hands 'as though impressed on wax'.[9] Such formulae should not be seen as examples of thinly disguised pagan recidi-vism; rather we need to recognize the extent to which Christi-anity itself embraced the notion of the immanence of the holy in the natural world and engendered its own sacred geography.[10] The locations in the landscape with which such stories became inti-mately connected attest to the vitality of devotion to local saints in the Middle Ages and point to tendencies that were implicitly in tension with the principle of the universal accessibility of these heavenly patrons promoted by the Church of Rome. While these trends were particularly pronounced in the Celtic regions of the

211, 261–62, 406 n. 17; John Blair, *The Church in Anglo-Saxon Society* (Oxford, 2005), 471–89.

[7] John Charles Arnold, 'Arcadia becomes Jerusalem: Angelic Caverns and Shrine Conversion in Monte Gargano', *Speculum* 75 (2000), 567–88.

[8] See S. Reinach, 'Les monuments de pierre brute', *Revue Archéologique* 21 (1893), 195–223; and Bord, *Footprints,* chs 4–5 for an overview. For examples, see *The Life of St Samson of Dol*, ed. Thomas Taylor (London, 1925), 96; and, in this volume, Raymond Gillespie, 'Devotional Landscapes: God, Saints and the Natural World', 217–36.

[9] *Rhigyfarch's Life of St David*, ed. J. W. James (Cardiff, 1967), 32.

[10] For sensitive treatments of these contentious themes, see Hippolyte Delehaye, *The Legends of the Saints,* trans. Donald Attwater (Dublin, 1998; first publ. 1955), ch. 6; Peter Brown, *The Cult of the Saints: Its Rise and Function in Latin Christianity* (Chicago, IL, 1981); John Howe, 'Creating Symbolic Landscapes: Medieval Development of Sacred Space', in John Howe and Michael Wolfe, eds, *Inventing Medieval Landscapes: Senses of Place in Western Europe* (Gainesville, FL, 2002), 208–23.

British Isles, they were also a significant feature of its Anglo-Saxon heartlands.[11]

Such relics not only served as visual reminders of the early Christian evangelists who had converted the ancient Britons and Gaels; often they also became the focus of thaumaturgic cults and a favourite destination of pilgrims eager to tap into the 'holy radio-activity' that was believed to emanate from them.[12] They were places where medieval people could quite literally touch and feel the divine. Thus by the early post-Conquest period a rock at Ebbsfleet on the coast of Kent, on which the abbess Mildreth had left an impression of her foot, was renowned for working cures and enclosed within a chapel. A similar shrine at Richborough commemorated the arrival of Augustine of Canterbury and was also widely visited on the anniversary of his burial in the hope of healing miracles.[13] A large granite slab preserved on South Ronaldsay, one of the Orkney Islands, was said to be the makeshift boat on which St Magnus had conveyed himself to the Scottish mainland and likewise bore the outline of his feet.[14] In Ireland and Scotland, stones with deep hollows were revered as the beds and chairs of Gaelic saints like Brigid, Kevin and Uinniau,[15] and in Cornwall many devout people travelled to sit in another piece of rock furniture on St Michael's Mount sacred to the memory of the archangel. As late as 1558, conservative parishioners in the same county were still making donations to St Piran's foot at Perranzabuloe.[16] Even Westminster Abbey boasted its own marble relic of

---

[11] See Alan Thacker and Richard Sharpe, eds, *Local Saints and Local Churches in the Early Medieval West* (Oxford, 2002), esp. the essays by John Reuben Davies, Thomas Owen Clancy, Catherine Cubitt and John Blair.

[12] To use Ronald Finucane's phrase, in his *Miracles and Pilgrims: Popular Beliefs in Medieval England* (London, 1977), 26.

[13] See D. W. Rollason, *The Mildrith Legend: A Study in Early Medieval Hagiography in England* (Leicester, 1982), 36, 67, 78, 132; Alan Smith, 'St Augustine of Canterbury in History and Tradition', *Folklore* 89 (1978), 23–28.

[14] See Martin Martin, *A Description of the Western Islands of Scotland* (London, 1703), 367.

[15] On Brigid and Kevin, see Ailbe Séamus Mac Shamráin, *Church and Polity in Pre-Norman Ireland: The Case of Glendalough* (Maynooth, 1996), 39–40; Bord, *Footprints,* 61–63. On Uinniau, see Thomas Owen Clancy, 'Scottish Saints and National Identities in the Early Middle Ages', in Thacker and Sharpe, eds, *Local Saints and Local Churches,* 397–421, at 412.

[16] Robert Whiting, *The Blind Devotion of the People: Popular Religion and the English Reformation* (Cambridge, 1989), 58, 64.

the footprint of the ascending Christ, which had been imported to England from the Holy Land by the Dominicans in 1249 and bestowed on the church by King Henry III.[17] While many such sites were endorsed and legitimized by the ecclesiastical authorities, others were situated in marginal locations in the rural world over which it was more difficult to exert official control. Hovering on the edges of orthodox piety, they were a source of anxiety to humanists and reformers worried by the crudely materialistic flavour of late medieval popular religion.

The Protestant Reformation presented a fundamental threat to the religious culture of which the sacred footprint was a constituent feature. Reformed theology was deeply hostile to the cult of saints and relics and to the practice of undertaking spiritual journeys in search of redemption from sin and supernatural help. It condemned what it saw as an ingrained human tendency to transform physical objects, whether natural or artificial, into idols. Jean Calvin launched a visceral attack upon the phenomenon in the scurrilous inventory or 'register' of relics he published in Geneva, which was translated into English in 1561. He poured scorn on the footmarks of Christ allegedly preserved at Rome, Poitiers, Soissons and Arles, dismissing them as fables and impostures. As for the alleged impression of his hips on a stone kept behind the altar of a church in Rheims, this was a 'blasphemie … so execrable' that he was ashamed even to mention it in passing. Such abominations exemplified the corruption of the papacy and the 'seae full of lyes' which it had fabricated to keep simple laypeople in thraldom.[18] William Lambarde's *Perambulation of Kent* of 1576 no less vociferously dismissed the story of St Mildreth's footprints as the work of 'Monkishe counselors' determined to make profitable 'marchandize of her myracles', just one among many instances of the 'deceivable trumperie' by which the antichristian Church of Rome had maintained its monopoly for so many centuries.[19] The Jacobean Protestant antiquary Robert Hegge was equally scathing about the claim that the cloven hoof of the devil could still be

---

[17] Cambridge, CUL, MS Additional 3041, Nicholas Roscarrock, 'Alphebitt of Saints', fol. 304[r].

[18] John Calvin, *A Very Profitable Treatise … Declarynge what Great Profit Might Come to al Christendome, yf there were a Regester Made of all Sainctes Bodies and other Reliques*, trans. Steven Wythers (London, 1561), sigs E1[r–v] and D5[v] respectively.

[19] William Lambarde, *A Perambulation of Kent* (London, 1576), 81–82.

seen on the banks of the Tweed at the place where St Cuthbert had given him a 'good cudgelling': to discern it, he commented mockingly, one would need to 'borrow an Opticke-glasse from Superstition'.[20]

Protestantism unleashed passions that made many such places of reverence the targets of an ongoing crusade to eradicate the stumbling blocks that stood in the path of the weak and ignorant. It is likely that a number of sacred footprints were casualties of the combination of official and spontaneous iconoclasm that marked the early decades of the Reformation. Others escaped the first wave of Protestant vandalism, only to suffer in later phases of the campaign to eradicate idols from the face of the landscape, which culminated during the bitter civil wars that engulfed the Three Kingdoms in the mid-seventeenth century. In 1632, for instance, a hallowed stone bearing the footprint of St Patrick was ordered to be defaced and thrown into Lough Derg by local officials charged with demolishing the famous pilgrimage shrine of Purgatory in County Donegal. So too was his 'bed' and a rock under the water upon which it was 'vainely' declared he had left the indentation of his knees while he said his devotions.[21] At Abbey Boile in Roscommon in 1641, a font stone bearing another replica of one of St Patrick's limbs was destroyed in the course of raids on St Mary's parish church, though this time, ironically, by a group of Catholic rebels themselves.[22] This seems to have been a case of collateral damage, but many such relics were the subject of deliberate attacks by puritan zealots and parliamentary soldiers convinced that there was no better way of suppressing the potent memories of medieval popery which they evoked than by smashing them to smithereens.

Nevertheless numerous objects of this kind remained intact and continued to provide a rallying point for conservative resistance to the imposition of Protestantism. The elderly papist women a foreign traveller saw muttering rote-learned prayers at a flintstone marked with the foot of St Finbar in the suburbs of Cork in

---

[20] London, BL, MS Sloane 1322, Robert Hegge, 'The Legend of St Cuthbert with the Antiquities of the Church of Durham', fol. 5[t].

[21] Henry Jones, *Saint Patricks Purgatory: Containing the Description, Originall, Progresse, and Demolition of that Superstition Place* (London, 1647), 130.

[22] Dublin, Trinity College, MS 830, Depositions concerning murder and robberies committed in the counties of Roscommon and Galway, fol. 28[r]. The page is fragmented at the edge, and it is unclear which part of the anatomy is under discussion.

1644 reflect a practice that was paralleled elsewhere: at Urney in County Tyrone four decades later people were still kissing a slab on which the face of St Brigid was said to have been miraculously imprinted.[23] Other committed Catholics endeavoured to preserve these endangered traditions by lovingly recording them in writing: the Elizabethan recusant gentleman Nicholas Roscarrock's voluminous 'Alphebitt of saints' includes a number of topographical tales of this type, including the legends of the knee-shaped impressions left by St Bega (or Bee) on a stone near Cockermouth in Cumbria and the hole created when the buttocks of the Irish evangelist St Fiacre sank into a rock upon which he sat during his missionary tour of France.[24] It would be a mistake to see the repetition of such stories as a function of simple nostalgia for a mythical Catholic past that was rapidly vanishing. The resurgent Counter-Reformation Church on the Continent enthusiastically promoted local landscape shrines of this kind, including pious visits to the bed of St Francis on the precipitous slope of Monte Verna in Piedmont.[25] It also issued thousands of printed pilgrimage tokens reproducing the outline of Christ's footprint on the Mount of Olives and an indulgenced Spanish image of the measure of Virgin's foot was among the many prohibited devotional aids smuggled into England in the reign of James I.[26] Despite the concerns to prune away superstitious accretions that animated the delegates who attended the Council of Trent, the process of Catholic renewal proved flexible and capacious enough to accommodate continuing devotion to this class of contact relics and their more ephemeral paper facsimiles.

More surprisingly, perhaps, stories about sacred footprints continued to be told in Protestant circles. Before proceeding to analyse this corpus of folklore, it is necessary to stress that the

[23] *The Tour of the French Traveller M. de la Boullaye le Gouz in Ireland, A.D. 1644*, ed. T. Crofton Croker (London, 1837), 30; John Richardson, *The Great Folly, Superstition and Idolatry of Pilgrimages in Ireland* (Dublin, 1727), 69.

[24] CUL, MS Add. 3041, fols 87ᵛ, 217ᵛ, and see fol. 314ʳ on St Brigid. Mildreth's footprints are recorded in a manuscript collection of the lives of women saints of Britain and Ireland compiled c. 1610–15: *The Lives of Women Saints of our Contrie of England*, ed. C. Horstmann, EETS os 86 (1886), 63.

[25] Schama, *Landscape and Memory*, 436–37.

[26] See Bord, *Footprints*, 38, for a reproduction of one such pilgrimage token, and Antony Wootton, *A Defence of M. Perkins Booke, Called A Reformed Catholike* (London, 1606), 390, for the Spanish image of the Virgin's foot.

notion that an omnipotent God could, if he wished, cause such impressions to be left in hard rock was entirely consistent with the Reformed doctrines of creation and Providence. Godly clergymen who wrote systematic treatises on these topics accepted the text of Genesis as a literal account of how the Lord had formed the earth and the heavens out of a confused chaos and void. Guided by Psalms 8: 3 and 102: 25, they thought of the world as his personal handiwork, a sculpture chiselled by a master craftsman, every square inch of which displayed his infinite care and unbounding beneficence. As often as 'we see and behold the visible outward workes' of creation, declared the London minister George Walker, 'let us in them behold the face of God, and remember his glorious attributes'.[27] Nature was his 'great booke in Folio' and 'every creature a severall page, in which we may read some instruction to further us in heavenly wisdome'.[28] The Scottish preacher Hugh Binning spoke of the 'great characters' he imprinted upon each of them and the Exeter divine Thomas Manton said that they all carried his distinctive 'signature and mark', not to say his very 'tract and footprint'.[29] The trope of tracing the footsteps of the Almighty in the theatre of nature was equally commonplace,[30] though we may note that for Calvinists who abhorred the depiction of God anthropomorphically it could only ever be a figure of speech. To conceive of, or represent, the supreme incorporeal force that was the Lord in visible bodily form was to defile his majesty by an 'impious lie' and 'an absurd and indecorous fiction'.[31]

---

[27] George Walker, *God Made Visible in his Workes, or, A Treatise of the Externall Workes of God* (London, 1641), 12. See also John Calvin, *A Commentarie … upon the First Booke of Moses called Genesis*, trans. Thomas Tymme (London, 1578), 25–49; Gervase Babington, *Certaine Plaine, Briefe, and Comfortable Notes upon Everie Chapter of Genesis* (London, 1592), fols 1ʳ–7ᵛ; William Pemble, *Workes* (London, 1635), 265–69. See also Susan E. Schreiner, *The Theater of his Glory: Nature and the Natural Order in the Thought of John Calvin* (Durham, NC, 1991).

[28] L. Brinkmair, *The Warnings of Germany* (London, 1638), sig. ★2ᵛ.

[29] Hugh Binning, *Fellowship with God* (Edinburgh, 1671), 19–20; Thomas Manton, *One Hundred and Ninety Sermons on the Hundred and Nineteenth Psalm* (London, 1681), 495. See also John Calvin, *Sermons … upon the X. Commandementes of the Lawe*, trans. I. H. (London, 1579), fol. 29ʳ⁻ᵛ.

[30] e.g. William Ames, *The Marrow of Sacred Divinity* (London, 1642), 28; John Ray, *The Wisdom of God Manifested in the Works of the Creation* (London, 1691), sig. A6ᵛ; William Borlase, *The Natural History of Cornwall* (Oxford, 1758), iv.

[31] John Calvin, *Institutes of the Christian Religion*, 1.11.1–2, trans. Henry Beveridge, 2 vols in 1 (Grand Rapids, MI, 1989), 1: 91.

Despite the latent ideological inconsistency entailed in doing so, Protestants also continued to use poetic licence in metaphorically tracing 'the finger of God' in his ongoing providential (and occasionally miraculous) intervention in the material world. They saw his hand at work in strange botanical, meteorological and geological wonders, interpreting these prodigies as judgements for sin and warnings to repent before more consuming punishments befell their communities or the nation at large.[32] They also ascribed anomalous phenomena to the malicious and devious activities of Satan, that master magician skilled in manipulating nature to seduce mankind to eternal damnation.[33] There was, then, no insurmountable obstacle to the idea that indentations in rock might be the product of super- or preternatural processes. Even Calvin himself could not deny that this was technically possible.[34]

It is against this backdrop that we may now turn to interpret the stories of miraculous footprints recorded by post-Reformation topographers, antiquarians and later folklorists. Many such tales were not recorded before the eighteenth or nineteenth centuries: it is often impossible to judge how far they had previously circulated orally or to assess accurately the extent to which they were distorted, contaminated or even created by the learned clergy and laymen who documented them for the benefit of posterity. The preoccupation with tracing their 'primitive' and 'archaic' origin that inspired many of these writers has fostered an enduring tendency to see them as throwbacks to paganism, with popery as an interim phase. Such stories certainly betray telltale signs of the syncretism of different belief systems, but there are dangers in dwelling on these elements at the expense of evidence of transformation and change. To see their endurance over time as an index of no more than 'minimal popular reception' may be unduly pessimistic. It runs the risk of eclipsing the role which Protestantism played in reconstituting social memory and creating a distinctively post-

---

[32] See my *Providence in Early Modern England* (Oxford, 1999).

[33] See Stuart Clark, *Thinking with Demons: The Idea of Witchcraft in Early Modern Europe* (Oxford, 1997), esp. ch. 11.

[34] Calvin, *Very Profitable Treatise,* sig. E^v: 'I dispute not weather Jesus Christ coulde have imprinted the fourme and fashion of hys fete on a stone. But I only dispute of the facte'.

Reformation tissue of legend.[35] These and other landscape legends need to be approached as embodiments of a culture in a state of constant and dynamic motion.[36]

There is space here to examine only a handful of examples. The first is the tradition explaining the curious cavity in a flagstone in the floor of Smithills Hall near Bolton, Lancashire. This is said to have been created by the Protestant George Marsh who was arrested and interrogated here in 1555 and burnt at the stake in Chester later that year. According to a story first recorded in 1787,

> provoked by the taunts and persecutions of his examiners, he stamped with his foot upon a stone, and, looking up to Heaven, appealed to God for the justness of his cause; and prayed that there might remain in that place a constant memorial of the wickedness and injustice of his enemies ...

This was a Protestant prodigy vindicating a man who made the ultimate sacrifice for the true faith. In everlasting honour of his martyrdom, it was reported to ooze blood occasionally. Divine anger at subsequent attempts to move it resulted in the house being troubled by poltergeist activity.[37] The fact that there is no warrant for this cluster of interrelated traditions in Foxe's *Actes and Monuments* or a printed local history of 1656 should not really trouble us.[38] Regardless of whether or not it existed in unwritten discourse before the late eighteenth century, it provides a revealing testimony of how long the memory of the Marian burnings lingered on in Protestant minds. The story may be seen as a by-product of the

---

[35] For a fuller exposition of this approach to folklore, see Walsham, *Reformation of the Landscape,* ch. 7. A more sceptical assessment of its value can be found in Robert W. Scribner, 'Luther Myth: A Popular Historiography of the Reformer', in his *Popular Culture and Popular Movements in Reformation Germany* (London, 1987), 301–22, at 321–22.

[36] For recognition of the role of pre- and post-Reformation Christianity in shaping such traditions, see Jacqueline Simpson, 'God's Visible Judgements: The Christian Dimension of Landscape Legends', *Landscape History* 8 (1986), 53–58; eadem, 'The Local Legend: A Product of Popular Culture', *Rural History* 2 (1991), 25–35.

[37] John Harland and T. T. Wilkinson, *Lancashire Folk-Lore* (London, 1882), 135–37; Christina Hole, *Traditions and Customs of Cheshire* (London, 1937), 206; Bord, *Footprints,* 145–46.

[38] John Foxe, *Actes and Monuments* (London, 1563), 1118–29; William Smith and William Webb, *The Vale-Royall of England. Or, the County Palatine of Chester Illustrated* (London, 1656), 197.

potent mixture of national pride and anti-Catholic prejudice that was one of the most lasting legacies of the Reformation.

A second footprint legend offers further insight into how this ancient cultural formula was affected by processes of religious confessionalization. This interprets a strange indentation in the wall of the parish church of Brindle in Lancashire as the consequence of a spirited confrontation between the Protestant vicar of the village and the Jesuit missionary Edmund Arrowsmith, who succoured the Catholic faithful in an area renowned for recusancy for a decade and a half before being captured and executed for treason at Lancaster in 1628.[39] Two competing versions of its origins, rooted in opposing sectarian outlooks, were in circulation in the nineteenth and early twentieth centuries. One saw the miracle as an act of approbation of the future priestly martyr, the other as a divine indictment of the false religion he taught. For Catholics it marked the spot where the Almighty had intervened in response to Father Arrowsmith's pious oath: 'If my religion is right, my foot will leave its impression on this stone'. To Protestants it was tangible proof of heavenly anger at his blasphemous request for the Lord to intervene to defend the embattled faith he preached. Upon the utterance of these words, it was asserted, 'the reforming stone instantly softened, and buried the papistical foot'.[40] Both confessions sought to commandeer the mysterious imprint to demonstrate that God was on their side. It is a testament both to the spontaneous consecration of places associated with Roman Catholic evangelists and martyrs and to the deep-seated Protestant conviction that the material world was a canvas upon which the deity inscribed important messages about his will for mankind.

The tradition of the sacred footprint also attached itself to evangelical and dissenting Protestants. The case of the Congregationalist John Flavell, who, ejected from his lectureship at Dartmouth, conducted services from a rock in the Kingsbridge estuary at low

---

[39] *ODNB*, s.n. 'Arrowsmith, Edmund'. The incumbent between 1603 and 1629 was William Bennett: William Farrer and J. Brownhill, eds, *VCH Lancashire*, 8 vols (1906–14), 6: 80.

[40] Bede Camm, *Forgotten Shrines: An Account of some Old Catholic Halls and Families in England and of Relics and Memorials of the English Martyrs* (London, 1910), 195; Edward Baines, *History of the County Palatine and Duchy of Lancaster*, 4 vols (London, 1836), 3: 498.

tide, provides a hint of the circumstances in which such myths might arise: in this instance, though, the incoming waters regularly washed away all trace of his footsteps.[41] By contrast, several stories about impressions left by John Wesley in the eighteenth century have acquired the status of enduring legends. Peculiar iron-coloured stains on the slab covering the grave of his father at Epworth in Lincolnshire were marks made when the founder of Methodism stood upon it to preach, having been refused access to the parish pulpit. He reputedly 'grew into such a fervour that his toes burnt hollows in the very substance of the stone'.[42] A similar tradition is linked with a famous early nineteenth-century lay preacher from East Yorkshire, Tommy Escritt, who stood overlooking the village of Hutton Cranswick and prayed daily for its conversion: grass refused to grow at the spot, which became 'sacred to his memory', and a 'holy place' frequented by pilgrims.[43] Such tales are illuminated by recent research revealing the magical and providential mentality that marked some wings of this movement.[44] Another story from the same era associated with Glen Moriston near Loch Ness in Scotland evokes the trope embodied in the legend of Edmund Arrowsmith's boot: heckled by locals who called him a liar, he called upon God to bear witness by permanently branding the land with his footprints.[45] It may well be that this version simply superseded an earlier aetiological myth about this unusual topographical feature.

An associated subset of stories attributes such phenomena to satanic agency. Parallelling a wider body of folklore that ascribes craggy outcrops and other ugly landmarks to diabolical activity, we find a variety of tales accounting for marks on wood, stone and rock that resemble the cloven feet which the devil was popularly

---

[41] Cited in Michael R. Watts, *The Dissenters*, 1: *From the Reformation to the French Revolution* (Oxford, 1978), 230–31.

[42] *Notes and Queries,* ser. 3, 9 (1866), 205, 277; ser. 3, 10 (1866), 189–90; ser. 4, 9 (1872), 494, 542; Mrs Gutch and Mabel Peacock, *Examples of Printed Folk-Lore Concerning Lincolnshire,* County Folk-Lore 5 (London, 1908), 3–4; Bord, *Footprints,* 47.

[43] John Nicholson, *Folk Lore of East Yorkshire* (London, 1890), 55.

[44] Among others, see John W. B. Tomlinson, 'The Magic Methodists and their Influence on the Early Primitive Methodist Movement', in Kate Cooper and Jeremy Gregory, eds, *Signs, Wonders, Miracles: Representations of Divine Power in the Life of the Church,* SCH 41 (Woodbridge, 2005), 389–99. Forthcoming work by John Walsh will also illuminate this theme.

[45] Bord, *Footprints,* 48.

believed to sport when he assumed tangible form. The menacing black dog that swept through the church of Bungay in Suffolk in 1577 is a case in point: in his moralizing pamphlet about this frightening incident, the Elizabethan divine Abraham Fleming pointed to the burn marks like 'clawes and talans' that could still be seen in its stones and door 'as testimonies and witnesses of the force which rested in this strange shaped thing'.[46] Interpreted as a terrible warning of impending punishment for sin, belief in this prodigy was wholly in keeping with the renewed emphasis which Protestantism placed on the terrifying power of the devil, and with the fears and anxieties that drove the witch-hunts of the period.[47] Older stories about landmarks arguably endured for the same reason. These include the tale of the large boulder on the ridge of Hood Hill in north Yorkshire allegedly dropped by Lucifer after he fled the scene of his trouncing by a missionary, and which bore the imprint of his infernal foot.[48] In a theological atmosphere antagonistic to the idea of a corporeal devil, such traditions might have withered; their persistence may be seen as a measure of how far the ideological climate of post-Reformation Britain favoured their survival. A comment made by a loquacious Irish lady in 1836, meanwhile, provides evidence of how some sites of this kind could undergo metamorphosis under the pressure of momentous events. Found praying in the churchyard of Cork Cathedral, she told a visitor of the stone footprint of St Finbar that had once resided there, adding, in a telling revelation of her attitude to the Anglo-Dutch invader, that after the arrival of William of Orange 'it changed into the mark of the devil's foot'.[49]

Finally, we may consider two post-Reformation permutations of the related and no less venerable theme of the miraculous hoof-print. One is the case of the ox foot stone at South Lopham in Norfolk, reputed to mark the providential appearance of a cow whose steady profusion of milk fed the local inhabitants during a great dearth in the town. Francis Blomefield, the antiquary who recorded this wonder in 1739, described it as a 'fable', but it was

[46] Abraham Fleming, *A Straunge and Terrible Wunder Wrought Very Late in the Parish Church of Bongay* (London, 1577), sig. A6[v].

[47] See also Walsham, *Providence*, 186–94.

[48] Mrs Gutch, *Examples of Printed Folk-Lore Concerning the North Riding of Yorkshire, York and the Ainsty* (London, 1901), 3–4.

[49] *Tour*, ed. Crofton Croker, 102–103.

widely believed by the 'Country People' and may be an example of a story from which an explicitly hagiographical dimension had gradually evaporated, leaving behind a more 'secular' deposit.[50] This is more clearly evident in a tradition regarding the horse-shoe-shaped indentations on a stone near Tedstone Delamere in Herefordshire. In 1812 a 'traditionary account' told how these had been left by a mare and colt stolen one night from a local farmer but restored after his daughter prayed to God to leave some sign by which they could be traced. Many 'pretended vestiges' of the animals' feet were pointed out in the channel of the brook by the 'credulous peasantry'; others had been 'cut away by the felon chisel to deck the simple mantel-piece of the rustic naturalist'. Originally linked with the life of the pious fourteenth-century anchorite Katherine Audley of Ledbury, the excision of the saint from the tale by the early nineteenth century was reversed in 1835, when William Wordsworth reinserted her in a sonnet invoking this piece of local folklore.[51] A salutary reminder of the role played by poets and scholars in the invention and reinvention of lapsed traditions, the evolution of the story also alerts us to the cyclical manner in which the landscape was repeatedly encrusted with fresh layers of religious significance.

★   ★   ★

Stories of footprints supernaturally deposited in stone and rock thus offer unexpected insights about the 'Reformation of the landscape' and the nexus between the Church and the natural world. They add weight to recent qualifications of the claim that the advent of Protestantism contributed to a profound shift in sensibility and played a critical role in the disenchantment of the material universe. Reformed theology was hostile to the idea that physical space or visible objects had inherent sanctity, but over time it nevertheless

---

[50] Francis Blomefield, *An Essay towards a Topographical History of the County of Norfolk*, 5 vols (London, 1739), 1: 157. On this process, see Daniel Woolf, *The Social Circulation of the Past: English Historical Culture 1500–1700* (Oxford, 2003), 191–97.

[51] John Duncumb et al., *Collections Towards the History and Antiquities of the County of Hereford*, 6 vols (Hereford, 1804–1912), 2: 196; Ella Mary Leather, *The Folk-Lore of Herefordshire* (Hereford, 1912), 6–7; Jennifer Westwood, *Albion: A Guide to Legendary Britain* (London, 1987), 319–20. For Roscarrock's Catholic account of the tale incorporating St Katherine, see CUL, MS Add. 3041, fol. 116[v].

fostered 'new sacred topographies' of its own.[52] Far from a measure of the resilience of popery or paganism, these hallowed places must often be seen as authentic products of a Protestant mindset steeped in assumptions about creation and Providence. Secondly, an examination of this category of legend highlights the way in which the landscape functioned as an archive and repository of multiple layers of local, national and ecclesiastical memory, as a continuing stimulus to the making of myths of geographical origin and as a visual mnemonic to popular knowledge of the past. The Reformation did nothing to halt this process; on the contrary, it gave it an additional fillip. It grafted new meaning onto natural phenomena and it transformed topographical landmarks into symbols of its moral and ideological priorities and of the confessional conflicts that unsettled Britain and Ireland throughout the sixteenth and seventeenth centuries.

University of Exeter

---

[52] Ulinka Rublack, *Reformation Europe* (Cambridge, 2005), 157.

NATURE, MUSIC AND THE REFORMATION
IN ENGLAND*

by JONATHAN WILLIS

THE story of music in the Elizabethan Church is, in many ways, an embodiment of the relationship between two larger, competing and often contradictory discourses: those of Renaissance and Reformation. As Alexandra Walsham noted in the introduction to *Providence in Early Modern England*, published in 1999,

> there is a growing conviction that too much ink has been spilt arguing about the pace, geography and social distribution of conversion and change and too little charting the ways in which the populace adjusted to the doctrinal and ecclesiastical revolution as a permanent fact.[1]

This 'post-revisionist' approach has been a fruitful one, and Reformation historians have examined diverse cultural practices in order to shed new light on processes of Protestant religious identity formation.[2] A part of this trend has been increased scholarly interest in the relationship between music and religious identity, and while there is still no post-revisionist monograph on music in the English Reformation, a number of essays and articles have treated aspects of the subject.[3] But while the practice of vernacular

* My thanks go to those who commented on earlier versions of this paper. It draws upon themes which are discussed in greater detail in my Ph.D. thesis, 'Church Music and Protestantism in Post-Reformation England: Discourses, Sites and Identities' (University of Warwick, 2009).

[1] Alexandra Walsham, *Providence in Early Modern England* (Oxford, 1999), 5.

[2] e.g. Tessa Watt, *Cheap Print and Popular Piety, 1550–1640* (Cambridge, 1991); Peter Lake, with Michael Questier, *The Antichrist's Lewd Hat: Protestants, Papists and Players in Post-Reformation England* (New Haven, CT, 2002); Peter Marshall, *Beliefs and the Dead in Reformation England* (Oxford, 2002); Ronald Hutton, *The Rise and Fall of Merry England: The Ritual Year 1400–1700* (Oxford, 1996); David Cressy, *Bonfires and Bells: National Memory and the Protestant Calendar in Elizabethan and Stuart England* (Berkeley, CA, 1989).

[3] Andrew Pettegree, 'Militant in Song', in idem, *Reformation and the Culture of Persuasion* (Cambridge, 2005), 40–75; Ian Green, '"All people that on earth do dwell, Sing to the Lord with cheerful voice": Protestantism and Music in Early Modern

congregational metrical psalmody has attracted the lion's share of historical attention, much less consideration has been given to the cultural discourse of music, primarily classical in its origins, which provided the context within which religious musical practices were conceived of, negotiated and implemented.

Music in sixteenth-century England was not simply an art: it was an ancient and potent science, discussion of which entailed the use of a complicated and multifaceted discourse. Sixteenth-century humanists and divines had access to an enormously rich intellectual musico-cultural heritage, and they were also bound by it in all their discussions of music, while the same tropes suffused culture at every level. This paper will argue that understanding this discourse, given new vigour by renewed Renaissance emphasis on the classical past, is fundamental to any attempt to understand music in the context of the English Reformation. The role of music in formal worship and private devotion was not simply shaped by a set of overriding religious imperatives. Rather, musical discourse helped shape the place of musical practice in the religious life of early modern Englishmen and -women, and therefore also helped to shape their very belief as it was practised. This paper begins by outlining briefly the classical context for Reformation-era attitudes to music. It goes on to explore one key aspect of the Elizabethan cultural discourse of music, that is, the relationship between music and the natural world. Finally, it sketches out some of the implications that this deeper understanding of early modern music has for our understanding of the place of music within the English Reformation as a whole.

The commonly acknowledged starting point for Graeco-Roman notions of the science of music was Pythagoras.[4] Inspired by the sounds of blacksmiths' hammers, Pythagoras's experiments with

England', in *Christianity and Community in the West: Essays for John Bossy*, ed. Simon Ditchfield (Aldershot, 2001), 148–64; Beat Kümin, 'Masses, Morris and Metrical Psalms: Music in the English Parish c. 1400–1600', in Fiona Kisby, ed., *Music and Musicians in Renaissance Cities and Towns* (Cambridge, 2001), 70–81; John Craig, 'Psalms, Groans and Dog-Whippers: The Soundscape of Sacred Space in the English Parish Church, 1547–1642', in Will Coster and Andrew Spicer, eds, *Sacred Space in Early Modern Europe* (Cambridge, 2005), 104–23.

4   Hans T. David, 'The Cultural Functions of Music', *JHI* 12 (1951), 423–39, at 425. See also John Hollander, *The Untuning of the Sky* (New York, 1970), 15–30; Kathi Meyer-Baer, *Music of the Spheres and the Dance of Death* (Princeton, NJ, 1970); Peter Webster, 'The Relationship between Religious Thought and the Theory and Practice

the tones produced by a vibrating cord yielded both mathematical and musical notions of harmony, or 'relative proportion'.[5] The 'harmony of the spheres' was an indication that the heavens were governed by similar mathematical proportions to those by which certain tonal sequences could be generated. In the *Republic*, Plato made explicit the relationship between the motion of the heavenly spheres and an actual audible music,[6] while a sixteenth-century translation of Aristotle's *Politics* noted 'that Musicke hath force to dispose the affections of the mind in diuerse sorts [and] many wise men affirme that the soule is an harmony, or that there is harmony in it'.[7] The ideas of the classical Greek authors were developed in the sixth century by the Roman statesman and philosopher Boethius, who spelled out the tripartite schema of *musica mundana*, *musica humana* and *musica instrumentalis*.[8] Following Pythagoras and Plato, Boethius asserted that *musica mundana* was the music of the heavens, and that which existed in macrocosm was replicated in microcosm: *musica humana* was the equivalent harmony within the human body. *Musica instrumentalis*, the actual audible music composed, performed and heard by man, was unquestionably the inferior variety, a pale shadow and reflection of the divine harmonies which underlay the joint miracles of human existence and the operation of the heavenly spheres. Body, soul and rational mind were all, therefore, held in harmony both between and within themselves through the mathematical proportionality of musical harmonies. It followed quite logically that if music had the power to speak directly to the human soul, then diverse musical stimuli would elicit differing emotional responses.

of Church Music in England, 1603 – c. 1640' (unpublished Ph.D. thesis, University of Sheffield, 2001), 72–89.

[5] Hollander, *Untuning of the Sky*, 15, 26–27. Boethius mentions Pythagoras's accidental discovery of musical harmony: 'while passing the workshop of blacksmiths, he overheard the beating of hammers somehow emit a single consonance from differing sounds': Boethius, *Fundamentals of Music*, trans. and intro. Calvin M. Bower, ed. Claude V. Palisca (New Haven, CT, 1989), 18.

[6] Meyer-Baer, *Music of the Spheres*, 12.

[7] Aristotle, *Aristotles politiques, or Discourses of gouernment*, trans. Loys Le Roy (London, 1598), 388.

[8] Boethius, *De institutione musica*, intro. Calvin M. Bower, ed. Claude Palisca (London, 1989), 9; Hollander, *Untuning of the Sky*, 24; David, 'Cultural Functions of Music', 426.

By the sixteenth century, notions concerning the affective powers of music had become detached from the particular musical forms or styles by which they were supposed to have been generated. This was useful for Elizabethan polemicists, who could indulge in a polite Platonic fiction, praising music in general while at the same time decrying contemporary usage as being more in line with the harmful Lydian or Mixolydian modes than the beneficial Dorian or Phrygian ones.[9] These classical modes may have been an anachronism by the sixteenth century, but the idea that certain forms of music could be beneficial or injurious to the human soul by virtue of their very audition was an important and enduring one.

Harmony was tangible proof of the divine in nature. Many of the musical tropes ubiquitous in Elizabethan England related to the harmony of the spheres. Bartholomeus Anglicus's mid-thirteenth century encyclopedia *De proprietatibus rerum*, printed in English during the 1580s, described the astronomical music of the stars.[10] Castiglione's *The Courtyer*, translated into English by Sir Thomas Hoby and printed in four editions during Elizabeth's reign, declared that the movement of the heavens produced melody,[11] while in his *Orchestra or A poeme of dauncing*, Sir John Davies noted that the starry wheels in 'the turning vault of heauen … doe a musick frame'.[12]

Elizabethan polemicists of all religious stripes subscribed to the same musical ontology. The crypto-Catholic Thomas Lodge defended music from an attack by the puritan theatre critic Stephen Gosson by referring him to the 'harmonie of the Heauens'.[13] But Gosson himself had charged those who would 'profite well in the Arte of Musicke' to put away their fiddles and to look instead to the heavens, to the order of the spheres, the movement of the

---

[9] Plato dismissed the 'Mixed Lydian' and the 'taut Lydian' modes as 'dirges', useless even to women. The Ionian and more relaxed Lydian modes made men 'drunk, soft and idle'. Only the Dorian and Phrygian modes were to be permitted, which could properly capture 'the tones and variations of pitch of a brave man's voice': Plato, *Republic*, trans. Robin Waterfield (Oxford, 1993), 96.

[10] Bartholomaeus Anglicus, *Batman vppon Bartholome* (London, 1582), fols 132ᵛ, 136ᵛ. ESTC records English editions in 1495, 1535 and 1582: <http://estc.bl.uk>.

[11] Baldassarre Castiglione, *The courtyer of Count Baldessar Castilio* (London, 1561), sig. I2ʳ. ESTC lists editions for 1561, 1577, 1588 and 1603: <http://estc.bl.uk>.

[12] Sir John Davies, *Orchestra or A poeme of dauncing* (London, 1596), sig. A6ʳ.

[13] Thomas Lodge, *Protogenes can know Apelles by his line* (London, 1579), 25.

planets, the course of the year and the concord of the elements.[14] In 1582, arguing against an opponent of a rather different confessional allegiance in *The Christian against the Jesuit,* Thomas Lupton also reached to the harmony of the spheres to defend music.[15] The harmony of the spheres existed in poetical language, but its effectiveness as simile and metaphor derived from the scientific knowledge that it was a real phenomenon. Sir Philip Sidney described the music of poetry as 'Plannetlike' in his *Apologie* (1595),[16] for example, while in Michael Drayton's *Matilda* love could fetch 'musick from the Spheres'.[17] Music's mathematical qualities also formed part of its more general character, as reflected by its status as one of the quadrivial liberal sciences. 'What other thing is in musicke entreated of', asked Euclid in one sixteenth-century translation of his *Elements of Geometrie,* 'then [*sic*] number contracted to sound and voyce?'[18] The composer John Dowland hence confessed to Sir George Carey, the dedicatee of his *First booke of songes or ayres,* that the power of harmony came about 'by reason of the variety of number & proportion' of which it consisted.[19] Through their shared mathematical basis, music could engender an understanding of space and time itself.[20]

A second rich strain for the discourse of music and the natural world lay in music's relationship not with the heavens, but with the earth. The world itself was considered to be harmonious: Bartholomeus Anglicus cited Isaiah 51: 3 in support of his claim that it was 'made in a certaine proportion of harmony'.[21] Thomas Campion likewise held that 'the world is made by Simmetry and

---

[14] Stephen Gosson, *The schoole of abuse* (London, 1579), fol. 8[r].

[15] Thomas Lupton, *The Christian against the Iesuite* (London, 1582), fol. 63[r–v].

[16] Sir Philip Sidney, *An apologie for poetrie* (London, 1595), sig. L3[r].

[17] Michael Drayton, *Matilda The faire* (London, 1594), sig. C1[r].

[18] Euclid, *The elements of geometrie,* trans. H. Billingsley (London, 1570), fol. 183.

[19] John Dowland, *The first booke of songes or ayres* (London, 1597), fol. 1[r].

[20] See, e.g., Lupton, *The Christian against the Iesuite,* fol. 63[v]: 'the Astronomical second, and the musicall semebreefe, are iust both of one time. And thus by this famous science of musicke we may finde out the merueylous motions of the Celestiall signes.'

[21] Anglicus, *Batman vppon Bartholome,* fol. 418[r]. See also ibid. fol. 119[r]: 'Then the world, of the which we speake at this time is not diuers in it selfe: neither departed in substaunce, though contrariousnesse be found in parts thereof touching contrarinesse of the qualities: for the world hath most needfull accorde in all it selfe, and as it were aecorde of musike'.

proportion, and is in that respect compared to Musick'.[22] The world itself was a musical creation, and assorted natural sounds were also considered to be musical. To Michael Drayton, for example, the 'gravell sound' of 'murmuring Springs' was 'like doleful instruments'.[23] This language was predominantly poetical, but its choice also reflected the deep-seated cultural significance of music in the *mentalité* of the Elizabethan Englishman and -woman. Harmony was elemental and, as well as water, music was often likened to air. For Michael Drayton, 'gentle Zephire[s]' whistled 'sweete musick'.[24] Puritan killjoy John Northbrooke, in trying to explain why certain forms of music could 'rapte and vanishe men in a maner wholy', cited Cicero's claim that even the rocks and wilderness gave sound and were subject to its powers.[25] Music was rooted in the air and the sea, the rocks and the rivers, and the composition of the earth itself was governed by musically determined harmonies.

One of the most important ancient proofs of the musicality of the world was the figure of Orpheus. Orpheus was an effective shorthand for the efficacy of music as laid out by classical antiquity: only the music of Orpheus, for example, could be powerful enough to comfort the most distressed individuals.[26] Some attributed the origins of music in antiquity to Orpheus,[27] while for lutenist and composer John Dowland, Orpheus was a convenient illustration of the notion that to 'that kinde of Musicke, which to the sweetnes of instrument applies the lively voice of man' was reserved the highest 'authoritie and power'.[28] The parallels between *musica instrumentalis* and the harmonies which governed the natural world meant that Orpheus's supreme musical abilities had affected the world around him in a number of ways. There was a recognition amongst Elizabethan authors that contemporary music rarely had quite the same miraculous effects, and consequently Elizabethans possessed a real sense that the potency of music had decayed from its zenith in

[22] Thomas Campion, *Obseruations in the art of English poesie*, (London, 1602), 31.

[23] Michael Drayton, *Endimion and Phoebe Ideas Latmus* (London, 1595), sig. C4ʳ.

[24] Michael Drayton, *Idea the shepheards garland* (London, 1593), 42. See also Christopher Marlowe, *Hero and Leander* (London, 1598), sig. K2ʳ.

[25] John Northbrooke, *Spiritus est vicarius Christi in terra. A treatise wherein dicing, daunting, vaine playes or enterluds with other idle pastimes [et]c. commonly vsed on the Sabboth day, are reproued* (London, 1577), 81.

[26] Robert Greene, *Philomela The Lady Fitzvvaters nightingale* (London, 1592), sig. G3ᵛ.

[27] Lodowick Lloyd, *The pilgrimage of princes* (London, 1573), fol. 112ᵛ.

[28] Dowland, *The first booke of songes or ayres*, fol. 1ʳ.

classical antiquity to a rather feeble simulacrum. Yet music's ability to affect the human mind was still universally recognised, and the ability of Orpheus to charm nature itself existed as a testament to the extent of its latent force. Quite apart from bewitching the underworld in his quest to free Eurydice from clutches of Hades, on earth Orpheus's music had had the power to make the trees dance, and to move stones, rocks and mountains.[29]

Orpheus was one convenient shorthand for the capability of music to master the creatures, elements and even the physical landscape of the natural world. Many other tropes current in the Elizabethan period related to the world of birds. In Richard Jones's *Arbor of amorous deuises* (1597), a choir composed of birds mourned the death of 'a Mayde forsaken' with 'dolefull musick'.[30] In the dedicatory epistle to his book of canzonets,[31] Giles Farnaby referred to Chaucer's poem *The Parliament of Birds*, which had described 'the straunge and sweete harmonie amonge the fowles of all kindes'.[32] While the music of nightingales was merry, the shrieks of owls were the 'poste of Death'.[33] Birdsong resonated with the echoes of the entire natural world, including the processes of birth and decease. The nightingale was, by common consent, the most musical bird. 'Who is he which heareth the sweete melodie of the Nightingal', Thomas Rogers asked, '& is not stroken with admiration?'[34] While birdsong itself could bewitch, birds themselves, as musical creatures, could also be affected by music, in the same way as the rocks and trees which danced for Orpheus.[35] According to Thomas Lupton, music was 'of such force, that birdes are catcht through the pleasure they have in melodious whistling',[36] while for Thomas Rogers, birds were actually nourished through the

---

[29] Edmund Spenser, *The shepheardes calender* (London, 1579), fol. 43[r]; Lloyd, *The pilgrimage of princes*, fol. 112[v]; Davies, *Orchestra*, sig. B2[v]; Thomas Naogeorg, *The popish kingdome, or reigne of Antichrist*, trans. Barnaby Googe (London, 1570), fol. 71[r].

[30] Richard Jones, *The arbor of amorous deuises* (London, 1597), sigs A5[v]–B1[r].

[31] Canzonets were short airy vocal songs of more than one movement.

[32] Giles Farnaby, *Canzonets to fowre voyces, with a song of eight parts* (London, 1598), fol. 2[r].

[33] Thomas Churchyard, *A pleasaunte laborinth called Churchyardes chance* (London, 1580), 16.

[34] Thomas Rogers, *A philosophicall discourse, entituled, The anatomie of the minde* (London, 1576), fol. 5[v].

[35] Naogeorg, *The popish kingdome*, fol. 71[r].

[36] Lupton, *The Christian against the Iesuite*, fol. 71[r].

'concent & sweete variety' of their music.[37] Birds were creatures of the air, and like the air itself they were harmonious. As with the harmonies described by the ancients, in Elizabethan England birds were affected and could affect through their song in numerous ways, some virtuous but others dangerous.

The discourse of music in sixteenth-century England also included the beasts of the earth and the fish of the sea. John Lane, in *Tom Tel-Troths message*, wrote that music's 'eare-bewitching melodie' could 'unto men and beasts such pleasure moue'.[38] Just as music had the power to calm the wilder aspects of human nature, it also, as a rational and harmonious force, had a great civilizing and pacifying power to tame animals. Robert Roche observed how 'the softest drops, do peirce the hardest stoanes' and that, in like manner, 'milde musick can, mad beastes allure and weild'.[39] Philip Stubbes observed that music 'dooth delight bothe man and beast'.[40] Leonard Wright, in his *Display of dutie* (1583), recorded an entire ontology of music's capacities to affect animals. 'The fiercenes of the Wolfe' was 'mitigated by the sound of the cornet: the Elephant delighted with the Organe: the Bee with the noyse of brasse: the Crane with the trumpet: and the Dolphin with the harpe'.[41] Numerous authors agreed that the dolphin was a particularly musical beast.[42] The main reason for this lay in the story of Arion, who, finding himself captured by pirates, had first lured and then tamed nearby dolphins by singing and playing the harp, and then jumped into the sea and escaped the pirates by riding the benevolent beasts to safety. This tale was related by, amongst others, both John Northbrooke and Thomas Lodge in their polemical wrangling over the value of music.[43] Music infused nature at every level: both the natural world itself, and the birds, beasts and fish which dwelt therein. This infusion was not simply a passive description, but an active quality facilitated by music's affective

---

[37] Rogers, *The anatomie of the minde*, fol. 5^v.

[38] John Lane, *Tom Tel-Troths message* (London, 1600), 16.

[39] Robert Roche, *Eustathia* (London, 1599), sig. F5^r.

[40] Phillip Stubbes, *The anatomie of abuses* (London, 1583), sig. O4^{r-v}.

[41] Leonard Wright, *A display of dutie* (London, 1589), 33.

[42] Ibid. 33; Anglicus, *Batman vppon Bartholome*, fol. 418^r; Lupton, *The Christian against the Iesuite*, fol. 63^r; Thomas Lodge, *Euphues shadow* (London, 1592), sig. D1^r.

[43] Northbrooke, *A treatise*, 82; Lodge, *Protogenes*, 26. See also Edwards, *The paradise of daintie deuises*, sig. H3^v; Naogeorg, *The popish kingdome*, fol. 71^r.

properties and the corresponding harmonies of God, the universe, nature and the world. If God could value the bellowing of oxen and the bleating of sheep,[44] and if music had such power over dumb beasts and inanimate objects, then its potential for human praise and for bewitching man was both wonderful and terrifying.

Music was a controversial subject in the Elizabethan period. It was also an extremely complex one. In his 1583 diatribe *The anatomie of abuses*, Philip Stubbes described music as both 'very il' and 'very laudable'; 'a cup of poyson' and 'a good gift of GOD'; which both 'stireth vp filthie lust, womannisheth ye minde rauisheth the hart ... and bringeth in vncleannes' but also 'reuiueth the spirits, comforteth the hart, and maketh it redyer to serue GOD'. Stubbes's intention was to write 'of Musick ... and how it allureth to vanitie', but his rhetoric was confused and contradictory, heaping praise upon his subject matter in equal degree to opprobrium.[45] Puritan polemicists like Stubbes did not usually struggle to get their point across successfully. But classical notions of the dignity, antiquity and potency of music meant that debates over the appropriate religious uses of music had to play out within a broader cultural context. Polemical discussions about the practice of church music during the English Reformation were conducted within the limits established by the discourse partially outlined above. Even someone as ardent as Stubbes could not utterly condemn music, in the same way that someone enthusiastic about its use, such as Thomas Lodge, had to concede that music could be harmful if abused. With the exception of Bullinger, most of the major Continental reformers accepted without question the God-given nature of music.[46] But the polyvalence of musical discourse allowed for wildly divergent interpretations of the appropriate use of music in a religious context.

The character of musical discourse also helps explain how and why music was seized upon so readily to fulfil such a wide range

---

[44] George Abbot, *An exposition vpon the prophet Ionah* (London, 1600), 471.

[45] Stubbes, *The anatomie of abuses*, sigs. O3^r–O4^v.

[46] See Walter E. Buszin, 'Luther on Music', *Musical Quarterly* 32 (1946), 80–97, at 83; Robin Leaver, *Goostly Psalmes and Spiritual Songs* (Oxford, 1991), 30; Charles Garside Jr, 'Calvin's Preface to the Psalter: a Re-Appraisal', *Musical Quarterly* 37 (1951), 566–77, at 570; Heinrich Bullinger, *The Decades of Henry Bullinger: Decade 5*, ed. Thomas Harding, PS (Cambridge, 1852), 191–97; Gottfried W. Locher, *Zwingli's Thought: New Perspectives* (Leiden, 1981), 1–30.

of polemical, didactic, propagandistic and devotional functions. The facet of musical discourse described here, concerning the natural world, performed several functions. Firstly, it underscored the divinity of musical harmony, and the ubiquity, fundamentality and embeddedness of that harmony in all of God's creation. It provided proof that divine harmony was fundamental to the makeup of audible harmonies, and consequently of the harmonies of the human body, the natural world and the universe itself. Secondly, this discourse was a description of the affective powers of music, simultaneously a testament and a warning. If Orpheus could charm with music the very ground upon which he walked, to what terrifying extent could the weak and corruptible form of man fall prey to those same seductive powers? Plato had taught that the wrong harmonies improperly used could completely dissolve away man's spirit.[47] But in language also redolent of Plato, St Basil had written that music had the power to 'fasten the fruite of godly doctrine in us'.[48] Religious attitudes to music were not only conditioned by religious discourses, such as liturgy and doctrine, but also by musical discourse. Belief did not simply shape religious uses of music, and neither did religious music simply shape belief. Instead, the two formed part of a powerful and ongoing dialectical process. Too often, perhaps, we forget that belief-as-practice was not simply expressed through cultural phenomena: it was also, in large part, their product. Considering the relationship between music, the natural world, and the nature of religious belief and practice helps to illuminate this. And music, as both discourse and practice, therefore provides a complex but vital lens through which we can more clearly observe key aspects of the negotiation of the English Reformation.

University of Warwick

---

[47] See note 9 above.
[48] Lupton, *The Christian against the Iesuite*, fol. 63ʳ; St Basil, 'Homily on the First Psalm', in Oliver Strunk, ed., *Source Readings in Music History: From Classical Antiquity through the Romantic Era* (New York, 1950), 64–65.

THE 'WONDERS IN THE DEEP' AND THE 'MIGHTY TEMPEST OF THE SEA': NATURE, PROVIDENCE AND ENGLISH SEAFARERS' PIETY, c. 1580–1640*

by SARAH PARSONS

THE religious beliefs of seafarers have not received a great deal of attention over the years. Contemporaries of early modern English seafarers stereotyped them as superstitious and irreligious, prone to turning to God only in times of danger. The Puritan William Perkins preached about 'the *Mariner*, who is onely good in a storme'.[1] The association of seafarers, irreligion and superstition was also reflected in popular literature. Edmund Spenser, in *The Faerie Qveene*, wrote of 'the glad merchant, that does vew from ground / His ship far come from watrie wilderness, / He hurles out vowes, and *Neptune* oft doth blesse'.[2] These stereotypes have coloured the historiography of maritime religion, which has drawn a division between 'superstition' and religion in seafaring culture.[3] However, recent work on religion and providentialism on land shows this to be a faulty paradigm.[4] In light of this research, this paper will explore the particular cast to maritime providentialism and piety. There are strong indications that

* I am grateful to my supervisors, Professors Alexandra Walsham and N. A. M. Rodger, and to the Editors of Studies in Church History for their comments on this article. I also wish to thank the Arts and Humanities Research Council for their generosity in funding my research.

[1] William Perkins, *A Godly and Learned Exposition or Commentarie vpon the three first Chapters of the Reuelation* (London, 1606), Epistle Dedicatorie.

[2] Edmund Spenser, *The Faerie Qveene disposed into twelve books, fashioning XII. morall vertues* (London, 1590), I. iii, stanza xxxii, lines 282–84.

[3] Fletcher S. Bassett, *Legends and Superstitions of the Sea and of Sailors in all Lands and at all Times* (Chicago, IL, 1885), 6–7; Raymond Lamont Brown, *Phantoms, Legends, Customs and Superstitions of the Sea* (London, 1972), 42–43; Bernard Capp, *Cromwell's Navy: The Fleet and the English Revolution, 1648–1660* (Oxford, 1989), 326–28; Cheryl Fury, *Tides in the Affairs of Men: The Social History of Elizabethan Seamen, 1580–1603* (Westport, CT, 2002), 91–92.

[4] Tessa Watt, *Cheap Print and Popular Piety, 1550–1640* (Cambridge, 1991); Christopher Marsh, *Popular Religion in Sixteenth Century England: Holding their Peace* (Basingstoke, 1998); Alexandra Walsham, *Providence in Early Modern England* (Oxford, 1999).

seafarers' responses to events were rooted in their understanding of those events and the extent of their own ability to influence them. The propensity to identify extraordinary providence in the world lay in seafarers' absence of knowledge and agency. When seafarers believed they understood what was happening, and could apply their skills to the situation, their identification of supernatural activity in the world steadily diminished. In these shifting responses can be seen seafarers' perceptions of Providence in the world and in their lives.

Life at sea opened up possibilities of seeing all sorts of strange things. Ministers preached to maritime congregations about the opportunities afforded by seafaring to see the world God had created. 'They that goe downe to the Sea in shippes, and occupy the great waters, these see the workes of the Lorde, and his wonders in the deepe.'[5] Thus did Richard Madox quote Psalm 107 as an encouragement to praise God. Venturing to sea, preachers might write glowingly of how 'our eies did behold the wonderfull workes of God in his creatures, which he hath made innumerable both small and great beasts, in the great and wide seas'.[6] Seafarers did take this to heart. In an account of his voyage to the South Seas in 1593, written later in his life, Richard Hawkins noted the health-giving powers of lemons and oranges. 'This is a wonderfull secret of the power and wisedome of God, that hath hidden so great and vnknowne vertue in this fruit, to be a certaine remedie for this infirmitie'.[7] Captain Richard Whitbourne observed a species of bird in Newfoundland which could be driven onto a boat a hundred at a time, 'as if God had made the innocency of so poore a creature, to become such an admirable instrument for the sustentation of man'.[8] The world was interpreted as having been created by a benevolent God for the help and use of man. Nature was an encouragement to piety just as preachers hoped. Hawkins

[5] Richard Madox, *A Learned and a Godly Sermon, to be read of all men, but especially for all Marryners, Captaynes and Passengers, which trauell the Seas* (London, [1591]), sig. A6[r].

[6] Francis Drake, *The World Encompassed By Sir Francis Drake … Carefully collected out of the notes of Master Francis Fletcher Preacher in this imployment, and diuers others his followers in the same* (London, 1628), 12.

[7] Richard Hawkins, *The Observations of Sir Richard Hawkins Knight, in his Voiage into the South Sea* (London, 1622), 54.

[8] Gillian T. Cell, ed., *Newfoundland Discovered: English Attempts at Colonisation, 1610–1630*, Hakluyt Society 2nd ser. 160 (1982), 122.

believed that all aspects of nature, even how ducks laid their nests, 'are motiues to prayse and magnifie the vniuersall Creator, who so wonderfully manifesteth his wisedome, bountie, and providence in all his creatures, and especially his particular loue to ingratefull mankinde, for whose contemplation and service he hath made them all'.[9]

There were also occasions in which early modern Englishmen saw God's hand at work in wonders and prodigies. For land dwellers, sea creatures might fulfil this role. 'Amongst many other prodigious accidents', wrote a pamphleteer, one 'terrible tempestuous day, the Maine-Ocean disgorged herself of a mightie Sea-monster or Whale'.[10] But seafarers, by contrast, did not perceive the majority of even 'monstrous' sea creatures to be marvels. James Welsh, the master of a voyage to Benin in 1590, identified 'a monstrous great fish (I think it was a Gobarto[11])' which came up to the ship's side and could have carried away the cook.[12] Whether or not his guess was factually correct, Welsh felt knowledgeable enough to identify this fish. John Walker was a preacher on a voyage of 1582 to Brazil and the South Seas. He wrote that a monstrous fish was brought aboard which, because it had a mouth like a cow, he and the seafarers gathered 'tooke it for a sea cowe'.[13] Neither the sea-cow nor the Gobarto were construed as special divine portents. Seafarers were used to encountering sea creatures of strange and monstrous appearance. They therefore did not perceive them with the same fear and awe which encouraged land dwellers to see a wonder.[14]

There was not always this clarity of perception within seafaring culture. Mermaids, unlike most other sea creatures, may have been viewed by seafarers as supernatural. Mermaids often elicited

---

[9] Hawkins, *Observations*, 74.

[10] Anon., *A True Report and Exact Description of a mighty Sea-monster, or Whale, cast vpon Langar-shore ouer against Harwich in Essex* (London, 1617), 10–11.

[11] A large ravenous fish, possibly a shark: W. H. Smyth, *The Sailor's Word-Book* (London, 1875), online at Project Gutenberg, <http://www.gutenberg.org/etext/26000>, accessed 1 March 2009.

[12] Richard Hakluyt, *The Principal Navigations, Voyages, Traffiqves and Discoveries of the English Nation made by Sea or ouerland*, 3 vols (London, 1598–1600), 2/2: 130.

[13] *An Elizabethan in 1582: The Diary of Richard Madox, Fellow of All Souls*, ed. Elizabeth Story Donno, Hakluyt Society 2nd ser. 147 (1976), 318.

[14] Walsham, *Providence*, 167–69; Barbara Benedict, *Curiosity: A Cultural History of Early Modern Inquiry* (Chicago, IL, 2001), 6–7.

fearfulness in seafarers. In 1642 the occasion of the sighting of a 'Man-fish' by a group of mariners was presented as a prodigious providence by 'a Gentleman'. How far his interpretation was shared by the seafarers who saw and reportedly conversed with the creature is difficult to tell. But, owing to its monstrous appearance, at 'first sight they were much dismayd'.[15] Their trepidation is consistent with another mermaid sighting, by Richard Whitbourne in Newfoundland. The mermaid approached him at a fast pace when he stood on land, and also advanced on and tried to climb into the boats of seafarers in the harbour. They all reacted fearfully.[16] This was partly a response to the creature's aggressive approach. But given seafarers' more pragmatic responses to other sea creatures, there may have been something abnormal about the identity of the mermaid itself that caused fear. Mermaids were hybrid forms, and bizarre hybrids tended to be associated with divine warning or demonic influence.[17] Equally, however, it was thought that the creatures of the land had counterparts in the sea.[18] Thus mermaids may have been accepted as natural creatures by seafarers. This would explain why a sighting in January 1602/3 prompted no amazement or prodigious conclusions. The seafarer concerned simply noted: '[t]hey say they are signes of stormy weather; and so we found it'.[19] These differing reactions suggest the mermaid may have had an ambiguous character, occupying a place in the margins between the natural and the supernatural.

The mermaid as a natural, rather than supernatural, portent of the weather is representative of seafarers' interpretations of most weather omens. Richard Madox was a minister for the same voyage of 1582 as John Walker. Various connections between animal behaviour and winds or tempests were introduced to him by seafarers on this voyage. 'Yn the after noon a poydrel which is a lytle black byrd cam to the ship, which M. Fayrwether sayd was

[15] John Hare, *The Marine Mercury* (London, 1642), sig. A2ᵛ.

[16] Cell, ed., *Newfoundland Discovered*, 194–95.

[17] Lorraine Daston and Katharine Park, *Wonders and the Order of Nature 1150–1750* (New York, 1998), 182.

[18] Anon., *Vox Piscis: or, The Bookfish Contayning Three Treatises which were found in the belly of a Cod-fish in Cambridge Market, on Midsummer Eue last, Anno Domini 1626* (London, [1627]), 1–2.

[19] Sir William Foster, ed., *The Voyages of Sir James Lancaster to Brazil and the East Indies, 1591–1603*, Hakluyt Society 2nd ser. 85 (1940), 138.

a token of wynd, and so yt was'.[20] It was the same with creatures of the sea such as porpoises. 'Ther appeared hear a great shole of purposes scowrging above water which som say ar forboders of a tempest'.[21] The sea itself might indicate what the weather would be; for example, 'when the waves of the sea sparkle or shine like twinkling flames, it is a sign of southerly winds as I learned from the master'.[22] John Smith's *A Sea Grammar* noted that 'commonly before any great storme' the sea would act contrarily to the present wind conditions.[23]

Certain atmospheric phenomena were also taken to be possible weather indicators. The Northern Lights, for example, were thought to presage storms.[24] In one particularly interesting instance, Arthur Gorges reported that he and his crew saw a strangely coloured rainbow at night near Florida in 1597. This 'made vs expect some extraordinary tempestuous weather'. However, 'it fell out afterward to be very calme and hot'.[25] Gorges then noted that such rainbows were actually common in those parts. Madox did not remark on any 'superstitious' leanings of the seafarers with regard to these beliefs. Rather he accepted them as practical weather knowledge, an area of natural lore to which the Church had no objection.[26] This knowledge was probably a product of seafarers' functional approach to the sea environment. In order to travel the oceans and to leave a record helpful to others, shipmasters and other seafarers noted their observations of the natural world. They recorded in logbooks and journals wind strength and direction, seabed depths, the presence of whales, seals and fish, and observations of the sky.[27] In doing so, seafarers built up a solid body of information on common animal behaviour and occurrences in the seas and skies,

---

[20] *An Elizabethan in 1582*, ed. Donno, 146.

[21] Ibid. 113.

[22] Ibid. 220.

[23] John Smith, *A Sea Grammar, With The Plaine Exposition of Smiths Accidence for young Sea-men, enlarged* (London, 1627), 41.

[24] Miller Christy, ed., *The Voyages of Captain Luke Foxe of Hull, and Captain Thomas James of Bristol, in Search of a North-west Passage in 1631–32. Vol. II*, Hakluyt Society 1st ser. 89 (1894), 327, 396.

[25] Samuel Purchas, *Purchas His Pilgrimes, In Five Bookes* (London, 1625), 4: 1949.

[26] Keith Thomas, *Religion and the Decline of Magic* (London, 1991), 303.

[27] London, BL, MS IOR/L/MAR/A/LXI, John Mucknall (mate), Journal on *Coaster* and *Jewel*, fols 5ʳ, 13ᵛ; MS IOR/L/MAR/A/LXIV, James Birkdell (mate), Journal on *London*, fol. 10ᵛ; Christy, ed., *Voyages of Foxe*, 276, 322; Smith, *A Sea Grammar*, 40, 42.

and how they might relate to conditions at sea. These omens were part of the patterns of the natural world; they were therefore not viewed as supernatural intrusions.

This interpretation of weather portents could shift, as in one particular case. St Elmo's fire, lights which clung to high points such as ships' masts, was caused by static electricity in stormy weather. There is little evidence of seafarers' reactions to the phenomenon; however, differing interpretations can be discerned. A more learned seafarer showed simple interest, noting '[i]f they be seene in the cheanes or shrowds of the ship, it is a signe the storme is of longer continuance, if in the highest toppes, it is likewise a signe the storme is ended. And so we found it for certain.'[28] This refers to the belief that the height of the fires signified the weather to follow – their number was another sign.[29] This man did not appear to perceive the fires to be supernatural, but others did explain the strange lights in supernatural terms. This was particularly the case with ordinary crewmen. William Strachy, a land dweller travelling aboard a ship, opined that the 'superstitious Sea-men make many constructions of this Sea-fire, which neuerthelesse is vsuall in stormes'. Not finding the phenomenon useful, he mocked the Roman Catholic reputation for seeing within it the miraculous, and dismissed it as a reliable sign of 'safety or ruine'.[30] But the seamen did believe in the fires' portentous properties. Moreover, despite the fact that their appearance in storms was normal, these seamen would seem to have interpreted them as extraordinary. These 'constructions' of the crew probably did not reflect the Roman Catholic belief that the fires were the ghost of St Elmo, returned to guide them.[31] It is unlikely Strachy, scathing as he was, would have been silent regarding such an interpretation by a crew of English Protestants. Possibly he was referring to beliefs similar to those of the crew of a ship in the Mediterranean in the 1670s. When the fires appeared then, the seamen characterized them as

---

[28] Foster, ed., *Voyages of Lancaster*, 138.

[29] George Carey, 'The Tradition of St Elmo's Fire', *American Neptune* 23 (1963), 29–38, at 33, 37.

[30] Purchas, *Pvrchas His Pilgrimes*, 4: 1736–37.

[31] Pablo E. Pérez-Mallaína, *Spain's Men of the Sea: Daily Life on the Indies Fleets in the Sixteenth Century*, trans. Carla Rahn Phillips (Baltimore, MD, 1998), 243–44.

'*Hobgoblins* or *Fairies*, or the inchanted Bodyes of witches'.[32] These apparitions did inspire story-telling rather than rituals to guard the ship. However, they demonstrate that when seafarers were faced with occurrences that they did not understand, especially in circumstances in which their mastery of the environment rapidly decreased, they resorted to explanations that transcended nature.

The shifting quality possible in seafarers' religious responses to their environment is thus further suggested by seafarers' experiences of and responses to danger. As highlighted by the contemporary caricature of seafarers' (im)piety, in dangerous circumstances seafarers did call on God with considerable intensity. 'This fulsome ugly morning presented the foulest childe that the whole voyage brought forth, with such variety and changes of the Elements, Ayre and Water, as if all had conspired to make our destiny fatall.'[33] Seafarers were confronted with such perils of the elements, and of ice, shoals and rocks, at frequent intervals. They approached them with great practicality and were well versed in the actions which had to be taken in such circumstances – but often those actions were not enough. In 1631–32 Thomas James commanded a search for a passage to the East Indies through the area of Greenland and Canada. He recorded the reaction of his crew to being trapped in ice there.

> Having now done all to the best of our vnderstandings (but to little purpose), we went all vpon a piece of Ice and fell to prayer, beseeching God to be mercifull vnto vs. … we did looke euery minute when she would ouer-set. Indeed, at one time, the Cables gaue way, and shee sunke downe halfe a foot at that slip; but vnexpectedly it began to flow, and sensibly wee perceiued the water to rise apace, and the Shippe withall. Then was our sorrow turned to ioy, and we all fell on our knees, praising God for his mercy in so miraculous a deliuerance.[34]

The elements, seabed and landscape which could put seafarers in jeopardy were not under their control. When they reached the limits of their own abilities to influence the situation, seafarers

---

[32] J. Theodore Bent, ed., *Early Voyages and Travels in the Levant*, Hakluyt Society 1st ser. 87 (1893), 127.

[33] Christy, ed., *Voyages of Foxe*, 272.

[34] Ibid. 468.

looked to divine intervention for aid and deliverance. There was a firm belief that God controlled the natural world. Thus ritualistic attempts to calm the elements focused on him, and the bypassing or overcoming of dangers was often attributed to his caring providence.[35]

However, before their efforts began to find success through God's beneficence, seafarers might identify their problems as ordained by God for the purpose of chastisement. Concomitant with the belief that God commanded the elements was the possibility that he was the cause of perilous occurrences, especially storms. It was a fairly common belief among land dwellers that tempests were a divine punishment for sin.[36] Some even wrote prayers to this effect for seafarers to use in storms.[37] Seafarers rarely commented on the content of their prayers, so the actual use of these is uncertain. However, there was in seafaring culture the idea of a 'Jonah'. When a storm blew up while he was on a Catholic ship in the Mediterranean in 1581, the English Protestant merchant Laurence Aldersey was thought by the Catholic crew to be a Jonah. They said 'that they, and the shippe, were the worse for me. I answered, truely it may well be, for I thinke my selfe the worst creature in the worlde, and consider you your selues also, as I doe my selfe, and then vse your discretion.'[38] This implies that he believed it quite possible that the storm had come as an affliction from God for their sins. Thus in instances where seafarers' capacity to exert control was diminished, seafaring providentialism could include moral interpretations of occurrences.

Immersed in a world of providence, seafarers usually assigned divine causation to events and turned to God for help. However, a smaller body of evidence gives us glimpses of a different approach to the hazards of the marine environment. As intimated with regard to St Elmo's fire, extraordinary providence was not the only mani-

---

[35] *The Journal of John Jourdain, 1608–1617, Describing his Experiences in Arabia, India, and the Malay Archipelago*, ed. Sir William Foster, Hakluyt Society 2nd ser. 16 (1905), 285–86.

[36] John Norden, *A Poore Mans Rest Founded vpon Motives, Meditations, and Prayers* (London, 1620), 349–50; David D. Hall, *Worlds of Wonder, Days of Judgement: Popular Religious Belief in Early New England* (Cambridge, MA, 1990), 73; Walsham, *Providence*, 125.

[37] Anon., *The Bookfish*, 36–43; Michael Sparke, *The Crvms of Comfort with godly Prayers* (London, 1628), no. 52.

[38] Hakluyt, *Principal Navigations*, 2/1: 151.

festation of the supernatural identified in precarious circumstances. Indeed, when endangered by storms seafarers might believe the cause of the threatening weather to be witchcraft or other wickedness.[39] On at least one occasion a group of seafarers reportedly turned to magic to overcome a witch-caused storm. Contemporary historian Edward Johnson wrote that, on a voyage in 1634, 'the Master, and other Sea men made a strange construction of the fore storme they met withall, saying, their Ship was bewitched, and therefore made use of the common Charme ignorant people use, nailing two red hot horseshoos to their mainemast'.[40] There is unfortunately little further corroboratory evidence of such rituals. Possibly the literate seafarers who wrote descriptive voyage accounts were somewhat less inclined to such beliefs. Opinions of the frequent bad weather suffered in the Bermudas exemplify this. According to the merchant Silvester Jourdain, the Bermudas, which had a reputation as 'a most prodigious and inchanted place, affoording nothing but gusts, stormes, and foule weather; which made every Nauigator and Mariner to auoide them', was actually a 'temperat' place.[41] Although Walter Raleigh wrote of the 'hellish' nature of the storms there, his language was customary rather than heartfelt.[42] Most merchants and ships' officers simply noted that the weather was foul.[43] No details about the possible beliefs of the crews, as hinted at by Jourdain, or rituals performed were included. Perhaps they were not thought appropriate or of interest in accounts written for business, propaganda or entertainment purposes. Johnson, on the other hand, a godly man recounting the foundation of a godly colony, did have reason to include what he regarded as impious practices. Johnson did not mention whether the seafarers of 1634 also prayed to God. However, their utilization of charms indicates that they believed there were supernatural forces other than God at work in the world. The evidence suggests that seafarers turned to a range of explanations and methods of intercession when they lacked control over their fate at sea. These

[39] Capp, *Cromwell's Navy*, 326–28; Peter Earle, *Sailors: English Merchant Seamen 1650–1775* (London, 1998), 106.

[40] Edward Johnson, *A History of New-England* (London, 1653), 65.

[41] Silvester Jourdain, *A Plaine Description of the Barmvdas, now called Sommer Ilands* (London, 1613), sigs B3ᵛ, B4ʳ.

[42] Hakluyt, *Principal Navigations*, 3: 661.

[43] Ibid. 2/2: 109, 3: 577, 573–74.

methods were not necessarily seen as antithetical to each other; rather, their use reveals an instrumental approach to religion.

This range of responses indicates why some contemporaries represented seafarers as 'superstitious', but the providence of God was central to most seafarers' reactions. However, the presence of God retreated when circumstances calmed. An episode related by Thomas Claybourne neatly illustrates this relationship. Claybourne was master's mate of the *Ascension*, a ship going to the East Indies in 1604. In his nautical observations he recorded that once a ship had brought itself to a certain latitude, 'so (by Gods helpe) you shall goe cleare betweene the shoales of Celebes and another shoale that lieth south-south-west from the shoales of Celebes'.[44] The habitual reference to God demonstrates that he was at the core of seafarers' worlds: it echoes God's role in seafarers' lives in times of peril. But Claybourne's technical approach to the issue also emphasizes that he did not believe divine intercession was essential to this piece of navigation. Extraordinary providence was distant for seafarers when they faced situations within rather than without the purview of their own agency.

Conditions and experiences at sea gave rise to subtle differences between seafarers and land dwellers in the area of providentialism. Seafarers' increased knowledge of the world constricted areas in which they identified supernatural activity. It was in situations of instability and anxiety – where they lacked understanding of the environment, or when their confidence in their ability to master the environment faltered – that the supernatural filtered into seafarers' perceptions of the world. This synthesis was probably something Roman Catholic maritime cultures experienced as well as Protestant ones, although their piety obviously had Catholic rather than Protestant tones.[45] This highlights how the seafaring context provides a highly focused example of the findings of historians such as Stuart Clark, of the eclectic and sometimes contradictory interpretations of phenomena, and of the shifting of supernatural

---

[44] *The Voyage of Sir Henry Middleton to the Moluccas, 1604–1606*, ed, Sir William Foster, Hakluyt Society 2nd ser. 88 (1943), 73.

[45] Pérez-Mallaína, *Spain's Men of the Sea*, 84, 226, 240, 242–44. See also, in this volume, Elizabeth Tingle, 'The Sea and Souls: Maritime Votive Practices in Counter Reformation Brittany 1500–1750', 205–16.

boundaries according to occasion and circumstance.[46] This research delineates another example of how the religious outlook of early modern people was essentially fluid and dynamic, the boundaries and character of the natural and the supernatural responsive to changes in circumstance.

University of Exeter

---

[46] Stuart Clark, *Thinking with Demons: The Idea of Witchcraft in Early Modern England* (Oxford, 1997); Daston and Park, *Wonders*, 187.

THE SEA AND SOULS: MARITIME VOTIVE PRACTICES IN COUNTER-REFORMATION BRITTANY, 1500–1750

by ELIZABETH TINGLE

If God had not given a natural inclination to some with regard to things of the sea, I do not believe that anyone would ever dare to go upon it. ... Barely has a long voyage begun when fresh water becomes so short that one is reduced to drinking so little that thirst is provoked rather than quenched ... Food shortages are so frequent that one is often forced to eat rats and ship's leather ... One has difficulty in deciding which is the more insupportable, the heat of the torrid zone or the cold of the north. Scurvy and the maladies of Guinea and the tropics are so painful and grievous that you would not believe the human body could suffer so greatly. The horror of maritime warfare and of storms cannot be explained to those who have not experienced them. I know of voyages where a third or a half of the crew have been lost.[1]

FEW human communities are as exposed to risk as those who make a living from the sea. More prone to the unpredictability of the natural world than those who live on land, sailors, fisherman and their families have always been greatly conscious of the fragility of life and of human powerlessness before the elements. Because the capriciousness of the sea is beyond the normal control of seafarers, during the historic past and no doubt long before, recourse was made to supernatural methods of management. By the later Middle Ages in Christian Europe, the most important form was invocation of divine protection through the intercession of the saints of the Church, by a process of vow and exchange.

While saintly intercession sought through veneration and votive gift exchange was a feature of terrestrial as well as maritime Europe

---

[1] Georges Fournier, *Hydrographie contenant la théorie et la pratique de toutes les parties de la navigation* (Paris, 1643), 112–13.

in the later medieval and early modern periods, there were nuances particular to coastal communities. There was also change over time, part of wider transformations in the cult of the saints observed by historians across the Reformation centuries.[2] The votive practices adopted to reduce the dangers of seafaring are the subject of this paper, with reference to the coastal regions of western Brittany. Here, maritime religious practices offer a case study of the relationship between popular devotions and the ideas of Catholic reformers. Votive offerings declined in the sixteenth century, under the influence of Protestantism and reformed Catholicism. They then underwent a resurgence from the mid-seventeenth century, coincident with missions to the west by Jesuits and other religious orders. As in other regions, the devotional culture that evolved on the western Breton coasts was a result of interaction between elites and local Catholics. There emerged a cult of saints more carefully managed by the clergy within a more firmly Marian context than had occurred in the past. But the prime objective remained the provision of effective protection in the daily struggle with the hostile environment of the sea.

Communities adjacent to and dependent on the sea were rich in ritual practices developed to help control the natural world. These did not always meet with clerical approval. The abbé Fournier summarized the views of many literate elites in early modern France, when he wrote that 'it has mistakenly been suggested that mariners are barbarous and incapable of leading sensitive and refined lives.'[3] Maritime communities were considered godless, where blasphemy and lack of observance were frequent. Sailors in particular were regarded as uncivil and brutal, living irreligious lives, with dubious morals. At sea, mariners often had little recourse to formal devotions and services, and they knew that they ran the risk of dying unshriven and coming to rest in unconsecrated ground, such as on the seabed itself.

The inaccessibility of remote maritime communities certainly mitigated against frequent contacts with the formal structures of

---

[2] See Trevor Johnson, 'The Catholic Reformation', in Alec Ryrie, ed., *The European Reformations* (Basingstoke, 2006), 190–211; Marc Venard, ed., *Histoire du christianisme*, 8: *Les temps des confessions (1530–1620)* (Paris, 1992); R. P.-C. Hsia, ed., *The Cambridge History of Christianity*, 6: *Reform and Expansion 1500–1660* (Cambridge, 2006), esp. chs 9, 12.

[3] Fournier, *Hydrographie*, 618.

the institutional Church. For example, the island of Ouessant off
the west coast of Brittany could only be reached by crossing a strait
notable for its many shipwrecks, a secure site for the inhabitants but
'not for their salvation'.[4] The extreme danger involved in visiting
this community meant that it had been many years without an
episcopal visit before the priest Michel Le Nobletz's mission in
the 1620s.[5] Similarly, the island of Sizun was without a priest when
Le Nobletz visited it a short time later. Such isolation was not
always a bad thing, however. For example, Le Nobletz observed of
Ouessant that 'the fury of the sea, which is continual in that place,
and which prevented [the inhabitants] from enjoying commerce
and the commodities of firm land, also exempted the people
from the faults ordinarily found [on land] and of the corruption
which reigned there' such that he 'never found any other people
so susceptible to the grace of the Gospels, nor less subject to the
vices which proved the greatest obstacles' to its reception.[6]

But even for the most charitably disposed of missionaries,
the religious practices of seafaring communities were rife with
superstition. In Cornouaille, Le Nobletz found large numbers of
women who would carefully sweep out their local chapel and,
having gathered up the dust, would throw it into the air, to ensure
a favourable wind for the return of their husbands and sons from
the sea. Others took images of the saints from these same chapels
and threatened them with harsh treatment if they did not grant the
prompt and safe return of their loved ones. The women would also
carry out these threats, beating the images or submerging them in
water, when they did not obtain what had been asked for.[7] These
were not godless communities, however. Everyday life on the coast
was filled with references to the divine, while maritime culture was
deeply permeated with religious sensibilities and practices. Ships
were frequently named after saints. For example, in Languedoc,
until the French Revolution, the great majority of vessels were
named for the patron or favourite saint of the captain or owner.
Before undertaking journeys or expeditions, sailors and fishermen

---

[4] 'Père Verjus' [A. de Saint-André], *La vie de Monsieur Le Nobletz, prestre et mission-aire de Bretagne* (Paris, 1666), 130–31.

[5] Ibid. 131.

[6] Ibid.

[7] Ibid. 184.

would begin by attending mass or offering prayers to the saints. Because of frequent shipwrecks at the entrances to harbours, port authorities often erected crucifixes at their mouths.[8] But these practices were frequently lay-initiated, local and archaic. There was too much familiarity with God and his saints. Louis Châtellier has argued that missionaries did not find a people without God, rather they were shocked by the ease with which he was appealed to: they had the difficult task of substituting a sense of divine transcendence for workaday familiarity with God and the saints, while also demonstrating God's omnipresence in the whole universe and in every person's life.[9]

For these reasons, the maritime communities of Brittany were the target of numerous missions by Jesuits and others in the early and mid-seventeenth century. There was at this time a wider interest in the faith of coastal populations and mariners in France, part of the educational and social disciplinary movement associated with Catholic reform. Thus, the Jesuit Georges Fournier, provost of the college of Caen and naval chaplain in Normandy, dedicated a section of his book *Hydrographie* to the devotions of men at sea.[10] Even the Protestant pastor of the Île de Ré, near La Rochelle, Théophile Barbauld, writing before the Revocation of the Edict of Nantes, made a collection of sixty-two prayers which were useful during dangerous sea voyages, including prayers for 'those who have fallen into the sea and work to save themselves', for 'when the ship is surrounded by ice and in danger of breaking up' and 'for those whom enemies threaten to throw into the sea'.[11]

In Brittany, Michel Le Nobletz began his work by visiting the offshore islands of Ouessant, Molène, Batz and Sein, in the footsteps of the sixth-century evangelist of northern Brittany, St Paul d'Aurélien. Although Le Nobletz undertook preaching campaigns in the interior, he spent the majority of his time in coastal towns, such as Douarnenez and Concarneau, and on the Saint-Matthieu peninsula around the port of Le Conquet.[12] Julien Maunoir, the Jesuit missionary, followed Le Nobletz's initial jour-

---

[8] Catherine Lopez, *Piété des gens de mer* (Pézenas, 1994), 18.

[9] Louis Châtellier, *The Religion of the Poor: Rural Missions in Europe and the Formation of Modern Catholicism c. 1500 – c. 1800* (Cambridge, 1997), 107.

[10] Fournier, *Hydrographie*, 671–704.

[11] Anon., *Ex-voto marins de la Charente-Maritime* (La Rochelle, 1979), 20.

[12] 'Verjus', *Monsieur Le Nobletz*.

neys to the Breton islands and again spent much time in the coastal settlements.[13] Preaching was adapted to local circumstances. For example, when visiting the island of Molène, where the majority of the inhabitants spent much of their time fishing, Le Nobletz sought them out at sea. He mounted the tallest of their boats and

> preached the truth of the Gospel with such vigour and repre-
> sented to them the sufferings of the Son of God, the enor-
> mity of their sins and the necessity of repentance in so lively
> a manner, that he saw them fall to weeping and take up the
> ropes of their boats in order to chastise themselves ...[14]

The primary aims of the missionaries were to educate the local inhabitants in Catholic doctrine, to enhance devotional practice and to improve moral comportment. This was the usual programme of reformed Catholicism, taught through the sacraments, the catechism, hell-fire sermons and theatrical performances on the themes of sin, penitence and redemption. But what is particular to seafaring communities is the explicit link between spiritual reformation and the better ordering of the natural world. Missionaries and local people were convinced that the harshness of the sea could be ameliorated by devout and correct observance. According to 'Verjus', after Le Nobletz's visit to the island of Sizun, the inhabitants began to behave as model Christians. They attended mass daily, except when at sea, they made monthly confession, there was morning and evening adoration of the Blessed Sacrament in the parish church, and everyone attended vespers on Sundays and feasts. One of the fishermen was persuaded to become a priest and sent off to the mainland to be trained. On his return, the sailor-priest introduced the singing of spiritual canticles to the island. These were adopted by the fishermen in place of their profane shanties. 'Verjus' recorded that after these songs were introduced to the island, for more than twenty years the fury of the sea abated and no-one from the community drowned, whereas before they had been accustomed to lose several of their boats every year.[15] When Julien Maunoir travelled and preached among the sailors and fishermen of Ouessant, while he journeyed

[13] R. P. Boschet, *Le parfait missionaire ou la vie du RP Julien Maunoir* (Paris, 1697).
[14] 'Verjus', *Monsieur Le Nobletz*, 133.
[15] Ibid. 202.

on the sea, singing sacred songs, the sea was calmed, the tides were gentler than they were normally in those places and the sailing was easier.[16] Conversely, those who disdained the missionaries and their teachings could suffer. At Île-Tudy, Le Nobletz celebrated mass and then entered the pulpit to preach a sermon, at which point several merchants left the church. At the end, Le Nobletz warned that there would be a divine visitation upon this community, where many had 'buried their hearts into the goods of the world'. After a short time, a third of the community's shipping was lost at sea.[17]

The most striking feature of seventeenth-century maritime religious practice was the revival of the ex-voto or votive offering in coastal sanctuaries. This was part of a wider Tridentine programme of reforming saints' cults by channelling veneration into churches, where it became systematized, observable and supervisable by local clergy. The ex-voto is one of the most common post-medieval religious objects found in the churches and chapels of coastal regions of Europe. The word 'ex-voto' means 'the consequence of a vow taken'. The letters V. F. G. A., often found on post-medieval votive offerings, stand for *Votum fecit, gratiam accepit*, 'a vow was made and grace was obtained'. A votive can either be an action made or an object deposited in a sanctuary, in accomplishment of a vow and in thanks for a received grace.[18] While propitiatory votives can be given in request for future favours, the majority of ex-votos were thanksgiving offerings, gestures of gratitude for the bestowing of divine aid or assistance. They were also commemorative, a souvenir of a past event.[19] Votive deposits and objects are known from the earliest periods of antiquity.[20] While votives were commonly deposited at healing and other shrines, maritime communities have been particularly prolific generators of ex-voto acts and objects.

---

[16] Boschet, *Le parfait missionaire*, 108.

[17] Julien Maunoir, *La vie du vénérable dom Michel Le Nobletz* (Saint-Brieuc, 1934), 214.

[18] F. and C. Boullet, *Ex-voto marins* (Paris, 1978), 12.

[19] Association pour la Sauvegarde du Patrimoine Religieux en Vie dans les Côtes d'Armor, *Ex-voto marins en Trégor-Goëlo* (Pérros-Guirec, 1991), 4; Colin Renfrew, 'The Archaeology of Religion', in Colin Renfrew and Ezra B. Zubrow, eds, *The Ancient Mind: Elements of Cognitive Archaeology* (Cambridge, 1994), 47–54, at 48–49.

[20] For votive practice in archaeological contexts, see Robin Osborne, 'Hoards, Votives, Offerings: The Archaeology of the Dedicated Object', *World Archaeology* 36 (2004), 1–10; Richard Bradley, *The Passage of Arms: An Archaeological Analysis of Prehistoric Hoard and Votive Deposits* (Cambridge, 1990).

For the most part, they result from experience of calamity at sea. The seafarer, in the presence of natural elements which he or she could not control, having exhausted all other possibilities of saving him or herself, turned to supernatural powers.[21] The votive, an acquittal of a debt towards the heavenly protector, according to a promise made, was deposited in a sanctuary – usually a parish church or chapel – as close as possible to the altar.[22] They are thus sacred objects, visible, material witnesses to the expression of invisible and infinite sacred power.[23] They also offer a continued representation of the donor to the saint, a means of prolonging the protection given, for they remained in the sanctuary, perceptible and tangible, long after their presentation.[24] By this means, the donor hoped for help and protection in the future from the saint who was well disposed to the gift-giver through delight at having received the votive offering.[25]

The two most common forms of maritime votive in France were the painting – seen more commonly in the Mediterranean – and the model ship, either scale models or half-hull reliefs. Maritime votive paintings generally record the scene and act of divine and saintly intercession. In the lower half of the picture, a shipwreck or disaster from which the donor or donors escaped through divine intervention is shown, while in the upper register, an image of the divine intercessor appears. Sometimes there is also a text, relating the circumstances of the vow and giving witness to the act of grace.[26] In Brittany, the commonest form of votive is the model ship. These were suspended from the vaults of churches and chapels, above altars, a memento of the 'site' where the vow and intercession took place.

During the Middle Ages, survivors of storms and disasters at sea frequently gave votives as thank-offerings, although few such objects survive. Jean de Joinville recounts (in his late thirteenth-

[21] Bernard Cousin, *Ex-voto de Provence* (Paris, 1981), 17.

[22] Ibid. 12; Lopez, *Piété des gens de mer*, 8, 12. Christine Peters comments that the votive was 'the greatest secular intrusion into sacred space' in her 'Access to the Divine: Gender and Votive Images in Moldavia and Wallachia', in R. N. Swanson, ed., *Gender and Christian Religion*, SCH 34 (Woodbridge, 1998), 143–62, at 143.

[23] Boullet, *Ex-voto marins*, 13.

[24] F. T. Van Staten, 'Gifts for the Gods', in H. S. Vernel, ed., *Faith, Hope and Worship* (Leiden, 1981), 65–151, at 69.

[25] Ibid. 72.

[26] Anon., *Ex-voto marins de Bretagne et Galicie* (Rennes, 1987), 12.

century history of the saintly King Louis IX) a vow taken by Queen Marguerite while returning from crusading in the Holy Land. Frightened by a storm while at sea off Cyprus, she promised St Nicolas a silver ship weighing five marks if he saved the party. An instant later, the wind fell. Once returned to France, the queen commissioned a silver boat with figures of the king, queen, three royal children and sailors. The Sieur de Joinville himself went to deposit the offering at the shrine of St Nicolas de Port in Lorraine.[27] Another known maritime votive from the same site was a mother-of-pearl and silver-gilt ship deposited by the Cardinal of Lorraine in the sixteenth century.[28]

During that century, however, votive practice declined. An important cause was Protestantism's attack on saintly intercession, upon which the vow and promise were based. But Catholic reformers also regarded the use of votives at shines with suspicion as superstitious practice, a degraded sort of piety, at the margins of religiosity, even as tainted with paganism.[29] The Council of Trent confirmed the validity both of the cult of the saints and of religious art, but it was concerned to regulate 'abuses'. In France during the early seventeenth century, François de Sales was one of several who ordered the destruction of popular works of art suspected of 'superstition' which probably included votives of various sorts.[30] In addition, in Brittany the religious wars of the later sixteenth century saw destruction of and damage to coastal and island churches and chapels, which were subject to piracy and raiding by Catholic and Protestant alike. All of this reduced traditional observance.

After 1600 the practice of votive offering underwent a resurgence, at shrines in general and in maritime communities in particular. There was a return to traditional means of controlling the elements of nature. In Provence, the earliest ex-votos date from the early seventeenth century, and Bernard Cousin argues that votive gifts were at first mainly the preserve of social elites, moving down the social scale to become more widespread after

[27] Boullet, *Ex-voto marins*, 21.
[28] Ibid. 22.
[29] Anon., *Ex-votos marins de la Charente-Maritime*, 26.
[30] Boullet, *Ex-voto marins*, 22.

1720.[31] Evidence from other regions suggests, however, that the 'middling sort' rather than the elites took up this devotion and that it took off more from the mid-seventeenth century. In Galicia in northwest Spain, the two earliest surviving votives, both paintings, are dated 1640 and 1685 and both result from disasters at sea. In the first, Jean dó Rio of Coruña was captured by Barbary pirates while out fishing, but released after he invoked the Blessed Virgin's help. In the second, the Virgin aided a woman washed overboard from a fishing vessel. Even more miraculously, Balthasar Lopez of Santiago, shipwrecked three times during a journey to Rome in the mid-seventeenth century, was saved by frequent invocation of the Mother of God.[32] In Brittany, in the region of Trégor in northern Brittany, the oldest surviving marine ex-voto is a model of the ship Maria, offered to the chapel of Notre-Dame-de-Kermouster in the parish of Lézardrieux 'by me, MM Le Guen, 1651', as the inscription records.[33] A similar chronology is found in Finistère and from the coasts of the Morbihan around Vannes.[34] There was clearly a renewed belief in the link between saintly intercession and human attempts to modify and control the natural world of the sea.

This resurrection and reaffirmation of traditional practice by Catholic reformers working in these coastal regions is further evidence of their accommodation with popular demand for devices with which to manipulate the sacred in the struggle with the natural world. This is a feature observed elsewhere in Europe, for example in the use of sacramentals by Jesuits in southern Germany, studied by Trevor Johnson.[35] However, this revival of ex-votos incorporated modernization as well, for the saints called upon to aid mariners changed over time. In the later Middle Ages, Saints Nicholas, Clement and Barbara were important in protecting seafarers. In seventeenth-century Spain, representations

---

[31] Cousin, *Ex-voto de Provence*, 18–19.

[32] Anon., *Ex-voto marins de Bretagne et Galicie*, 13.

[33] *Ex-voto marins en Trégor-Goëlo* (Pérros-Guirec, 1991), 4.

[34] For Finistère, see the special edition of the *Bulletin de la société d'archéologie de Finistère* 102 (1973); there was an exhibition of marine votives in the Musée Cohue de Vannes in 2007.

[35] Trevor Johnson, 'Blood, Tears and Xavier-Water: Jesuit Missionaries and Popular Religion in the Eighteenth-Century Upper Palatinate', in Bob Scribner and Trevor Johnson, eds, *Popular Religion in Germany and Central Europe, 1400–1800* (Basingstoke, 1996), 183–202, 272–75, at 185.

of the crucified Christ became common.[36] But what is evident all over Catholic Europe is the overwhelming role of the Virgin Mary in votive acts. In Languedoc, almost all votives represent a Marian piety.[37] In Brittany, Mary, under a multitude of dedications, was again the most important. Saint Anne, the virgin's mother, was also prominent. The cult of Saint Anne took off particularly in southern Brittany after the founding of a shrine at Auray under the guidance of the local Capuchins, following the miraculous discovery of an ancient statue by Nicolas Rouzic in 1624. Here there grew up – and remains – a great deposition centre for maritime votive objects. It may have been Breton sailors who took this cult to Québec where a century later eighteen out of twenty-six known votive paintings show St Anne as intercessor with her chapel as their repository.[38] This practice is clearly in line with the Counter-Reformation tendency to pay 'more attention to saints recognised by all the church and so to bring out more effectively its universality'.[39] Using the votive tradition for a new repertoire of saintly intercessors, the Church sought to end abuses associated with the veneration of saints while reasserting their intercessory power and their roles as models of the Christian life.[40] The move towards universal saints seems to have been efficacious. The main objective of Breton maritime devotions remained reassurance and protection when in danger on the sea. To be so widely adopted, the new practices must have proved efficacious in the battle with the forces of the natural world.

The deposition of votives in churches and chapels was also part of a wider campaign to channel devotions into formal sanctuaries, overseen by clergy. It was a testamentary act, a public witness to and tangible proof of the gratitude of the supplicant towards his or her protector.[41] Votives were deposited in pilgrimage shrines or chapels, some, such as that of Auray, newly favoured by maritime

[36] Boullet, *Ex-voto marins*, 30.

[37] Lopez, *Piété des gens de mer*, 24. In Malta, the Virgin, followed by our Lord and then Saints Joseph and John the Baptist, predominated: A. H. J. Prins, *In Peril on the Sea: Maritime Votive Paintings in the Maltese Islands* (Valletta, 1989).

[38] Pierre Berthiaume and Emile Lizé, *Foi et legends: La peinture votive au Québec (1666–1944)*, (Québec, 1991), 18.

[39] Robert Bireley, *The Refashioning of Catholicism 1450–1700* (Basingstoke, 1999), 107.

[40] Ibid. 113.

[41] Van Staten, 'Gifts for the Gods', 72.

communities, while new sites and sacred spaces were added to the local geography of coastal regions. For example, after a naval battle in the mid-seventeenth century, the community of Arzon took a vow to make a pilgrimage to the shrine annually.[42] As Johnson remarks, in these sacred places in a small way 'there was a sense of managed and controlled devotion … accompanied by an increase in clerically organised and directed pilgrimage'.[43] Victory over the sea and the natural world was brought firmly under the supervision of the Church.

In conclusion, Hsia comments that 'in subordinating … popular religious practices to the linear authority of the ecclesiastical hierarchy, Tridentine Catholicism reinforced all forms of institutional central authority at the expense of informal social power … with their dispersed world views that had appropriated religion for their own uses'.[44] But what we have in early modern maritime votive practice is evidence for what Johnson calls a 'local culture of the miraculous', another example of the engagement of elite beliefs and popular practices typical of the Catholic reformation.[45] Clericalism and renewed emphasis on saintly intercession – largely that of the Virgin Mary and her mother Saint Anne – blended with a resurrected older practice of votive offering to create something that looked new and different in maritime communities. Such changes in popular practice in the Counter-Reformation period came from a fusion of elite and popular religiosity. There were fundamental common assumptions underpinning the world-views of sailors and clerical reformers, 'chief of these being a universal faith in the immanence of the divine and of the possibility at any moment of supernatural eruption into the earthly world'.[46] Both sought effective means to control the natural world in their favour. Enhanced devotional practice and moral discipline did help mariners to control the natural world around them. Singing sacred songs calmed the sea. Mary and her mother provided efficacious intercessors for seafarers who were in peril on the waves, evidenced

[42] Anon., *Ex-voto marins de Bretagne et Galicie*, 13.

[43] Trevor Johnston, '"Everyone should be like the people": Elite and Popular Religion and the Counter Reformation', in Kate Cooper and Jeremy Gregory, eds, *Elite and Popular Religion*, SCH 42 (Woodbridge, 2006), 218–19.

[44] R. P.-C. Hsia, *The World of Catholic Renewal 1540–1770* (Cambridge, 1998), 55–56.

[45] Johnson, '"Everyone should be like the people"', 222.

[46] Ibid. 224.

by the range of gifts and commemorations devoted to them. As Hsia comments, 'Tridentine Catholicism succeeded in the long term not by suppressing "superstitions" but by grafting orthodoxy onto traditional and popular spirituality.'[47] The miracles wrought at sea, attested by votives in the churches of maritime Brittany, were clear evidence of God's power over the natural world, mediated through the saints and harnessed for the devout seafarer in peril.

University of Plymouth

---

[47] Hsia, *World of Catholic Renewal*, 201.

DEVOTIONAL LANDSCAPES: GOD, SAINTS AND THE NATURAL WORLD IN EARLY MODERN IRELAND

by RAYMOND GILLESPIE

RECONSTRUCTING the relationship of the inhabitants of early modern Ireland with the natural world and its Creator is both a difficult and a straightforward task. At one level those who lived in Ireland, both Catholic and Protestant, had much in common with other contemporary Europeans, and they shared similar ideas about the existence of God, his actions in creating the world and how that world worked. At another level the relationship between the inhabitants of early modern Ireland and the natural world is rather different from that observable in other places. In terms of pilgrimage, the inhabitants of Ireland before the Reformation in the early sixteenth century had little interest in visiting corporeal relics, and body parts of saints were in short supply in Ireland by comparison with other European countries. Rather, the devout preferred to visit places in the natural world that had reputed associations with a saint, such as a well created by a saint or a cave where he had lived. Why this should be so is difficult to explain, but it certainly created an experience of the natural world which, though not unique to Ireland, was certainly more intense there. In turn, this affected local religious experiences as they were reshaped through the process of religious change in the early modern period, giving a particular hue to the local forms of religious devotion practised by both Catholics and Protestants. This essay aims to reveal something of the distinctive traits of local religion that formed as a result of the conscious interaction of the inhabitants of Ireland with God's creation.

I

Before the Second Vatican Council (1962–65), the first formal contact that most Irish Catholic children had with religious doctrine was through the catechism. The first question of the most commonly used catechism asked 'Who made the world?', to which the approved answer was 'God made the world'. Subsequent questions elicited the fact that the world was made from nothing, to show God's power and for man's benefit.[1] Thus, even for those who did not get beyond the first question, they acquired the idea that the world around them was God's work and, perhaps more importantly, that God could be revealed in the natural world. For the generation of catchumens on the eve of Vatican II this was hardly a new doctrine. The catechism that they repeated by rote, the Maynooth Catechism, was an 1882 revision of a catechism of 1777 composed by Archbishop Butler of Cashel and the opening question on creation had survived all the revisions of that text from its inception. Butler's catechism contained the most strident statement of a theology of creation, but the subject of religion and the natural world had not evaded other catechists. However, they approached it in a slightly different way, more in line with the structure of the official Roman Catechism produced by the Council of Trent (1545–63), by way of commentary on the first article of the Creed declaring God to be maker of heaven and earth. Fr Augustine Kirwan's catechism, written in the late eighteenth century but not published until the 1830s, enquired 'What do you understand by "Creator of heaven and earth?"', to which the correct response was 'I understand that he [God] created heaven and earth, all that is in them and between, out of nothing.' This included 'the sea, the fish of the sea, the birds of the air, the dumb beasts and man himself'.[2] Again this was not new. The same questions and responses can be traced back through Andrew Donlevy's Irish language catechism published in Paris in 1742 to Bonabhentura Ó hEodhasa's *An Teagasg Críosdaidhe* of 1611, compiled in the Franciscan house at Louvain for the Irish mission. Donlevy proclaimed that God was 'maker of heaven and earth and sovereign lord of all things' and was 'in heaven, and on earth and in every part of the world'.[3] This was a fairly minimalist approach but Ó hEodhasa's *An Teagasg Críosdaidhe* is somewhat more revealing of the ideas

---

[1] Most easily accessible in James Butler, *Who Made the World? The Catechism we Learned in School* (Cork, 2001), 19, 21.

[2] *Doctor Kirwan's Irish Catechism*, ed. William J. Mahon (Cambridge, MA, 1991), 22, 23.

[3] Andrew Donlevy, *The Catechism of Christian Doctrine* (Dublin, 1848), 41, 43.

being conveyed to the catchumens since it includes a versification of the catechism, no doubt to make it more easily memorized. Ó hEodhasa's aim was to use the concrete world to reveal God in a very solid and almost tactile way. Thus he explained that while the Creed simply stated that God created heaven and earth, he really created the whole world and everything in it: heaven, and all the angels and the souls of the blessed now in it, the earth with its trees and living things, as well as people and hell with the devils and souls of the damned. God also created everything between heaven and earth, the waters and fish, the air and birds, fire, and the seven planets above and the five heavens above them. Moreover God did not just create these but he continued to protect and preserve them, and they could not survive without his protection.[4] More concise were the comments of the Irish secular priest Theobald Stapleton, whose Latin and Irish catechism of 1639 contented itself with pointing out that God made everything, heaven and earth, angels and men, and preserved his creation through his goodness.[5]

If early seventeenth-century Irish Catholics had some sense of the relationship of God to the natural world, what of their Protestant counterparts? Archbishop Ussher's catechism, *The Principles of Christian Religion*, published in 1654 and widely used in late seventeenth-century Dublin, enquired 'In what manner had all things their beginning?', to be answered 'In the beginning of time, when no creature had any being, God by his Word alone, in the space of six days, created all things'. The Calvinist-inspired Ussher continued his exploration of the theology of the created world with the question 'What doeth God after the creation?', to be answered 'By his providence he preserveth and governeth his creatures, with all things belonging to them.' In an unpublished catechism Ussher amplified these views and added that God's decree for the world was revealed 'in the works of creation and providence'.[6]

---

4 Bonabhentura Ó hEodhasa, *An Teagasg Críosdaidhe*, ed. Fearghall Mac Raghnaill (Dublin, 1976), 5, 13. For the importance of the concrete in traditional belief and pilgrimage, see Bernadette Cunningham and Raymond Gillespie, 'The Lough Derg Pilgrimage in the Age of the Counter Reformation', *Éire-Ireland* 39.3–4 (2004), 167–79, at 170–72.

5 Theobald Stapleton, *Catechismus seu doctrina Christiana Latino-Hibernica* (Brussels, 1639), 16–17.

6 *The Whole Works of the Most Revd Father in God James Usher [sic] Lord Archbishop of Armagh and Primate of All Ireland: With a Life of the Author and an Account of his Writings*, ed. C. R. Elrington and J. H. Todd, 17 vols (Dublin, 1847–64), 2: 183, 203–4.

For Ussher the world did shine with the glory of God. In the late seventeenth century those in the Church of Ireland tradition who did not share Ussher's Calvinistic theological position and had a less providentalist mindset would dilute Ussher's formulation. The 1696 edition of the Church catechism with notes by Edward Wetenhall, Bishop of Cork, glossed on the Creed that God had created the 'worlds that we see and the world that we cannot' and accepted that all things depended on God, but went no further.[7] From a Dissenting perspective the catechism compiled in Dublin during 1680 by Robert Chambers (who had begun his ministry in the Church of Ireland but during the 1650s had gravitated to Presbyterianism) showed a much more Calvinistic and providentialist strain. Using the Shorter Catechism of the Westminster Assembly as his model, Chambers discoursed for some five pages on the ninth question of the catechism that asked 'What is the work of creation?'[8] Much of what Chambers had to say was unremarkable. He gathered together much of what his predecessors had set out: that nothing existed before creation, that God created the world out of nothing without tools or instruments, and that God made the world not out of compulsion but because it pleased him to do so. As a result creation was good and that goodness extended to even toads, serpents and other 'venomous creatures' who became hurtful through man's sin in a way that was not specified. Chambers's most significant contribution to the understanding of God and the natural world came in his discussion of the question of things that were not made in the first six days of creation. In dealing with the shaping of the natural world, Chambers stressed that this later creation was also by God since the forces at work had been created originally by God, that the power to reproduce was from God, and 'because the preservation of things by God in their being is, as it were, a continual creation'. Thus for Chambers the natural world was in flux and always regenerating itself under God's influence. In this way he linked God's providence, that is the 'preserving and governing of all His creatures and all their actions', as the eleventh question of the Westminster Shorter Catechism

---

7 Edward Wetenhall, *The Catechism of the Church of England* (Dublin, 1696), 13.
8 Belfast, Union Theological College, MS Robert Chambre [*sic*], 'An explanation of the Shorter Catechism of the Rev Assembly of Divines', 79–83.

put it, with the appearance of the natural world and made explicit what other catechetical writers, such as Ussher, had only hinted at.

II

By the seventeenth century, Irish catechisms of both the reformed and Tridentine traditions allotted considerable space to the subject of God and his creation and displayed considerable agreement on the basic principles of a theology of creation. This is hardly surprising. The use of the historic credal formulae as a basis for the catechisms, especially in the Catholic tradition, required some comment on the role of God as Creator of the natural world. However the implications of this went rather further than simply a commentary on the text of the Creed. It presented a natural world suffused with God's power but distinct from God. In this cosmology the natural world was a symbol of cosmic order, maintained by God. As such, contemporaries looked to the natural world not as inanimate but as suffused with divine meaning that required decoding.

In this context the natural world became an important way of divining cosmic order or, as the Church of Ireland Bishop of Derry, Ezekiel Hopkins, observed in the 1670s, God revealed himself in two books, the Bible and the 'book of creatures' or the natural world.[9] Interpreting what these revelations meant was a difficult subject and was filtered through cultural and social lenses.[10] It is well known that godly Irish Protestants, particularly in the first half of the seventeenth century, looked to the natural world, and particularly to abnormalities in that world, for hints as to how the sort of cosmic order set out in their catechisms could be seen in nature around them. Their Catholic counterparts also peered into the murky glass of nature to divine God's will for them. A case in point is the episode in Drogheda in 1617–18 when the plants from a vegetable garden, formerly a Franciscan friary, were found to have roots in the shape of a man's hand. For some this was a curiosity but for others it was a sign of God's anger that a Fran-

[9] *The Works of the Rt Revd and Learned Ezekiel Hopkins, Lord Bishop of Londonderry* (London, 1710), 315–16.
[10] Raymond Gillespie, *Devoted People: Belief and Religion in Early Modern Ireland* (Manchester, 1997), 63–83, 107–26.

ciscan house should be profaned and they asserted that the hand of judgement was suspended over the town.[11] That the appearance of this natural wonder could sustain a diversity of interpretations is an indication of just how vital the debate over the natural world and its meaning was, in confessional terms, in seventeenth-century Ireland.

The linkage in the catechisms of the seventeenth century between natural order and cosmic order meant that the understanding of the natural world could be a profoundly divisive area for discussion as both Protestants and Catholics claimed divine sanction for their actions. Not surprisingly this appeared most acutely when relationships were at their most stressed. The wars of the 1640s and the 1690s produced crops of stories, both Protestant and Catholic inspired, about abnormalities in the natural world: rivers running red (apparently as with blood), strange lights in the sky, and swarms of rats all feature in the contemporary reportage. Perhaps unsurprisingly the supernatural, in the form of ghosts and other walking spirits, also made an appearance to demonstrate the upset in cosmic order and confirm the divine underpinning of a particular confessional standpoint.[12]

The significance of the natural world in religious discourse in seventeenth-century Ireland rested on two important ideas, both of which brought wider agreement on the natural world than might be expected. The first was that the idea of the revelation of God in creation was a common one among Protestants or Catholics regardless of their social status. On this was built a series of devotions that attracted interest from diverse sources. A case in point is the holy well, a prominent sacralized feature of the natural landscape, which served to draw people of all social backgrounds together. In the late seventeenth century the scientifically minded Sir William Petty might have doubted this proposition. He observed that the better sort of Catholics 'are as such Catholics are in other places' while the poorer 'have a great opinion of holy wells, rocks and caves which have been the reputed cells and receptacles of men, reputed saints'.[13] Yet, earlier in the century the position

---

[11] 'Brussels Ms 3947', ed. Brendan Jennings, *Analecta Hibernica* 6 (1934), 12–138, at 29–31.

[12] Gillespie, *Devoted People*, 46–47, 50–54, 109–10.

[13] William Petty, *The Political Anatomy of Ireland* (London, 1691), 94–95.

was much less clear cut. The holy well at Brideswell in County Roscommon, which still survives, is contained within a well-house erected by the Scottish Catholic settler Randal MacDonnell, first Earl of Antrim, in 1625 and is adorned with his arms. From within the Anglo Irish tradition in County Dublin, Sir John Plunket of Dunsoghly walled St Margaret's well in the early seventeenth century for the benefit of pilgrims, and Patrick Fagan of Feltrim constructed a complex of highly decorated buildings around the well at St Doulagh's, near Baldoyle, on his County Dublin estates.[14] Indeed, so powerful was this holy well tradition for the Catholic landowner Sir John Talbot of Malahide that he returned from banishment to Connacht to attend the annual patronal day festivities at St Marnock's well at Portmarnock, County Dublin.[15] By contrast, one Dublin Carmelite described those who flocked into the city in 1629 to go to St Stephen's well on 16 December to drink the water as 'country clowns'.[16] The sacralized natural world thus became a common point at which those from different social groups could interact.

A second belief concerning the created world shared by Protestants and Catholics was that it was the result of God's actions alone. Yet, it would be overstating the case to see the natural world as the catalyst for an outburst of seventeenth-century ecumenical activity. There were distinct differences in the ways in which Catholics and Protestants looked at nature, albeit with some embarrassing overlaps. Catholics, drawing on history and tradition, were prepared to admit that there were different densities of sanctity, often revolving around the actions of a saint or holy man in the landscape, while Protestants held to a more diffused sense of God's power in the natural world. However, shared belief in divine creation of the natural world may be of importance as a site of 'confessional leakage' around which the normal confessional boundaries

---

[14] Petra Skyvova, *Fingallian Holy Wells* (Swords, 2005), 45, 64. For the popularity of some well sites with the elite in pre-Reformation Wales, see Alexandra Walsham, 'Holywell: Contesting Sacred Space in post-Reformation Wales', in Will Coster and Andrew Spicer, eds, *Sacred Space in Early Modern Europe* (Cambridge, 2005), 211–36, at 212–14.

[15] 'A Rhapsody on the Carved Oak Chimney Piece of the Assumption of the Blessed Virgin in the Oak Room at Malahide Castle', ed. Joseph Byrne, *Archivium Hibernicum* 52 (1998), 24–29, at 25.

[16] London, BL, Harley MS 3888, fol. 110.

may have been relaxed. This by its nature is much more difficult to detect than common social interaction. There are certainly nineteenth-century examples of this phenomenon. At the beginning of the twentieth century in County Clare, T. J. Westropp recorded one story of how butter refused to churn for one woman; 'the mistress of the house (a Protestant woman of good birth and fair education) as she told me herself about 1878 took some of the refractory milk to the well [of St Mochuda], made the sign of the cross over it, said the Lord's prayer, dug a hole in the mud at the well with her left hand and went away without looking back', and the butter duly churned.[17] From a different confessional position, the authors of the 1838 Ordnance Survey memoir on the parish of Ballymartin, in south Antrim, noted that here was a holy well with curative powers for rheumatism in the townland of Ballymartin and which formerly had attracted a pilgrimage. They continued: 'There are two old men (Presbyterians) who still believe in the properties of this well and are in the habit of using it, but from a dread of incurring the character of being superstitious, they resort to it privately and deny having done so'.[18] This sort of activity, indicative of lingering belief in the efficacy of Catholic practices which were rooted in the natural world, had a long history. In the 1580s, for instance, one poet accused the Protestant third Earl of Thomond of visiting holy wells, although here independent evidence is lacking.[19] However the evidence in the case of Cranfield well, in County Antrim, is clearer, for there 'most of the Irish and many other people' visited the well in the 1680s.[20] None of this amounted to conversion or even proselytism, and may add up to nothing more than curiosity, but it does suggest that Protestants puzzled over some of the features of the natural world and at times were prepared to lend credence to local religious devotion towards what might otherwise have been seen as only natural features.

[17] T. J. Westropp, 'A Folklore Survey of County Clare', *Folklore* 21 (1910), 180–99, at 195–96.

[18] Angélique Day and Patrick McWilliams, eds, *Ordnance Survey Memoirs of Ireland*: vol. 2, *Parishes of County Antrim 1* (Belfast, 1990), 12. For contemporary attitudes to wells in Protestant England, see Alexandra Walsham, 'Reforming the Waters: Holy Wells and Healing Springs in Protestant England', in Diana Wood, ed., *Life and Thought in the Northern Church, c. 1170–1700: Essays in Honour of Claire Cross*, SCH S 12 (Woodbridge, 1999), 227–55.

[19] *Measgra Dánta I*, ed. Thomas F. O'Rahilly (Cork, 1927), 43, 80.

[20] Dublin, Trinity College, MS 883/1, fol. 197.

III

What lay behind this sense of a religious commonality with the natural world is difficult to determine. Clearly the experience of the local was important here as individuals constructed their own sense of local religion in order to interpret everyday experiences. In this process Irish Catholics may well have had an advantage over their Protestant contemporaries since they drew on an older tradition of local religion stretching back into the late Middle Ages. Religious reform may have modified that, but its integration into the natural world made it impossible for reformers to shatter it completely, hence the survival of common ideas on God and nature which are clear in the catechisms discussed above. The natural world before the reform process of the 1530s was not regarded as uniformly revealing the wonder of God's creation but was seen as having different densities of sanctity, thicker in some places than others, depending on the level of its contact with the friends of God (the saints). In response to this experience, the Church and popular actions created a varied ritualized landscape, marking out areas of the densest sanctity.

Stories of saintly intervention in the natural landscape abounded in this world. Saints' lives written in early sixteenth-century Ireland, mostly in the north-west of the country, provided such stories in abundance and are an important, if neglected, body of evidence in understanding how local religion was articulated and how it related to the natural world. Admittedly this evidence is far from perfect and tends to focus on the lives of individual saints, from which almost incidental materials must be gleaned. Nevertheless these saints' lives provide an important way into the articulation of local religion and its links with the natural world before the reform process.[21] In the 1530s Manus O'Donnell, who would succeed as lord of the O'Donnells within a few years, compiled a life of Colum Cille, the saint most associated with the O'Donnells. He combined formal older hagiographies with popular traditions about the saint explaining how Colum Cille was associated with various parts of the country. The result was a linking of the local natural world with the power of the saint, creating tangible indi-

---

[21] For the dates of the Lives that are used here, see Raymond Gillespie, 'Saints and Manuscripts in Sixteenth-Century Breifne', *Breifne* 11.44 (2008), 533–56.

cations of faith and points of devotion but also explaining something of the organization of local worlds. Thus at Gartan there
was a flagstone with a figure of a cross on which Colum Cille
was born, which remained at that place 'working miracles and
wonders'. Nearby, where he was baptized was another flagstone
that was supposed to help the sick but the family who maintained
the local church hid it because of the demand for it. Close by there
was another stone where he played and which made those who
came near to it sterile to commemorate Colum Cille's chastity;
'*Leac na Geanmnaidheachta* [stone of chastity] is the name of that
flagstone to this day'. To the west of Gartan was another stone
from which Colum Cille gave water to a grieving man; so that
'*Leac na Cumhadh* [stone of the sorrows] is the name of that stone
today, in memory of that great miracle'.[22]

A similar cluster of stories, all with topographical and place-name
references, commemorated Colum Cille's visit to Tory Island; many
of these contained common folkloric elements.[23] Thus within a few
miles in north Donegal an early sixteenth-century visitor could
see topography, place names and hagiography working together to
explain the apparently natural world. Manus O'Donnell's Life of
Colum Cille was not unique in its interest in the natural world
and how it connected to saintly lives. In the prose Life of St Caillin
in the Book of Fenagh, written in 1516 at the religious house
at Fenagh in County Leitrim, the turning of Druids into stone
columns (although the earlier verse Life incorporated in the 1516
text simply says they were turned to stone) at Fenagh by Caillin
is probably related to the fact that the largest standing stones in
Leitrim are located there and Caillin's actions provided a suitable
explanation for these.[24] Again, the sixteenth-century register of
Clogher recorded the existence of a stone on which St Patrick's
head had rested in Fermanagh: 'the stones … consecrated by the
saint's touch are now placed in front of the church [at Pobal]

[22] Manus O'Donnell, *The Life of Colum Cille*, ed. Brian Lacey (Dublin, 1998), 32–35,
61. On the role of holy stones, see Christine Zucchelli, *Stones of Adoration: Sacred Stones
and Mystic Megaliths of Ireland* (Cork, 2007), 65–92, 157–70.

[23] O'Donnell, *Life of Colum Cille*, 62–64; Joesph Szövérffy, 'Manus O'Donnell and
Irish Folk Tradition', *Éigse* 8 (1956–7), 108–32, at 119–21.

[24] *The Book of Fenagh*, ed. William Hennessy and D. H. Kelly (Dublin, 1875, facsimile
repr. 1939), 116–17, 128–29; Michael Moore, *Archaeological Survey of Leitrim* (Dublin,
2003), 23.

which have miraculously given and indeed give health of body to many'.[25] Perhaps not surprisingly some of these sites became places of pilgrimage. In the 1680s, for instance, it was noted that at Loughshane, in Urney parish in County Cavan, there was said to be a stone that was like St Brigid and there people would congregate on St Brigid's Day to pray and walk around the piles of stones that had accumulated near the stone.[26] While such stories certainly boosted the power and image of particular saints, they also shaped local religiosities. The most striking of these unusual features in the landscape was, undoubtedly, the holy well. Such wells were an important part of Manus O'Donnell's story of Colum Cille. Thus, for instance, when Colum Cille visited Termonmagurk in Tyrone 'he blessed it and left the right of sanctuary there from then on. He delivered three strokes to the ground with his staff and a well sprang up from each of the three strokes'.[27] Stories of holy wells and their origins were legion in the early sixteenth century. The register of the early sixteenth-century bishop of Clogher, for instance, contained not only a list of the previous incumbents of the office but a list of the holy wells that some of the more pious had created.[28] Thus the number of holy wells in early sixteenth-century Ireland was continuously shifting, and it is impossible to say how many wells existed at any one point in time since they fell in and out of use over time. A list of churches in the diocese of Kilmore, probably written by a Franciscan in the early seventeenth century, identifies a *fons miraculosus* at Rossinver, Inishmagrath and Ballaghmeehan, but these are clearly only the most important of those that existed.[29] In the 1640s Monsignor Massari, chaplain to the papal nuncio G. B. Rinuccini, visiting a former ecclesiastical site on Lough Oughter in the diocese of Kilmore, found 'a well of the clearest water which, as many of the islanders told me, had been miraculously discovered in the days of a saintly abbot when

---

[25] 'The Register of Clogher', ed. K. W. Nicholls, *Clogher Record* 7.3 (1971–2), 361–431, at 400–01.
[26] John Richardson, *The Great Folly, Superstition and Idolatry of Pilgrimage in Ireland* (Dublin, 1727), 68–70.
[27] O'Donnell, *Life of Colum Cille*, 72–73.
[28] 'Register of Clogher', ed. Nicholls, 378–79.
[29] Canice Mooney, 'Topographical Fragments from the Franciscan Library', *Celtica* I (1946–8), 64–85, at 65–67.

his monks were suffering greatly for want of water' and those present drank from the well.[30]

Holy wells attracted pilgrims from both local parishes and wider regions. Events at the well shaped local religiosities, although the detail of how this happened is very rarely recorded. There are relatively few accounts before the nineteenth century of what went on at local holy well pilgrimages. Nineteenth-century accounts usually describe pilgrims walking clockwise around a site or devotional object, reciting prayers as they moved.[31] Such rounding rituals were certainly known in the early sixteenth century and are best documented in connection with the pilgrimage to the renowned St Patrick's Purgatory in the diocese of Clogher.[32] Rounding rituals were not confined to this site. The second Irish Life of Maedoc, written at Rossinver in north-west Leitrim in the 1540s, mentions them in a number of places. According to this Life, which contained an account of the inauguration of a lord, the main reliquary of the saint, the *Breac Maedoc*, was to be carried round the lord; it was also to be carried clockwise around the men of Breifne in battle for their protection. Some of this may be the result of copying such rituals from the Book of Fenagh and the Life of Colum Cille, which also describe how secondary relics, including the *Cathach*, or battle book of the O'Donnells, should be carried around armies going into battle. Again, when Maedoc cursed the local lord of Rossinver for grudging him land on which to build his church, he cursed him with the Breac Maedoc reliquary by carrying it around him three times anticlockwise, the reverse of the direction for pilgrimage and other rituals.[33] These rounding rituals with prayers were not the only practice at holy wells. An early sixteenth-century Life of Naile, written at the church at Kinawley in Fermanagh, seems to imply that the primary objects of the pilgrimage were to wash using water from the well and to

---

[30] Msgr Dino Massari, 'My Irish Campaign', *Catholic Bulletin* 7 (1917), 246–49, at 248.

[31] Patrick Logan, *The Holy Wells of Ireland* (Gerrards Cross, 1980), 21–37.

[32] e.g. the poem edited in Próinséas Ní Chatháin, 'The Later Pilgrimage Irish Poetry on Lough Derg', in Michael Haren and Yolande de Pontfarcy, eds, *The Medieval Pilgrimage to St Patrick's Purgatory* (Enniskillen, 1988), 202–11; and the detailed description of the pilgrimage by Mícheál Ó Cléirigh reproduced in Peter Harbison, *Pilgrimage in Ireland* (London, 1971), 62.

[33] *Bethada Náem nÉrenn*, ed. Charles Plummer, 2 vols (Oxford, 1922), 1: 236; 2: 229.

say a prayer.[34] There are many parallels to this sort of pilgrimage activity. In the eighteenth century washing in the holy well was the main activity at the pilgrimage site of Struell Wells in County Down, and the main rituals at the late-medieval pilgrimage to St Mullins in County Carlow were to drink the water from the saint's mill race and to wash in it.[35]

Perhaps the most detailed account of how local religion related to the natural world and how it drew its inspiration and justification from it occurs in the early sixteenth-century Life of Naile of Kinawley, that tells of the saint's part in creating a holy well. According to the Ordnance Survey memoirs of the 1830s, there were two holy wells in the parish of Kinawley but according to one early eighteenth-century history of Fermanagh one of these was a recent creation and was dedicated to St Patrick.[36] The older well, apparently dedicated to Naile, was that beside the now ruined late-medieval parish church. In the early sixteenth-century Life of the saint, the third section is largely given over to the narration of an origin legend for the cult of Naile at Kinawley and an explanation of the holy well at the site.[37] This section explains how St Maedoc from the adjoining diocese of Kilmore met Naile at Kinawley, then called Disert na Topar and occupied by a saint called Ternoc, but previously known as Cluain Caem and the location of a fort.[38] According to this version of the legend, Naile sat with his back to a pillar stone on the height above the church and sent one of his servants to Ternoc to ask for a drink of water. This Ternoc refused, challenging Naile to produce his own water. Naile was furious and threw his finely carved *bachall* [staff] so that it hit stones nearby and then dispatched his servant with a cup to the spot where the *bachall* landed. There the servants found the staff stuck in a rock and a 'pure-cold stream of blue water burst instantly and spontaneously after it' from which he filled the cup

[34] Charles Plummer, *Miscellanea Hagiographia Hibernica* (Brussels, 1915), 106–7, 133.
[35] Walter Harris, *The Antient and Present state of the County of Down* (Dublin, 1744), 25–26; Máire B. de Paor, *Saint Moling Luachra* (Dublin, 2001), 140–41.
[36] Angelique Day and Patrick McWilliams, eds, *Ordnance Survey Memoirs of Ireland*: vol. 4, *Parishes of County Fermanagh I* (Belfast, 1990), 116; Patrick Ó Maolagáin, ed., 'An Early History of Fermanagh', *Clogher Record* 1.3 (1955), 133–49, at 136–37.
[37] Plummer, *Miscellanea Hagiographia*, 131–36. I take paras 16–28 of Plummer's edition as comprising the second section.
[38] The name Kinawley derives from Cill Naile, 'church of Naile'.

and brought it to Naile. Naile then declared the well to have healing powers, entrusted it to the care of the *erenagh* and seized the opportunity to impose a curse on anyone who did anything against his church or the associated lands. Faced with this, Ternoc admitted defeat, proceeded on his knees from the well to where Naile stood, and was duly expelled from the site. After some curses from Naile and counter-curses from Ternoc, Ternoc was expelled and Naile renamed the place and established his church and well there.

The motifs here are all well-established hagiographical ones based on Exodus 17 and Numbers 20, in which Moses strikes a rock to provide water for the children of Israel in the desert. This analogy was certainly known to early sixteenth-century hagiographers in Ulster. Manus O'Donnell in his Life of Colum Cille, for instance, had drawn the analogy explicitly noting that when Colum Cille blessed a rock water flowed out 'and it is clear from this that God made Colum Cille similar to Moses at the time that the children of Israel were in need of water in the desert'. By imitating the Old Testament patriarch the saint at least confirmed his holy credentials, but as O'Donnell pointed out: 'not alone did He make Colum Cille like Moses, but a degree above him because Moses had the help of all his followers in getting the water from God … Colum Cille had help from no one when he himself got the water from God'.[39] However, in the case of the story in the Life of Naile the analogy with Moses is not the main point of the story. The episode was intended as an origin legend for what was probably an existing holy well in the middle of the sixteenth century. The nineteenth-century Ordnance Survey map for Kinawley shows that the topographic features mentioned in the Life were still visible in the landscape. The well was located to the south-east of the then ruined medieval church and to the north on higher land is a standing stone known as the 'Station Stone' where the Ordnance Survey memoir recorded that 'stations [gatherings for prayer at traditional sites which mostly involved circling the sites with prayers] were formerly held by the Roman Catholic inhabitants [of Kinawley]'.[40] To the east of this lay a substantial rath (a circular earthen fort), presumably the fort mentioned in the

---

[39] O'Donnell, *Life of Colum Cille*, 77–78.
[40] Day and McWilliams, eds, *Ordnance Survey, Fermanagh I*, 108.

Life. If these elements in the archaeological landscape were there in the 1830s, they were there in the sixteenth century also. What the Life provided was an explanation for these unusual features in the landscape.

The story as it was recorded in the Life may well have originated as an oral tradition. The colophon to the Life makes it clear that Mícheál Ó Cléirigh did not acquire a copy of the Life of Naile until January 1630. Yet in 1628, when he compiled the first recension of his Martyrology of Donegal, he was able to include an entry for Naile under his feast day on 27 January, despite the fact that there was no entry for Naile in any of the older martyrologies that Ó Cléirigh had access to, including the Martyrology of Gorman which was his main source for the Donegal martyrology. The entry in the new martyrology described the legend of the origin of the holy well:

> It was to him God gave water from the hard stony rock, when great thirst had seized him and Maedog of Ferna with the monks of both. When he made a distant cast of his crozier at the hard stony rock so that a stream of pure spring water gushed there from; just as this spring is now to be seen at Cill Naile …[41]

When Ó Cléirigh revised his text of the Martyrology in 1630, he had acquired the Life and other material and was able to expand the entry with a genealogy of Naile, a reference to his Life and material from other lives that Ó Cléirigh had acquired.[42] It seems, therefore, that in 1628 Ó Cléirigh was drawing on a source or sources other than the written Life. The form of the entry in the first recension of the Martyrology suggests that this may have been an oral tradition, particularly in the linking of the story to a specific site that could be seen and that apparently offered proof of the story. There is certainly rather later evidence to suggest that such oral stories circulated widely and were often never incorporated into any of the Lives. In the 1790s an antiquarian, Daniel Grose, observed of Fenagh in County Leitrim:

---

[41] Brussels, Bibliothèque Royale, MS 4639, fols 14–14ᵛ.
[42] *The Martyrology of Donegal*, ed. J. H. Todd and William Reeves (Dublin, 1864), 28–29.

the country people show a well, about half a mile from the ruins [of the abbey at Fenagh] of which they relate the following wonderful tradition. The founder of this abbey (St Caillin or Kilian) was one day walking with some of his holy brotherhood over this spot, and feeling himself fatigued and thirsty he stooped down to pick up a small tuft of rushes in order to moisten his mouth, when wonderful to relate, a spring immediately burst up in the place, from whence he had pulled the rushes at which the holy man quenched his drouth [thirst] without further trouble.

To commemorate this miracle the saint immediately ordained that this holy well should become a station and endowed it with many wonderful qualities, especially that of curing pains and aches, which it is supposed to retain to this day. A patron or festival is held here annually in honour of the saint on St John the Baptist's day, stations and penance is [*sic*] then performed and vast numbers of people attend.[43]

The story does not appear in any of the Lives of the saint and hence probably circulated mainly in oral tradition before it was recorded by Grose, but, like so many of these stories, its ultimate origin cannot be determined.

Stories such as these, linking the natural world and cosmic order, served to shape, and were shaped by, local identities and needs in late-medieval Ireland in the same way that such stories would be shaped by a confessional tradition in the seventeenth century. Sites such as wells or stones made holy by the activities of saints were important foci where earth and heaven met in a natural feature. As such they were places of power. Hence at least some holy wells may have had their origin as baptismal places in early Christian Ireland, reflecting their importance as places of power.[44] As such they needed to be controlled and continually reinterpreted by associating them with saints in order to use the natural world as a way of reflecting cosmic order.

---

[43] Daniel Grose, *The Antiquities of Ireland: A Supplement to Francis Grose,* ed. Roger Stalley (Dublin, 1991), 149.

[44] See, e.g., Niamh Whitfield, 'A Suggested Function for the Holy Well?', in Alistair Minnis and Jane Roberts, eds, *Text, Image and Interpretation: Studies in Anglo Saxon Literature and its Insular Context in Honour of Eamon Ó Carragáin* (Turnhout, 2007), 495–514.

A case in point is the treatment in Manus O'Donnell's *Life of Colum Cille* of the waterfall at Assaroe on the border of the O'Donnell lordship. This is certainly one of the places most associated with the saint according to the *Life*. Even before the birth of Colum Cille, the *Life* records that St Patrick visited the site, blessing the O'Donnell side of the river while cursing the side belonging to their main political rivals, the O'Neills, so that no fish could be caught on the southern side of the river. Colum Cille himself duly visited the site and, using the staff of a local holy man, created a holy well there 'so that there is a well of fresh water in that place today'. This was further reinforced with a piece of local place lore explaining the origin of the well. The saint then proceeded to lower the rocks at the waterfall so that fish could pass along the river despite Patrick's curse, demonstrating the superior power of Colum Cille over Patrick, 'and in memory of that great miracle the fishing of Assaroe on Colum Cille's feast day, from then till now, belongs to his successor'.[45] The Assaroe stories make a number of points underpinned by the reality of the natural world. These are clearly stories about property rights, and this technique of attaching stories to the landscape as a way of underpinning local rights, especially for tithes and church land, is used in other places in the *Life*.[46] However, there are also larger issues at stake here for, as the *Life* itself points out, Assaroe had a political significance, being on the western end of the border of the O'Donnell lordship which ran between the River Bann and Assaroe which it was also the southern border of the diocese of Raphoe.[47] To associate Colum Cille, as the patron of the O'Donnell family, with such a place was to make an important political statement about the saint's control, and hence his family, of access to both Ulster and Connacht. Thus stories about the natural features at Assaroe in the *Life of Colum Cille* helped to shape not only local religiosities but also local political identities, and as such became an important way for organizing particular places.

Space was not the only variable that such religious stories could be shaped to define. Stories of saints and their interaction with the natural world could also shape and be shaped by the ways in which

---

45 O'Donnell, *Life of Colum Cille*, 21, 76–77.
46 e.g. ibid. 55–57.
47 Ibid. 188.

local communities understood the passage of time. A case in point is the story of St Caillin of Fenagh discussed above. While the feast day of St Caillin falls on 13 November, and presumably was marked by some form of liturgical commemoration at his church at Fenagh on that date, the pattern (i.e. patronal day celebration) in the version of the story recorded by Grose was held on the feast of St John the Baptist. This might have been either 24 June or 29 August but it is most likely the former date which also marks midsummer in the traditional Irish calendar. What this suggests is that the liturgical calendar had been reshaped to meet local needs. This date shifting has a parallel in the cult of Naile, whose Life, with its story of the creation of a holy well, has been discussed above. There is something of a problem in establishing the feast day of Naile. The earliest Irish martyrology, the Martyrology of Tallaght, compiled in the early ninth century, has no entry for Naile under 28 January. It does, however, have an entry under 27 January for a Noele of Inver, and this entry is repeated in the twelfth-century Martyrology of Gorman.[48] The name is also a Gaelicized form of the Latin name of St Natilis of Kinmanagh in Kilkenny, who does appear in the earliest martyrologies under 31 July, and this suggests some cult splitting.[49] In the seventeenth century the Irish hagiographer John Colgan included the feast of Naile in his *Acta Sanctorum* of 1645 under 27 January. However, the Ordnance Survey memoirs in the 1830s recorded that the pattern of St Naile was kept at the church on the last Sunday in July.[50] Maire MacNeill, in her study of the traditional festival of Lughnasa, recorded this as an example of the celebration of Crom Dubh, or the pagan god Lug, usually held on the last Sunday of summer, and noted the disjunction between the feast day of the saint and the date of the pattern. She speculated:

> might it be that the celebration of a patronal feast falling in midwinter was transferred to a day in the summer months, that a stone on the hill already had Lughnasa associations and

[48] *The Martyrology of Tallaght*, ed. R. I. Best and H. J. Lawlor (London, 1931), 12. The Martyrology of Oengus gives this saint at 14 January: see *The Martyrology of Oengus the Culdee*, ed. Whitley Stokes (London, 1905), 42.

[49] *Martyrology of Tallaght*, ed. Best and Lawlor, 59.

[50] Day and McWilliams, eds, *Ordnance Survey, Fermanagh I*, 112.

that in a district rich in Lughnasa celebrations, the appropriate day would seem to be the last Sunday of Summer?[51]

The more likely explanation is the confusion of the dates of patronal festivals between Noele on 27 January and Natalis on 31 July, from which it was easy and more convenient to move to the last Sunday of July. Again, as with the cult of Caillin discussed above, there appears to have been local reorganization of a liturgical event to meet the needs of the local sense of time. The phenomenon was not uncommon. Even at one of the most significant Patrician pilgrimage sites in Ulster, Struell Wells, the pilgrimage to the well was, according to Walter Harris in 1744, made on Midsummer Eve or on the Friday before Lammas rather than on the feast day of the saint.[52] This date shifting for such gatherings at local sites was possible because these places of pilgrimage lay outside official liturgical control. Their validity did not depend on doctrine (whether orthodox or not) or theological discussion but on the concrete reality of their existence together with their origin legend, often circulating in oral form rather than as formal, written hagiography. In that way origin legends about time or place could be easily manipulated to suit local communities and so serve in creating a sense of local religion and in aligning a community's sense of time (marking out the key points in the economic or cultural year) with that of the saint.[53] In such ways did religion and local identities reinforce themselves.

IV

For those who lived in early modern Ireland the natural world was not inanimate. Later generations might see the might of God in the dramatic, but in the sixteenth and seventeenth centuries even the everyday was full of signs and pointers to his will. The natural world provided a common language, mental imagery and (perhaps most importantly) a set of experiences of God for those who inhabited that world. Thus they observed the natural world carefully and with an eye to its meanings for their daily life, equating

---

[51] Máire MacNeill, *The Festival of Lughnasa* (Oxford, 1962), 118.

[52] Harris, *County of Down*, 25–26.

[53] For the linkages between liturgical time and community time, see Sean Ó Duinn, *Where Three Streams Meet: Celtic Spirituality* (Dublin, 2000), 222–46.

natural order with cosmic order. As such the natural world shaped popular religiosities in a very powerful way. It was all the more significant because of the important part that natural features in the world had played in forming local religious customs in the early sixteenth century, which determined practice for later generations. The Irish landscape was dotted with natural features that had acquired sacred legends that linked them to saints and other holy men. Such sites and stories, crafted to meet local needs and priorities, came to have a central position in defining who one was in that world. From that point of view, the natural world was far from pristine and was carefully crafted with social, cultural and religious messages for contemporaries to read. The linking of particular landscapes with the cult of saints was a local religious expression of a wider sense of the linkage of the order of the natural world with a wider cosmic order. In that sense, the story of natural landscapes transcends the merely local by both universalizing the particular sense of place and particularizing the universal power of God at one place through the saint. As such, the natural world played a key part in shaping the beliefs and local religious practices and identities of the inhabitants of early modern Ireland.

National University of Ireland Maynooth

NATURE'S SCOURGES: THE NATURAL WORLD AND SPECIAL PRAYERS, FASTS AND THANKSGIVINGS, 1541–1866[*]

by ALASDAIR RAFFE

FROM the sixteenth to the nineteenth centuries, special prayers, fasts and thanksgivings were an important means by which the Established Churches of England, Scotland and Ireland responded to natural occurrences. Although war prompted the largest number of special religious observances in this period, environmental calamities – instances of plague, famine, drought, earthquakes and storms – led civil and ecclesiastical authorities to order prayers, or to call national fast days, requiring subjects to cease work and attend worship on a specific day. Natural blessings, such as seasonable rain, successful harvests and the abatement of plague, were also marked by prayers, and sometimes by days of national thanksgiving. In Reformation England, the appointment of special observances can be traced back to 1541, when Henry VIII ordered Archbishop Cranmer to organize prayers in response to drought.[1] Henry's successors developed the practice of ordering special prayers and days in response to natural events and man-made calamities. In Scotland, national fasts were observed at the appointment of the church courts from 1566;[2] they were not regularly under the control of the Crown until the Restoration period. The first national thanksgiving in Scotland was appointed in 1600 after James VI survived an apparent attempt on his life by the Earl of Gowrie.[3] In Ireland, the first special observance was

[*] The research for this paper derives from the project on 'British State Prayers, Fasts and Thanksgivings, 1540s–1940s', funded by the Arts and Humanities Research Council. The project team is preparing an edition of all the orders and prayers relating to fasts, thanksgivings and other special observances from the Reformation to the twentieth century. I am grateful to my collaborators, Philip Williamson, Natalie Mears and Stephen Taylor.

[1] London, LPL, MS. Cranmer Register, I, fol. 18ʳ.
[2] W. Ian P. Hazlett, 'Playing God's Card: Knox and Fasting, 1565–66', in Roger A. Mason, ed., *John Knox and the British Reformations* (Aldershot, 1998), 176–98.
[3] *The Register of the Privy Council of Scotland*, 1st ser., ed. J. H. Burton and D. Masson, 14 vols (Edinburgh, 1877–98), 6: 156–57.

a fast day called in 1625. From 1651, the Irish authorities quite regularly appointed special prayers in response to natural events.[4]

Most previous historians of these religious observances have concentrated on short series of prayers or days, usually illustrating a particular political context.[5] This paper surveys the full history of those special prayers, fasts and thanksgivings called in response to disease, meteorological events, fire, earthquakes and successful or failed harvests. It is based on the little-studied proclamations and acts appointing special days, and the prayers issued to be read in English, Welsh and Irish Churches.[6] These provide new evidence of the continuity into the modern period of ideas concerning God's providential government of the natural world. Some historians, notably Keith Thomas, Alexandra Walsham and William Burns, have argued that in the late seventeenth century Providence was marginalized as a means of explaining natural events.[7] This interpretation should be qualified. While the use of providential language to report individuals' experiences – what Nicholas Guyatt has called 'personal providentialism' – was in decline, civil officials and clergymen continued to explain events of national and global significance in terms of Providence. Special prayers used the rhetoric of 'national providentialism'[8] to describe natural processes, with surprisingly little change through the eighteenth and nineteenth centuries. Frank Turner was incorrect to assert that 'the Anglican church of the eighteenth century issued no special prayers during national disasters'.[9] And Richard Janet's claim that English

---

[4] Robert Steele, *A Bibliography of Royal Proclamations of the Tudor and Stuart Sovereigns, 1485–1714*, 2 vols (Oxford, 1910), 2: nos 266, 481, 485, 554.

[5] The most recent investigation of this subject, which discusses much of the previous literature, is Philip Williamson, 'State Prayers, Fasts and Thanksgivings: Public Worship in Britain 1830–1897', *P&P*, no. 200 (August 2008), 169–222.

[6] In Scotland, a form of prayer written for the fast of 1566 was used until the 1630s, after which the Established Church eschewed set forms.

[7] Keith Thomas, *Religion and the Decline of Magic* (Harmondsworth, 1973), 126–28; Alexandra Walsham, *Providence in Early Modern England* (Oxford, 1999), 333–34; William E. Burns, *An Age of Wonders: Prodigies, Politics and Providence in England, 1657–1727* (Manchester, 2002).

[8] Nicholas Guyatt, *Providence and the Invention of the United States, 1607–1876* (Cambridge, 2007), 5–6, 14–17, 60.

[9] Frank M. Turner, 'Rainfall, Plagues, and the Prince of Wales: A Chapter in the Conflict of Religion and Science', *JBS* 13 (1974), 46–65, at 49.

fast days between 1721 and 1832 were called only for military purposes is misleading:[10] the fast of 1756 responded to the Lisbon earthquake as well as to war, and a fast in 1801 was prompted in part by shortages of food. Natural events also inspired Scottish fasts, and thanksgiving days in all parts of the British Isles, during this period. None of the special prayers and days between 1759 and 1796 was provoked by natural events, but in some degree this reflects the greater significance of war in public life in these years.

It is increasingly clear that ideas of Providence remained widespread in the eighteenth century. Most people believed in God's superintendence of the natural world and saw his hand in particular events, though opinions varied as to whether divine interventions temporarily suspended the natural order.[11] The evangelical climate of the first half of the nineteenth century made Providence more prominent in public life,[12] but it was not necessary for Evangelicals to rediscover a defunct concept. Moreover, the orders and prayers for special observances illustrate how divine and natural explanations could coexist.[13] They show how religious occasions could be used to convey news, instructions and justifications of government policies from the political centres to worshippers in the parishes.

In the period from from the first observance in 1541 to the last in 1866, natural events prompted the appointment of at least 103 fasts, thanksgivings and special prayers.[14] This total includes

[10] Richard J. Janet, 'Providence, Prayer and Cholera: The English General Fast of 1832', *Historical Magazine of the Protestant Episcopal Church* 51 (1982), 297–317, at 308.

[11] J. C. D. Clark, 'Providence, Predestination and Progress: Or, Did the Enlightenment Fail?', *Albion* 35 (2003), 559–89; Robert J. Ingram, '"The Trembling earth is God's Herald": Earthquakes, Religion and Public Life in Britain during the 1750s', in Theodore E. D. Braun and John B. Radner, eds, *The Lisbon Earthquake of 1755: Representations and Reactions* (Oxford, 2005), 97–115; Boyd Hilton, *The Age of Atonement: The Influence of Evangelicalism on Social and Economic Thought, 1785–1865* (Oxford, 1986), 13–14.

[12] Boyd Hilton, 'The Role of Providence in Evangelical Social Thought', in *History, Society and the Churches: Essays in Honour of Owen Chadwick*, ed. Derek Beales and Geoffrey Best (Cambridge, 1985), 215–33.

[13] Cf. Françoise Deconinck-Brossard, 'Acts of God, Acts of Men: Providence in Seventeenth- and Eighteenth-Century England and France', in Kate Cooper and Jeremy Gregory, eds, *Signs, Wonders, Miracles: Representations of Divine Power in the Life of the Church*, SCH 41 (Woodbridge, 2005), 356–75, at 357.

[14] The main sources used to compile this list were William Keatinge Clay, ed., *Liturgical Services: Liturgies and Occasional Forms of Prayer set forth in the Reign of Queen Elizabeth*, PS (Cambridge, 1847); David Calderwood, *The History of the Kirk of Scotland*, ed. Thomas Thomson and David Laing, 8 vols, Wodrow Society (1842–49); *Acts of the*

40 prayers and days observed throughout England and Wales, 27 exclusively Scottish occasions, 5 Irish, and 25 eighteenth- and nineteenth-century occasions that were observed in at least three of the four nations. A further 2 prayers (in 1543 and 1560) seem to have been used in Canterbury province alone, and 4 observances were restricted to capital cities. In addition to these 103 observances, other fast and thanksgiving days appointed in response to man-made events sometimes inspired clergy to refer to natural phenomena.[15] The Book of Common Prayer contained prayers relating to the weather, harvest and disease, used at ministers' discretion in England and Wales throughout the period.

Human and animal diseases prompted fifty-one of the occasions. The major English plague outbreaks between 1563 and 1665 occasioned national fasts or the issuing of forms of penitent prayer. Indeed, the order and prayers issued for the fast of 1563, the first such national day in England, were the basis for forms of prayer appointed in response to the plague in 1593, 1603, 1625 and 1636. And in 1563–64, 1604, 1625, 1658 and 1666, the waning of epidemics prompted the Crown to call for prayers or days of thanksgiving. In 1720 and 1721, special prayers and fasting were part of the government's attempt to prevent an outbreak of plague, which was then affecting Continental Europe. Prayers continued to be issued in response to epidemic disease: after 1830, outbreaks of cholera helped to bring about an increase in the overall frequency of special prayers and days.[16] Cattle disease also prompted prayers. A collect for the relief of cattle mortality was added to the Anglican service in 1748 and used daily for eleven years. In 1865–66, an outbreak of bovine disease, combined with a cholera epidemic, inspired three special prayers.

Weather conditions, the threat of dearth and the success or failure of harvests were marked by forty-nine of the special prayers and days. Indeed, the first two special prayers (in 1541 and 1543) responded to unseasonable weather. Weather – in most cases heavy rain – also prompted observances in England and Wales in 1560,

---

General Assembly of the Church of Scotland, MDCXXXVIII MDCCCXLII (Edinburgh, 1843); Steele, *Bibliography of Royal Proclamations*; ESTC, <http://estc.bl.uk>; the LPL catalogue; and the *London Gazette*.

[15] See, e.g., *The Cavses of this General Fast, to begin the first Sabbath of August nixt, 1595* (Edinburgh, 1595).

[16] Williamson, 'State Prayers, Fasts and Thanksgivings', 172–73.

1613, 1646, 1648 and 1661–62. The stormy winter of 1703–04 led to fast days in the three kingdoms. Dearth inspired prayers throughout the period, but the most important famine, judged from the five fasts it prompted, afflicted Scotland in the late 1690s. After the improved harvest of 1699, a national thanksgiving was called, but continuing dearth was mentioned in the acts appointing fasts in 1700 and 1701. Ireland's potato famine led the government in England to appoint a prayer in September 1846 and a general fast in the following March.

Earthquakes prompted observances in 1580, 1750 and 1756. Yet of all the devastating fires in the period, it is interesting that only the great fire of London (1666) and fires in Edinburgh in 1700 and 1701 were marked on a national basis. This casts doubt on whether all the most severe disasters and greatest blessings inspired special observances. Moreover, there was a tendency for prayers and days to be called in cycles. This is particularly apparent with respect to thanksgivings for abundant harvests, which were often appointed immediately after times of scarcity, as in 1699, 1796, 1801 and 1847. One of the prayers issued in 1847 made the relationship clear, being addressed to 'Merciful God, at whose bidding the earth hath withholden her increase, and again hath rendered her fruits in their season'. The lesson – 'our entire dependence on Thee [God] for the supply of our daily bread' – was no doubt easier to apprehend in the context of greatly fluctuating agricultural yields.[17]

Fasts, thanksgivings and the other special prayers examined here were meant as acknowledgements of divine Providence, its scourges and blessings, and also as pleas for God's mercy and favour. The form of prayer for the English fast of 1563 contained a preface justifying the practice of fasting which was adapted and republished several times over the following century. As this preface made clear, God manifested his anger against sin by sending 'perticuler punyshementes, afflictions, and perylles'. These called the people to repent of their sins, reform their lives and crave a respite from their danger. The example of the successful prayers of King David 'in the time of plague and pestilence which ensued upon

---

[17] *A Form of Prayer and Thanksgiving to Almighty God; to be used in all Churches and Chapels in England and Wales … on Sunday the Seventeenth Day of October 1847* (London, 1847), 5.

his vayne numbrying of the people' (2 Samuel 24) was invoked.[18] Throughout the period, orders and prayers alluded to Old Testament stories of providential scourges. A form of prayer for the fast called in response to heavy rain in 1661 specified that the account of Noah in Genesis 8 be read.[19] After the Lisbon earthquake of 1756, English and Welsh congregations were to be put in mind of God's violent punishment of the world as described in Isaiah 24.[20] The form of prayer for the equivalent fast day in Ireland specified as a lesson Ezekiel 14, with its account of judgements inflicted on Jerusalem.[21] Yet fast day services also aimed to instil the hope that God would treat England, Scotland and Ireland with the mercy seen in his dealings with Israel. Thus a prayer for the fast held after the cholera outbreak of 1832 recalled the relief brought by King David's worship, and told how the 'repentance of Nineveh didst spare that sinful city'.[22] Although the forms of prayer also specified readings from the New Testament, it was Old Testament texts – permitting typological comparisons between Israel and England, Scotland, Ireland or Britain – that did most to describe the roles of Providence and the natural world.

The practice of fasting and praying in response to natural events exemplifies what Keith Thomas has called the 'self-confirming quality' of the doctrine of Providence.[23] Some observances were quickly followed by relief from danger or disease. In July 1658, Oliver Cromwell appointed a thanksgiving to celebrate the defeat of an invasion attempt and the end of an outbreak of plague. In his declaration, Cromwell saw the decline in deaths as a response to earlier prayers: 'tis not without remark, that the two weeks Bills of Mortality, immediately after the Fast upon that occasion

---

[18] *A Fourme to be used in Common Prayer Twyse Aweke, and also an Order of Publique Fast, to be used every Wednesday in the Weeke, during this Time of Mortality* (London, 1563), sig. Aii[r].

[19] *A Form of Prayer, to be used upon the Twelfth of June* (London, 1661), sig. [B4][v].

[20] *A Form of Prayer, to be used … upon Friday the Sixth Day of February next* (London, 1756), 7.

[21] *A Form of Prayer, to be used in all Churches and Chappels throughout the Kingdom of Ireland, upon Friday the Sixth Day of February next* (Dublin, 1756), 7.

[22] *A Form of Prayer, to be used in all Churches and Chapels throughout those Parts of the United Kingdom called England and Ireland, on Wednesday the Twenty-first Day of March 1832* (Berwick-upon-Tweed, 1832), 4.

[23] Thomas, *Religion and the Decline of Magic*, 95, 137.

[of the plague], were brought to the half of what they were the week before, and did amount not to more discernably then in the healthiest times'.[24] On some occasions, however, national humiliation was seen to have little effect. When successive fasts failed to remove the famine afflicting Scotland in the late 1690s, this was attributed to insufficiently sincere fasting and repentance. As the commission of the General Assembly lamented in December 1696, 'few have been duely humbled' for the nation's sins, and 'few have joyned suitable Reformation with their professed Humiliation'. God's anger continued to be 'visible in the Judgment of frequent Sickness, and great Mortality, Dearth inflicted, and Famine threatned'.[25] In subsequent years, the Church of Scotland's fast acts repeatedly complained that sins had been 'not yet sufficiently mourned for', or that divine mercies had been forgotten.[26] In 1757, an English preacher published his sermons on the previous fast days, so 'that the Fast, though gone, may not be forgotten. That We may remember the Sins We confessed, and the Miseries We deprecated.'[27] An ungrateful people continually had to be urged to repent, pray and appease God's anger.

With respect to the plague, however, providential beliefs could conflict with the desire of the civil authorities to restrict contagion. Some forms of prayer for English plague-time observances, together with the government's plague orders, sought to prevent clergy from teaching that no practical measures could counter the disease, or that only the sinful would be infected.[28] It was also necessary to ensure that, by assembling congregations for worship, special observances did not contribute to the spread of the disease. The order for the fast of 1563 requested that 'prudent' measures be taken to segregate infected people from the healthy.[29] In 1625,

---

[24] *A Declaration of His Highnesse the Lord Protector for a Day of Publick Thanksgiving* (London, 1658), 5.

[25] *Causes of a Solemn National Fast and Humiliation, unanimously agreed upon by the Commission appointed by the late General Assembly* (Edinburgh, 1696).

[26] *Acts of the General Assembly*, 290, 435 (1700 and 1709 respectively).

[27] James Hervey, *The Time of Danger, and the Means of Safety; to which is added, the Way of Holiness. Being the Substance of Three Sermons, Preached on the Late Public Fast-Days* (London, 1757), iii.

[28] Paul Slack, *The Impact of Plague in Tudor and Stuart England* (London, 1985), 230–31; Thomas, *Religion and the Decline of Magic*, 101–02.

[29] *Fourme to be used in Common Prayer*, sig. Aii[v].

clergy were instructed not to keep the people in church too long, both to prevent misunderstanding of the religious merit of fasting, and also to reduce the chance of contagion.[30] In 1636, the fast was to be 'no otherwise Celebrated in publike ... then by a Devout and Religious use of the Prayers in the Printed Booke'.[31] These restrictions on preaching can certainly be set in the context of the Caroline church's struggles with its puritan critics.[32] Yet there was also a public health rationale for limiting the length of congregational worship in infected areas.

Thus orders and prayers conveyed the civil government's instructions for responding to the plague, at the same time as they propagated providential narratives implying that God was the chief source of respite. One collect for use in the fast of 1563 suggested that sufferers should abandon 'all confidence in our selues or any other creature', and depend on the mediation of Christ.[33] This prayer was reprinted in the form for the fast of 1603. Yet the homily provided in 1603 taught that 'though it be true that all things are guided by God's prouidence', yet 'hath he ordained the Phisition and created many medicinable and comfortable things to procure and preserue the health of man'.[34] In 1832, the prayers for the fast day called in response to cholera also sought to balance divine intervention and human effort, calling for God's assistance 'that we may neither neglect the means of preservation, nor look for success in the use of them, without Thy blessing'.[35]

Special prayers and days often mixed providential and political messages; these were not necessarily in conflict. In Scotland, for example, fast days called in response to the threat of plague were occasionally used to provide explanations and justifications of government policies. In 1665, a fast proclamation explained that plague in England had led the government to forbid trade with

---

[30] *A Forme of Common Prayer, together with an Order of Fasting* (London, 1625), sig. [O3]ʳ.

[31] James Larkin, ed., *Stuart Royal Proclamations. 2: Royal Proclamations of King Charles I, 1625–1646* (Oxford, 1983), 539.

[32] Walsham, *Providence*, 164–65.

[33] *Fourme to be used in Common Prayer*, sig. Biiiʳ.

[34] *Certaine Prayers collected out of a Forme of Godly Meditations* (London, 1603), sig. [C4]ʳ.

[35] *Form of Prayer ... on Wednesday the Twenty-first Day of March 1832*, 5.

the southern kingdom, so as to prevent the spread of disease.[36] Even the Presbyterians, who played a role in the appointment of special days after the re-establishment of their church polity in 1690, helped to account for government policy. In November 1711, the commission of the General Assembly called for a fast in response to the threat of plague, then raging on the Continent, 'For preventing wherof, Her Majesty hath Exercised such a wise and tender care'.[37]

The religious significance and social functions of fast days intersected in another way when parishioners were instructed to make charitable donations for the relief of the poor, the starving or those afflicted by disease. The order of 1563 specified that the wealthy should reduce their ordinary expenditure and increase their almsgiving.[38] In 1625, they were explicitly encouraged 'to bestow the price of the meale forborne, vpon the poore'.[39] In 1666, the English government used a national fast day as a means to collect donations for those left destitute and homeless by the great fire of London.[40] Most of the funds raised to relieve victims of the Irish potato famine were collected on the fast day held in March 1847.[41] Moreover, prayers issued after successful harvests sometimes encouraged churchgoers to enjoy the plenty with an eye to social responsibility. In 1796, English worshippers asked for grace 'to employ the gifts of Thy bounty to Thy glory; neither squandering them in riot and luxury, nor hoarding them for greediness of sordid gain'.[42]

More generally, the orders and prayers issued for special religious observances helped to convey news of natural events. The

---

[36] *A Proclamation, for a Publick General Fast throughout the Kingdom of Scotland* (Edinburgh, 1665).

[37] Edinburgh, NAS, Commission of the General Assembly registers, CH1/3/11, fol. 282.

[38] *Fourme to be used in Common Prayer*, sig. Ciii[r].

[39] *Forme of Common Prayer, together with an Order of Fasting*, sig. O2[v].

[40] *By the King. A Proclamation for a General Fast through England and Wales, and the Town of Barwick [sic] upon Tweed, on Wednesday the Tenth of October next* (London, 1666).

[41] Peter Gray, '"Potatoes and Providence": British Government Responses to the Great Famine', *Bullán* 1 (1994), 75–90, at 84.

[42] *A Prayer of Thanksgiving to Almighty God; for the great Blessing, which, in His Mercy and Goodness, he hath Vouchsafed to this Nation, in our Favourable and Abundant Harvest* (London, 1796), 4.

form of prayer produced in response to the earthquake of 1580 provided an account of the disaster, suitable for reading from the pulpit.[43] Following the great fire of London, the royal proclamation appointing a fast gave a brief but authoritative description of the devastation, a 'Visitation so dreadful, that scarce any Age or Nation hath ever seen or felt the like'.[44] Proclamations and prayers also helped to explain the consequences of natural occurrences. In 1661, the royal proclamation for a fast in England and Wales cautioned that recent heavy rain might lead to 'scarcity, and famine, and sickness, and diseases'.[45] Indeed, on occasion special prayers emphasized secular losses and gains more than providential explanations. This was more common with prayers inspired by military victories than those responding to the natural world. Yet in 1754 a clerical correspondent of the *London Evening Post* complained that the prayer for the relief of disease in cattle had 'nothing of the Spirit of the Gospel in it', and was an invitation to the congregation 'to be carnally minded'.[46]

Special prayers, fasts and thanksgivings reflected nature's scourges and its benefits. They demonstrate that political and ecclesiastical authorities promoted providential interpretations of natural processes throughout the three centuries after the Reformation. Yet from the start, special prayers and days regularly combined providential language with more secular or political messages. By studying the orders and prayers on which this paper is based, historians will learn more about how public worship could respond to environmental and political conditions. This paper has investigated beliefs and practices prescribed by the Established Churches of England, Scotland and Ireland, and has not tested the responses of parishioners to fasts and thanksgivings. Nor has there been space to consider why special prayers and days, which continued until the mid-twentieth century, were not called in response to epidemic disease and other natural events after 1866.[47] These reli-

---

[43] Clay, ed., *Liturgical Services*, 567. See also Natalie Mears, *Queenship and Political Discourse in the Elizabethan Realms* (Cambridge, 2005), 163–66.

[44] *Proclamation for a Fast on the Tenth of October.*

[45] *By the King, A Proclamation, for a General Fast throughout the Realm of England* (London, 1661).

[46] *London Evening Post*, no. 4126, 20–23 April 1754.

[47] Individual bishops in the Church of England responded to natural events by appointing prayers in their dioceses after this date: see, e.g., *The Times*, 29 June 1882, 8e.

gious observances raise a number of questions for future research, which will cast further light on Protestant attitudes to the natural world.

University of Durham

'THE MIRACULOUS MATHEMATICS OF THE WORLD': PROVING THE EXISTENCE OF GOD IN CARDINAL PÉTER PÁZMÁNY'S *KALAUZ*

by TADHG Ó HANNRACHÁIN

THIS paper offers a brief examination of Cardinal Péter Pázmány's meditation on the role of the beauty and wonder of the natural world in leading to the true knowledge of God, which is placed at the beginning of his most important work, the *Guide to the Divine Truth* (*Isteni Igazságra Vezérlő Kalauz*). Pázmány's treatment of this subject offers an insight into the Catholic intellectual milieu which ultimately rejected the Copernican cosmology championed by Galileo in favour of a geocentric and geostatic universe. In this regard, the confidence with which Pázmány asserts the harmony and compatibility between secular knowledge and apprehension of nature and the conviction of the existence of a creator God is of particular importance. An analysis of this section of his work also points up a surprising contrast with Calvin's treatment of the same subject in the *Institutes of the Christian Religion*.[1] Pázmány was raised within the Reformed tradition until his teenage years and as a Catholic polemicist he devoted great attention to Calvin's writings. Indeed, to some extent it can be suggested that the *Institutes* served as both target and model for his own great work. Yet his handling of the topic of nature as a proof of the existence of God, an area where relatively little difference might have been expected in view of its non-salience as a polemical issue, not only offers a revealing insight into the confident intellectual perspective of seventeenth-century Catholicism, but also suggests some additional ramifications of the great *sola scriptura* debate which split European Christianity in the early modern period.

Although the subject of constant scholarly attention in Hungary, Pázmány (1570–1637) remains a largely neglected figure in modern

---

[1] J. Calvin, *Institutes of the Christian Religion*, 1.1.6.

English-language historiography.[2] This is particularly unfortunate as Pázmány can be considered the single most important figure in the Catholic revival in early modern Hungary, a kingdom which comprehended present-day Hungary as well as much of modern Slovakia, Croatia and (after the expulsion of the Turks) some of Romania. From his elevation to the primatial archbishopric of Esztergom in 1616, he played a key role in the creation and funding of Catholic educational establishments, including in 1635 a university at Nagyszombat. Politically his influence was immense. Arguably the key development in seventeenth-century Hungarian Catholicism was the gradual recatholicization of the magnate order and its subsequent cooperation with the Habsburg monarchy in promoting Catholic reform. Pázmány was personally involved in up to thirty conversions of Protestant magnates and his influence was critical within the Hungarian diet or parliament in securing the election of the combative Counter-Reformation zealot Ferdinand II as king of Hungary in 1618. The sometimes volatile cocktail of sturdy Hungarian patriotism and confessional loyalty to the Habsburg dynasty which Pázmány personally epitomized became the dominant pattern of the Magyar aristocracy during the course of the century.[3] Yet it is arguable that Pázmány's chief contribution to Hungarian Catholicism was literary and intellectual rather than in his role as ecclesiastical organizer and politician. A veritable tide of books, both polemical and devotional, flowed from his pen from the 1590s until his death in 1637. Much of this output was in Latin but his most influential works, most notably the *Kalauz*, were undoubtedly those in the Hungarian vernacular.[4] The first version of the *Kalauz* appeared in 1613 and it was subsequently revised and updated on several occasions before the publication of a final edition in the year of his death. In its definitive version, the *Kalauz* was a massive work, running to over

---

[2] For an excellent, though unpublished, examination of his career and of the history and reception of the *Kalauz*, see Peter Schimert, 'Péter Pázmány and the Reconstitution of the Catholic Aristocracy in Habsburg Hungary, 1600–1650' (unpublished Ph.D. thesis, University of North Carolina, Chapel Hill, NC, 1989).

[3] The best English-language analysis of the Habsburg system in Hungary, including some pertinent observations on Pázmány's role, remains R. J. W. Evans, *The Making of the Habsburg Monarchy 1550–1700: An Interpretation* (Oxford, 1979), 235–74.

[4] Miklós Őry and Ferenc Szabó, 'Pázmány Péter (1570–1637)', in *Pázmány Péter Válogatás Műveiből*, eds Miklós Őry, Ferenc Szabó, Péter Vass, 3 vols (Budapest, 1983), 1: 11–84.

a thousand pages of often highly polemical argumentation, aimed at proving the divinely instituted status of the Catholic Church and the impious and heretical nature of other religious doctrines, particularly Lutheranism and Calvinism. It had the effect of shifting the centre of gravity of religious debate in Hungary.[5]

At the beginning of the work, however, was a short section on how observation of the natural world leads to the cognition of God. This section is deserving of attention for two principal reasons. Firstly, despite his intellectual brilliance, Pázmány did not claim any particular originality for his work. His preoccupation was above all with a forceful statement of Catholic orthodoxy. To that end, he read voraciously and adopted and adapted the arguments of his contemporaries, especially those of Bellarmine, under whom he had studied at Rome, and of his predecessors, with a particular emphasis on patristic sources.[6] His concern with representing the orthodoxy of Catholicism was heightened by his position as chief Hungarian ecclesiastical representative in the multi-national domains of the Habsburg dynasty. His great synthesizing abilities, therefore, have the effect of introducing a certain typicality of contemporary Catholic thought into his work.

Secondly, Pázmány was no ivory-tower intellectual. He engaged in constant longrunning literary battles with a number of adversaries but, unlike many other contemporary Catholic polemicists domiciled in securely Catholic jurisdictions, he also interacted in an everyday fashion with Protestants. Particularly in the *Kalauz*, his arguments were intended to convince rather than merely to score intellectual points and his career indicates a marked degree of success in converting individuals to the Catholic faith. The ideas which he expressed in the *Kalauz*, therefore, can justifiably be seen as having been grounded in, and to a considerable extent validated

---

5 Őry and Szabó, 'Pázmány Péter', 39–40, 57.

6 From Bellarmine, Pázmány naturally draws mostly on *Disputationes de controversiis Christianae fidei adversus huius temporis haereticos*, 3 vols (Ingolstadt, 1586). Thomas Stapleton was also a very important source: it is not clear if Pázmány possessed Stapleton, *Opera Omnia*, 4 vols (Paris, 1620), but he refers frequently to Stapleton's *Principiorum fidei doctrinalium relectio scholastica et compendiaria, per controversias, quaestiones et articulos tradita. Accessit per modum appendicis triplicatio inchoata adversus Gulielmum Whitakerum, anglo-calvinistam, pro authoritate Ecclesiae …* (Antwerp, 1592). Another important authority was Martin(us) Becanus, *Quaestiones miscellaneae de fide haereticis servanda, contra Batavum Calvinistam* (Mainz, 1609); I have only seen the version of that text in Becanus, *Opusculorum theologicorum tomi quattuor* (Mainz, 1610).

as convincing by, his own pastoral experience. It is this combination of typicality and belief in the efficacy of his arguments which lends a notable interest to the points which Pázmány elected to stress in his treatment of various issues.

★　★　★

Pázmány's opening statement on the subject of the knowledge of God was a forceful and conscious restatement of Lactantius's argument that, although wisdom (*sapientia*) and religion were inseparable, wisdom (which led to the knowledge of God) preceded religion (defined as worship of God).[7] Having asserted the great importance of correct belief, he benignly observed that the easy and harmonious witness of both faith and intelligence to the truth of Christianity would act as a source of comfort to the faithful. Not merely from Scripture but from the wise and ordered structure of creation, from its power, beauty and usefulness, a clear knowledge of God's lordship and careful direction of the world was apparent.[8] The contrast here with Calvin is striking. Certainly, Calvin equally argued that God 'revealed himself and daily discloses himself in the whole workmanship of the universe' and that the 'marks of his glory' were 'so clear and prominent that even unlettered and stupid folk cannot plead the excuse of ignorance'.[9] But, for Calvin, God's manifestation in nature was ultimately in vain. Where Pázmány confidently referred to Romans 1: 20 ('Invisibilia enim ipsius, à creatura mundi, per ea quae facta sunt, intellecta, conspiciuntur: sempiterna quoque eius virtus & divinitas[10]) as clear proof of his contention,[11] Calvin instead argued that this passage did not indicate a manifestation which men's intelligence could discern but rather one which rendered men's inability to see it inexcusable. He stressed a different scriptural text, Hebrews 11: 3 ('Through faith

---

[7] Péter Pázmány, *Hodoegus. Igazságra vezérlő Kalauz* (Nagyszombat, 1637), 1; cf. Lactantius, *Divinarum Institutionum* 4.4.

[8] Pázmány, *Kalauz*, 2.

[9] Calvin, *Institutes*, 1.5.1, ed. John T. McNeill, trans. Ford Lewis Battles, LCC 20–21, 2 vols (London, 1960), 1: 52.

[10] *Biblia Sacra Vulgatae Editionis Sixti V & Clementis VIII Pont. Max. auctoritate Recognita Editio Novo Notis Chronologicis et Historicis Illustrata* (Paris, 1666). We may translate this as: 'For the invisible things of him from the creation of the world are clearly seen, being understood by the things that are made: his eternal power also and divinity'.

[11] Pázmány, *Kalauz*, 2.

we understand that the world was ordeined by the worde of God, so that the thinges which we se, are not made of thinges which dyd appeare')[12] to argue that humanity lacked the eyes to detect God's divinity in nature, unless already illumined by the inner revelation of God through faith.[13] In a striking metaphor, Calvin argued that faith acted as the spectacles which allowed the previously blurred apprehension of God in nature to be brought into focus: without the gift of Scripture this was impossible.[14]

Such qualification is absent in Pázmány. The cardinal would certainly have accepted the hierarchical supremacy of the scriptural witness but his text dwells instead on the harmony between worldly intelligence and biblical knowledge, a position intellectually consistent with other Catholic theological rejections of *sola scriptura*. In a cognate fashion to the manner in which the traditions of the Church illuminated the meaning of the Gospel, so nature harmoniously supported faith in its testimony. In the second part of the first book of the *Kalauz* he expanded on how the beautiful creations of the world allowed God's power and wisdom to become apparent. Elaborating from Isaiah 40: 12 (who hath poised with three fingers the bulk of the earth?')[15] he declared that in God's direction of the world three of his wondrous characteristics were made manifest, namely his benevolence; the careful wisdom through which he found ways to bring his goodwill to fruition; and his almighty power by which he ordained whatever was necessary for the useful functioning of the world.[16]

In addition, he identified another triad of insights which intelligent contemplation of the order of creation could confer on the observer. The first was a slightly repetitive expansion on his previous thoughts concerning the proof of the existence of God. He commenced with Gellius's anecdote of how Pythagoras reconstructed Hercules's height from his footprint[17] before meditating

---

[12] *The New Testament of our Lord Jesus Christ Conferred Diligently with the Greek and Best Approved Translations – A Facsimile reprint of the Celebrated Genevan Testament (Geneva, 1558)* (London, 1842).

[13] Calvin, *Institutes*, 1.6.1 (ed. McNeill, trans. Battles, 1: 69).

[14] Ibid.

[15] 'Quis appendit tribus digitis molem terrae': *Biblia Sacra Vulgatae*.

[16] Pázmány, *Kalauz*, 9.

[17] Gellius, *Noctes Atticae* 1.1.

on Wisdom 13: 3 to conclude that, in a similar fashion, from the beautiful and orderly condition of the world humanity could deduce the almighty power and wise governance of God. Wisdom and the Psalms (especially Psalm 99: 3) were significant sources of inspiration for Pázmány's arguments in this section, but his greatest intellectual debt was clearly to the *Homilies on the Hexaemeron* of St Basil. These he quoted approvingly and at length, drawing on the first homily to emphasize that creation was a book which taught knowledge of God: by its beauty demonstrating the greater beauty of its Creator, by its vastness his infinitude. Thus the natural order was both a mirror of his power, wisdom and benevolence, and a flight of stairs which led to cognition of God.[18]

St Basil's sixth homily[19] was also a critical source for the second insight, namely that contemplation of the physical universe inspired love of God, because creation was for the use of man. The argument is unabashedly human-centred. The grass on the hills exists not for itself, nor for God, nor for the angels, but for the service of mankind, by nourishing the animals which provide meat, leather and labour. But contemplation of this Providence led further, for the grass could not flourish without rain, and rain without the sea and the rivers providing clouds, which could not exist without the sun. Thus the simplest human requirement depended on the generous and providential arrangement of the entire world.[20] Nor was this the end of benevolence, for creation provided for sensual delights as well as necessities, which led Pázmány to St Augustine's observation concerning what wonders might be expected for the recipients of eternal life, if God was prepared to pour out such bounty even for those who were predestined to damnation.[21] The lesson to be derived from this particular insight was, of course, the need to give thanks. Only an animal or a child could fail to express their gratitude at such munificent bounty.

The third great usefulness of observing the natural world was the (rather trite) lessons to be derived from the example of subordinate orders of creation. Once again St Basil, on this occasion

[18] Pázmány, *Kalauz*, 10; cf. Basil, *Hexaemeron* 1.11.
[19] Basil, *Hexaemeron* 6.1.
[20] Pázmány, *Kalauz*, 11.
[21] Augustine, *De civitate Dei* 22.24.

the fifth homily on the Hexaemeron, was a critical source.[22] The contemplation of a flower should properly concentrate the mind on the transience and fragility of joy and life in this world, for, like flowers, human beings swiftly wither, lose their beauty and become desiccated. Grapes should recall the need for fruitfulness, the protective instincts of animals our own need for spiritual watchfulness, storks the need for filial care of declining parents and – returning to flowers again – just as they unfurled their petals with constant attention to the sun, so should human beings constantly fix their gaze on the centre of their universe, namely God.[23]

In the most interesting section of his discussion, Pázmány next turned to space for further proof that the natural world was the product of an intelligent maker. Not surprisingly, Ecclesiasticus 43 provided him with an initial starting point with its catalogue of the wonders of creation and of the manner in which God exceeded all such natural magnificence. The biblical references were supplemented from the book of Job (12: 7) and the Psalms (99: 3). The human form had been created to view the heavens and not the ground and therefore it behoved mankind to consider the lessons which the firmament could teach. What renders this section particularly striking is the evident influence of Jesuit mathematician and astronomer, Christopher Clavius.[24] Pázmány had almost certainly come into contact with Clavius in Rome and this part of the *Kalauz* suggests an enduring influence from the great Jesuit mathematician on his erstwhile colleague. This first becomes evident when he addresses the miraculous magnitude of the skies. Drawing initially on Seneca and St Basil, he comments on the optical illusion that the sun and the stars are smaller than the world. From Clavius he then draws the exact figure that the 1,022 stars in the eighth heaven which are perceptible to human eyes are each 1,007 times larger than the earth, despite appearing no greater than a pinprick. He then repeats Clavius's calculation that the starry firmament revolving around the earth is 22,612 times greater than the world, which from Ptolemy (whose estimate

---

[22] Basil, *Hexaemeron* 5.2, 6.

[23] Pázmány, *Kalauz*, 12.

[24] James M. Lattis, *Between Copernicus and Galileo: Christopher Clavius and the Collapse of Ptolemaic Cosmology* (Chicago, IL, 1994), 1–29.

is presented with slightly less respect) he places at 22,500 Italian miles (33,148 kilometres). Pausing briefly to endorse the moralistic observations of Pliny and Seneca on the vanity of those who puffed themselves up on the basis of puny mortal possessions in such a vast universe, he then emphasizes how God exceeded in magnitude even these extraordinary dimensions.[25]

Clavius was invoked again to supplement Aristotle concerning the miraculous speed of the firmament in its orbit around the world. Pázmány, evidently convinced of the impressive nature of these figures for his audience, deliberately attempted to present this mathematics in the most accessible form possible. Each part of the firmament revolved in an hour a distance which a man travelling ten Hungarian miles a day (about forty-eight kilometres), would need 2,904 years to accomplish. Or to illustrate the point in another way, in the time that it took to say an Our Father, the firmament travelled as far as a bird would, if in the same time it circled the entire world seven times.[26]

The Clavian figures were not merely presented for the pleasure of exactitude but helped to anchor and illustrate an important argument concerning the providential and miraculous nature of the universe. For why did the firmament revolve with such stupendous speed, unless by God's ordination to divide day from night and, by alterations in the orbit of the sun, to create the order of the seasons? Without such providential care, the planet's life would perish. Drawing once again on St Basil's third homily,[27] Pázmány hammered home this point at length: eternal day would be as harmful to humans and the plants and animals on which they depended as eternal night.

It is revealing that Clavius is the only contemporary author used by Pázmány to supplement the frequent biblical, patristic and classical references in his entire discussion of the natural world.[28] His

---

[25] Pázmány, *Kalauz*, 14; cf. Seneca, *Naturales Quaestiones* 1.3.10; Basil, *Hexaemeron* 6.9. Pázmány was evidently drawing on Christophorus Clavius, *In Sphaeram Ioannis de Sacro Bosco, Commentarius. Nunc quarto ab ipso Authore recognitus & plerisque in locis locupletatus*, 4th edn (Lyons, 1593, repr. 1602). He may, however, have also used other editions: see Lattis, *Between Copernicus and Galileo*, 44.

[26] Pázmány, *Kalauz*, 14–15, citing Clavius, *Sphaeram*, fol. 236.

[27] Basil, *Hexaemeron* 3.7.

[28] There was an abundant literature which could have been looked at if Pázmány had truly been interested; cf. Brian W. Ogilvie, *The Science of Describing: Natural History in Renaissance Europe* (Chicago, IL, 2006).

manner in presenting the figures suggests his personal enthusiasm for the uses to which they could be put. It is hardly surprising that the *Kalauz* makes no mention of Galileo but his deployment of Clavian cosmology does suggest some interesting insights into the Catholic intellectual culture which ultimately proved unreceptive to the Galilean revolution.[29] In his early university career, Pázmány was very much the product of the profoundly influential Jesuit intellectual culture of the 1590s in which Robert Bellarmine was the single most important individual and in which Clavius also figured significantly. This was the intellectual milieu which produced the *Ratio Studiorum* and Clavius played a key role in ensuring that mathematics was to play a key role within future Jesuit curricula.[30] Clavius was personally convinced of the spiritual as well as the practical utility of mathematics.[31] As Pázmány indicates in this section of the *Kalauz*, one of the attractions of Clavius's work was the manner in which it could subtly refresh the providentialist discourse effectively inherited from late Christian antiquity. Particularly seductive was the manner in which Clavius's calculations were not merely the product of common sense or close observation, which could be performed by anyone. Rather, they partook of a difficult knowledge which used the power of the mind to penetrate the secrets of God's universe but, unlike Galileo for instance, produced results exactly in harmony with the received world-view. Through mathematics, human beings could gain an enhanced understanding of the extraordinary power which God had deployed on behalf of his creatures. A subtle contrast with Calvin in the *Institutes* is again apparent here. Calvin certainly accepted that education in the liberal arts enhanced men's appreciation of 'the secrets of divine wisdom',[32] but he made this observation in passing with something approaching apathy.

Pázmány, on the other hand, eagerly incorporated the advanced mathematical geocentricism of the late sixteenth century into his text for providential purposes. On this reading, it might be

[29] In this regard, see also Richard J. Blackwell, *Galileo, Bellarmine and the Bible* (Notre Dame, IN, 1991).

[30] Lattis, *Between Copernicus and Galileo*, 1–29; Dennis C. Smolarski, 'The Jesuit *Ratio Studiorum*, Christopher Clavius, and the Study of Mathematical Sciences in Universities', *Science in Context* 15 (2002), 447–57.

[31] Lattis, *Between Copernicus and Galileo*, 36, 135–36.

[32] Ibid. 53; cf. Calvin, *Institutes*, 1.5.2.

suggested that for Pázmány the chief intellectual difficulty with heliocentricism was not likely to have been its contradiction of the letter of Scripture. The cardinal was perfectly comfortable with the position that certain biblical passages required a metaphorical interpretation, although he castigated a variety of reformers for resorting to such interpretation at the behest of their own fancies. Rather, heliocentricism would have threatened three aspects of the world-view, all emblematic of seventeenth-century Catholic thought in general, demonstrated in his treatment of the natural world.

The first of these was the human-centred nature of the universe which he outlined. It was of course possible to reconcile heliocentricism with the idea that all creation existed for the benefit of humankind. But such a cosmology had far greater potential to render humanity's role incidental rather than central. The grandeur of the universe orbiting the tiny human biosphere, which was at the bottom of the cosmos because of its gross nature,[33] made very satisfyingly manifest both the greatness of God and his providential care for his creatures. The earth orbiting the sun subtly altered this teleological framework, coarsening its explanatory elegance.

The second and third points relate to the intellectual strategies utilised by Catholic polemicists, such as Pázmány, to legitimize their confession in the face of the Protestant challenge. One of the heaviest guns in the Catholic arsenal in this regard concerned issues of continuity. Their unmatchable lineage of a visible church was constantly foregrounded by Catholic apologists, such as Pázmány himself, as a key mark of Roman superiority. The claim to continuity and the validity of tradition as a source of legitimation of doctrine and practice made the Catholic claim to the Fathers of the Church particularly urgent.[34] This could require a deal of mental gymnastics, and the Protestant traditions certainly were not prepared to concede patristic sources, but Catholic investment in their reading of the Fathers was particularly heavy.[35] The assertion,

[33] Lattis, *Between Copernicus and Galileo*, 120.

[34] See Pontien Polman, *L'Élément historique dans la controverse religieuse du XVIe siècle* (Gembloux, 1932).

[35] Jean-Louis Quantin, 'The Fathers in Seventeenth Century Roman Catholic Theology', in Irena Backus, ed., *The Reception of the Church Fathers in the West*, 2 vols (Leiden, 1997), 2: 951–86; G. Thils, *Les notes de l'église dans l'apologetique catholique depuis la Réforme* (Gembloux, 1937).

for instance, of Pázmány's Hungarian contemporary, the Lutheran preacher Johannes Hodik, whose views were alleged to contradict those of St Augustine, that even the bishop of Hippo could be wrong, was not an available option for the cardinal or his Catholic contemporaries.[36] As mentioned earlier, one of the evident reasons for Pázmány's embracing of Clavius's mathematics in his discussion of nature in the *Kalauz* was the ease with which it harmonized with his own presentation of a patristic position, principally conscripted from St Basil.

Third, and most important, is the issue of rationality in Catholic belief. As noted previously, Pázmány firmly asserted the complementarity of intelligent observation of nature and the revealed truth of Scripture in demonstrating both the existence and the almighty and benevolent nature of God. This was very much in harmony with the wider contours of the mental universe which he and his contemporaries inhabited, which placed a great emphasis on the role of reason in confirming the truth of Catholic doctrine.[37] Central to Pázmány's own arguments in the *Kalauz*, for instance, was that only a tyrant God could demand worship from human beings without creating clear and rationally apprehensible signs to denote which was his one true Church. This was not to deny the central mysteries of Christianity, but rational pathways led to the appreciation of those mysteries. This mindset was inherently hospitable to scientific observations which could be used to confirm providentialist convictions but was potentially hostile to ideas which raised any challenge to its formidable consensus.

Pázmány continued his discussion of nature with a brief discussion of the providential organization of the Earth's atmosphere and seas. With the exception of a single reference to St Thomas Aquinas, he invokes no source which would not have been available to late antiquity. Briefly he runs through the wondrous nature of natural phenomena such as wind, rain and snow, the astonishing providential fact that the middle heavens though closer to the sun are colder than the lower, without which rain would be impossible; the fixing of the earth in the sky and the waters of the sea

---

[36] 'Ex diario Johannis Hodik Delineatio Mensalis Colloquii', in László Szelestei, ed., *Naplók és útleírások a 16–18 századból* (Budapest, 1998), 143–69, at 155, 157.

[37] In this regard, see, e.g., G. B. Rinuccini, *Della Dignita et Offitio dei Vescovi*, 2 vols (Rome, 1651).

from the land; the inexhaustible flow of rivers; and the plenitude of sea creatures, including the amazing stingray, whose numbing power he had personally witnessed.

The section concludes with a discussion of human beings and their natural bodies in which Pázmány is once again happy to echo St Basil. The human body teaches three important lessons. Firstly, it was created out of earth and this should serve as a constant reminder of its vileness. Secondly, the physically upright nature of the human form differs from that of animals and this upward directed condition should call to mind the object of human life, which is in heaven and not on earth. Thirdly, because God created humans to be lords of nature, this confers the responsibilities to be higher in morality than animals. The final statement is a suggestive but unamplified reference to Macrobius's *Saturnalia* which refers to the world as God's temple which requires humanity to live in it as priests in a church.

In conclusion, therefore, Pázmány's treatment of nature in the *Kalauz* represents a very forceful, didactic, and, in many ways typical, early modern Catholic statement of a geocentric universe providentially ordered for the benefit of humankind. As such it raises a series of interesting insights and questions concerning the contours of the mental universe of Catholic intellectuals on the eve of the Galilean revolution. The text is also notable in the light of the differences which emerge between Pázmány's and Calvin's treatment of the natural world. The topics covered by the opening sections of the *Kalauz* and the *Institutes* are in many respects star-tlingly similar and there can be no question that the Hungarian cardinal was deeply familiar with Calvin's work. But, although he does not polemically engage with Calvin in this section of the text, very different emphases on a common intellectual inheritance are evident, most importantly concerning the relationship between reason and revelation.

University College Dublin

'GOD HATH PUT SUCH SECRETES IN NATURE': THE REFORMED KIRK, CHURCH-BUILDING AND THE RELIGIOUS LANDSCAPE IN EARLY MODERN SCOTLAND*

by ANDREW SPICER

A LTHOUGH the Reformed tradition advocated the primacy of the Word of God, the writings of Calvin and other theologians also emphasized the importance of the natural world for revealing the glory of God.[1] As early as 1534, Calvin argued that God had

> raised everywhere, in all places and in all things, his ensigns and emblems, under blazons so clear and intelligible that no one can pretend ignorance in not knowing such a sovereign Lord, who has so amply exalted his magnificence; who has in all parts of the world, in heaven and on earth, written and as it were engraved the glory of his power, goodness, wisdom and eternity ...[2]

The revelation of God's glory through the natural world recurs in Calvin's sermons and biblical commentaries; in his exegesis of Romans 1: 20, for example, he argued: 'God is invisible in Himself, but since His majesty shines forth in all His works and in all His creatures, men ought to have acknowledged Him in these, for

---

* Jean Calvin, *Sermons of Maister Iohn Caluin, vpon the booke of Iob*, trans. Arthur Golding (London, 1580), 476. I am grateful to the Marquess of Linlithgow and the archivist of Hopetoun House, Patrick Cadell, for permission to consult and quote from the Hopetoun House Archives, South Queensferry [hereafter HHA]. This paper is a fruit of an Arts and Humanities Research Council Research Project, 'The Early Modern Parish Church and the Religious Landscape', at Oxford Brookes University.

[1] For Calvin's thought on the natural world, see R. Stauffer, *Dieu, la création et la Providence dans la prédication de Calvin* (Berne, 1978); Susan E. Schreiner, *The Theater of His Glory: Nature and the Natural Order in the Thought of John Calvin* (Grand Rapids, MI, 1991).

[2] Jean Calvin, *Calvin: Commentaries and Letters*, ed. J. Haroutunian, LCC 23 (Philadelphia, PA, 1958), 59–60 (preface to Olivétan's New Testament, 1534).

they clearly demonstrate their Creator'.[3] Even the heavens stood 'as witnesses and preachers of the glory of God'. The Almighty was therefore acknowledged as the 'great Author of Nature', 'Artificer' and 'the supreme Architect, who has erected the beauteous fabric of the universe'.[4] A synthesis of Calvin's perception of the natural world, the way in which God is manifested, and its implications appeared in the 1559 edition of the *Institutes of the Christian Religion*, which included a chapter entitled 'The Knowledge of God shines Forth in the Fashioning of the Universe and the Continuing Government of it'.[5]

Despite the importance of the natural world, it was surpassed by the power of the Word of God which remained steadfast and transcended the vicissitudes and vulnerability of the earth.[6] Furthermore, while God might call mankind to himself through the contemplation of heaven and earth, or by his 'awesome voice, which strikes the earth in thunder, winds, rains, whirlwinds and tempests, causes mountains to tremble, shatters the cedars', the unbelievers still remain in ignorance and deaf to his calls. It is only through being 'aided and assisted by his Sacred Word' that a knowledge of God could be attained: 'Scripture can communicate to us what the revelation in the creation can not'.[7] The higher importance accorded to the Word of God can also be seen in the attacks that Calvin launched upon some radical sects which he regarded as adopting a pantheistic perception of the natural world.[8]

Although the revelation of God's glory provided by the natural world was secondary to the Word of God, according to Calvin, just as man had dominion over the beasts of the earth, its natural resources were also placed at the disposal of mankind. He believed

---

[3] Jean Calvin, *The Epistles of Paul to the Romans and Thessalonians*, trans. R. Mackenzie (Edinburgh, 1960, repr. Grand Rapids, MI, 1973), 31.

[4] Jean Calvin, *Commentaries on the First Book of Moses, called Genesis*, trans. John King, 2 vols (Edinburgh, 1847–50), 1: 104–05 (on Gen. 2: 2); idem, *Commentary on the Book of Psalms*, trans. James Anderson et al., 5 vols (Edinburgh, 1845–49), 1: 267, 309, 480 (on Pss 18: 7; 19: 1; 29: 5–8 respectively).

[5] Jean Calvin, *Institutes of the Christian Religion*, ed. J. T. McNeill, trans. F. L. Battles, 2 vols, LCC 20–21 (Philadelphia, PA, 1960), 1: 51–69.

[6] Calvin, *Psalms*, 4: 468–69 (on Ps. 119: 89–90).

[7] Calvin, *Institutes*, 1.6.4 (ed. McNeill, trans. Battles, 1: 73–74).

[8] Schreiner, *Theater*, 17–18. See Jean Calvin, *Treatises against the Anabaptists and against the Libertines*, trans. and ed. B. W. Farley (Grand Rapids, MI, 1982), 230–32 (*Against the Fantastic and Furious Sect of the Libertines who are called Spirituals*).

that 'the earth is put here for its inhabitants', it could be plundered for the needs of man but this did require that 'every one regard himself as the steward of God in all things that he possesses'.[9] The exploitation of the earth by mining is something on which Calvin had little to say, but Theodore de Bèze suggested that the ingenuity of men had exceeded their station and threatened creation itself. In his commentary on the Book of Job he wrote:

> There lie hid in the bottome of the earth mines of siluer and golde out of which they are digged, and afterward purified and made perfite. Men haue deuised a way to draw iron out of the dust, and melt brasse out of the stone quarries …
>
> And surely I acknowledge, that labour & industrie of men is so great and wonderfull in this behalfe, that they do extreme violence to nature her selfe. For they have gone beyond the bounds & limits which God hath set. I meane beyond those hidden & secret caues in the earth, and being nothing at al dismaied in respect of that great depth, they neuer leave of searching, til such time as they find those minerall stones, which lie hidden in the lowest & farthest parts of the earth, & as it were in the verie bosome of death.[10]

This interpretation was at odds with that of other Reformed divines such as the Edinburgh minister George Hutcheson, whose approach in his interpretation of the same chapter was closer to that of Calvin, regarding the discovery of metals as providing further evidence of the revelation of God in nature while arguing that these minerals had been placed in the earth by God for the needs of mankind.[11]

Beyond the theological discussions, the exploitation of natural resources and expansion of the early modern industrial landscape provided new opportunities for extending the religious landscape. The attempts to establish a church at Leadhills in what is now South Lanarkshire provide a useful case study through which to examine Reformed attitudes towards the natural world. At Leadhills the exploitation of natural resources through mining led to efforts

---

[9] Calvin, *First Book of Moses*, 1: 125, 253 (on Gen. 2: 15; 6: 11).
[10] Calvin, *Iob*, 475–77 (Job 28: 1–9); Théodore de Bèze, *Iob expounded by Theodore Beza* (London, 1589), ch. 28.
[11] George Hutcheson, *An exposition of the book of Job* (Edinburgh, 1669), 362.

to establish the preaching of the Word of God. While the Kirk supported these endeavours, its stance towards the natural world, however, was more at odds with the teachings of the Genevan Reformer. This essay will therefore consider firstly the attempts to establish a church at Leadhills, but will then use the issues raised by this mining community to assess the attitudes of the Kirk towards the natural world.

The development of lead and silver mining in the Lowther Hills, on the borders of South Lanarkshire and Dumfriesshire, by Sir Bevis Bulmer and Thomas Foulis began in the late sixteenth century with royal encouragement and support.[12] It was Foulis who established a highly profitable lead mining concern at Leadhills which came into the possession of Sir James Hope, through inheritance, after his marriage to Anna Foulis. Hope had a keen commercial and personal interest in mining, metals and technology which not only provided the basis of his fortune but also led to his preferment; he was appointed Master of the Mint in 1641 and played a prominent role in the radical politics of mid-seventeenth century Scotland.[13] Besides his business interests, Hope's concern for the spiritual provision for his workers at Leadhills prompted him to petition the Scottish Parliament for a minister and to erect a parish church in this isolated mining community. In 1649 Parliament agreed to the request and the following year Hope asked the Presbytery of Lanark that one John Browne 'might be authorized to expone the Scripture, pray and use and exercise such other dueties in his house, to his familie and workfolkes'.[14] The General

---

[12] *ODNB*, s.n. 'Bulmer, Sir Bevis'; 'Foulis, Thomas'; R. W. Cochran-Patrick, ed., *Early Records Relating to Mining in Scotland* (Edinburgh, 1878); T. C. Smout, 'The Lead Mines at Wanlockhead', *Transactions of the Dumfriesshire and Galloway Natural History and Antiquarian Society* 39 (1960–61), 144–58.

[13] 'The Diary of Sir James Hope, 1646–1654', ed. J. Balfour Paul, *Miscellany of the Scottish History Society III*, SHS 2nd ser. 19 (1919), 97–168; 'The Diary of Sir James Hope, 1646', ed. P. Marshall, *Miscellany of the Scottish History Society IX*, SHS 3rd ser. 50 (1958), 127–97; A. H. Williamson, 'Union with England Traditional, Union with England Radical: Sir James Hope and the Mid-Seventeenth-Century British State', *EHR* 110 (1995), 303–22; *ODNB*, s.n. 'Hope, Sir James, of Hopetoun'.

[14] Edinburgh, NAS, CH2/234/1, Minutes of the Presbytery of Lanark, 1623-1657, 437, 439; *The Acts of the Parliament of Scotland, 1124–1707*, ed. T. Thomson and C. Innes, 12 vols (London, 1814–75) [hereafter *APS*], 6/2: 292–94; *The Records of the Commissions of the General Assemblies of the Church of Scotland*, ed. A. F. Mitchell and J. Christie, SHS 25 (1896), 222–25. On John Browne, see Hew Scott, *Fasti Ecclesiæ Scoticanæ*, 7 vols (Edinburgh, 1915–28), 2: 239.

Assembly 'thankfully acknowledged the pious undertaking of the petitioner, praying the Lorde to bless the same', while the minister Robert Birnie, on behalf of the presbytery, praised his 'zeall to the honour of God and cair for the well [being] of the soulls of your poore people for whom ye ar contented to be at so much charges' and prayed that 'ye fall not from your pious purpose of erecting a ministrie their, a place needfull as I know none moir'.[15]

In spite of the enthusiastic response from the Kirk, agreement on provision for the ministry at Leadhills proved to be a more protracted process. Hope intended that the church should be financed from the profits of lead extraction, the exploitation of the earth's natural resources thereby supporting the preaching the Word of God. He offered to provide an endowment of ten thousand marks in return for the waiving of his feu duties from the extraction and production of lead on his estates. This had been outlined in the initial recommendation from Parliament, but it took almost a decade of financial wrangling and prolonged petitioning before the matter was resolved. The situation was no doubt complicated by the English military occupation of Scotland, which meant that such matters were referred to the government in London, and Sir James Hope had himself during that time become 'disengaged from public employment'.[16] Nonetheless during this period Hope himself paid for a minister to serve the community, claiming to have done so for nine years, although by October 1656 the presbytery was looking for a new minister.[17] On 29 June 1658, Oliver Cromwell ordered:

> And as to his ffew dutye which he desires to be applyed towards the maintenance of a Preacher at the said Mines: We are willing the same be allowed as to the time past, and for the future continued to such as you shall approve of to preach at the said Mynes ...[18]

[15] HHA, Bundle 652, Robert Birnie to Sir James Hope, 6 May 1650; *Records of the Commissions of the General Assemblies*, 225.

[16] HHA, Bundle 648, Sir James Hope to Oliver Cromwell, January 1656; *Calendar of State Papers, Domestic Series, 1649–1660*, ed. M. A. E. Green, 13 vols (London, 1875–86), 10: 242; 12: 76; Williamson, 'Union with England', 320–21.

[17] HHA, Bundle 648, Sir James Hope to Col. Lambert, 3 February 1657; Bundle 652, Petition to the Council in Scotland, 24 November 1658; NAS, CH2/234/1, 529, 553.

[18] HHA, Bundle 648, Oliver Cromwell to the Council in Scotland, 29 June 1658.

Despite agreement being reached on financing preaching from lead production, the scheme for a church at Leadhills ultimately faltered, partly no doubt due to the death of Sir James Hope in November 1661 but also for religious reasons. When the scheme was revived in 1690 in the name of his grandson Charles Hope, the earlier failure to establish a church was regarded as being due to 'the inquitie of the tymes and the great troubles and revolutiones that thereafter followed' the initial petition.[19]

While the exploitation of mineral reserves at Leadhills and the use of the profits for the ministry of the Word would seem to accord with Calvin's theology, the attitude of the Kirk towards the natural world was contradictory. Theologically, the ministers of the Kirk accepted the understanding of the natural world which had been outlined by Calvin and other Reformed writers. John Knox had quoted extensively from Calvin's treatise against the Libertines in his *An answer to a great nomber of blasphemous cauillations written by an Anabaptist and aduersarie to God's eternal predestination*, citing passages emphasizing the role of God as not only the Creator but also as governing and maintaining his will through his creatures.[20] The Genevan reformer's commentaries were respected by ministers and theologians studying the Scriptures; there were relatively few Scottish exegetes, but the works that were produced by scholars such as David Dickson adopted a Calvinist perspective.[21] This understanding of the natural world as revealing the glory of God and his continued government of the world is evident in Dickson's commentaries on the Psalms and the New Testament.[22]

In spite of the broad acknowledgement of the theological precepts relating to the revelation of God through the natural world, at a practical level the delivery of the Word of God could be impeded by features in the landscape and past associations which meant that some aspects of the natural world were regarded with

[19] NAS, GD26/10/40, Petition to General Assembly by Lady Margaret Hope in name of Charles Hope of Hoptoune [Hopetoun], her son, for erecting a church for the convenience of his workers at the mines of Leadhill.

[20] *The Works of John Knox*, ed. D. Laing, 6 vols, Bannatyne Society (1846–64), 5: 172–78.

[21] G. D. Henderson, 'The Bible in Seventeenth-Century Scotland', in idem, *Religious Life in Seventeenth-Century Scotland* (Cambridge, 1937), 22–25.

[22] e.g. David Dickson, *A brief explication of the first fifty Psalms* (London, 1655), 39, 101, 103, 164, 219, 302; idem, *An exposition of all St. Pauls epistles* (London, 1659), 3, 40, 262.

suspicion by the Reformed Kirk. Into the seventeenth century, it struggled to suppress and eradicate what it regarded as superstitious and idolatrous activities amongst its congregations. A number of these religious practices focused on landscape features such as caves, springs, trees and wells which in the past had been regarded as sacred sites. The links between these sacred sites and local saints or miraculous cures heightened the opposition of the Kirk to natural features which it associated with the pre-Reformation Catholic Church. Far from providing evidence of God's glory, they were regarded as hindering the suppression of papistry and idolatry.[23] The Presbytery of Stirling, for example, attempted to halt pilgrimages to Christ's well where people went in search of miraculous cures for the sick, left votive offerings and 'usis gret idolatrie or superstitioun thairat expres againis Godis law'.[24] Parliament passed a statute in 1581 imposing fines for those 'passing in pilgrimage to chappells, wells and croces'.[25] Despite this legislation, pilgrimages to these wells persisted into the seventeenth century and the General Assembly was forced to take further steps in 1649; three years later the Synod of Aberdeen requested that special notice should be taken of 'all superstitious persones frequenting that well [at Seggett], and upon the notorietie theroff to censure them'.[26] Although the Kirk continued to regard these natural springs with suspicion, there was an attempt made by some writers to explain their existence, mineral content and healing properties in both scriptural and scientific terms; a pamphlet on Saint Catherine's well at Liberton accused the English invading forces under Cromwell of 'defacing such rare and antient monuments of *Natures* hand-

---

[23] *Acts and Proceedings of the General Assemblies of the Kirk of Scotland*, ed. T. Thomson, Bannatyne Club 81 (1839–45), 1120.

[24] *Stirling Presbytery Records, 1581–1587*, ed. J. Kirk, SHS 4th ser. 17 (1981), xxxiv–xxxv, 115–16, 120, 128, 130, 132–37, 139–40, 144, 147, 149–51, 154–55, 161. See also *Acts and Proceedings*, ed. Thomson, 462, 721, 1120; *Visitation of the Diocese of Dunblane and Other Churches, 1586–1589*, ed. J. Kirk, Scottish Record Society ns 11 (1984), 3, 12, 41–42; *The Records of Elgin, 1234–1800*, ed. W. Cramond, 2 vols, New Spalding Society 27 (1903), 35 (1908), 2: 97, 202; *Selections from the Records of the Kirk Session, Presbytery and Synod of Aberdeen*, ed. J. Stuart, Spalding Club 15 (1846), 110–11; M. Todd, *The Culture of Protestantism in Early Modern Scotland* (London, 2002), 204–9, 219–20.

[25] *APS*, ed. Thomson and Innes, 3: 212–13.

[26] Todd, *Culture of Protestantism*, 220; *Selections from the Synod of Aberdeen*, ed. Stuart, 221. On pilgrimages to wells, see also, in this volume, Raymond Gillespie, 'God, Saints and the Natural World in Early Modern Ireland', 217–36.

work, but also the *Synagogues* of the God of *Nature*.[27] Springs
were not, however, the only natural features in the landscape
which attracted the attention of the kirk sessions. A cave known
as Dragon's Hole in Kinnoull Hill, for example, caused concern for
the Perth authorities because of possible promiscuity among the
young men and women that gathered there in the early 1580s.[28]
The natural world therefore harboured a number of sacred sites
or landscape features which were regarded by the ecclesiastical
authorities as preserving superstitious practices or encouraging
irreligious behaviour, so that rather than aiding in the revelation
of his glory, it hindered the furtherance of the Word of God.

It was not only the religious associations of natural features in
the landscape that posed problems for the furtherance of God's
Word. At the Reformation, the Scottish Kirk inherited a religious
landscape which had been shaped by the practices and organization of its Catholic predecessor. While it sought to suppress
some religious buildings and sacred sites, the parochial system
provided the vehicle for spreading the Word of God but this was
at times inhibited by features in the landscape and aspects of the
natural world. There were some 1,100 parishes spread across the
country, some encompassing vast areas of remote wilderness and
difficult terrain. While the evolution of the parochial structure in
southern Scotland reflected the Anglo-Norman influences that
had led to the establishment of parishes in England with the
link between the parish and the manor, in parts of the north it
was more closely linked with the Celtic saints. Their association
with monastic and missionary settlements meant that the parishes
established covered wide areas. Furthermore the Celtic saints had
tended to favour remote locations for their religious buildings and
churches, reflecting their eremitic and contemplative lifestyle, such
as the inlets of the Western Isles or other islands.[29] This parochial

---

[27] Gilbert Skeyne, *Ane breif descriptioun of the qualiteis and effectis of the well of the
woman hil besyde Abirdene* (Edinburgh, 1580); Matthew Mackaile, *Moffet-well, or, A topo-
graphico-spagyricall description of the minerall wells* (Edinburgh, 1664), 118. The latter tract
lamented Hope's death for halting further investigation into mineral springs: ibid. 136.

[28] Todd, *Culture of Protestantism*, 203–4.

[29] I. B. Cowan, 'The Development of the Parochial System in Medieval Scotland',
ScHR 40 (1961), 43–55, at 50–51; A. MacQuarrie, 'Early Christian Religious Houses in
Scotland: Foundation and Function', in J. Blair and R. Sharpe, eds, *Pastoral Care Before
the Parish* (Leicester, 1992), 110–33, at 110, 112–13, 117–18, 129–33.

landscape posed real problems for the Reformed Kirk, especially
in view of the expectation that congregations should gather in
church every Sunday to hear the Word of God.[30]

The accessibility of these churches was often hampered by the
weather or landscape features, particularly rivers which could flood
or become impassable. (Calvin argued that God prevented the
natural tendency of waters to cover the world, but drew attention
to recent flooding.)[31] During the seventeenth century, the Kirk
attempted to redraw the parochial landscape in order to overcome the problems posed by these natural obstacles. Permission
was given for the erection of a new kirk at Greenock in 1592
because the parishioners 'having ane greit river to pas over to the
samyn May haif ease in winter seasoun and better commoditie
to convene to goddis seruice on the sabboth day'. At Gullane the
church was 'incommodiouslie situate besyde the seasand', so that
the churchyard was 'continewallie overblawin with sand' thereby
'staying the saidis parochiners in tyme of storme and vnseason-
able weather to convene at the said kirk'. The Commission for
the Plantation of Kirks and Valuation of Teinds, first set up in 1617
but reconstituted regularly during the seventeenth century, sought
to deal with not only the financial problems of the Church but
also the problem of accessibility to the parish church where 'the
interiectioun of wateris betuix thair roumes and ye kirkis whiche
often tymes and in speciall in winter ar not passable'.[32]

The problems caused by weather and geography likewise affected
the establishment of Reformed worship at Leadhills. A sense of the
isolation of these hills was provided by a visitor to the region in
1658, who described the area around Sanquhar as 'besieged with
Mountains that are rich in Lead-Mines. The Planets I fancy them
very benevolent to influence this swompy Rocky Earth, and shine
Mettallick Blessings into them, to commode the indigent and

[30] J. Dawson, 'The Origin of the "Road to the Isles": Trade, Communications and
Campbell Power in Early Modern Scotland', in R. Mason and N. MacDougall, eds,
People and Power in Scotland (Edinburgh, 1992), 74–103, at 84–86; eadem, 'Calvinism and
the Gaidhealtachd in Scotland', in A. Pettegree, A. Duke and G. Lewis, eds, *Calvinism
in Europe, 1540–1620* (Cambridge, 1994), 231–53, at 243–45.
[31] Calvin, *Psalms*, 4: 152 (on Ps. 104: 9).
[32] *APS*, ed. Thomson and Innes, 3: 550, 4: 490, 605.

almost uncultivated Native'.[33] Sir James Hope had petitioned the Scottish Parliament because his lead works employed

> a great number of workmen both natives and strangers who with wives and children makes up a considerable number amongst whom (to the said supplicant his no small greiff) there is nothing but impiety and want of the knowledge of god occasioned through the great distance of the said works from the nearest church thereabout whereunto they cannot so conveniently repair because of the great stormes that are frequent in those mountainous places ...

Parliament responded by ordering that 'ane paroshe kirk maybe established and erected at the said works in the most convenient place'.[34] A sense of the difficulties posed by the remote location can be seen in the examination of several witnesses about the need for a church at Leadhills. Being asked 'How farre the said workes ar distant from the nearest parish churche', one resident answered: 'the workes will be foure miles from the churche in the summer tyme and five in winter'.[35] The community was therefore 'many myles distant from all occasions of hearing the word', an opinion endorsed by the presbytery.[36] The difficult terrain and winter weather prevented the faithful of Leadhills from reaching the nearest parish church at Crawford, thereby inhibiting the furtherance of the Word of God, a problem which could only be resolved by establishing a new parish.

The Kirk was also at odds with Reformed teaching on the natural world when it came to the use of particular buildings or sites as the only designated and appropriate locations for worship. Calvin's understanding of the natural world had led him to reject the claims of those who sought to restrict the revelation of God's glory to specific places or buildings. In particular he rejected the heightened importance given to the Temple of Jerusalem, speaking of

---

[33] Richard Franck, *Northern Memoirs, Calculated for the Meridian of Scotland* (London, 1694), 81.

[34] *APS*, ed. Thomson and Innes, 6/2: 292–94.

[35] HHA, Bundle 652, Interrogators ... to the erecting of a Churche at the Mines, 1652.

[36] HHA, Bundle 648, Petition from Sir James Hope, 22 September 1655; NAS, CH2/234/1, 529.

the foolish boasting of the Jews, who thought that the glory of God was nowhere to be seen but among themselves, and wished to have it shut up within their own temple. But Isaiah shows that it is so far from being confined to so narrow limits, that it fills the whole earth …[37]

Similarly, in expounding the expression 'the gate of heaven', Calvin attacked the role ascribed to Catholic places of worship:

The Papists, however, foolishly misapply this passage to their temples, as if God dwelt in filthy places. But if we concede, that the places which they designate by this title, are not polluted with impious superstitions, yet this honour belongs to no peculiar place, since Christ has filled the whole world with the presence of his Deity …[38]

The manifestation of God's glory was therefore present throughout the earth and could not be constrained within the limits of a building. Furthermore, when it came to worship, while Calvin recognized the convenience of a specific building in which to gather, he rejected that the notion that any particular building had any greater sanctity than any other place.[39] In the preface to the *Institutes*, he quoted from Hilary of Poitiers: 'It is wrong that a love of walls has seized you; wrong that you venerate the church of God in roofs and buildings … To my mind, mountains, woods, lakes, prisons, and chasms are safer'.[40]

For the Kirk, the natural world did not provide suitable places for worship; in fact, during the seventeenth century, worship outdoors was more often associated with religious nonconformity. During the 1620s and 1630s, religious dissent prompted by the Five Articles of Perth and the reintroduction of kneeling to receive communion had resulted in the spread of private prayer meetings across the south-west of Scotland and large outdoor gatherings to hear sermons delivered by evangelical preachers. These ministers, in advancing their opposition to the Crown's religious policies, were keen to stress that worship and the administration of the sacra-

---

[37] Jean Calvin, *Commentary on the Book of the Prophet Isaiah*, trans. William Pringle, 4 vols (Edinburgh, 1850–53), 1: 205–06 (on Isa. 6: 3).

[38] Calvin, *First Book of Moses*, 2: 118 (on Gen. 28: 17).

[39] Calvin, *Institutes*, 3.20.30 (ed. McNeill, trans. Battles, 2: 893).

[40] Ibid., Prefatory Address (ed. McNeill, trans. Battles, 1: 25).

ments need not be confined to particular places.[41] To an extent the comments of David Calderwood echoed those of Calvin quoted earlier: 'The Sacraments are not tyed to the materiall Kirks made of dead stones but the Kirk made of lively stones [i.e. the faithful]. If therefore the congregation bee in a woode, a house or a Cave, the Sacraments may bee ministred in a house, a woode or a cave'.[42] Although gathering in conventicles did not mean the complete abandonment of the parish church, it nonetheless represented a radical departure from the notion of the church as the single place of worship, and for the authorities the unacceptability of gathering in the natural landscape.[43]

The conventicles revived after the restoration of the monarchy and the re-establishment of the episcopate in the 1660s, as ministers who opposed the new order were ejected from their churches and gathered with their congregations in private houses or barns, or in the open air in fields and sometimes churchyards.[44] Resistance was strongest in the south-west of Scotland but while the movement gradually declined through a combination of government suppression and accommodations, the area around Sanquhar continued into the 1680s as a bastion of dissent and radicalism. Men from Crawfordmoor had been amongst those who had intimidated and expelled a minister and his family at Glenholme in Tweeddale; a group of prisoners captured at a conventicle were set upon and released while being taken under military escort from Dumfries to

---

[41] L. E. Schmidt, *Holy Fairs: Scottish Communions and American Revivals in the Early Modern Period*, (Princeton, NJ, 1989), 22–29; D. Stevenson, 'Conventicles in the Kirk, 1619–37: The Emergence of a Radical Party', *RSCHS* 18 (1972), 99–114; A. Spicer, '"What kinde of house a kirk is": Conventicles, Consecrations and the Concept of Sacred Space in Post-Reformation Scotland', in W. Coster and A. Spicer, eds, *Sacred Space in Early Modern Europe* (Cambridge, 2005), 81–103, at 95–98.

[42] [David Calderwood], *Perth assembly Containing 1 The proceedings thereof. 2 The proofe of the nullitie thereof. 2 [sic] Reasons presented thereto against the receiving the fiue new articles imposed. 4 The oppositenesse of it to the proceedings and oath of the whole state of the land. An. 1581. 5 Proofes of the unlawfulnesse of the said fiue articles, viz. 1. Kneeling in the act of receiving the Lords Supper. 2. Holy daies. 3. Bishopping. 4. Private baptisme. 5. Private Communion* (Leiden, 1619), 97.

[43] D. Stevenson, 'The Radical Party in the Kirk, 1637–45', *JEH* 25 (1974), 135–65, at 136–37.

[44] I. B. Cowan, *The Scottish Covenanters, 1660–1688* (London, 1976), 50–63; Schmidt, *Holy Fairs*, 32–41; E. Hannan Hyman, 'A Church Militant: Scotland, 1661–1690', *Sixteenth Century Journal* 26 (1995), 49–74.

Edinburgh at the Enterkin Pass in 1684.[45] Among those executed in the ensuing government retribution was Andrew Clark from Leadhills.[46]

One commentator later reflected on the resistance to episcopacy and the radicalism preached at the open-air conventicles around Leadhills:

> so little do they regard the Ordination and Ministerial Authority of Episcopal men, that it has been declared frequently in their Sermons, that all the time of Episcopacy, people have been without a Ministry, and without Sacraments. Some two or three years ago, there was one who preached up this Doctrine so warmly, in and about the Lead-Mines of Hopton, that, as was reported, he prevail'd with many to suffer themselves to be Re-baptized, and Re-married, and had twelve pence from each of them for so doing.[47]

One of the ministers particularly active in the area was James Renwick, who was reported in 1683 as having preached and baptized about twenty children. In his *Informatory Vindication*, written at Leadhills in 1687, Renwick praised 'the faithful Ministers of Christ in preaching the Gospel in the Fields' contrasting them with those who succumbed to the authorities.[48] He went further in a sermon justifying open-air preaching on theological grounds, albeit in defiance of government policy, in a manner akin to Calvin's writings: 'it is a Practical Asserting of this principle,

---

[45] John Sage, *The Case Of the Present Afflicted Clergy in Scotland Truly Represented … by a Lover of the Church and his Country* (London, 1690), 66; Cowan, *Scottish Covenanters*, 119.

[46] *A Cloud of Witnesses, for the Royal Prerogatives of Jesus Christ: or, the Last Speeches and Testimonies Of those who have suffered for the Truth in Scotland, since the Year 1680. …* 5th edn (Glasgow, 1751), 243–44. Another of the rebels sought in July 1684 was Watson from Glengonner, near Leadhills: *The Register of the Privy Council of Scotland: Third series*, ed. P. H. Brown et al., 16 vols (Edinburgh, 1908–70), 10: 218.

[47] John Cockburn, *A Continuation of the Historical Relation of the late General Assembly in Scotland …* (London, 1691), 8.

[48] NAS, GD406/1/9414, William Paterson (Edinburgh) to the Duke of Hamilton, referring to the conventicles in Lanark 'whereon Mr. James Renwick, a notorious trator, preached and baptised about 20 children'; James Renwick, *An Informatory Vindication of a Poor, wasted, misrepresented remnant of the suffering, Anti-popish, Anti-prelatick, Anti-erastian, Anti-sectarian, true Presbyterian Church of Christ in Scotland. … Written at the Leadhills in the Year 1687, conjunctly by Mr. James Renwick and Mr. Alexander Shiells …;* (Edinburgh, 1744), 30–31. See also *ODNB*, s.n. 'Renwick, James'.

That God is to be worshipped everywhere. That place is an indifferent Circumstance in the Worship of God and that we are no more to be restricted Now than in the Dayes of Christ and his Apostles.'[49]

Renwick was the last of the Covenanters to be executed and in a sermon following his death, the minister Alexander Shields used nature and in particular the weather, not as evidence of God's revelation but as a warning for his congregation:

> The last time that I was with you not far from this place, we got such a Cold Stormy Day as this we might look upon as a presage of what we have met with since; It was like the spittings before the Storm: For since we are trysted with a sad Stroak. We have lost a Famous Standard Bearer, Mr James Renwick who was with us that Day, whose voice used to cry out to you amongst those Hills ... he was as the voice crying in the Wilderness who preached the Gospel freely and faithfully to you.[50]

Even after Renwick's death and the abolition of episcopacy following the Glorious Revolution, Leadhills remained a centre of religious radicalism; a meeting there in April 1690 resulted in 'The Humble Petition of the Persecuted People of the West and Southern Shires'.[51]

It is unclear how far the efforts to establish a church at Leadhills made by Lady Margaret Hope and her son Charles Hope in the 1690s, were related to the religious troubles in the area. In their petition to the General Assembly they attributed the failure of the earlier attempt to religious and political difficulties, but also argued that 'the usurpers and their ministers under them had so much regaird to the forsaid destination and the necessite of that place That they ordered out of the publict revenue ane equivalent sum for the maintenance of a preacher'. There is also a sense that the time was propitious following the abolition of episcopacy, the accession of William III and 'the resolution of the ancient government of this

---

[49] James Renwick, *The Church's Choice or a Sermon on Canticles Ch. 1 v. 7* ([London?], 1705), 51.

[50] Alexander Shields, *Some Notes Or Heads Of A Preface And Of A Lecture Preached at Distinckorn-Hill, In The Parish of Gaastoun. April 15. 1688. By Master Alexander Shields Preacher of the Gospel* ([Edinburgh?], 1688), 2.

[51] *Faithful contendings displayed* (London, 1780), 428–33.

Church'.[52] As in the first petition, the ministry was to be financed by the extraction of lead ore at Leadhills. The presbytery was also concerned that there should be adequate pastoral provision for Leadhills during the 1690s and into the eighteenth century, occasionally lobbying the Hope family to finance a minister, as well as sending pastors to preach to the community.[53] While there were other reasons for building a parish church at Leadhills, such as the increased size of the community (which had doubled since the mid-seventeenth century), it is certainly suggestive that this might also have been related to an attempt to establish worship focused on the parish church in the area rather than open-air conventicles. Nonetheless, this attempt to plant a church also faltered, possibly due to doubts about the viability of the mines in the mid-1690s.[54] It was not until the eighteenth century that a building was finally erected. Almost a century after the initial efforts to build a church, Charles Hope agreed in 1738 to make provision for a schoolmaster and catechizing 'and being inclined to be at the expense of building a convenient house for their attending Divine Worship, sermon and catechising. And also to furnish and set apart a piece of ground where they may burie their dead'.[55]

The scheme to build a church at Leadhills was a reflection on the expansion of the religious landscape through the industrial development of lead mining in a remote and desolate part of south Lanarkshire. The scheme attempted to finance the preaching of the Word of God through the income derived from the extraction of the earth's natural resources. In his commentary on Job, Calvin reflected on how, in the case of gold and silver, 'the metal is mingled with the earth, it hath not so much as colour, yea and it seemth

[52] NAS, GD26/10/43, Information for Charles Hope of Hoptoun [Hopetoun] regarding the erecting of a church at his lead mines at Hoptoune with petition to King for gift of the tack duty of 1000 merks due yearly for said mines. Reference is made to 'after the happy settlement of this Church' but this might refer more to the success of the petition than the post-1689 religious settlement: GD26/10/40, Petition by Lady Margaret Hope. See also *APS*, ed. Thomson and Innes, 9: 454.

[53] NAS, CH2/234/3, Minutes of the Presbytery of Lanark, 1691–1699, 189, 216, 240; CH2/234/4, Minutes of the Presbytery of Lanark, 1699–1709, 3, 4, 6, 8, 10, 17, 30, 32, 35, 45, 56, 139, 145, 151. For religious discipline, see CH2/234/3, 229, 234, 238.

[54] HHA, Accounts, volume 1, memorandum of 5 March 1696.

[55] HHA, Bundle 116, Extract Act of Assembly 1738 Respecting the chaplain at Leadhills; NAS, CH1/2/76, General Assembly Papers, Main Series (1738), fols 299–303. See also CH1/2/106, General Assembly Papers, Main Series (1765), fols 304–305.

too bee utterly vnprofitable' but it nonetheless is evidence of God's revelation, which should move man to acknowledge his glory and inestimable power. It was something that was brought out of the darkness into the light.[56] While the appeals made for establishing the ministry at Leadhills repeatedly emphasized the importance of making the Word of God known to these mineworkers and their families, Sir James Hope may have seen this endeavour in similar terms to the Genevan reformer. He recorded a dream in which he saw himself walking into the darkness en route to church carrying a candle which he put out to confront the darkness, only to see 'many lights as it wer people repaireing to church wth candles in ther hands with much zeall and rejoiceing thogh in darknesse'.[57] While the natural world provided evidence of divine revelation, it alone was insufficient as it required Scripture to bring mankind to a closer understanding of God and his wonders. In this respect the work of the Kirk closely reflected some of the writings and themes relating to the natural world explored by Calvin in his sermons and Biblical commentaries. More generally, however, the implications of the Genevan reformer's perception of the world posed problems for the Kirk when it came to the regular round of worship. The natural landscape was regarded more often with suspicion and its features as, at times, either encouraging Catholic survivalism and idolatry or as impeding congregations from receiving the Word of God. Furthermore, while the Kirk acknowledged that no one place was more sacred or holy than another,[58] in practice non-parochial worship and the open-air conventicles as centres of religious radicalism meant that for the authorities the natural world, rather than furthering the revelation of God's glory, threatened to undermine the preaching of his Word.

Oxford Brookes University

---

[56] Calvin, *Iob*, 476–77 (on Job 28: 1–9).

[57] 'Diary of Sir James Hope', ed. Balfour Paul, 153–54. For an alternative political interpretation, see Williamson, 'Union with England', 315.

[58] See Spicer, ' "What kinde of house" ', 87–98.

NATURE, HISTORY AND THE SEARCH FOR ORDER: THE BOYLE LECTURES, 1730–1785*

by ROBERT G. INGRAM

HISTORY supplanted nature as the most important apologetical language among English polemical divines during the mid-eighteenth century, but not for the reasons usually adduced. The triumph of history over nature owed everything to the power of orthodox patronage and to nature's demonstrable apologetical efficacy, and nothing to natural theology's supposed failure sufficiently to prove God's existence. Put another way, by the late 1720s orthodox apologists had come to believe that the popular argument from design in nature applied equally to history. Moreover, the argument from design in history appears to have been an apologetical strategy which accorded more closely with the disposition of an increasingly orthodox episcopate during the mid-century period. Little evidences the mid-century historical turn – a shift either missed or ignored by most historians – more clearly than the second generation (1730–1785) of the Boyle lectures, a series of public sermons founded by Robert Boyle in order to defend Christianity from the attacks of unbelievers. For whereas the first generation of lecturers founded their defences of Christianity on natural theology, the second built on Christianity's historical record.

Among the most notable of the second-generation lecturers was Thomas Newton, the future Bishop of Bristol. '[T]here is nothing inconsistent in science and religion', he pronounced in January 1756 at the outset of his Boyle lectures. 'True philosophy is indeed the handmaid of true religion: and the knowledge of the works of nature will lead one to the knowledge of the God of nature'.[1] Nature's design provided trustworthy evidence of a Creator's exist-

* I wish to thank William Gibson, Scott Mandelbrote, Johannes Wienand, Stephen Snobelen, Melanie Barber and Clare Brown, as well as the Editors of Studies in Church History, for help in the preparation of this paper.

[1] Thomas Newton, *Dissertations on the Prophecies*, 9th edn, 2 vols (London, 1793), 1: 298. For a complete list of the Boyle lecturers from 1730 to 1785, see the appendix to this paper.

ence. History, though, illuminated even more. 'Prophecy is … history anticipated and contracted; history is prophecy accomplished and dilated'. In particular, the prophecies of Daniel and St John 'may really be said to be a summary of the history of the world, and the history of the world is the best comment upon their prophecies'.[2] Such was the correlation of prophecy and history that the incredulous rejected the authenticity of prophecies, arguing instead 'that they must have been written after the events, which they are pretended to foretell'.[3] In order to rebut such sceptics, Newton aimed to prove the authenticity of the sources for and to explicate the meaning of 'only such [prophecies] as relate more immediately to those later ages, and are in some measure receiving their accomplishment at this time'.[4] Newton aimed, in other words, to prove that history, no less than nature, embodied God's carefully wrought providential plan. Put another way, Newton took the argument from design in nature and extended it into history. 'What stronger and more convincing proofs can be given or required of a divine providence and a divine revelation, [than] that there is a God who directs and orders the transactions of the world', he asked rhetorically.[5] The God who designed nature to fulfil his divine plan and to provide evidence of himself, then, did the same thing in history. Thus we have in Newton's Boyle lectures a vision of the world in which history, no less than nature, is God-imbued, an enchanted world in which its immanent Creator purposefully executes his plan. Yet, it must be noted, Newton's immanent God – though no absentee deity who left his creation to work out things on its own – was less forthrightly interventionist and less clearly transparent in his communications than he had been in the early days of his Church.[6] So, God remained providential but was more remote and more mysterious.

Thomas Newton's conception of God and his creation is not one we might normally associate with the mid-1750s. Even if we were to discount David Hume's influence and to stipulate that the eighteenth century gave birth neither to modernization

---

[2]   Ibid. 2: 413.
[3]   Ibid. 1: 219.
[4]   Ibid., prefatory dedication.
[5]   Ibid. 2: 414.
[6]   Ibid.

nor to secularization, immanence and enlightenment still seem an unlikely pair.[7] They seem such mainly because of our current confusion about the relationship of nature and history in the era's mindset.

Some scholars simply ignore the eighteenth-century apologetical turn to history. Historians generally reckon that nature and history had an inversely proportional relationship during the century: when the use of one waxed as an apologetical tool, the other was supposed to have waned.[8] Scholars explain this hydraulic relationship in one of two ways. They argue instead that, aside from a few stalwart Tories and misguided Hutchinsonians (anti-Newtonian followers of John Hutchinson),[9] enlightened Christians quickly accepted the marriage of nature and religion – natural theology steamrollered 'baroque mysticism' until Charles Darwin 'expose[d] the scientific failings in the argument from design' in nature.[10] In this view, the Boyle lectures were '*the* major vehicle disseminating Newtonian natural philosophy', which itself served 'as the cornerstone of a liberal, tolerant, and highly philosophical version of Christianity'.[11] Others, though, reckon that it is better to pay heed to the evidence and so to acknowledge and explain

[7] But see Robert G. Ingram, '"The Weight of Historical Evidence": Conyers Middleton and the Eighteenth-Century Miracles Debate', in William Gibson and Robert Cornwall, eds, *Politics, Religion and Dissent, 1660–1832* (Aldershot, forthcoming); Alexandra Walsham, 'The Reformation and "The Disenchantment of the World" Reassessed', *HistJ* 51 (2008), 497–528.

[8] For a succinct overview of apologetics during the era, see M. A. Stewart, 'Revealed Religion: The British Debate' and idem, 'Arguments for the Existence of God: The British Debate', in Knud Haakonssen, ed., *The Cambridge History of Eighteenth-Century Philosophy*, 2 vols (Cambridge, 2006), 2: 683–709, 710–30.

[9] Christopher Wilde, 'Hutchinsonianism, Natural Philosophy, and Religious Controversy in Eighteenth-Century England', *History of Science* 18 (1980), 1–24; Geoffrey N. Cantor, 'Revelation and the Cyclical Cosmos of John Hutchinson', in Ludmilla Jordanova and Roy Porter, eds, *Images of the Earth: Essays in the History of Environmental Sciences* (Chalfont St Giles, 1979), 3–22.

[10] Margaret Jacob, 'Christianity and the Newtonian Worldview', in David C. Lindberg and Ronald L. Numbers, eds, *God and Nature* (Berkeley, CA, 1986), 238–55, at 253.

[11] Ibid. 243 (emphasis mine). Margaret C. Jacob, *The Newtonians and the English Revolution, 1689–1720* (Ithaca, NY, 1976), esp. 143–200, is the *locus classicus* for her case regarding the character and aims of the early Boyle lectures. Cf. Geoffrey Holmes, 'Science, Reason and Religion in the Age of Newton', *British Journal for the History of Science* 11 (1978), 164–71; John Gascoigne, 'From Bentley to the Victorians: The Rise and Fall of British Newtonian Natural Theology', *Science in Context* 2 (1988), 219–56, at 224–25.

the evident rise of a historically grounded apologetics during the century. They account for the apologetical sea-change in varying ways.[12] Most reckon that natural theology was a double-edged sword. In the late seventeenth century, Christian apologists – hoping to wrong-foot sceptics and to emphasize the broad areas of agreement among Christians – turned to natural philosophy in order to defend their religion in the language and on the ground of their opponents.[13] However, many soon found that the natural philosopher's God of nature looked a little too much like the deist's clockmaker God.[14] In response, Christian apologists, keen to emphasize a voluntarist understanding of God (stressing the primacy of his will),[15] turned their attentions to historical proofs of God's existence – miracles and prophecies most prominent among them – which emphasized God's activity in his creation.[16] There is a sense, though, that the eighteenth-century proponents of a historically grounded Christian apologetics had unwisely hopped astride an already dying horse, one which German biblical critics and Edward Gibbon would mercifully soon put out of its misery.

Yet there is Thomas Newton uncomplicatedly and, as it were, unapologetically combining the insights from both nature and history to prove that God exists and that he is immanent in his creation. Was Newton anomalous? No. Indeed, he and the entire

---

[12] Cf. David S. Katz, *God's Last Words: Reading the English Bible from the Reformation to Fundamentalism* (New Haven, CT, 2004), esp. 74–211; J. G. A. Pocock, 'History and Enlightenment: A View of Their History', *Modern Intellectual History* 5 (2008), 83–96; Justin Champion, *Republican Learning: John Toland and the Crisis of Christian Culture, 1696–1722* (Manchester, 2003); Joseph M. Levine, 'Deists and Anglicans: The Ancient Wisdom and Idea of Progress', in Roger Lund, ed., *The Margins of Orthodoxy: Heterodox Writing and Cultural Response, 1660–1750* (Cambridge, 1995), 219–39.

[13] Scott Mandelbrote, 'The Uses of Natural Theology in Seventeenth-Century England', *Science in Context* 20 (2007), 451–80; Gascoigne, 'Bentley to the Victorians', 219–56.

[14] Roy Porter, *The Creation of the Modern World* (New York, 2000), 96–129; Gascoigne, 'Bentley to the Victorians', 228–30.

[15] Peter Harrison, 'Voluntarism and Early Modern Science', *History of Science* 40 (2002), 63–89.

[16] Jane Shaw, *Miracles in Enlightenment England* (New Haven, CT, 2006), esp. 144–73; Peter Harrison, 'Miracles, Early Modern Science and Rational Religion', *ChH* 75 (2006), 493–510; Neil W. Hitchin, 'The Evidence of Things Seen: Georgian Churchmen and Biblical Prophecy', in Bertrand Taithe and Tim Thornton, eds, *Prophecy: The Power of Inspired Language in History, 1300–2000* (Stroud, 1997), 119–39.

second generation of Boyle lecturers (1730–85)[17] show that there were powerful enticements for Christianity's proponents to defend its historical truths. To begin with, the historical turn testifies to the power of patronage in setting the boundaries and, indeed, at times dictating the agenda of enlightened clerical debate during the eighteenth century. In addition, clerical apologists did not flee to history because the argument from design in nature was a hazardous solvent to Christian orthodoxy: rather, they turned to history precisely because the argument from design was so effective. Nature evidenced clearly God's providential design. If history could be shown to be similarly ordered, perhaps the mystery of the present could be made more bearable, if not more explicable, because an immutable God might change his methods of interposition but not surely his reasons for it. Perhaps his divine plan could even be glimpsed through an examination of his actions in the past. The Boyle lectures of the eighteenth century, then, should be understood as a collective search for the order in God's creation, a search which focused initially upon nature and latterly upon history.

I

Those doing the searching stood at the forefront of England's clerical Enlightenment, and their arguments reflected the broad centre of enlightened thinking about the world and its Creator. In part, this may be explained by the lecturers' remit. As importantly, the move from natural theology to a historically grounded apologetics in the second generation of the Boyle lectures exemplified the success of the Duke of Newcastle's policy of packing the episcopal bench with the stolidly orthodox and the degree to which the members of that bench shaped the parameters of enlightened clerical debate.[18]

Just before his death in July 1691, Robert Boyle added a codicil to his will to endow an annual lecture series 'for proving the Christian religion against notorious infidels, viz. Atheists, Theists, Pagans,

---

[17] John Hunt, *Religious Thought in England from the Reformation to the End of the Last Century*, 3 vols (London, 1873), 3: 121–24, 283–85, 334–36.

[18] S. J. C. Taylor, '"The Fac Totum in Ecclesiastical Affairs"? The Duke of Newcastle and the Crown's Ecclesiastical Patronage', *Albion* 24 (1992), 409–33.

Jews, and Mahometans, not descending lower to any controversies, that are among Christians themselves'.[19] The Christian virtuoso of Boyle's age – who 'by manifold and curious experiments searches deep into the nature of things' – was, he thought, ideally suited to bring his experimental knowledge to bear in Christianity's defence.[20] The very early Boyle lectures bore the influence of England's most eminent Christian virtuoso, Isaac Newton, who assured Richard Bentley, the inaugural lecturer, '[w]hen I wrote my Treatise about our System, I had an Eye upon such Principles as might work with considering Men, for Belief in a Deity, and nothing can rejoice me more than to find it useful for that Purpose'.[21] The first generation of Boyle lecturers (1692–1730) likewise consistently employed the argument from design in nature.[22]

We should not, though, conflate the first and second generation of the Boyle lecturers.[23] Instead, we should recognize that governing structures and personnel shaped and reshaped the lectureship's character. Boyle placed the choice of lecturer in the hands of a board of trustees, which initially included his friends John Rotheram, Henry Ashurst, John Evelyn and Thomas Tenison. Though they may have heeded Isaac Newton's advice on the choice of lecturers in the very early days of the series, there is no evidence that he

[19] Robert E. Maddison, *The Life of the Honourable Robert Boyle* (London, 1969), 257–82.

[20] *The Works of Robert Boyle*, 5 vols (London, 1744), 5: 43. Cf. Jan W. Wojcik, *Robert Boyle and the Limits of Reason* (Cambridge, 1997). For the context, see John Marshall, 'Some Intellectual Consequences of the English Revolution', *European Legacy* 5 (2000), 515–30; Michael Hunter, 'Science and Heterodoxy: An Early Modern Problem Reconsidered', in David C. Lindberg and Robert C. Westman, eds, *Reappraisals of the Scientific Revolution* (Cambridge, 1990), 437–60.

[21] Isaac Newton, *Four Letters from Sir Isaac Newton to Doctor Bentley. Containing Some Arguments in Proof of a Deity* (London, 1756), 1. Cf. Stephen D. Snobelen, '"God of gods, and Lord of lords": The Theology of Isaac Newton's General Scholium to the *Principia*', *Osiris* 16 (2001), 169–208.

[22] Andrew Pyle, 'Introduction', in *A Defence of Natural and Revealed Religion: Being an Abridgement of the Sermons preached at the Lecture founded by Robert Boyle*, ed. Gilbert Burnet, 4 vols (Bristol, 2000), 1: x–liii. Cf. Jacob, *The Newtonians and the English Revolution*, 162–200; John J. Dahm, 'Science and Apologetics in the early Boyle Lectures', *ChH* 39 (1970), 172–86.

[23] Alister McGrath, 'A Blast from the Past? The Boyle Lectures and Natural Theology', *Science and Christian Belief* 17 (2005), 25–33; Pyle, 'Introduction', esp. l.

had any sustained influence in the selection process.[24] Late in 1711,
Tenison, the last original trustee, appointed the Earl of Burlington,
Edmund Gibson, Charles Trimnell, White Kennett and Samuel
Bradford to the board.[25] In March 1750, Burlington, again the only
surviving Boyle trustee, named William Cavendish (later Duke of
Devonshire), Richard Arundell, Thomas Sherlock, Martin Benson
and Thomas Secker to the board.[26] Finally, in August 1765, Secker
himself appointed Robert Hay Drummond, Richard Newcombe,
Frederick Cornwallis and the late Duke of Devonshire's three
brothers as trustees.[27] The board, then, became less Latitudinarian
and more stolidly orthodox as the century wore on.[28]

As importantly, the choice of lecturers fell almost wholly either
to the senior cleric on the board or to the senior board member
in consultation with the senior cleric,[29] so that Gibson, Sherlock,
Secker, Drummond and Cornwallis, all unmistakably orthodox in
their theology, either virtually controlled or decisively shaped the
choice of second-generation lecturers. These bishops were neither
adept at nor sympathetic to metaphysics,[30] and, not surprisingly, the
eighteen lecturers chosen between 1730 and 1785 clearly reflected

[24] Henry Guerlac and Margaret C. Jacob, 'Bentley, Newton and Providence: The
Boyle Lectures Once More', *JHI* 30 (1969), 307–18. Of the initial trustees, only Tenison
was a cleric.

[25] London, LPL, MS 2958, fols 20–21: Nominations to Boyle Trustees, 18 December
1711; Newton, *Dissertations*, 1: 287–88 n. 1. Of Tenison's appointees, Gibson, Trimnell,
Kennett and Bradford were all clerics, and all would serve as bishops in the Church
of England.

[26] MS 2958, fols 23–25: Nominations of Boyle Trustees, 21 March 1750. See also
Newton, *Dissertations*, 1: 288 n. 1. At the time of their appointment, Sherlock, Benson
and Secker all sat on the episcopal bench.

[27] London, LPL, Secker Papers, vol. 4, fol. 273: Thomas Secker's nominations of
Boyle Trustees, 1765. See also ibid. fol. 272: Secker to Drummond, 1 August 1765.
Drummond, Newcombe and Cornwallis were all bishops at the time of their appoint-
ment.

[28] On orthodoxy, see Robert G. Ingram, *Religion, Reform and Modernity in the Eighteenth Century: Thomas Secker and the Church of England* (Woodbridge, 2007), 11–14.

[29] See, e.g., Secker Papers, vol. 4, fols 267, 272: Nicholls to Secker, 20 November
1755; Secker to Drummond, 1 August 1765.

[30] On Gibson's theological views and his patronage of orthodox clerics, see S. J. C.
Taylor, '"Dr. Codex" and the Whig "Pope": Edmund Gibson, Bishop of Lincoln and
London, 1716–1748', in Richard W. Davis, ed., *Lords of Parliament: Studies, 1714–1914*
(Stanford, CA, 1995), 9–27. Sherlock published two of the most influential orthodox
defences of miracles and prophecies during the eighteenth century: for an exami-
nation of his orthodox polemics, see Edward Carpenter, *Thomas Sherlock 1678–1761*
(London, 1936), 294–322. For the stable of prominent orthodox polemicists nurtured
by Secker, see Ingram, *Religion, Reform, and Modernity*, esp. 71–113. For Drummond and

the dispositions of their ecclesiastical patrons.[31] The historical turn, in short, proved the power of patronage in eighteenth-century English intellectual life.

II

The historical turn in the mid-century lectures also reflected shifts in the era's intellectual winds. The second generation of Boyle lecturers spanned just over half a century, from 1730 when William Berriman took to the pulpit of St Mary-le-Bow to preach on God's gradual revelation until 1785 when East Apthorp finished his lectures on the prevalence of Christianity. Much changed during that time, but there is nevertheless a distinctive coherence to the lectures, for they cast God as eternally immanent in his ordered creation, a view which the lecturers reached and defended by way of the argument from design in both nature and history.

The lecturers began from the premise that human reason is insufficient either to prove God's existence or to illuminate his providential plan. With Descartes and Samuel Clarke in his sights, Ralph Heathcote argued that knowledge of God's existence is intuitive knowledge which is not subject to rational proof. 'The Philosopher (Descartes) has shewn here, what will always be found true, that Intuitive knowledge cannot be made more intuitive, nor self-evident truths still more evident, by Logic and Argumentation', Heathcote reckoned.[32] In the 1750s, prior to giving his

Cornwallis, see *ODNB*, s.n. 'Drummond, Robert Hay (1711–1776)' and 'Cornwallis, Frederick (1713–1783)'.

[31] The average Boyle lecturer (1730–85) graduated from Cambridge, served as a royal chaplain, embraced orthodoxy, and was firmly ensconced within the clerical establishment. Cf. Scott Mandelbrote, 'Eighteenth-Century Reactions to Newton's Anti-Trinitarianism', in James E. Force and Sarah Hutton, eds, *Newton and Newtonianism: New Studies*, International Archives of the History of Ideas 188 (Dordrecht, 2004), 93–112, at 101–03 for the composition of those who delivered the Lady Moyer's lectures, another prestigious forum for promoting orthodoxy. Only two of the second-generation Boyle lecturers (John Jortin and Ralph Heathcote) would not have counted themselves among the orthodox: see, e.g., John Jortin, *Remarks on Ecclesiastical History*, 5 vols (London, 1751–73), 1, esp. xi–xxxii; John Nichols, *Literary Anecdotes of the Eighteenth Century*, 9 vols (London, 1812–16), 3: 531–44: 'Memoir of Rev. Dr. Ralph Heathcote'. Nevertheless, both Jortin and Heathcote gave lectures which defended the historical facts of Christianity, and Jortin owed his nomination to the Boyle lecturership to Thomas Sherlock's lobbying: John Jortin, *Tracts, philological, critical, and miscellaneous*, 2 vols (London, 1790), 1: x.

[32] Ralph Heathcote, *A Discourse Upon the Being of God* (London, 1763), 26.

Boyle lectures, Heathcote had decried what he perceived to be the Hutchinsonian rejection of reason, but he did so not because he doubted the historical proofs from revealed religion but rather because he thought the Hutchinsonians had stepped down the slippery slope to Bayle's fideism (the belief that revealed religion's truth transcends human reason).[33] '[B]y discarding Natural Light', he argued, the Hutchinsonian 'has no means left of knowing, either what a Revelation imports, or whether it be, in truth, a Revelation or not'.[34]

William Berriman was far more typical of the Boyle lecturers in his explanation of reason's insufficiency in apologetics.

[A]ll Men are naturally in a depraved and sinful Estate; so that whatever Knowledge they may have of their Duty either from the Dictates of Reason, or from the external Benefit of Revelation, yet they perceive a vehement Attachment to the contrary, which they are neither able to root out, nor in any tolerable Degree to regulate, till assisted by the gracious Aid and Succours of the Gospel ...[35]

'How then is this Difficulty cleared up by Revelation?', he wondered. 'Not by any nice and philosophical Deductions, but by a plain and rational Account of Fact, sufficient to preserve the Honour of God, and the Influences of Religion.'[36] That 'Fact' was the Genesis account of the Fall.[37]

The Fall was a type of evidence, and all of the mid-century Boyle lecturers reckoned that evidence – what many simply called 'facts' – was the only sufficient ground on which to attempt to prove God's existence. William Worthington, a clerical Gradgrind,

---

[33] Ralph Heathcote, *The Use of Reason Asserted in Matters of Religion* (London, 1756). Cf. Nigel Aston, 'From Personality to Party: The Creation and Transmission of Hutchinsonianism, c. 1725–1750', *Studies in History and Philosophy of Science* 35 (2004), 625–44. Fear of fideism was common among the Boyle lecturers: Richard Biscoe, *The History of the Acts of the Holy Apostles*, 2 vols (London, 1742), 1: 4; Jortin, *Ecclesiastical History*, 1: 89; Henry Owen, *The Intent and Propriety of the Scripture Miracles*, 2 vols (London, 1773), 1: 5. On Bayle's fideism, see Richard H. Popkin, *History of Scepticism: From Savonarola to Bayle* (Oxford, 2003), 283–302.

[34] Heathcote, *Use of Reason*, 5.

[35] William Berriman, *The Gradual Revelation of the Gospel*, 2 vols (London, 1733), 1: 8–9.

[36] Ibid. 23.

[37] Ibid. 23–27. See also Henry Stebbing, *Christianity Justified upon the Scripture Foundation* (London, 1750), 22–54, 289–90; Owen, *Intent and Propriety*, 1: 28–30.

mercilessly made the distinction between 'facts' and mere argument the crux of his Boyle lectures. 'Facts are the best foundation of all knowledge, and all truth, in general', he insisted.[38] Facts
he defined as 'objects of sense', on the belief that 'if man cannot
trust their senses, they can trust nothing'.[39] A century and a half
earlier, Worthington assured his listeners, Francis Bacon had recognized the illusory claims of metaphysics for what they were and
had, in response, outlined an 'experimental philosophy' whose end
product was a body of incontestable facts. Ever since, the great
English natural philosophers

> grounded their reasons on experiments: and they have reasoned
> from them with certainty, and raised conclusions upon them,
> which are not to be denied or doubted of; among whom,
> none hath made greater discoveries and improvements in
> the knowledge of nature, by these means, than the judicious
> founder of these lectures ...[40]

Just as facts explicated nature's mysteries, so too did they under-
gird Christianity. 'Fact ... is a deeper and safer foundation for
religion, than reason itself', Worthington contended, '... for
our reasoning never proceeds upon such firm grounds as when
we have facts to ground it upon'.[41] Citing Joseph Butler as his
authority, Worthington concluded that 'the belief of the first, and
consequently of all succeeding Christians, is to be resolved into an
attestation of facts'.[42] His fellow Boyle lecturers were less pedantic,
but no less insistent, than Worthington that concrete evidence
provided the only sure foundation of all truth and none of the
lecturers provided any extended metaphysical proof of God's existence.[43]

All agreed that the first place to look for facts about God was
nature. 'The visible World ... is as truly and properly the Organ

---

[38] William Worthington, *The Evidence of Christianity Deduced From Facts,* 2 vols
(London, 1769), 1: 6–7. See also idem, *An Impartial Enquiry Into The Case of the Gospel
Demoniacks* (London, 1777), 2–5.
[39] Worthington, *Evidence of Christianity,* 1: 14.
[40] Ibid. 9.
[41] Ibid. 12–13.
[42] Ibid. 26–27.
[43] See Biscoe, *Acts of the Apostles,* 1: 11; 2: 466–67, 540–41, 563–65; Stebbing,
Christianity Justified, 255–56; Heathcote, *Use of Reason,* 16, 25–34; Owen, *Intent and
Propriety,* 9.

of the eternal Mind which resides in it, and pervades it in every Part, as the human Body is the Organ of the human Mind', Henry Stebbing argued during the late 1740s. 'And as when I see the dull, passive Instrument moved, and directed with Aptness to some End, ... I conclude that there must be some intelligent Being, which directs the whole, and which is, as it were, the Soul of this immense Organ'.[44] John Jortin, a Latitudinarian to Stebbing's hyper-orthodox, concurred that the natural world evidenced God's existence, noting in particular that 'natural Religion has received so much friendly aid from natural Philosophy, and from the excellent Newtonian System'.[45] So too did Ralph Heathcote reckon that 'we can no more contemplate the Creation, without associating the idea of a Creator, than we can contemplate an Orrery or any curious piece of Mechanism, without associating the idea of a Mechanic'.[46] Likewise, a decade later Henry Owen observed that 'the frame of the world speaks God for its author', noting in particular that 'the stupendous grandeur and astonishing immensity of the whole fabric point his supreme power' and that 'the beautiful symmetry, regular disposition, and admirable propriety of the several parts, are manifest indications of his infinite wisdom'.[47]

Yet for all that nature might to do prove God's existence and to illuminate his plan, the Boyle lecturers agreed that history had even greater explanatory power. Writing in response to Gibbon's *Decline and Fall*, East Apthorp asserted that '[t]he historical evidence is the true and proper demonstration of the divine truth of the Christian religion: and this evidence of a kind, which admits not of doubt, mistake, or ambiguity'. For historical evidence did not depend 'on the minuter circumstances of historic tradition, in which there is often room for a prudent scepticism; but on such facts as are evident and certain from the actual state of the world, as well as fully authenticated by all ancient records'.[48] In his lectures, Jortin aimed to use historical scholarship to strip away the harmful philosophical and superstitious accretions which had turned Christianity into a 'bulky system'. His targets were not so much the sceptics

---

[44] Stebbing, *Christianity Justified*, 261.

[45] Jortin, *Ecclesiastical History*, 1: 84.

[46] Heathcote, *Use of Reason*, 33.

[47] Owen, *Intent and Propriety*, 1: 5.

[48] East Apthorp, *Letters on the prevalence of Christianity* (London, 1779), vi.

who chipped away at Christianity's foundations, but popish and dogmatical divines who had corrupted Christianity from its primitive purity. To blame, in particular, were 'the loquacious and ever-wrangling Greeks; … the enthusiastic Africans, whose imagination was sublimed by the heat of the sun; … [and] the superstitious Egyptians, whose fertile soil, and warm climate produced monks and hermits swarming like animals sprung from the impregnated mud of the Nile'.[49] If only ecclesiastical history could point up the origin of these errors, Jortin reckoned, then Christianity could revert to its original, unadorned simplicity.

Ecclesiastical history derived from two sources, the Bible and other written records. The former was – had to be – infallible, for in the eighteenth century the Bible remained the religion of Protestants. Most of the lecturers devoted considerable space to proving the historical authenticity and accuracy of the Bible, because, as Richard Biscoe noted in his examination of the Acts of the Apostles, 'If the matters of fact contained in these historical relations be admitted as true, it can be no longer doubted whether the Christian religion be a divine revelation.'[50] While the Bible was the pre-eminent source of Christian history, the rest of the written historical record was also important to scrutinize since it might reveal the fulfilment of a biblical prophecy, illuminate a perversion of original Christian teaching, or simply confirm history as it was related in the Bible. 'Had we all the records and histories of that time now extant, I am persuaded we should see an abundant confirmation of every particular contained in the book of Acts', Biscoe confidently predicted.[51]

The great evidences of God from ecclesiastical history were miracles and prophecies. The second generation of lectures spilled tens of thousands of words proving – relentlessly, methodically and exhaustively proving – that the biblical examples of miracles and prophecy were literally and historically true. There is nothing original about their arguments, and many took their analytical frameworks straight from Thomas Sherlock's *The Use and Intent*

---

[49] Jortin, *Ecclesiastical History*, I: xii. Cf. J. G. A. Pocock, *Barbarism and Religion*, 4 vols (Cambridge, 1999–2006), which explores the perceived corruption of Christianity by philosophy in some detail; idem, 'History and Enlightenment', 83–96, states his thesis succinctly.

[50] Biscoe, *Acts of the Apostles*, I: 26.

[51] Ibid. 39.

of Prophecy (1725) and *The Tryal of the Witnesses of the Resurrection of Jesus* (1729).[52] Even Hume's *Essay concerning Human Understanding* (1748) failed to stop lecturer after lecturer from subjecting the evidences of Christian miracles and prophecies to historical scrutiny and finding them ultimately to be true. Why did the Boyle lecturers keep mining this one apologetical vein for half a century when it yielded little new? One possibility, of course, is that the lecturers were, as a group, a rather dull lot. It might also be, though, that Providence had boxed them into a corner. To understand why this might be the case, we might keep in mind three things about miracles and prophecies: their definition, their chronology and their purpose. Firstly, one could recognize a miracle or a prophecy: Leonard Twells uncontroversially defined miracles as 'Performances above the Power or Sleight of Man to effect' and prophecies as 'Knowledge of future Events'.[53] Secondly, in the minds of the Boyle lecturers, at least, both miracles and prophecies had long ago ceased.[54] The last prophecies any lecturer treated as authentic were those contained in the Book of Revelation, and the last Christian miracle was wrought sometime during the first four centuries of the Christian Church. Finally, and most importantly, miracles and prophecies illuminated: they proved that God existed, that he became incarnate, that he was crucified and that he was resurrected; but they proved something else, as well, for they were the best evidence that God had created everything in the universe with an end in mind, one that he would, one way or another, ensure was fulfilled.

Proving God's existence, then, meant illuminating his providential design. But what *was* Providence? How could one recognize a providence? How could one know if it was providential? In the light of the lecturers' confident specificity about the mechanics and intent of miracles and prophecy, they were notably vague about the mechanics of Providence. Jortin, for instance, argued that for the 'excellent end and purpose' of leaving proofs, 'the divine Providence seems to have preserved ecclesiastical records, and has

[52] Stebbing, *Christianity Justified*, 289–90; Owen, *Intent and Propriety*, 33.
[53] Leonard Twells, *Twenty-Four Sermons*, 2 vols (London, 1742), 1: 3, 86.
[54] Cf. Shaw, *Miracles*; Alexandra Walsham, 'Miracles in Post-Reformation England', in Kate Cooper and Jeremy Gregory, eds, *Signs, Wonders, Miracles: Representations of Divine Power in the Life of the Church*, SCH 41 (Woodbridge, 2005), 273–306.

commanded devouring time to respect them, that posterity might receive instruction from those venerable and silent monitors, and not want examples to shun and to follow'.[55] But how exactly had Providence ensured their survival? On this Jortin was silent, though he was able elsewhere in his lectures to enumerate twenty reasons why Christ's miracles were self-evidently real.[56]

Jortin's fellow Boyle lecturers were similarly reticent to discuss the mechanics of Providence, and in their unwillingness to explicate precisely how Providence worked, they were entirely in tune with their fellow enlightened clerics of the mid-eighteenth century.[57] This does not mean that they thought God was no longer immanent in his creation. When a war went well or poorly, when an earthquake rumbled underneath London or Lisbon, when a rival claimant failed to seize the throne, when someone survived a terrible illness, when a house collapsed during a strong wind, the clergy immediately put it down to Providence.[58] In some ways, God had never been so active – or so opaque. It took a character like William Warburton, though, to attempt an explanation of the precise physical mechanisms by which God providentially controlled men's thoughts. Suffice it to say that he rushed in where other polemical divines feared to tread.[59]

If the Boyle lecturers could not explain the mechanisms of Providence, they could, at least, know its intent. And here is where the arguments from design in nature and history proved so instructive. For if nature and history both evidenced and embodied God's divine plan for his creation, so too surely did Providence. Not surprisingly, then, the theme which binds together all of the lectures is that of order and meaning. Everything had a purpose

---

[55] Jortin, *Ecclesiastical History*, 1: xi.

[56] Ibid. 258–67.

[57] London, LPL, Sion Arc. L40.2/E34 (2): Manuscript notes for eleven of Joseph Roper's Boyle lectures, 1744–45, unpaginated, is the lone Boyle lecture to confront, even briefly, the inscrutability of the mechanics of Providence.

[58] J. C. D. Clark, 'Providence, Predestination and Progress; Or, Did the Enlightenment Fail?', *Albion* 35 (2003), 559–89; Robert G. Ingram, '"The Trembling Earth is God's Herald": Earthquakes, Religious and Public Life in Britain during the 1750s', in Theodore E. D. Braun and John B. Radner, eds, *The Lisbon Earthquake of 1755: Representations and Reactions* (Oxford, 2005), 97–115.

[59] Robert G. Ingram, 'William Warburton, Divine Action and Enlightened Christianity', in William Gibson and Robert Ingram, eds, *Religious Identities in Britain, 1660–1832* (Aldershot, 2005), 97–118.

because everything had a creator, and creation implied design. But where Richard Bentley might have looked to nature for evidence of God's design, the mid-century Boyle lecturers looked to both nature *and* history for such evidence. They found the same order in nature which Bentley had observed, but they also found in, for example, the fate of the Jewish people further evidence of God's providential plan.[60] 'And is not every Jew we meet with in our streets an evidence of the truth of the Mosaic revelation?', Richard Biscoe asked rhetorically.

Evidence like this of God's presence in the streets of London helped to make sense of his providential care for his creatures. Henry Owen's thoughts on the matter reflect those of his fellow lecturers. Owen reckoned that God continually accommodated his providential interpositions to man's historical condition and that he continually watched over his creatures. And if we accept this, Owen thought, then the mysterious now became knowable, if not explainable: 'we may reasonably presume, that all the subsequent dispensations of his providence, though frequently of an extraordinary and miraculous kind, were planned and conducted with equal wisdom; and were perfectly adapted to the various necessities, which they afterwards laboured under'.[61] Or, as Thomas Newton put it, 'Wisdom, in the mysterious things of God, and especially in the mysterious things of futurity, will still adhere to the words of Scripture; and having seen the completion of so many particulars, will rest contented with believing that these also shall be, without knowing *how* they shall be.'[62]

Ohio University

---

[60] Stephen D. Snobelen, '"The mystery of this restitution of all things": Isaac Newton on the Return of the Jews', James E. Force and Richard H. Popkin, eds, *The Millenarian Turn: Millenarian Contexts of Science, Politics and Everyday Anglo-American Life in the Seventeenth and Eighteenth Centuries* (Dordrecht, 2001), 95–118.

[61] Owen, *Intent and Propriety*, 36.

[62] Newton, *Dissertations*, 1: 397–98 (emphasis mine).

APPENDIX: BOYLE LECTURERS, 1730–1785

The lists of lecturers in Johannes Wienand, 'The Boyle Lectures: St. Mary-le-Bow and the Origins of an Institution', in Michael Byrne and G. R. Bush, eds, *St. Mary-le-Bow: A History* (Barnsley, 2007), 222–47, and Nichols, *Literary Anecdotes*, 6: 453–56, both contain errors and omissions.

YEARS	LECTURER
1730–1732	William Berriman, *The Gradual Revelation of the Gospel* (1733)
1733–1735	Dr. [??] Hay[63]
1736–1738	Richard Biscoe, *The History of the Acts of the Holy Apostles* (1742)
1739–1741	Leonard Twells, *Twenty-Four Sermons* (1742)
1742–1744	John Thomas (1696–1781)
1744–1746	Joseph Roper[64]
1747–1749	Henry Stebbing, *Christianity Justified upon the Scripture Foundation* (1750)
1750–1752	John Jortin, *Remarks on Ecclesiastical History* (1767)
1753–1755	Samuel Nicolls[65]
1756–1758	Thomas Newton, *Dissertations on the Prophecies* (1754–1758)[66]
1759–1762	Charles Moss
1763–1765	Ralph Heathcote, *A Discourse Upon the Being of God* (1763)[67]
1766–1768	William Worthington, *The Evidence of Christianity* (1769)

[63] Secker Papers, vol. 4, fol. 268: Samuel Nicolls to Thomas Secker, 5 May 1758. Neither Wienand nor Nicholls list a lecturer for the years 1733–35.

[64] Roper could not complete his course of lecturers because he died in March 1746: John and J. A. Venn, *Alumni Cantabrigienses*, 10 vols (Cambridge, 1922–58), Part I, 3: 486. For manuscript notes for eleven of them, see Sion Arc. L40.2/E34 (2).

[65] Secker Papers, vol. 4, fol. 267: Nicolls to Secker, 20 November 1755; *London Evening Post*, no. 3923 (19 December 1752). Neither Wienand nor Nicholls list a lecturer for the years 1753–55.

[66] Newton, *Dissertations*, 1: 288–89.

[67] Though he published only two of his lectures, Heathcote, *pace* Wienand and Nicholls, preached the full course of twenty-four Boyle lectures: *Literary Anecdotes*, 2: 538.

1769–1771 Henry Owen, *The Intent and Propriety of the Scripture miracles* (1773)
1772–1774 Glocester Ridley
1775–1777 William Barford
1778–1780 James Williamson, *An argument for the Christian religion* (1783)
1781–1785 East Apthorp[68]

---

[68] *Literary Anecdotes*, 3: 96, 99 note that Apthorp's *Letters on the prevalence of Christianity* earned him an immediate D.D. and a subsequent nomination to present the Boyle lectures. They also intimate that Apthorp reworked his volume as his Boyle lectures for the years 1781–85. Certainly, his understanding of Christian history and his critical method did not change between 1779 and the publication of his *Discourses on prophecy: read in the chapel of Lincoln's-Inn, at the lecture founded by the Right Reverend William Warburton*, 2 vols (London, 1786). As such, for the purposes of this paper, the general historical principles which Apthorp spelled out in the initial chapters to *Letters on the prevalence of Christianity* are taken to reflect accurately the theoretical foundation for his subsequent Boyle lectures.

AUSTRALIAN ANGLICAN CLERGYMEN, SCIENCE AND RELIGION, 1820–1850*

by MICHAEL R. GLADWIN

THE second quarter of the nineteenth century has long been recognized as a formative period for public discussion of the relationship between science and religion, particularly in emerging sciences such as geology, where new evidence raised questions about the interpretation of the Bible.[1] Recent scholarly studies of scientific publishing, theologies of nature and links between missionaries and scientific endeavour have drawn attention to various ways in which the relationship between religion and science was understood during the period.[2] A common theme has been the key role of clergymen in public discourse. A lacuna in this literature, however, has been analysis of colonial sites in which these debates took place. In colonies such as New South Wales, for example, public discussion of these issues was dominated by Anglican clergyman-scientists. Yet they have attracted little attention from scholars.[3] The purpose of this paper is therefore to assess, by analysis of the journalism of the Australian colonies' most

* Thanks are due for the support of the Australian Research Theology Foundation and the Cambridge Commonwealth Trust, without which this paper could not have been written, and to Professor David Bebbington for helpful comments and criticisms.

[1] For a useful overview and bibliography, see Nicolaas A. Rupke, 'Christianity and the Sciences', in Sheridan Gilley and Brian Stanley, eds, *Cambridge History of Christianity. 8: World Christianities c. 1815 – c. 1914* (Cambridge, 2006), 164–80; Boyd Hilton, *A Mad, Bad and Dangerous People? England, 1783–1846* (Oxford, 2006), 248–49, 339–41, 440–60, 694–96.

[2] David N. Livingstone, D. G. Hart and Mark A. Noll, eds, *Evangelicals and Science in Historical Perspective* (Oxford, 1999); Geoffrey Cantor et al., *Science in the Nineteenth-Century Periodical: Reading the Magazine of Nature* (Cambridge, 2004); Aileen Fyfe, *Science and Salvation: Evangelical Popular Science Publishing in Victorian Britain* (Chicago, 2004); Sujit Sivasundaram, *Nature and the Godly Empire: Science and Evangelical Mission in the Pacific, 1795–1850* (Cambridge, 2005).

[3] Notable exceptions include Ann Mozley's seminal 'Evolution and the Climate of Opinion in Australia, 1840–76', *Victorian Studies* 10 (1967), 411–30; C. M. Finney, *To Sail beyond the Sunset: Natural History in Australia, 1699–1829* (Adelaide, 1984), 184, 187; idem, *Paradise Revealed: Natural History in Nineteenth-Century Australia* (Melbourne, 1993), 6–9; Tom Frame, *Evolution in the Antipodes: Charles Darwin and Australia* (Sydney, 2009), ch.6.

important clergyman-scientists, the contribution of Australian
Anglican clergymen to local debates about scientific knowledge
and religious understanding in the years between 1820 and 1850.
Their efforts, I argue, did much to frame that discourse in Christian terms, and fostered an intellectual climate which promoted
both scientific endeavour and Christian orthodoxy.

I

The first Australian journal dedicated to discussing issues related
to science and religion was the work of the Rev. Charles Wilton
(1795–1859), a Cambridge-trained geologist and member of the
Ashmolean and Cambridge Philosophical Societies. Seeking to
invigorate the embryonic intellectual life of New South Wales
and to attract English interest in the Australian colonies, in 1828
Wilton founded and edited the *Australian Quarterly Journal of
Theology, Literature and Science* (hereafter the *Quarterly*). Although
it lasted for only one year, the *Quarterly* reveals how the colonies'
first clergyman-scientist viewed the relationship between scientific
knowledge and religious understanding; and how he set about
educating the nascent public mind of the Australian colonies.

The *Quarterly*'s subject matter ranged widely, but the pervasive theme was, as Wilton put it in the first article, the ways in
which 'Religion and Science may well go hand in hand together'.[4]
Although religion was doubtless the 'chief thing', it was the true
Christian's 'bounden duty' to improve his mind and his knowledge of God by surveying 'the countless wonders of the world …
created for his use and instruction'.[5] Science further enabled the
use of the earth's resources for prosperity, commerce and national
expansion, while the order in creation demonstrated God's providential order in church, society and state.[6]

These themes were expanded upon in several articles, poems
and reviews, in which Wilton set forth his understanding of natural
theology and its application to a touchstone of scientific and religious debate during the period: the reconciliation of Genesis with
the advances of scientific – and especially geological – knowledge.

[4] *Quarterly* 1.1, 4.
[5] *Quarterly* 1.1, 3.
[6] *Quarterly* 1.1, 7–15.

Geology had gained a prominent place in English life by the 1820s. The 'whole country', wrote Wilton, had 'run mad' after caves of hyena and mammoth bones, while every drawing-room had its 'little cabinet and museum', and every lady her *Outlines of Geology*, her bag and her hammer.[7] This was accompanied by considerable debate about the age of the earth and geological evidence for the Noahic flood, a debate which turned on whether human remains accompanied fossils supposedly destroyed by such a deluge. In the Australian context, landholder Alexander Berry applied to New South Wales Hutton's earlier uniformitarian ideas (that geological change occurred gradually and continuously over millions of years, rather than as a result of catastrophic events such as floods), as did explorer Peter Cunningham in 1827.[8]

Wilton responded to Cunningham by invoking Oxford professor Rev. William Buckland's 1820 *Vindiciae Geologicae*, an influential attempt to fit evidence for a catastrophic flood with Genesis.[9] In contrast with the views of some so-called 'Scriptural Geologists', whose literal readings of Genesis and suspicions of science were gaining currency after the mid-1820s, Buckland had suggested that 'leading difficulties' presented by geological evidence could be reconciled in at least three ways: first, with recourse to non-literal days of creation; second, by adopting an interpretation known as the 'gap theory', which posited a long period of geological history between the first two verses of Genesis (i.e. before the six days of creation); and third, with the retention of God's miraculous intervention as a first-cause explanation of the Noahic flood.[10]

In his *Quarterly* articles Wilton agreed with Buckland on the latter point.[11] Wilton also rejected the 'hypocrisy and cant in the present day – that the Bible [was] the only book man ought to peruse' and that 'human learning' was 'to be disclaimed as useless and hurtful'. Rather, declared Wilton, 'the Bible was designed

---

[7] *Quarterly* 1.2, 192.

[8] Alexander Berry, 'On the Geology of Part of the Coast of New South Wales', in Barron Field, ed., *Geographical Memoirs on New South Wales* (Sydney, 1825); Peter Cunningham, *Two Years in New South Wales*, 2nd edn (London, 1827). For Hutton's early uniformitarian ideas, see James Hutton, *A Theory of the Earth* (London, 1785).

[9] *Quarterly*, 1.2, 133–34.

[10] William Buckland, *Vindiciae Geologicae* (London, 1820), 25–33; see also *Geology and Mineralogy considered with reference to Natural Theology*, 3rd edn, 2 vols (London, 1858), 1: 13–31.

[11] *Quarterly*, 1.4, 376–77.

not to teach Geology, but Religion – not the structure of the earth, but the way to heaven'.[12] Nevertheless, Wilton's linguistic and biblical deductions convinced him that creation occupied six 24-hour days and that the age of the earth was only a few thousand years, *contra* Buckland's schema of non-literal days.[13] And while Wilton conceded the '*possibility*' of the gap theory, he doubted its '*probability*'.[14] In short, Wilton presented to the Australian colonies a conservative catastrophist position (changes in the earth's geology had been caused by violent events such as the Noahic flood) which affirmed the pursuit of science, but in the end was more akin to the Scriptural Geologists in its literalist interpretation.

Although the *Quarterly* ran for only four issues throughout 1828, its reach may be gauged from subscription lists which included the Colonial Office, Oxford and Cambridge, and eighty of the elite of New South Wales and Van Diemen's Land.[15] It was also received warmly in the press: the *Austral-Asiatic Review* was pleased with Wilton's reconciliation of geology and Genesis, while *The Tasmanian* praised the *Quarterly* as a 'useful, instructive and scientific work'.[16]

By the early 1830s, however, Wilton's views were becoming difficult to maintain in the wake of Charles Lyell's influential 1830–33 *Principles of Geology*, a devastating uniformitarian critique of the gap theory, although some debate persisted as to whether geological changes might have resulted from several catastrophic events.[17] Nevertheless, Wilton stuck to his diluvial guns, maintaining in a popular almanac of 1833 that there was evidence for minor catastrophes and for 'that one grand convulsion of nature, the Noachic Deluge'.[18]

The vacuum left by the *Quarterly*'s termination in 1829 was filled briefly by the short-lived *New South Wales Magazine,* which lasted only from 1831 to 1833. Mechanics' Institutes and debating

---

[12] *Quarterly*, 1.2, 3, 194.

[13] Ibid. 194–98.

[14] Ibid. (emphasis in original).

[15] *Quarterly*, 1.1, v–vi. The subscription list included the governors of New South Wales and Van Diemen's Land, the Chief Justice, scientists such as Alexander Macleay, all major newspaper editors and the leading gentry of New South Wales.

[16] *Murray's Austral-Asiatic Review*, August 1828; *The Tasmanian*, 1 August 1828.

[17] Charles Lyell, *Principles of Geology*, 3 vols (London, 1830–33).

[18] *1833 Calendar and Directory of New South Wales* (Sydney, 1833).

societies began to proliferate, while Presbyterian ministers such as J. D. Lang and John Lillie occasionally published sermons and lectures on science and religion; yet there were still few avenues in the colony for the dissemination of scientific discoveries and the discussion of their religious implications.[19] The sciences were 'all very good things', argued one Sydney newspaper editor in 1833, but hardly warranted the taxes that could support the more immediate concerns of wool production, agriculture and commerce.[20] As in 1828, however, it was an Anglican clergyman who would seek to remedy this situation.

II

W. B. Clarke (1798–1878) was by far the most accomplished of Australia's parson-scientists. Before taking his B.A. at Cambridge in 1817 he had come under the aegis of geology professor Rev. Adam Sedgwick, and after ordination went on to combine clerical appointments with substantial scholarly achievements in geology, zoology and meteorology.[21] A moderate Evangelical, in 1839 he took up a position in New South Wales which was sponsored by the Society for the Propagation of the Gospel, by now the largest provider of clergymen for the Australian colonies.[22]

Upon his arrival Clarke threw himself into parish and scientific work. Within three years he was leading the Australian Museum; combining geological fieldwork with parish work and itinerant preaching; and writing scholarly articles for journals in Tasmania, Britain and Europe. Clarke also established the Church of England Clerical Book Society, which held public lectures (reviewed at

---

[19] For the contributions of Presbyterian ministers to colonial intellectual life, see Michael Roe, *Quest for Authority in Eastern Australia, 1835–1851* (Melbourne, 1965), 140–81. In contrast, Roman Catholics and Nonconformists, both clerical and lay, contributed relatively little during this early period to public discussion of religion and science.

[20] *Sydney Monitor*, 13 and 20 July 1833, quoted in John Gascoigne, *The Enlightenment and the Origins of European Australia* (Cambridge, 2002), 89–90.

[21] The best introduction to Clarke and his scholarship is Ann Moyal, ed., *The Web of Science: The Scientific Correspondence of the Rev. W. B. Clarke, Australia's Pioneer Geologist*, 2 vols (Melbourne, 2003).

[22] The best account of the Society's role in providing Australian clergymen, both High Church and Evangelical, is G. P. Shaw, *Patriarch and Prophet: William Grant Broughton, 1788–1853* (Melbourne, 1978), chs 6–9.

length and often published in colonial newspapers) and accumulated the colony's most extensive scientific library.

Clarke is known among Australian historians as the 'father of Australian geology', as well as for his correspondence with a large international network which included many of the eminent scientists and explorers of the period.[23] Almost ignored, however, is Clarke's unusually influential role in shaping public discussion of science and religion.[24] As features editor and reviewer for the *Sydney Morning Herald* (hereafter the *Herald*), the colony's first daily (from 1840) and most widely read newspaper, Clarke wrote on an extraordinary breadth of issues, including religion, politics, geology, astronomy, botany, meteorology, Aboriginal anthropology and exploration. His 250 contributions to Australian newspapers between 1839 and 1850 – almost solely to the *Herald* – comprise mostly lead articles, as well as lectures, reviews and letters to the editor. Clarke's impact was magnified by the fact that during his editorship the *Herald* served as the colony's major forum for scientific discussion, in the absence of a scientific journal until the early 1850s. Also remarkable is the length of Clarke's articles, which often ran unabridged over several issues and took up thousands of words of editorial space. In short, Clarke's views were difficult to avoid in colonial New South Wales.

Like Wilton's earlier efforts, Clarke's writings between 1839 and 1850 are notable for their dissemination of contemporary scientific developments and their attempts to demonstrate the congruence of scientific endeavour and Christian orthodoxy. The latter was of especial importance in a decade in which that synthesis came under increasing pressure from biblicist Scriptural Geologists on the one hand and heterodox publications such as Robert Chambers' sensational *Vestiges of the Natural History of Creation* on the other.[25] The 1840s were also a particularly important decade for the maturing of Australia's intellectual life, in which an expansion of the periodical press paralleled increasing scientific endeavour,

[23] Moyal, *Web of Science*, 1: 15–16, 51–54. Correspondents included luminaries such as Adam Sedgwick, Charles Darwin, Richard Owen and the American geologist James Dwight Dana.

[24] The only scholarly analysis of Clarke's journalism is Michael Organ, 'W. B. Clarke as Scientific Journalist', *Historical Records of Australian Science* 9 (1992), 1–16; cf. Moyal, *Web of Science*, 1:10–13.

[25] Robert Chambers, *Vestiges of the Natural History of Creation* (London, 1844).

exploration and political independence. Throughout the decade Clarke argued that powerful theological, moral and social imperatives underlay scientific enquiry. In a lecture published in the *Herald* during 1841, he insisted that scientific pursuits played a key role in 'the promoting of a right knowledge of God, and of genuine religion', which, in turn, helped to 'fight the infidel tendency of the age', ennoble the mind, and inculcate morality and social order. It was far better, he added, 'to search out grounds for admiring and loving your Creator in a herb or a pebble, than to swell the throng of dissipation and vice, or suffer your faculties to be dormant when they ought to lead you to adoration and worship'. The present life was a 'preparation for immortality' and a knowledge of nature a means of gathering truth and fitting us 'better for the enjoyment of eternal bliss'. More radically, Clarke echoed Thomas Dick, author of the *Christian Philosopher*, in speculating that, in the light of Adam's skill in natural history before the Fall, such pursuits 'may belong to the saints in glory, and therefore ought now to be pursued on earth'.[26] Accordingly, the true scientist was defined in Christian terms as one who exchanged 'the ordinary pursuits and pleasures of life for the patient and self-denying investigation of the works of God', while what were often called 'human discoveries and inventions, [were], in their real character, gifts and revelations from God'.[27]

Like Wilton, Clarke insisted that the disciplines of science and theology recognize their limitations. Science, argued Clarke in a *Herald* editorial of 1841, was concerned with facts and empirical research rather than with theoretical speculation. Revelation should be 'exclusively directed to moral and religious purposes, and not as a guide in physical investigations'.[28] Additionally, Clarke placed limits on the extent to which knowledge of God could be obtained by natural reason independent of revelation. As in the 1820s, geology provided a touchstone for reconciling Genesis with the advances of scientific knowledge. In a lecture published in the *Herald* during 1843, Clarke suggested that geologists disagreed about interpretations of evidence because they were merely 'pioneers in the march of truth' and explored but '*part* of the ways

---

[26] *Herald*, 23 October 1841.
[27] *Herald*, 16 March 1846. See also 27 March and 3 April 1846.
[28] *Herald*, 18 November 1841.

of God'. Great harm would be done to divine truth if Scripture 'were to be brought in to build up theories which observation of the eye could refute, or to explain what it was never intended to explain'. Thus Clarke gave short shrift both to biblicist arguments against science and to the procrustean tendencies of the Scriptural Geologists. Clarke also echoed earlier statements of Archbishop Sumner and Buckland in his plea that theory be left 'till a time when some Newton should arise to put together the scattered elements of what was truth, and frame therefrom the only true history of the Earth'. This, Clarke earnestly believed, 'would be in strict accordance with the written records of creation'.[29] Consequently, Clarke was untroubled, unlike Wilton, by the idea that the earth was far older than literal biblical interpretations had suggested – a position which long been mainstream in British intellectual circles by the 1840s.[30]

Nevertheless, Clarke's own theoretical commitments were clear. In 1842 he wrote a series of lengthy lead articles on the discovery of fossil bones in New South Wales and their relevance to a Noahic flood.[31] Clarke saw insufficient evidence of fossilized human remains to claim man's contemporaneous existence with extinct species and therefore evidence of a flood. Although, wrote Clarke, persons 'of strong faith in revelation, and still stronger prejudices as to the province of faith' might consider 'the Diluvial Theory the most prudent and only certain one', religion gained nothing from such views,

> which could not be independently followed out; and therefore, knowing that *Truth* cannot be subverted by a *want* of evidence, and that the arguments against a *diluvial theory* are actually not to be found in geology (which deals with *several such catastrophes*), it does not establish any charge of being 'wise above what is written,' to be found content to review facts, without drawing conclusions from them, for or against that Word, which bears within itself its own credentials …[32]

[29] *Herald*, 7 April 1843 (emphasis in original).

[30] Compare Clarke's developing views on the age of Australia: *Herald*, 8 October 1842; 3 January, 7 April 1843; 27 March, 3 April 1846; 6 December 1847.

[31] *Herald*, 8 October 1842 (emphasis in original). See also 19, 26 October, 11, 19 November, 9 December 1842.

[32] *Herald*, 8 September 1842 (emphasis in original).

Thus while Clarke argued for proper detachment from theory, he nevertheless revealed his own (and his mentor Sedgwick's) belief that geology provided evidence for many catastrophes rather than one Noahic flood.[33] Clarke's catastrophist assumptions were reiterated in series of articles in 1847.[34]

Clarke also drew a line in the sandstone when scientific claims threatened orthodoxy.[35] Accordingly, after the publication in 1844 of Chambers' sensational *Vestiges* – which *inter alia* left no place for a superintending God – Clarke lamented in a book review that such 'mischievous and unphilosophical works ... are rashly considered as exponents of truth'.[36]

A final striking feature of Clarke's journalism is his discussion of science within a providential framework. 'Providence', wrote Clarke in a *Herald* article of 1846, 'never allowed man to be menaced by his other instruments, without teaching him how to avoid the danger'.[37] Thus scientific endeavour was a partnership with divine providence to benefit one's fellow man in a fallen world, whether it concerned discovering which Australian snakes were venomous; delineating the laws of weather patterns to avoid storms; or creating lightning conductors to protect buildings and ships.[38] Regarding the latter, Clarke added that young ladies who wore corsets with steel stay-plates made particularly good lightning conductors. Such ladies, he added wryly, invited 'fires to their hearts' and died to show that 'too much attraction is dangerous'.[39]

Science was also prominent in Clarke's wider providential vision. For example, geological research into the vast coal deposits of New South Wales was a means of extending 'the boundaries of civilization, arts, and manufactures, and in assisting the spread of scriptural truth'. It was no accident, he added, that such 'depositaries[*sic*] of fossil fuel' were found to exist 'wherever the Anglo-Saxon race have established themselves'.[40] Clarke thus repeated a familiar trope

[33] John Willis Clark, *The Life and Letters of Adam* Sedgwick, 2 vols (London, 1890), vol. 1, ch. 8.

[34] *Herald*, 30 November, 6 December 1847.

[35] *Herald*, 7 April 1846.

[36] *Herald*, 3 October 1846.

[37] *Herald*, 10 November 1846 .

[38] *Herald*, 10 January, 12 February 1842; 10 November, 1 December 1846.

[39] *Herald*, 10 November 1846.

[40] *Herald*, 27 March 1846.

of providential imperialism, though for him this was tempered by the equally familiar notions of trusteeship and divine accountability. Similarly, in one of his many editorials advocating scientific exploration in Australia, Clarke declared that Britain, 'a maritime, commercial nation', had received 'a fifth of the globe' (Australia) and its wider empire 'in trust from Providence'. At the same time, scientific developments and their applications, notably steam ships and locomotion, represented 'a revolution of the human mind' and 'the unopposable progress of intellectual expansion', and were a means of lessening prejudice and fostering commerce and peace between foreign nations. Given these developments, it was

> impossible not to see what … must be the destiny of Australia. It will be the civilization and evangelization of thousands and tens of thousands of immortal beings, and the extirpation of many of the crimes which, in these distant regions of the ocean, are as much national as individual.[41]

Clarke's optimism about the social, economic and moral benefits of science and technology reflect that of Dionysius Lardner, editor of the *Cabinet Cyclopaedia* and author of popular scientific works which Clarke had elsewhere recommended.[42] It also echoed a wave of providential enthusiasm in English missionary circles during these years, not least due to Britain gaining a freer hand in China in the wake of the Nanking Treaty (1842).[43] To the popular missionary slogan of 'Christianity, commerce and civilization' Clarke thus added science.

The impact of Clarke's journalism is evinced in the considerable criticism, debate and scientific activity generated by his pen. This ranged from running battles in the editorial and letter columns to public debates with other colonial scientists.[44] In 1847, for example, Clarke used the *Herald*'s columns to criticize friend and zoologist W. S. Macleay, the other first-rank scientist in the Australian colonies, for the latter's suggestion that ancient animal species had

---

[41] *Herald*, 1 January 1847.

[42] *Herald*, 23 October 1841.

[43] Brian Stanley, 'Commerce and Christianity': Providence Theory, the Missionary Movement, and the Imperialism of Free Trade, 1842–1860', *HistJ* 26 (1983), 71–94, at 78.

[44] For examples of criticism and debate generated by Clarke's articles, see *Herald* letters and editorials for 21 December 1841, 10 January 1842, 31 January 1847.

become extinct gradually rather than as a result of violent catastrophes.[45] Elsewhere, Clarke used book reviews to challenge both
the scientific analysis and the religious interpretations of scientists,
explorers and authors.[46] At other times Clarke trained his occasionally withering fire on radical papers such as the bishop-baiting
Atlas, which Clarke described on one occasion as 'puerile and
Quixotic' for its 'burlesque upon bishops' and its virulent criticism
of his *Herald* articles on scientific exploration.[47]

Other Anglican clergy before 1850, including Wilton, presented
a more conservative approach to science and faith than Clarke;
yet all publicly affirmed the value of scientific pursuits. Bishop
Broughton supported his clergy's scientific endeavours, granting
his clergymen permission to geologize while itinerating, and
writing that the Church bore 'no hostility to the pursuit of
science' and willingly 'received the homage of its professors'.[48] Yet
Broughton held that 'science alone could not lead to truth', and so
he favoured Paley's *Natural Theology* and a solid classical education
over science in his educational plans.[49] A similar teleological stamp
was evident among other Australian clergymen when the Church's
own monthly journal, the *Sydney Guardian*, was published from
1848 to 1850.[50]

III

Clearly Anglican clergymen played a key role in Australian debates
about science and religion in the formative second quarter of the
nineteenth century. Wilton and Clarke mediated metropolitan
debates to the colony through a distinctly Christian understanding

[45] *Herald*, 30 November, 6 December 1847. It should be noted, however, that after
the 1850s Clarke moved towards a uniformitarian position, in part due to Macleay's
influence and friendship.

[46] See, for example, Clarke's criticisms of Polish explorer Strzelecki's geological
conclusions: *Herald*, 16, 27 March, 3 April 1846.

[47] *The Atlas*, 16, 30 January 1847; *Herald*, 31 January 1847.

[48] W. G. Broughton, *The Present Position and Duties of the Church of England: A
Sermon Preached in Canterbury Cathedral, on Thursday September the 17th, 1835* (London,
1835), quoted in Mozley, 'Evolution', 417.

[49] Mozley, 'Evolution', 418; Shaw, *Patriarch and Prophet*, 29–30. See also, in this
volume, Keith A. Franics, 'William Paley, Samuel Wilberforce, Charles Darwin and the
Natural World: An Anglican Conversation', 353–65.

[50] Full title: *The Sydney Guardian: A Journal of Religion, Literature and Scientific Information* (Sydney, 1848–50).

of scientific endeavour. Influenced by their establishment Anglican mentors in England, they attacked biblicist suspicions of science and affirmed science as a providential gift for deepening spiritual understanding and for benefiting individual and society. At the same time they sought to delineate the limits of both theology and science. Both men were measured in their embrace of natural theology's claim to provide knowledge of God through natural reason independent of revelation. While insisting that the Bible was not a scientific textbook, they recognized a tension between scientific evidence and scriptural truth. Their differing hermeneutical schemes nevertheless reflect a spectrum within the broader liberal Anglican view of science.

Clarke's hearty embrace of science as an Evangelical provides colonial support for David Bebbington's assertion of the 'tight bond' between science and moderate Evangelicalism, in contrast with an earlier scholarly perception of evangelical indifference or hostility towards science.[51] The congruence of the moderate evangelical world-view, science and contemporary social thought has also been recognized in the metropolitan milieu by Boyd Hilton, and in the colonial Australian milieu by John Gascoigne (*contra* C. M. H. Clark's earlier epic schema of the Enlightenment and Anglican Evangelicalism as antithetical intellectual currents in Australian history).[52]

That Anglican clergymen took on such a role should not be surprising, given their strong establishment links, university connections and enhanced influence in a relatively small intellectual stratum. This was, after all, a period in which amateurs and clerics still wielded significant influence on scientific theory and practice. More striking is the use made by Wilton and Clarke of the popular literature of journals, newspapers and almanacs to

---

[51] David W. Bebbington, 'Science and Evangelical Theology in Britain from Wesley to Orr', in Livingstone et al, *Evangelicals*, 120–41, at 124. For evidence of Clarke's evangelical views, see W. B. Clarke, *The Dead Which Are Blessed: A Sermon Preached in the Church of St. Thomas, Willoughby, N. S. W., on Sunday, 2nd March, 1856* (Sydney, 1856); Elena Grainger, *The Remarkable Reverend Clarke: The Life and Times of the Father of Australian Geology* (Oxford, 1982).

[52] Boyd Hilton, *The Age of Atonement: The Influence of Evangelicalism on Social and Economic Thought, 1785–1865* (Oxford, 1988), 1–10; idem, *A Mad, Bad and Dangerous People?*, 174–86; C. M. H. Clark, *History of Australia*, 6 vols (Sydney, 1962–87), esp. 1: 91–110; 3: 383–414, 456–62; Gascoigne, *Enlightenment*, 96, 99.

present their views; as is the extent to which their efforts sprang from voluntary energy and initiative, rather than from formal agencies such as the Religious Tract Society, the British Association for the Advancement of Science or the Society for the Diffusion of Useful Knowledge. Such agencies, and especially the evangelical RTS, sought to ensure that the sciences were, as Aileen Fyfe puts it, 'properly interpreted' by an increasingly literate public.[53] In this sense the work of Wilton and Clarke sheds further light on the ways in which the periodical press mediated science and religion to a popular British audience.[54]

In her seminal assessment of the climate of opinion which prevailed in the Australian colonies until the 1850s, Ann Mozley concluded that, despite minor radical murmurings, 'faith in Mosaic cosmogony prevailed widely in educated circles in Australia'.[55] Similar trends in scientific and religious thought were evident in Britain and her wider empire, where the general tendency before 1850 was to harmonize science and religion and to delay any absolute break with teleology or the Genesis account.[56] In the colonies this was also partly a reflection of the derivative nature of colonial science, which tended to act as a source of raw scientific materials and to leave theorizing to the metropolitan elite.

This conservative tradition of integrating orthodox faith and science persisted in the Australian colonies well after the sound and fury of Darwinian debates after 1859.[57] While Anglican clergymen contributed significantly to the institutional and scholarly development of Australian science, it is also clear that they did much to create the climate of opinion which prevailed before 1850.

A recent flowering of critical scholarship on Australian Anglicanism has brought nuance to an earlier historical tradition which severely criticized the pre-1830 generation of Anglican chaplains

---

[53] Fyfe, *Science and Salvation*, 3.

[54] See Fyfe, *Science and Salvation*; Cantor et al., *Science in the Nineteenth-Century Periodical*.

[55] Mozley, 'Evolution', 419.

[56] See Rupke, 'Christianity and the Sciences', 163–68; John Barrett, *That Better Country: The Religious Aspect of Life in Eastern Australia, 1835–1850* (Melbourne, 1966), 192–95.

[57] Mozley, 'Evolution', 419; cf. Frame, *Evolution*, ch. 6.

for their role as magistrates and 'flogging parsons'.[58] Perhaps, in light of the journalism of Wilton and Clarke, the second generation might be better described as *blogging* parsons.

University of Cambridge

---

[58] For a succinct overview of past debates and recent scholarship, see Bruce Kaye, ed., *Anglicanism in Australia: A History* (Melbourne, 2002) 7–51.

THE MOUNTAIN AND THE FLOWER: THE POWER AND POTENTIAL OF NATURE IN THE WORLD OF VICTORIAN EVANGELICALISM

by MARK SMITH

IN the middle decades of the nineteenth century a new wind could be felt rustling in the branches of the Church of England. The transforming effect of the Oxford Movement on the High Church tradition is the most prominent example of this phenomenon but also well established in the literature are the transformations in contemporary Anglican Evangelicalism. David Bebbington in particular has stressed the impact of Romanticism as a cultural mood within the movement, tracing its effects in a heightened supernaturalism, a preoccupation with the Second Advent and with holiness which converged at Keswick, and also an emphasis on the discernment of spiritual significance in nature.[1] But how did this emphasis play out in the lives of Evangelicals in the second half of the century and how might it have served their mission to society? This paper seeks to address the evangelical understanding of both the power and potential of nature through the example of one prominent Anglican clergyman, William Pennefather, and one little-known evangelical initiative, the Bible Flower Mission.

William Pennefather was born in Dublin in 1816 into a wealthy Anglo-Irish family eminent in the legal profession and well connected to the hotter sort of Irish Anglican Evangelical including John Nelson Darby and Lady Powerscourt.[2] After an educational career interrupted by bouts of severe illness, Pennefather was ordained in 1841 and served a number of cures in Ireland.

---

[1] D. W. Bebbington, *Evangelicalism in Modern Britain: A History from the 1730s to the 1980s* (London, 1989), 81–171; The Keswick conventions, which began in 1875 in the romantic surroundings of the Lake District, brought together a theology of sanctification by faith with an emphasis on the imminence of the personal return of Christ; they were foundational for much mainstream evangelical spirituality in the succeeding decades. See also, in this volume, Andrew Atherstone, 'Frances Ridley Havergal's Theology of Nature', 319–32.

[2] For this context, see Alan Acheson, *A History of the Church of Ireland 1691–1996* (Blackrock, 1997), pt 4, ch. 1; Timothy C. F. Stunt, *From Awakening to Secession: Radical Evangelicals in Switzerland and Britain 1815–35* (Edinburgh, 2000), ch. 7.

Like many of his evangelical countrymen, however, he ultimately chose to make his career in England – the homeland of his wife Catherine, whom he married in 1847. There he served incumbencies at Aylesbury; Christ Church, Barnet; and St Jude's, Mildmay Park, in north London; but he exercised a wider influence through the annual pan-evangelical conferences he hosted from the mid-1850s, notable for their emphasis on holiness and for their adventism. A key element in Pennefather's world crystallized in the 1830s when as a teenager he went to study with a private tutor at Levens in Westmorland. There over the course of a three-year stay the young William, like other contemporaries, fell in love with the English Lake District, where to the attractions of mountains and flowers was added the lustre of Romantic poetry.[3] His appreciation of landscape was as passionate as that of any Romantic but the spiritual insights he drew from it were those characteristic of evangelical biblical orthodoxy. Viewing the fells around Windermere in 1847, he wrote: 'The rugged mountains come precipitously down to the water-side, and beyond rises summit above summit, with the sun sinking behind them. … Oh! To be ever rising, ever springing up in thought and affection towards Him, the eternal One, from whom all beauty and blessing flow!'[4]

This spiritual aesthetic drew Pennefather frequently to mountain scenery in both England and Ireland. It also filled him with a desire to see the Alps so intense that when, in 1865, an opportunity finally offered he hardly dared to contemplate the prospect, lest the gratification of the desire should draw his heart away from, rather than towards, his Saviour. The concern is characteristic of the finely drawn nature of Pennefather's spiritual sensibility but he need not have worried. One of Catherine's lingering memories of her husband was of sitting beside him observing the mountains, 'with his hand laid on mine to impose silence, the tears streaming down his cheeks, and his soul rapt in a communion with the Creator which I dared not break'.[5] His was not a pre-scientific

---

[3] M. A. Smith, 'William Pennefather', in T. Larsen, ed., *Biographical Dictionary of Evangelicals* (Leicester, 2003), 514–16; Bebbington, *Evangelicalism*, 159–61. For Pennefather, Lakeland and the Romantic poets, see R. Braithwaite, *Life and Letters of Rev. William Pennefather* (London, 1878), 12–13, 27, 400.

[4] Braithwaite, *Pennefather*, 206.

[5] Ibid., 31, 308, 399. For mountains as a site of communion with God, see also W. Pennefather, *The Bridegroom King: A Meditation on Psalm XLV* (London, n.d.), 16.

Romantic spirituality. Pennefather devoured studies of the effects of glaciation and could move seamlessly from a reflection on the 'throes of nature' that had produced the mountains to the assertion that 'all this loveliness and grandeur is the product of the *mind of God*'.[6] His love of the natural world was, however, given additional force by his eschatology. Pennefather was, like many other historicist premillennialists, devoted to the notion of the restitution of all things. This doctrine, as Martin Spence has recently pointed out, tended towards a highly positive appreciation of the value of the natural world.[7] Matter was for Pennefather never to be treated as of necessity evil and would in future 'yet again be fitted for the glorious presence of Jehovah'.[8] His joy in nature, whether at the beauty of a garden in spring or the grandeur of an Alpine range, was charged with promise – the sense that it represented a foretaste of the glories of a renovated earth at the millennium.[9]

Of course the danger of a spirituality of the mountains, especially for a clergyman based in an English city, was its relative inaccessibility to anyone outside a leisured elite. In Pennefather it was balanced by an equally intense appreciation of the beauty of flowers. Where mountains spoke to him of the might and magnificence of the Creator, flowers, whether in a mountain valley, an English hedgerow or a town garden declared God's care and tenderness. 'Flowers', Pennefather wrote in 1853, 'are tender tokens of a Father's love just to refresh His children by the way. What will the flowers of a renewed earth be, when in a blighted world like ours they are so fair and fragrant!'[10] The mountain would not come to Aylesbury or Barnet and the vast majority of Aylesbury or Barnet could never go to the mountain but the flower might easily be found or brought there and for Pennefather, as his biog-

[6]   Braithwaite, *Pennefather*, 400, 440.

[7]   The doctrine of the restitution of all things was the notion that God, at the physical return of Christ, would restore the whole of his creation to its primitive perfection and that a restored earth would be the home of a redeemed humanity. See Martin Spence, 'The "Restitution of All Things" in Nineteenth-Century Evangelical Premillennialism', in Peter Clarke and Tony Claydon, eds, *The Church, the Afterlife and the Fate of the Soul*, SCH 45 (Woodbridge, 2009), 349–59.

[8]   Braithwaite, *Pennefather*, 165.

[9]   Ibid. 131–32, 440. The concept of nature as promise among these Evangelicals stands in marked contrast to the emphasis on a lost Eden characteristic of some other Christian traditions.

[10]   Ibid. 277.

rapher noted, flowers, along with music and pictures, 'always had their place in the mission-work over which he presided, at a time when the power of these things was far less appreciated than is now the case'.[11]

If the mountain represented the power of nature for Evangelicals like Pennefather, then the flower represented its potential, and one of the leading ways in which this potential was realized in the late Victorian period was through a substantial yet little-known evangelical enterprise – the Bible Flower Mission. The initial concept of flower missions seems to have originated in the circles of the metropolitan Broad Church elite. In *The Flower Mission*, published in 1874 with an introduction by Dean Stanley, the initiative is attributed to a 'Lady in Belgravia' who

> knowing from experience what a love the poor have for the beauties of nature [was] led to a consideration how far this wholesome and innocent taste could be extended, and whether it would not be possible to procure a weekly supply of cut flowers from country friends to distribute amongst the various classes to whom they would be such a boon.[12]

The idea was simple. People with access to flowers would send supplies to a central point where they could be distributed in hospitals and workhouses and by district visitors to the homes of the poor. Two years of private experiment had revealed the potential of the idea and the 1874 publication, which was backed by the Stanleys and Octavia Hill,[13] was an attempt to extend its scope among the population of the great cities more generally:

> What a pleasure a parish depot of flowers well supplied each week would be! District Visitors would know where to send for nosegays for their sick, and it might benefit a higher class. How many an invalid in the middle and even upper ranks of life would rejoice in finding flowers within their reach, – single ladies, reduced in circumstances, who never can afford

---

[11] Ibid. 203.

[12] *The Flower Mission* (London, 1874), 7.

[13] For Hill's similar involvement with the Kyrle Society, which aimed to bring beauty into the lives of the urban poor, see N. Boyd, *Josephine Butler, Octavia Hill, Florence Nightingale* (London, 1982), 113–17.

in the lonely hours of their latter days the luxury of what they had in profusion in their youth, when all was bright.[14]

The project was entirely congruent with the civilizing mission and organic conception of society espoused by contemporary Broad Churchmanship. It aimed to create 'a bond of sympathy' between rich and poor and 'between town and country, through God's own gift of simple flowers'. It brought to bear the 'innocent gifts of the country in cheering and refining the habitations of the town poor'.[15] Moreover, the presence of the flowers, suggested the anonymous author of *The Flower Mission*, might have an even more powerful moral influence: 'truly God's natural beauties preach sermons to the hearts of the poor. "I was walking in the park last Sunday," said an old woman, "and when I saw all the trees budding out, I could not but ask myself, is there any good budding out in me?"' To first-generation city dwellers, in particular, the sight of country flowers evoked a former life uncorrupted by the town. Drawing inspiration from a recent initiative to place flowers as a humanizing influence on the floor of the New York Stock Exchange, *The Flower Mission* noted, many of the younger stockbrokers remarked 'that the flowers would remind them of the green fields of their youth, and of the days when they were young and innocent. If the flowers upon the table are the means of giving a pleasing sentiment to a simple broker, surely their mission is not in vain.'[16]

However pleasing the idea, it was not in its Broad Church form but in an evangelical one that this initiative was to blossom in the later 1870s, and not as the Flower Mission but as the Bible Flower Mission. The latter, which traced its own origins to the use of flowers by an East End district visitor in 1874, shared much of its methodology with the former.[17] Hampers containing cut flowers were sent from all over the country to a depot at the House of Industry in Spitalfields where lady volunteers made up bunches for later distribution – by the ladies themselves to hospitals and infirmaries and by Bible Women and London City Missionaries

---

[14] *Flower Mission*, 14.

[15] Ibid., 5–30. The idea that nature needed to be brought in to lighten the darkness of urban life was also characteristic of evangelical supporters of flower missions.

[16] Ibid. 16.

[17] *Woman's Work in the Great Harvest Field* [hereafter *Woman's Work*] 5 (1876), 80–81.

to the tenements and lodging houses of the East End.[18] This evangelical enterprise was, however, altogether different in scale. In
1882, for example, the East London depot alone distributed 110,125
bouquets and at least three other depots had been established in
the metropolitan area including one at the Mildmay Conference
Hall. Bible Flower Missions also spread rapidly to other British
cities and, through contacts made at Mildmay conferences, to other
locations in Europe and the Empire.[19] Depending as it did entirely
on gifts of flowers and on volunteer labour, the mission could
operate effectively on a very slender financial base: the East End
depot, for example, managed to conduct its entire business for less
than £50 in 1882. It was also a reflection of the energy and organizational genius of late Victorian evangelical networks in procuring
a steady supply of both materials and workers and even arranging
cut-price or free transport of the flower hampers on the railways.
At Spitalfields, the mission was run by the formidable Miss Annie
Macpherson – a close friend of the Pennefathers and a regular
attender and occasional speaker at the Barnet and Mildmay conferences – supported by her adjutant, the appropriately named Miss
Stock.[20] Their efforts were reinforced by a no-nonsense appeal to
evangelical concepts of stewardship,

> If this little record should fall into the hands of those who
> have hot house flowers at their disposal, we would ask them
> to remember the sick poor of our great city, and to spare them
> some of the choice blossoms. We are sure they will doubly
> enjoy their happy country homes, and the beauty of their
> conservatories, by sharing some of the rich produce with their
> poorer brethren and sisters; and if this service is rendered for
> Jesus' sake, it will have a full reward.

The less fortunate could still take a share in the work, however, and
even those who could not gather wild flowers could be equipped

---

[18] E. Murray, *A Day at the Bible Flower Mission* (London, n.d.), 4–13.
[19] *Report of the Bible Flower Mission East End Depot 1882* (London, 1882), 21;
Braithwaite, *Pennefather*, 530–34; *First Report of the Flower Mission in Connection with the
Manchester Evangelisation Committee March 1876–7* (Manchester, 1877); *Woman's Work* 4
(1875), 227–28.
[20] C. M. S. Lowe, *God's Answers: A Narrative of Miss Macpherson's Work* (London,
1882), 2–10; L. M. Birt, *The Children's Home-Finder* (London, 1913), 122.

by the mission with seeds to plant from packets provided gratis by Mr Martin Sutton.[21]

It was not only in scale and organizational capacity that the Bible Flower Mission differed from its Broad Church counterpart but also in its purpose and practice. The Evangelicals did not eschew a civilizing mission but theirs was first and foremost an evangelistic one. For them a general moral message conveyed by flowers was inadequate – what was needed was a clear statement of the gospel adapted to the needs of the recipients. The answer adopted by the Bible Flower Mission was simply to attach to each of the bouquets a card bearing a text of Scripture – not printed or mass-produced – but handwritten, again by volunteers, as a personal message. As the East End Depot report put it,

> we may never forget that our errand to the abodes of sorrow and suffering is to proclaim the good news of salvation to sin-stricken men and women. We have a warfare to wage against sin in the heart and sinful practice, and we dare not go without the texts our 'Weapons of warfare, … mighty through God to the pulling down of strongholds.' A large proportion of the poor we meet with in the Hospitals and Unions are lamentably ignorant of all Gospel truth, and in putting a text into their hand, we are using, perhaps the only opportunity we may have of giving them a clear statement as to *how they may be saved*. Next week when we go the bed may be empty, the patient may have passed into eternity, or have sufficiently recovered to mingle again in the busy scenes of life, and be lost in the crowd of those who throng our streets or who toil unseen in the dark recesses of our innermost courts and alleys. How necessary then that the words given should contain the message of salvation.

Some of the early efforts may have been defective, as Mrs Ashby, author of *Wonderful Words of Life. A Manual for Flower Missions*, explained,

> Too often passages from Scripture have been sent in for the Flower Mission which, taken by themselves, have no special application, and are, therefore, in no way likely to rouse,

---

[21] *East End Depot 1882*, 21–24.

313

convert, comfort, or restore. Sometimes again a prayer only without a reply is written, such as, 'God be merciful to me a sinner;' or a warning with no way of escape, such as, 'The wicked shall be turned into hell.' Thus the aim of the mission is completely frustrated.[22]

Hence the production of her manual designed so that 'each selection or collection of texts may come as a definite, concise, and pointed message of grace, as, so to speak, a telegram from God to the individual to whom the text bouquet is given'.[23]

The ideal was a pair of texts that combined a promise or a warning with an invitation. Mrs Ashby, for example, recommended associating: 'Sorrow and sighing shall flee away' (Isaiah 35: 10) with 'Ask, and ye shall receive, that your *joy* may be full' (John 16: 24).[24] The delivery of the texts was not entirely random and if the eighteenth-century Evangelicals had pioneered discriminating preaching their Victorian successors might be credited with discriminating bouquet delivery. As the East End report for 1882 noted,

> We need special texts for the anxious and the timid, the words of Him whose 'lips like lilies drop sweet smelling myrrh'. 'Come unto Me, all ye that labour and are heavy laden, &c.' ... 'Him that cometh to Me, I will in no wise cast out.' ... Lastly our basket will not be complete without some cheering gracious words of promise for the suffering believer; Oh, how often have the little texts – 'Fear thou not for I am with thee.' 'I will not fail thee nor forsake thee.' ... brought joy and rejoicing to tried and weary hearts.[25]

Reports from the flower missions were replete with instances of the effectiveness of the texts and the tendency of the recipients to preserve the cards long after the flowers had faded. But the texts themselves were only the beginning because the delivery of the bouquets naturally opened the door to conversation – what Miss Murray described as 'the precious opportunity to read the little text; to tell the story of "Jesus and His love," and to bid the weary

---

[22] E. Ashby, *Wonderful Words of Life: A Manual for Flower Missions* (London, c. 1882), 5.
[23] Ibid. 5.
[24] Ibid. 78.
[25] *East End Depot 1882*, 21.

and heavy laden go to Him for rest',[26] and the author of the East End Depot report as 'EARNEST WORK FOR SOULS'. Visits were therefore carefully prepared for, and Murray's account of the prayer meetings that preceded each round paints a vivid picture of the Romantic Keswick spirituality that fuelled the mission:

> A portion from God's word is read, and then kneeling around the mercy seat we spread our wants and work before the Lord. Those are indeed holy and happy moments, as one sister follows another in short earnest prayers for more entire consecration to Jesus, and meetness for his service; so that out of full hearts we may speak of 'His mighty love' to the sick and dying.[27]

To the written word on the cards and the spoken word in conversations – sometimes extended over several visits – the Bible Flower Mission added the third element in the nineteenth-century evangelical verbal armoury – the word sung. As Murray put it, with entirely unconscious irony, 'When the patients are able to bear it we sing softly one or two of Sankey's hymns – "The Home over there," "I left it all with Jesus," and "The great Physician now is near," are special favourites.'[28] Singing on the wards does in fact seem to have been particularly popular with the patients and was certainly effective in securing a welcome for the visitors. The Manchester branch, which began to use singing in 1878, summed up its impact in the words of Frances Ridley Havergal's 'Ministry of Song':

> When you long to bear the message
> Home to some troubled breast,
> Then sing with loving fervour,
> 'Come unto Him and rest,'
> O, would you whisper comfort,
> Where words bring no relief,
> Sing how 'He was despised
> Acquainted with our grief,'
> And, aided by His blessing

---

[26] Murray, *Flower Mission*, 9.
[27] Ibid. 6–7.
[28] Ibid. 10.

The song may win the way
Where speech had no admittance,
And change the night to day.[29]

The particular emphasis of the *Bible* Flower Mission on the word written, spoken and sung might raise a question about the value of the flower. At one level it is clear that the flowers were valued simply as a door opener – a universally acceptable gift that might open the way for the gospel message. The acceptability of such gifts to the poor and the sick had long been recognized and it constituted, as Miss MacPherson put it, 'a simple unostentatious way of bringing us in contact with those who in health and engaged in work, scarcely hear anything about the Saviour',[30] but they were far from unaware of its possible wider application. Mrs Ashby noted:

> Everyone acknowledges the great difficulty of bringing the simple gospel before unconcerned people in the middle and upper classes, and that it is comparatively rare for them to read or even willingly to accept a book or a tract on the subject. But the little floral offering of even a casual acquaintance can hardly be refused, and though the accompanying text may be apparently ignored, we have God's own promise to rely upon, 'My word shall not return unto me void' … Are there not many Christians cultivating conservatory and hothouse flowers who, if these were regarded as part of their stewardship, would see that they possess an invaluable ticket of admission into homes otherwise closed against the word of God?[31]

Nevertheless, as in the case of Pennefather, the flowers were also seen as possessing an intrinsic as well as a merely instrumental value. For Miss MacPherson, they might need the text to give them voice but 'Sweet and precious … are the blossoms which our heavenly Father has created to be silent messengers of His love and tenderness,' and 'The beautiful aphorism of our Lord's, that King

---

[29] *Third Report of the Manchester Bible Flower Mission March 1878–9* (Manchester, 1879), 6.

[30] *East End Depot 1882*, 9. For an earlier example, see the relationship between Margaret Hale and Nicholas and Bessy Higgins established by a gift of flowers in E. Gaskell, *North and South* (London, 1855), ch. 8.

[31] Ashby, *Wonderful Words*, 7.

Solomon, in all his glory, was not arrayed like one of the sweet lilies, might have included that with all his power, he could not wield an influence like one of these little flowers.'[32] Just as with the Broad Churchmen, the Evangelicals recognized the capacity of flowers to evoke a less sullied existence: 'A little buttercup or sprig of honeysuckle, will bring back memories of a happy childhood in the country home; and hearts are softened that have been hard and stony for years';[33] 'are not the flowers one of the first links in that chain of love which draws the poor, wearied, sinful heart up to God and heaven?'[34] For Mrs Henry, one of the earliest workers at the East End depot, 'we know that the little flowers have accomplished their mission, pointing from their own beauty, with silent though powerful voice, to Him who made them for his glory, to speak of Himself'.[35] For Catherine Pennefather, the work might often be 'the only opportunity of opening before eyes soon to close in death the two books which tell God's love to a sinful sorrowful world – creation in its living beauty, revelation with its glorious salvation'.[36] A renewed sense of the revelatory power of 'creation in its living beauty', especially (though not solely) among those who held to the world-affirming doctrine of the 'restitution of all things', should therefore be restored to our picture of late nineteenth-century Evangelicalism which has too often been dominated by a caricature of oppositional logocentric philistinism. From the life and ministry of William Pennefather to the work of his associates in the Bible Flower Mission and the Keswick-inspired spirituality of the visitors we can trace not just a continuity of delight in the beauty and power of the natural world but also an urgent desire to harness its potential to draw people back to their Creator and Redeemer, both of which were genuinely evangelical in character.

> I would not of course depend on these things, or carry them too far, [noted Pennefather,] nothing can satisfy the soul of man but 'the Bread of Life, which came down from heaven and of which if a man eat, he shall live for ever.' But man is

---

[32] *East End Depot 1882*, 6, 20.

[33] Murray, *Bible Flower Mission*, 9.

[34] *Woman's Work* 4 (1875), 141.

[35] *Woman's Work* 3 (1874), 158.

[36] C. Pennefather, 'Preface', in Ashby, *Wonderful Words* (unpaginated).

a compound being, and God has met his nature at all points. He has given food for the body, the intellect and the affections; He has surrounded us with forms of beauty and man is permitted to copy and represent and delight in these works of His Father's hand.[37]

University of Oxford

---

[37] Braithwaite, *Pennefather*, 202.

FRANCES RIDLEY HAVERGAL'S THEOLOGY
OF NATURE

by ANDREW ATHERSTONE

HISTORIANS of the nineteenth-century Keswick holiness movement have long observed, though seldom analysed, its theological appropriation of the natural world. With annual conventions held from 1875 in the Lake District, home territory of Wordsworth and Southey, the movement's love of nature was one of its most obvious 'Romantic affinities' and marked it out from other streams of contemporary Evangelicalism, as David Bebbington has recently shown.[1] Yet much of the early theological inspiration behind the Keswick Convention was drawn not from the Lake Poets, but from the devotional writings of Victorian England's best-known evangelical poet, Frances Ridley Havergal. The Keswick emphases upon absolute surrender to God and 'entire consecration' in his service, with a deep christocentric piety and a passion for spiritual transformation, pervade her teaching. Although Havergal's brief career lasted only two decades, being cut short by her untimely death in June 1879 at the age of 42, her output was prodigious. Alongside indefatigable letter-writing and the production of numerous evangelistic booklets, she published several collections of poetry and hymnody in a short space of time, notably *The Ministry of Song* (1869), *Under the Surface* (1874), *Loyal Responses* (1878) and, posthumously, *Under His Shadow* (1879). Her popular hymns, such as 'Take My Life' and 'Like a River Glorious', became synonymous with Keswick spirituality.

As this paper will seek to demonstrate, Havergal's own spiritual life and teaching were significantly influenced by her engagement with the natural world. In Britain she loved to explore the Lake District, Snowdonia and the Scottish Highlands, while in the last

---

[1] See esp. David Bebbington, *Holiness in Nineteenth-Century England* (Carlisle, 2000), 73–90 (quotation at 79); idem, *Evangelicalism in Modern Britain: A History from the 1730s to the 1980s* (London, 1989), 151–80; Charles Price and Ian Randall, *Transforming Keswick* (Carlisle, 2000); M. E. Dieter, *The Holiness Revival of the Nineteenth Century*, 2nd edn (Lanham, MD, 1996).

decade of her life she discovered the Swiss Alps, enjoying five extended visits there between 1869 and 1876. She found both Wales and Switzerland pleasurable in their own ways, like a forget-me-not compared to a rose,[2] but as her biographer Janet Grierson observes, 'it would be no exaggeration to say that she had a love affair with the Alps'.[3] Those tours amongst the mountains left a deep impression, giving new inspiration for her poetry and theologizing, which in turn influenced the Keswick movement. This paper will argue that Havergal's theology of nature had three major strands, which we will examine under three headings – nature's sanctity, nature's futility and nature's analogy.

NATURE'S SANCTITY

Havergal's intense encounter with the natural world began in early childhood, growing up in rural Worcestershire. She was born into an evangelical family, the youngest daughter of an Anglican clergyman, and her explorations of the large rectory garden and the local countryside were a vital preparation for her teenage spiritual awakening. Writing her secret autobiography in 1859, she recalled:

> I think I had a far more vivid sense of the beauty of nature as a little child than I have even now; and its power over me was greater than any one would imagine. I have hardly felt anything so intensely since, in the way of a sort of unbearable enjoyment. Especially, and I think more than anything else, the golden quiet of a bright summer's day used to enter into me and do me good. What only some great and rare musical enjoyment is to me now, the shade of a tree under a clear blue sky, with a sunbeam glancing through the boughs, was to me then. But I did not feel happy in my very enjoyment; I wanted *more*.[4]

At the age of seven or eight she read *The Task* (1785) by the evangelical poet, William Cowper, and was especially struck by its portrayal of true liberty for the Christian who encounters nature

---

[2] Maria V. G. Havergal, *Memorials of Frances Ridley Havergal* (London, 1880), 116.

[3] Janet Grierson, *Frances Ridley Havergal: Worcestershire Hymnwriter* (Bromsgrove, 1979), 114.

[4] Maria Havergal, *Memorials*, 15.

as God's bounty. She wanted to be able to join with Cowper in proclaiming of nature's wonders, 'my father made them all'.[5] Those words 'teased' her each time she looked upon a lovely country scene, and at springtime she could not get Cowper's poem out of her mind

> and a dozen times a day said to myself, 'Oh if God would but make me a Christian before the summer comes!' because I longed so to enjoy His works as I felt they could be enjoyed. And I could not bear to think of *another* summer coming and going, and finding and leaving me still 'not a Christian'.[6]

The natural world, according to Havergal's recollection, made a greater impact upon her nascent spiritual life than evangelical sermons and family prayers. She remained unmoved even by being taken to see the corpse of a dead child in her father's parish. Yet she was alert to nature's voice: 'the quiet every day beauty of trees and sunshine was *the* chief external influence upon my early childhood. Waving boughs and golden light always touched and quieted me, and spoke to me, and told me about God.'[7]

Throughout her later life, Havergal felt closer to the divine when enjoying the solace of nature. She described natural beauty as 'visible music'.[8] It stimulated her poetic talent and composition of sacred songs, the means by which she so often expressed her Christian devotion and her spiritual longings. Sometimes Havergal even saw her interaction with nature as a worthy substitute for her normal religious duties. Although a strict Sabbatarian, on one occasion she was content to spend Sunday in the isolated Swiss village of Göschenen (near Andermatt), at 3,500 feet, without attending divine service because 'I really think it will be as good as going to church just for once!'[9] The following summer she was prevented from attending William Pennefather's Mildmay Confer-

---

[5] *The Poems of William Cowper, 2: 1782–1785*, ed. John D. Baird and Charles Ryskamp (Oxford, 1995), 230.

[6] Maria Havergal, *Memorials*, 15.

[7] Ibid. 16–17.

[8] 'A Seeing Heart' (1872), in *The Poetical Works of Frances Ridley Havergal*, 2 vols (London, 1884), 2: 205.

[9] Havergal to J. Miriam Crane, 30 June 1871, in F. R. Havergal, *Swiss Letters and Alpine Poems*, ed. J. Miriam Crane (London, 1882), 128.

ence in London[10] due to illness and fatigue, so decided to climb Mount Snowdon instead, where the air was more bracing. Yet she anticipated that walking in the hills would be as much a spiritual blessing as listening to evangelical exhortations at Mildmay, and prayed 'that Wales might be *my* conference'.[11]

Havergal protested at human intrusions upon the natural world. During her tours of Switzerland she resolved 'systematically to let the towns alone & reserve myself for the "beauties of nature"'.[12] Likewise, while dashing through the grand scenery of the Rhône Valley by steam train she 'rather wished George Stephenson had never been born'.[13] Back in England, in an unfinished poem from 1872, she pleaded:

> Oh! give to me
> A pierless and paradeless sea,
> With a shore as God made it, grand and free,
> And not a mere triumph of masonry …

In the same verses she reflected upon the miraculous healing power of nature as nurse and physician:

> Oh! I could tell,
> For I know so well,
> How the unstrung nerves are tuned again,
> And the load rolls off from the tirèd brain,
> And strength comes back to the languid frame,
> And existence hardly seems the same.
> Her process is surer far and shorter,
> When out of reach of bricks and mortar![14]

Havergal experienced that psychological and spiritual refreshment during her Alpine adventures. She felt like the psalmist whose 'youth is renewed like the eagle's' (Psalm 103: 5) and her friends remarked on her unusually good health when she returned

---

[10] On Pennefather, see, in this volume, Mark Smith, 'The Mountain and the Flower: The Power and Potential of Nature in the World of Victorian Evangelicalism', 307–18.

[11] F. R. Havergal to Elizabeth Clay, 16 July 1872 (Maria Havergal, *Memorials*, 117).

[12] Worcester, Worcestershire Record Office, Havergal MSS, Swiss Journal, 10 June 1869.

[13] Ibid., 8 July 1869.

[14] 'Fragments' (1872; *Poetical Works*, 1: 199).

home.[15] She joked that in a previous existence she must have been a ptarmigan or a chamois, such was her agility and vivacity in the mountains.[16]

In her poems and letters, Havergal often invested the natural world with sacred and celestial imagery. She likened the unfolding of a flower to 'a wing-veiled seraph' uncovering its face.[17] Again, the blooms of spring, 'freed from snowy sepulchres', spoke with angelic voice of the resurrection of Christ.[18] Havergal had particular recourse to the language of sanctity upon discovering Switzerland. She described the Alps as 'God's great mountain temple'[19] and 'like a glimpse of the Celestial City ... so pure, so peaceful, so saintly, so solemnly, gloriously beautiful!'[20] Lausanne Cathedral was said to be the finest in the country, though Havergal considered it 'a plain awkward affair'. Yet she observed that they need not bother with 'architectural beauty' because 'The Swiss have natural temples ... in contrast with the Belgians who have cathedrals instead of mountains.'[21]

Havergal's first sighting of the Alps, keenly anticipated, occurred at five o'clock in the morning on 12 June 1869. As the sun rose and the mists lifted, she jumped out of bed and rushed to the window of her hotel bedroom in Berne. There stood the mountains in clear view, like 'mighty guardian spirits' keeping watch while people slept:

> Anything less ethereal & less holy than such they could scarcely be – the very mist was a folding of wings about their feet & a veiling of what might be angel brows, grand & serene. It is no use laughing at 'fancies' – wait till you have seen what we did from the roof of the Berner Hof!'[22]

That afternoon she sailed with her companions upon Lake Thun for a closer view of the Alpine trio – the Jungfrau, the Eiger and the Mönch – and Havergal was in ecstasy:

---

[15] Havergal to Charlotte Havergal, 2 October 1874 (*Swiss Letters*, ed. Crane, 302).
[16] Havergal to Crane, 20 July 1871 (ibid. 169).
[17] 'New Year's Wishes' (1858; *Poetical Works*, 1: 129).
[18] 'Easter Echoes' (1876; ibid. 1: 399).
[19] 'The Col de Balm' (1869; ibid. 2: 138).
[20] F. R. Havergal, 'Lucerne', *The Dayspring* (June 1874), 62.
[21] Swiss Journal, 3 July 1869.
[22] Ibid., 12 June 1869.

So now the dream of all my life is realized, & I have seen snow-mountains. ... It may be rather in the style of the old women who invariably say 'it's just like heaven' whenever they get a tolerably comfortable tea meeting, but really I never saw anything material & earthly wh[ich] so suggested the ethereal & heavenly, which so seemed to lead up to the unseen, to be the very steps of the Throne; & one could better fancy them to be the visible foundations of the invisible Celestial City, bearing some wonderful relation to its transparent gold, & crystal sea ...[23]

Havergal was impressed not just by the grandeur of the Alps, but also by the 'marvellous lavishment of beauty God has poured upon the *details* of His works', especially the carpets of flowers.[24] She told her siblings: 'I don't believe all the Botanic gardens in Europe could give so much actual pleasure.'[25] Nevertheless, as she exclaimed upon encountering Mont Blanc for the first time,

Mountains − real ones − are more to me than any other created thing − the gentle loveliness of lake scenery, or forest, or pastoral picturesqueness, is delightful, but nothing sends the thrill all through one's very soul that these mountains do. It is just the difference between the Harmonious Blacksmith on a piano, & the Hallelujah Chorus from a grand orchestra.[26]

Surveying Mont Blanc, the Dôme du Goûté and the Aiguille du Midi, Havergal portrayed them as 'robed in that singular holiness of light, utterly calm & pure, entirely celestial ... There is nothing like it except the smile of holy peace on the face of one asleep in Jesus.'[27] On a summit above the Col de Balm, revealing 'one of the most sublime & perfect panoramas in the world ... far away from the clatter and chatter of tourists',[28] she imagined herself one day standing with friends upon another mountain, 'the mountain of our God', enjoying the 'bliss of heaven'.[29] A few days later she

23 Ibid.
24 Ibid., 15 June 1869.
25 Ibid., 10 July 1869.
26 Ibid.
27 Ibid.
28 Ibid.
29 'Col de Balm' (*Poetical Works*, 2: 138−39).

wrote about the 'strange unique solemn beauty' of the mountains, almost oppressive, weighing 'one's soul down into awe ... If one were borne on an angel's wings up to Pierre Pointue, one would hardly dare speak in the sudden presence of the snow-glory'.[30] There was strong resonance in Havergal's mind between the 'snow-glory' of the Alps and the 'shekinah-glory' of the Holy of Holies.

Two years later, in July 1871, Havergal witnessed her first Alpine dawn, from a hillside overlooking the Aletsch glacier. Her description again resounds with language from the Apocalypse, where from 'a great and high mountain' the Apostle John witnessed the New Jerusalem descending out of heaven, shining with the glory of God (Revelation 21: 10). This Alpine dawn, for Havergal, was a foretaste of that final consummation of all things:

> In the east was a calm glory of expectant light, as if something altogether celestial must come next instead of a common sunrise. In the south and west, 'clear as crystal' [Revelation 21: 11], stood the grandest mountains, white and saintly, as if they might be waiting for the Resurrection, with the moon shining in paling radiance over them, and the deep Rhone [*sic*] Valley, dark and grave-like, below. Suddenly the first rose flush touched the Mischabel, then Monte Leone was transfigured by that wonderful *rose-fire*, delicate yet intense. When the Weisshorn came to life – most beautiful of all, more *perfectly* lovely than any earthly thing I ever yet saw – the Matterhorn caught the same resurrection-light on its dark and evil-looking rock-peak. It was like a volcano, lurid and awful, and gave the impression of a fallen angel, impotently wrathful, shrinking away from the serene glory of a holy angel, which that Weisshorn at dawn might represent if any material thing could.[31]

Elsewhere Havergal described the Matterhorn as 'the weirdest, most unreal looking spectre of a mountain you can imagine ... the snow mountains glimmered like ghosts'.[32] Here is a rare counter-

---

[30] Swiss Journal, 15 July 1869.

[31] F. R. Havergal, 'Holiday Work', *Woman's Work in the Great Harvest Field* 1 (1872), 184–85. For a similar description, see Havergal to Crane, 8 July 1871 (*Swiss Letters*, ed. Crane, 143).

[32] Havergal to Crane, 13 July 1871 (*Swiss Letters*, ed. Crane, 152, 155).

point to her general habit of representing nature in sacred terms. The images of 'spectre' and 'fallen angel' are spiritual ones, but convey the converse of sanctity.

NATURE'S FUTILITY

In July 1848, when Havergal was just eleven years old, her mother died. Alongside that devastating bereavement came for the first time a realization of nature's transience and futility, and 'a strange new sense of the vanity of life'. She confessed to her autobiography: 'As the beautiful spring came on there was a mist of melancholy over the very flowers: they had opened, well, what matter? they would fade again, and so would everything! I did not enjoy that spring as I had others, its charm was gone.'[33] That loss of childhood innocence is movingly portrayed in her poem 'Clouds in Prospect' (1854), and later in *The Four Happy Days* (1874), a devotional book about another eleven-year-old girl, Annie, coming to terms with her mother's death. Annie's vivid imagination and escapist joy concerning the natural world was undermined by reading a science textbook which gave her the molecular facts. The clouds, Annie discovered, were not 'snow mountains that could be climbed and rested upon', but 'only dismal thick mist and rain'.[34]

The natural world's inability to satisfy the longings of the human heart is a dominant feature in Havergal's theology. She draws attention to its fleeting beauty – whether snowflakes that melt or flowers that wither – compared to the enduring loveliness of heaven.[35] Furthermore, nature is not just passing, but fallen. In 'Earth's Shadow' (1855), she reflects upon the corruption of creation where 'sin pervades Earth's loveliest bowers':

> Like Italy's fair sunny vales
> With unknown deathly vapours teeming –
> Or like Sahara's sand-charged gales
> Beneath a sun unclouded beaming, –
>
> Such is our Earth. Roam where you will,
> Seems loveliness the eye entrancing;

[33] Maria Havergal, *Memorials*, 28–29.
[34] F. R. Havergal, *The Four Happy Days* (London, 1874), 23.
[35] 'Colossians 3: 2' (1854; *Poetical Works*, 1: 167–69).

The silent glen, the breezy hill,
The sun-tipped wavelet blithely dancing.

But gaze again. Each zephyr's breath
Uplifts a veil, dark truths revealing;
For all is stained with sin, and death
The fairest buds is grimly sealing.[36]

In Havergal's theology, access to beauty was a barometer of spiritual receptivity. Yet the natural world, even unsullied by human intrusion, could be barren rather than beautiful. For example, in January 1851 Allen Gardiner, evangelical missionary to Patagonia, died of starvation along with his companions on Picton Island, off Tierra del Fuego. In a poem to mark the tragedy, Havergal made much of the natural desolation of the South American coastline. Was it any wonder that a landscape so physically barren was inhabited by pagans who were resistant to the gospel?

No flowerets spring that barren land to cheer,
No waving trees salute that stormy sky
With graceful bend; scarce grass and herbs appear,
Or aught of greenery, to soothe the wearied eye.

O who in such a dreary clime could dwell?
Who would abide on such a desert shore?
Save the wild natives, who, our sailors tell,
No Saviour know, no Deity supreme adore.[37]

Here were people living far away from the urban slums of the industrialized West, yet their natural environment was still no Paradise, in fact the reverse. Elsewhere, Havergal concluded that even German dust, which limited her pleasure in touring the Black Forest region, must be a result of God's curse upon creation: 'surely there could have been no *dust* in Eden'.[38]

The inability of the natural world, even of the Swiss Alps, to bring true satisfaction, features in 'Zenith' (1877), which explores the futility and fragility of earthly zeniths. One section encapsulates the exhilarating thrill of mountaineering, and yet also its unhealthy attraction, the lure of 'that Alpine witchery'. It describes

[36] 'Earth's Shadow' (1855; ibid. 1: 171).
[37] 'On the Death of Captain Allen Gardiner' (1852; ibid. 1: 183).
[38] Swiss Journal, 7 June 1869.

an intrepid adventurer who at last achieved his great ambition to conquer the heights:

> He stood upon a long-wooed virgin-peak,
> One of the few fair prizes left to seek;
> Each rival pinnacle left far below!

Yet as he stood in triumph, there were tears in his eyes because still he remained unsatisfied. The poem climaxes with the affirmation that only through faith in Jesus Christ is 'perpetual zenith' attained.[39] A related lesson, from a different angle, is taught by 'The Splendour of God's Will', composed at Ormont-Dessous during her Swiss tour of 1874. It portrays a young invalid confined to her couch, barred from enjoying the springtime outdoors; yet through that deprivation she comes to a deeper appreciation of God's sovereign love.[40] Here again is a counterpoint to the general thrust of Havergal's teaching – an example of spiritual sensitivity heightened by enforced absence from the natural world, not by interaction with it. Similarly, she lauded her American contemporary Fanny Crosby (1820–1915), the evangelical hymn-writer, for her ability to compose poetry of such spiritual depth even though she was blind and therefore unable to experience natural beauty.[41] Ultimately, in Havergal's theological framework, nature by itself was futile. It could act as a spiritual stimulus, but was neither necessary nor a substitute for relationship with God himself.

NATURE'S ANALOGY

While meditating upon the natural world, Havergal constantly sought new spiritual insights and biblical illustrations. A passion for evangelism and discipleship was the keynote of her ministry, and nature provided a rich source of material to convey Christian truth. Often she taught these lessons by way of analogy.

For example, holidaying in July 1855 at Langland Bay on the Gower Peninsula looking out across the Bristol Channel, Havergal reflected upon the ocean waves, both dangerous and yet delightful. By analogy, the trials of life could be viewed from two perspec-

---

[39] 'Zenith' (1877; *Poetical Works*, 2: 310–11, 328).
[40] 'The Splendour of God's Will' (1874; ibid. 2: 360–64).
[41] 'Seeing Heart' (ibid. 2: 205–07).

tives, as 'awful messengers of ire' and yet as heavenly blessings.[42] On another occasion, Havergal was walking in Snowdonia and dark clouds shrouded the mountains until a reviving breeze blew in from the Irish Sea. This led her to portray God's faithfulness as a mountain, firmly established but sometimes veiled.[43] Other aspects of the natural world – sunshine and shadows, blossom and birds, fruit and forests, rain and rivers, the changing seasons and the animal kingdom – provided an endless store of imagery to convey biblical lessons. Just as springtime had made a spiritual impact upon Havergal as a young girl, so in her later poetry it was often synonymous with conversion, restoration or resurrection. Nor did it escape her attention that the Treaty of Paris (1856), which brought the Crimean War to an end, was signed in the early spring, and she turned to nature and the cosmos for pictures to describe the arrival of peace.[44]

Once again, Havergal's Alpine adventures considerably expanded her range of illustrations, while also enhancing her understanding of the biblical texts. For example, the snow on the Jungfrau, with its 'wonderful intensity of whiteness', gave new force to the Psalmist's prayer to be washed 'whiter than snow' (Psalm 51: 7).[45] The raging torrents of glacier water cascading down Alpine gorges brought deeper meaning to the thunderous 'voice of many waters' heard upon Mount Zion (Revelation 14: 2, 19: 6).[46] Likewise the dangerous waves suddenly whipped up on Lake Lucerne by the föhn wind coming off the mountains, while Havergal was boating across, gave her a fresh appreciation of the storm on Lake Galilee.[47] Elsewhere she meditated upon the ways in which walking as a Christian disciple along the 'narrow way' (Matthew 7: 14) could be a pleasure:

> Narrow indeed it is! Who does not choose
> The narrow track upon the mountain side,
> With ever-widening view, and freshening air,
> And honeyed heather, rather than the road,

[42] 'Two Points of View' (1855; ibid. 1: 194).
[43] 'July on the Mountains' (1872; ibid. 2: 207–208).
[44] 'Peace' (1856; ibid. 1: 196–98).
[45] Swiss Journal, 14 June 1869.
[46] 'The Voice of Many Waters' (1878; *Poetical Works*, 2: 381–87).
[47] Havergal to Caroline Havergal, 3 June 1873 (*Swiss Letters*, ed. Crane, 224).

> With smoothest breadth of dust and loss of view,
> Soiled blossoms not worth gathering, and the noise
> Of wheels instead of silence of the hills,
> Or music of the waterfalls? Oh, why
> Should they misrepresent Thy words, and make
> 'Narrow' synonymous with 'very hard'?[48]

Havergal's Swiss travels also offered many analogies of biblical principles. For example, in July 1869 her party boated across Lake Geneva from Montreux to Bouveret, where the River Rhône enters the lake. At first their passage was

> utterly tranquil & innocent, all at once … you are in the midst of a mighty wild brown roaring wicked current. The boatmen say 'Don't be afraid, only sit still' & pull with all their might. In a minute or two you shoot into uncontaminated, still, blue again. The current is so impetuous that it flows thus unmingled for a mile & a half.[49]

The experience suggested 'plenty of analogies' to Havergal's mind, though she did not commit them to paper – probably about the need to trust in Christ as the divine boatman for protection from spiritual assault. At Ormont-Dessous she penned 'The Thoughts of God' (1874), described by Grierson as a poem in which 'her heightened spiritual awareness seems to fuse with her aesthetic sensitivity to the Alpine scene'.[50] It is a meditation upon divine omniscience and ineffability, contrasted with weak and fallible human thinking. Again Havergal returned to the image of a mountain climber to express the impossibility of reaching up to God's holy transcendence:

> Or like the traveller, toiling long to gain
> An Alpine summit, white and fair,
> With far-extending view; but still withheld,
> And to the downward track with fainting step compelled
> By an intangible barrier; for the air
> Is all too rare,

---

[48] 'The Two Paths' (1878; *Poetical Works*, 2: 365–66).
[49] Swiss Journal, 7 July 1869.
[50] Grierson, *Havergal*, 152.

> Too keenly pure
> For valley-dweller to endure.[51]

A further analogy was drawn from Havergal's alpenstock on which, following mountain-climbers' tradition, she carved a record of locations she had visited. In the same way Christians were urged to engrave upon their hearts a record of God's faithfulness and answers to prayer.[52] Elsewhere, she theologized pain as a proof of God's love, by illustration from an Alpine rescue: 'He inflicts or permits it, that He may rouse, and warn, and check, and *save*. What thousands have blessed Him for the pain that came like a rough hand catching them as they fell over a precipice, hurting and pinching their very flesh, but *saving* their lives!'[53]

The analogy which Havergal developed at greatest length was that of the Swiss mountain guide. In the evangelical *Sunday Maga-zine* she elucidated the many ways in which the guide was a model of Jesus Christ – carrying the burdens of the English travellers, showing the safest route up the mountain, leading by example, caring for the weak and sick, and putting his own life in danger to protect them. Those following the guide were wise to remain close, literally standing in his footsteps and heeding his every instruction.[54] Havergal's favourite guide was Joseph Devouassoux from Chamonix at the foot of Mont Blanc,[55] and she reminded her readers that in biblical typology Jesus Christ is 'our true Joseph'. She was also impressed by the rope which the guide fastened around the mountaineers when in danger from hidden crevasses or sudden avalanches. The authentic Alpine Club rope, known to be the safest in Switzerland, was identified by a scarlet thread amongst the strands – strikingly reminiscent of Rahab's scarlet cord (Joshua 2: 18), which was widely interpreted as a typological foreshadowing of the blood of Christ.[56]

---

[51] 'The Thoughts of God' (1874; *Poetical Works*, 2: 332).
[52] 'Our Red-Letter Days' (1877; ibid. 1: 423–24).
[53] Maria Havergal, *Memorials*, 228.
[54] F. R. Havergal, 'Our Swiss Guide', *Sunday Magazine* 4 (1874–75), 47–51.
[55] *Swiss Letters*, ed. Crane, 318.
[56] Havergal, 'Swiss Guide', 47, 50.

CONCLUSION

As has been argued in this paper, the natural world played a significant part in Havergal's theology, one of the key foundations of the Keswick holiness movement. At one level, nature provided an abundant source of memorable and attractive illustrations and analogies to help Havergal convey biblical lessons to her readership. Yet she did not view nature merely as a teaching tool to serve her own didactic and evangelistic ends. At a deeper level, she understood nature itself to be the teacher – awakening her spiritual longings, stimulating her poetic instinct, helping her to hear the voice of God and giving her a foretaste of heaven. Both the delicious pleasures and the frustrating transience of the created world spoke of the need to seek ultimate satisfaction only in the Creator.

Wycliffe Hall, Oxford

DARWIN'S CHURCH*

by PAUL WHITE

> From the war of nature, from famine and death ...
> endless forms most beautiful and most wonderful have
> been, and are being, evolved.
>
> (Charles Darwin, *On the Origin of Species*)

MUCH has been made of the roots of Darwinian theory in the work of Thomas Malthus, who argued for the inevitability of strife, suffering and death following on the scarcity of resources and the tendency of populations to multiply without limit. It has been noted that a Malthusian pessimism about human nature re-emerged in the 1830s, darkening the political discussions surrounding the welfare of the poor, and informing the legislation of the Poor Laws in those crucial years in which Darwin formulated his natural selection theory.[1] Historians have also focussed on the harshness of the social Darwinism that was taken up by theorists later in the century, in contrast to the more optimistic, Lamarckian evolution of Herbert Spencer, Peter Kropotkin and others.[2] Yet in the closing passage of *Origin of Species*, Darwin extended his famous metaphor of the entangled bank, offering a form of redemption through struggle toward higher forms of life.[3] Darwin often dwelt upon, and used to calculate

---

* I would like to acknowledge my indebtedness to Elizabeth Smith for research on Darwin's involvement in the parish church of Downe, and to the ground-breaking scholarship of James Moore on Darwin and religion.

[1] Thomas Malthus, *An Essay on the Principle of Population* (London, 1789). On Darwin's reading of Malthus, see Robert Young, *Darwin's Metaphor: Nature's Place in Victorian Culture* (Cambridge, 1985), 23–55. On the revival of Malthus in the 1830s, see Adrian Desmond and James Moore, *Darwin* (London, 1991), 153–54, 196–97, 264–68; A. M. C. Waterman, *Revolution, Economics, and Religion: Christian Political Economy, 1798–1833* (Cambridge, 1991).

[2] Peter Bowler, *The Eclipse of Darwinism: Anti-Darwinian Theories of Evolution in the Decades around 1900* (Baltimore, MD, 1983); Diane B. Paul, 'Darwin, Social Darwinism, and Eugenics', in J. Hodge and G. Radick, eds, *The Cambridge Companion to Darwin* (Cambridge, 2003), 214–39.

[3] On the redemptive strain in Darwin's theory, see Robert Richards, 'Darwin on Mind, Morals and Emotions', in Hodge and Radick, eds, *Cambridge Companion*, 92–115.

precisely, the months, days and hours he had invested in each of his works, a process he described not as invention or creation, but as hard labour.[4] For Darwin, the economies of nature and human society were both driven by labour, and marked by hardship and loss, but also by an enormous wealth of productions, generative force, abundance and proliferation without end.

This paper explores the ways in which Darwin and some of his contemporaries sought an accommodation between a human life of toil and hardship and a natural world of bounty and grandeur. The suggestiveness of some of Darwin's language of natural law and the power of selection facilitated readings in which the books of nature and God could be incorporated within various church traditions, and the visions of fallen man and the prelapsarian garden reconciled. It is also significant that in Darwin's own daily life and that of his family, the ameliorative role of the Church remained crucial. Darwin did not abide a selfish individualism or an aggressive secularism, but rather supported the Church as a social institution through a variety of charitable and custodial activities in his own parish of Downe. The history of Darwin and the Church is thus one of entanglement, mutual accommodation and incorporation.

I

That Darwin and his work achieved some rapprochement with the Church may be surprising. The view of religion and science locked in battle, with the Church and its bishops on one side and the proponents of evolution on the other, is a persistent one in the public sphere, despite having been substantially overturned by three decades of scholarship.[5] The responses to Darwin were wide-ranging, and many show an active engagement and appro-

---

[4] See, e.g., Charles Darwin, *Autobiography: With Original Omissions Restored* (London, 1958), 122. The time spent on each of his publications was tallied in his journal: Gavin de Beer, 'Darwin's Journal', *Bulletin of the British Museum (Natural History), Historical Series* 2 (1959), 1–21.

[5] John Hedley Brooke, *Science and Religion: Some Historical Perspectives* (Cambridge, 1991); idem, *Reconstructing Nature: The Engagement of Science and Religion* (Edinburgh, 2000); Thomas Dixon, *Science and Religion: A Very Short Introduction* (Oxford, 2008); James Moore, *The Post-Darwinian Controversies: A Study of the Protestant Struggle to Come to Terms with Darwin in Great Britain and America, 1870–1900* (Cambridge, 1979).

priation of Darwinian ideas for a variety of religious ends. One of the best sources for this material is correspondence, for it shows the religious reception of Darwin in the making, with reader and author engaged in conversation over the moral meaning and theological implications of the text at hand. Darwin's work relied to an unusual degree on correspondence, his research and reputation resting upon an extensive network of contacts with breeders, gardeners, travellers, military and colonial officials, and leading specialists in various branches of natural history, all of whom fed him information, specimens and ideas.[6]

One of Darwin's most avid readers was the Anglican cleric, Charles Kingsley. Kingsley wrote to Darwin shortly after the publication of *Origin*:

> I have gradually learnt to see that it is just as noble a conception of Deity, to believe that he created primal forms capable of self development into all forms needful pro tempore & pro loco, as to believe that He required a fresh act of intervention to supply the lacunas which he himself had made.[7]

At the time of writing, Kingsley was best known for his role in the Christian Socialist movement and as the author of *Alton Locke*, but he had also acquired a reputation as a naturalist and popular science writer through works such as *Glaucus, or the Wonders of the Shore* (1855). In letters, sermons and children's literature, Kingsley would expound a version of Darwinian theory and beneficent design.[8] Kingsley was not atypical in his liberal theological accommodation of Darwinism, drawing on science to promote a less doctrinal, unfolding revelation, and a catholicity of outlook deemed essential to the maintenance of the Church of England.[9] Clergymen were

---

[6] Janet Browne, *Charles Darwin: The Power of Place* (London, 2002), 10–13; James Secord, 'Darwin and the Breeders: A Social History', in David Kohn, ed., *The Darwinian Heritage* (Princeton, NJ, 1985), 519–42; Paul White, 'Correspondence as a Medium of Reception and Appropriation', in T. Glick and E.-M. Engels, eds, *The Reception of Charles Darwin in Europe*, 2 vols (London, 2008), 1: 54–65.

[7] Letter from Charles Kingsley, 18 November 1859, in *The Correspondence of Charles Darwin*, ed. F. Burkhardt, S. Smith et al., 17 vols so far (Cambridge, 1985–), 7: 379. Volumes 1–14 are available online at <http://www.darwinproject.ac.uk/>.

[8] John Beatty and Piers Hale, '*Water Babies*: An Evolutionary Fairy Tale', *Endeavour* 32 (2008), 141–46.

[9] On liberal Anglican theology and the Broad Church movement, see E. R. Norman, *The Victorian Christian Socialists* (Cambridge, 1985); B. M. G. Reardon, *Liberal*

among the largest professional groups with whom Darwin corresponded. In his publications, Darwin was generous and precise in acknowledging the support of his correspondents, and was keen to incorporate their authority as well as their expertise when warranted. Darwin made striking use of Kingsley's letter in order to secure religious authority, specifically clerical sanction, for his work. After obtaining permission from Kingsley, he inserted the above sentence (translating the Latin) in the second edition of *Origin*, as issuing from 'a celebrated author and divine'.[10]

In the period immediately following the publication of *Origin*, Darwin sought to diffuse polemical debate and encourage religious readings of his work. He enhanced the Old Testament language of the book itself, adding the word 'Creator' in his concluding remarks,[11] in spite of the fact that his close scientific colleague, Charles Lyell, had criticized him for deifying natural selection.[12] He encouraged one of his correspondents, Asa Gray, a botanist, devout Presbyterian, and leading proponent of Darwinism in America, to reissue a series of reviews he had written for the *Atlantic Monthly* as a separate pamphlet in Britain, with Darwin financing the re-publication. The pamphlet was titled *Natural Selection Not Inconsistent with Natural Theology*. According to Gray, Darwin wrote only of secondary causes, not of first causes. He left questions such as the origin of life and the design of nature's laws open for theologians to answer as they might. Gray also offered his own suggestions as to how a benevolent and all-knowing God might operate in accordance with natural selection, directing the process of variation along favourable lines.[13] The correspondence between Darwin and Gray is rich in discussions of design in nature, and it is clear that Darwin had strong reservations about the particularities

---

Theology in the Nineteenth Century (Cambridge, 1982); Charles Sanders, *Coleridge and the Broad Church Movement* (Durham, NC, 1942). On accommodation with Darwinism, see, in this volume, William Sheils, 'Nature and Modernity: J. C. Atkinson and Rural Ministry in England, c. 1850–1900', 366–95.

[10] Charles Darwin, *On the Origin of Species*, 2nd edn (London, 1860), 481.

[11] The changes to Darwin's text can be traced in *The Origin of Species: A Variorum Text*, ed. Morse Peckham (Philadelphia, PA, 1959).

[12] Letter from Charles Lyell, 15 June 1860 (*Correspondence*, ed. Burkhardt, Smith et al., 8: 255).

[13] Asa Gray, *Natural Selection Not Inconsistent with Natural Theology: A Free Examination of Darwin's Treatise On the Origin of Species and of Its American Reviewers* (London, 1861).

of Providence as suggested by Gray, fearing the implication that such Divine activity rendered natural selection superfluous:

> I have lately been corresponding with Lyell, who, I think, adopts your idea of the stream of variation having been led or designed. I have asked him (& he says he will hereafter reflect & answer me) whether he believes that the shape of my nose was designed. If he does, I have nothing more to say.[14]

Darwin's nose loomed large in these discussions of the absurdity of specific design, along with the rudimentary *mammae* of man and his peculiarly constructed bladder, 'drained as if he went on all four legs'. Yet Darwin would typically retreat from theological engagement with a profession of ignorance: 'You say that you are in a haze; I am in thick mud; – the orthodox would say in fetid abominable mud. I believe I am in much the same frame of mind as an old Gorilla would be in if set to learn the first book of Euclid.'[15]

This charming withdrawal from religious subjects became a fixture of Darwin's correspondence, resting most often on a division of authority between science and theology. During his most active period of speculation on species theory, Darwin had read widely in philosophy and theology during the late 1830s and 1840s. The impression he gives in letters is of respect and deference to such authors as he would show an expert on any scientific subject. At times this professional division of labour was supplemented, or even supplanted, by a methodological one, as Darwin hinted that there were some questions that were closed to scientific investigation. Darwin's views on such matters were drawn out by correspondents who looked to him for answers to various questions of religious belief or doctrine. In December 1866, Darwin received a letter from Mary Boole, an educator and writer who was supporting her five daughters as a librarian after her husband, the mathematician George Boole, died in 1864.

---

14 Letter to Asa Gray, 17 September [1861] (*Correspondence*, ed. Burkhardt, Smith et al., 9: 266).
15 Letter to Asa Gray, 11 December [1861] (ibid. 9: 368).

Dear Sir

Will you excuse my venturing to ask you a question to which no one's answer but your own would be quite satisfactory ... Do you consider the holding of your Theory of Natural Selection to be inconsistent ... with the following belief:

That God is a personal and Infinitely good Being ...

That the effect of the action of the Spirit of God on the brain of man is especially a moral effect.

My own impression has always been ... that you had supplied one of the missing links, – not to say *the* missing link, – between the facts of Science & the promises of religion.[16]

Letters of this sort, written to Darwin by persons unknown to him, became more frequent from the late 1860s onward, as his international fame grew. Young naturalists, sceptical writers and evangelical solicitors wrote to him inquiring about his personal beliefs, and seeking direction for their own. Darwin's replies to such communications were always polite and brief. To Boole he wrote: 'It would have gratified me much if I could have sent satisfactory answers to yr. questions. These as it seems to me, can be answered only by widely different evidence from Science, or by the so called "inner consciousness".' He reiterated the view suggested in *Origin of Species* that to regard the pain and suffering of the world as an outcome of universal laws, rather than of the direct will of God, was for him a source of consolation.[17]

Darwin is of course famous for his public reticence on matters of religious belief. Letters became an important medium through which readers sought to explore the religious implications of his work. But there is also often an attempt in these letters to invest Darwin himself with religious authority, and in so doing gain support for religious heterodoxy. Boole had written to Darwin directly, she remarked, because she had been dissatisfied with the reviews of his work, though they were written by persons 'cleverer and wiser' than herself. For some, Darwin the author became a

---

[16] Letter from Mary Boole, 13 December 1866 (ibid. 14: 423–24). For biographical details on Boole, see M. Ogilvie and J. Harvey, eds, *The Biographical Dictionary of Women in Science*, 2 vols (London, 2000), 1: 158–59.

[17] Letter to Mary Boole, 14 December 1866 (*Correspondence*, ed. Burkhardt, Smith et al., 14: 425–26).

scientific apostle, who alone could provide authoritative commentary on his sacred text.

> I greatly admire your Book, which I have read twice & which I shall read as I do the precepts of Christ & the parable of the prodigal son ... You have enlarged my mind, filled it with power, given an upward direction to my thoughts, & conciliated my respect for humanity ... you demand of me a faith 'in the substance of things not known & the evidence of things not seen' – which requires all those dispositions of mind which faith implies. So far, my faith has been individual & personal. I have a profound reverence for Abraham & Moses & Jesus Christ, & I have much of the same reverence for you, whom I look upon as the High priest of nature. But the Church would condemn me to the stake for my religious creed.[18]

This letter was from Francis Boott, a physician, botanist, and secretary to the Linnean Society of London, the leading natural history society in England. He was a close friend of Asa Gray, and had some previous correspondence with Darwin on botanical subjects. Boott was certainly earnest in regarding Darwin's theory of descent by natural selection as an article of faith. He explains to Darwin that he could follow the modifications in *Carex*, a genus of grasses of which he was the leading expert, 'but when you bring millions of years into play, & ask me to believe in a common ancestor to the Sedge-palm, Oak &c you are like the Church, which demands of me a faith I have no elements for'. Boott described his religion as 'an orthodoxy of its own'. His doubts about natural selection notwithstanding, he placed Darwin in his 'self-consecrated Temple ... Your altar close to that of Linneus & Gilbert White'.[19]

Such reverential regard for Darwin might seem highly eccentric and marginal were it not borne out by a variety of other sources, and entirely consistent with more elaborate movements of secular religion and scientific humanism elsewhere.[20] Only such manifest adoration could provide raw material for tongue-in-cheek repre-

---

[18] Letter from Francis Boott, 29 February 1860 (*Correspondence*, ed. Burkhardt, Smith et al., 8: 113).

[19] Letter from Francis Boott, 26 December 1862 (ibid. 10: 627).

[20] See, for example, the discussion of the cult of Comtism and the religion of humanity in Thomas Dixon, *The Invention of Altruism: Making Moral Meanings in Victorian Britain* (Oxford, 2008); also Edward Royle, *Victorian Infidels: The Origins of the*

Fig. 1. T. H. Huxley's sketch of Darwin, 20 July
1868 (courtesy of the Syndics of Cambridge
University Library). Cambridge University
Library. Darwin Archive, DAR 221,254.

sentations as the sketch in a letter from Thomas Huxley in 1868
(figure 1), in which Darwin appears as a holy man giving solemn
audience to a believer in the form of a German naturalist, Wilhelm
Kühne. A bishop's staff or crozier appears in Huxley's drawing as
a collector's net and reads 'Variation', while the mitre is stamped
with the word 'Pangenesis', Darwin's theory of inheritance recently
unveiled in his book *Variation in Animals and Plants under Domestica-*

British Secularist Movement, 1791–1866 (Manchester, 1974); idem, *Radicals, Secularists, and
Republicans: Popular Freethought in Britain 1866–1915* (Manchester, 1980).

340

tion. Devoted naturalists did indeed make pilgrimages to Darwin's home in Downe, though they might be granted but an hour's audience. As Huxley wrote, 'The great Saint though always kind to worshippers is not always in a condition to be worshipped.'[21] Several years later Darwin's cousin Francis Galton would portray Darwin as an exemplar of hereditary genius, the leader of a scientific priesthood: new ministers of nature who would guide human destiny toward perfection.[22]

Darwin resisted these efforts to invest him with religious authority, and asserted that the religious beliefs of even so public a figure as himself were a private matter: 'What my own views may be is a question of no consequence to any one except myself.'[23] He refused to be recruited by movements of secular religion, and discouraged the tactics of some of his more ardent supporters, who sought to make Darwinism a weapon against the power of the Church and its clergy. We are familiar with the picture of Darwin working quietly in his study at Downe, avoiding the fray of scientific and social controversy, allowing others like Huxley to battle on his behalf. Darwin did express gratitude for, and occasionally glee at, the combativeness of his colleagues and supporters. But he was also concerned that such controversial styles would alienate potential allies and disturb old allegiances. Darwin once admonished his German crusader Ernst Haeckel:

> I know that it is easy to preach & if I had the power of writing with severity I dare say I shd triumph in turning poor devils inside out & exposing all their imbecility. Nevertheless I am convinced that this power does no good, only causes pain. I feel sure that our good friend Huxley, though he has much influence, wd have had far more if he had been more moderate & less frequent in his attacks.[24]

According to Darwin, it was better for society and for the cause of science to be adopted by the Church than to oppose its authority

[21] Letter from Thomas Huxley, 20 July 1868 (*Correspondence*, ed. Burkhardt, Smith et al., 16: 634–35).

[22] Francis Galton, *English Men of Science: Their Nature and Nurture* (London, 1874).

[23] Letter 12041, to John Fordyce, 7 May 1879 (Darwin Correspondence Project, <http://www.darwinproject.ac.uk/>, accessed 4 January 2009).

[24] Letter to Ernst Haeckel, 12 April [1867] (*Correspondence*, ed. Burkhardt, Smith et al., 15: 219).

as the founder of a rival sect. The voice of science should not be one of absolute conviction, but rather of openness and criticism, or even sometimes of confessed ignorance. The diversity and collaborative nature of Darwin's network, the persons on whom he relied and whose observations and authority he incorporated into his texts, favoured such provisionality and humility. In 1864, Darwin received a long letter from Leo Lesquereux, a Swiss emigré to the United States, an expert on coal formations, and a Lutheran. He had written several critical articles on *Origin of Species* in American natural history journals.

> I can not explain … the antagonistic repulsion which I felt against your system when I read its exposition for the first time. I considered it then as hostile to every kind of religious faith and religious feelings … By and by this mistrust has passed away; I have read your book again and again and now I find that your system not only does not contradict any of the Dogmas of my Christian faith; but on the contrary that it satisfies my reason far better than any other human explanation could have done, concerning some of the most obscure points of the biblical teachings; the miraculous birth of Christ, a new being the first species of a higher and Divine type; the doctrine of grace, &c. [25]

Darwin remarked to his close friend, Joseph Hooker: 'I have had an enormous letter from Lesquereux … he wrote some excellent articles … against [my] views; but – he says now … he is a convert! But how funny men's minds are; he says he is chiefly converted because my book makes the Birth of Christ – Redemption by Grace &c plain to him!!'[26]

II

Alongside the appropriation of Darwin by the Church and its faithful, we find a reciprocal manoeuvre, less visible to the public eye, namely the incorporation of the Church into Darwin's own social life, his circle of activity and his responsibility in the local community. Such ties had characterized his upbringing. From at

[25] Letter from Leo Lesquereux, 14 December 1864 (ibid. 12: 463).
[26] Letter to J. D. Hooker, 19 January [1865] (ibid. 13: 29).

least the mid-eighteenth century, formal adherence to the Church of England had been combined with Unitarian belief in the Darwin household. The same may be said of the Wedgwood family, closely bound to the Darwins through marriage, including that of Darwin himself and Emma Wedgwood, his first cousin. Darwin's parents attended a Unitarian chapel throughout his childhood, yet both Charles and his older brother Erasmus were christened in the Church of England.[27] A nominal adherence to Anglican teachings remained essential for admittance to many of England's elite institutions. It was required to enter Oxford and Cambridge, and an Oxbridge degree was often crucial, in turn, in securing a position in the most prestigious professions.[28]

During Darwin's lifetime, Oxford and Cambridge continued to be the main training ground for Anglican clergy. After several years at Edinburgh in an unsuccessful turn at medicine, Charles followed his brother to Cambridge in 1828 with the aim of becoming a clergyman. Relatively few parsonages paid enough to support even a small family in comfort, and the possession of an independent income was essential to enjoy a gentlemanly lifestyle. For Darwin, who could rely on the financial support of his wealthy father, and who anticipated a substantial inheritance, the clerical life offered the prospect of a highly respectable and comfortable existence that was also compatible with the pursuit of scientific interests. His Cambridge friend and cousin William Darwin Fox, like Darwin a great beetle collector, settled into a clerical living in Cheshire after taking his degree.

Darwin set off on the *Beagle* intent on returning to his religious studies, and wrote to his sister Caroline in 1832, 'I find I steadily have a distant prospect of a very quiet parsonage, & I can see it even through a grove of Palms.—'[29] Darwin's sisters were supportive of his desire to enter the Church. His brother, however, wrote to the contrary: 'I am sorry to see in your last letter that you still look forward to the horrid little parsonage in the desert.

---

[27] On religious belief and practice in the Darwin and Wedgwood families, see Randal Keynes, *Annie's Box: Charles Darwin, His Daughter, and Human Evolution* (London, 2001).

[28] Arthur Engel, *From Clergyman to Don: The Rise of the Academic Profession in Nineteenth-Century Oxford* (New York, 1983).

[29] Letter to Caroline Darwin, 25–26 April [1832] (*Correspondence*, ed. Burkhardt, Smith et al., 1: 225).

I was beginning to hope I should have you set up in London in lodgings somewhere near the British Museum or some other learned place.'[30] Writing to Fox in 1835 from Lima, Peru, Darwin reflected on the rewards of a clerical life, and yet distanced himself from it: 'To a person fit to take the office, the life of a Clergyman is a type of all that is respectable & happy: & if he is a Naturalist and has the "Diamond Beetle", ave Maria; I do not know what to say.— You tempt me by talking of your fireside, whereas it is a sort of scene I never ought to think about—'.[31] Darwin's growing doubts about orthodox belief and his speculations about the nature of religion are evident in his scientific notebooks from the late 1830s and in correspondence with his fiancée, Emma Wedgwood, in 1838 and 1839.[32]

In 1842, within six years of his return from the *Beagle* voyage, Darwin moved to Down House, in the village of Downe, Kent. There was no Unitarian chapel in the vicinity, and the family attended the local Anglican church, St Mary's, each Sunday. All the children were baptized and confirmed in the Church of England. The whole family took the sacrament, although Emma used to make the children turn around and face the back on occasions when the rest of the congregation recited the Athanasian Creed. Around 1850, Darwin himself stopped attending services. He would accompany the family to church and would often wait outside, chatting with the village constable, or would stroll around the village until the service ended.[33] Yet despite absenting himself from worship, Darwin was actively engaged in church affairs. He took a lead in local charities, supervised church and school finances, and worked to uphold the status of the church in the community.

Darwin's biographers have emphasized his traditional social role in Downe. James Moore has argued that Darwin's patronage of the church was largely a by-product of his hereditary wealth and desire

---

[30] Letter from E. A. Darwin, 18 August [1832] (ibid. 1: 258).

[31] Letter to W. D. Fox, [9–12 August 1835] (ibid. 1: 460).

[32] *Charles Darwin's Notebooks, 1836–1844*, ed. Paul Barrett et al. (Cambridge, 1987); letters from Emma Wedgwood, [21–22 November 1838], [23 January 1839], and [c. February 1839] (*Correspondence*, ed. Burkhardt, Smith et al., 4: 122, 169, 173). See also Darwin's retrospective account in *Autobiography*, 85–96, and James Moore, 'Of Love and Death: Why Darwin "Gave Up Christianity"', in idem, ed., *History, Humanity, and Evolution* (Cambridge, 1989), 195–229.

[33] See Keynes, *Annie's Box*, 113–22, 222.

for social respectability in a small agricultural village.[34] Although he was not the principal landowner in Downe, Darwin was a gentleman of means and might have been expected to share some of the pastoral responsibilities of the village with the local parson. But Moore has also noted the parallel callings of the clergyman and naturalist. Darwin had studied the example of the Reverend Gilbert White, whose *Natural History of Selborne* inspired many field naturalists. Darwin greatly admired his own mentor at Cambridge, the Professor of Botany John Stevens Henslow, who presided over the parish of Hitcham in Suffolk, and taught the Linnean system of classification, based upon the sexual parts of plants, to labourers.[35] That Darwin so readily assumed a number of pastoral responsibilities in the village may be seen as a fulfillment of the traditional vocation of the clergyman-naturalist, but without religious office or religious conviction.

In these activities, Darwin worked closely with the Anglican incumbent, John Brodie Innes, who became Perpetual Curate of Downe in 1846. A Tory and High Churchman, Innes preached eternal torment in the 1850s: the worm that never dies, the bitter remorse of a conscience that had awakened too late, a doctrine Darwin would later describe as 'damnable'.[36] But their political and doctrinal differences were glossed over, it would seem, in their shared sense of duty toward the community, especially its poor. They collaborated on the running of village charities, a Coal and Clothing Club, and a Friendly Club (an insurance fund). Darwin served as treasurer of both organizations, and would read out the accounts to members, who assembled on his lawn for regular meetings.[37] At a Church Congress in Dundee in 1878, Innes remarked that the men 'never attacked each other. Before I knew Mr Darwin I had adopted ... the principle that ... the Book of Nature and Scripture came from the same Divine source, ran in parallel lines, and when properly understood would never cross.' Darwin, for

---

[34] James Moore, 'Darwin of Down: The Evolutionist as Squarson-Naturalist', in D. Kohn, ed., *The Darwinian Heritage* (Princeton, NJ, 1985), 435–81.

[35] S. M. Walters, *Darwin's Mentor: John Stevens Henslow* (Cambridge, 2001).

[36] J. B. Innes, *Five Sermons Preached in Advent and on the Festival of the Holy Innocents, 1851 in the Parish Church of Downe, Kent* (London, 1852), 3–4, 12–13, 62; Darwin, *Autobiography*, 87.

[37] Letter 7776, to J. B. Innes, 29 May [1871] (Darwin Correspondence Project, <http://www.darwinproject.ac.uk/>, accessed 4 January 2009).

his part, is reported to have said: 'I am a Naturalist, the lines are separate. I endeavour to discover facts without considering ... the Book of Genesis. I do not attack Moses, and I think Moses can take care of himself.'[38] To the end of his life, Innes remained unpersuaded by Darwin's theory of evolution.

In 1862, Innes inherited an estate in Scotland and left the village. Darwin wrote regularly, apprising him of village affairs, the passing of agricultural labourers and the health of Innes's old dog: 'Today poor old Spearing was buried and I think before a year or two is over, young Mr Smith will follow all his family to the grave. Your old terrier Tartar is awfully venerable in all his movements. I do not believe a word about the toad stories.'[39] Innes, always keen to pass on useful facts of natural history, had reported on toads found in the stone cuttings of the new railway. Despite his move to Scotland, Innes retained the advowson of the village, and was thus responsible for the appointment of a resident curate and the maintenance of a local parsonage. The village of Downe did not fare well under this system. The living was comparatively small, and the local parsonage had been sold. In fact, some years before the Darwins arrived, the parsonage had actually been Down House. The details are not known, but Innes evidently had property of his own in the village, and did not need a parsonage. When he left for Scotland, he tried to secure the purchase of land for a new parsonage, but was unsuccessful.

Beginning in 1867, Downe's parishioners experienced troubles securing the services of a reliable replacement for Innes. Darwin complained of the prolonged absence of the curate at the time, Samuel James O'Hara Horsman, and reported that, owing to difficulties in accessing church funds under Horsman's care, he had had to advance the salary of the schoolmaster. Darwin also acted as intermediary for Horsman, who excused his long absence as due to his needing a 'change of air' and being invited by some friends, 'who kindly took me about in their yacht & otherwise made it pleasant to me'. In addition, 'the wretched & miserable lodgings at Downe' and all kinds of 'wicked reports & misrepresenta-

[38] Letter 11768, from J. B. Innes, 1 December 1878 (Darwin Correspondence Project, <http://www.darwinproject.ac.uk/>, accessed 4 January 2009).
[39] Letter to J. B. Innes, 1 September [1863] (*Correspondence*, ed. Burkhardt, Smith et al., 11: 616).

tions' induced him to stay away.[40] Darwin examined the school account books, advancing the required sum for the school and in the process discovered that Horsman appeared to have made off with the church's organ fund: 'He was curiously anxious to get up a subscription for the new organ & some ... have suggested that he may have pocketed the money ... no one seems to know what the organ really cost.'[41]

But if Horsman had turned out to be a 'complete & *premeditated* swindler', his replacement, John Warburton Robinson, proved no better.[42] Darwin first voiced concern when the curate absconded to Ireland for three months, leaving Downe entirely without a clergyman. Shortly upon his return, Robinson was rumoured to have walked with young women from the village at night.

> I did not mention this before, because I had not even moderately good authority; but my wife found Mrs Allen very indignant about Mr. Rs conduct with one of her maids. I do not believe there is any evidence of actual criminality. As I repeat only second hand my name must not be mentioned— Our maids tell my wife that they do not believe that hardly anyone will go to church now.[*sic*][43]

In reporting the incident to Innes, Darwin was concerned about exposing himself to charges of defamation of character. He complained that the eyewitnesses either would not come forward, or on questioning could not be certain of the parties involved, or whether the alleged walks occurred in daylight or after dark. Innes advised Darwin on a possible course of action, noting that he himself was powerless on the matter.

> You may not be aware that a vicar has no power over a licensed curate. To cause his removal the Bishop must revoke his licence, which he can do summarily without any legal judicial proceeding ... He would desire the Rural Dean to enquire, and act at once on his report. I much hope there

---

[40] Letter from S. J. O'H. Horsman, 2 June [1868] (ibid. 16: 556).
[41] Letter to J. B. Innes, 15 June [1868] (ibid. 16: 581).
[42] Letter to J. B. Innes, 1 December 1868 (ibid. 16: 871).
[43] Letter to J. B. Innes, 10 December 1868 (ibid. 16: 888).

may very soon be a resident vicar, and the services of a Curate dispensed with.[44]

Such letters can almost make us believe in the characters of Trollope's Barchester novels: the scandal that attends the poor and defiant Reverend Crawley, accused of passing a bad cheque, or the domestic chaplain Mr Slope, who consoles and consorts with women of the cathedral city. Because of the problems of clerical vacancy associated with absentee incumbents, and because the system of appointments was liable to abuse by unscrupulous agents and even clerical impostors, some within the Church of England had called for an elimination of multiple livings, and increased action on the part of bishops over the sale of advowsons and the appointment of curates.[45]

The scandals of Horsman and Robinson also indicate the considerable pastoral role that Darwin had assumed in Innes's absence. Already in charge of accounts for the charities, he now kept the books of the Sunday School and the National School as well, and took personal charge of raising money for the upkeep of church buildings, as well as overseeing the repairs. 'The Church will be lowered in the estimation of the whole neighbourhood', Darwin warned.[46] Innes tried to discharge his duties as patron upon the archbishop, and even offered the advowson to Darwin himself, together with his neighbour, John Lubbock. Though Darwin refused, Innes was very grateful for his efforts on behalf of the church, the school, and local charities: 'I do not forget that you have taken, and are taking, a great deal of trouble as a labour of love, having no responsibility but the desire to do good, and help an old friend out of a most distressing dilemma.'[47]

This assumption of pastoral responsibilities by Darwin later proved to be a source of great tension when the curacy passed to George Sketchley Ffinden in 1871. Like Innes, Ffinden was a Tory High Churchman, but unlike his predecessor he was unwilling to

---

[44] Letter from J. B. Innes, 18 December 1868 (ibid. 16: 901).

[45] Owen Chadwick, *The Victorian Church*, 2 vols, 3rd edn (London, 1971), 1: 207–13; Frances Knight, *The Nineteenth-Century Church and English Society* (Cambridge, 1995), 116–41.

[46] Letter to J. B. Innes, 1 December 1868 (*Correspondence*, ed. Burkhardt, Smith et al., 16: 871).

[47] Letter from J. B. Innes, 14 December 1868 (ibid. 16: 890).

share parish leadership with the likes of the Darwins. A series of conflicts ensued, leading quickly to an impasse. Emma Darwin's regular use of the village schoolroom as an evening reading room for workers was opposed by Ffinden on grounds that the space, so used, would not be left in salutary condition for scholars. Darwin appealed directly to the School Committee, prompting this curt reply from the curate: 'As I am the only recognized correspondent of the School according to rule 15, Code 1871, I deem such a proceeding quite out of order.'[48]

Darwin's authorization of five pounds' worth of repairs to the Infant School, whereas the Committee had only sanctioned an expenditure of four, was similarly regarded by Ffinden as an intentional slight, and brought a similar appeal to the law. Emma privately referred to Ffinden as the 'fiend', complaining that 'he cuts every member of our family when we meet', and that at any rate he had no influence over anyone in the village.[49] For his part, Ffinden appealed to the leading landowner, John Lubbock, regarding the insults he suffered from the Darwins, adding 'of one thing I am convinced that neither Socinians nor Infidels can feel *quite sure* of their ground'.[50]

Darwin's clash with Ffinden might be attributed to ideology. Despite his deep respect for established authority, including that of the Church, Darwin's theories ran counter to the traditional rationale for such authority. Ffinden did indeed write to Lubbock of the 'harmful tendencies to the cause of revealed religion of Mr. Darwin's views', adding that he trusted 'that God's grace might in time bring one so highly gifted intellectually & morally to a better mind'.[51] Yet such theoretical differences, though manifest, had not divided Darwin and Innes, who shared Ffinden's High Church training and outlook. That Darwin's involvement in parish charities and education should be regarded as a threat to the leadership

---

[48] Letter 9122, from Darwin to the Down School Board, [November–December 1873] (Darwin Correspondence Project, <http://www.darwinproject.ac.uk/>, accessed 4 January 2009); Letter from G. S. Ffinden to Emma Darwin, 24 December 1873, cited in Moore, 'Darwin of Down', 471.

[49] Letter from Emma Darwin to J. B. Innes, in R. M. Stecher, 'The Darwin-Innes Letters: The Correspondence of an Evolutionist with his Vicar, 1848–1884', *Annals of Science* 17 (1961), 201–58, at 239.

[50] Letters from Ffinden to John Lubbock, 1875, cited in Moore, 'Darwin of Down', 471–72.

[51] Ibid.

of the church may reflect some of the social changes that it was undergoing over the course of the nineteenth century, particularly as they bore upon rural parishes from the 1850s onwards. As Frances Knight has argued, one of the effects of the gradual secularization of English institutions was that Church of England clergymen came to see their pastoral role as limited to the care of their own denomination, rather than as extending to the village as a whole.[52] The involvement of non-Anglicans (and Ffinden clearly regarded the Darwins in this light) in local church business would have been viewed as an encroachment, and the use of church property like the school building by persons who were not members of the congregation would be regarded as a trespass.

It is perhaps because of this more narrowly denominational role of the local Anglican church that the Darwins partly shifted their attention and patronage to Nonconformity. Darwin's annual contributions to the church dropped from £50 in 1872 to £10 in 1873 and less thereafter; but he continued to give large sums for restoration work.[53] Toward the end of 1880, he supported the use of the proverbial reading room, which he now rented to a young Brethren evangelist, James Fegan:

> May I have the pleasure of handing the Reading Room over to you? ... You have done more for the village in a few months than all our efforts for many years. We have never been able to reclaim a drunkard, but through your services I do not know that there is [one] left in the village.[54]

Members of Darwin's family sometimes attended Fegan's services, altering their dinner hour to do so. Owing to this original sponsorship, Nonconformist services continued in what became known as the Gospel Room for more than fifty years.[55]

---

[52] Knight, *Nineteenth-Century Church*, 70–74.

[53] Moore, 'Darwin of Down', 473.

[54] Letter 12879, to J. W. C. Fegan, [December 1880 – February 1881] (Darwin Correspondence Project, <http://www.darwinproject.ac.uk/>, accessed 4 January 2009).

[55] Moore, 'Darwin of Down', 473.

III

The relationship between Darwin and the church remained pluralistic and contentious following his death in 1882. A broadsheet entitled 'Our National Church' (figure 2) depicts various religious parties beneath a great dome, pulling in different directions, while Roman Catholics, Dissenters and Secularists stake out the surrounding territory. In the upper left-hand corner, Darwin appears as the presiding figure of a new dawn, the age of protoplasm, with other scientific authorities held in tow by the tail of a monkey. A more sober and literal incorporation was performed by the Church of England, in Darwin's burial in Westminster Abbey.

The suggestion of a Darwin memorial had apparently been made by Frederic Farrar, Master of Harrow and a Darwin correspondent, who described having broached the subject with Huxley in the Athenaeum: 'we clergy are not all so bigoted as [you suppose]'.[56] Farrar preached the funeral sermon, and served as one of the pallbearers, along with Huxley, Lubbock, Alfred Russel Wallace and others. The Abbey had been a place of convergence for men of science and clergymen from the mid-1860s, when the liberal Anglican Arthur Stanley was appointed dean. Men of science, Stanley later explained, had no special corner in the Abbey, but rather 'penetrated promiscuously into every part, much in the same way as science had imperceptibly influenced all our social and literary relations elsewhere'.[57] In a sermon given on the eight-hundredth anniversary of the foundation of the Abbey by King Edward the Confessor, Stanley declared that in its walls and pavements, the commonwealth in all its history, were embedded: 'Roman, puritan, non-conformist and doubting sceptic hard by the enthusiastic believer, opposing parties both in Church and State co-existing, neutralizing, counteracting, completing each other, neither by the other subdued, each by the other endured'.[58]

There was some discussion in the Darwin family about the appropriateness of this site. Some favoured burial in the village where Darwin had lived and worked for forty years, the local

---

[56] R. Farrar, *The Life of Frederick Farrar* (London, 1904), 109. See the account of the burial in Desmond and Moore, *Darwin*, 664–77.

[57] A. P. Stanley, *Historical Memorials of Westminster Abbey* (London, 1868), 292.

[58] A. P. Stanley, *Dedication of Westminster Abbey: A Sermon* (Oxford, 1866), 19–20.

Fig. 2. Our National Church (detail), c. 1882 (courtesy of the Syndics of Cambridge University Library). Cambridge University Library, Darwin Archive, DAR 141.12.

parish that he had served, the landscape in which he had walked, observed, and experimented so vigorously, near the site of Orchis Bank, where Darwin had marked the local varieties and studied the remarkable mechanisms of competitive advantage and of co-adaptation in plants and insects: the inspiration for his closing metaphor in *Origin of Species*. But we conclude with Darwin's work immortalized, and his body given over to worms, within the larger corporation of the Church, part of the entangled bank of a broad Anglican culture.

University of Cambridge

WILLIAM PALEY, SAMUEL WILBERFORCE, CHARLES DARWIN AND THE NATURAL WORLD: AN ANGLICAN CONVERSATION

by KEITH A. FRANCIS

SOAPY Sam[1] and the Devil's Chaplain: even for an age in which public figures were regularly lampooned, the epithets are evocative.[2] To call the recipients of the epithets, Samuel Wilberforce and Charles Darwin respectively, controversial figures of the nineteenth century is the intellectual equivalent of noting that the sky is blue. Without seemingly trying, both men were involved in controversy. Whether it was the Church of England's response to *Essays and Reviews* or the creation of a government policy with regard to vivisection, for various reasons both men were regularly in the national spotlight in the mid-Victorian period.[3] As a 'couple', they are inextricably linked by the supposed debate between Wilberforce and Thomas Huxley at the meeting of the British Association for the Advancement of Science held

---

[1] See David Newsome, 'How Soapy was Sam? A Study of Samuel Wilberforce', *History Today*, September 1963, 624–32, for an assessment of Bishop Wilberforce's somewhat notorious eponym. For assessments written soon after his death by contemporaries, see Lucy Phillimore, *Bishop Wilberforce: A Sketch for Children* (London, 1876); Thomas Pinches, *Samuel Wilberforce. Faith: Service: Recompense. Three Sermons* (London, 1878), 16–76, 157–59; John William Burgon, *Lives of Twelve Good Men*, 2nd edn (London, 1888), 1: viii, 2: xii, 1–70; George W. Daniell, *Bishop Wilberforce* (London, 1891); S. Baring-Gould, *The Church Revival: Thoughts thereon and Reminiscences* (London, 1914), 174–76. For a twenty-first-century assessment, see Alistair Redfern, 'Oversight and Authority in the Nineteenth-Century Church of England: A Case Study of Bishop Samuel Wilberforce' (unpublished Ph.D. thesis, University of Bristol, 2001).

[2] The latter name was given to the radical clergyman Robert Taylor (1784–1844). Adrian Desmond and James Moore apply it to Darwin, who was a student at Cambridge when Taylor challenged members of the University to a debate on the merits of Christianity in 1829: *Darwin* (London, 1992), 70–73, 84–85, 677.

[3] *Essays and Reviews*, published in 1860, was an attempt by seven Anglican authors to reconcile contemporary knowledge in science, philosophy and theology with the traditional understanding of the truths of Christianity. Wilberforce wrote a review of the book and was a leader in the formulation of an episcopal condemnation of it: Standish Meacham, *Lord Bishop: The Life of Samuel Wilberforce 1805–1873* (Cambridge, MA, 1970), 220–23, 241, 247–50; Reginald G. Wilberforce, *Life of the Right Reverend Samuel Wilberforce. D.D. Lord Bishop of Oxford and afterwards of Winchester with Selections from His Diaries and Correspondence*, 3 vols (London, 1882), 3: 1–11.

in Oxford from 27 June to 4 July 1860.[4] That fact is ironic in itself: Darwin did not attend the meeting – only his proxies.[5] (Darwin was ill: this was convenient because he did not want to go.) Further, Huxley only attended the Botany and Zoology Section meeting on 30 June because he was persuaded to do so by a supporter of evolution, Robert Chambers.[6] Wilberforce only spoke because he was invited to do so by the platform chairman, John Stevens Henslow.[7] The speeches by Wilberforce and Huxley nearly did not happen.[8]

Although they did not meet physically, Wilberforce and Darwin 'encountered' each other in their writing. Wilberforce wrote a review of the *Origin of Species* for the *Quarterly Review* which was published in July 1860 and Darwin commented on the review and on the British Association meeting at Oxford in letters to his friends.[9]

---

[4] Perhaps Wilberforce was one of those who advised Queen Victoria not to give Darwin a knighthood in 1859. This is stated in Desmond and Moore, *Darwin*, 488, but the authors admit that they could not find the evidence used by their source, James Bunting, *Charles Darwin: A Biography* (Folkestone, 1974), 88; Wilberforce's supposed interference is not recorded by any of his biographers.

    Several historians have attempted to describe and analyse the Oxford incident; see Josef L. Altholz, 'The Huxley-Wilberforce Debate Revisited', *Journal of the History of Medicine* 35 (1980), 313–16; J. Vernon Jensen, 'Return to the Wilberforce-Huxley Debate', *British Journal for the History of Science* 21 (1988), 161–79; and John Hedley Brooke, 'The Wilberforce-Huxley Debate: Why did it Happen?' *Farmington Papers*, Science and Christianity 15 (Oxford, 2001). I use the word 'incident' because, as most historians now recognize, there was not a debate in the sense that the word is commonly used.

[5] A contemporary report of the meeting is in *The Athenaeum*, 14 July 1860, 64–65.

[6] Chambers (1802–1871) had written *Vestiges of the Natural History of Creation* (London, 1844), the first major work in English advocating a theory of evolution.

[7] Henslow (1796–1861) was Regius Professor of Botany at Cambridge and an Anglican clergyman. He had recommended Darwin for the position of ship's naturalist on the *Beagle*: Keith A. Francis, *Charles Darwin and The Origin of Species* (Westport, CT, 2007), 22–23.

[8] See Altholz, 'Huxley-Wilberforce Debate', 315–16; Jensen, 'Return', 165–69.

[9] [Samuel Wilberforce], 'Art. VII. – *On the Origin of Species, by means of Natural Selection; or the Preservation of Favoured Races in the Struggle for Life*. By Charles Darwin, M.A., F.R.S. London, 1860', *Quarterly Review* 108 (1860), 225–64; Letter 2700, Charles Darwin to Charles Lyell, '15th' [February 1860]; Letter 2853, Darwin to Joseph D. Hooker, 'Monday night' [2 July 1860]; Letter 2854, Darwin to Thomas H. Huxley, 'July 3^{d}' [1860]; Letter 2855, Darwin to Asa Gray, 'July 3^{d}' [1860]; Letter 2860, Darwin to Lyell, 'Thursday, 5th' [July 1860]; all online at the Darwin Correspondence Project, <http://www.darwinproject.ac.uk>, accessed 12 July 2008.

The aforementioned facts are well known. Darwin did indeed call Wilberforce's review 'uncommonly clever' and Wilberforce did say: 'We think it difficult to find a theory fuller of assumptions; and of assumptions not grounded upon alleged facts in nature, but which are absolutely opposed to all the facts we have been able to observe.'[10] Wilberforce, despite the claims to the contrary by Huxley and his associates, left the Natural History Museum, where the Oxford meeting was held, believing that he had 'thoroughly beaten' Huxley.[11]

The overall impression left by a story in which Darwin and Wilberforce are antagonists representing opposite sides, pro- and anti-science, does an injustice to both men. As with most matters historical, and this is certainly the case in the history of science, the picture is more complex.[12] Noting that there was a mid-century debate about the theory of evolution and stating nothing else about the attitude of both men to nature and science is to paint a one-dimensional picture of Darwin and Wilberforce for two reasons. First, it ignores large portions of their careers. In the case of Darwin, he was already a renowned scientist before 1859. He had written the best scientific explanation for the formation of coral reefs, and a definitive series of monographs on barnacles; in addition, his account of the voyage of HMS *Beagle* was a best-selling book.[13] Darwin had been elected a Fellow of the Royal Society, the Geological Society and the Zoological Society by the time he was thirty. After 1859, Darwin would publish ground-

---

[10] Letter 2873, Darwin to Huxley, 'July 20th' [1860], Darwin Correspondence Project, <http://www.darwinproject.ac.uk>, accessed 13 July 2008; ['Wilberforce'], 'Art.VII', 237.

[11] Oxford, Bodl., Wilberforce Family Papers, MS. Wilberforce d.29, Samuel Wilberforce to Sir Charles Anderson, 3 July 1860.

[12] This point has been made most forcefully by John Hedley Brooke, in *Science and Religion: Some Historical Perspectives* (Cambridge, 1991).

[13] The books were *The Structure and Distribution of Coral Reefs; Being the First Part of the Geology of the Voyage of the* Beagle, *under the Command of Capt. Fitzroy R.N. during the Years 1832 to 1836* (London, 1842); *A Monograph on the Fossil Lepadidae, or, Pedunculated Cirripedes of Great Britain* (London, 1851); *A Monograph on the Sub-Class Cirripedia, with Figures of All the Species: The Lepadidae; or, Pedunculated Cirripedes* (London, 1851); *A Monograph on the Sub-Class Cirripedia, with Figures of All the Species: The Balanidae, (or Sessile Cirripedes); The Verrucidae, etc., etc., etc.* (London, 1854); *A Monograph on the Fossil Balanidae and Verrucidae of Great Britain* (London, 1854); *Journal of Researches into the Geology and Natural History of the Various Countries Visited by H.M.S. Beagle, under the Command of Captain Fitzroy, R.N. from 1832 to 1836* (London, 1839).

breaking research on orchids, insect-eating plants, and tropism in plants.[14] As Wilberforce acknowledged in his review of the *Origin of Species*: '[Darwin's] scientific attainments, his insight and carefulness as an observer ... and his clear and lively style, make all his writings unusually attractive.'[15] In the case of Wilberforce, he had become a bishop at the age of forty, having already held the positions of Archdeacon of Surrey, Chaplain to Prince Albert, Canon of Winchester, and Dean of Westminster. After 1859, Wilberforce was a major force behind the reform of Convocation and the most vocal episcopal supporter of Anglican foreign missions, both through his preaching and his fundraising.[16]

Second, Darwin and Wilberforce were much more than representative figures in a debate about evolution or human origins; a joke about Huxley's relationship to an ape or Huxley's supposed desire to be an ape rather than a bishop should only be a small part of any analysis of the nineteenth-century attitude to nature and science. The Victorian discussion about nature and whether it worked with or without the help of divine guidance was more than a monkey debate. Further, the debate predated Wilberforce and Darwin, and even the Victorians. The philosophers George Berkeley (1685–1753) and David Hume (1711–1776) participated in it, as did the doyen of nineteenth-century natural theology, William Paley (1743–1805).

Paley studied theology at Cambridge, Wilberforce and Darwin at Oxford; these two universities were bastions of Anglicanism as well as premier sites of debates about the writings of philosophers such as Berkeley and Hume on nature, existence and God. Whether God ordered and sustained the universe was a question which interested Christians of every denominational stripe but Anglican dominance of the major universities meant that Anglicans framed and led the debate. Thus the debate about the natural world was a very Anglican conversation.

Intriguingly, the language, style, and construction of argument used by participants such as Wilberforce and Darwin were the

[14] *On the Various Contrivances by which British and Foreign Orchids are Fertilised by Insects, and on the Good Effects of Intercrossing* (London, 1862); *Insectivorous Plants* (London, 1875); *The Power of Movement in Plants* (London, 1880).

[15] [Wilberforce], 'Art. VII', 225.

[16] Meacham, *Lord Bishop*, 236–46. I am grateful to Bob Tennant, Honorary Fellow of the University of Glasgow, for drawing my attention to this latter point.

same. Darwin noted in his autobiography that he could have written out 'the whole of the "Evidences" with perfect correctness but not … in the clear language of Paley';[17] ironically, a review of his major scientific books demonstrates that he adopted several 'Paleyisms'. The language all three men used about nature, particularly in praise of nature, was similar: the agency that Darwin gave to nature was different. While Darwin's undirected and seemingly purposeless natural selection was radically different from Paley and Wilberforce's designed universe, all three men viewed the natural world as 'wonderful'. Change a word here or there and it is nearly impossible to differentiate between Paley, Wilberforce and Darwin.

Before illustrating the similarities between the three men, a word or two about the sources is necessary. There are more than one hundred of Wilberforce's sermons in print, the majority of these are in five volumes.[18] If episcopal charges and sundry addresses are included, the number rises to a figure between 150 and 200.[19] As Wilberforce was a popular preacher and speaker, much in demand, these represent a small portion of the sermons he preached or the addresses he gave. Nonetheless, it is possible to gain a sense of Wilberforce's thinking from the extant corpus. Themes such as his interest in missions, foreign and domestic, his concern for the spiritual lives of students at Oxford University, and his desire that his hearers experience God for themselves are very obvious.

As for the natural world, there is only one published sermon on the topic, 'The Relation of Man to the Natural World', which Wilberforce preached before the Fellows of the Royal Society on 13 May 1856 at St Leonard's, Shoreditch. There are numerous references to nature and the natural world in his other sermons

---

[17] Francis Darwin, ed., *The Life and Letters of Charles Darwin, including an Autobiographical Chapter*, 3 vols (London, 1887), 1: 47.

[18] *Sermons Preached before the University of Oxford in St. Mary's Church, in the Years MDCCCXXXVII., MDCCCXXXVIII., MDCCCXXXIX* (London, 1839); *Sermons Preached and Published on Several Occasions* (London, 1854); *Sermons Preached before the University of Oxford: Second Series, from MDCCXLVII. TO MDCCCLXII* (Oxford, 1863); *Sermons Preached before the University of Oxford: Third Series, from MDCCCLXIII to MDCCCLXX* (Oxford, 1871); *Sermons Preached on Various Occasions* (Oxford, 1877).

[19] The exact number is difficult to ascertain as there is no formal list of Wilberforce's published sermons; individual sermons published as tracts can be found in several libraries. This lack of a database of published sermons for Wilberforce (or any other preacher) will be corrected in the soon-to-be-created British Pulpit Online web site.

and addresses but no mention after 1859 of Darwin, Darwinism or evolution.[20] On the other hand, the proper use of knowledge, particularly scientific knowledge, was a theme Wilberforce addressed on a regular basis, both before and after 1859.[21]

Wilberforce also wrote three articles for the *Quarterly Review* in which he discussed nature and the natural world. Apart from his review of the *Origin of Species*, Wilberforce wrote reviews of two books by Arthur E. Knox: *Ornithological Rambles in Sussex, with a Systematic Catalogue of the Birds of that County, and Remarks on their Local Distribution* (1849) and *Autumns on the Spey* (1872).[22] These reviews indicate that by nineteenth-century British standards Wilberforce was a typical amateur scientist, more than competent in terms of knowledge even though scientific study was merely a hobby.

In the case of Darwin, the *Origin of Species* is the obvious place to find his comments on nature and the natural world.[23] Additionally, his other major published works are a useful source of his views. Particularly after 1859, Darwin used the preface, introduction, and conclusion of his books to comment on wider questions about the development of life. *Origin of Species* was supposed to be an 'abstract' (Darwin's word), but he never found the opportunity to write a full-length edition; thus his other books became the forum for a discussion of the subject of nature and the natural world.

How, then, did Darwin imitate Paley (and Wilberforce)? First, in the rhetorical approach that he used to argue for natural selection. The genius of Paley's argument in *Natural Theology* was his assertion that the agglomeration of all the phenomena in the natural world had meaning. As anyone who knew anything about the new

---

[20] This is not a surprise; my analysis reveals that few preachers from the different denominations addressed the subject of evolution directly: 'Nineteenth-Century Sermons on Evolution and *The Origin of Species*: The Dog that Didn't Bark?' in Robert Ellison, ed., *A New History of the Sermon: The Nineteenth Century* (forthcoming).

[21] e.g. 'The Temper of Mind in which to Receive the Christian Mysteries', *Sermons in St. Mary's Church*, 65–97; 'Pride a Hindrance to True Knowledge', *Sermons: Second Series*, 1–19; 'Personal Affiance in Christ the Soul's Safeguard', *Sermons: Third Series*, 89–104.

[22] Samuel Wilberforce, *Essays Contributed to the 'Quarterly Review'*, 2 vols (London, 1874), 1: 1–22, 23–51.

[23] For this paper I have used the first edition, which is entitled *On the Origin of Species*.

industrialism would realize, complex machines (and their components) did not create themselves; in the same way, the eye and ear were complex machines which must have had a designer and a creator.[24] Darwin used the same artifice in the first four chapters of the *Origin of Species*. Phenomena such as the ability of horticultur ists and animal breeders to create new varieties demonstrated that nature was not static; further, the observed changes in the natural world, both domestic and wild, were evidence of a much larger scale of changes over thousands of generations, similar to those which geologists had already proven. For both men, the natural world was governed by discoverable laws. As Wilberforce put it, 'redeemed man' has the right 'to scrutinize and interrogate the mysteries of nature' and 'read in all her marvel the rule by which His reconciled Father has ordered the material universe'.[25]

Second, Paley and Darwin chose similar subjects on which to make their argument. That both men discussed the complexity of organs such as the eye is well known; less well known is that both discussed comparative anatomy and morphology, the physiology of small or unusual animal organs, adaptation and co-adaptation, and instinct.[26] (Wilberforce discussed the same subjects also; in reviewing the *Origin of Species*, he had no choice but to comment on the subject matter chosen by Darwin.[27]) This similarity is not odd. The argument of either man could only succeed by the persuasive accumulation of a large number of facts, particularly unusual phenomena which did not fit an easily recognizable pattern or law.

Third, the language of the conversation is surprisingly similar (particularly for those who think of Darwin as departing radically from orthodoxy). The following is Paley's description of avian adaptation:

> The covering of birds cannot escape the most vulgar observation. Its lightness, its smoothness, its warmth; the disposition of the feathers all inclined backward, the down about their

---

[24] William Paley, *Natural Theology: or Evidences of the Existence and Attributes of the Deity, Collected from the Appearances of Nature* (London, 1802), 1–52.

[25] Samuel Wilberforce, 'The Relations of Disease to Man', *Sermons on Various Occasions*, 155–68, at 165.

[26] Paley, *Natural Theology*, 19–41, 227–71, 282–314, 324–45; Darwin, *Origin of Species*, 186–200, 207–44, 434–39. Paley used the word 'compensation' for co-adaptation.

[27] [Wilberforce], 'Art. VII', 231–46.

stem, the overlapping of their tips, their different configuration in different parts, not to mention the variety of their colours, constitute a vestment for the body, so beautiful, and so appropriate to the life which the animal is to lead, as that … we should have had no conception of any thing equally perfect, if we had never seen it, or can now imagine any thing more so.[28]

But how different is it in style from Darwin's description of cows in his book on domestication? 'The whole subject of inheritance is wonderful', he notes, and then asks:

what can be more wonderful than the well-ascertained fact that the minute ovule of a good milking cow will produce a male, from whom a cell, in union with an ovule, will produce a female, and she when mature, will have large mammary glands, yielding an abundant supply of milk, and even milk of a particular quality?[29]

And Wilberforce, when explaining why birds are a pleasure to study, says:

their voice, from the rich melody of our warblers to the laughing taunt of the gull or the solemn hooting of the owl; their habits, from the domestic familiarity of the robin to the wild soar of the Falconidae, – all tend to secure for birds an interest and regard which is shared with them by few of the quadrupeds.[30]

For all three men, nature was fascinating and could best be described in the language of fascination.

Further, it is the language of men who loved nature. Even though he pressed his argument about design frequently, Paley clearly loved nature. He could not have written chapters 12 to 22 of *Natural Theology* in the style that he did if it were otherwise. The detailed explanation of instincts, the survey of the life of plants, and the analysis of the laws of astronomy all have a sense of wonder underpinning them and would not have been out of

---

[28] Paley, *Natural Theology*, 231.
[29] Charles Darwin, *The Variation of Animals and Plants under Domestication*, 2 vols (London, 1868), 2: 2. Paley makes a similar point in *Natural Theology*, 273–74.
[30] Wilberforce, 'The Naturalist in Sussex', in idem, *Essays*, 1: 5–6.

place in the *Origin of Species*.[31] Darwin himself marvelled at nature. In the *Origin of Species* he used a variant of the word 'astonished' eight times, a variant of 'beautiful' fourteen times, and a variant of 'wonderful' fourteen times.[32] The eye, a favourite of Paley's, has a 'wonderful structure' and beehives are 'wonderfully perfect'.[33] Wilberforce, commenting on a point of Darwin's about bumble bees,[34] talked in his review about the 'wonderful interdependence of nature'. 'Who,' Wilberforce asked:

> as he listened to the musical hum of the great humble-bees, or marked their ponderous flight from flower to flower, and watched the unpacking of their trunks for their work of suction, would have supposed that the multiplication or diminution of their race, or the fruitfulness and sterility of the red clover, depend as directly on the vigilance of our cats as do those of our well-guarded games-preserves on the watching of our keepers?[35]

Both Paley and Darwin would have been proud to write such a description. As most of his biographers note, Wilberforce too loved nature.[36]

One reason Darwin's writing was 'unusually attractive', as Wilberforce put it, was because he seemed to revel in nature. The impression a reader receives is that Darwin enjoyed his research and took pleasure of a layman's kind in describing his experiments and their results.[37] Thus, at the conclusion of his book on climbing plants, Darwin describes the actions of tendrils this way:

---

[31] Compare Paley, *Natural Theology*, 324–97, 409–38 with Darwin, *Origin of Species*, 207–44, 312–45.

[32] Paul H. Barrett, Donald J. Weinshank, and Timothy T. Gottleber, eds, *A Concordance to Darwin's Origin of Species, First Edition* (Ithaca, NY, 1981), 57, 60, 824.

[33] Darwin, *Origin of Species*, 172, 227. In his other works, see, e.g., *Cross and Self Fertilisation in the Vegetable Kingdom* (London, 1876), 2, 5; *The Differing Forms of Flowers on Plants* (London, 1877), 3–4.

[34] See Darwin, *Origin of Species*, 73–74.

[35] [Wilberforce], 'Art. VII', 226.

[36] See Burgon, *Twelve Good Men*, 2: 68; Daniell, *Wilberforce*, 147.

[37] For an analysis of Darwin's writing style and organization, see Gillian Beer, *Darwin's Plots: Evolutionary Narrative in Darwin, George Eliot, and Nineteenth-Century Fiction* (London, 1983); eadem, 'Darwin's Reading and the Fictions of Development', in David Kohn, ed., *The Darwinian Heritage* (Princeton, NJ, 1985), 543–88.

The tendril strikes some object, and quickly curls round and firmly grasps it. In the course of some hours it contracts into a spire, dragging up the stem, and forming an excellent spring. All movements now cease. By growth the tissues soon become wonderfully strong and durable. The tendril has done its work, and has done it in an admirable manner.[38]

Had Darwin added a phrase or two about 'the beauty of creation' or 'the work of the Creator', his comments would have been appropriate in any Anglican church on a Sunday morning.

Naturally, Wilberforce did add the appropriate phrase. In his sermon before the Royal Society in 1856, Wilberforce painted the following word picture:

[A person walking] amidst the beauties and harmonies of rejoicing nature, gladdening his own spirit with the song of birds and the hum of insects, with the sighing of the breezes and the thunder of the waves; or with the glorious lights of moon and sunset, with the deep shadow of forests, with the magnificence of the everlasting hills, with the bright painting of the flowers of the field, and the variety and gracefulness of that animal life, which, with the glad pulsations of its exuberant joyfulness, is ever throbbing round him [ought to have] a general sense of God's goodness …[39]

And that was the crux of the matter: nature was a teacher but what was the lesson a student or admirer should learn? For Wilberforce (and Paley), the answer was simple:

Nature is a parable of grace, and grace an interpreter of nature: man's intellect is most exalted when it is humbled the most, and the deep waters of Nature are fathomed by him in whose steady hand is held the plummet-line, wherein a steadfast observation of God's *works*, and a humble faith in His *Word*, are wound into one indissoluble thread.[40]

---

[38] Charles Darwin, *The Movements and Habits of Climbing Plants*, 2nd edn, revised (London, 1875), 206.

[39] Wilberforce, 'The Relation of Man to the Natural World', *Sermons on Various Occasions*, 182–94, at 185.

[40] Ibid. 194.

Wilberforce's thinking is consistent throughout his career: he made the same point in the 1830s and in the 1870s.

Whether it was caution, his writing style or genuine uncertainty, Darwin was not so clear in 1859. In the *Origin of Species* there are seven occasions when Darwin uses the term 'the Creator' which sound as though he is describing the Christian God.[41] Conversely, there are seventy-three occasions when Darwin expresses doubt about or mentions the impossibility of special or independent creation.[42] But then 'nature' is anthropomorphized no less than twenty-four times in phrases that Paley himself would have little trouble adopting; for example, it is 'the hand of Nature' which gives humankind the ability to produce varieties of species.[43] Perhaps more important for understanding his thought, as more time passed after 1859, Darwin said much less about 'the Creator' and far more about laws of nature and natural causes in his comments about origins. Nature was still wondrous and worthy of admiration but not because someone made it so.

Given the significance of Darwin's theory of natural selection – evolution based on demonstrable natural phenomena – it is not a surprise that Paley, Wilberforce and Darwin disagreed about the agent of the creation of nature. In Paley's famous example, a watch required a watchmaker and the complexities of nature required a creator (ultimately with a capital 'C').[44] While agreeing with Paley in the main, Wilberforce recognized the importance of law in a Darwinian sense – regular, dependable, fathomable. In his sermon 'The Relation of Man to the Natural World', Wilberforce noted that while 'Man might have been cast amongst the works of God as on a heap of disconnected facts, bearing no impress of mutual relations, and exhibiting no marks of any special law of order, or general and pervading principles, as directing their construction', the opposite had occurred. 'In the world in which man actually finds himself, there is on every side the highest conceivable rule of regularity and order', he argued.[45]

---

[41] Darwin, *Origin of Species*, 186, 188, 189, 413 (twice), 435, 488.
[42] e.g. ibid. 6, 129, 138, 159, 167, 185, 244, 483, 487, 488.
[43] Ibid. 61; see also ibid. 30, 73, 82, 83, 147, 194, 242, 292, 390, 467, 469.
[44] Paley, *Natural Theology*, 1–19.
[45] Wilberforce, *Sermons on Several Occasions*, 188.

Unsurprisingly, Darwin would have been more comfortable with Wilberforce's position. After commenting on the 'beautiful contrivances' of his favourite flower, the orchid, Darwin noted that his book on orchids

> affords me ... an opportunity of attempting to show that the study of organic beings may be as interesting to an observer who is fully convinced that the structure of each is due to secondary laws, as to one who views every trifling detail of structure as the result of the direct interposition of the Creator ...[46]

Paley might argue that 'a law presupposes an agent'[47] but Darwin would counter that sometimes a law is simply a law, not requiring anything or anyone to make it operate.

Unlike some of his contemporaries and acolytes, Darwin did not intend his theories to exalt the position of humans in the universe. In fact, in a style Paley and Wilberforce would have praised, Darwin suggested that the laws of nature should make humans more humble. Darwin famously ended *The Descent of Man* by acknowledging that 'Man still bears in his bodily frame the indelible stamp of his lowly origin.'[48] Three years earlier, Darwin made an equally strong point about humans' lack of power over nature:

> Man has no power of altering the absolute conditions of life ... he cannot change the climate of any country; he adds no new element to the soil ... It is an error to speak of man 'tampering with nature' and causing variability. If organic beings had not possessed an inherent tendency to vary, man could have done nothing.[49]

Darwin's theory of evolution did not put humans apart from or above nature: the same was true of Paley's natural theology.

Sheridan Gilley has suggested that 'the *Origin* is Paleyism inverted' because 'Darwin explains as an advantage in the struggle

---

[46] Darwin, *Contrivances by which Orchids are Fertilised*, 2.
[47] Paley, *Natural Theology*, 7.
[48] Charles Darwin, *The Descent of Man, and Selection in Relation to Sex*, 2 vols (London, 1871), 2: 405.
[49] Darwin, *Variation under Domestication*, 1: 2.

for survival whatever Paley attributes to intelligent design.'[50] Perhaps 'Paley with the core substituted' is a more appropriate characterization. While discussing the contributions of the German botanist Julius von Sachs (1832–1897) and Dutch botanist Hugo de Vries (1848–1935) to contemporary knowledge about climbing plants, Darwin notes that certain tendril-bearing plants 'display as beautiful adaptations as can be found in any part of the kingdom of nature': typical Paley. Darwin then adds: 'It is ... an interesting fact that intermediate states between organs fitted for widely different functions, may be observed on the same individual plant of Corydalis claviculata and the common vine; and these cases illustrate in a striking manner the principle of the gradual evolution of species': not Paley at all.[51] Conversely, when Wilberforce described adaptation in his sermon 'The Relation of Man to the Natural World', these were 'unquestionable and innumerable instances of intelligent design' which 'of necessity imply the previous existence of an intelligent Designer'.[52] Darwin's 'designer' was of a very different order from Wilberforce's – perhaps it was Nature (with a capital 'N'), perhaps there was no designer at all. Both men used Paleyesque language but the underlying teleology was very different.

Peter Bowler suggests that 'by persuading scientists to only talk about the natural world in terms of natural processes, Huxley triumphed over the supporters of design, even if in a less dramatic fashion than the popular image of his confrontation with Wilberforce would imply'.[53] Huxley's 'win' has had another consequence: by talking less about Darwin's love of flowers, Wilberforce's love of birds or Paley's wonderment at the beauty of nature, twenty-first-century historians appreciate less the character of all three men and understand imperfectly their nineteenth-century 'conversation'.

Baylor University

[50] Sheridan Gilley, 'The Huxley-Wilberforce Debate: A Reconsideration', in Keith Robbins, ed., *Religion and Humanism*, SCH 17 (Oxford, 1981), 325–40, at 328.

[51] Darwin, *Climbing Plants*, v–vi.

[52] Wilberforce, *Sermons on Various Occasions*, 183, 184.

[53] Peter Bowler, *Monkey Trials and Gorilla Sermons: Evolution and Christianity from Darwin to Intelligent Design* (Cambridge, MA, 2007), 108.

NATURE AND MODERNITY: J. C. ATKINSON AND RURAL MINISTRY IN ENGLAND c. 1850–1900

by WILLIAM SHEILS

THE impact of industrialization and urbanization in the second half of the nineteenth century, and the Churches' responses to it, in terms of meeting pastoral needs and devotional impulses, has produced an extensive literature since Owen Chadwick's magisterial study of forty years ago.[1] Much of that has focussed on the social mission of the Church, but the publication of Darwin's *Origin of Species* and the rapid transformation of parts of the physical landscape following industrialization and urbanization in the later nineteenth century also raised issues about humanity's relationship to the natural world and in particular, for the purposes of this paper, the English countryside.[2] Questions about that relationship have become even more pressing as industrialization has made a global impact and our use – and abuse – of the world's natural resources threaten to deplete those life-giving assets upon which our future depends: clean air and clean water. Historians have much to contribute to the debate and the publication of *The Oxford Handbook to Religion and Ecology* in 2006 indicates the contemporary importance of the theme to theologians also.[3] It is a timely topic for this volume to address. This paper will take a micro-historical approach to what are large

---

[1] Owen Chadwick, *The Victorian Church*, 2 vols (London, 1966, 1970). More recently, Frances Knight, *The Nineteenth-Century Church and English Society* (Cambridge, 1995) has provided a fresh survey of the Established Church. S. J. D. Green, *Religion in the Age of Decline: Organisation and Experience in Industrial Yorkshire 1870–1920* (Cambridge, 1996) examines urban England at this time; the best study of rural England remains J. Obelkevich, *Religion and Rural Society: South Lindsey, 1825–1875* (Oxford, 1976); D. W. Bebbington, *Evangelicalism in Modern Britain: A History from the 1730s to the 1980s* (London, 1989) is the best survey of that tradition.

[2] Raymond Williams, *The Country and the City* (London, 1973), esp. 221–58, 297–315; B. Short, 'Images and Realities in the English Rural Community: An Introduction', in idem, ed., *The English Rural Community: Image and Analysis* (Cambridge, 1992), 1–18.

[3] R. S. Gottlieb, ed., *The Oxford Handbook to Religion and Ecology* (London, 2006).

questions by analysing the writings and ministry of a little-known figure in a little-known place during the latter half of the nine-teenth century, in the hope that it will illustrate contemporary understanding of the relationship between religion and the natural world at a time of rapid economic, social and intellectual change.

Our subject takes us to an 'area of outstanding natural beauty', the North York Moors, and in particular to the parish of Danby in Cleveland on its northern edge, for it is in that place that the subject of this paper, John Christopher Atkinson, worked as both curate and vicar from 1847 until his death in 1900 at the age of 86. What frames this paper is the account he wrote of his life and ministry there, *Forty Years in a Moorland Parish*, published in 1891.[4] This account gained for its author a belated celebrity among those literate middle classes of the towns who avidly sought their own versions of the rural idyll, that 'land of lost content' which they entered on their holidays or through rail excursions. It also brought Atkinson academic honour, after a life of extensive schol-arly endeavours, in the form of a DCL from Durham University, and ecclesiastical recognition as a canon of York Minster.[5]

Atkinson's book brought him to the attention of metropolitan literary circles, and its sympathetic evocation of rural life in the later nineteenth century has resulted in it being used, or mined, by successions of historians and writers on rural life, most notably for our purposes by Owen Chadwick in an equally sympathetic portrayal of rural religion, his chapter on 'The Village Church' in *The Victorian Church*.[6] The opening of this chapter bears quotation:

> In 1860 the idea of a village church was still embodied in some country parishes. The squire was in his pew, his friend the parson in his stall, respectable farmers in pews, and on benches the labourers in smock frocks, delicately embroidered at front and back, their wives often in scarlet shawls. The men sat passive, not following in books, some unable to read, but silent with a stolid attentiveness, not liking to be absent because of

---

[4] J. C. Atkinson, *Forty Years in a Moorland Parish*, 2nd edn (London, 1891). The third edition contained a memoir of Atkinson by his publisher, George Macmillan: 'A Memoir', in *Forty Years*, 3rd edn (London, 1907), vii–xxvi.

[5] See my article in *ODNB* [online edn, 2007], 'Atkinson, John Christopher' (1814–1900)', <http://www.oxforddnb.com/view/article.849>, accessed 10 July 2008.

[6] Chadwick, *Victorian Church*, 2: 151–217.

the squire or the farmer or habit, but in no way sorry to be there, men without hostility and with quiet acceptance. ...

In some country parishes this time honoured structure continued to the end of the century and beyond.[7]

In support of this position Chadwick called on Atkinson's account of his ministry, concluding that in this remote area of rural England, Atkinson, 'looking back, ... could not see that his parish or people altered during the Victorian age so markedly as his questioners seemed to expect them to have altered'.[8] I would like to suggest that the issue was more complex than that, and that Atkinson's account of his ministry, read alongside his other published works and his manuscripts, reveals a mind grappling with the consequences, spiritual, intellectual and material, of modernity. Three issues, all of which are relevant to the concerns of the volume, reveal that complexity and uncertainty: Atkinson's response to the landscape and to 'nature'; his engagement with scientific advances, especially those in natural history, in which he was a skilled practitioner; and his assessment of his ministry in the light of the spiritual and cultural expectations of his congregations.

But first we should return to the man, and to the place, for they are central to the argument. John Christopher Atkinson was born in his mother's home parish of Goldhanger in Essex on 9 May 1814 into an evangelical clerical family of Yorkshire origin. Among its members it claimed an early associate of John Wesley, and subsequently Atkinson's grandfather had employed the Evangelical Charles Simeon as a curate in his Cambridge parish. It was into this style of churchmanship that John Christopher was born, and his university career, at St John's College, Cambridge, where he was a wrangler, confirmed the family tradition. After ordination in 1841 Atkinson, like many other scholarly young clerics, spent some years as a private tutor, in Suffolk and at Berwick-upon-Tweed, before taking a curacy at Scarborough on the Yorkshire coast where he attracted the attention, and the friendship, of William Henry Dawnay, Viscount Downe, a close contemporary who had recently inherited the title along with an extensive estate of over thirty thousand acres in the North Riding. It was

---

[7] Ibid. 151.
[8] Ibid. 181.

through Downe's patronage that Atkinson was appointed to the living of Danby in 1847. In many respects the match between scholarly pastor and rough, moorland parish with its scattered farming settlements and small-scale extractive industrial activity was an unlikely one, and there is no suggestion in the early years that either pastor or patron thought it likely to lead to a lifelong commitment. Situated at the northern end of the North Yorkshire Moors, Danby comprised scattered hill farms of modest size, providing dairy produce and honey for the local market at Whitby, and some mining and quarrying at Castleton, at the northern end of the parish and two miles from the church. The living was not well endowed and Atkinson was a man of some ambition, professional and intellectual.[9] He had published a sermon in 1847 while at Scarborough, and his star seemed to be in the ascendant when, in 1851, as chaplain to the High Sheriff, he was chosen to preach the Assize Sermon at York Minster.[10]

This was a set-piece occasion which gave the preacher the opportunity to reach a wide and influential audience and, for his text, Atkinson chose Revelation 20: 12, 'And the books were opened', on which to base a sermon affirming Christ's redemptive victory over human sinfulness, a sinfulness manifested in the unfolding of the human past. Memory, or history, was essentially the record of human frailty, 'so that there is nothing forgotten that has come to pass, or unregistered in the Archives of Heaven', but Christ's sacrifice had overcome that sinfulness. The message was unexceptional and broadly evangelical in tone, and Atkinson's treatment somewhat dense. If it was hoped that the sermon might lead to greater things, that hope remained unfulfilled and Atkinson returned to Danby, there to remain until his death on 31 March 1900.[11]

To judge from his account, however, his life at Danby was far from unfulfilled. In that place he was a scholar among rustics, as were many of his clerical contemporaries elsewhere, and the reference to archives in his sermon was to be prophetic in the scholarly,

---

[9] J. C. Atkinson, *The History of Cleveland: Ancient and Modern*, 2 vols (Barrow-in-Furness, 1872–77), 1: 278–79.

[10] *ODNB*; J. C. Atkinson, *Repentance: A Sermon* (London, 1847).

[11] J. C. Atkinson, *A Sermon Preached at York Minster before the Judges of Assize, 9 March 1851* (York, 1851).

if not the spiritual, sense. Once established in his parish, Atkinson did not neglect his intellectual interests and he embraced the region and its history, editing the cartularies of the abbeys at Rievaulx and Whitby, chronicling human frailty in the five volumes of Quarter Sessions records he produced for the North Riding Record Society (a learned body established by him and which did not survive its founder's death), engaging in philological studies on the local dialects, and embarking on an unfinished *History of Cleveland*. Although essentially a traditional antiquarian account of the parishes in the area which concentrated on archaeological and architectural features, the *History* included an account of more recent developments in economy and society and was dedicated to the elected member for the newly enfranchised parliamentary borough of Middlesbrough, the fastest growing urban concentration in mid-Victorian England and, as 'Ironopolis', the crucible of much of its industrial development.[12] Unlike some rural clergy, however, in Atkinson's case this scholarly activity did not represent a withdrawal from the open world of the parish to the closed world of the study. Any distance which his learning placed between him and his flock was more than compensated for by the fact that Atkinson was a countryman among country folk, and his writings on natural history, both learned and popular, revealed a practical and lively engagement with the everyday lives of his neighbours, both human and animal. For example, in the course of a lengthy text to which we will return, which was devoted to the study of behaviour in the animal kingdom, Atkinson illustrated his discussion of the impact of experience and training on the mind with a homely and familiar example, contrasting the fearful response of a newly born lamb with the calm indifference of its mother as each became aware of Atkinson's presence while he was out walking on the moors.[13]

This vignette leads us naturally to consideration of place. Danby was a moorland parish with a number of settlements divided by

---

[12] J. C. Atkinson, ed., *Cartularium Abbathiae de Whiteby*, 2 vols, Surtees Society 69, 72 (1879); idem, ed., *Cartularium Abbathiae de Rievalle*, Surtees Society 83 (1889); idem, ed., *North Riding Quarter Sessions Records*, 5 vols (London 1883–86); idem, *History of Cleveland*, dedication. For Middlesbrough, see W. Lillie, *A History of Middlesbrough* (London, 1968).

[13] J. C. Atkinson, *Sketches in Natural History: With an Essay on Reason and Instinct* (London, 1861), 336.

deep valleys formed by tributaries of the River Esk, which ran through to meet the sea a few miles downstream at the busy fishing port of Whitby. From 1861 the railway passed through the northern end of the parish, at Castleton and Glaisdale, transporting modest tonnages of coal to the surrounding towns of Stockton and Whitby and iron and stone from the quarries for the industrial north-east. These were never very profitable and had closed by the mid-1870s, so that in the years following the railway was as significant for its human cargoes as for its goods, taking emigrants out of the parish to the rapidly growing industrial centre of Middlesbrough and beyond, and bringing the professional classes and day trippers, usually in church or chapel parties, into the parish as tourists seeking respite from industrial life in the dramatic, but sparsely populated scenery. To that degree, at least in the later half of Atkinson's ministry, the parish was in more regular contact with the modern world than it had ever been before.[14] It was not quite the self-sufficient or isolated rural community envisaged in Atkinson's account, or in the pastoral ideal as expressed in contemporary commentary, whether in the fiction of Charlotte Yonge or the pastoral writings of Richard Wilson Evans, another cleric working in an upland northern parish,[15] and these facts were to prove problematic to Atkinson's understanding of his ministry.

Nor did the geography of the region assist the already difficult task of giving institutional expression to the ideal Christian community that the parish was taken to represent in much contemporary pastoral theology.[16] Some essentials were present; a church and rectory, albeit in some disrepair when Atkinson arrived, and a landlord who, if not resident, kept a shooting box on the estate which he visited regularly. Other features of the place were less helpful to the rural priest; scattered moorland farms spread about a wide and dramatic but often impassable terrain, new settlements growing at some distance from church and rectory around the coal and iron workings at Castleton and Glaisdale, and the presence

---

[14] M. Stainsby, *More than an Ordinary Man: Life and Society in the Upper Esk Valley, 1830–1910* (Helmsley, 2006), 17–22.

[15] Charlotte Yonge, *The Daisy Chain* (London, 1856); R. W. Evans, *The Bishopric of Souls* (London, 1844), a popular pastoral text reprinted five times within thirty years. For Evans, see *ODNB*.

[16] J. C. Hammond, *The Parson in the Victorian Parish* (London, 1977), 132–51; A. Haig, *The Victorian Clergy* (London, 1984), 282–83.

of Nonconformity, and in particular Methodism, with its long-established tradition in the area, among both farmers and industrial workers. Indeed, at the start of his ministry Atkinson endorsed his patron's view, expressed on his acceptance of the living, that had it not been for the Wesleyans 'religion would practically have died out altogether in these parts'. By the mid-seventies, however, Atkinson had begun to see their success, and the particular mode of worship which they followed, now more Primitive than Wesleyan Methodism, as among the chief obstacles to his own ministry.[17] Danby was not fertile terrain for the Established Church, and Atkinson never really understood the changing religious register from established to associational (or voluntary) congregations which marked the last half of his ministry. For this representative of the Established Church the task was not so much the preservation of a well-established traditional Christian community, but rather the edification of one whose social and economic well-being was being threatened by rapid change at national and global level. This change resulted in a growth in Nonconformity and a decline in the population of the parish so that, by the time of his death, many residents attended chapels rather than the church and had younger family members living not only in the major industrial cities of England but also in Canada, the USA and Australia.[18]

It is these geographical and social contexts which make Atkinson's life and writings such useful channels through which to explore some of the key themes of this volume, and we can add to them the intellectual consequences following the publication of Darwin's *Origin of Species* in 1859, which Atkinson, as a skilled natural historian, could not ignore.

★ ★ ★

We will turn first to the geographical context, and in particular the landscape. It has already been suggested that the rough upland terrain of Danby posed problems for parochial ministry as conventionally understood, but this drawback had its compensation in the

---

[17] Atkinson, *Forty Years*, 42–45, Stainsby, *More than an Ordinary Man*, 66–69.

[18] Stainsby, *More than an Ordinary Man*, 1–21; Obelkevich, *Religion and Rural Society*, 168–72. For the problems of the church in rural society more generally, see A. Digby, 'Social Institutions', in E. J. T. Collins, ed., *The Agrarian History of England and Wales*, 8 vols (Cambridge, 2000), 7/2: 1466–86.

landscape to which Atkinson, in the tradition of rural writing shared by mystics such as Richard Jefferies and by fellow clerics like his Lake District contemporary Canon Hardwicke Rawnsley, turned for spiritual sustenance.[19] In describing the moorland scenery of his parish Atkinson created a 'mystical geography' which represented a moral and spiritual universe for his readers.[20] The work of visiting his parishioners, a task which Atkinson regarded as central to his ministry, in itself involved him in what, by his estimation, was a walking ministry of over seventy thousand miles, described by him in two vigorous chapters focusing on the winter landscape of the moors and dales.[21] In these pages the author made much of his indefatigable labours in coping with the hardships of traversing the snow-clad moors, in the process setting himself up as an example to his parishioners and to his readers of the way in which physical courage and stamina could be construed as outward signs of moral and spiritual strength. These passages provided a pastoral reflection of that Romantic pedestrianism and muscular Christianity which was to prove so beguiling to so many. One example will suffice, dating, be it noted, from the late 1880s, when Atkinson was already in his seventies.

Having walked four miles in fine weather across a snow covered moor in order to visit a distressed young farmer whose bride-to-be had just been buried on her planned wedding day, Atkinson set off on a further three mile walk to visit

> the widow of another old and staunch friend, who had been ailing lately … It was still perfectly fair overhead, the sun shining brightly at times; and the snow – no great thickness of it anywhere; perhaps two to three inches where it was thickest – was crusted over, as I said. But the wind grew colder and colder as it increased momentarily in force; and long before I got to my widowed parishioner's house the crusted snow had begun to be broken up by the force of the wind, and

---

[19] For Jefferies and Rawnsley, see *ODNB* and accompanying bibliographies. Rawnsley was a founder of the National Trust.

[20] The phrase is taken from John Lowerson, 'The Mystical Geography of the English', in Short, ed., *English Rural Community*, 152–74, esp. 152–62. It was coined by Terence Ranger in his study of African Christianity: 'Taking Hold of the Land', *P&P* no. 117 (1987), 158–94.

[21] Atkinson, *Forty Years,* preface, xi, 348–83; for the importance of visiting, see Obelkevich, *Religion and Rural Society*, 164.

to drive along in most incisive fragments ... when I got to within a field or two of the house, drifts formed in parts of the road approaching it such that the wheels of a recently-passing vehicle had cut through some of them to a depth of eighteen inches. I did not prolong my visit for things were looking badly for my walk home – a more than four miles walk the nearest way ...

It was time I was afoot. Some idea may be formed of the fury of the wind from the fact that, as I passed at the corner of the second field, up which the drift of the snow-crust had pursued me with cutting sharpness ... the sharp-edged particles driven with the full force of the wind against the nape of my neck and the more exposed ear and cheek, inflicted such acute pain that it required some nerve to bear it and keep busy with getting over the nasty, dangerous place. Once over, the worst was also over. There were still two more walls to surmount, but then downhill, across a sloping field ... On reaching the castle the direction of my march altered, and I had the wind behind me. But there was a difficulty at the first gate across the road I came to. There was a drift just through it, nearly four feet thick, and it reached several yards along the road. And I have known things easier of doing than plunging through three or four feet of utterly loose snow ...

All this time not a flake of fresh or soft snow had fallen. It was perfectly fair overhead, thickening up from half-hour to half-hour with a prophetic intimation of what was yet to come. And come it did, though not for two or three hours after I reached home, and had at last got the snow out of my hair and beard.[22]

These difficulties were not without their compensations, and the play of light on winter landscape is a recurrent descriptive trope, both in conjuring up the large vistas of the moors and in describing the detailed structures of the elements. First the large vistas, described by Atkinson as those 'wonderful creations by nature's jeweller'. Looking across Danby Moor on a winter evening he revealed the 'wonderful display of nature's lights and colouring' in the following terms:

---

[22] Atkinson, *Forty Years*, 349–50.

This strangely beautiful succession of rose tints and steel-blue tones of deepening intensity has been witnessed by me once and again ... At your feet and in the foreground your eye rested in the unsullied snow; in the mid distance, or on the deep slopes of the moor banks you saw the tones and tints of the rose, and in the far-distance, or above the braes of the walls of the dales, you gazed out upon the matchless blues, the colours might be fainter ... but they were all there; and waited there to be gazed on with a sort of reverent admiration until the sun had sunk too low.[23]

Just as the expansive landscape described in this passage could inspire reverence for its Creator, so could the detailed structure of its constituent parts inspire awe. In contemplating the frozen surface of the snow while out walking he noted:

Every step I had taken had crushed and destroyed myriads of frost gems, all symmetrically perfect and beautiful, and set as no jeweller on earth could set them. Still, though these glimmered with a sort of pearly lustre in the sunbeams, the sources of the flashing, lustrously-hued diamond rays were not in them; but set among them in infinite numbers were facets of such reflecting and refracting power as only nature herself could produce ... I no longer wondered that the brightness and the splendour were so dazzlingly glorious to behold when I came to regard the enginery [*sic*] from which they resulted.[24]

In his reaction to (and descriptions of) the landscape, Atkinson created a moral universe encapsulated in his own unremitting pastoral labours and in the qualities of those people among whom he lived, qualities which he most frequently characterized through the adjective 'staunch', a term which combined in the people those enduring features of the landscape. His accounts of his journeyings around the parish, to visit the sick, to offer comfort, and to hold services, record the solitariness and smallness he felt in the face of nature, the fear of losing the way, and the fidelity of those few parishioners who shared these hardships in their determination to serve their God. They were compensated for their travail, for the

---

[23] Ibid. 368.
[24] Ibid. 370.

landscape was a God-given gift, a mystical geography, which both demanded virtue from those who had to cope with it, and created virtue in the characters of those who had to toil within it. In recompense it offered to those with eyes to see, fleeting glimpses of a beauty which revealed the Creator (jeweller or engineer in Atkinson's words) behind it.[25]

This was the lesson drawn by Atkinson from the passages quoted above, and in both of them it was the combination of nature, and the act of walking through it, which revealed God's grandeur, through contemplation of the changing stimuli which such movement provoked. It was the movement of mankind within nature which revealed its God-given qualities, not just nature itself, and that was a crucial point in his argument. Atkinson's response to the colours on the moor was an essentially emotional response to the play of light on landscape and, as such, it revealed him, like so many other Evangelicals, as a follower of the Romantic poets whose works would have dominated his youth and for whom walking, and particularly the act of passing through upland scenery, moved the imagination from the terrestrial to the celestial.[26] If Wordsworth was, in Seamus Heaney's telling phrase, truly a 'pedestrian poet' then Atkinson was, by his own account, a 'pedestrian priest'.[27] That pedestrianism was an essential element in his imaginative and spiritual response to nature and to his vocation but, as the second passage revealed, it also stimulated his observational and scientific curiosity, where God was no longer the artist, but the engineer. It is this engagement with science, and in particular with natural history, that we must now address.

★   ★   ★

Like many nineteenth-century parsons, Atkinson was an accomplished naturalist, who published in 1859 a 'Nature Study' reader

---

[25] Ibid. 348–82.

[26] See, in this volume, Andrew Atherstone, 'Frances Ridley Havergal's Theology of Nature', 319–32; Mark Smith, 'The Mountain and the Flower: The Power and Potential of Nature in the World of Victorian Evangelicalism', 307–18. For the influence of Wordsworth on the Evangelicals, see Bebbington, *Evangelicalism*, 80–81.

[27] Seamus Heaney, *Preoccupations: Selected Prose Writings 1968–78* (New York, 1980), 68; for walking and culture generally, see A. D. Wallace, *Walking, Literature and English Culture: The Origins and Uses of Peripatetic in the Nineteenth Century* (Oxford, 1993), esp. 166–99.

entitled *Walks, Talks, Travels and Exploits of Two Schoolboys*, which was framed as an account of a holiday taken by two boys journeying and sailing up the east coast of England. In the course of their travels the varying landscapes and the differing farming practices observed between, say, the Essex marshes and the Yorkshire coast were linked to, and used to explain, the diversity of flora and fauna found in each region. As such the book follows that tradition of natural history writing that was located in what one might call an ecological rather than a classificatory mode, where habitat was the dominant explanatory influence. This was Atkinson's preferred mode of writing, and set him firmly in a long tradition of natural history writing, much of it by clergymen, and even when he did adopt the alternative classificatory method in another illustrated handbook published two years later, *British Birds' Eggs and Nests*, environment and location remained central to his account.[28]

By that date, of course, the *Origin of Species* had been published, its ideas circulated, and the infamous clash between Huxley and Bishop Wilberforce had taken place at the Oxford meeting of the British Association in 1860. For the scientifically minded clergyman, natural history could no longer be an essentially descriptive science, as Atkinson's earlier works had been, albeit with, perhaps, an underlying religious message. Although the conflict between science and religion was far from being partisan in the 1860s and would not gather momentum until after the appearance of *The Descent of Man* in 1871, the publication of *Origin* meant that the implications of the arguments contained within it could not be ignored by a clergyman of scientific interests such as Atkinson was.[29] Accordingly, in 1861 Atkinson took up his pen and wrote his

[28] D. Elliston Allen, *The Naturalist in Britain: A Social History* (London, 1976), demonstrates the extensive publication on natural history by clergymen, mostly of the Church of England; J. C. Atkinson, *Walks, Talks, Travels and Exploits of two Schoolboys* (London, 1859); idem, *British Birds' Eggs and Nests, Popularly Described* (London, 1861). These were popular books with further editions, some of them capitalizing on Atkinson's fame after the publication of *Forty Years*.

[29] See Adrian Desmond and James Moore, *Darwin* (London, 1991), 485–99, for the immediate row; for overviews of the topic, James Moore, *The Post Darwinian Controversies: A Study of the Protestant Struggle to Come to Terms with Darwin in Great Britain and America, 1870–1900* (Cambridge, 1979); J. Hedley Brooke, 'Darwin and Victorian Christianity', in J. Hodge and G. Radick, eds, *The Cambridge Companion to Darwin* (Cambridge, 2003), 192–213. For Darwin's relations with his own rector, see, in this volume, Paul White, 'Darwin's Church', 333–52.

Sketches in Natural History, with an Essay on Reason and Instinct. In this text, in which he combined his descriptive mode with analytical method drawn from philosophical enquiry and from recent publications, not only in natural history but in what might be termed psychological science, Atkinson wrestled with the implications of the questions prompted by Darwin's book, without mentioning it directly, and it may have been the catalyst for a longer process of internal debate.[30]

In accordance with his usual practice, Atkinson sought to draw his conclusions from essentially familiar, even homely examples, as the story of the sheep and the newborn lamb referred to above suggests. Firstly, he challenged Locke's assumption, widely held at the time, that it was the power of abstraction which separated man from the animals, referring to recent psychological research to support his case and employing the example of a dog raising the alarm to warn of fire to demonstrate, as he thought, that the abstract idea of danger was inherent in the animal kingdom, and that animals also understood, and had the capacity to communicate these ideas to others.[31] The first part of the book, the 'Sketches on Natural History', was designed to demonstrate the rationality of the animal kingdom, and to challenge the arrogance of humanity in its relations with it. His concluding section on the snipe makes his point well; having acknowledged the skill with which the bird can conceal itself, even from a countryman as watchful as he was, Atkinson continues:

> I know that man is 'fearfully and wonderfully made', and I believe that the inferior orders of animate creation are also, and with a startling amount of truth in the words, wonderfully made; and it is with feelings of distaste that I sometimes hear whole species of them vilipended [denigrated] as to their common sense, as we should term it in our own case, and even as to their qualifications for discharging the functions or objects of their creation. It seems to me that they who speak

[30] Atkinson, *Sketches,* in which he refers to several articles published in the *Journal of the Society for Psychical Research* as well as standard theological works such as Joseph Butler's *Analogy of Religion,* which had been reprinted several times in mid-century, and David Livingstone's *Missionary Journeys,* published in 1857. See also the letter he wrote towards the end of the century, quoted below at 382.

[31] Atkinson, *Sketches*, 164.

so slightingly of the creatures formed, neglect to think of the Wisdom which created them …

For my own part, I have the most entire conviction that the more closely we observe the ways and habits of the various members of animal creation, the more thoroughly and intimately we become acquainted with the laws of their being; the more searchingly we trace and investigate the characters legibly, and to the true inquirer not unintelligibly, impressed upon them by the Author of their existence, the more, even among the most contemned and despised races, shall we find to admire, to wonder at, and reverently to pronounce compatible only with the possession by their Maker of nothing short of Infinite Wisdom, Infinite Power, and Infinite Goodness.[32]

Reason, then, was found throughout created nature, and was God-given. As such it required humility from a humanity currently over-conscious of its own power to effect progress and improvement. So far, so good, but the question of reason also posed its own problems, and especially so when Atkinson came to consider the higher primates in the second part of the book, the 'Essay'.

After a discussion of the means whereby species can transmit experience and practical knowledge down the generations, Atkinson then sought to identify a point of fundamental discontinuity between humankind and the animals. While he noted that animals had a 'soul or spirit' (in the light of the quotation which follows, one wonders what he had in mind), and even an 'imagination', Atkinson found the crucial break in conventional theological understanding, that is to say, in 'the immortality of the soul'. He wrote, at the end of a section on the orang-utan.

To the mere animal there is the love of life: – to man, the desire after immortality. The instinctive longing, yearning even, of the latter is for something commensurate with the capacity and the duration of 'the conscious living agent himself', and which he feels rather than simply knows or believes, is reserved only, but surely, in the mysterious recesses of Eternity. But the craving of the former reaches no further than food, well being,

---

[32] Ibid. 174–75.

safety – the mere requisites of the right fleeting life that now is ...

He then continued:

As facts are fairly stated, and boldly brought forward, the more all investigation goes to establish the ancient opinion of man before it was confirmed by revealed religion, that brutes are of this world only; that man is imprisoned here only for a season to take a better or a worse hereafter as he deserves it. This old truth is the fountain of all goodness and justice and kindness among men; may we all feel it intimately, obey it perpetually, and profit by it eternally.[33]

Atkinson's appeal here to the connection between reason and revealed religion directed him to the Bible and especially to Genesis, and to an attack on those who retained a literal interpretation of the beginnings of the world. As a discussion of the authority of the Bible as a scientific text, by a clergyman of broadly conservative social views but liberal, if not advanced, theological understanding, the passage deserves quotation at some length:

reference should be made to the pages of the Bible, as speaking authoritatively, if speaking at all – which it is assumed to do – upon the subject in hand. I certainly do not wish to dispute, and still less to ignore, the existence of certain passages in the Bible, which seem, at least, to bear upon the question: and I am quite disposed to admit that, having such apparent applicability, they both challenge inquiry and demand attentive consideration.

But still, however willing to consent to the course here indicated, I desire at once to state my conviction that no information or instruction of the kind anticipated is reasonably to be looked for or expected in the Bible. The object with which that volume was given to man was to teach him his relations with his Maker; and in such a way that nothing might be more plainly seen than that the highest and best human interests coincided precisely with entire and uncompromising observance of the Creator's requirements. In order to do this,

---

[33] Ibid. 254–55.

it might be and really was necessary that a brief introductory sketch of man's origin, and that of Creation at large, should be given; but only so far that man, thoroughly understanding into what an abyss he had plunged himself 'by transgression', might, the more willingly, as well as the more readily, comprehend the nature of the means of extinction, which it was the business of the Bible, in all its several stages towards completion, to set forth and explain, and so recommend. Room for scientific disquisition or philosophical explanation of any sort there was none, therefore, in the scope of the Volume itself, any more than in the mental culture or intellectual adaptability of those to whom it was progressively delivered; and hence, I expect to find in the Bible no information, properly so called, on Geological matters, and in so far as philosophical research and inquiry are mentioned in the Sacred Writings, whether directly or in the way of allusion, they are constantly spoken of in what must be termed a popular manner; with no attempt at or even thought of scientific accuracy, or precise exactness of expression.[34]

Atkinson's scientific background therefore led him to the view, not that science and religion were in opposition, but that they comprised entirely separate fields of knowledge. Not only did the Bible have nothing to say of scientific value, in the strictest sense of the word, but he also thought that those who sought to claim scientific authority for the Scriptures proved a stumbling block in the way of understanding the true purpose of the text. For him such a view would have had humanity still believing that the earth was flat, that the sun and not the earth was in motion, and that there had never been, in his own words, 'a stupendous series of ecological epochs, of almost inconceivable duration, countless ages before man was sent to be an inhabitant of the Globe'.[35] For Atkinson such biblical literalism actively diminished the role of God who, through the mysteries of nature, would raise humanity to a greater understanding of its purposes and those of its Creator. In so far as Atkinson expressed himself on these issues in 1861, it was the obscurantism of biblical literalism, and not the views

---

[34] Ibid. 192–93.
[35] Ibid. 196.

of the supporters of evolution, which undermined true religion, and he adopted the more liberal theology expressed in *Essays and Reviews,* the publication of which soon produced a vigorous debate between liberals and conservatives within the Church which, during the 1860s at least, placed the row over evolution into the background.[36]

This early response to the debate thrown up by Darwin's ideas and his own scientific researches was not repeated by Atkinson in print, but newspaper reports and records of his lectures, and his sermon notes, indicate that he remained firm in the views he expressed in that text, sharing them with his parishioners from the pulpit as well as with his professional and clerical colleagues at gatherings of local literary and philosophical societies, where he was a frequent and popular speaker.[37] Reflecting on the ways in which his scientific training had influenced his theology, he wrote to a friend in December 1896:

> I remember seeing some large earthworms which had come unwarily out of their holes one rainy night, and which had been caught by a sharp frost imminent on the rain and put to death thereby. I was told that 'by sin came death' and that this accounted for the miserable death of these worms. I think that and things like it which I got from some among the strictest sect of the 'Evangelical' (!) School of my young associations set me revolting, thinking, enquiring, and I have never left off. My aunts on my father's side and their husbands were eminently good people, and all but one who had been a Missionary were as eminently 'narrow' and did not know how to deal with an enquiring boy. ... Ryle, Kirkpatrick and Co. would have had a free ticket, booked through, express at the hands of the good people I refer to — and they were good: and I should have been 'damned' like a hopelessly reprobate free-thinker, if they had ever dreamed of Darwin and his 'issue' and that I should think there was (not might be) 'something in it' ...[38]

---

[36] Chadwick, *Victorian Church*, 2: 75–97; for a reference to the Colenso case being discussed at Danby, see Atkinson, *Forty Years*, 16–17.

[37] Whitby, Whitby Museum, Literary and Philosophical Society, Atkinson papers, press cuttings.

[38] Atkinson, *History of Cleveland*, 1: 244.

This is a caricature, of course, and unfair to his evangelical roots. As David Bebbington and others have shown us, many Evangelicals were to find Darwin's theories compatible with their understanding of God's purposes and were not the biblical literalists of Atkinson's memory.[39] As the letter suggests, the caricature probably stems from Atkinson's own theological journey, and the distance he sought to put between his present views and those of his youth. During the 1850s Atkinson's theology moved from its origin in the parsonage of his evangelical father to a position more closely associated with the liberal theology of F. D. Maurice;[40] and in this shift, Atkinson's scientific interests were crucial. For Atkinson and other clergymen like him, Darwin's ideas as set out in the *Origins* were liberating, providing better solutions than biblical literalism could ever do to the problems encountered in understanding the actions of 'God-in-Nature' (not only in historical and scientific terms but also on key theological issues such as the questions of suffering and judgement). It was a view he was prepared to share with his correspondents and to commit to print in forcible terms.

★　★　★

Mention of F. D. Maurice brings us to the purpose of ministry and, in particular, to the social gospel, through which the kingdom of God was revealed by the Christian's endeavour to create in this world a society of justice and freedom. It was not solely a this-worldly religion, but in Maurice's case, his liberal theology led him to a practical and political expression of Christian Socialism, encapsulated in the foundation of the Working Men's College in 1854.[41] Atkinson's theology, which from the 1860s and possibly earlier seems to have been increasingly influenced by the approach to Scripture and authority expressed in *Essays and Reviews*, also led him to a social gospel, but in a very different direction.

We have already noted his imaginative connection to the Romantic poets through his response to landscape, and also his natural historian's approach to the animal kingdom, in which

[39] Bebbington, *Evangelicalism*, 142–43.
[40] For Maurice's career, see *ODNB*.
[41] See J. Morris, *F. D. Maurice and the Crisis of Christian Authority* (Oxford, 2005), 130–61, esp. 153–58, for the appeal of his 'universal Christian society' to those of conservative views.

habitat and the way in which different species adapted to their environment provided the basis for his essentially observational way of understanding behaviour. These two impulses came together in Atkinson's ministry, producing in his case an approach to social, political and religious questions (it would go too far to describe it as a philosophy) which, on the surface, looked very much like the 'romantic conservatism' which David Eastwood and others have identified as the defining characteristic of the later writings of the Romantic poets, and in particular those of Robert Southey.[42]

Atkinson shared much of Southey's scepticism about the virtues of industrialization, and certainly endorsed his view of the superiority and strengths of agrarian society, held together as it was, in his view, by a network of reciprocal ties between landlord and tenant, pastor and people. To these could be added the natural affections which bound communities through long-established familial relationships.[43] By the time Atkinson was ministering in Danby, however, and certainly in his later years, this was breaking down under the pressures of agricultural depression and emigration. The problem of emigration from the countryside was a matter for national debate by the 1890s, especially in the context of the perceived deterioration in the physical standards of the labour force, and the plight of those who were left in the countryside also attracted the attention of social commentators from this time. Like many rural communities, Danby experienced declining population in these years though, as we shall see, the environment, in respect of facilities such as housing, had improved for those who remained. In this context Darwin's ideas combined with Atkinson's own 'observational' approach to natural history to produce in his writing about the parish what might be best described as an early example of social anthropology in his description of the lives and behaviour of his parishioners.

Two-fifths of Atkinson's text is occupied by sections entitled 'Folklore' and 'Manners and Customs', and in these sections he treated questions of belief and of healing in essentially functionalist

---

[42] D. Eastwood, 'Robert Southey and the Intellectual Origins of Romantic Conservatism', *EHR* 104 (1989), 308–31.

[43] W. J. Sheils, 'Church, Community and Culture in Rural England, 1850–1900: J. C. Atkinson and the Parish of Danby', in *Christianity and Community in the West: Essays for John Bossy*, ed. Simon Ditchfield (Aldershot, 2001), 260–77.

terms, that is to say, by relating them to the social and historical circumstances in which they were deployed rather than engaging in any systematic analysis of their intellectual or scientific basis. His views and methods in this respect can be understood most clearly from his treatment of witches and wise men. Although he was at pains to make clear that, on this issue, he was describing a passing world (part of the intellectual advance he had seen more generally), it was a world that had only recently passed. If he did not know the witches and wise men personally, he knew those who had known them. In describing their activities his method was the descriptive one of the fieldworker, and he employed oral testimony in local dialect to bring life to his narratives, but what is more important to our purpose is the interpretation. Unlike the armchair folklorists of the day (classifiers who interpreted this material in what he considered to be mechanistic terms as a demonstration of the march of progress from primitivism to modernity), Atkinson brought a profound sympathy for his subjects to his interpretation.[44] After a lengthy description of the cures and wonders attributed to 'old Wrightson', a local wise man of some renown earlier in the century, Atkinson was content to place him alongside, if not quite among, the local professional medical and clerical resources available in the neighbourhood, concluding thus:

> the impression I was unconsciously led on to receive of Wrightson was – setting aside the inevitable circumstance that, like all the others of his class, he was, up to a given degree, a charlatan and an impostor – that of a man of not unkindly nature, with a pungent flavour of rough humour about him, shrewd and observant, and with wonderfully well-devised and well-employed means of information at his command … he possessed, in common with many others then and since, wide and deep acquaintance with herbs and simples, and he used his knowledge with skill and judgement. No doubt also he knew the properties and uses of what we more usually speak of as 'drugs' and employed them accordingly. No doubt either that he possessed the power of influencing men's minds and

[44] J. Ashton, 'Beyond Survivalism: Regional Folklorists in Late-Victorian England', *Folklore* 108 (1997), 19–23.

imaginations, and knew it right well, and used it of set purpose and intention.

He went on to close this passage by remarking that he had never once heard him spoken of as a man of mischief.[45]

Benevolent witchcraft was one thing, but Atkinson also had to address the propensity of the people, or many of them, to believe in the power of witches to do harm. In this discussion Atkinson made three major points, each of which directly challenged contemporary perceptions of the various intellectual establishments – folklorists, conservative biblical scholars, and the medical and scientific professions. Firstly, he rejected the folklorists' concept of superstition as an explanation for such belief, as it was a concept which was by definition in opposition to understanding or knowledge. Instead he produced a concept of his own, which he called 'over-trow' or 'believing over-much'. Unlike superstition, these terms were not in opposition to knowledge but rather reflected a distorted level of understanding. They thereby made the survival of such beliefs within modern society more intelligible, requiring a major rethinking of the relationship between traditional beliefs and the modern world which challenged the teleological assumptions of the Folklore Society, whose members saw these as survivals from a past age which had no place in modern society.[46]

His second conclusion, drawn from a comparison between some of the witchcraft tales and Baden Powell's study of the miracles in St Paul in James Maurice Wilson's *Essays and Addresses*, challenged conservative biblical readings. He wrote of the alleged witchcraft cases that 'there is really no valid reason why whole sentences from the former, with only slight verbal alteration, should not be transferred from the subject of the Christian miracles'.[47] Not only would this have scandalized his more conservative clerical colleagues, but perhaps even exponents of the new theological criticism would have been taken aback by the ease with which

[45] Atkinson, *Forty Years*, 111–15; quotation at 113.

[46] Ibid. 69 72; for the establishment view, see G. L. Gomme, *Ethnology in Folklore* (London, 1892), esp. 192–93. R. M. Dorson, *The British Folklorists* (London, 1968), 266–315, shows that those who espoused this 'evolutionary' approach to folklore were losing their dominant position after 1891.

[47] *Atkinson, Forty Years*, 76–78; J. M. Wilson, *Essays and Addresses: An Attempt to Treat some Religious Questions in a Scientific Spirit* (London, 1887).

he applied the higher criticism they espoused to the folk world of witchcraft.

Finally, in his discussion of witchcraft he issued the following challenge to the medical and scientific community who dismissed such tales as far-fetched, suggesting that the reasons underpinning belief in so-called magic were no less fanciful than many of the explanations given for the success of some branches of modern scientific experimentation: 'All this is every day experience now, and indeed is very much short of many of the experiences detailed in any memoir or treatise on the subject of electro-biology or animal-magnetism ... Is it possible to deny, or rather is it not imperative on us to assume, that in some quite sensible propor- tion of the hundreds of persons credited with the power of the witch, there may or must have been an exact analogy to the exam- ples afforded in the experiences of the magnetic or biological professor!'[48]

Atkinson's account has been used extensively by social histo- rians as a source for the survival of custom and traditional beliefs in industrial England,[49] but the consequences of his approach to these questions have not been properly treated. The immediate fame of the book as a chronicle of a rapidly disappearing England, and its subsequent celebrity as a representation of a particular mode of English country and provincial writing, have obscured his under- lying argument.[50] This is not entirely surprising, as it is largely an argument from silence. There is a huge and revealing gap at the heart of the book. If you were to look for an account of Atkin- son's ecclesiastical activities, or of the history of the worshipping community during his time at Danby, you would find only the most fleeting references to them in *Forty Years*.

After the remarks about the failings of his predecessor there are a few accounts of baptisms, marriages and burials, and especially of

[48] Atkinson, *Forty Years*, 79–80. For general discussion of this topic, see A. Winter, *Mesmerized: Powers of Mind in Victorian Britain* (Chicago, IL, 1985); J. Oppenheim, *The Other World: Spiritualism and Psychical Research in Britain, 1850–1914* (Cambridge, 1985).

[49] J. A. Sharpe, *Instruments of Darkness: Witchcraft in England, 1550–1750* (London, 1996), 276–77, 283; B. Bushaway, 'Tacit, Unsuspected but still Implicit Faith: Alternative Belief in Nineteenth-Century England', in T. Harriss, ed., *Popular Culture in England, c. 1500–1850* (Basingstoke, 1985), 189–215; O. Davies, *Witchcraft, Magic and Culture, 1736– 1951* (Manchester, 1999), 23, 190.

[50] e.g. J. G. O'Leary, ed., *A Countryman on the Moors* (London, 1967); T. J. Burns, *Canon Atkinson and His Country* (Guiseley, 1986).

the last, when the church or, more accurately perhaps, the churchyard could still be seen, at the larger gatherings, to stand at the heart
of the community. These accounts occasionally make remarks on
worship, as when Atkinson records the tolerance he chose to show
over the custom of men wearing hats in church when attending
funerals or the way in which he gradually replaced the Wesleyan
hymn book with, to him, more orthodox hymns, but in general
the nature of church worship at Danby, and the religious life it
was supposed to express, remains a mystery.[51] Likewise those other
pillars of Victorian pastoral endeavour, the school, Sunday School,
choir and parochial officers get no more than a passing mention,
and the chapels at Fryup and Castleton are merely recorded as part
of the adventure in getting to and from them in winter weather
to minister to their modest congregations.[52] As an insight into the
workings of parish institutions in the Victorian countryside the
book is decidedly lacking. Equally elusive is any assessment of relations between the Established Church and other denominations;
the only references to any other minister (and in this case not
even a minister, as William Hartas was a Quaker) was to his social
purpose as a peacekeeper and settler of disputes. Reflecting on the
death of Hartas, Atkinson commented, that he (Hartas)

> was often called upon to act as arbitrator and peacemaker in
> cases which might otherwise have led on to litigation. He was
> a man of shrewd, sound sense and judgement; and it was with
> the feeling of having lost a personal friend and helper in all
> efforts for the good of the parish and the district, that I heard
> of the death of old William Hartas.[53]

Relations with other denominations were not so harmonious and,
especially with the Methodists, they proved a source of real conflict
(over such questions as control of the village school) and anxiety,
as Atkinson compared the growing strength of their congregations
at Castleton with the dwindling numbers attending the parish
church, but his book is silent on these matters.[54]

---

[51] Atkinson, *Forty Years*, 225–26, 233.
[52] Ibid. 352–53, 360–62, 370–71.
[53] Ibid. 224.
[54] Stainsby, *More than an Ordinary Man*, 63–70.

Just as in Atkinson's assessment of the ministry of William Hartas, so too in the account of his own ministry: in so far as he came to record it in his book he did so in essentially civil rather than religious terms. Of all the changes and improvements that he recorded, and in which he, with the support of the landowner Viscount Downe, played a significant part, the most dramatic and significant was in the domestic living conditions of the people. Improved housing led to improved morals, with better sleeping arrangements for children and servants. This was achieved with the help of the landowner, but it was also successful because 'the people themselves were awake to the shame and indecency and the certainty of moral degradation' which arose from overcrowding and promiscuous sleeping arrangements.[55] It was to that fundamental decency, or humanity, that Atkinson addressed his ministry. Thus, since his arrival in the parish, he notes a greater regard for what he called moral decency, marked among the young by less rowdyism at public and social events and among the general population by less drunkenness and more civility between the sexes. That civility was given domestic expression in the parlours, which, with their pianos and harmoniums, had proliferated among the more prosperous farmers and tradesmen in the parish and which provided opportunities for neighbourly and familial sociability within a domestic environment. At more public occasions also 'the pipe and beer', to use Atkinson's phrase, were now reserved until after the business had been transacted and, though the passing of old traditions was regretted, there was now 'certainly less of the exuberant festivity on the occasion of a wedding that there used to be, – festivity which so continually degenerated into downright debauchery, – and the people have learnt to respect decency of expression and conduct'.[56]

The people had also begun to participate in more productive and profitable leisure pursuits. Land was secured for allotments for the labouring classes at Castleton; a village cricket team had been formed by the vicar for the young men; and the farming community had benefited from the establishment of an Agricultural Society in 1872, promoted by Atkinson himself, which held an annual show, as a result of which stock and stock-keeping had

---

[55] Atkinson, *Forty Years*, 28–29, 212.
[56] Ibid. 26–31.

improved to the commercial advantage of the community.[57] This was of course a record of considerable achievement, but it was not quite what the hopeful young clergyman who arrived in the parish seeking to make the church the centre of his community and to place God at its heart had originally aspired to. Atkinson could see for himself Hopkins' 'grandeur of God' whilst walking the moors, and provided testimony that 'God-in-Nature' could move other hearts and minds as well, but what he could not do was to get his parishioners to come to church, at least not in sufficient numbers to represent a reasonable proportion of the people. Herein lies the silence in the text, and Atkinson knew it. If his reports on the parish at episcopal visitations are an accurate reflection of his views, then from the 1870s onwards he viewed his ministry at Danby with a profound sense of failure, a failure which he attributed not only to his own shortcomings but also to those of the institutional Church and its structural inability to respond to changes in population density or to face the challenges posed by Methodism, which in Atkinson's analysis had come increasingly to fill the vacuum left by the Established Church. The growth of voluntary and associational religious congregations posed problems for Atkinson and created anxiety in him about the value of his own ministry in which, paradoxically, he was also trying to create similar associational communities in the civil sphere, through the Agricultural Society and the cricket club he founded. His failure, when compared to the perceived success of the Methodists, in establishing a flourishing religious community at the parish church produced a bleak assessment of his ministry in the return he made at the bishop's visitation of 1894, and reveals a depressing self-assessment on his life's work.[58]

Notwithstanding the assistance of a curate by then, he had proved unable to assemble a class to prepare for communion, and although two laymen assisted in the reading of the lessons at Danby and Fryup there was no lay involvement, beyond that of the parish schoolmaster, in the running of the Sunday School. The young still left the parish and, with it, the practice of churchgoing, and 'there was no suggestion of hidden talent in [the] congrega-

---

[57] Ibid. 11, 19–27; Obelkevich, *Religion and Rural Society*, 37.
[58] Stainsby, *More than an Ordinary Man*, 54–58; Sheils, 'Church, Community and Culture', 265–68; Green, *Religion in the Age of Decline,* 182–200.

tion'. Atkinson was by now only one and, in terms of attracting a congregation, by no means the most successful of 'several preachers' of differing denominations living in the parish. In summary he turned once again to geography, declaring that the isolated position of the parish church was not so much the chief impediment to ministry but an insurmountable obstacle, 'enforcing the utter waste of the parson's time and work'.[59]

This was not surprising, and nor was Atkinson alone in this. By the 1890s the decline in church attendance generally was a source of comment at national level and there was widespread concern for the problems of ministry in a rapidly depopulating countryside, where the material opportunities available to the poor were deteriorating and where the cultural needs of the people were rarely being met by the Established Church.[60] However, it was not only his apparent failure when compared to the Methodists which led Atkinson to his devastating judgement. He had already noted in *Forty Years* that the essentially secular achievements of his ministry contained within them the seeds which were to undermine his true vocation, that of placing God and the church at the heart of the community. In one sharp and prophetic passage, written almost in passing and therefore overlooked by contemporary and subsequent readers, he commented on the rising tide of secularism: 'The religious fervour and earnestness of the old days seems to have lost warmth and energy, and to have been in part replaced by more secular feelings and objects. And the change will be fatal in the end.' In Atkinson's view the increasing penetration of the modern world into the dale, through newspapers and varieties of secular pastimes, challenged not only the church but the Methodists also who, despite their vigorous numbers, were 'barely holding their own at present'.[61]

This, of course, questioned the achievements of his denominational rivals, and reflected the loss of authority over information and access which many Established Churchmen experienced at this time as both the state, through taking on many functions

[59] York, Borthwick Institute, V1894/Ret. Danby.
[60] Digby, 'Social Institutions', 1470–71; Haig, *Victorian Clergy*, 287–96; M. Freeman, *Social Investigation and Rural England, 1870–1914* (Woodbridge, 2003), 62, 67–68, 133–58.
[61] *Atkinson, Forty Years*, 15; cf. Obelkevich, *Religion and Rural Society*, 330–31. But see C. Brown, *The Death of Christian Britain* (London, 2001), 49–55, for the vigour of cheap religious publications at this time. Atkinson himself started a parish magazine.

previously dominated by the Church, and the rapidly expanding flow of cheap sources of information and entertainment, increasingly challenged their position. Nevertheless, in these brief remarks Atkinson can be seen to anticipate a process of secularization which cut across denominational boundaries and which emigration and industrial living would only hasten, especially among the inhabitants of the settlement which grew up around the railway at Castleton.

★　★　★

On that, for him, depressing note, it is time to draw some conclusions from this case study of a lengthy ministry located in one place, removed from recognized centres of learning and in a community situated in the hinterland of, but not benefiting from, rapid economic growth and social change. How far can this microcosm reveal the complexities of the wider responses of churchmen to the Romantics, to Darwinism and to modernity, if by that we mean the consequences, both social and cultural, of economic growth?

Atkinson was undoubtedly a conservative Romantic, who saw in the natural world the glory of God revealed, both in its grand vistas and its intricate details. His response to the landscape, as described in his account of life in Danby, and in his sermon notes, was not just a personal one, but a means of bringing others to an imaginative and informed understanding of their place in God's plan. That understanding was also informed by his observation of the relationships which peopled that landscape, social, biological and geological. It was through his long personal history of experimentation and observation that Atkinson came to see the significance of Darwin's early work. For him, and for many broad and liberal churchmen, the *Origin of Species* still left space for God, and indeed, provided humanity with the means to understand 'difference', not only among species but also, in terms of race and circumstance, among humanity. This was an understanding which, for him, much contemporary Christian teaching did not assist and often actively hindered.[62] Atkinson's case illustrates the extent to which Darwin's earlier writings sharpened the boundaries and

---

[62] Atkinson, *Sketches*, 295–323.

widened the gap between biblicist Christians and Broad Church liberals, but more than that, it turned him (or maybe it merely confirmed his already ecologically-based scientific instincts) into something of an anthropologist whose observations on the society in which he lived and whose writings on the religion of his parishioners were, against his own instincts, largely expressed in sociological or anthropological language

And in that lies the paradox: for in his description of his ministry, and of the lives of those to whom he ministered, God was conspicuously absent. It seems that, whether he recognized the fact himself (and I think he did not), religion as it was experienced by the general run of humanity had become largely a matter of social practice and moral behaviour, and that is what he chose to record. Not only that, but in commenting on the lives of the younger members of his parish, Atkinson could also foresee a time when people might no longer feel the need to describe or justify those practices by reference to religion or to God. For Atkinson that would have been a disaster, hence the damning judgement he passed on his own life's work in 1894: 'an utter waste of … time'.[63]

That brings me to my final point. Atkinson's text was, and has been, celebrated as a vindication of the values inherent in what was recognized even then as a rapidly disappearing world. In this context I would suggest that the book was more of an elegy than a vindication for his world and parish, and that, to a regular preacher on biblical themes, the title itself, though broadly accurate in historical terms, might perhaps have had a further meaning. 'Forty Years' is a significant time in biblical terms, recalling the time spent by the Israelites in the wilderness, and perhaps Atkinson had something of this in mind. For Danby must have seemed like exile to a scholarly figure such as he was, as did rural ministry to many other graduate clergy ministering in rural England in these years to increasingly empty pews whose former occupants had either transferred their loyalties to other denominations or abandoned regular attendance at church.[64] 'Perhaps' is, however, a word of which the critical reader should be wary, and I may have put

---

[63] York, Borthwick Institute, V1894/Ret. Danby.
[64] See Knight, *Nineteenth-Century Church*, 150, for an earlier example of this sense of failure; Haig, *Victorian Clergy*, 283–89, for examples from northern upland parishes such as Danby.

too heavy an interpretative weight on a conventional choice of words, but his deeply pessimistic judgement on his ministry makes the comparison a plausible one, without, in his case, any collective sense of a promised land at its end. What his text does show, through Atkinson's work and life, is how the 'Victorian Crisis of Faith' was played out in the ministry of a scholarly, if otherwise undistinguished, clergyman in a remote corner of the realm. Its unexceptional quality is what makes Atkinson's ministry and his record of it such a valuable source.

The natural world sustained his faith, and could sustain that of others if they had the eyes to see. Scientific enquiry, far from undermining that faith, could enhance it and make sense of it, but the balance was a difficult one to maintain. Atkinson could hold both elements together in his own life, but when it came to providing an account of his ministry, the balance sheet was almost entirely in favour of the affairs of this world; civility, decency and tolerance had all improved – not unworthy objects – but he had far less success with his congregation's souls, and indeed, could foresee a time when people might forget that they ever possessed them, never mind that they represented their essential identity. For Atkinson these shifts in religious and cultural expectations were bewildering and represented a disaster, whether it manifested itself in the strengthening hold which associational religious activities, in his case Methodism, had among the people, or in the drift away from churchgoing which he observed among the young. Thus, despite his own conviction of the presence of 'God-in-Nature', it seemed that the world had overcome eternity, if not for Atkinson himself, then for the majority of those among whom he lived and worked. If nature had not yet overcome God, modernity had relegated religion to a set of social observances. It was that essentially secularizing conclusion which Atkinson grappled with in his thoughtful response to the advances of biology in the 1860s, and which he became aware of through looking back on the history of his own ministry and observing the lives of his young parishioners in the 1890s.[65] As he looked back on his lengthy ministry it must

---

[65] Recent studies of religion in industrial England have challenged the long-term interpretation of secularization: M. Smith, *Religion in Industrial Society: Oldham and Saddleworth 1740–1865* (Oxford, 1993), 274; Green, *Religion in the Age of Decline*, 380–83,

have seemed to a priest like Atkinson, socially conservative but theologically liberal, that the material values of modernity were triumphing over the transcendental values of nature in the minds of those he had sought to serve for so long.

University of York

---

demonstrates the vitality of voluntary, or associational, religion in the later nineteenth century, an argument also developed nationally in Brown, *Death of Christian Britain*, 9–13.

HEAVENS ON EARTH:
CHRISTIAN UTOPIAS IN NINETEENTH- AND
TWENTIETH-CENTURY AMERICA

by CHRISTOPHER CLARK

IN the rich and complex history of American Christianity, utopias in one form or another have played a constant part. From the early puritan settlements onwards, North America has played a distinctive role in the Christian imagination – as a place of refuge, as a place for experimentation, as the founding-spot for new sects, churches, and denominations. Among the experimenters have been many groups of Christians in America who have, over more than two centuries, gathered themselves into communal organizations – what participants and commentators now call 'intentional communities'.[1] Their numbers have been almost impossible to measure accurately; one authoritative listing counts about six hundred communal groups with over fifteen hundred separate settlements in the USA before 1965, and there will have been thousands more communes formed since then. Membership figures are even harder to pin down, but it is certain that the numbers of people who have at one time or another lived in an American intentional community runs into the hundreds of thousands.[2]

Inspired by the communal gathering of Christ's disciples described in Acts 2, Christians of various denominations have gathered together to share a life 'all in common' on the pattern of the early Church. Some groups were actually communistic, abolishing private property and living from a common purse; others adopted various arrangements for co-operation, co-residence, or sharing. But in forming their 'intentional communities' all went beyond the practices of mainstream congregations, some for only short periods and with little success, but others in organizations

---

[1] David Yount, *America's Spiritual Utopias: The Quest for Heaven on Earth* (Westport, CT, 2008); Jyotsna Sreenivasan, *Utopias in American History* (Santa Barbara, CA, 2008).
[2] Donald E. Pitzer, comp., 'Appendix: America's Communal Utopias Founded by 1965', in idem, ed., *America's Communal Utopias* (Chapel Hill, NC, 1997), 449–94.

that have lasted for centuries. Such groups have usually offered challenges, implicit or explicit, to prevailing conventions about church organization, worship, or belief; about social and political structures; and about human relationships to nature. Some have even presented themselves, more or less seriously, as models of heavenly life on earth. Studying them throws light both on humans as social beings and on conceptions of humans as part of a 'natural world' that does not merely lie around them, but includes their own bodies, sexuality, health and wellbeing. The survey of their history that follows will note this dual aspect of their thinking about 'nature' as both external to human beings and inherently connected to humans' relationships with one another.

A large historical literature has built up around Christian intentional communities, but their variety has been so great as to defy easy categorization. While the results will be imperfect, this paper will identify four principal types of American Christian communal group, though it will focus chiefly on the last of them, and to a lesser degree the second. First, and of great importance, North America played a large role in the nineteenth-century revival and expansion of Christian monasticism, particularly of Catholic men's and women's orders; and these various communities remained significant for much of the twentieth century also. But monastic communities are arguably not 'utopian'; they focus on the afterlife and on service to a wider Church, rather than on separating from the Church to realize some form of social ideal, so they will not be discussed here.[3] Secondly, from German-speaking Anabaptist and Pietist traditions came a range of important communal movements that either migrated to or were established in North America, some of which have become the largest and most durable of Christian intentional communities there. Thirdly, premillennialists have, from the early nineteenth century to the present, sometimes gathered in communities to await the Second Coming. Finally, and most significant, Christian social reformers have chosen communalism as a means for furthering their visions of an ideal society. In the nineteenth century, such groups were particularly associated with

---

[3] Lawrence J. McCrank, 'Religious Orders and Monastic Communalism in America', in Pitzer, ed., *America's Communal Utopias*, 204–52; John J. Fialka, *Sisters: Catholic Nuns and the Making of America* (New York, 2003).

postmillennialism – a conviction that the world had to be improved to prepare the way for Christ's return. In the twentieth century eschatological themes have been less important in shaping these movements than broader currents of progressive social thought. German communities and reform communities, the second and fourth of these categories, both draw a contrast with the conditions of contemporary society, and construct an ideal by which an imperfect world might be measured. But while German communities have provided successful models of communal society, it is the social reform communities that can most readily be termed 'utopian', putting forward their ideals as inspiration for social transformation or improvement.

Thomas More of course coined the term *Utopia* as a pun, meaning both 'good place' and 'no place'. Hostile commentators have perennially seen 'utopias' as 'bad', or at best as 'impossible' places. Usually small, usually short-lived, and inherently unconventional, intentional communities also earned the disdain of many scholars. In twentieth-century America, a strong anticommunist tradition and Cold War-era social conformism made communal movements appear malignant, 'extremist', or at best marginal to mainstream religion and society. Even the great revival of communalism associated with the counterculture of the 1960s at first reinforced this interpretative tendency. Newly sympathetic commentators and historians, who now viewed utopias as 'possible' places and 'hopeful' places, nevertheless regarded communal groups as countercultural 'alternatives' to a dominant 'mainstream'. Only more recently, as the passions of the Cold War and the counterculture cooled, did many scholars begin to evaluate utopian communities in a fresh light.

Recognizing the paradox that utopias seek to change society but are inevitably rooted in its character and concerns, historians are now less likely to see them merely as marginal or eccentric, and more likely to examine them as part of broader patterns on which they can shed light. Historians are less preoccupied than once they were with tracing 'progress' or with the achievements only of 'winners', while a multicultural society is less confident than its predecessors in declaring what 'the mainstream' is, or was. Accordingly, writing on American utopias over the last three decades has drawn us towards a new paradigm that recognizes both their distinctiveness and their congruency with wider social and religious currents.[4] 'Utopia' also presents another paradox, that if it represents the ideal, then its realization should also mark the end of change, 'the end of history'. Older scholarly interpretations of intentional communities, often drawing (appropriately enough) on the testimony of men and women who formed them, frequently ascribed to them a kind of timelessness or stasis, in which change had either no place or appeared potentially destructive. The newer paradigm in utopian studies better captures the elements of communal change and adaptability, and suggests that quite often it was these elements that made the difference between a community's success and failure. The overview of America's Christian utopias that follows will keep these two themes of congruency and adaptability in view.

★   ★   ★

Though the first examples dated from the eighteenth century, a succession of German Separatist-Pietist and Anabaptist groups migrated from Europe in the nineteenth century, to build what has remained one of the strongest communal movements anywhere in the Christian West. Some five hundred members of the Harmonist Society, who had gathered in Württemberg in the 1780s, followed their leader George Rapp to Pennsylvania from 1805 on, and adopted celibacy and community of property in their settlement at a place they called Harmony, while they awaited the Second Coming. Concerned at backsliding as the community began to prosper, Rapp moved the group five hundred miles west in 1814 to build a new settlement on the Indiana frontier, named New Harmony. Ten years later, Rapp decreed yet another move, sold New Harmony to the British reformer Robert Owen for his own utopian project, and returned to Pennsylvania, to settle at a site near Pittsburgh the Harmonists called Economy. Long surviving Rapp's death in 1847, the community continued until financial irregu-

---

[4] Among early exponents of this reinterpretation were Edward K. Spann, *Brotherly Tomorrows: Movements for a Cooperative Society in America, 1820–1920* (New York, 1989); and Donald E. Pitzer, 'Developmental Communalism: An Alternative Approach to Communal Studies', in Dennis Hardy and Lorna Davidson, eds, *Utopian Thought and Communal Experience*, Middlesex Polytechnic Geography and Environmental Management Paper, 24 (Enfield, 1989). Pitzer, ed., *America's Communal Utopias*, extended the theme.

larities forced its abandonment in 1905.[5] Wilhelm Keil, a Prussian émigré, led a splinter group from Rapp's Economy to found the Society of Bethel, establishing communities in Missouri and in Oregon that lasted into the 1870s. Other emigrant communities survived longer. Another Separatist group, the Society of True Inspiration, founded around 1716 and scattered across southern Germany, Switzerland and Alsace, followed its leader Christian Metz to America in the 1840s and 1850s and established the Amana Society in seven villages in Iowa which retained a communal form of organization until 1932. During the 1870s, the Hutterite Brethren, a radical Anabaptist sect which originated about 1530 and had first been scattered eastward from Moravia during the Thirty Years War, migrated to North America after Tsarist Russia withdrew their exemption from military service.[6] They established communal settlements in South Dakota and Montana, later moving also into Canada. With some 36,000 members in 390 communities, the Hutterites became the largest and longest lasting of all Christian communal groups in North America.[7]

Following charismatic leaders who had separated from Churches in Europe, these groups adopted communalism partly to establish themselves with limited means, but chiefly to live out a vision of Christian brotherhood and material asceticism. Though they are gatherings of the faithful to await Christ's return, they have been governed by quietist patience rather than by apocalyptic expectation. In some cases this has enabled generation after generation to live a communal life envisioned as a model of heaven on earth, and scholars now stress the adaptability that has allowed the Hutterites and others to sustain this seemingly static position.[8] But their continued attachment to the German language for worship, teaching and home-life has also contributed to their longevity,

[5] For a brief overview, see Karl J. R. Arndt, 'George Rapp's Harmony Society', in Pitzer, ed., *America's Communal Utopias*, 57–87. Arndt was the author of ten monographs published between 1971 and 1994 that provide a definitive account of the Harmonists.

[6] John A. Hostetler, *Hutterite Society* (Baltimore, MD, 1974), 112–13.

[7] Robert P. Sutton, *Communal Utopias and the American Experience: Religious Communities, 1732–2000* (Westport, CT, 2003), chs 3, 5; for statistics, see ibid. 101. Scholars usually distinguish communal groups, such as those mentioned here, from Amish and Mennonite settlements of privately-owned family farms.

[8] William P. Thompson, 'Hutterite Community: Its Reflex in Architectural and Settlement Patterns', *Canadian Ethnic Studies* 16 (1984), 53–72.

and has helped keep them apart from other communitarian movements. Only incidentally have these communities been part of a wider 'utopian' tradition. That, of course, has not been their purpose. Taking the imperfection of the world for granted, and preparing for the afterlife, German sects have used communalism chiefly for otherworldly, rather than earthly purposes.

Anglophone Christian communal groups have had more engagement with wider reform movements, and generally less long-term stability, but have remained a consistent presence in the American religious scene. In the nineteenth century, they were almost invariably Protestant and often aimed to build a better society on earth. Twentieth-century communalism became more pluralistic, in some cases ecumenical, and had more varied purposes. Social reform efforts became more pragmatic, less dedicated to changing the world than to making incremental improvements. These shifts in Christian communalism reflect changes in the religious and ideological contexts that gave rise to utopian aspirations.

The most powerful influence on nineteenth-century communities was a pervasive millennarian climate that had roots in Europe and especially the British Isles, and had been strengthened by the expectations and anxieties of the American and French Revolutions. Some premillennialists, the best known of whom were the followers of William Miller in the early 1840s, expected an imminent Second Coming and withdrew from society to await it. Though most of Miller's flock, disappointed at the failure of the apocalypse to arrive in 1843 or again the following year, drifted to other churches or rallied to build the Adventist movement, a few founded communes to watch for Christ's delayed return. Some of these proved unstable: a Millerite community founded at Uriah Adams's farmhouse in Avon Township, Michigan, late in 1844 at length broke up after Adams was jailed amid accusations of adultery and incest. Others were more durable: Millerites in Groton, Massachusetts, who had already formed a loose-knit commune, moved after 1844 to Wisconsin, where their community functioned for another half-century.[9]

---

9   Maureen Thalmann, 'A Millenarian Family: Uriah Adams and a Private Second Coming', *Michigan Historical Review* 28 (2002), 173–80; Peggy Sands, 'Till the End of Time: Awaiting the Millennium in Wisconsin', *Wisconsin Magazine of History* 83 (1999), 2–29.

Like the German communities, these premillennialist groups had relatively little engagement with wider reform movements; they were awaiting divine action. But the postmillennialist impulses in American Protestant culture did, by contrast, bring forth communities whose members were determined to reshape existing society, and to become actors clearing the way for Christ's triumphal return to a perfected world. There were several strands to this desire for social action. Quakers had already established a tradition of social activism, especially over slavery in the later eighteenth century, and were enduring divisions over this and other issues in the 1820s and 1830s.[10] Meanwhile, the post-revolutionary reaction against orthodox Calvinism produced various forms of Universalism and also ignited powerful evangelical revivals that emphasized individuals' free will and the need for self-control. An 'immediatist' determination to root out social evils such as slavery and intemperance marked reform campaigns that achieved great prominence in the northern states during the 1830s. Partly as a result of the conflicts that these campaigns prompted in politics and in the Churches, some activists proposed forming communities as a way of furthering their ideals. Schemes for such communities proliferated in the Christian and reform press, and at least sixty actual examples were founded in the USA during the 1840s, a majority of them between 1841 and 1845. Even those that were nominally secular tended to advance Christian ideals as justification for their plans.[11]

In Massachusetts, four communities founded by different groups between 1841 and 1843 all emphasized Christian principles. Of the Transcendentalist Brook Farm community, established outside Boston, the reformer Elizabeth Palmer Peabody wrote in early 1842 that it was 'an attempt to realize in some degree this great Ideal ... of Christ's Idea of Society'.[12] The Northampton Association of Education and Industry, a community established in 1842

---

[10] Ryan P. Jordan, *Slavery and the Meetinghouse: The Quakers and the Abolitionist Dilemma, 1820–1865* (Bloomington, IN, 2007).

[11] For an overview of the millennialist climate, see Daniel Walker Howe, *What Hath God Wrought: The Transformation of America, 1815–1848* (New York, 2007), ch. 8. Carl J. Guarneri, *The Utopian Alternative: Fourierism in Nineteenth-Century America* (Ithaca, NY, 1991), discusses the religious dimensions of a secular utopian movement.

[12] [Elizabeth Palmer Peabody], 'Plan of the West Roxbury Community', *The Dial* 2.3 (January 1842), 361.

by radical abolitionists who were also exponents of Christian non-resistance, sought to 'raise the banner of reform and separate from existing evils, to assert ... the all-embracing law of love so emphatically taught by true Christianity'. One of its founders wrote that the community would be a base for preaching 'godliness and its collaterals' – abolition, temperance, and the doctrine of nonresistance.[13] At Milford, Massachusetts, meanwhile, founders of the Hopedale Community, led by the Universalist minister Adin Ballou, proposed what they called 'Practical Christianity': 'faith in the religion of Jesus Christ, ... according to the Scriptures of the New Testament', and 'subjection to all the moral obligations of that Religion'. Naming their venture 'Fraternal Community No. 1', they intended it as a prototype for others, 'the parent of a numerous progeny of Practical Christian Communities'.[14] The Fruitlands community, led by Bronson Alcott and Charles Lane, proposed to model the 'consociate family', and pursue a vision of social harmony that also included avoiding harm to all living creatures. In addition, eight communes in New York, Ohio and Indiana, formed by the Society for Universal Improvement and Reform, which had Quaker roots and abolitionist and moral reform connections, abolished private property among members.[15] Except for Hopedale, which lasted until 1856, none of these communes survived more than six years, and some of them only a matter of weeks or months. The economic weakness of idealistic but impoverished members, and the shifting political contexts in which such ventures existed, undermined efforts to sustain them.

Two longer-lasting Christian communal groups had less connection with reform movements but adopted more radical social arrangements than those we have just looked at. They also took further the contemporary reform emphasis on the possibility of human perfectibility, because they each had distinctive interpretations of the millennium. The United Society of Believers in Christ's Second Appearing, known as the Shakers, initiated by English

---

[13] Northampton Association of Education and Industry, 'Preamble and Articles of Association' ([Northampton, MA], 1843); Christopher Clark, *The Communitarian Moment: The Radical Challenge of the Northampton Association* (Ithaca, NY, 1995), 87.

[14] *The Hopedale Community* (Milford, MA, [1851]), 2–3, 8; Edward K. Spann, *Hopedale: From Commune to Company Town, 1840–1920* (Columbus, OH, 1992).

[15] Thomas D. Hamm, *God's Government Begun: The Society for Universal Inquiry and Reform, 1842–1846* (Bloomington, IN, 1995).

immigrants in the 1770s and organized into communally owned villages from the late eighteenth century, had nearly four thousand members living in eighteen communities in New England, New York, Ohio, Indiana and Kentucky at its peak around 1850. The Oneida Perfectionists, first organized in Putney, Vermont, in the early 1840s but resettled in Oneida, New York, in 1848, had three hundred or more members there (and in branches in Connecticut and Brooklyn, New York) until the early 1880s.

The Shakers (so called because they used dance movements during worship) had originated in a charismatic sect founded in Lancashire and brought to New York by their leader Ann Lee (1736–84), usually known as Mother Ann, at a time when prophetic and millenarian sects flourished on both sides of the Atlantic. Shakers organized themselves into communities in the years after Lee's death, and their theology crystallized by the early nineteenth century. Rejecting more conventional millennialist doctrines, Shakers believed that God was both male and female, and that the life of Ann Lee – Jesus's female counterpart – had marked the Second Coming. Now living in the promised millennium, Shakers were enjoined to give up their earthly possessions, adopt celibacy, and to join communities where men and women functioned as equals, though assigned to distinct and separate roles and subject to strict rules restricting contact. Governed by male and female hierarchies of ministers and elders, Shaker communities aimed to keep their members in what they called 'gospel order', a state as close to perfection as could be accomplished on earth. Though proselytizing, especially among New Light Baptists and Presbyterians, recruited many early Shakers, the movement had only an intermittent commitment to missions, relying on kinship and personal connections, and on its reputation, to attract members. After 1850, membership declined, aided of course by the Shakers' celibacy, though the process has been a gradual one. The first village to close did so in 1875, and after 1961 only two remained; but one of these, at Sabbathday Lake, Maine, still continues today after more than two hundred years of existence.[16]

John Humphrey Noyes (1811–86), leader of the Oneida Community, also held that the Second Coming had already occurred. His

---

[16] Stephen J. Stein, *The Shaker Experience in America* (New Haven, CT, 1992), is the fullest of many studies.

deductions from Scripture convinced him that the millennium had commenced at the fall of the Temple in Jerusalem in AD 70. For Noyes, as for the Shakers, life in the millennium entailed the adoption of community and of communal property, but Noyes went beyond the Shakers' conviction that they should live in a heaven-like manner, to argue that humans could live in a state of perfection on earth. '*[S]in was to be abolished* in this world', explained an Oneida Community text of 1853, 'Christ … was without sin. He came to introduce into the world the Constitution of the kingdom of heaven; and as there is no sin there, his mission necessarily involved the abolition of it here.' Like the Shakers, too, Noyes reasoned that 'in the kingdom of heaven they neither marry nor are given in marriage', but deduced from this not that members should be celibate but rather that all members of the community were married to all others, 'that they *all* [not two and two] may be one'.[17] In a system he called 'complex marriage', which his opponents condemned as 'free love', but which was in fact a highly regulated succession of male-female pairings, Noyes sustained a community around a pattern of generalized and non-exclusive intimacy. Men and women were prohibited from forming sustained attachments, and were initiated into sexual practice by elders of the opposite sex. Men were trained to practice *coitus reservatus*, which Noyes called 'male continence', and which he intended to prevent pregnancies, to foster sexual pleasure for women, and as an exercise in male self-control. Oneida's complex marriage system, which worked smoothly for over twenty years, came under increasing pressure in the 1870s as outsiders voiced more strident objections, and as generational changes began to affect the community. But the greatest single weakening of Oneida derived from the adoption after 1869 of a method of selective child-breeding intended to perpetuate the community in the future. Influenced by his reading of Darwin, and especially of Francis Galton, Noyes introduced what he called 'scientific propagation' or 'stirpiculture', in which couples he chose for their religious and moral superiority were

---

[17] *Bible Communism: A Compilation from the Annual Reports and other Publications of the Oneida Association and its Branches; Presenting, in Connection with their History, a Summary View of their Religious and Social Theories* (Brooklyn, NY, 1853), 67, 68–69, 58 (emphases in original); Spencer Klaw, *Without Sin: The Life and Death of the Oneida Community* (New York, 1993).

permitted to conceive children to be raised by the community.[18] The stresses induced by this, although it took them a decade to mount up, led to the abandonment of community property and complex marriage at Oneida once Noyes had been obliged to flee to Canada to evade immorality charges in 1879.

The long decline of Shakerism, the abandonment of complex marriage at Oneida, and the collapse of most other social reform communities led contemporaries, and many historians since, to regard the era of small-scale communes as having passed. Looking back in 1867 to the Northampton community's founding a quarter-century before, one of its leaders commented, 'We had … an idea that the Associative movement would generally obtain and would ultimately revolutionize the old system, but we were shortsighted. It takes much longer to bring about such results than we anticipated. The millennium we thought so near seems a good way off now.'[19] I have written of the passing of 'the communitarian moment', as the communes of the 1840s dwindled, while the historian Howard P. Segal cited 'a change in form and purpose' in later nineteenth-century utopianism, as reformers came to doubt the effectiveness of communes at radically reforming society.[20]

Nevertheless, other scholars have correctly stressed that communalism never died out. Robert S. Fogarty identified 140 communal groups, many of them religious, founded in the USA between 1880 and 1914. Various German communities continued to thrive. Premillennialist sects continued to spring up also. What perhaps changed most during the late nineteenth and early twentieth centuries was that communal efforts became less associated with grand plans for sweeping social reform. For reform-minded Christians, postmillennialist expectations dissolved into the Social Gospel[21] and other patterns of activism in which intentional communities played at most a partial role. Few modern Christian communities still expressed their predecessors' hope that they could model

---

[18] John Humphrey Noyes, *Essay on Scientific Propagation* (Wallingford, CT, [1872]).

[19] Clark, *Communitarian Moment*, 185.

[20] Ibid. 220–23; Howard P. Segal, 'From Utopian Communities to Utopian Writings: A Change in Form and Purpose', *Communal Societies* 3 (1983), 93–100.

[21] The Social Gospel movement encompassed the efforts of many liberal Protestants in late nineteenth- and early twentieth-century America to reform housing, public health, labour and other social issues.

a complete social transformation.[22] When some Christian Socialists founded the Christian Commonwealth Colony in Georgia in
1896, others criticized the effort as unwise, urging them – as one
put it – to 'be brave enough and patient enough to live out their
ideals in their homes, in business, in politics'. When the under
capitalized community folded in 1900, its leader acknowledged
its material failure, though he insisted that its spiritual accom-
plishments had exceeded what would have been possible 'through
regular channels of religious work'.[23]

Two examples located near Lake Michigan help illustrate the
variety of Christian communes at the beginning of the twentieth
century. Scots-born John Alexander Dowie (1847–1907) had built
a following as an evangelist in Australia before moving to the USA
in 1888, and organizing his Christian Catholic Church in Chicago
some seven years later. One of many contemporary exponents of
divine healing, Dowie preached that illness was the fruit of sin
and of distance from God. He acquired 6,600 acres some forty
miles north of Chicago, named the property Zion City, and began
turning it into a Christian town and headquarters for his movement.
Followers settled there from 1901, buying houses on 1,100-year
revocable leases and accepting rule by an autocratic town government. Residents had to be born-again Christians, were expected
to tithe, and were prohibited from drinking, dancing, swearing,
and other indulgences. Physicians and druggists were kept out,
and denounced from the pulpit. Dowie advocated pacifism, racial
integration and toleration for Jews; he condemned imperialism
and the antagonism between capital and labour. But he focused
increasingly on millennialist prophecy; by 1904 he was claiming
to be Christ's 'first apostle' (i.e. the first apostle of a restored apostolic Church) and preaching the imminence of a 'rapture' that
would return Christ to Jerusalem and make Zion City, Illinois,
the center of world government. Already facing financial troubles
and rumours (which he denied) of sexual impropriety, Dowie lost
control over his followers when he fell ill in 1906 and failed to

---

[22] Robert S. Fogarty, *All Things New: American Communes and Utopian Movements,
1860–1914* (Chicago, IL, 1990).
[23] John O. Fish, 'The Christian Commonwealth Colony: A Georgia Experiment,
1896–1900', *Georgia Historical Quarterly* 57 (1973), 213–26.

invoke the healing powers he had preached about.[24] Meanwhile, across the lake at Benton Harbor, Michigan, another millennialist group, the House of David, arrived from Ohio in 1903 and also purchased a large property, in this case for an imminent gathering of the tribes of Israel and the Second Coming of Christ. Its leader, Benjamin Purnell (1861–1927), claimed to be the seventh and last of a series of messengers bringing news of these events (the first had been Joanna Southcott), and that his settlement would eventually house 144,000 people – 12,000 members of each of the twelve tribes. Purnell eventually fell into disgrace; he was tried for sexually abusing girls, but died before a verdict could be reached. The House of David divided, about half the members following Purnell's wife Mary to an adjacent site, which they called the City of David. Both communities continued to function in the 1990s; the schismatic group, now called Mary's City of David, claims descent from the seventeenth-century English mystic and millennarian Jane Lead (1623–1704), whose writings and example have influenced various Christian communalists in the USA and elsewhere since the eighteenth century, and to be America's third oldest religious community.[25]

Communal movements found themselves disfavoured during periods of anti-communist fervour – often supported by Churches – between World War I and the 1960s. But there were always exceptional Christians willing to counter the trend. Quakers gathered a progressive rural community at Celo, North Carolina, from the late 1930s, employing the uncontentious device of forming a land trust to accomplish communal ends. Some Mormon families in northern California formed the Harmony Hills Cooperative in 1946, which they farmed with shared labour until 1970. A few went further to breach social and political taboos. Two white Southern Baptist pastors purchased land in Georgia in 1942, named it Koinonia Farm, and established a community consisting of black and white members, who shared a common purse and farmed

---

[24] Grant Wacker, 'Marching to Zion: Religion in a Modern Utopian Community', *Church History* 54 (1985). 496–511; Philip L. Cook, *Zion City, Illinois: Twentieth-Century Utopia* (Syracuse, NY, 1996).

[25] Robert S. Fogarty, *The Righteous Remnant: The House of David* (Kent, OH, 1981); Clare Adkin, *Brother Benjamin: A History of the Israelite House of David* (Berrien Springs, MI, 1990); House of David Museum, <http://www.houseofdavidmuseum.org/>, accessed 14 July 2008.

successfully.[26] In 1948 a number of communal groups, religious and secular, organized the Fellowship of Intentional Communities, a loose affiliation that has succeeded over six decades in giving public shape to an infinitely varied and shifting movement.[27]

The revival of communalism in the 1960s helped set what has remained a pluralist pattern for Christian communities over the past forty years. Christians were among the many thousands who formed rural and urban communes during the peak of the counterculture. A *Time* magazine article of 1970, entitled 'Street Christians: Jesus as the Ultimate Trip', featured Christian hippies who spread the Gospel at rock concerts and other venues in major cities, and who 'build their lives on the Book of Acts, living in common like the early Christians'.[28] A dozen Christian students at Michigan State University formed the Sunrise Communal Farm on cheaply purchased land in 1971, and conducted it until 1978.[29] Quaker peace campaigners formed a commune in Portland, Oregon, in 1972, called their collective home 'Terrasquirma', organized pioneering recycling campaigns, and protested against the construction of a nearby nuclear power plant.[30] Though many such communes were short-lived, others such as Reba Place and Jesus People USA, both founded in Chicago, have continued to the present.[31]

[26] George L. Hicks, *Experimental Americans: Celo and Utopian Community in the Twentieth Century* (Urbana, IL, 2001); Jessie L. Embry and Janiece Johnson, 'Harmony Hills: A Twentieth Century Mormon Cooperative', *Communal Societies* 23 (2003), 75–94; Tracy Elaine K'Meyer, *Interracialism and Christian Community in the Postwar South: The Story of Koinonia Farm* (Charlottesville, VA, 1997).

[27] The FIC 'incorporated' (the US equivalent of founding a limited company) in 1986 as the Fellowship for Intentional Community.

[28] 'Street Christians: Jesus as the Ultimate Trip', *Time*, 3 August 1970, <http://www.time.com/time/magazine/article/0,9171,876689,00.html>, accessed 9 March 2009.

[29] Caroline Hoefferle, '"Just at Sunrise": The Sunrise Communal Farm in Rural Mid-Michigan, 1971–1978', *Michigan Historical Review* 23 (1997), 70–104.

[30] Alexander Patterson, 'Terrasquirma and the Engines of Social Change in 1970s Portland', *Oregon Historical Quarterly* 101 (2000), 162–91.

[31] For the Reba Place Fellowship, founded in 1957, see <http://www.rebaplacefellowship.org>, accessed March 9, 2009; Dave Jackson and Neta Jackson, *Glimpses of Glory: Thirty Years of Community, the Story of Reba Place* (Elgin, IL, 1987); Perry Bush, 'Anabaptism Born Again: Mennonites, New Evangelicals, and the Search for a Usable Past', *Fides et Historia* 25 (1993), 26–47. Jesus People USA, founded in 1972, has a website at <http://www.jpusa.org>, accessed 9 March 2009, and maintains archives of its now defunct periodical *Cornerstone* (1971–2003) at <http://www.cornerstone.com>, accessed 9 March 2009. See also David DiSabatino, *The Jesus People Movement: An Annotated Bibliography and General Resource* (Westport, CT, 1999).

Public attention has most focused on communal disasters, such as the mass suicide by members of the California-based People's Temple in Guyana in 1978, and the fire that destroyed the Branch Davidian compound in Waco, Texas, in 1993. Most Christian communities live undramatically, out of the limelight, and there are currently signs that their numbers are growing again. In March 2008 the Intentional Communities Directory listed a total of 109 groups in the United States that referred to themselves as 'Christian'; of these, no fewer than 54 described themselves as 'forming'.[32] Though the list includes communities that have existed for decades, it is likely that most will not last long. Yet this communalism is a movement of constant renewal, and the variety among Christian communes is probably greater than at any time in the past. There are groups of Catholics, Russian Orthodox and Anabaptists; there are mixed communities of Lutherans, Quakers and Catholics; many call themselves 'Christian based' or 'Bible believers'. Some continue to prepare for the Second Coming; a man in southern California recently formed the Christian Soldiers Fellowship, a community of believers who will settle (in 'separate residences') 'to await the tribulation' referred to in Matthew 24. But most appear to reflect the broader change we have noted, from the nineteenth-century desire to reshape society to the more recent impulse to offer modest improvement and useful, practical services. The several US branches of the worldwide Camphill community movement include adults with disabilities among their members.[33] The six members of the Bethlehem Farm community in West Virginia describe themselves as 'Progressive Catholics', raise some of their own food, and undertake 'low-income home repair' in the surrounding area. Though a few communities have dozens or even hundreds of members, most are small, consisting of only a handful of individuals or families. And they continue to reflect tendencies in American society at large. Some have websites or toll-free phone numbers. There are communities that serve as bases for the Christian home-school movement (in which children are educated at home, not in conventional schools), or for environ-

[32] Fellowship for Intentional Community, 'Community List', <http://directory.ic.org/iclist/>, accessed 13 March 2008.
[33] On the Camphill communities, see Dan McKanan, *Touching the World: Christian Communities Transforming Society* (Collegeville, MN, 2007), esp. 22–27.

mental activism; early in 2008 a group calling itself the 'Anabaptist Eco-Village (USA)' was recruiting members for a community that would form 'a collective of Christ-Centric Earth Stewards'. An increasing number of Christian 'co-housing' schemes (communities in which families live in private houses but also share common activities and facilities) help pool resources for the poor or elderly, or overcome the isolation of modern living. A group of Methodists started one in Oakland, California, in 1996,[34] and others have since been developed elsewhere. One such project, in Orange County, New York, cites its 'desire to build strong Christian living communities, as in the days of Acts, living in close proximity to each other in a Christian co-housing environment within our community'.[35] The perennial desire to emulate the early Church has found yet another fresh iteration.

★   ★   ★

Our survey has revealed 'communities' as vehicles for a variety of spiritual and social purposes. Equally, they present no single perspective on the relationships between God, humans and 'nature'. Like 'utopia' itself, these questions have often been double-edged in intentional communities. Human societies are constructions *in* nature, to which the 'natural world' is counterposed, but humans are also themselves part *of* nature and take steps to realize, amplify, regulate or control their characteristics as natural creatures. Intentional communities have often been places where the two aspects of this human relationship with nature, and the tensions between them, have been consciously addressed and played out.

Various communal groups, especially but not exclusively in the nineteenth century, sought to separate themselves from the world, conceiving this primarily in human terms. They hoped to improve upon the world by constructing social arrangements superior to those prevailing around them. From the early Pietists and Shakers to the present, members of Christian communities have expressed a desire to build 'heaven on earth'. According to Clarence Jordan, its co-founder, Koinonia Farm, the interracial community established

---

[34] Temescal Commons Cohousing, Oakland, CA, <http://www.cohousing.org/directory/view/6221>, accessed 15 July 2008.
[35] Orange County Community Builders, <http://www.actsliving.com/>, accessed 13 March 2008.

in Georgia in 1942, was 'a demonstration plot for the Kingdom of God', and the organization continues to use this motto today.[36] The Hutterite Elmendorf Christian Community in Minnesota consisted in 2006 of some fifty adults and seventy-five children 'seeking to live out the Kingdom of Heaven as Jesus taught'.[37]

Such expressions are, of course, to a large extent figurative; they relate to human behaviour and relationships. But communes exist in the material world, and concepts like 'heaven on earth' inevitably call forth speculations about what this might look like in a concrete sense. Commune members or sympathizers have frequently invoked images of Eden or Paradise. One abolitionist brimmed over with enthusiasm when he visited the Northampton Community in 1844: 'Nothing short will be adequate to describe the paradisiacal nature of that lovely spot,' he wrote. 'It is Eden, Jr, to say the least.' 'We had "dreams of future bliss"', wrote one young woman after an evening spent discussing plans for a new building and landscaping at Northampton.[38] Part of the House of David's property in early twentieth-century Michigan was a park called 'Eden Springs'.

Such sensibilities mirrored the perfectionist impulse that underlay much nineteenth-century American Christian thinking. On one hand perfectionism embodied a belief in the human ability to dominate and reshape nature; as the historian David E. Nye has written, it embraced the notion that the occupation of the American continent marked a 'second creation', an opportunity for humans to take God's natural world and improve upon it.[39] Shakers began mostly as modest, even impoverished, families and individuals, but through devoted collective effort built substantial, prosperous farms, successful craft industries, and residences of impressive size and quality of construction. Members of the Oneida community also created a solid, comfortable communal home, and businesses substantial enough to sustain them and their

[36] Koinonia Partners, <http://www.koinoniapartners.org/>, accessed 4 July 2008.
[37] Fellowship for Intentional Community, 'Community List', <http://directory.ic.org/iclist/>, accessed 13 March 2008.
[38] Clark, *Communitarian Moment*, 109; Almira B. Stetson to James A. Stetson, 26 May 1844, in Christopher Clark and Kerry W. Buckley, eds, *Letters from an American Utopia: The Stetson Family and the Northampton Association, 1843–1847* (Amherst, MA, 2004), 35.
[39] David E. Nye, *America as Second Creation: Technology and Narratives of New Beginnings* (Cambridge, MA, 2003), esp. 1–8.

successors for some considerable time. Oneidans even claimed that the weather was better in community, not because the weather itself was different but because communal life made its vagaries easier to contend with.[40]

On the other hand, perfectionism drove a desire to regulate humans' potentially uncontrollable impulses to succumb to the vagaries of their own 'nature', and so put themselves at odds with their conception of God's will. Intentional communities offered frameworks for reconciling the tensions between human nature and God's 'natural world'. Like most Shakers, Isaac Newton Youngs was torn between his convictions and the demands of celibacy, expressing his struggle in striking naturalistic metaphors. Writing to fellow Shaker Garret Lawrence in 1826, he expressed the hope that his friend was untroubled: 'that the sun shines bright, the sky looks blue, and the waters run clear with you; … while with a fair wind, smooth sea, flowing sails and streaming colors, you are sweetly and swiftly sailing for the celestial land'. But confessing that he himself faced difficulties ('poor me is a beating the briny billows against wind and tide'), Youngs invoked Shaker 'gospel order' as the safeguard that kept him true to his faith:

> I perseveringly stem the tide of nature. … I have a good compass firmly placed in the binnacle, and the needle has lately been touched with the heavenly magnet, and feels the invisible attractions of gospel love, and though it may sometimes vary, when passing over extensive beds of <u>natural</u> & <u>attracting</u> ore, yet in the main it points toward the true polar star.[41]

Numerous communities, in the nineteenth century and since, promoted health reform, dietary controls and regulation of sexual relationships as means of resolving the tensions between 'nature' and social order. Oneida's complex marriage system, nineteenth-century reformers' fascination with water-cure and other medical remedies, and the perennial communal interest in vegetarianism, have all represented efforts to channel the belief that it is not

[40] William B. Meyer, 'The Perfectionists and the Weather: The Oneida Community's Quest for Meteorological Utopia, 1848–1879', *Environmental History* 7 (2002), 589–610, esp. 594–97.

[41] Glendyne R. Wergland, *One Shaker Life: Isaac Newton Youngs, 1793–1865* (Amherst, MA, 2006), 97–98.

'nature' that needed improving, but humans themselves. Such efforts did not always work. Louisa May Alcott, later famous as the author of *Little Women*, found herself as a ten year-old enduring the rigours of her father's strictly vegetarian Fruitlands community. Cautionary mottoes appeared on the meal table ('Vegetable diet and sweet repose. / Animal food and nightmare'), and the children's tutor was dismissed for eating fish. After leaving Fruitlands, Alcott wrote in her journal, 'Life is pleasanter than it used to be, and I don't care [i.e. worry] about dying any more.'[42]

Indeed, the pastoral image conjured up by the term 'Eden' was often belied by the activities communal societies engaged in. By the mid-nineteenth century Shakers were manufacturing a range of items for sale, including furniture and other woodenwares. The Oneida Community thrived for a time on making metal animal traps, and then adopted cutlery manufacture (which its successor company still produces). The Amana Society manufactured textiles and then household appliances (which, again, its successor still makes). Community industries did not always succeed: the Northampton Association failed to make silk manufacture its principal source of income, and the Christian Commonwealth Colony in Georgia lost much of its scarce capital in a poorly-run towelling mill.[43] But in other cases, communities adapted well to changing circumstances. Like many other communes the House of David in Michigan ran a farm and developed a lumber business, but it also contributed to the emerging world of commercial public entertainment. Located near a pier used by Lake Michigan excursion steamers, the community ran a hotel and an amusement park with ornamental gardens, a miniature railroad, and other attractions. It also fielded travelling baseball teams which brought the community regional and national prominence in the 1920s. Existing in the world, even if they sought to distance themselves from it, communes were often more convergent with contemporary social patterns than their ideologies might have suggested.

---

[42] *The Journals of Louisa May Alcott*, ed. Joel Myerson and Daniel Shealy (Boston, MA, 1989), 51–52.

[43] M. Stephen Miller, *From Shaker Lands and Shaker Hands: A Survey of the Industries* (Hanover, NH, 2007); Clark, *Communitarian Moment*, 140–60; Peter Hoehnle, 'Machine in the Garden: The Woolen Textile Industry of the Amana Society, 1785–1942', *Annals of Iowa* 61 (2002), 24–67; Fish, 'Christian Commonwealth Colony'.

Even so, they often incorporated features into buildings or spatial arrangements that reflected distinctive beliefs and practices. Each Hutterite community or *Bruderhof* was 'was laid out to "a geometric plan based on the points of a compass to represent a miniature model of the universe"'.[44] Shakers were less rigid, but still laid out buildings in neat groupings to express their ideals of simplicity and order. Work buildings were usually segregated by gender, but Shaker dwellings and meetinghouses were designed for the needs of communal life and worship, and relied more on symbolic than on physical means to keep the sexes apart. These buildings had separate entrance doorways for men and women, but the spaces within them were segregated only by self-discipline. Men and women ate and worshipped on opposite sides of dining rooms and meetinghouses; hallways were made wide, so that members could use them without coming into contact. The most striking feature of the large Mansion House the Oneida Community built in the 1860s was a communal sitting room on an upstairs floor surrounded by doorways into numerous small bedrooms. Designed to facilitate the practice of complex marriage, this arrangement reflected both the public regulation of sexual assignations and their temporary nature, since the small rooms discouraged dalliances other than for essential intimacy.[45] Comparable building practices may be found today. The polygamist Fundamentalist Latter-day Saints' Yearning for Zion ranch, from which the state of Texas temporarily removed hundreds of children in April 2008, includes sizeable residences with living and sleeping rooms evidently designed for occupation by multiple mothers and their offspring. The Oakland co-housing project started in 1996, by contrast, consists of a group of houses arranged around a green, together with a common dining room for meals and gatherings and a barn for the use of teenage members. The separate family houses reflect the fact that the group does not see itself as a commune. Wanting to avoid what they see as the naïve mistakes of the counterculture, these Christian co-residence members balance the privacy of

---

[44] Sutton, *Communal Utopias and the American Experience: Religious Communities*, 93.
[45] Dolores Hayden, *Seven American Utopias: The Architecture of Communitarian Socialism, 1790–1975* (Cambridge, MA, 1976), chs 4, 7.

families with being what they call 'a living faith community within a neighborhood'.[46]

As the architectural historian Dolores Hayden argued in a book on utopian communities more than thirty years ago, though spatial arrangements were important in any commune's life, interactions among members themselves have been most crucial to communal success or durability. Hayden drew from a Shaker hymn the striking metaphor of community itself as a building, the purposive action of creating which could shape a viable communal life:

> Leap and shout, ye living building
> Christ is in his glory come
> Cast your eyes on Mother's children
> See what glory fills the room!

Shakers, already living in the millennium, held 'two simultaneous visions of an ideal community', the 'earthly' and the 'heavenly' spheres, in which heaven would be built on earth and earthly members would come to live as in heaven. The metaphor of the 'living building' sustained Hayden's broader argument that utopian communities succeeded to the extent that they were able to grow organically, rather than from imposed authority, and to develop in ways that were improvised by members, not predetermined by blueprints.[47]

Accordingly, adaptability rather than stasis was often a hallmark of communal life. Though this was not always sufficient for a community's success or longevity, it was usually necessary. Of the four Massachusetts communities of the 1840s, Brook Farm, Hopedale and Northampton all altered their modes of operation at least once. Only the Fruitlands community did not, and it was the shortest-lived. Mid-twentieth-century historical interpretations of the Shakers dwelt on the group's timelessness, but more recent scholarship has stressed the extent to which Shakers modified their practices in the light of shifting circumstances. The same has been true of modern communities. Koinonia Farm in Georgia survived hostility and violent attacks because of its inter-

---

[46] Tom Sine, 'Not Your Father's Commune' *Re:generation Quarterly* 6.1 (Spring 2000), at <http://www.beliefnet.com/story/38/story_3853.html>, accessed 13 March 2008.

[47] Hayden, *Seven American Utopias*, 64, 67.

racial composition in the 1950s, sheltered civil rights activists in the 1960s, reorganized itself later that decade, and in the early 1990s again carried out significant reforms to empower its poorer, black members. Koinonia Partners, as it has been known since 1968, has fostered housing and development schemes, including Habitat for Humanity, and established an international reach.

Hayden's insight turned out to be much deeper than merely a spatial or architectural observation. Indeed it could be said to denote the single most important development in studies of intentional communities in the past three decades. Many scholars since have implicitly taken up Hayden's themes, shaping a fresh historiography of utopias that shifts our focus from communal leaders and their ideas to communal members and their experiences. In 1972, in his great work on American religion, Sydney E. Ahlstrom, wrote of communal utopias as 'so often but the lengthened shadow of some charismatic leader', but the best recent works have altered this view, by paying attention to the expressed thoughts of ordinary Shakers, Oneidans and members of other communes.[48] Even studies of German communities have now also modified the once common focus on charismatic leadership. George Rapp, Christian Metz and others are now given more modest credit for the achievements of their followers, as scholars emphasize communal organization, family patriarchy and kinship to explain the fact that such communities often long outlived their founders.[49] Followers can tell us as much as leaders about how communities sustained the faith and attachment of their membership, or how they failed to do so. We now have, for example, the letters of women who lived at the Northampton community, and at least two extensive journals and memoirs of Oneida Community women, whose writings throw much fresh light on the loyalty inspired by John Humphrey

---

[48] Sydney E. Ahlstrom, *A Religious History of the American People* (New Haven, CT, 1972), 491.

[49] Michael Taylor, 'Changing Pilots in Mid-Stream: How German-American Communitarian Societies Successfully Handled the Deaths of their Founders', *Communal Societies* 26 (2006), 135–45; see also Christoph Brumann, 'The Dominance of One and its Perils: Charismatic Leadership and Branch Structures in Utopian Communes', *Journal of Anthropological Research* 56 (2000), 425–51; Timothy Miller, ed., *When Prophets Die: The Postcharismatic Fate of New Religious Movements* (Albany, NY, 1991).

Noyes, and the demands on faith that complex marriage imposed.[50] And there is a growing body of oral and written testimony that will provide comparable insights into the beliefs and experiences of late twentieth-century communalists.

Hayden drew attention to the literal and metaphorical senses in which the concept of 'building' could harness and express collective effort: the actual construction and laying out of community premises; the nurturing of spiritual practice and commitment; and the effort to ensure that commitment might be sustained into the future. Groups that were able to focus on the constant processes of renewal implied in the metaphor of a 'living building' have been among those that have lasted longest. This concept, too, appears appropriately to embody the combination of material and spiritual efforts that members of Christian communities have sought to expend in the constantly varied and changing world of American utopias. Though from the eighteenth century onwards many communities have sought closer relationships to (external) nature by establishing relatively self-sufficient communes in rural environments, to some extent all have also had to address the complexities embodied in humans' own 'nature' and their relationships with one another.

University of Connecticut

---

[50] Clark and Buckley, *Letters from an American Utopia*; *Special Love, Special Sex: An Oneida Community Diary*, ed. Robert S. Fogarty (Syracuse, NY, 1994), *Desire and Duty at Oneida: Tirzah Miller's Intimate Memoir*, ed. Robert S. Fogarty (Bloomington, IN, 2000).

METHODISM, SCIENCE AND THE NATURAL WORLD: SOME TENSIONS IN THE THOUGHT OF HERBERT BUTTERFIELD*

by MICHAEL BENTLEY

IT is no longer a name that everyone knows. At the height of his fame as historian and broadcaster, Herbert Butterfield (1900–1979) reached into homes and schools through his varied activities and established a public reputation far beyond Cambridge University, where he spent the entirety of his working life from 1923 to his retirement in 1968, and among people who knew nothing of his small and idiosyncratic college, Peterhouse, to which he had arrived as an undergraduate in 1919 and with which he would be associated for the rest of his career. The Chair of Modern History at Cambridge, which he held from 1944 to 1963, and the Regius Chair to which he was relocated for the remaining five years of his professional life, offered major platforms for one determined to communicate to a wider audience. His tenure of the Mastership of his college after 1955 offered another by lending him the possibility of hosting individuals and colloquia. Through less than a dozen major works of history – *The Whig Interpretation of History* (1931) and *Christianity and History* (1949) come at once to mind as the best-regarded – Butterfield established a *persona* considerably more influential than a fairly modest literary production might imply. Only when one stands back from that *oeuvre* and examines its internal consistencies does it become clear that it engenders in the reader a certain discomfort. For if his thought does not often become mired in outright contradiction, it frequently displays moments of inner tension.

Tension is not a new ingredient in Butterfield's life. Indeed a glorious typographical error in a recent study of him persistently located the family's Tenison Road house in 'Tension Road'. But we tend to think of that tension, domestic dramas apart, as a

---

* Some of the argument and material offered here anticipates my biography of Butterfield which it is hoped will appear in 2010.

feature of the relationship between Butterfield's notion of 'technical history' as a professional procedure and his Christian stress on meaning-within-narrative and the place within it of the individual soul's journey towards death and beyond – a place where methodology conflicts seemingly with eschatology. Science and the nature of the physical universe come less naturally to an observer of how Butterfield's mind worked; but they played an important role in his intellectual and emotional make-up and suffered related tensions of their own. In part that importance follows from the way in which 'technical history', looked at from one angle, resembles a conception of 'scientific history'. In later life Butterfield made that connection pretty explicit in his frequent talk of 'historical science' and the need to retain it as some form of control. But there is far more to it than that. From his teens Butterfield engaged with technology – mills and how to work them was what one learned at Keighley Trade and Grammar School – and his occasional reflections during the 1920s, multiplying through the 1930s, carry a continual concern with and knowledge about astronomy, mechanics and the physical sciences. At the same time that science burgeoned, formal Methodist commitments receded: not many of them remained in any traditional form by 1937, though he retained a 'cultural Methodism' that produced some of his more knee-jerk reactions, especially to the Church of England. A close engagement with the nature and implications of Christian thought and life more generally understood persisted to his death, however, and informed his responses both to historical writing and to formulating his ideas about what it was to be human.

A scientific approach to theological matters – one that reminds modern readers of Reinhold Niebuhr and which he amended in the chilling light of Rudolf Bultmann in the 1960s and his determination to strip liturgy down to a minimum – is often evident.[1] Our picture of him has clouded because his formative years, say between the age of twenty and forty, usually do not enter into accounts of his experience for the excellent reason that

---

[1] Intimate friend Martin Wight drew attention to the Niebuhr dimension in 'History and Judgement: Butterfield, Niebuhr and the Technical Historian', *The Frontier: A Christian Commentary on the Common Life* 1 (1950), 301–14. Bultmann became part of Butterfield's preparations for delivering the Gifford Lectures in Glasgow in 1965–66.

nobody knows anything about them apart from what he himself let fall in later life.[2] As a result his writing a book about the history of science – a very important book for its generation and one crucial to understanding its author's view of life after the Second World War – often appears in modern accounts as a *non sequitur*, thrust upon Butterfield by an importunate collection of scientists looking for a lecturer, rather than a genuine sequel to much earlier reflection. His thinking centred, moreover, on wider considerations than the offering of insights about appropriate methods of intellectual enquiry. Butterfield manifested throughout his life an intense communing with the world of nature and its lessons tugged constantly at the constructions he made about history, the intellect and the point of being alive. It provoked serious worries in his mind about the usefulness of history as *Wissenschaft* (a word he believed English the poorer for lacking); it led to an emotional reaction against intellectualizing the universe, present or past; and it stimulated some very bad poetry. His engagement remains important for the relationship it implied between nature and human nature, science and bastard science, religion and deformed religion. These were antinomies characterized by creative tension and they are my subject in this paper. It will not be possible to report fully on the range of Butterfield's tensions or on the evidence that illuminates them, but I hope to clarify and extend the suggestions made here in my biography of this very complicated man.

The natural world compelled Butterfield by its God-given beauty. He published little about it: one has to turn to the unpublished meditations and jottings to feel its force but that does not detract from its importance for him since many of his most personal statements never reached print. Perhaps one should say 'natural worlds' because Butterfield began with the cosmos, tutored by Sir James Jeans whose popularizations of astronomy he read, though he would also have come across Sir Arthur Eddington in Cambridge. Variants of the Big Bang hypothesis interested him, presumably because of their theistic possibilities, and he had some elementary grasp of the general theory of relativity. Indeed when experiment showed what Einstein said it would show – the gravitational force of the sun bending light from Mercury and fractionally displacing

---

2   Many recollections were put on tape by C. T. McIntire in the 1970s and used in his *Herbert Butterfield: Historian as Dissenter* (New Haven, CT, 2004).

its observed image – the thought found its way into an essay on, of all things, the writing of official history, in a scintillating passage urging historians to look for their own perihelion of Mercury to revise their narratives in the way scientists had revised their theories.[3] He loved the colours of stars, the mystery of other planets, the idea that we all float about in space on a ball; but the point of his interest did not reside in the physical objects themselves but in the universe as a dynamic backdrop to human intellect and the miracle of personality. Among Butterfield's papers is a single sheet which is plainly a title page. It reads 'Man and the Universe'. He never wrote the book (a familiar story in Butterfield's career) but his jottings about it take us into his perception of what mattered cosmically; and that was not bits of rock or gravitational fields.

> For since the earth holds human life it holds that wonder which we call Intellect; and without Intellect, what does it matter how many things roll in empty space – what does it matter how seethingly hot or how incredibly bleak they are? Modern science may have widened the responsibilities and magnified the power of the human intellect ... But if we value Mind, then so far as we know at present, the earth must still remain the centre of the great drama that takes place in time – the hub or the capital of the universe.[4]

He did not deny that 'seething, soaring globes of merely luminous matter' deserved their students,[5] but he wanted to say that they mattered in human terms only when they contained the mind of man. His own natural world was therefore a smaller place than that proclaimed by a Jeans or even that analyzed by other scientific friends such as Joseph Needham or Max Perutz. It touched him through its visual proximity as a beacon of God. When emotionally disturbed, as he was in 1926, he became notoriously capable of seeing God as an elf in a bush on Cambridge's Trumpington

---

[3] 'Official History', in Butterfield, *History and Human Relations* (London, 1951), 182–224, at 210–11.
[4] 'For since the earth holds ...', Fragment, Later Writing, Miscellany. The latter is a small collection of unpublished material currently in my care and not available for research. Most documents in it are untitled, and I give their opening words instead.
[5] Ibid.

Street.[6] He knew perfectly well that it was a trick of light but it was a fertile trick that brought its own light and, judging from the smudges, some tears to the page of his journal. Years later he found himself again on Coe Fen and the wonder stole back. At ten o'clock in the evening of a hot July day:

> ... I stood still and held my breath as I watched the moon not far above the willow-trees, when the blue of the sky was turning grey and the waters of the Cam were black with occasionally a broken light. I found that I was unconsciously trying to see this as I saw it in my childhood, or as the ploughman saw it a thousand years ago – as man would see it before he knew much of science and the reeling worlds of heaven and the speed of the rolling earth. I tried to see it as something still, something which stood steadfast while Time speeds ahead and generations of men come and go – instead of thinking of a universe in which all was in perpetual motion, perpetual flux ...[7]

The first tension comes into view – one between a scientistic appreciation of the universe as an object of empirical study and Butterfield's humanized natural world, 'a timeless picture of man under his own piece of sky', in which the essence of what may be valuable loses itself in the method of appraising it.

Butterfield's worries about translating the scientists' understanding of the natural world into the world of human relations preoccupied his thoughts about how history should be written but also his everyday perceptions. One trope concerns the buttercup of field and lawn, not unnaturally when the young Cambridge undergraduate had once acclimatized himself to being called Buttercup by public-school hearties.[8] Not only the flower's symmetrical beauty but its essence – the thing that makes it what it is – consists in its harmonious wholeness of colour and texture and location. Leach its colour, disturb its close formation of petals or wrench the plant from the soil and you no longer have the

---

[6] Butterfield's Journal, 4 February 1926. The entry was published by C. T. McIntire in 1979: see Herbert Butterfield, *Writings on Christianity and History*, ed. C. T. McIntire (New York, 1979), xxiv.

[7] 'Out in Coe Fen ...', 3 pages, Later Writing, Miscellany.

[8] McIntire, *Herbert Butterfield*, 16.

thingliness of the thing – not that Butterfield had read Heidegger, but there are intriguing echoes. Then the scientist arrives and his first act is to pull off a petal and press it on a glass slide in his microscope, discovering constituent chemicals but obscuring the entity of which they comprise a part.[9] It is the same, but worse, with *human* nature. Those who do not understand or respect the sanctity of the individual soul come along and pull off arms and legs as they might those of an insect, making the individual a mere object caught up in some wider scheme of evolution. Many readers of *Christianity and History* may have forgotten that in its early pages Butterfield turns to Hitler as a malevolent force in the history of humanity by relating him, not to sin or ideology, but to a disastrous misunderstanding of man in the natural world:

> The historian does not treat man as the student of biology seems to do – does not regard him as essentially a part of nature or consider him primarily in this aspect. He picks up the other end of the stick and envisages a world of human relations, standing, so to speak, over against nature – he studies that new kind of life which man has superimposed on the jungle, the forest and the waste ... And if we take our bearings from this as we make our judgments on life ... it will carry us far from the stark, bleak nature-fallacies of a Hitler.[10]

Thus the natural world, conceived as Butterfield would like to conceive it, does not so much emerge from scientific results as a sort of collective noun, but rather act as a recalcitrant resistance to human analysis, created and impregnated by a God whom scientists, Needham apart, often wish to exclude from their conclusions.

Again, however, that conclusion itself runs into friction as one thinks about Butterfield's relationship to science as a discipline over a long period of his life. For it was not consistent and, again, one must be prepared for tension or even contradiction. During the black hole of the 'thirties, the Cambridge atmosphere of excitement in the natural sciences that reached so many dons and students working there also enveloped Butterfield to a striking degree. His own *entrée* came through his close friendship with the

---

[9] It is a trope with him. One example is 'When the scientist has torn the buttercup to pieces ...' Single sheet, Later Writing, Miscellany.
[10] *Christianity and History* (London, 1949), 6–7.

high Anglican Marxist biochemist Joseph Needham of Gonville and Caius College which brought him into the Committee on the History of Science Lectures and the society of people he would not normally have met, and introduced to him the subject that would become a book in 1949.[11] Less well-known, indeed unknown, is Butterfield's own political radicalization in the direction of a mild and controlled corporatism and a willingness to bring a more analytical focus to his social theory. In the few years before the Second World War we have a Butterfield who has abandoned the Methodist circuit; developed painful and aggressive doubts about Methodists themselves; advocated, at least in private, the abolition of marriage; and discussed the virtues of a society in which children would be brought up in common in large barracks that sound distinctly like those housing the camps of the *Hitlerjugend*.[12] We have a Butterfield whose historical world took a related turn away from the study of political elites and towards the history of economic and intellectual life, civilization and art, especially in the sixteenth and seventeenth centuries, as a basis for a more scientific understanding of how societies in the West had developed. This Butterfield leaves a sense that he is a man of the left out of conscience, of the right out of sympathy with the home of all civilization, his beloved Germany, and above all of having become 'advanced' in many areas of his intellectual life. It is not that he had espoused the laboratory as the place of serious work: he retained his distance from all forms of laboratory work and was later criticized for having neglected it in his study of *The Origins of Modern Science*. But he had come to think that Descartes or Fontenelle had more to say about what made the seventeenth century tick than had Richelieu or Louis XIV and that students of history ought to know about them.

That the mood did not last did not mean that it did not matter and the evangelistic zeal he brought to the history of science after the war, with its explicit mission to set the subject on its feet as a serious subdiscipline, commented on how far he had come

---

[11] Anna-K. Mayer, 'Setting up a Discipline: Conflicting Agendas of the Cambridge History of Science Committee 1936–1950', *Studies in History and Philosophy of Science* 31 (2000), 665–89.

[12] These views are conveyed in a series of confidential letters to Joy Marc between 1935 and 1938 (Private collection).

since the mid-thirties. His determination to do so depended on two imperatives: the need to show that man's view of the natural world had played a fundamental role in bringing about the 'scientific revolution' of the early modern period in ways that the East, and especially China, had proved unable to replicate; and a more methodological mission to save the subject from the scientists who, left to themselves, would perpetuate its current primitivism as a new type of Whig history resting on linear progress of the kind he had lambasted in his essay on the *Whig Interpretation* almost two decades before.

The undertows of both these commitments can be felt throughout *The Origins of Modern Science*, which has rarely been given the place it deserves in Butterfield's thought. Whatever its impact on the scientific community (and it was considerable) it made a great impact on Butterfield himself and illustrated how far his thinking had moved since the 1920s. What the book does is to take the lessons of the *Whig Interpretation* and then use the history of science as a test case in their implementation. Beginning with the concept of motion as a denial of Aristotelian stasis, the text concentrates on the sixteenth and seventeenth centuries and treats the period declared in the title (1300–1800) as prefix and suffix. Astronomy and cosmology play an important role with Kepler as a sort of Reformation hero; anatomy features strongly with Harvey as totemic; the 'scientific revolution' – a concept he inherited and did not invent but which he certainly popularized – is seen as their legacy and as the apogee of significant change, with Fontenelle (1657–1757) its prophet for the masses who developed discussion of the universe for an eighteenth-century audience. He does not say explicitly that the Reformation of Luther has the Reformation of Kepler as its complement but the originality of the book's argument certainly implies that the history of religion and social thought cannot be divorced from views of the natural world – a position that Keith Thomas would entrench in scholarship in 1983.[13] A more spectacular foreshadowing concerns Thomas Kuhn. The paper that would grow into *The Structure of Scientific Revolutions* (1962) must have struck Butterfield – who was probably among the audience – as one that he could have written

---

[13] Keith Thomas, *Man and the Natural World: Changing Attitudes in England 1500–1800* (London, 1983).

rather more elegantly himself.[14] For, although he did not have the concept of a 'paradigm shift', his entire thesis turned on scientific non-progress and the place of the mistakes, wrong turnings and blind alleys that modern scientists dismissed as 'errors' before identifying 'advances'. Butterfield saw and animadverted on the historical misunderstanding behind this position. It was important to see that views from alchemy to flat-earthery rested on assumptions that contemporaries found entirely sensible. Each age lay equidistant from eternity – his beautiful translation of Ranke – and that meant taking each period seriously and in its own terms. *The Origins of Modern Science* might have been called *The Origins of Modern History* without too much loss.

In the world of science the book's importance did not depend on what it *said* but on what it *was* – the first rounded attempt to place the history of science within a broader history of European civilization. It contained many errors of both omission and commission which an extra fifty pages in the second edition of 1957 did something to remedy,[15] but the mistakes were hardly the point. A distinguished historian of science, Bernard Cohen of Harvard, said that much of it was mistaken but that the argument overall was brilliant.[16] The great polymathic guru of Paris, Alexandre Koyré, sent a lordly offprint by way of encouragement. Meanwhile Butterfield had succeeded in manipulating his History of Science Committee in Cambridge into appointing into a lectureship on the subject an expert on seventeenth-century ballistics – an unknown young man called Rupert Hall[17] – beginning the building of what is now the Department of the History and Philosophy of Science and turning it into a rival of J. B. S. Haldane's department at University College, London. Even as his

---

[14] Kuhn had acknowledged the influence of Butterfield on his *The Copernican Revolution* (London, 1957) and Butterfield commented on the papers delivered in Oxford in 1961. There is no journal for the latter year and the appointment diaries do not confirm an Oxford visit; but see Keith C. Sewell, *Herbert Butterfield and the Interpretation of History* (Basingstoke, 2005), at 163, 242 n. 59. Kuhn's book quoted a 'perceptive historian, viewing a classic case of a science's reorientation by paradigm change': *The Structure of Scientific Revolutions* (London, 1962), 85.

[15] Review by J. D. Bernal, *New Scientist*, 31 October 1957.

[16] Review by Bernard Cohen, *Isis* 41 (1950), 231–33.

[17] Professor A. Rupert Hall was later to become one of the most distinguished historians of science of his generation and for many years a senior professor in the University of London.

fame spread from America to Japan, however, Butterfield found himself in internal tension over the ability of science and scientists to address the evils of the present world: indeed he thought them guilty of producing some of the most serious among them. 'About the scientists my complaint is a fundamental one,' ran an undated postwar note; 'they perfected and actualised the atom-bomb before they gave similar effort to the prevention of starvation ... If they say that it was not their fault – that they were under some such system of necessity – that is what I complain about.'[18] After 1950 he continued his interest in the academic history of the subject and attended international conferences on it. He was even invited to contribute to Koyré's Festschrift.[19] But the spark of idealism in his thinking about science had died. 'We are slaves of science,' he had decided by 1952, 'and have sold our souls to it. The real issue is whether we have a spiritual view of life or not.'[20]

In the mature thinker of the 1950s and 1960s the bedrock of existence on the planet was that life was a spiritual fact first and a scientific curiosity second. He retained the language of scientific analysis in his historical writing and was happy to see in the historiographer that he found himself becoming something of the biochemist (nodding towards Needham) 'employ[ing] particular techniques but on a wide range of subject matter'.[21] His unfortunate notion of 'technical history' moved closer to the phrase he now used often, that of 'historical science'. But the natural world itself meant little to him unless it rested on a Coleridgean wholeness of vision and inner meaning:

> Stay here with me beside the stealthiness of water,
> Till the moon dwindles and the starlight filters away.
> They have left open a door for love to enter,
> And the trees are still, for the trees are pondering.
> It is so quiet now, with no wind to wake the waters
> And comb ripples and whisperings out of summer leaves
> That set the hills and hollows murmuring;
> But there is a note on the air to trouble a mind,

---

[18] Commonplace Book, n.d., Fragment, Later Writing, Miscellany.
[19] Herbert Butterfield, 'The History of History and the History of Science', *Histoire de la Pensée*, 12/13 (1964), 13: 57–68.
[20] Cambridge, CUL, Commonplace Book, 1952, Butterfield MSS BUTT/520.
[21] Herbert Butterfield, *Man on his Past* (London, 1955), 8.

And there is magic here that would baffle the song-makers.
You could not choose but listen to the voice that lies
Under the silence and secrecy of these hills.[22]

Too clumsy for Coleridge, too banal for Auden, and yet the voice is his own and argues that some reconciliation between the tensions of the natural world as a collection of objects and the human faculty of synthesis need not remain a chimera.

What made it more possible was time itself and the easing of another, ultimate tension, not one between human nature and the natural world but within human nature itself. That had been the discomfort with which his pre-war Methodism had not coped. He had said that the human being must stand over against nature; but he knew all too well that human beings were part of that nature through their own animality. Butterfield participated self-consciously in the world of creatures through a powerful sexuality – something often found in spiritual and romantic people – which internalized the natural world in confusing and conflicted ways. Abandoning the Methodist pulpit and withdrawing later from Wesley House, of which he had been a lifelong supporter, followed from an internal tension that no church seemed likely to release; and it would remain Butterfield's complaint that the Methodism of his youth had achieved no theology of sexual relationships beyond that of condemnation, narrow-mindedness and inhumanity. It seemed to him that a starting point for any such discussion rested on an acceptance of universal sin, certainly, but also of God's chosen instrument of corporeality. To put it at its harshest: if God had not wanted us to be sexual creatures he would have given us different bodies.[23] Thus Butterfield resolved one tension in his image of religion's relation to the natural world, but he did not resolve it in religion's favour, or at least not in a form that Methodists could readily accept. 'Hold to Christ, and for the rest be totally uncommitted' had more edge to it than readers of *Christianity and History* may nowadays suspect and the edge had been honed on a sense that God's creation deserved more respect than man's ecclesiologies.

---

[22] Extract from an untitled and undated poem, Early Writing, Miscellany.
[23] The evidence for these contentions is sensitive but I shall discuss and quote from it in my biography.

Those who seek consistency should write little or die young and Butterfield did neither. Tensions, changes of mind, even near-contradictions become par for the course when the course extends over half a century. Nor should one pretend that the triangular arguments between Methodism, science and images of the natural world over-determined the rest of Butterfield's thinking about the nature of history, the role of historiography or the idea of an international order. On the other hand, these concerns make less sense when one leaves his commitment to relating the history and nature of science as an optional side-dish. Their flavour has largely disappeared through treating Butterfield as a Methodist avatar – a role he liked to assume in public writing and interviews – rather than one deeply troubled by what human agency had done to faith and to religion's contact with the physical universe. He could have said so much more about that but left his ideas scattered in a hundred notes and meditations. We lament his never having written the life of Charles James Fox, the book that would have transformed his reputation as a productive historian. There are grounds for wondering whether his failure to write *Man and the Universe* might not prove, from a more ultimate standpoint, the greater pity.

University of St Andrews

WHICH NATURE? WHOSE JUSTICE? SHIFTING MEANINGS OF NATURE IN RECENT ECOTHEOLOGY

by PETER MANLEY SCOTT

R EVIEWING the diversity of responses in English-language ecotheology over the last forty years or so, what impresses the reader is the vigour of the response of theology to ecological concerns. Of course, every undergraduate who has studied in this area can quote Lynn White's 1967 judgement that 'Christianity is the most anthropocentric religion the world has seen'.[1] Yet, as you review the material, that is hardly the only impression the reader is left with. Mostly, what strikes home is the range and energy of the theological responses. Of course, some adherents of theology proper might regard ecotheology as without standing. Is not environmental concern after all properly a matter for Christian social ethics? However, for those who consider that environmental concern presents the need for the construction or reconstruction of Christian commitments, ecotheology names that theological effort. In what follows, three ways are identified in which nature enters into theology as a way of presenting how ecotheology proceeds. Moreover, a narrative of development is offered in the sense that ecotheology has unfolded by drawing on immanentist themes in theology that stress the presence of God. As difficulties have emerged with this procedure, ecotheology has sought to attend to emerging issues and problems. Finally, this essay concludes by bringing the story of ecotheology up to date: the final topic of consideration is the ecotheology of climate change.

What is ecotheology? As a preliminary identification, ecotheology may be understood as that style of theological enquiry which responds to environmental or ecological concerns; ecotheology emerges from the impact of environmental questions upon theology. Dating the beginning of that impact is not easy: US Lutheran theologian Joseph Sittler addressed the World Council of

---

[1] Lynn White, 'The Historical Roots of our Ecologic Crisis', *Science* 155 (1967), 1203–07, at 1205.

Churches on the theme in 1961 in a well-known address entitled 'Called to Unity'.[2] And, as already noted, by 1967 Lynn White could publish a now notorious and negative critique of Christianity's ecological credentials which suggests that by the mid-1960s the issue was being actively debated. Certainly, by the publication of the Club of Rome report *The Limits to Growth* in 1972, ecological concerns come to be debated widely in the culture and so also in theology.[3]

By using the descriptions of response and impact, a methodologically neutral statement is intended – although, as we shall see, different methodologies are operative in this area. This will become clearer later, when we consider the matter of natural theology. Ecotheology engages in the critical assessment of the sources of ecological degradation and seeks to strengthen the ecological promise of Christianity.[4] Ecotheology is thereby both directed towards its ecological context and towards the reformulation of theology. In this sense, for ecotheology, ecology has a double meaning: (1) the interweaving of the human into a wider order as a theme for theological engagement, and (2) the ecology or dynamic organization of theology itself as this interweaving is incorporated comprehensively and systematically into theological enquiry. We might call this double hermeneutic the dialectic of engagement and the dialectic of repair, in which the movement of theological interpretation moves outwards in a constructive phase of ecological engagement and yet is also concerned with the repair of Christian faith in the light of ecological concerns. By way of engagement and repair, ecotheology emerges.

Ecotheology has been called a sort of contextual theology. Ernst Conradie offers a summary along these lines: 'Ecological theology may be regarded as a next wave of contextual theology'.[5] Given that any theology is marked by its conditions of production, perhaps the adjective 'contextual' is superfluous. Conradic offers a version of this concession: 'all theologies reflect the contexts

---

[2] Joseph Sittler, *Evocations of Grace: Writings on Ecology, Theology and Ethics* (Grand Rapids, MI, 2000), 38–50.

[3] D. H. Meadows et al., *The Limits to Growth* (London, 1972).

[4] The phrase is H. Paul Santmire's; cf. his *The Travail of Nature: The Ambiguous Ecological Promise of Christian Theology* (Philadelphia, PA, 1985).

[5] Ernst Conradie, *Christianity and Ecological Theology: Resources for Further Research* (Stellenbosch, 2006), 3.

within which they are situated'[6] – yet this is deeply ambiguous as the phrasing of this concession could mean that theology is a creature of its context. Moreover, 'contextual' is sometimes used in theology as a coded word of criticism against something called abstraction.[7] Yet ecotheology at its best is abstract because, as we shall see, of the difficulties in the concept of nature. A profound problem for ecotheology is the competition between the concepts of God and nature. The effort to free theology from this competition is not well caught by the adjective 'contextual'. The adjective 'natural' is the older – but also deeply ambiguous – term. Yet the employment of this older term indicates the importance of considering how ecotheology *transcends* its context. That is, ecotheology of course makes reference to ecological issues but it also attends to the universal claim to an unconditioned transcendence that is present in the use of the word 'God'.

It is also possible to locate ecotheological enquiry within the infrastructure of theology proper. For example, in her 2008 survey, Celia Deane-Drummond explores the relationships between ecology and a range of theological topics. These topics include Christ, the Spirit, the problem of evil and the end times as well as the relationship between ecological theology and the Bible.[8] There are also examples of ecotheology that eschew the term, especially those theologians whose methodological approach privileges doctrines or who prefer the term 'theology of nature'.[9] Moreover, some work in the theology of technology might also merit the description 'ecotheology'. That is, the technology associated with, for example, genetic manipulation has been of profound interest to ecotheologians, raising as it does matters to do with human power over and control of nature and who benefits from such power and control. Thus the matter of justice is raised: justice between

---

[6]   Ibid.

[7]   In other words, 'contextual' serves as a rebuke to styles of theology that appear to pay little attention to issues emerging out of a particular context or setting, or that fail to consider how context or location impinge upon theology. Conradie does *not* use it in this pejorative sense.

[8]   Celia Deane-Drummond, *Eco-Theology* (London, 2008).

[9]   e.g. Jürgen Moltmann, *God in Creation: An Ecological Doctrine of Creation* (London, 1985); George S. Hendry, *Theology of Nature* (Philadelphia, PA, 1989); Sigurd Bergmann, *Creation Set Free: The Spirit as Liberator of Nature* (Grand Rapids, MI, 2005).

humans, and the matter of the intelligibility or otherwise of justice between humans and, say, non-human animals.

The reference to justice brings to mind two other theological styles that are also concerned with justice: liberation and feminist theologies. With these theologies ecotheology may usefully be compared. (Indeed, these styles have sometimes also been called contextual theologies.) Liberation, feminist and eco-theologies do share an interest in justice and a concern with the category of the natural. For feminist and liberation theologies there is a concern that the natural functions as an oppressive category designed to support certain social arrangements and conceal the power interests that are 'naturalized' in those arrangements. The narratives of liberation proposed by liberation and feminist theologies are concerned with emancipation *from* something. Ecotheologies are here more cautious: of course, ecotheology is also concerned about the way that the natural presents itself as an account of the given. There can be notions of givenness that are deeply unecological; the claimed givenness of processes of globalization as these inform and support anthropogenic climate change is an obvious, contemporary example.

More than this, however, and in distinction from liberation and feminist theologies, ecotheology is cautious about narratives of emancipation *from*. That is, to borrow a little from Bruno Latour, ecotheology is sceptical about the human desire to free ourselves from our attachments.[10] By this we mean not only our artificial attachments – our technologies, for example – but also attaching animals and the biosphere on which we rely to breathe, on which our corporeal existence depends. Ecotheology wants, then, to speak not of emancipation *from* but instead of emancipation *into*; not emancipation from nature but emancipation into nature. The problem of course – and it is a problem for our way of life as well as for our ways of thinking – is whether it makes any sense to speak of 'emancipation *into*'.

We can explore this a little further if we note Rosemary Radford Ruether's affirmation of the critical interpretative principle in feminist theology. For Ruether, the non-negotiable interpretative

---

[10] Bruno Latour, 'Is there a Cosmopolitically Correct Design?', Fifth Manchester Lecture on Environment and Development, delivered at the University of Manchester, 5 October 2007.

434

principle is 'the full humanity of women'.[11] All feminist theological criticism and construction is to be tested against this principle. From an ecological point of view, we can discern an immediate tension: the denial of the full humanity of women tends to locate 'woman' outside the human. And what is 'outside the human'? Traditionally, this is 'the animal'. Those struggling for liberation know this well enough: in such struggles effort is expended to move the oppressed group practically and rhetorically within the pale of the human: we are people, not animals; we are agents, not property; we are persons, not non-persons. Yet, this struggle to be emancipated from the sphere of the 'not-human' is predicated upon the human/animal duality. And, of course, it is this duality of human/animal that it is one of the tasks of ecotheology to inter-rogate because – so ecotheology argues – the emancipation of the human cannot at some basic level always be at the expense of the non-human.

Let us amplify this point a little by noting how difficult it is to offer for ecotheology an interpretative principle that corresponds to Ruether's for feminist theology. What is ecotheology's variation on 'the full humanity of women'? Perhaps we could accept: 'the full naturality of the human'. Yet we can appreciate immediately that this phrase raises a difficult question. To speak of the 'full humanity of women' is to relate two terms that refer to the same class of 'thing': women and human may be understood as pointing towards the same species or to the same class; women can readily be seen to be a division of the human species. Indeed, to refuse this relation is to call into question the interpretative force of Ruether's principle.

It is one of the difficulties in this area that it is not clear that nature and human relate in the same way. The 'full naturality of the human' assumes a commonality between these two terms but it is just this commonality that is disputed – even within ecothe-ology. Just what is the relation between the natural and the human that would provide some semantic resources to give the expres-sion 'the full naturality of the human' some interpretative force? Because nature and human are not necessarily of the same class,

---

[11] Rosemary Radford Ruether, 'Feminist Interpretation: A Method of Correla-tion', in Letty M. Russell, ed., *The Feminist Interpretation of the Bible* (Oxford, 1985), 111–24, at 115.

435

and precisely because the relation between the two is in dispute, we can also see that this eco-principle can be extended only with difficulty. We may propose the 'full naturality of the human' and thereby also propose the 'full humanity of nature'. Yet it is not clear whether the consideration is intelligible let alone comprehensible: what is the 'full humanity of nature'? We might make a little more sense of the phrase if we dropped 'full'. We might then speak in some anthropomorphic idiom of the 'humanity of nature'. Yet it would need further elucidation to show that such a manoeuvre is not just another turn in anthropocentrism.

We can see this difficulty one more time by noting that it is a little easier to develop an interpretative principle for ecotheology if we restrict our concerns to a theology of animals. Our interpretative principle in its short form now becomes: the 'full animality of the human'; and in its longer version we would append the 'full humanity of the animal'. Thus no work in the theology of animals would resile from the principle of the 'full animality of the human and the full humanity of the animal'. This principle enjoys greater *prima facie* intelligibility and perhaps goes a little way to explain ecotheology's interest in a theology of animals. 'Animal' and 'human' in some traditions are of the same class and thereby it is intelligible to speak of the human's 'animality'; human is here considered to be a subset of animal. It is less clear what it means to speak of the 'humanity of the animal', full or otherwise. Nonetheless, we can see now why much effort is being expended in closing the gap between the human and the 'higher' animals because by means of that rapprochement some account of the humanity of the animals might be given. For example, if higher animals possess even a rudimentary capacity for language, then some content can be given to the affirmation of the 'humanity of the animal'.

HOW DOES NATURE ENTER THEOLOGY?

Rather than responding to these conceptual difficulties located in the notion of nature, let us ask instead how it is that nature enters theology. How is nature produced as knowledge for theology?

In surveys or other attempts to characterize the area of ecotheology, one common way is to proceed methodologically: that is, to situate the development of ecotheology as part of a methodological discussion between theology and ecology or environmental science (sometimes natural sciences).[12] Even apologetic approaches, as identified by Ernst Conradie – that is, those theological approaches that stress that the basic problem is not the Christian message itself but its presentation[13] – are vulnerable to the criticism of what C. S. Lewis called the 'methodological idiom'.[14] In other words, what nature is may be grasped by how it is treated by an academic discipline; and then a conversation between two disciplines, with their different meanings of nature, is conducted. The effect, intended or not, is a sort of stabilization of meanings. And, when it comes to the consideration of nature (with the attendant instabilities of that term), this may not be the wisest approach.

In what follows, something different is attempted: we shall be asking how it is that nature enters into and recedes from theology; how nature waxes and wanes in theology, so to speak. This is not simply a logical and interpretative process but a movement in reality also. In other words, what at its best ecotheology describes is a movement in life and thought that is both social and natural, in and through which both the human and the non-human are changed. Both the social and the natural are dynamic, materially and epistemologically. We are in the middle of a profound conflict, both material and intellectual.[15] What is the content of this conflict? An approximate and provisional characterization would be to note the independence and value of nature that is accompanied by an ever more comprehensive and deeper mixing of the human and the non-human. The alterity – that nature is not the result of human willing – of nature is accompanied by human-natural hybridity; the otherness of nature is accompanied by the mixing of the human and the natural. We are of course in a period in which nature's alterity is being emphasized. Yet its hybridity cannot be overlooked. (Moreover, if changes in our lifestyle will require the re-localizing of our hybridity or the reworking of our transformation of nature, then that re-localizing cannot overlook otherness.) Nor can we overlook that such alterity and such hybridity impacts on humans as individuals and communities in a diversity of ways. Power emerges now as an important theme in the sense that refer-

---

12 See my article, 'Types of Ecotheology', *Ecotheology* 4 (1998), 8–19.
13 Conradie, *Christianity and Ecological Theology*, 123–33.
14 C. S. Lewis, *Studies in Words*, 2nd edn (Cambridge, 1967), 69.
15 A. D. Lindsay, *Karl Marx's* Capital (London, 1925), 17–26.

ence to nature involves reference to access to nature's goods, hence the reference to justice in the title of this paper.

Elsewhere I have borrowed some terms from Dietrich Bonhoeffer's Lutheran Christology[16] in order to set this out in a little more detail, writing of nature as *extra nos*, *pro nobis* and *in nobis*. This threefold classification is an attempt to specify that in the interpretation of nature we are confronted with nature's alterity, its hybridity and matters of equity.

If this seems unnecessarily complicated, perhaps what is at issue here can be reprised by presenting Erica Fudge's threefold typology of historical approaches to the consideration of animals. She argues that there are three types of animal history: intellectual history, humane history, and holistic history. In an intellectual history of animals, Fudge argues, the story of animals is retold by the historian in order to explicate human attitudes; animals exemplify what is already considered to be true of a historical period. In humane history, relations between the human and the animal are the focus but the task now is to discern something new about the human. A holistic history of animals builds on humane history with the addition that, as Fudge puts it, 'what is at stake here is the status of the human itself'.[17] Of holistic history, she asserts: 'Recognizing the centrality of the animal in our understanding of ourselves as human forces us to reassess the place of the human.'[18] In this paper, something similar is being attempted: an exploration of the ways in which the contrast between nature and the human – that shores up and defends a certain construal of the human – is present in, and challenged by, ecotheologies over the last forty years or so.

THREE WAYS INTO ECOTHEOLOGY

Conradie argues that the trajectory of ecotheology is marked at the beginning by its pressing into service those aspects of Christian

---

[16] For a helpful discussion, see Martin Rumscheidt, 'The Formation of Bonhoeffer's Theology', in J. de Gruchy, ed., *The Cambridge Companion to Dietrich Bonhoeffer* (Cambridge, 1999), 50–70.

[17] Erica Fudge, 'A Left-Handed Blow: Writing a History of Animals', in Nigel Rothfels, ed., *Representing Animals* (Bloomington, IN, and Indianapolis, IN, 2002), 3–18, at 9.

[18] Ibid. 11.

tradition that seem most ecologically serviceable.[19] In other words, the stress at first has been on engagement rather than repair. Only as theological difficulties have emerged subsequently have matters of repair then acquired greater importance. As we review the three areas of practice, doctrine and natural theology in the following section, we shall encounter this dynamic of engagement and repair.

(i) *By Practice: Stewardship*

A principal mode of engagement has been by referring to practice. What is responsible Christian practice in the face of ecological distress? One important answer has been the affirmation of the theme of stewardship. Christopher Southgate goes so far as to maintain that stewardship is the default Christian response in this context: 'That human beings are called to be stewards of creation tends to be the default position within ordinary Christian groups. The concept of stewardship is affirmed in recent major documents in both the evangelical and catholic traditions'.[20] In an otherwise strong rejection of stewardship, Clare Palmer similarly notes its citation by John Paul II in 1985 and in an official report by the Church of England in 1990.[21] And we can note its more recent deployment in a 2005 Church of England report, *Sharing God's Planet*, from the Council of Mission and Public Affairs.[22] Richard Bauckham makes a comparable comment: 'The understanding of the human dominion over nature that has become popular among Christians, in the context of a new consciousness of ecological responsibilities, is the idea of stewardship'.[23] And although there has been some reaction against it – for example, the development without reference to stewardship by Christian Aid of its theology for climate change – stewardship remains important. It is also

[19] Conradie, *Christianity and Ecological Theology*, 107–08.

[20] Christopher Southgate, 'Stewardship and its Competitors: A Spectrum of Relationships between Humans and the Non-Human Creation', in R. J. Berry, ed., *Environmental Stewardship: Critical Perspectives Past and Present* (London, 2006), 185–95, at 185.

[21] Clare Palmer, 'Stewardship: A Case Study in Environmental Ethics', in Ian Ball et al., eds, *The Earth Beneath: A Critical Guide to Green Theology* (London, 1992), 67–86, at 68; repr. in Berry, ed., *Environmental Stewardship*, 63–75, at 64.

[22] Council of Mission and Public Affairs, *Sharing God's Creation* (London, 2005), esp. 16–28.

[23] Richard Bauckham, 'Modern Domination of Nature', in Berry, ed., *Environmental Stewardship*, 32–50, at 42.

evident that even among proponents of stewardship there is some disagreement on the meaning of the concept. Which understandings of nature and justice are present in stewardship?

To begin, we may note that there is in ecotheology more than one biblical warrant cited for stewardship. For some, it is a way of drawing out the ecological implications of the *imago dei* language articulated in Genesis 1: 26–28. As the language of dominion is present there, it is fair to say that stewardship emerges as a way of reinterpreting the term 'dominion'. There is no substantive support, we may conclude, amongst ecotheologians for dominion itself. It is true that Thomas Sieger Derr, in a polemical argument, employs the term but the model with which he operates is one of stewardship.[24] The subtitle of one of Douglas John Hall's books captures the majority opinion: dominion *as* stewardship.[25]

How might we characterize the difference between dominion and stewardship? Theologically, dominion by the human over other creatures may be understood by analogy with God's action towards God's creation. That is, if God can be understood as free in relation to the creation and thereby as transcendent over it, human dominion imitates such freedom and transcendence. Secured here is a type of anthropocentrism which we can identify by reference to the concept of will. As Gordon Kaufman has pointed out, this interpretation of dominion tends to associate humanity with divinity in that both humanity and divinity are agents with the capacity to will; nature (that is, non-human nature) is held not to have such volitional capacity. As Kaufman concludes: 'Nature is not conceived primarily as man's proper home and the very sustenance of his being but rather as the context of and material for teleological activity by the (non-natural) wills working upon and in it'.[26] Value is here associated with volition; only artificers have moral considerability; value is sourced to action and non-human nature does not act in the precise sense required here.

By contrast, the model of stewardship interprets humanity less as over creation and more as within it. The performance of stew-

---

[24] Thomas Sieger Derr, *Ecology and Human Need* (Philadelphia, PA, 1975), 68–70.

[25] Douglas John Hall, *Imaging God: Dominion as Stewardship* (Grand Rapids, MI, 1986).

[26] Gordon D. Kaufman, 'A Problem for Theology: The Concept of Nature', *HThR* 65 (1972), 337–66, at 353.

ardship is part of the human vocation, so to speak, and the steward is regarded more in terms of management or administration. This connects with a second biblical source, the parables of the steward told by Jesus (Matthew 21: 33–41; 24: 45–51; 25: 14–30). In this view, humanity does not enjoy the rights of dominion but has the responsibilities of a steward.

Perhaps this double source in Scripture goes some way to explaining why there is a disagreement in ecotheology over the emergence and first occurrence of the concept of stewardship. According to Richard Bauckham, for example, it is relatively recent, dating in English from the second half of the seventeenth century. For Bauckham, stewardship is a response to the developing sense of human control over nature that emerges in the early modern period. The work of the steward was directed to taming an unruly nature; the task of the steward was dedicated to the improvement of nature. And although responsibility towards a creation that has its own value is central to stewardship, for Bauckham the stress is on the steward over nature. Nonetheless, a new note is sounded: human rule over nature now requires an acknowledgement of 'nature's inherent value'.[27]

For Robin Attfield, by contrast, what he calls the 'key components' of stewardship predate the early modern period and certainly go back to Scripture. And, although he concurs with Bauckham that Matthew Hale's contribution in the seventeenth century is important, yet Attfield regards it as one in a long series. He quotes a Church of England report with approval: 'Stewardship implies caring management, not selfish exploitation; it involves a concern for both present and future as well as self, and a recognition that the world that we manage has an interest in its own survival and well being independent of its value to us'.[28] It is this caring management that Attfield regards as ancient.

Bauckham's reference to 'vertical' and 'horizontal', and his concern that stewardship stresses the vertical relation with God at the expense of the horizontal relations that the human enjoys

---

[27] Bauckham, 'Modern Domination of Nature', 43.

[28] Robin Attfield, 'Environmental Sensitivity and Critiques of Stewardship', in Berry, ed., *Environmental Stewardship*, 76–91, at 78–79, citing *Christians and the Environment: A Report by the Board of Social Responsibility*, General Synod Miscellaneous Paper 367 (London, 1991).

with a wider creation, remind us of the unsettled concept of nature that is operative here. It is in the work of Douglas John Hall that we find the theologically most adventurous effort to explore the meanings of nature in stewardship. Hall notes that the human can neither be seen as in or above nature; instead, he proposes that the human must be seen *with* or *alongside* nature and performs the functions of a steward from that position. Most interestingly, he associates dominion with the lordship of Jesus, the *dominus*, and thereby connects lordship with the themes of service and self-sacrifice. As Hall puts his case, 'The "lordship" of the Crucified ... radically transforms our preconception of dominion, exchanging for the concept of a superior form of being one of exceptional and deliberate solidarity (being-with), and for the notion of mastery a vocation to self-negating and responsible stewardship.'[29] Preservation of the other goes hand in hand with self-sacrifice and thereby reworks what we mean by justice in order to include a solidarity with nature.

If it is already evident that there is a diversity of meanings of nature in the interpretation of stewardship, the matter of justice is also present. 'The value of the notion of stewardship', Bauckham proposes, 'was that it formally introduced the notion of justice into the human relationship to nature'. And he continues: 'As steward responsible to the divine King, humanity has legal obligations to administer the earth justly and without cruelty'. In an extended quotation from a church report, Attfield concurs: 'Good stewardship requires justice, truthfulness, sensitivity, and compassion. It has implications ... for individuals, organisations, and states.'[30]

We can immediately see that the insertion of justice by ecotheology into theological thinking about the management of nature is a highly important development. Bauckham claims that Hale even raised the matter of cruelty to animals and queried whether animals should be killed for food. Such a seventeenth-century development would reach its apogee in the development of nineteenth-century utilitarianism and in the twentieth century in utilitarianism's bringing of animals within the sphere of the human by means of their capacity to suffer or flourish. Yet, we can also begin to see the difficulties. If justice refers mainly to care of a

---

[29] Hall, *Imaging God*, 186.
[30] Attfield, 'Environmental Sensitivity', 78–79.

garden against chaos and in favour of order, then the central theme here is the balance of nature.

Although of course it can never be the original balance, the steward improves nature in order to recover a balance. And now the critical questions crowd in: what is this balance, and who decides when it has been achieved? Answering these questions is made more difficult if we note that mercantilist capitalism with its bourgeois property relations emerges from the seventeenth century. And this, if Bauckham is right, is coincident with a greater confidence in human control over nature and the emergence of the terminology of stewardship. A sense of nature as wealth in common, of common ownership, now begins to be called into question. Justice now develops in relation to property and its defence.

This matter is further complicated if we note that in English-language discussion justice has tended to refer to acts both punitive and compensatory; punishment and rectification are key themes. Yet we can see that these themes relate uneasily to the non-human in that for the punitive and the compensatory to be operative, all relevant agents must be regarded as part of the same moral community. Does stewardship speak of the moral community of the human and non-human? The answer is not obvious. 'Balance of nature', in the sense of a sort of natural equilibrium, usually points away from the human towards the non-human in which the non-human suffers from a lack, a dis-ease. Additionally, we may bear in mind that the discourse of balance occurs in the context of an emerging discussion of property rights and how the owner comes to hold property with legitimacy. What justice means here is, then, perhaps not immediately clear; the introduction of justice into discussions of stewardship seems belied by the new economic context and a focus on the human. To put the matter differently, we are presented with the question as to how dialectical is the engagement: for stewardship, does nature wane more than wax?

And we may note the matter of repair also. For the discussion of justice raises the intertwined issues as to how the actions of God in Christ are themselves acts of God's justice. To be sure, the tradition has maintained something of this, not least by its maintenance of justice as one of the key metaphors of the doctrine of the atonement. Presumably, then, some sense will have to be made of what it means to say that God's creating is an act of justice, and in what sense this engages the non-human. Moreover, it will need some theological repair to understand how it is that the theme of eschatological justice relates to the non-human. When Bonhoeffer writes that in redemption nature is not reconciled from sin but set free from its curse, he intends to be generous: redemption addresses non-human nature, albeit in a different way from the human. Thus he writes: 'Nature stands under the curse which God laid upon Adam's ground. ... Nature, unlike man and history, will not be reconciled, but it will be set free for a new freedom.'[31] Yet looking past the generosity, we may note that the difference in justice between the non-human and the human is once more being presented.

It seems likely, then, that the presentation by ecotheology of stewardship as an ecological ethic will require attention not only to ethical aspects but also to the theology in which the account of the steward is embedded. In other words, an account of God's actions in creation and redemption will be needed. And such an account will require some discussion of the justice of God for God (how do justice and injustice impinge upon the life of God and how does God 'process' injustices and resource justice-making?), and will thereby require some attention to God as a justice-making God of nature. It is doubtful that the restriction of ecotheology to immanentist or worldly concerns will be theologically adequate to this task.

Given this theological uncertainty, perhaps we should characterize stewardship as a moral attitude rather than as a system of moral norms. It points to a Christian commitment to take ecological responsibility seriously rather than a fully worked-out way of understanding and exercising that responsibility. It then becomes understandable why some argue for its retirement.[32] And perhaps this very 'openness' of stewardship goes some way to explaining its popularity: stewardship can be interpreted in a variety of ways and thereby attracts a range of supporters. Part of the reason for the hardiness of stewardship may be best understood if we regard it as an atonement metaphor of a subjective and exemplarist type.[33] If

---

[31] Dietrich Bonhoeffer, *Christology* (London, 1978), 64.

[32] See H. Paul Santmire, 'Healing the Protestant Mind: Beyond the Theology of Human Dominion', in D. T. Hessel, ed., *After Nature's Revolt: Eco-Justice and Theology* (Minneapolis, MN, 1992), 57–78, at 75.

[33] Peter Scott, *A Political Theology of Nature* (Cambridge, 2003), 213–18.

this is correct, such an interpretation would connect nicely with the stress on vocation and an ethic of prudence and caution that have been so important in certain traditions of Reformed Protestant thinking.

(ii) *By Doctrine: Creation and Eschatology*

Ethics is traditionally located in Christian doctrinal thinking under the rubric of the doctrine of creation. And it is to the doctrine of creation to which we shall turn next. What has hopefully been shown in the brief exposition of stewardship is the way that it raises theological issues concerning the doctrines of creation and eschatology. One such issue is that of how the steward is to be understood in relation to nature. If the human creature forms some kind of community, some kind of common realm with other creatures, how are we to understand that relation?

If the 'directive meaning'[34] of theology is God, we may readily appreciate that the God of ecotheology is often understood in immanentist terms; a God of the economy (*oikonomia*). And some ecotheologians, like some feminist and liberation theologians, are impatient with the technical issues associated with inquiries after the otherness of God, God in God's own life. Is not such technicality a distraction from practical tasks? Thus the God we are presented with by theologians who hold such a view is construed as God-with-us; given this, we can safely bet our last carbon credit that a construal of incarnation is not far behind.

The tendency of this God-with-us analysis is clear enough: if the world or nature may be understood as God's presence, the value of creation is increased or enhanced. The following axiom is at work here: the de-divinization of the world is synonymous with its de-sacralization. In other words, the otherness of God to the world is considered to be a withdrawal of God from the world that is considered to be synonymous with a reduction in the sacredness (for which, read 'value') of the world. To speak, for example, of the world as God's body (as Sallie McFague does) is to argue that God is present by way of non-human nature. It is to claim furthermore that God is present to nature in ways that ought to mean that we respect nature more. Nature is one of the forms of

---

[34] I owe this phrase to Daniel W. Hardy, in conversation.

God's presence to us and this form cannot be altered or degraded without in some way dishonouring God. Such a presentation is often called panentheism.

A good example of such a presentation can be found in McFague's *Models of God* in which she proposes the world as God's body as a way of picturing the relationship between God and world in immanentist terms. This is presumably a metaphysics of parental presence: a doctrine of God's creation in which the continuities between creation and Creator are affirmed in such a fashion that God has a stake in the materiality of the world. There is no opposition between 'spirit' and 'matter'. She pursues this project in *The Body of God* in which she argues that the key theological task is the development of Christian symbols that are congruent with the findings of postmodern science and its stress on the organic nature of reality.

Such a synonymy of de-divinization and de-sacralization has largely been denied by theological tradition. The transcendence of God is not usually elided with the de-sacralization of the world. Instead, theology has preferred to recommend that the denial that the world is the site of local gods or warring divines is the refusal of *parochial* divinity; the transcendence of the monotheistic God is the criticism of local gods. Such refusal permits the identification of God as present to creation in non-parochial fashion out of God's otherness to creation; without such a radical transcendence – a *sui generis* alterity – then the presence of God to God's world is imperilled. The relation of transcendence and immanence is not a zero-sum game therefore; the relation is not one of competition. The sort of ecological doctrine of creation presented here is suspicious of this traditional sort of transcendence – as has been argued, such an ecological doctrine equates de-divinization with de-sacralization and often regards transcendence and immanence as being in competition – and prefers instead a strong account of the immanence of God in which God is present through all parts of the universe.

A different construal of incarnation would not be far behind, as I have already suggested. And so we find: the traditional concentration in Christology of the immanence or presence of God in that scandal of historical particularity – a Son of a Father – becomes a scandal of anti-ecological particularity – a solitary, independent individual without an environment. It is this sense of an independent individual that needs revision, so runs the critique. A change in the meaning of incarnation follows quite naturally. Incarnation is transferred from the doctrine of Christ to the doctrine of God. Or, as McFague puts it, we need in ecotheology to make two moves: 'the first is to relativize the incarnation in relation to Jesus of Nazareth and the second is to maximize it in relation to the cosmos'.[35] To put the matter less kindly: Jesus becomes an instance or result of God's relationship with the world rather than the content of that relationship.

If such claimed anti-ecological particularity is to be overcome, it must additionally be achieved by re-presenting the relations between the human and the non-human. Powerful disciplines are available to provide information on this matter and to these disciplines in the natural sciences theology turns. In a profound irony, a strong emphasis on the presence of God concludes in the occlusion of theological resources for interpreting the interweaving of God's life in creaturely life. Once more the concept of nature proves slippery. Affirming the importance of humanity's relations with nature is not the same as giving a theological account of those relations, nor are accounts of these relations in other disciplines necessarily congenial to those offered by theology. Moreover, it is not immediately clear how laws of nature, as proposed by the natural sciences, may be understood as an account of a worldly order that mediates the presence of God.[36]

To stress the immanence of God in this fashion is to close the gap between the human and otherkind by locating both the human and otherkind in the immanence of God. We might say that nature is here being reformulated thereby to encompass the human; a type of theological naturalism is being offered to us. Whereas stewardship sometimes speaks of the human *with* nature, on this more immanentist view the human is located *within* nature. Justice is no longer concerned with right care and correct management but rather is directed at identifying and rectifying ill-judged efforts at separation. That is, ecological injustice is identified with efforts to deny the mutual dependencies and interweaving of nature and humanity. Injustices occur when the human overlooks

---

[35] Sallie McFague, *The Body of God* (London, 1994), 162.
[36] Peter Scott, 'Nature in a "World Come of Age"', *New Blackfriars* 78 (1997), 356–58, at 362.

such dependencies and seeks to advance without nature, so to speak. We are working with what Kathryn Tanner calls 'a vision of cosmic justice in which all beings are due equal consideration at some basic level of moral concern'.[37]

With the emphasis on creation comes an emphasis on redemption. Certainly, we may agree that the theme of redemption and the matter of eschatology are very important routes whereby nature enters into ecotheology. There are at least two reasons for this. First, redemption has been interpreted as body- and world-denying: redemption has been criticized as referring to an other-worldly rescue that undermines any world-affirming tendencies in Christianity.[38] Second, in its reference to a Kingdom, eschatology is the most political and certainly the edgiest of Christianity's doctrines. For various political and liberation theologies, eschatology has been the nerve of political engagement calling into question, as it does, the status quo. Ecotheology has struggled with these two emphases which we may grasp, following Jürgen Moltmann, as differing construals of personal, socio-historical and cosmic eschatologies.[39]

As we might now expect, eschatology has been reworked within ecotheology along strongly immanentist lines: for example, Rosemary Radford Ruether has over-written eschatology in terms of a conversion to the earth.[40] In other words, she has been concerned to reject a recurrent tendency to see eschatology as the translation of individual, human life into a divine realm reserved solely for humans. By contrast, Jürgen Moltmann has appealed to the unruly aspect of eschatology and stressed that eschatology is about hope in the present on the basis of a coming future that calls into question the present. In this view, eschatological fulfilment is concerned with the surpassing of life but not the denial of creatureliness; such fulfilment transcends rather than obliterates.[41] Indeed, the matter

---

[37] Kathryn Tanner, 'Creation, Environmental Justice, and Ecological Justice', in Rebecca Chopp and Mark Lewis Taylor, eds, *Reconstructing Christian Theology* (Minneapolis, MN, 1994), 99–123, at 118.

[38] For an extended treatment of this point, see Santmire, *Travail of Nature*.

[39] Jürgen Moltmann, *The Coming of God* (London, 1994).

[40] Rosemary Radford Ruether, *To Change the World: Christology and Cultural Criticism* (London, 1981), 67–70.

[41] See Peter Scott, 'The Future of Creation', in David Fergusson and Marcel Sarot, eds, *The Future as God's Gift: Explorations in a Christian Eschatology* (Edinburgh, 2000), 89–114.

of the eschatological fulfilment of nature beyond the human is the denial that matter is merely transient; this natural matter is of such importance to God that it is redeemed by God rather than passing out of existence.[42]

For ecotheology, then, the vital question is: what is the redemption of nature, and what sense does it make to say that the human is co-redeemed with the non-human? Yet, as Celia Deane-Drummond argues, the difficulties here are immense, for how are we to think of the redemption of nature?[43] For those such as Moltmann who wish to stress that all nature is redeemed a useful stress on the materiality of redemption is maintained. At the least, we might say that the human will needs some supporting infrastructure in being redeemed; at the most, even the nature unrelated to the human will be preserved. Yet, in some eschatological state, will all nature exist together? What of features such as predation – will this be lifted from a nature released by redemption from its curse? Of course, such issues are not new. Any theology of redemption has had to face whether, for example, human redemption includes or overcomes human disability; the matter of predation is analogous. Yet, in that extrapolation seems unwise in this matter, our picture of this redeemed state is necessarily obscure.

Moreover, efforts by some theologians to address these difficulties by reducing the materiality of the eschatological state seem undermined by the resurrection. For example, arguing that God preserves nature 'only' in God's memory seems less than persuasive. Is it theologically plausible to suggest that resurrection means that God holds Christ in God's memory? That hardly seems consonant with tradition. If then we respond to this difficulty by arguing that the non-human is held in God's memory but the human is materially present to God, does that not reintroduce a duality between the human and the non-human of an unhelpful sort in that it renders the non-human a second-class citizen in redemption, an idealized memory rather than redeemed matter?[44]

In drawing these reflections on eschatology to a close, we may also note that the organizing themes of justice and nature are present once more. Traditionally, the Last Judgement has been part

---

[42] Conradie, *Christianity and Ecological Theology*, 103.
[43] See Deane-Drummond's fascinating discussion in her *Eco-Theology*, 169–77.
[44] Ibid.

of eschatology. So in the consideration of eschatology, ecotheology is faced with the issue of the moral considerability or standing of nature. What does it mean to say that nature appears as an agent in the justice of God, that God addresses nature as judge? What does the bestowal of mercy on nature mean? The destiny of the human and the non-human is a moral notion; by fulfilment the human and the non-human enter into their respective joys, and their true natures are for the first time disclosed by the love of God enacted in judgement. And this matter of fulfilment is vitally important in the consideration of the manipulation of human bodies and the non-human nature. For eschatological discourse is a teleological discourse. This teleology is important to us as we proceed to manipulate both our own bodies and our environment. How do we know that we are manipulating in continuity with a fulfilment bestowed by God? We can only answer this question by attending to eschatological discourse.

Yet our intelligence is poor here. And if our best clue in this matter is the Resurrection of Jesus Christ, we should perhaps highlight Holy Saturday as a kind of caesura, an epistemological warning against too much speculation about the Resurrection. Nonetheless, we may note that the ubiquity of the resurrected Jesus Christ comes under the forms of the sacraments of bread and wine. If the resurrected Jesus is *more* available than he was before his death, his life has a new, precisely institutional, form; that institution is called the eucharist, in which Christ's presence is available as before yet differently. And as freshly re-institutionalized, present in a different set of social conventions, his availability is qualitatively changed so as to become generative. Indeed, this generative power creates a new community. Bizarrely, we are forced to the conclusion that the resurrected Christ, under the forms of bread and wine in the institution that is called the eucharist, has a more concrete presence than before. This intensified availability is sourced to God's action, as the Father and the Spirit render this Christ available once more in a new institution.[45]

It is perhaps along lines something like this that we could imagine the redemption of ourselves and the non-human: as God's

---

[45] These reflections are my own, yet are prompted by responses given by Terry Eagleton at the conclusion of his Wickham Lecture, 'Was Jesus a Revolutionary?', delivered at Manchester Cathedral, 15 May 2008.

work to re-institutionalize in order to make God's creatures newly and freshly available, for God and for others. It follows that an axiom which Deane-Drummond quotes approvingly from the work of Denis Edwards – 'God relates to each creature on its own terms' – must be refused. There can be no eschatological state of a creature 'on its own terms'. For what divine judging secures is the revealing of who the creature truly becomes in the purposes of God; it is to the *redeemed* creature that God relates, in continuity and discontinuity. This also allows a fresh look at concerns over the redemption of, say, cancers and viruses – to take two of Deane-Drummond's examples. Cancers are corruptions of good flesh and in a redeemed circumstance can be understood to pass away; these are not really 'life' but the negation of life and thereby are part of the transience of creatureliness that is surpassed in redemption. Viruses are not corruptions in that sense but perhaps these will be re-institutionalized so that only their goodness will remain; viruses will be made freshly available, so to speak, but only as a contribution to the glory of God. The freedom of creatures does not outrun the freedom of God.

The primary category here is word, communication: creatures are available to be addressed and to address. Communication requires institutions and so we, as well as the non-human, perhaps should expect to be re-institutionalized to be radically available for communication. It seems to me that from this point of view we could imagine that, for example, predation would be lifted, and animals that are currently predators would require a different sort of infrastructural support. Further detail at this point may be unwise and quickly leads to questions such as: will the dinosaurs be redeemed? if all the animals return will the earth be big enough? It is not quite clear to me where we would have to stand in order to answer these questions.

(iii) *By an Independent Route: Natural Theology*

A third way that nature enters theology is by way of natural theology. This is a highly contested area of discussion and we cannot really hope to do justice to it. Yet it should be an important strategy for ecotheology, even if there is not much discussion on the topic in that discipline.

Why is natural theology important? Fundamentally, the function of natural theology is the criticism of idolatry. Why is the critique of idolatry important for ecotheology? Because the greatest potential idol in ecotheology is Nature, and the task of natural theology in this context is to offer a protocol for theology to ensure that theology does not unwittingly construct a competition between God and nature. How, you may ask, does nature function as an idol? The short answer is that God and nature compete for the status of a comprehensive whole. The task of natural theology is negative or critical: natural theology functions to recover the transcendence of God as that which is not identifiable as a 'whole', and so as comprehending all wholes and parts.

Natural theology has not had a good press, even in recent Catholic theology, and has suffered from a certain narrowing. For some, the notion of the natural appears to function in opposition to grace and thereby natural theology is held to be working with an independent notion of reason.[46] Thus some are happier with working with a theology of nature. As George Hendry puts the matter: if 'to establish a knowledge of nature in the light of God … may be taken as a rough definition of a theology of nature', then this is to be contrasted favourably with a natural theology that seeks to 'establish a knowledge of God in the light of nature'.[47] And we may now appreciate the strength of appeals to God's two books – Nature and Scripture – in that the appeal to the book of nature may be identified as a part of a theology of nature.[48]

Yet natural theology remains vitally important. Consider only the phrase that is part of this volume's theme: 'natural world'. What do these words mean in this context and for theology? 'World', like nature, is a troublesome term; indeed, it functions somewhat like nature. When we refer to world, precisely what do we identify? In part of its biblical provenance, world refers to all that is created by God. In the David Attenborough sense, natural world refers to activity that is not to be sourced to human willing. Nature has a similar, troubling, unruliness: does nature refer to some whole of which humanity is a part? Or should we prefer to say that nature identifies that which is not human? Neither option seems attractive. To affirm that humanity is a part of nature seems to deny the

---

[46] For further discussion, see Peter Scott, 'Blessing and Curse: "The Natural" as a Theological Concept', *Modern Believing* 28 (1997), 15–23.

[47] Hendry, *Theology of Nature*, 14.

[48] R. J. Berry, *God's Book of Works: The Nature and Theology of Nature* (London, 2003).

ways in which we are different from the non-human, and might
be thought to have the effect of undermining our moral responsibility. To stress our difference from nature, to assert that nature
is for us only alterity, suggests that we are separate from, and so
independent of, the non-human.

Natural theology is not the attempt to establish knowledge of
God in the light of nature. Instead, natural theology is best understood in my view as the effort to establish knowledge of God
by creation. That is, natural theology is not concerned with the
rational 'deduction' of God but instead with the effort to interpret nature as a whole for theology. It is the effort to free us in
theology from being mesmerized by the pressures to confuse God
and world. Thereby natural theology is fundamentally concerned
with the correct use of the word 'God'. As I have put it elsewhere:
'In its Thomist version, natural theology has been concerned with
what God is *not* in order to avoid confusion between God and the
world.[49] And in its Protestant version, we may borrow some words
by Moltmann: natural theology is concerned with 'the universal
claim bound up with the word, "God" '.[50] So natural theology
relates talk of the unconditioned God to the conditioned world
in order to avoid a confusion of the two.

Why there is so little discussion in ecotheology of natural
theology is unclear. There have been a few calls to reconsider
natural theology: for example, Ernst Conradie has argued in favour
of a natural theology but with a focus on the hermeneutical matter
about pre-understandings given in language, culture and location.
Instead, here we are focussing on what Wolfhart Pannenberg calls
'criteria for a positive definition of the concept of God'.[51] Such
an effort to specify the conditions of God-talk is important to
ecotheology as part of the effort to engage theologically with the
many dimensions of climate change. That is, natural theology is
important to ecotheology not least because climate change seems
to offer us the universal of a change in global weather coupled
with the universal character of the phenomenon of economic
globalization. In this context, natural theology aims to distinguish
between universals, to deny that these universals compete with

[49] Scott, 'Blessing and Curse', 19.
[50] Moltmann, *God in Creation*, 58.
[51] Wolfhart Pannenberg, *Systematic Theology*, 3 vols (Edinburgh, 1991–98), 1: 73.

God, and so to deny that the world can wag the god. As such, the task of natural theology is critical: the scrutiny of universals.

ECOTHEOLOGY'S CHANGING CLIMATE?

So far, it has been argued that nature enters theology by one of three routes: by practice, by doctrine, and independently. Furthermore, whichever way nature enters into theology, issues both theoretical and practical follow from difficulties in the interpretation of the concepts of nature and justice. In this final section, we turn to the topic of theological engagement with climate change and will find that issues to do with nature and justice arise here also. As always, we shall be obliged to explore with which nature and whose justice we have to do.

For Michael Northcott in *A Moral Climate: The Ethics of Global Warming*, theology makes a persuasive contribution to understanding the sources of climate change and resisting that change. The theme of stewardship is important to this act of persuasion. Northcott understands global capitalism as an alienated way of living that departs from and overstresses the 'natural' structures of the earth. Beginning from the claim that climate change is earth's judgement on the 'global market empire',[52] Northcott connects this to the disastrous effects of empire as narrated in Christian Scripture. This leads to the theological judgement that informs the remainder of his argument: the relationships between earth, humans and God are 'intrinsically moral' such that justice cannot be restricted to the human. For earth and humans to flourish, in other words, will require a rescaling of human activities in order to conform better to earth's given structures and capacities. This flourishing must be developed theologically – that is, by reference to a particular doctrine of creation in which a notion of the 'natural' is privileged. And the rescaling will require new policies and practices.

Given that anthropogenic climate change is *earth's* judgement, the moral case against such change is that the consequences of such change affect the poorest most who are also those who pollute least; the least culpable bear more of the burden of climate

---

[52] Michael S. Northcott, *A Moral Climate: The Ethics of Global Warming* (London, 2007), 7.

change. In addition, climate change is encouraging the extinction of species. Such reduction in species diversity reduces the earth's imaging of the Creator in that such diversity reflects the nature of God. It is this moral climate – a double acknowledgement of the immorality of climate change – that the book seeks to commend.[53]

For Anne Primavesi in *Gaia and Climate Change: A Theology of Gift Events*, matters are rather different; indeed, we are reminded of the writings of Sallie McFague. Stewardship and notions of naturalness are displaced by a stress on the history of events and their effects, together with an appeal to the 'authentic' sayings of Jesus (those deemed highly likely to have been spoken by him) as the basis of a corrective practice of forgiveness. Despite the title, there is not much detailed discussion of climate change; indeed, the book reads more like an ecological doctrine of creation which is then drawn from to engage with the issue of climate change. And the prescriptions proposed would, we may think, be recognizable even if the present ecological crisis did not include anthropogenic climate change.

More than any other theologian known to me, Primavesi has engaged with, and been influenced by, the Gaia hypothesis of James Lovelock.[54] That influence is evident throughout, as when she states that:'The name Gaia ... brings us up to the present when the event of this self-regulation is seen to maintain earth's climate in a state of dynamic equilibrium that enables us to describe her as a living organism'. Primavesi continues:

> Looking forward, it [Gaia] draws us out into a future where the global climate that emerged from these Gaian feedback systems and planetary relational processes is so compromised by human-led events that it may not continue to provide the life support that makes our lives, and indeed all their lives, possible ...[55]

[53] For a fuller response to Northcott, see my review of his book in *Theology* 112 (2009), 68–70.

[54] This hypothesis has a range of interpretations but at its boldest proposes the earth as a sort of self-regulating organism in which earth's *biota* – its living beings – function to maintain the conditions for life: James Lovelock, *Gaia* (Oxford, 1987).

[55] Anne Primavesi, *Gaia and Climate Change: A Theology of Gift Events* (London, 2009), 25.

This Gaian theory helps us to reconsider the event of God's creating by arguing that 'God, the people, the land and all its inhabitants coexist in interconnected networks of life-giving relationship'.[56]

From this theological position, Primavesi takes issue with notions of transcendent divinity, images of God that promote violence, otherworldly readings of salvation, accounts of redemption that are restricted to the human, penal-substitutionary theories of atonement with their inappropriate understanding of gift, and dualistic anthropologies. The key term here is alienation: the alienation of the human from its wider context. Primavesi trawls Christian tradition in order to privilege theological resources which might draw attention to this alienation and seek to reduce that alienated and alienating distance. Exploring the gift event – the complex interplay between giver, gift and recipient – that is called Jesus, she draws heavily on the latest 'quest for the historical Jesus' (the methodologically diverse – and non-theological – effort to establish historically verifiable data on Jesus and thereby reconstruct his context) to privilege Jesus's call to love your enemies; this injunction Primavesi regards as historical bedrock. Loving your enemies connects to climate change in two ways. First, the ecology of love here includes the non-human. The logic must go something like this: we are enjoined to love even our enemies; the non-human is not our enemy so must be included in our loving. Second, Jesus, according to this quest of the historical Jesus, spoke from a 'low social situation' to those in a similar situation. In that climate change affects the poorest first and more severely – their efforts at adaptation to the effects of climate change will be hampered by lack of resources – Gaian theology sides with the poorest and commends practices that will reduce burdens on these poorest.

The problems being explored in terms of justice and nature crowd in once more. Does stewardship presuppose a balance of nature that in fact is denied by the dynamics of climate change? Can species diversity be affirmed and protected by grounding such diversity in the nature of God? What is the relationship if it is to be understood as more than semantic? Should we accept the reduction of the Jesus event to a set of Jesus-sayings? And why should these sayings rather than others be granted authority? Of course,

[56] Ibid. 17.

we may accept that they are helpful in developing an ethics of justice for climate change but do they have any authority apart from such ethical functioning? Is such a 'sayings-Christology' sufficient?

For contemporary ecotheology, then, the bounty of God is given with nature and justice and requires both engagement and repair. The generosity of God engages the human in part through a set of natural relations; nature is one of the forms of God's way to the human and with the human; by nature God approaches the human and shapes the human. If we are co-participants in the community of creation, theological repair work is required to explore how this 'animal' community is to be understood. In other words, any account of the distribution of the goodness of God, and God's efforts to redistribute that goodness against its distortions, requires a presentation of community; not least, we need a way of refusing the opposition of nature and humanity and the positing of nature in competition with God. Stewardship is less concerned with this issue. Yet, to give it its due, stewardship presses the matter of justice, even if it is not clear how notions of justice developed for human communities relate to a common realm of nature and humanity. More repair work is signalled. Moreover, in the consideration of justice some attention will need to be paid to how nature may have some sort of moral considerability. What sort of independence, and what sort of volitional capacity, does nature enjoy? A moral attitude emerges that finds liberality in the mutuality of asymmetrical dependencies between the human and nature and seeks to find a way of responding to this liberality with its own modes of generosity. It is to the articulation of this liberality, this bounty, lived from and before God, that ecotheology is dedicated.

University of Manchester

457